A LIFE OF
JAMES BOSWELL

Peter Martin was born in Argentina of English parents and educated there and in America. He has taught English literature in both England and America and written extensively on eighteenth-century British and American literature and culture. His most recent book (1995) is a biography of Edmond Malone, the greatest of eighteenth-century Shakespeareans and (after Dr Johnson) James Boswell's most intimate friend. He lives half the year in America where he lectures at Principia College, Illinois, and half the year in West Sussex.

Also by Peter Martin

Pursuing Innocent Pleasures:
the Gardening World of Alexander Pope

British and American Gardens in the Eighteenth Century
(editor)

From Jamestown to Jefferson:
the Pleasure Gardens of Virginia

Edmond Malone, Shakespearean Scholar:
a Literary Biography

A LIFE OF
JAMES BOSWELL

Peter Martin

PHOENIX
PRESS

5 UPPER SAINT MARTIN'S LANE
LONDON
WC2H 9EA

A PHOENIX PRESS PAPERBACK

First published in Great Britain
by Weidenfeld & Nicolson in 1999
This paperback edition published in 2000
by Phoenix Press,
a division of The Orion Publishing Group Ltd,
Orion House, 5 Upper St Martin's Lane,
London WC2H 9EA

© 1999 Peter Martin

A CIP catalogue record for this book is available
from the British Library.

Printed and bound in Great Britain by
Butler & Tanner Ltd, Frome and London

ISBN 1 84212 167 7

For Cynthia

Contents

List of Illustrations   ix
Preface   1
Prologue   13

PART I: JOURNEY TO THE PROMISED LAND
1740–1763

1   A World of Chimeras   23
2   Edinburgh Gloom   43
3   Escape to London   66
4   Early Scribblings   75
5   Harvest Jaunt   91
6   London: The Promised Land   103
7   'The Johnsonian Æther'   124

PART II: TRAVEL AND MARRIAGE 1763–1769

8   Utrecht: Acquiring a Noble Character   143
9   Zélide   155
10   'Let Me Be Boswell':
Touring Germany and Switzerland   163
11   'Above the Vulgar Crowd':
Meeting Rousseau and Voltaire   175
12   O Italy!   190
13   'Like Embroidery upon Gauze':
Corsica, Law, and Propaganda   214
14   'Happy as an Unmarried Man Can Be'   235
15   'The Rage for Matrimony'   246

PART III: STAGNATION: THE MIDDLE YEARS
            1769–1782

      16   Settling Down: 'The Antechamber of His Mind'   265
      17   'The Down upon a Plum'   277
      18   The Hebrides   299
      19   Post-Hebrides: Ominous Edinburgh Flatness   327
      20   Picking Up Fragments   347
      21   'Inexplicable Dilatory Disease'   377
      22   Later Thirties: 'The Author and the Gentleman
            United'   398
      23   No Considerable Figure: Politics, Family, and
            Hypochondria   415
      24   The Road to Ulubrae–Auchinleck   432

PART IV: BIOGRAPHER AND LAIRD OF AUCHINLECK:
            TRIUMPH AND DESPAIR 1782–1795

      25   The Cracked Enamel   449
      26   From Death to Biography   468
      27   'Oh, If This Book of Mine Were Done!'   488
      28   Painful Progress   511
      29   The *Life of Johnson* and Its Aftermath   526

EPILOGUE   The Children   549

            Acknowledgements   550
            Abbreviations   553
            Bibliography   556
            Notes   562
            Index   597

List of Illustrations

Between pages 310 and 311

James Boswell (*Oil on canvas by George Willison, 1765. Scottish National Portrait Gallery, Edinburgh*).

Alexander Boswell, Lord Auchinleck, Boswell's father (*Oil on canvas by Allan Ramsay, 1754. Yale Center for British Art, Mellon Collection*).

Edinburgh in 1780 (*Drawing by John Gabriel Steadman, National Galleries of Scotland*).

The Old Tolbooth, Edinburgh (*Drawing by Henry Duguid, late eighteenth century. National Galleries of Scotland, Edinburgh*).

Old Parliament House and St Giles, Edinburgh (*Drawing by Henry Duguid, late eighteenth century. National Galleries of Scotland, Edinburgh*).

Auchinleck House (*Photograph courtesy of Mrs Christina Wilson*).

Samuel Johnson (*Oil on canvas by Sir Joshua Reynolds, 1756. National Portrait Gallery, London*).

John Wilkes and Mrs Corradini (*Oil on canvas by Louis Carrogis. Private Collection, Scotland*).

Jean-Jacques Rousseau (*Oil on canvas by Allan Ramsay, 1766. National Galleries of Scotland, Edinburgh*).

James Boswell in the Dress of an Armed Corsican Chief (*Engraving by J. Miller, after S. Wade, 1769*).

Mrs Hester Thrale (*Oil on canvas by Robert Edge Pine, 1781. Courage, Barclay, and Simonds Ltd*).

Margaret (Montgomerie) Boswell (*Oil on canvas attributed to George Willison. Photograph courtesy of Scottish National Portrait Gallery. Hyde Collection, USA*).

Fanny Burney (*Drawing in pencil and colour crayons by her cousin Edward Francis Burney. The Brooklyn Museum of Art, Carll H. de Silver Fund*).

'Tea' from *The Picturesque Beauties of Boswell* (*Etched by Thomas Rowlandson after a sketch by Samuel Collings, 1786. Department of Prints and Drawings, British Museum, London*).

'Sailing Among the Hebrides' from *The Picturesque Beauties of Boswell* (*Etched by Thomas Rowlandson after a sketch by Samuel Collings, 1786. Department of Prints and Drawings, British Museum, London*).

The visit of Dr Johnson and James Boswell to Flora MacDonald (*Artist unknown, 1773. Dr Johnson's house, Gough Square, London*).

Oliver Goldsmith (*Oil painting by Sir Joshua Reynolds, c.1769. National Portrait Gallery, London*).

'Revising for the Second Edition' from *The Picturesque Beauties of Boswell* (*Etched by Thomas Rowlandson after a sketch by Samuel Collings, 1786. Department of Prints and Drawings, British Museum, London*).

'Thou art a Retailer of Phrases' (*English School, 1800*).

James Boswell and his family (*Painting by Henry Singleton, late 1780s. Scottish National Portrait Gallery*).

A Literary Party, at Sir Joshua Reynolds's house (*Engraving by W. Walker after James E. Doyle, nineteenth century. Dr Johnson's house, Gough Square, London*).

David Garrick and his wife, Eva Maria (*Sir Joshua Reynolds, 1773. National Portrait Gallery, London*).

Sir Joshua Reynolds (*Self-portrait, c.1780. Royal Academy of Arts, London*).

Samuel Johnson (*Oil, artist unknown, c. 1784. James P. Magill Library, Haverford College, Pennsylvania*).

Edmund Burke (*Oil on canvas by Sir Joshua Reynolds, 1774. National Library of Ireland*).

Edmond Malone (*Oil on canvas by Sir Joshua Reynolds, 1779. National Portrait Gallery, London*).

The Biographers (*Engraving in British Museum Catalogue of Political and Personal Satires, no. 7052, 1786. Courtesy of the Lewis Walpole Library, Yale University.*)

First page of Boswell's manuscript of *The Life of Johnson* (*Beinecke Rare Book and Manuscript Library, Yale University*).

Preface

Thomas Carlyle wrote, 'Boswell has given more pleasure than any other man of this time, and perhaps, two or three excepted, has done the world greater service.' For Robert Louis Stevenson, Boswell's *Life of Johnson* was a way of life: 'I am taking a little of Boswell daily by way of a Bible. I mean to read him now until the day I die.' And Professor Chauncey Tinker, the first to bring to the public's notice the rich hoard of Boswell manuscripts at Malahide Castle in Ireland earlier this century, observed in the 1920s, 'Probably no English publication of the last hundred and thirty years has made more friends or kept them longer' than the great biography. 'The devotees of Boswell's *Johnson* are of both sexes and of all ages.'

The monumental and astonishing *Life of Dr Samuel Johnson LL.D.* (1791), which went through forty-one English editions in the nineteenth century alone, is still regarded as one of the greatest biographies ever written – many say *the* greatest. Boswell wrote two other books that in his day earned him literary fame across Europe, the *Account of Corsica* (1768) and *Tour to the Hebrides with Dr Samuel Johnson* (1785), but by comparison with his *Life of Johnson* they are like silvery minnows swimming around a majestic whale.

However, in the nineteenth century, or certainly at least until Boswell's personal papers were discovered in the 1920s, the *Life* was grudgingly celebrated as a work of genius mysteriously conjured up by a gregarious buffoon, neurotic, and sot. Thomas Babington Macaulay, trading on Boswell's posthumous reputation as an exhibitionist who could not control his huge sexual appetites or his consumption of alcohol, established the standard view when in 1831 he described him as the first of biographers, with no equal in ancient and modern literature, but added ruthlessly that 'if he had not been a great fool, he would never have been a great writer'. Boswell had his lucid moments as writer, the complacent argument went, but given his dissipation these were few and far between, making it nothing short of miraculous and even 'immoral' that he should have come up with one of the most famous literary works of the eighteenth century. He was 'utterly wanting' in 'logic, eloquence, wit, taste, all those qualities which are generally considered as making a book valuable'.[1]

Macaulay's few paragraphs on Boswell's character blackened his name. They were squeezed gratuitously into a review of an edition of the *Life*, surely one of the most resounding pieces of *ad hominem* criticism that ever found its way into print. For almost a century afterwards, he was the butt of jokes and an object of revulsion to those occupying the moral high ground. In fairness to Macaulay, however, even in Boswell's own lifetime he was pilloried in the press and laughed at by the powerful and the great as well as by the more humble.

Even today, Boswell's name conjures up vague images of immorality, amorality, exhibitionism, egotism, and vanity. With the exception of Frederick A. Pottle and Frank Brady, and the editors of the Boswell Research Editions, biographers of Boswell have tended to treat him as a neurotic and a buffoon, as 'Bozzy' the convivial companion whom nobody took seriously, often adopting the tone of jocular after-dinner banter.

This would have profoundly distressed Boswell. His desire to please others was sincere, his ability to do so uncanny. Most people found him very attractive, though the reasons for that are complex. Like an actor, in which guise he frequently saw himself, he put himself on show. He made no attempt to conceal his feelings and identity, partly out of naïvety and partly because he knew it would have interfered with his interaction with others. But if he was anything, he was a student of human nature, constantly sacrificing his dignity, respectability, and restraint to that end. In print especially, this openness and recklessness embarrassed many, and it is a short step from embarrassment to resentment. Why did he not abide by certain rules of decorum and social restraint as most of us do? Paradoxically, this lack of self-defensiveness was exactly what drew many people to him, a freedom that made them feel pleased to be in his company.

Boswell is the best example in the history of English literature, perhaps in the literature of any nation, of how the discovery of personal papers after an author's death can radically change his reputation. After the sensational discovery of his journals, letters, memoranda and literary manuscripts at Malahide Castle in Ireland and of other priceless manuscripts at Fettercairn House in Scotland, Boswell emerged as a very different person. And once Yale University acquired its massive collection in the late 1940s and began to publish Trade Editions of the journals in 1950, Boswell became something of a household name in Britain. Possibly to the disbelief of Professor Pottle, the brilliant general editor of the Boswell papers whose career was spent beavering away in a cluttered room on the third floor of the Sterling Library at Yale University, one million copies were sold of his edition of Boswell's *London Journal.*

At first the journals appeared to confirm the nineteenth-century perception of Boswell as a compulsive womanizer, drinker and gambler, a habitual gallant who only seemed happy when acting the fool. But readers soon began to see him as a highly complex figure, someone they thought they understood and with whom they were prepared to travel the extra mile. His honesty, sincerity, geniality, sensitivity, and desire to become a better human being are partly responsible for this change of perception. His journals also show him to be a conscientious and talented writer. Perhaps most importantly, they reveal the degree of mental suffering he endured for most of his lifetime.

What makes Boswell an interesting and challenging subject for the biographer is that, as a figure of paradoxes, opposites, and extremes, he defies classification. A prominent theme in this book will be to trace the link between his contradictory and confused self and his hypochondria or melancholia which, from adolescence onwards, set in motion causes and effects that often wrecked his behaviour. His sentiment and motivations, writing, relationships, social and professional conduct, persona as a Scottish laird, and general anxiety, were all tied to this mental disorder in one way or another.

As Boswell once said of himself, he was like an actor on a stage surrounded by mirrors, each reflecting back at him the multiple aspects of his mind. He was intrigued by his own character and strove mightily to stabilize his behaviour by trying to assess what he was and why. He failed most of the time, as we should if we sought to reduce him to measurable dimensions.

The discoveries of huge amounts of Boswell manuscripts earlier this century would seem improbable even in a work of fiction.[2] They have to be ranked among the most fabulous in world literary history. Their mystery and surprise are an ironic extension of the enigma that was Boswell himself.

The romantic story begins just after Boswell died in London in 1795. His friend and executor Edmond Malone almost despaired over what to do with the mountain of personal papers he found in Boswell's lodgings. Hoping to find something immediately publishable among them, he started hunting through the volumes of journals, hundreds of letters, and seemingly endless notes and memoranda. He was used to the massive labour required to search out archives, but this was too much even for him. He soon gave it up on the grounds that the papers (especially the journals) were too personal to publish anyway, and sent them to William Forbes at Pitsligo in Scotland, another executor and long a friend of the Boswell family. Forbes was even more conservative than Malone, refusing to allow any of the papers to see the light of day.

Here is where the mystery begins. First, in spite of the huge number of manuscripts that have been found, very few of the Boswell–Johnson letters have been recovered. Someone appears to have combed through the piles of correspondence and removed them. Did Boswell do this himself when he was writing the *Life*? Or was it Malone, or someone much later, a resourceful descendant of Boswell perhaps? A bundle of such importance is not likely to have been accidentally thrown away. Most probably someone tucked it away, too well as it happened, and possibly it still awaits discovery.

As for the rest of the papers Malone sent to Forbes, or that were already at Auchinleck, the Boswell family estate in Ayrshire, according to romantic legend of the nineteenth century Forbes forwarded a pile of papers to Auchinleck, where, with all the rest, they were crammed into a black ebony cabinet and its key as good as thrown away. The family, so the legend went, were so embarrassed by the contents of the papers that they declined all requests to see them; there were even rumours that the papers had been burnt.

The first large discovery of manuscripts was made during the lifetime of Boswell's grandson, Sir James. In the late 1830s, a Major William Stone of the East India Company stopped at a grocer's in Boulogne just long enough to make a purchase which was wrapped in a manuscript letter bearing Boswell's name. He rushed back to the shop to ask if the proprietress had any more of this paper. The answer thrilled him: she had been using it but still had plenty left. A hawker had sole it to her. Stone gathered all the papers in his trembling hands and later counted out ninety-seven autograph letters from Boswell to one of his oldest friends, William Temple, dating from his university years up to his death – two-thirds of all the correspondence between them now known to exist. For seventy years these letters, which were published in 1856 by Philip Francis, a barrister, were the most important existing biographical tool, apart from Boswell's published writings, yet scarcely anyone took sufficient note of them to counter Macaulay's denigration of Boswell.

The greatest discoveries still lay ahead. Boswell's great-granddaughter Emily (his last descendant from the male line) married an Irish peer, the fifth Lord Talbot De Malahide, and took up residence at Malahide Castle near Dublin. After her mother's death in 1884, Auchinleck remained unoccupied until it was sold in 1920. Beginning in 1905, Lord and Lady Talbot emptied Auchinleck and removed many of the papers to Malahide, including the family archives which Boswell took such pains to preserve. Whether or not they were then in the famous black ebony cabinet is anyone's guess. Apparently the Talbots had a slight literary bent, for in 1911 they took enough interest in the journals to have them typed out – leaving out the more scandalous passages – with a view to publication. The publisher they approached, Sir John Murray, was overwhelmed both by their volume and by their depiction of Boswell as 'an incurable sot and libertine'. While acknowledging that the journals were not historically 'devoid of interest', he could not bring himself to publish what were essentially 'trivialities'. Macaulay's ghost still haunted Boswell. For years after this the papers rested undisturbed at Malahide, though the Talbots were not at all secretive about their existence.

Enter Professor Chauncey B. Tinker of Yale University, then the world's leading Boswell scholar. Put on to the scent by two correspondents (one anonymous) who responded to his call for help in the *Times Literary Supplement*, in 1921 Tinker wrote to the sixth Lord Talbot who had succeeded to the estate asking if he had any Boswell manuscripts. He was blandly denied access but went on to publish his milestone edition of Boswell's letters in 1924, making no mention of Malahide and believing that most of the journals had been destroyed.

Things finally began to happen when Lord Talbot married in 1924. The new Lady Talbot also tried to have the journals published, but publishers still were not interested. However, rumours of their existence began to circulate more widely in London and in the United States. At this point, the great American collector of Johnsoniana, A. Edward Newton, picked up the scent and encouraged Tinker to pay a visit to Malahide to secure the journals – which was all that was thought to be there – 'against all comers'. With help from the American Consul-General in Dublin and a local archdeacon who was a friend of Lord Talbot's, Tinker was invited to tea at Malahide in July 1925. His heart leapt when he was shown into the Oak Room and his eyes fell on the black ebony cabinet. He said later that he felt like Sinbad in the valley of the rubies when he opened one of the drawers, crammed with papers 'in the wildest confusion'. Picking up a letter from Boswell to his son Alexander, Tinker realized in that instant that 'a new day had dawned for Boswellians'.[3]

Lady Talbot assured Tinker that there were, in addition, two cases of papers from Auchinleck that they had not even opened since their arrival in Ireland. On the spot, he offered to edit whatever there was, but Lady Talbot declined. He left empty-handed and without a commission, although at least he now knew that the Auchinleck archives had not perished in flames.

Exit Tinker; enter Lieut.-Col. Ralph Heyward Isham. Isham was an American book collector of limited means whose fascination with Boswell began as a student at Yale University. A dashing figure of thirty-five, charming, handsome and very persuasive, he enjoyed a wide circle of influential English friends. After several not entirely successful overtures to the Talbots on his behalf, Isham visited Malahide in June 1926. His charm worked instantly on Lady Talbot, on whom he depended to persuade her husband to sell the papers. He advised her objectively on how they might be published, offering guarantees of money and censorship that would allow her ultimate control. After that first meeting she was definitely on Isham's side, in spite of rival offers. By November, when Lady Talbot had gone through all the papers – apparently the first person to do so since Malone and Forbes – she indicated to Isham that her husband could be persuaded to sell all or part of the journals and letters to him. She suggested that he make an offer of £10,000 for the letters alone. Isham wanted the journals more than the letters, however, and wrote back offering that sum for the all the material. Two months later she replied that Lord Talbot would not hear of selling the journals. She repeated the offer of £10,000 for the letters and invited him back to Malahide.

That invitation was the turning point. Isham arrived at the castle on 19 August 1927 and for several days they went through everything except the journals, agreeing on a price of £13,585. The collection was remarkable: about 150 letters from Boswell; over 200 to him from the likes of Burke, Burns, Johnson, Goldsmith, Rousseau, and Voltaire. There was also the complete manuscript of his *Account of Corsica* and a very small amount of the manuscript of the *Life of Johnson*. That was the disappointing part: where was the rest of the *Life*? They concluded it must have been destroyed. Isham wrote out a cheque and left with one of the choicest treasures in English literary history – the entire Malahide Boswell collection except for the journals. The Talbots had also agreed to give him publishing rights.

Isham still badly wanted the journals, and after some additional coaxing Lady Talbot agreed to look at them again, decide what should be kept from the public eye, and try to convince her husband to relinquish them. In the meantime, Isham ran into Tinker in a London bookshop and offered him the job of editing the collected papers for a de luxe private edition. Shouting 'You have stolen my mistress,' Tinker declined, pleading bad eyesight, though the real reason was his realization that to do the job properly he would have to give up his highly successful academic career at Yale. Isham then offered it to T. E. Lawrence, who was serving in the RAF in Karachi. Lawrence had no taste for such a devotional literary mission, however, and also declined. A few days later at Simpson's-in-the-Strand, Isham accidentally met up with Newton who recommended Geoffrey Scott, the author of *Portrait of Zélide* (1925), a masterful and imaginative study of one of Boswell's first great loves. In a matter of hours he was excitedly arranging for Scott to come to the United States to work on the edition. For his part, Scott (who examined the papers in Isham's room at Claridge's Hotel) trembled at the sacredness of the commission. Isham knew he needed the journals to complete the edition but such was his confidence in Lady Talbot that he proceeded as if he already had them.

By November 1927, Lady Talbot had offered Isham all of the journals for £20,000. Having already spent about £15,000 and now feeling the financial pinch, Isham arranged to borrow the money from his kindly friend James H. Van Alen. Heavily censored, as that was the only way she could persuade her husband to part with them, the manuscript journals were then sent to Isham in batches during December and January. When they arrived in New York, Isham was appalled to find the manuscripts defaced with black paint and carbon ink. Fortunately it proved possible to read most of the excised words and passages by shining light through the pages. After agonizing over whether he should break his promise to Lady Talbot, he decided that the literary value of the manuscripts must be respected in his de luxe edition. Lady Talbot, of course, was angry and disappointed when she discovered the truth. To their credit, however, she and her husband eventually forgave Isham and cordial relations were restored.

By the summer of 1929 six volumes of the de luxe so-called Malahide Edition had appeared, to public acclaim. Scott's editorial work and introductions were widely celebrated. Isham was heavily in debt, but he had the satisfaction of knowing that the edition was an example of some of the best literary scholarship in existence and that he had managed to keep the Boswell papers together.

Exit Scott; enter Professor Frederick A. Pottle, Sterling Professor of English at Yale University. When Scott died tragically of pneumonia, he was succeeded by Pottle who was in favour of expanding the project significantly by including all Boswell's memoranda and journal notes. Even though this would mean delaying publication and would aggravate Isham's financial plight, he did not hesitate to give it his approval for the sake of the completeness of this great human document. He had already sold much of his collection of seventeenth- and eighteenth-century books to pay for the Boswell manuscripts, and he would lose more in the years to come. His obsession with Boswell eventually broke up his marriage and compelled him to sell his home in Long Island.

Another jolt came in April 1930 when Lady Talbot sent word that she had discovered at Malahide a cardboard box stuffed with additional Boswell papers instead of the expected croquet balls. The papers included 150 more pages of the journal, 110 pages of the manuscript of the Life, letters to and from Boswell, and almost the entire original manuscript of his *Tour to the Hebrides*. All this Isham could have for £4,000, bringing the total expenditure on the Malahide papers up to £40,000. Isham again borrowed the money from Van Alen, despite the further extensive delay to the edition that the addition of these new papers would cause. The problem worsened, when, in 1932, still more Boswell papers were put up for auction at Sotheby's by a family descendant. Isham could not buy any of these, but he secured the agreement of the purchasers to let him publish them in the de luxe edition. When Pottle finally finished the work in 1936 – eighteen volumes plus an index volume, an incredible scholarly achievement in a relatively short time – Isham looked poised to recoup his financial losses.

Enter C. Colleer Abbott. Just as the Malahide Edition was about to be published, the fruit of years of self-sacrifice and devotion, Isham was stunned to hear of another fantastic discovery of Boswell papers at Fettercairn House in Kincardineshire. Abbott's find was even more sensational than the ones at Malahide because it was so completely unexpected. Abbott, then a lecturer at the University of Aberdeen, had visited Fettercairn in 1930 in search of documents relating to James Beattie, a minor poet and acquaintance of Boswell's. What he found was another massive Boswell treasure trove about half the size of Isham's total Malahide collection.

The provenance of these papers was so simple that many were surprised they could have remained undiscovered for so long. William Forbes did not, it seems, return a substantial amount of Boswell papers to Auchinleck. When he died in 1806, they were still at Pitsligo, his home, but eventually found their way to Fettercairn, which had passed into the Forbes family through the marriage of his son. When Abbott (following a lead) visited Fettercairn in pursuit of Beattie, the house was owned by Forbes's great-great-grandson, the twenty-first Baron Clinton of Maxtock and Saye.

Abbott's account of his discoveries on several visits to Fettercairn between October 1930 and March 1931 reads like a scholar's archetypal fantasy. It seems that everywhere he turned in the house, in cupboards, libraries, nurseries, attics, chests and dusty sacks, he came up with remarkable finds. In the furthest recesses of the attic, for example, wedged between old furniture, he found an old sack or mailbag 'with rents here and there from which letters were ready to drop':

> Quickly I dragged it out. A loose letter fell. It was written to Boswell. Down the winding stairs I hurried the sack, wondering whether all the contents could possibly concern Boswell ... Soon I knew the truth. The sack was stuffed tight with Boswell's papers, most of them arranged in stout wads, torn here and there, and dirty, but for the most part in excellent order. Neither damp nor worm nor mouse had gnawed at them.[4]

Virtually all the papers were of the highest importance. Among them were the complete manuscript of Boswell's London journal of 1762–3, fragments of other journals, all the letters between Boswell and Forbes, 287 drafts or copies of letters from Boswell, over 1,000 letters written to him, and 119 letters from Johnson to various correspondents – letters which the recipients had sent to Boswell when he was writing the Life and which he had never returned. There were more than three times as many letters to and from Boswell at Fettercairn than among the Malahide papers.

Immediately, doubt arose over who was the legal owner of the Fettercairn papers. Whatever was Boswell's property belonged at Auchinleck, so perhaps the Talbots had a claim to it. The chief rival claim to these papers was made by the Cumberland Infirmary, a hospital in Carlisle, which as residuary legatee of Boswell's great-granddaughter maintained that it had a right to half of the papers. Legal advice was taken and a lengthy lawsuit ensued. In the meantime, Abbot began to work slowly on a catalogue but Lord Clinton refused to publicize the discovery until it was completed. There were also other legal reasons for 'Operation Hush', as his secrecy was dubbed, but the end result was that for six years Isham and Pottle struggled along with the Malahide Edition, in their ignorance fancying that it would be complete. R. W. Chapman, the Johnson scholar, was intimately involved with the Fettercairn papers yet never told Isham, a close friend of his, anything about them, even though he was also Isham's English publisher at the Clarendon Press.

When Isham found out in March 1936, he was devastated. Now he not only owned just two-thirds of the known Boswell papers, but he also feared that the saleability and authority of the Malahide Edition would be undermined by this fact. Moreover, the legal wrangle over ownership and publication rights of the Fettercairn papers promised to drag on for at least a year, and he had a vital stake in a decision in favour of the Talbots, who had agreed to let him have the papers at no extra cost if they were granted ownership.

In his efforts to help the lawyers, in March 1937 Isham ransacked Malahide Castle again looking for pertinent family papers. Astonishingly, he came up with more Boswelliana in a tin dispatch box in the strong-room, including a small diary of Dr Johnson's, more journal fragments, and a few letters. The Talbots generously gave all of it to him. He and Lady Talbot were now convinced that there were no unexamined corners left at Malahide.

The Court of Session eventually judged that the Talbots were entitled to half of the Fettercairn papers, and the Cumberland Infirmary the other half. This was a partial victory for Isham and a reason to rejoice, especially as the Cumberland Infirmary seemed interested in selling their share to him. But their ambivalence delayed things, as did the outbreak of war and Isham's financial difficulties, which now included a debt to Van Alen of almost $150,000 and a precipitous decline in his income from investments.

Then, in January 1941, word came from Lady Talbot that in a grain loft in one of the farm buildings at Malahide two large packing cases had surfaced, stuffed with Boswell papers. Isham was shattered by the news, especially when he was told that the find included nothing less than the complete manuscript of the *Life of Johnson* (except for the fragments he already owned) as well as many more letters. Lady Talbot wished to sell the former for the benefit of air-raid victims in Ayrshire, but Isham, desperate, insisted on his right to this El Dorado of manuscripts according to previous legal agreements. But he had a very weak case and only managed to antagonize the Talbots in the process. This new discovery also muddied the legal waters relating to the Cumberland Infirmary, and Isham unfortunately was persuaded to back off from a reasonable deal to acquire the other half of the Fettercairn papers for the time being. The Infirmary decided to auction their papers, and the Talbots, although they understood and felt for Isham's troubles, decided to do nothing about their priceless manuscript until the end of the war. The whole business was, in Isham's words, 'a damnable mess'.

After the war, Isham bought the new papers (except for the *Life*) from Lady Talbot for the ridiculously low price of £1,750. They included about 250 letters from Boswell and well over 500 letters to him, as well as valuable miscellaneous documents such as the nearly complete manuscript of Dr Johnson's *The Vanity of Human Wishes* and eighty-five more pages of the journal. Such numbers and documents are numbing, especially after all the previous discoveries, and one has to pinch oneself to comprehend the vastness of what was still turning up. Isham could not have paid even this modest amount without the appearance of a new collector-hero, Donald F. Hyde, a lawyer, who with his wife Mary went on to create one of the most precious libraries of eighteenth-century works in the world at Four Oaks Farm in Princeton, New Jersey. Hyde became a great defender and supporter of Isham and immediately began to lend him interest-free money. When Isham and the Hydes opened the trunk of papers in a hotel room in New York, they enjoyed what was described as a 'collector's orgy'. This batch alone rivalled the bulk of the Fettercairn papers.

The *Life* manuscript remained at Malahide. In the meantime, Isham again set about trying to prise the Fettercairn papers from the Cumberland Infirmary. Without it, no university would be willing to buy his collection, which he badly needed to sell to save himself from bankruptcy. 'What a lot of headaches and heartaches Mr Boswell has given us!' he wrote to his lawyer in Scotland.[5] In May 1947 he completed the purchase for £2,250. After twelve years of financial struggle and delicate negotiations, all the Fettercairn Boswell papers were finally his. They were despatched on the *Queen Mary* on 23 July. When their arrival in New York on the 28th was announced on CBS News all the main newspapers carried stories about it. Isham's photograph appeared on the front page of the *New York Times* and Herman W. Liebert of Yale described his acquisition as 'the greatest collection of manuscript material that has ever been assembled about a single man or a single period'. The material was not, he wrote, just old letters and papers, 'but the potentiality of growing

wise beyond the dreams of scholarship about one of the greatest periods
in human history'.[6] Isham finally received wide public acknowledgement
of his enormous service to literary scholarship.

On 28 June 1949, Isham sold his entire collection, except for a few
items which he sold to Hyde or kept as mementos, to Yale University for
$450,000. In 1950 Yale was also delighted to acquire the thousand-plus
pages of the *Life* from Lady Talbot for the extremely low price of £8,000.
And when the Hydes went to Ireland to pick up the priceless manuscript,
they discovered that Lady Talbot had still more Boswell papers for Isham:
important and totally unexpected additions to the journals and the *Tour
to the Hebrides*, more than two hundred letters to and from Boswell, and
other significant documents. These were part of the grain-loft discovery
that she had forgotten about and they were bought by Yale for £2,500.
Boswell manuscripts have continued to trickle in ever since.

Almost immediately an editorial committee, headed by Pottle, was
formed to supervise the vast Yale Boswell project in the so-called 'Boswell
Factory' in Sterling Library. Boswell's *London Journal*, the first of the
Trade Editions of the journals, was published in 1950. There would be
thirteen more, the last of which appeared in 1989. The volumes in the
Research Edition of the letters and other documents, models of modern
literary scholarship, continue to appear half a century later.

Prologue

'I was born with a melancholy temperament. It is the temperament of our family.' With these words, James Boswell at the age of twenty-four began the 'Sketch' of his early life for Jean-Jacques Rousseau.[1] Although the immediate objective of the 'Sketch' was to win him an interview with the great man at his home in Môtiers in Switzerland, there is no reason to doubt Boswell's sincerity on the matter of his melancholy. Education had aggravated, even caused, much of the problem, but the misery was the melancholy itself, beside which all other problems paled. The 'black demon' or 'English sickness' was indefatigable, never far away, always preying on him, always affecting the way he lived his life. Life was horrible when he had an attack, and even when his mind was clear he spent much of the time thinking about the disease, fearing it, speculating on how to cure or lessen it, defining and describing it, writing about it in his journals. If he could only suppress it, he could plan and live his life like a normal human being. But nothing worked. He had other distinct character flaws that vied for supremacy with his sincerity and good nature, but it may safely be said that melancholy determined the course of Boswell's existence. It is therefore crucial, before beginning his story, to pause to consider of what stuff his melancholy was made.

From the sixteenth to the eighteenth centuries, melancholy appears to have been, in one form or another, a uniquely English affliction. It was popular and mysterious enough to prompt Robert Burton to write *The Anatomy of Melancholy* (1621), an eccentric, ingenious, encyclopaedic account of all that was known of the ailment by the mid-seventeenth century. In the eighteenth century there was an epidemic of the sickness, as well as an increasingly scientific grasp of melancholy as people with some medical and clinical experience began to write about it. But the descriptive terms that are called up, among them depression, the vapours, the spleen, and hypochondriasis, all terms for milder states of gloom, were used loosely and interchangeably, so that one is not always certain how grievous a person's affliction was, how close to 'madness' it brought him.[2] The incidence of suffering writers and artists led to the documentation of many cases of melancholy. From personal experience, Matthew Green wrote a popular poem, *The Spleen*, on the subject and William Cowper, who suffered painfully and acutely throughout his poetic career, commiserated over it in letters to friends who were also victims and poeticized it in his long poem, *The Task*. Edward Young, famous for his Gothic masterpiece, *Night Thoughts*, often deployed images of melancholy that he drew from his own encounters with the malady. Another hostage to melancholia was the poet William Collins, whom Dr Johnson described as languishing 'some years under that depression of mind which enchains the faculties without destroying them, and leaves reason the knowledge of right without the power of pursuing it'.[3]

Next to Cowper and Boswell, perhaps the most famous depressive is Samuel Johnson himself. From an early age he dreaded that his 'vile melancholy' would one day slide him irrevocably into insanity. This explained much of his behaviour, such as his disinclination to be alone and his horror of indolence and vacant thought which he believed were fertile soil for rapacious fancy and pernicious self-consciousness. A friend and one of Johnson's first biographers, Arthur Murphy, feelingly pictured his misery:

> Indolence was the time of danger: it was then that his spirits, not employed abroad, turned with inward hostility against himself ... He tells us that, when he surveyed his past life, he discovered nothing but a barren waste of time, with some disorders of body, and disturbances of mind, very near to madness. His life, he says, from his earliest youth, was wasted in a morning bed; and his reigning sin was a general sluggishness, to which he was always inclined, and, in part of his life, almost compelled, by morbid melancholy and a weariness of mind. This was his constitutional malady, derived, perhaps, from his father, who was, at times, overcast with a gloom that bordered on insanity.[4]

In *Rasselas*, Johnson stressed that overactive fancy and imagination incite much of the victim's misery – 'All power of fancy over reason is a degree of insanity' – and wraps him in an inescapable cycle of vain hopes, crushing despair, and an unutterable sense of waste:

He then expatiates in boundless futurity and culls from all imaginable conditions that which for the present moment he should most desire, amuses his desires with impossible enjoyments, and confers upon his pride unattainable dominion. The mind dances from scene to scene, unites all pleasures in all combinations, and riots in delights, which nature and fortune, with all their bounty, cannot bestow.

Johnson's definition of melancholy in his *Dictionary* leaves us in no doubt that he regarded it as a physical disease: 'a kind of madness, in which the mind is always fixed on one object'; 'a disease, supposed to proceed from a redundance of black bile; but it is better known to arise from too heavy and too viscid blood: its cure is in evacuation, nervous medicines, and powerful stimuli'; 'a gloomy, pensive, discontented temper'. He defines hypochondriacal as 'disordered in the imagination'. In common with Boswell and most melancholics, for Johnson the affliction was compounded by a religious guilt. In some way the mental infirmity was God's punishment for sins, rendering the victim unworthy of Christ's redemption. The latter fear was in itself blasphemous, which in turn deepened the guilt and dejection. At the very least, thinking of melancholy as a sin clouded religious optimism.

In Boswell's view, though, Johnson did not understand the affliction as well as he did and was insufficiently informed about it. He devoted countless entries in his journals to examining and mourning his own states of depression, comparing them to each other and to those of fellow sufferers. 'I am really an instrument very easily put out of tune,' he wrote; 'I require the nicest and most delicate management.'[5] He wrote essays about melancholy and his letters are full of the subject. Neither Boswell nor Johnson, however, in common with the wisdom of their day, understood the difference between psychotic and non-psychotic depressive states. Boswell was aware that his gloom was either more or less severe than that of others, but he had little sense of the gradations in the milder forms or how they differed from manic states, melancholia, or madness. It was all rather impressionistic and his futile efforts to heal himself seem to us pathetic and pitiable. He called his mental disorder hypochondria or 'hyp' for short, and himself a 'hypochondriack', not to be confused with what we associate with psychosomatic or psychoneurotic illness today. In one of several essays on hypochondria Boswell wrote for the *London Magazine* between 1777 and 1783, drawing on his own experience, he observed somewhat vaguely, 'Perhaps there is a distinction between Melancholy and Hypochondria ... In my opinion, however, they are

only different shades of the same disease, for I know that what ... poets
[have] so strongly painted has been felt by the same person in the
gradations of his continued distress.'[6] William Cullen, who differentiated
scientifically between hypochondriasis and the more severe melancholia
or insanity, summarized the former in this way:

> In certain persons there is a state of mind distinguished by a concurrence of
> the following circumstances: A languor, listlessness, or want of resolution
> and activity with respect to all undertakings; a disposition to seriousness,
> sadness, and timidity; as to all future events, an apprehension of the worst
> or most unhappy state of them; and therefore, often upon slight grounds, an
> apprehension of great evil. Such persons are particularly attentive to the state
> of their own health, to even the smallest change of feeling in their bodies.[7]

Boswell did not think of himself and other hypochondriacks as diseased with melancholia, or psychotic states of madness or insanity. He
saw his affliction as milder, a loose-knit malaise consisting of illness,
worry and depression, though as we shall see, several of his severer attacks
are distinguishable as the more furious 'vexations of madness'. Anyone
like himself with a melancholy temperament, inherited as his was from
relatives or, as was also his fate, aggravated by upbringing and education,
was vulnerable at any time, without warning, to the odd thought, recollection, or association. A smell could set it off, a sound, a sight. A
happy visit to Oxford, for example, could be turned to 'flattened spirits'
by the sight of ancient academic buildings: 'from my old notions of a
college taken from those at Edinburgh and Glasgow, I had a kind
of horror upon me from thinking of confinement and other gloomy
circumstances.'[8] He knew that if he exerted himself, these wretched
attacks of blackness would pass eventually and could be controlled, if
never permanently cured: 'There is not the least doubt that Hypochondria, as well as fire, may be checked, if diligence, sufficiently early
and sufficiently vigorous, be used.' He admitted that 'the smoke and the
melancholy' may with their intensity at times incapacitate the poor
tortured soul, but cheerful companions can then come to the rescue 'by
playing their pleasantry upon the mind' and thus dispelling the 'dreary
clouds'. Although any amount of amusement or business would often
prove fruitless and only divine intervention seemed likely to help, Boswell
courageously insisted, 'We should ... guard against imagining that there
is a volcano within us, a melancholy so dreadful that we can do nothing
in opposition to it.'[9]

Another aspect of Boswell's suffering was the abrupt alternation of unnatural depression and very high spirits. This frenzy or mania typically showed itself in extravagant conduct and drunkenness, a 'conflagration' of the spirits.[10] As smoke breaks into flame, so the blackness of melancholy erupts into the brighter and more fruitful realm of extreme and irrational energy. This pattern explains much of Boswell's volatility, his incarnation of opposites. He worried about it but he was also proud of it. He opened his first essay on hypochondria for the *London Magazine* with this question from Aristotle: 'Why is it that all men who have excelled in philosophy, in politicks, in poetry, or in the arts, have been subject to melancholy?'[11] Indeed, Burton had touched on a common Renaissance theme that survived into the eighteenth century when he reminded his readers that melancholy was a mixed blessing. Imaginative souls are most prone to attacks, for (again to use Boswell's image) fire burns most greedily where there is much combustible material to feed it. At the same time, the fire heats the imagination, rousing it almost manically into periods of intense creativity. The intellect soars and fancies it is a prolific image-maker. At such moments, Boswell often said he was 'heated', though he also used the word to describe the effects of too much wine or of sexual arousal.

There is an element of smugness in this notion: that it is chiefly superior minds and souls which experience the exhilaration; inferior minds may be subject to melancholy, but they are ensnared only in the vaporous, cold, flat, dull, grey, smoky caves of inertia. Imaginative minds are restless minds, and Boswell was nothing if not restless. Here he anticipated the Romantic ethos of mingled brilliance, energy, and destructiveness in the imagination, the flaming taper that consumes itself. As he told John Johnston of Grange (whom he knew as 'Grange'), one of his dearest friends from Edinburgh University days and (he thought) a more severe hypochondriac than himself: 'when we consider what infinite pleasure we feel in our hours of Juvenility, we ought to be content with our fate; as upon the whole we have much more satisfaction than the dull Sons of Equality [i.e., unruffled equanimity] ... O Johnstone Johnstone! what a lively fertile Imagination I have.'[12]

In more studious moods, he denied that there was much to celebrate in being 'exquisitely miserable'. He begged to differ from Aristotle that hypochondriacs were marked by 'superiority': 'many who might have prevented the disease from coming to any height, had they checked its first appearances, have not only not resisted it, but have truly cherished it, from the erroneous flattering notion that they were making sure of

the undoubted though painful characteristick of excellence, as young
ladies submit without complaint to have their ears pierced that they may
be decorated with brilliant ornaments.'[13] Like fever or gout, hypochondria
was no respecter of persons, attacking the dull, the coarse, and the
brilliant alike.

Boswell knew at first-hand that the fire might easily burn out of
control. He constantly had to be on guard against too much 'wildness of
fancy and ludicrous imagination', 'a load of huge imagination'.[14] This
manic exuberance more often than not resulted in dissipation, and then
expired suddenly, leaving little behind in the cold and ashen aftermath
except a painful sense of guilt over his excesses – 'a grief without a pang',
as Coleridge put it: 'We should be particularly careful against resigning
ourselves to the mental distemper, when it vents itself in immoral acts.'[15]
The guilt from dissipation aggravated and, in Boswell's case, often
induced depression. After one such period he complained to Grange: 'I
have of late been rather too dissipated. It is a very unhappy situation of
mind. It debases the soul; deprives it of sollid [sic] Enjoyment, and feeds
it only with frivolous amusement. And yet a Man on whom the gloomy
Daemon of Melancholy takes strong effect is often glad to fly to Dissipation for relief.'[16]

Although he felt that the hypochondriac frequently could not tell
what was depressing his spirits because the symptoms did not 'settle
themselves with any permanent regularity in the memory', in his 'Hypochondriack' essays in the *London Magazine* Boswell made a good stab at
summarizing his particular brand of the black demon for the general
reader. In them he offered a totally honest 'personal testament' of the
medley of distress from which he never escaped and which pervaded his
existence both as a son and a father, from legal practice to politics, writing
to praying, matrimony to whoring, and sycophancy to lairdship. Languor punished him the most. His letters and journals unremittingly
bear witness to this. He was frozen in his tracks by it, which
for a man of his vivacity of imagination, as he puts it, was especially
grievous:

While in that situation, time passes over him, only to be loaded with regrets.
The important duties of life, the benevolent offices of friendship are neglected
... To pay a visit or write a letter to a friend, does not surely require
much activity; yet such small exertions have appeared so laborious to a
Hypochondriack, that he has delayed from hour to hour, till friendship has
grown cold for want of having its heat continued ...

The worst effect of languor on a man of Boswell's extremely convivial nature was his irritability towards even his closest friends: 'the company of those whom he loves and values is a burthen to him ...'[17] At such times, he would say and do things that later filled him with remorse and deepened his dejection. His intimate friends understood his temperament and made huge allowances for it.

Notwithstanding his open character and audacious and spirited conquests of great men, Boswell lacked self-confidence. Hypochondria lay at the root of this too. Self-deprecation became second nature to him. His account of how, during depression, he could be assaulted by disordering thoughts of inferiority and failure is dismal. Such a multitude of black thoughts left a heaviness in his self-image; it was not like a bad dream from which he could awaken:

His [the hypochondriack's] opinion of himself is low and desponding. His temporary dejection makes his faculties seem quite feeble. He imagines that every body thinks meanly of him. His fancy roves over the variety of characters whom he knows in the world, and except some very bad ones indeed, they seem all better than his own. He envies the condition of numbers, whom, when in a sound state of mind, he sees to be far inferior to him. He regrets his having ever attempted distinction and excellence in any way, because the effect of his former exertions now serves only to make his insignificance more vexing to him. Nor has he any prospect of more agreeable days when he looks forward. There is a cloud as far as he can perceive, and he supposes it will be charged with thicker vapour, the longer it continues.

Because he could not get down to anything, he felt shame and a fear of being despised. The fear could be more general, too, 'horrible imaginings', so that he easily 'starts into the extremes of rashness and desperation' as he ruminated on all the evils that could befall him. The more he thought, the more miserable he became. His 'corrosive imagination' blinded him to good anywhere, even in others: 'All that is illustrious in publick life, all that is amiable and endearing in society, all that is elegant in science and in arts, affect him just with the same indifference, and even contempt, as the pursuits of children affect rational men.' The only help in sight, remote as it may appear to the foundering victim, was piety, and this Boswell recommended vigorously. But piety helped only those who had already firmly grounded themselves in 'holy religion'. They at least had some hope of realizing that the present distresses were only trials for 'the other world'. Dreadful must be the fate of the hypochondriac who, like the brilliant David Hume, had only his religious scepticism and denial of a future state to comfort him. Boswell trembled on behalf of such poor souls.[18]

The unhappy fact about Boswell's history as a hypochondriac is that his extensive reflections on it in essays, letters, and journals did little to improve his condition. He could never write himself out of it. He looked at it from every angle but never really understood it. He sometimes escaped it by escaping from his self, by doing something remarkably out of character or by a dramatic change of scene. His writing, however, even when describing just such a shift, brought him into contact with his self but without being able to lift it out of its gloom. The ultimate dilemma, and what he feared most, was that inertia would block him from writing about his suffocating gloom, from sharing it with others. For Boswell, to whom writing about himself gave reality to existence, to be cut off from personal communication was the greatest curse of hypochondria. He might say bravely to his closest friend, William Temple, 'I have said to the Demon of Hypochondria, as the bold Highlander in *Fingal* says to his Deity of fanciful conjecture, "show yourself to me and I will search thee with my spear",'[19] but his spear (the language of reflection and introspection) could never strike its target.

PART I

Journey to the
Promised Land

1740–1763

ONE

A World of Chimeras

I

'What a world of chimeras had I when young! it is impossible to give a notion of this to others.'[1] This was Boswell's view in 1780, at the age of forty, a year when his imagination was particularly active explaining his early memories and persona, real and imaginary, to his mature mind. But he made such observations throughout his life. His journals and letters are filled with references to his youth, explaining his current behaviour and attitudes in terms of it, romanticizing, fictionalizing, defending, or accusing and lamenting it. His recollections on the whole were unpleasant or tinged with remorse and regret, not because he was obviously mistreated as a child though he had a far from ideal father – but because he was an unconventional boy with an unusual temperament. He never completely outgrew his youth or grew into manhood. He was ever the boy, as Samuel Johnson once put it.

He was an unusual youth partly because, as he wrote in an auto-biographical 'Sketch' for Jean-Jacques Rousseau in 1765, he was 'born with a melancholy temperament ... the temperament of our family'.[2] This made him an easy prey for aggressive sense impressions, both physical and imaginary, not only because pre-adolescent sickliness con-spired with strict Presbyterianism to perpetuate a strong morbid streak in him, but also because he had a highly active and poetic imagination, a sense of enchantment, charming and endearing to many but which no one in his family had the capacity to share. What is clear is that he suffered greatly during his childhood and adolescence.

In 1780 Boswell recalled two kinds of parental influence that plagued him for much of his life: his mother's religious strictness and his father's coldness. He was at this time suffering especially painful periods of self-doubt and hypochondria that coincided with the return of his younger brother David from Valencia after an absence of twelve years. David's return focused his thoughts back to his youth, as if he were trying both to account for how he came to have such an extraordinary personality and to snatch at visions of the boyhood he had somehow lost in the course of his travels, ten years of married life, and drudgery as an Edinburgh advocate.

The New (or High) Church in Edinburgh, part of the old choir of St Giles's Church, the 'shamefully dirty' (in Dr Johnson's judgement) Boswell family house of worship, was being renovated in 1780 with new pews and other improvements. This was the church where, on endless gloomy Presbyterian Sundays through infancy and adolescence, James had sat rigidly and silently in the family pew, haunted with persistent Calvinist fears of the afterlife. Always on the lookout for poignant and personally historic moments that could spur his imagination and which he could record in his journal, but drawn even more by the compulsive memories of his youth, in June he attended the last service before the church closed for repairs.

As he sat in his father's seat, he was caught off-guard. Instead of attending to the service, 'I meditated curiously on my remembering this seat almost as far back as my memory reaches – of my pious mother sitting at the head of it – of my dreary terrors of hell in it – of my having an impression of its being so connected with the other world as to be permanent.' Terrors and superstitions instilled by his mother's scrupulous and suffocating Calvinism mingled with recollections of her saintly and tender warmth. The image of the old seat propelled 'a multitude of ideas ... through my mind'. The cold terrors in the church, even at the age of forty, lived on 'inwardly dark and cold' in his memory and imagination, yet on this occasion his happy mood prevailed and he hoped that the demolition of the family pew would somehow exorcise his fears of death – 'not a vestige of it to be left'.[3]

A sign of his ambivalence towards his mother is evident in his almost complete failure to mention her in his copious journals. One of the two or three exceptions was in August 1780, after listening to four hours of sermons with David before the Sacrament: 'In the evening, retired to my closet and seriously meditated and prayed of my dear mother and prepared for commemorating the death of Christ.' Even his brother, with 'a degree of our family melancholy', was 'cold in spirit' from the service. Though Boswell suffered from Calvinist terrors of the afterlife, a few months earlier he had uncharacteristically frightened his own children with stories of black angels and devils dragging bad people down to hell:

'they were all three suddenly seized with such terror that they cried and roared out and ran to me for protection.' The incident 'vexed' Boswell because he saw that he could not help himself: he had to inflict on his children his own religious nightmares.[4]

Another early memory was revived after he beat his eldest son Sandy for telling a lie. Boswell's father had beaten into him the need for truth and integrity; now he was doing the same to his son:

> I do not recollect having had any other valuable principle impressed upon me by my father except a strict regard for truth, which he impressed upon my mind by a hearty beating at an early age when I lied, and then talking of the *dishonour* of lying. I recollect distinctly having truth and honour thus indelibly inculcated upon me by him one evening in our house...

Paradoxically, here a secular insistence on the truth mingled with memories of cold discipline and fear. If his mother was a warm saint who none the less encouraged in him morbid fears of hell and damnation, his father's coldness and severity ingrained in him candour and accuracy, or to put it negatively, a fear of lying. Boswell's truthfulness as a biographer and autobiographer would bring him fame at home and across Europe, but his father's legacy was not without a codicil of gall. 'He is oak. I am finer but softer wood,' he wrote. His resentment over the beating still lay deep. As in the incident when he terrorized his children with spectral images from hell, he was still the slave of his childhood traumas.[5]

2

Boswell was born into an ancient family which for two-and-a-half centuries had had as its seat the estate of Auchinleck in Ayrshire. Set in a pastoral landscape of rolling hills and green fields twelve miles east of Ayr and the Irish Sea, and within view of the Lanarkshire hills further to the east, Auchinleck House and its more than 20,000 acres inspired virtually all of Boswell's Scottish pride. The ancient heart of Auchinleck was down by the ruins of the Old Castle, in Boswell's time reduced to a ruined keep. This twelfth- or thirteenth-century fortification was the dwelling of the first Auchinleck Boswells, conferred on Thomas Boswell (of the even more venerable Balmuto Boswells in Fife) with extensive Auchinleck lands by James IV of Scotland in 1504 in reward for his valiant services to the Crown.[6] A barony, that also came with the gift,

lasted well into the nineteenth century. Thomas Boswell later fell with
the King on Flodden Field, a heritage that was the stuff of romance for
the young James. The ruins of the keep hung high over steep gullies
carved out by the joining of the Lugar Water and its tributary Dipple
Burn. Today all that is left are a few mounds of stone. It is a dark and
quiet spot, precarious to climb and hidden among thick foliage, shrubs,
exposed roots, and dead and dying trees. The streams below flow quietly,
forgotten. In Boswell's day the place must have been equally remote and
hauntingly dramatic, for in 1789 the antiquary Francis Grose found it
interesting enough to include an engraving of the ruined castle in his
Antiquities of Scotland.

Boswell's pride over his ancestry was underlined every time he took a
walk down to the ruins from the new mansion, or when he showed the
Old Castle to friends or a potential wife. As he wrote to Jean-Jacques
Rousseau in 1764, whom he knew would appreciate the wildness of the
spot, '[From ages 8–12] I read the Roman poets, and I felt a classic
enthusiasm in the romantic shades of our family's seat in the country.'[7]
He impressed Dr Johnson with a similar thought several months after
first meeting him in London: 'He said, "I must be there, and we will live
in the Old Castle; and if there is no room remaining, we will build
one." '[8]

When Boswell triumphantly brought Johnson to Auchinleck in 1773,
it was the environs of the Old Castle that impressed the sage: 'I was . . .
less delighted with the elegance of the modern mansion, than with the
sullen dignity of the old castle.' Boswell's fullest and proudest description
of the ancient scene came years later in his account of showing it to
Johnson in *The Journal of a Tour to the Hebrides* (1785). After informing
Johnson that the name 'Auchinleck' means a 'field of flagstones', not 'a
stony field', he continues:

> On one side of the rock on which its ruins stand runs the river Lugar, which
> is here of considerable breadth, and is bordered by other high rocks, shaded
> with wood. On the other side runs a brook, skirted in the same manner, but
> on a smaller scale. I cannot figure a more romantic scene.
>
> I felt myself elated here, and expatiated to my illustrious mentor on the
> antiquity and honourable alliances of my family, and on the merits of its
> founder, Thomas Boswell . . .[9]

A few yards away, another spot of 'consecrated earth' also spoke of the
past, 'the foundations of an ancient chapel, dedicated to St Vincent,

where in old times "was the place of graves" for the family'. In the *Tour*, he grieves over how his father violated 'the remains of sanctity' there by dragging away stones to build the new mansion in the early 1760s. 'Perhaps this chapel may one day be restored', he reflects. But there were still plenty of 'venerable old trees under the shade of which my ancestors had walked'. And with a truly romantic iconographic instinct, Boswell promises, if he survives Johnson, to add to the *genius loci* by erecting a monument to him there.[10]

This was the romantic-classical Boswell, even as a young boy defining his youthful landscape by merging two traditions: a boy whose neo-classical tastes were acquired through his Edinburgh schooling, but who already felt uncomfortable with his father's cold rationality and felt the compulsion to 'expatiate' in nature's more expansive realm, to roam mentally and physically in larger world of his own image-making. Two hundred and sixty years (and eight generations) of the Boswell lairds of Auchinleck fed his fertile mind. In *Young Boswell* (1922), Chauncey Tinker suggested that Boswell was an early Romantic bound uneasily to the analytical and rational traditions of the eighteenth-century Enlightenment.[11] Auchinleck satisfied his boyish dreams of building castles in the air, inhabiting regions of enchantment, while his Edinburgh boyhood, by his own admission, narrowed his sights and pressed them into the service of Enlightenment civilization, its education, religion, salons, clubs, and family life.

3

Boswell's mother's ancestry contributed another strain of his romantic mythologizing. She and his father, ten years her senior, were cousins, both descended from the second Earl of Kincardine and the Dutch countess Veronica van Aerssen of the distinguished Sommelsdyck family. Boswell would make much of that link with the Dutch aristocracy, especially when he reached Holland in 1763, but there was more. Born Euphemia Erskine, his mother was descended from a minor branch of Scottish royalty: she was the daughter of Lieut.-Col. John Erskine, Deputy Governor of Stirling Castle, and through him the great-grand-daughter of the second Earl of Mar, whose second wife was the daughter of the Duke of Lennox, a first cousin of the Earl of Darnley, King James VI's father. If that is difficult to follow, none the less it is a royal descent. Boswell made much of his royal blood, presenting himself as the future

laird of a family established by a Scottish monarch. His father, so far as
we know, never spoke of such tenuous family connections, at least not
in public, and it is perhaps fortunate that he died three years before
Boswell advertised his royal connection to the world when, in the *Tour
to the Hebrides*, he recalled showing Dr Johnson around the Old Castle:

> in the glow of what, I am sensible, will, in a commercial age, be considered
> as genealogical enthusiasm, [I] did not omit to mention what I was sure my
> friend would not think lightly of, my relation to the Royal Personage,
> whose liberality, on his accession to the throne, had given him comfort and
> independence. I have, in a former page, acknowledged my pride of ancient
> blood, in which I was encouraged by Dr Johnson; my readers therefore will
> not be surprised at my having indulged it on this occasion.

He even planned to include a genealogical table in the *Tour* 'showing the
collateral lines of descent of Me and of both the House of Stuart and the
family now on the throne . . . to point out at one glance my consanguinity
to Royalty past and present'. He added, 'I have the pride of blood in me
to the highest pitch.'[12] While such enthusiasms, privately indulged, were
acceptable in a youth with a romantic outlook, they were unquestionably
embarrassing when publicly aired by a man of forty-five. Fortunately,
the table never appeared.

When Boswell was born in Edinburgh in October 1740, his grandfather James, the seventh Laird of Auchinleck, was still alive. Old James,
as we shall call him, a highly successful advocate who in the wake of the
Revolution dedicated himself to no-nonsense Whig principles and to the
successful aggrandizement of the estate, was once described to young
James, his namesake, as a 'big, strong, Gothic-looking man', a 'man of
weight' and courage. He too was somewhat given to melancholy, and
there was much about him with which young James identified – infinitely
more than with his father. As Boswell wrote in his 'Sketch' of 1765, Old
James 'inherited from his mother a degree of hypochondria. When he
was young he was idle, but his father forced him by beating him with a
rod to apply himself to his studies . . . He was often overcome with a
dark melancholy and as he had been brought up to hide his bad moods
and not to rise above them when he no longer had his father to fear, he
no longer hid them.' He wanted nothing more than to withdraw from
the world, but his wife, 'more healthy and gay', prevented him. After her
death, though, he became something of a recluse at Auchinleck, to his
death plagued with 'a dark mood and . . . rigid religious beliefs', 'doleful

presbyterian dogmas' learned in childhood. In these passages, Boswell embraces a spiritual kinship with his grandfather. He always remained proud of him.[13]

4

In his earliest years Boswell only knew the Old Castle from the occasional visit, but after Old James's death in 1749 he lived at Auchinleck House during holidays. It was an early-seventeenth-century Renaissance mansion built by Thomas Boswell's son David, an appropriate residence for the 'Gothick-looking' grandfather, Boswell may have thought. Curiously, he never spoke of his boyish life and adventures in this house with David and his youngest brother John. His only surviving remark about his early life there was a troubled one, made at the age of fifteen, about the death of a newborn brother. It is the earliest surviving writing in his own hand, a polished, very well-written letter from Auchinleck to his 'mamma' in Edinburgh. After comforting her, he changes the subject abruptly: 'I sometimes try the shooting, and have shot two sparrows, which I know will disoblige my Lord, but as I am sorry for my fault and am henceforth to shoot at other birds, such as magpies and crows, I hope his Lordship will pardon me.'[14] Even in this rural paradise, his father's strictness invaded his romantic dream.

Situated about two hundred yards from the Old Castle and Lugar Water, the house was L-shaped with a tower that may have accommodated the main entrance and a small hall. The top floor of the tower served as a lookout point, with an eye more to local civil disputes and skirmishes during the violent Scottish Reformation than to English incursions since James VI of Scotland assumed the throne of England as James I in 1603. Boswell and his brothers must have relished the watchtower, gazing over miles of Auchinleck acreage and out to the Lanarkshire hills, imagining a wilder and more dangerous time when the Lowlands were particularly vulnerable to English raids.

The residence, surrounded by high walls, was a comfortable and secure laird's house, with a grotto and fine gardens, but its romantic associations apparently were insufficient compensation for its inconvenience and incommodiousness by the time Boswell's family took it over. Neither did its antique and archaic character measure up when, in 1754, Alexander Boswell became Lord Auchinleck, one of the Lords of the Justiciary, an important figure in Scotland's cultural and legal world. His image as a modern man of property required a classically solid and modern mansion in which to welcome society.

The new house, completed in 1762 when Boswell was twenty-two, while not grand was impressive enough for the eminent new judge. Built in the mid-century Adam style with a large central pediment and flanked by curving wings terminating in large stone gazebos, it is decently long, but its narrowness is disappointing. 'It is but a middling house,' wrote the Duchess of Northumberland in 1760, 'but justly, it is a romantick spot.'[15] The dining and drawing rooms were stately, with lovely plaster ceilings, but the staircase was not memorable, and except for the library where Boswell's father and Dr Johnson had a furious argument in 1773, the rooms on the second floor were small. Even so, Catherine Blair, one of Boswell's Scottish matrimonial hopes in 1767, had her head turned by it, telling him bluntly, 'I wish I liked you as well as I do Auchinleck.'[16]

While he admired the elegance of the new mansion, Boswell never outgrew his reverence for the antiquity of the old one which began to crumble with a speed that fed his ready appetite for nostalgia. By the time Francis Grose visited the scene in 1789, the 'old place' had already lost its roof. Just a month after leaving home for his first extended stay in London in the autumn of 1762, for example, he comforted himself that someday he would live with 'serene felicity at the delightful Auchinleck, the ancient seat of a long line of worthy ancestors. Here will I end my days in calm devotion.' He told Lady Northumberland, 'Indeed, Madam, there are more romantic beauties there than at any place I know.' Later, in July 1765, revelling in the Virgilian iconography at Mantua, his thoughts flashed back:

> when I am at Auchinleck in a sweet summer season, my imagination is fully persuaded that the rocks and woods of my ancestors abound in rural genii. There is hardly a classical spot which I have not upon our own estate, and even after having travelled the enchanted land itself, I shall not be deprived of my romantic dreams.[17]

5

But Boswell was born in Edinburgh, not at Auchinleck. He was educated and lived most of his life there. He always had a romantic affection for the city, as revealed in this passage from his first London journal:

O Arthur Seat, thou venerable mountain! whether in the severity of winter thy brow has been covered with snow or wrapped in mist; or in the gentle mildness of summer the evening sun has shone upon thy verdant sides diversified with rugged moss-clad rocks and rendered religious by the ancient Chapel of St Anthony. Beloved hill, the admiration of my youth! Thy noble image shall ever fill my mind! Let me travel over the whole earth, I shall still remember thee; and when I return to my native country, while I live I will visit thee with affection and reverence![18]

Yet he disliked living there. He thought the town was 'narrow' and insular, dull and coarse, oppressive, and depressing, but this, it is well to remember, was the Edinburgh of the Scottish Enlightenment, the 'Athens of the North'. It was an intellectually exciting centre of philosophy, history, medicine, geology, chemistry, political economy, and sociology, and it 'represented the *avant garde* of European thought in these and other subjects, much more so than London'.[19] Even so, the city was simultaneously dark, dirty, cramped, and smelly, not the spaciously beautiful and salubrious metropolis it is today.

The 'Old Town', as Daniel Defoe described it in the 1720s, only about fifteen years before Boswell's birth, was laid out along 'the narrow ridge of a long ascending mountain', with the ground falling off steeply to its north and south. The Castle, perched on the massive Castle Rock, is at the upper west end of the long street which runs along the ridge; a mile away at the east end is Holyrood House, which sits at the base of the famous extinct volcano, Arthur's Seat. In Boswell's youth most of the shops, many of the public buildings, and the general mad bustle of civic life were to be found in the High Street. It overwhelmed the novelist Tobias Smollett when he saw it in 1776, 'all the people of business in Edinburgh, and even the genteel company ... standing in crowds every day, from one to two in the afternoon' hawking their wares, talking commerce, gossiping, commissioning water-caddies or errand-boys, planning the evening's entertainments. Most of the people gathered either at the Market Cross in the middle of the street, or at Parliament Square next to the medieval St Giles's Church, or around the Luck-enbooths, the row of four-storey buildings that ran down the middle of the High Street just a few feet to the north of St Giles's, creating a narrow and tenebrous footpath for pedestrian traffic. Defoe described Edinburgh High Street as 'perhaps, the largest, longest, and finest street for buildings and number of inhabitants, not in Britain only, but in the world'. It was an impressive thoroughfare, to be sure, but not without its incon-veniences, as Defoe saw: 'which way soever you turn, either to the right, or to the left, you go down hill immediately, and that so steep, as is very troublesome to those who walk in those side lanes which they call wynds, especially if their lungs are not very good'.[20]

'Proposals' in 1752 to expand the city to the north compared its layout to a turtle, 'of which the castle is the head, the high street the ridge of the back, the *wynds and closes* the shelving sides, and the palace of Holyroodhouse the tail'.[21] The wynds were very narrow and dark, by day almost always shrouded in half-light and by night impenetrably black except when lighted by the occasional lamp. They descended northward towards the North Loch and southward towards the next major east–west street, the not very healthy Cowgate, where Boswell lived briefly as a married man.

With an increasing shortage of land within the town's medieval walls and a population by the mid-eighteenth century that had reached between thirty and fifty thousand, one of the city's dominant and unique impressions was of towering tenement buildings, mid-eighteenth-century 'skyscrapers' squeezed together, defying light and air to enter in. The only access to the upper floors was by common flights of stairs, up and down which the water-caddies clambered and all manner of goods and waste had daily to be carried – except for what was chucked out of the windows on to the streets and wynds below at around ten in the evening, with a cry of 'Gardyloo!' According to an Englishman A. Topham in 1775, the Town Guard's announcement of that hour was 'a sort of licence for deluging the streets with nuisances and warning the inhabitants home to their beds'. The smell was revolting. There was little exaggeration in the description of such detestable living conditions in the 1752 'Proposals':

The narrow lanes leading to the north and south, by reason of their steepness, narrowness, and dirtiness, can only be considered as so many unavoidable nuisances. Confined by the small compass of the walls, the houses stand more crowded than in any other town in *Europe*, and are built to a height that is almost incredible. Hence necessarily follows a great want of free air, light, cleanliness, and every other comfortable accommodation. Hence also many families, sometimes no less than ten or a dozen, are obliged to live overhead of each other in the same building; where, to all the other incon-veniences, is added that of a common stair, which is no other in effect than an upright street, constantly dark and dirty.

'In no city in the world [do] so many people live in so little room as at Edinburgh,' Defoe concluded.[22] 'Total stagnation', 'narrow notions', 'local prejudices', 'meanness', and pervasive 'ruins' are phrases the 'Proposals' used to whip up the indignation of the populace and foster support for the idea of a fresh, neoclassic, Enlightenment New Town on a blissfully level plain beyond the North Loch. It worked, and in the early 1760s work began swiftly on the expansion according to James Craig's plan. By 1770 people were already leaving the Old Town for the New Town. David Hume, for example, one of the luminaries of the Scottish Enlightenment, moved into an elegant house in St Andrews Square in 1771.

6

Boswell was born on 29 October 1740 in his father's residence on the fourth floor of an old tenement, Blair's Land, in Parliament Close (later renamed Parliament Square). Blair's Land was south of St Giles's in the High Street, around the corner from the law courts. For his father, a member of the Faculty of Advocates since 1729 and appointed in 1754 one of the fifteen distinguished Lords of Session, the family's Edinburgh home could not have been more conveniently situated. Boswell's earliest recollection of Edinburgh was of 1745 when Bonnie Prince Charlie's army 'occupied' the city and he was taken out to see the 'bold' Highlanders camped colourfully beneath Arthur's Seat. He also saw German troops in the streets, brought over by the Government to stem the Jacobite Rebellion. In Germany almost twenty years later he was reminded of them as he watched Hessian troops doing their military drills and wrote a poem to mark the occasion:

> Behold, ye Hessians, from the Shire of Ayr
> A laird whom your moustaches have made stare!
> While a mere child, nor yet advanced to taw [not old enough to
>   play marbles]
> You in Edina's ancient town he saw,
> When the Rebellion you came o'er to quell
> And send, forsooth, the monster back to hell;
> While Arthur's Seat resounded with your drums,
> I saw you buying breeches for your bums;
> But, with your breeches, you were not so stout
> As the bold Highlanders who went without.

Dr Johnson liked to repeat a more personal recollection of Boswell's: 'Boswell, in the year 1745, was a fine boy, wore a white cockade, and prayed for King James, till one of his uncles gave him a shilling on condition that he should pray for King George, which he accordingly did.' The white cockade hints at his fascination with military dress, even at the age of five.[23]

Another more poignant image of his Edinburgh childhood returned in the summer of 1782 when Boswell revisited Parkside, the country house at Newington, a mile or so south of Edinburgh, to which he and his family retreated during the Rebellion. He was dining there with the present resident:

> I went early, that I might walk about the place, where I had not been for thirty-seven years. I was in a calm, pleasing frame, and though I had a very imperfect reminiscence of the particulars, I had much satisfaction in surveying the spot. I went into a park which I clearly recollected, and lay upon a little green rising ground where I had lain when a child; and for a few moments I was as calm and gentle as at that time.

In 1792, during some of the most despairing days of his entire life, he dreamed of the house again: 'A confused jumble of being in a garden and gathering fallen pears, of being at my Father's old house at Parkside, now an inn.' The age of five seemed to him a warm, golden, pastoral dream of innocence. The clouds were gathering, however, over the idyll of youth. The dream was about to darken; he was about to begin school.[24]

7

At five or six, Boswell's father enrolled him in a private academy run by James Mundell, a well-respected institution in the West Bow, the street that twisted its way from the Lawnmarket down to the Grassmarket where public executions were held. The West Bow no longer exists as a connection between the Lawnmarket and Grassmarket, but in Boswell's day it was the only link between the High Street and the residential and commercial areas one hundred feet below. It was also the main route along which condemned prisoners were carried between the Tolbooth above (Edinburgh's city prison, the 'Heart of Midlothian' in Sir Walter Scott's novel), which was a prominent and unsavoury part of the Luckenbooths, to the place of execution at the bottom. Robert Chambers, in his *Traditions of Edinburgh* (1823), described the West Bow as a 'curious, angular, whimsical looking street of great steepness and narrowness',[25] replete with legends of ghosts, apparitions, witches, and the like. A famous story dating from the late seventeenth century that particularly struck Sir Walter Scott concerned a Major Weir and his sister who were accused of incest and witchcraft. He was murdered and she was hanged in the Grassmarket, but their apparitions were believed to linger around the entrance to the court of their house that little James, clinging fearfully to a servant or his mother, had to pass every day to and from school.[26]

It was not only the West Bow that terrified him. Any of Edinburgh's dark and forbidding streets, wynds, and passageways could also arouse his fear. Even before he began school he was a nervous and timid child, as well as delicate and superstitious. As he acknowledged in a portion of his autobiographical 'Sketch' (in French) in December 1764 that did not find its way into the final version for Rousseau, his acute fear of ghosts and darkness plagued him from his Mundell days right up to his late teens: 'Spirit crushed, no noble hope. Terribly afraid of ghosts. Up to eighteen could not be alone at night. Got over it by a habit of not thinking, not by reasoning about it. Afraid of the cold and everything else. A complete poltroon in the streets of Edinburgh.' He attributes his insecurity to the family's melancholy strain that he inherited: 'Black ideas even at that age. Ignorant – terrified by everything I did not understand.'[27] It is just as likely, however, that the servants in Blair's Land had something to do with his fear of ghosts and darkness since for years they tormented him with what for a young boy were harrowing tales of goblins, murders, and witches, many of them taken from Scottish lore and history.

The school got him off to a good start in Latin, English, writing, and arithmetic, but he hated it for all of the two or three years he attended. He found it too boisterous and robust. He certainly was not spared the rod there, just as he was not later when tutored at home. For boys of a nervous disposition like himself, Boswell writes, there was a danger either that they 'will fall into a debility which will completely destroy them, or that they will form a habit of viewing everything in such colours as to make their lives miserable'. He recalled of this period:

> I was brought up very tenderly. Consequently I began at any early age to be indisposed, and people pitied me as a very delicate child. My mother was extremely kind, but she was too anxious when I had some small ailment. If I did not feel well, I was treated with excessive attention. I was not made to go to school, which I detested. She gave me sweetmeats and all sorts of pretty

things to amuse me. When my health was restored, my slavery would begin again. I knew it, and I preferred being weak and ill to being strong and healthy.

The little actor played his part too well, and his main audience was his mother. Instead of feeling misery in illness, he exulted in it; he did not struggle against real or imaginary sickness, for this would have brought an end to his mother's nursing and landed him back at school. He 'encouraged' his illnesses, 'and instead of jumping and running about, I lolled in an arm-chair. I was discontented and capricious.' Such were his father's stern lessons on honesty that the one thing he would not do was lie by saying he was ill when he was well. Instead, 'I hung my head down towards the floor until I got a headache, and then I complained that I was ill.' He fooled everyone but also found himself in a no win scenario with his relentlessly negative prospects.[28]

Boswell's mother was his major accomplice in Blair's Land, and his devotion to her knew no bounds. She 'lovingly' brought him up, he wrote in a working draft of his 'Sketch', but in a passage he deleted from the final version he stated flatly that his own emotional instabilities developed out of hers. Ten years younger than his robust father, she married him when she was 'a very delicate young lady who was very melancholy ["hypochondre"] and who had been raised completely away from the world with scrupulous pious and visionary notions'. Boswell thought of telling Rousseau that, remarkably, she once wept 'when they forced her to go to the theatre, and she never went back there'. Though she was 'the most admirable mother of a family' because, unlike her husband, she concerned herself with 'temporal things' and thus made sure 'the interests of the family were looked after, and my dear mother had none of the ill nature of the idle devout', the end result was that he was very 'badly raised'.[29]

It was during this time that her Calvinism conspired with James's superstitions and fears to produce an essentially gloomy and withdrawn boy. Writing of his early years, he aimed his lamentations on childhood repression at what he was sure would be Rousseau's sympathetic ear. Still, there is no reason to doubt the veracity of his 'Sketch' since he reiterated many of these unhappy recollections throughout his life. His 'extremely pious' mother inspired him with 'devotion', but her Calvinism also inspired the 'gloomiest doctrines of that system'. His first 'great idea' as a boy was the 'eternity of punishment'.[30]

'I should have wished to go to heaven if there had been any other way of not going to hell. I imagined that the saints passed the whole of eternity in the state of mind of people recently saved from a conflagration, who congratulate themselves on being in safety while they listen to the mournful shrieks of the damned.' This is not an easy burden for any small boy to bear, and in eighteenth-century Presbyterian Edinburgh it was not uncommon. Euphemia Erskine Boswell, according to her son, was 'of that sect which believes that to be saved, each individual must experience a strong conversion. She therefore entreated me often to yield to the operations of Divine Grace: and she put in my hands a little book in which I read of the conversions of very young children.' One of these children, he remembers, was only three. 'O enlightened philosopher', he appealed to Rousseau in another passage he deleted from the final version:

tell me, how can a child conceive that millions deserve to be punished for the sin of only one? Profound theologians. Confess like men. Would this idea not shock the natural spirit? You have reasonings to make it fit divine justice. But do you think that a child is capable of understanding them? But you say it's always good to fix important truths in tender minds and when your pupil is capable of believing them he will have the advantage of having them printed in his memory. But, friends, let's leave that. Don't be afraid that important truths will be rejected because the words haven't been memorized. No, when a young man who has a sound mind hears the truth he recognizes it at once. He takes hold of it with virile joy. He will keep it all his life if you are careful not to confuse his memory by piling a lot of things one on top of the other.

Like Blake's chimneysweep, he was 'taught to sing the notes of woe' as parents and theologians 'make a heaven of our misery'. 'My imagination was continually in a state of terror. I became the most timid and contemptible of beings.'[31]

8

In 1749 Old James died and Alexander Boswell became the eighth Laird of Auchinleck. Now during the holiday periods between the court sessions the family retreated to Auchinleck instead of remaining in Edinburgh or residing nearby at Newington or elsewhere. As these were long holidays, a total of six months from August to November and March to June, Lord Auchinleck naturally desired his family to be with him and did not want his movements to be cramped by school terms. In March 1748 he was appointed Sheriff Depute of Wigtownshire, which required him to stay for some weeks in that county, and he wanted his family to be with him there too. For these periods, therefore, the children were withdrawn from school and educated at home.[32]

As a father, Alexander Boswell was inflexible and cold, without much love to draw on when any of his sons, especially James, tested his patience. A successful advocate (the Scottish term for barrister) and one of the fifteen Lords of Session, he was among the most highly respected men of law in Scotland and also well known in England. Wearing a full-bottomed wig and arrayed in a gown of purple cloth and crimson velvet with long white cravats, he stood the picture of perfect authority, highly intimidating to his sons. James never ceased to be proud of him and to respect him deeply. Like any normal son, he wanted nothing more than to please his powerful father. But the two were as different as father and son could be, and from those differences of disposition and temperament – one 'sollid and composed', the other 'light and restless'[33] – sprang deep antipathies that traced one of the most disastrous and sorrowful patterns in the son's life. In his journals, until his father's death in 1782 and even afterwards, Boswell is constantly angry and desperately disappointed with his father, but at times he touchingly sees, or tries to see, his father's good qualities. His opinions veer endlessly between love and hate, pride and disgust, forgiveness and blame. To be fair, his father always wanted the best for his eldest son, but their ideas on this differed so widely that they might as well have been living on different planets.

Boswell's ambivalence towards his father is evident in his 'Sketch': he protected his father's image by virtually leaving him out of it. All he said was, 'My father, who is one of the ablest and worthiest men in the world, was very busy and could not take much immediate care of my education. He did as others do and trusted me to teachers.' In one of the earlier drafts of the 'Sketch', he wrote that while his father had 'the happiest of temperaments' and 'the most robust of bodies', with (unlike his two brothers) no trace of melancholy, he was nevertheless 'not concerned immediately with my upbringing'. That was aggravated by his marrying a 'delicate young lady' with hypochondria.[34]

9

Life improved for James when he began his schooling at home. His first tutor was John Dun, a handsome minister of twenty-five. A man of sentiment and sensibility, and of some learning though of little imagination and few elegant manners, Dun introduced his eight-year-old ward to the Roman poets and Joseph Addison's civilizing *Spectator* papers. 'He began to form my mind in a manner that delighted me', with 'notions of taste' and the pleasures of reflecting on 'the variety of human nature'. But equally important was Dun's lighter approach to religion, his descriptions of heaven as a desirable place with beautiful music where the boy would acquire 'sublime knowledge' from God and meet up with all his dear friends and the authors he had studied. The warming Christian Humanist influence of this gracious message was balm to the boy's soul. He fell in love with heaven and began to think of religion more in terms of hope than damnation. His health also improved.

But Sundays remained miserable. Three gloomy sermons in the New Church with painfully dull impromptu prayers and tediously sung Psalms, 'all rendered in a stern and doleful manner', replaced Ovid and the *Spectator*. In the evening, it was all topped off with catechisms and more Psalms recited in the 'vilest doggerel'. He was prevented from doing his work, speaking his own words, and thinking his own thoughts – 'A fine exercise for a child's mind!' The only way to bring an early end to this misery was to go to bed early.[35] For the rest of Boswell's life a cloudy and lonely Sunday would guarantee an attack of hypochondria and render him listless and despondent.

A setback occurred when he was twelve, in the autumn of 1752. After more than three years, Lord Auchinleck promoted Dun to the living at Auchinleck and replaced him as tutor with Joseph Fergusson, 'a big lout, good man with book learning [but with] no taste – no delicacy', as Boswell put it. A man in his early thirties who still had not landed a parish living and would not for several years, Fergusson was learned enough but lacked Dun's warmth of feeling for the arts and literature. He was also a harsh mentor in religion, a disastrous and insensitive choice for a boy of twelve who ached to travel widely with the poets and luxuriate in the achievements of the human mind. In a letter (in 1763) to his college friend John Johnston, Boswell remembered Fergusson delivering his dull dinner benedictions 'stiff as the lofty tree in the forest' in 'phrase correct as ever issued'. In another letter to Johnston that year, he reminded his friend cuttingly of Fergusson's 'velvet bretches, his grizly wig ... his systematical morality ... [and] his excellent equivocations'. He quickly discovered that if Fergusson enjoyed literature, he surely did not show or share it:

> He made me read the ancient authors, but without getting any pleasure from them. ... When I asked him questions about the poets, for instruction or amusement – and why should I not have looked for amusement? – he lost his temper and cried out with a schoolmaster's arrogance, 'Come, come, keep at work, keep at work, don't interrupt the lesson. Time is flying.'

He blamed Fergusson for teaching him Latin and Latin authors well but without pleasure: 'It was enough to say that I had read such and such an author.'[36]

Fergusson appears to have brought on in his ward another psychosomatic illness. Before long he lost him to Moffat in the Lowlands, a small and then unsophisticated watering-place north of Dumfries, where James was sent to take the curative sulphurous waters. This illness began with a severe cold, but strong medicines and a weak stomach led to serious digestive problems. The boy's aversion to his tutor and the soulless lessons did the rest, as he told his confessor Rousseau:

> The greatest doctors in Scotland were called in. I was naughty enough to take measures to prevent their medicines from having any effect on me. I could somehow or other control the operations of my stomach, and I immediately threw up everything they made me take. I even endured blisters, congratulating myself on not having to *work*.

While the Faculty of Medicine at Edinburgh University was deciding he was suffering from a mysterious nervous illness, Boswell laughed inwardly at their consultations, lolled about in armchairs, and prayed for deliverance. He grew ever weaker in body and mind, contracting anaemia and scurvy from malnutrition and allowing his 'natural melancholy' to increase dangerously.[37] The twelve-year-old was cutting himself off from mother and father and, painful as it was, retreating into his own pitiable counterfeit refuge.

Moffat was the only solution anyone could come up with. It does not take much imagination to suspect that Boswell's father was not displeased to get him out of the house for a while and end the continual moping and groaning. Perhaps even his mother was glad of a little peace and quiet. Fergusson, whom Boswell a few years later describes as his 'supervisor' at

Moffat, 'a barbarian of a Presbyterian preacher', accompanied him. In spite of Fergusson's dour presence, this visit to Moffat turned out to be a very bright interval for James.

Amid spectacular hills and lochs in the Border country, Moffat provided his first taste of freedom from family and claustrophobic Edinburgh. It was only a village, with a couple of inns and little else in the way of a social life, but Boswell drank from the springs, bathed in the warm baths, enjoyed the company, and quickly got better. He had always liked to soak his feet in warm water, but here he could immerse his whole body like the Romans. He was not exactly pampered, as he recalled in October 1763:

> Truly, without exaggeration, one cannot imagine anything more consoling than after a day of annoyance and fatigue to undress and stretch one's self out at full length in fluid warmth, to have one's nerves gently relaxed, to enjoy indolent ease and forget all one's cares. I experienced a little of that enjoyment when I was at Moffat in Scotland for the mineral waters. But my pleasure was very crude because I was taking the baths for my health, and there were no conveniences for bathing for pleasure. I was put into a horrible tub, a scanty covering was thrown over me, and in that state I was obliged to remain for half an hour. Even worse, Fergusson was watching the whole time, calling out to me from time to time in a harsh voice, 'Take care, you rogue! If we see the least disobedience to our orders, we shall proceed to instant punishment.' And that is why I kept quiet, though I was extremely bored.[38]

As his scorbutic complaint disappeared, his melancholy gave way to a taste for liveliness. He savoured his freedom. He was permitted 'a great deal of amusement' with convivial people and probably a good deal of card-playing. It was there, too, that he discovered sexual sensation, as he wrote in some cancelled notes for Rousseau: 'Already pleasure in climbing trees. could not conceive it. thought of heaven (the sky) – returned often climbed – thought letting myself drop from the high branches in ecstasy – quite natural. Talked to the gardener about it. He, rigid, did not explain it.'[39]

Trees were one thing, girls another. He fell 'deeply' in love with a Miss Mackay who was staying in Moffat for a spell. When he met her again – 'a pretty, agreeable creature' – in 1763 after she had married, she asked him whether he remembered her from Moffat. She said she would not tell him her name if he could not remember her. He racked his brain and, never one to forget a pretty face even if he had first seen it when he was only thirteen, came up with the first letter of her name, which was good enough for her. He also remembered that Fergusson had discovered his passion and 'ridiculed [it] most roughly by setting his teeth together and giving hard thumps on the knees of his breeches'. It was 'the pleasing anguish of a genuine flame', although he did not tell Miss Mackay that. Later he interpreted for Rousseau these early sensual stirrings on behalf of 'the rites of Venus': 'Melancholy temperaments are given to love. I swear to you that before the age of twelve I felt all that the soul can know of this passion. Carnal desires had not yet their full strength. They would develop in the most singular fashion.'[40]

TWO

Edinburgh Gloom

I

James returned to Edinburgh from Moffat to endure his 'surly tutor' for only a few months more. The summer came and passed, and in October 1753, around the time of his thirteenth birthday, he enrolled in Edinburgh University, or the Old College of James VI, as it was called after its founder. His entrance at that age did not mean he was especially precocious, thirteen then being the normal age for admittance. Nor did he enter the university as we know it today. Robert Adam's classical designs, commissioned and begun in 1789 but not completed (in altered style) until the early nineteenth century by William Playfair, transformed out of all recognition what Boswell would have known. He attended classes in 'a mass of ruined buildings' built in the sixteenth century, thought by many scarcely a fit place to educate the youth of Scotland. The classrooms were spare and austere, the library in a restored upper gallery, with a handful of meagre chambers for resident students and equally shabby rooms for the professors. William Robertson, the historian of Scotland later much admired by Boswell, who in 1762 began his brilliant tenure as Principal of the College, described the three disconnected 'paltry' buildings as easily mistakable for 'almshouses for the reception of the poor'. There were about one thousand students studying there in 1753.[1]

It was not long after James walked through the doors of the College that he realized his 'narrow education' at home for the past four years had bred in him a social inferiority complex. His retrospective remarks on his two tutors in an early draft of the 'Sketch' are so scathing on account of this that he decided he could not show them even to Rousseau; and perhaps he was also reluctant to admit to a feeling of inferiority that he feared might make Rousseau lose interest in him. He was freer in College than he had ever been, and in good health, though from time to time a little melancholic, but he suffered acutely from lack of confidence:

> My tutors had both been unmannered people, men of the lowest sort of breeding. They were like my father's servants. They ate at our table but hardly dared open their mouths. I noted that they were held in scorn. And yet they had sufficient influence to inspire in me cowardly, lowly feelings. I believed that all those who were a bit better dressed and could speak without fear were my superiors. I trembled before a lord and would have felt honored to be the coachman of a duke. Such puerile and unworthy notions occupied the mind of a university student.

Paradoxically, his family's history also promoted an adolescent sense of social superiority to the 'vulgar throng' around him. He matriculated convinced that he was 'a little different from my companions' who, he found, had none of that 'high-mindedness and delicacy of taste which I believed existed in mankind and which I hoped might exist in me one day'.[2]

A student at the College of Edinburgh matriculated in 'public' classes as part of a course leading to an MA, which is the degree still awarded to all undergraduates at Scottish universities. Few students at the College in the eighteenth century actually took a degree, however, as the main purpose of the instruction was to prepare a student for a more specialized course such as the law or medicine, the equivalent of a university degree today. In addition to the 'public' classes in which students formally matriculated, professors offered 'private' classes at a higher standard, for which the students paid them directly. Students studied mostly Greek and Latin in 'public' classes during their first two years, continuing them in the 'private', more advanced, classes in the later years, when they would be supplemented chiefly by logic and natural and moral philosophy as well as other 'electives' such as astronomy and mathematics.[3]

Boswell was well prepared and successful academically. His father, a well-known classicist with a fine library at Auchinleck, had given him a shilling for every ode of Horace he learned by heart, and at one point he could repeat 'upwards of forty of them'. He distinguished himself right away in Latin, if we can believe his own words on the subject: 'I liked languages. I applied myself and my professors praised me highly and put it into my head that I was an extraordinary genius, that I would surely be a very great man who would do great honour to his country.'[4]

The 'public' classes in Latin were probably all he attended during the first two years. He continued with private Latin and mathematics and began public Greek in his third year; studied logic, private Latin, and private Greek in his fourth; and natural philosophy (physics), moral philosophy and French in his fifth.[5] It was an ideal course of study for someone earmarked by recent family tradition for the law. Indeed, while he was completing the arts course in his fifth year, he may even have begun studies in civil law, which he continued in a dilatory and chequered sixth year.

Neither George Stuart nor Robert Hunter, the Latin and Greek professors, was particularly inspiring, though they were competent. Stuart was known as a sound and tasteful scholar who encouraged his students to see the beauties of the classics, but who failed to stimulate them into critical discussions. Hunter was one of the finest classical scholars in Scotland, but taught like a dull country schoolmaster. His interest in the boys was minimal and for years Boswell could not expel his provincial accent from his mind – 'jeel' for 'jelly', he jeered in a letter to his friend William Temple, 'O fie! O fie!'.[6] Stuart and Hunter failed to stir in him a taste for systematic learning and deep reading, a deficiency he fretted over for the rest of his life.

When he was fifteen, this uninspired teaching led Boswell to flirt briefly with the idea of joining up with the Highlanders (the Black Watch) and going over to Pennsylvania to fight the Indians and French in the Seven Years' War: 'Although timorous where firearms were concerned, set in a flame, wished to go among the Highlanders to America. It was a frenzy. My father prevented it.' His father had no trouble killing the idea, but he had not heard the last of his son's military fantasies. Even at twenty-five, having bought a gun while travelling in Italy, Boswell was still vulnerable to this sort of seductive Byronic escapism, translating himself into a hero of a sublime time and cause, lifting himself out of the doldrums of hypochondria:

So young is still this fancifull head of mine that I had no sooner bought my Gun than the ideas returned which used to stir my blood at Auchinleck when I was eager to be a Soldier; I brandished my Gun (if the sword will permit me for once that expression) I slung it carelessly over my left arm like a handsome fowler or a Captain of a marching Regiment and I must own that I even shoulder'd my firelock like any bold Brother Soldier in his Majesty King George's service; all these motions I performed to an English march which I whistled and upon the honour of a man who is not ashamed to discover the simplicity of his sentiments at times I do declare I was as happy

as I could wish and giving my broad old-lac'd hat a gracefull turn to one side
of my head I thought myself a very great Man.[7]

The brightest light among his teaching mentors was John Stevenson,
who taught him logic and metaphysics in the 1756–7 academic session.
Boswell was one of a couple of generations of students who worshipped
Stevenson and were deeply influenced by his classes. By the time Boswell
found himself in these classes, Stevenson had been teaching at the College
for thirty-five years, and was already a legend. Alexander Carlyle, who
studied with him in the 1730s, remembered him fondly in his *Autobiography*:

> I went to the Logic class, taught by Mr John Stevenson, who, though he had
> no pretensions to superiority of learning and genius, yet was the most popular
> of all the Professors on account of his civility and even kindness to his
> students, and at the same time the most useful ...

All his students, Carlyle adds, felt the same thing happen to them, 'that
our minds were more enlarged, and that we received greater benefit from
that class than from any other'. Stevenson delivered Latin and English
lectures, philosophical debates and arguments, and assigned discourses
on rhetoric, metaphysics, and logic.[8]
    Stevenson finally ignited Boswell's intellectual curiosity. In the literary
vein, he introduced him to the history of philosophy, especially Longinus
on the sublime and John Locke's *Essay on Human Understanding*, and
the *belles lettres*: Aristotle, Homer, Cicero, and Quintilian, among the
ancients, and Sir William Temple, Dryden, Addison, and Pope, among
the English moderns. These classes unlocked the door to an undreamed-
of universe of rhetoric and its possibilities; from them Boswell developed
his love of letters and the writing skills that he began to use in public
ways even while he was still a student. For the first time, he also began
to think independently and critically of the perplexing patriarchal and
matriarchal complexities and tensions at home in Blair's Land and,
especially, of the Presbyterian doctrine and its hellfire lovingly administered by his mother. But Stevenson's effective teaching also caused
problems. Metaphysics, drawn from Devries's *Ontologia*, made a deep
impression and started him worrying about the problems of God's foreknowledge and man's free will, about the whole question of determinism.[9]

2

One very positive effect of Boswell's period of study at the College was that he began to shed some of his sense of inferiority and reach out for encouraging friendships. In Hunter's 1755–6 Greek class he launched out on what became, Samuel Johnson apart, two of the most important and intimate friendships of his life: with the mature John Johnston, 'a manly and cordial Scot', and the 'worthy and pleasant' William Temple.[10] These three never outgrew their friendships, in spite of the major vicissitudes they all experienced.

Johnston, called 'Grange' after the name of his family's estate in Dumfriesshire, in the lovely upland valley of the River Milk, a tributary of the Annan, had inherited the property in about 1750. It was only a small estate, a farm really, but it brought him a small independent income of about £100 per year and the title of laird. He also inherited a romantic family history, for the Johnstons were once one of the most formidable Border country clans, well-known for its violent outlawry and defiance of the government as recently as the end of the seventeenth century. He was full of the lore of his clan, and like Boswell belonged to 'the first generation of romantic revolt ... nostalgic for the freer, wilder, gayer times associated with an earlier age; converting in his fancy, no doubt, all the gruesome Johnston history of robbery and bloodshed into an epic of heroism and romance'. Grange was not shy of talking about his ferocious ancestry, and in his young and impressionable new friend – Boswell was fifteen to his twenty-six – he found an admiring listener.[11]

Deciding that he needed a wider and more adventurous canvas than life on a small farm and an obscure lairdship in the Border country had to offer, in 1756 Grange suddenly left his estate in the hands of his young brother, said farewell to his mother and numerous brothers and sisters, and made his way to Edinburgh and the College to study law. It was a brave, some would say reckless, act for an eldest son. Another reason he left home, however, and one that provided a further emotional link with Boswell, was his hypochondria. Especially during the winter months, life on a remote farm could be very depressing. The bleakness, the narrow moral standards, the unambitious prospects of half-a-century more of unrelieved sameness, and the limited society could even make one feel suicidal.

Boswell warmed first to Johnston's dashing figure, an older 'genteel Gentleman' with 'a straw-coloured lining to your coat'. Here was an older student with a refreshingly unconventional image, with whom friendship could be taken as an implied rebuke to his father's stern and respectable authoritarianism. What is less clear is what attracted Johnston to the fifteen-year-old. Ever since Moffat, Boswell's morbid timorousness had been giving way to a robust cheerfulness. That appealed to Grange, as did Boswell's endless questions about his 'heroic' Scottish ancestry, and he was undoubtedly impressed by his young friend's connections in the legal world. Soon Boswell was inviting him up to Blair's Land to while away the time. Or they wandered together through the town and took rambles into the surrounding countryside, talking, reflecting, railing, commiserating.

This was a happy period that they often revisited nostalgically in later, more troubled years. 'O Johnson! Johnston! Youth early youth is the season of joy,' Boswell wrote to him in February 1763. 'Then it is that we taste pleasure and relive the good things of this life. We never have such stomachs afterwards, as we had when at College.' He reminded Grange of 'the many tea-drinking afternoons' in each other's rooms, 'both in the Lawn market [and] Don's Close and the Parliament Close'; and of walks on careless Saturdays – that best of days – to Leith, returning to Parliament Close via 'Mrs Bird's tarts' where his comrade-in-arms would sit in an easy chair, 'stretching out your legs [and] with a pleasing languor look out at the Window to the lofty Arthur-Seat on which the silver moon would softly shine; while a pleasing mixture of Edinburgh and Annandale ideas would fill your mind'. Grange would regale his young friend with 'ideas' or visions of Scottish kings, the old lairds of Johnston, 'lovely Women with lines of black hair down their backs', 'buxom lasses milking their ewes on the banks of the Water of the Milk', and so on. There were 'loud laughs, the serious romantic conversations, and the indolent luxurious morning Slumbers which we then enjoyed'. All of this was a mighty tonic to the developing spirit of Grange's young accomplice.[12]

These evocations of 'auld lang syne' were part of Boswell's rhetoric of friendship, an elegiac tribute to their vanished youth.[13] When Boswell wrote to Grange about them they even settled on their own private language to refer to melancholia, 'antiquity', 'antique', and 'antiquarian', by way of intimately invoking each other's gloomy kinship – 'a little less than kin and more than kind'. 'We are both Antiquarians,' Boswell wrote from Auchinleck in September 1762, 'I can argue in this manner, which tends to alleviate, tho' not to remove my distress.' Thoughts of their College years and 'the ancient days of Scottish Grandeur' shielded them against their want of hope.[14] From London, Boswell implored Grange to take Saturday walks and recapture their 'warmth of heart and romantic feelings' for Arthur's Seat, St Anthony's Chapel (the ruined chapel and hermitage on the north slope of Arthur's Seat), the Firth of Forth, the Abbey of Holyrood, and 'Edina's [Edinburgh's] lofty towers the ancient Capital of your Country. What a grotesque heap of Building! What a Smoak. See how the City Stretches away to the Southeast while new houses are every day rising to increase it."[5]

Grange found the club and tavern life of Edinburgh perfectly to his taste. He hastened Boswell's maturing by introducing him to places such as Thom's, a popular haunt owned by Thomas Nicolson in the West Bow. Grange may also have been the one to nudge Boswell in the direction of Edinburgh's embryonic theatre life, which started him thinking of writing a play. He scribbled out (c. 1755) several adolescent pages about a young hero named Sam whose obsession with horses and the stable upsets his grandmother and tutor who wish him to make a good impression on his uncle, Mr Wealthy.[6]

A companion appreciates agreeable qualities a man may have, Boswell later wrote, but 'a friend loves the man himself'. If he were going to be married, it was Grange and Temple he would want shut up in a room with him, 'with the door locked, a piece of cheese, two moulded candles, and a bottle of claret upon the mahogany table, round which we would sit in quiet attention consulting and examining the settlements'.[7] The proof that Boswell thought of Grange as a 'true' friend, as distinct from a mere companion, is that he shared his first journals with him. In fact, he wrote the earliest ones for him, to entertain and lift his friend out of hypochondria with their 'warmth of heart and romantic feelings'.

Temple, whose grandson and great-grandson became Archbishops of Canterbury, was roughly the same age as Boswell, and a more intimate friend. He was born and grew up in the town of Berwick at the mouth of the River Tweed three miles south of the Scottish border. His father was a successful merchant who provided his son with as much comfort, culture, and education as a respectable and well-to-do merchant's family in such a 'frontier' community could expect. His Berwick education was not inferior to that which Boswell had received at Mundell's and at home. Temple stayed at the College only for two years, moving on from there to Trinity Hall, Cambridge, in the autumn of 1757 to study law.

Temple was not exactly cosmopolitan in his tastes, but at least he was English and his mind liked to travel on the Continent. When Boswell led him up Arthur's Seat, they talked not of Scottish history and lore but of France, Switzerland, and their Continental philosopher-heroes.

'Voltaire! Rousseau! immortal names,' they shouted from the top. That became a rallying cry between them in the future, which for Boswell gradually turned into an ambition to travel and meet those icons of the Enlightenment. Aware of Boswell's restiveness, Temple suggested that he study in Geneva during the summer of 1759: 'You may study the law better there than at Edinburgh. If your father knew this, perhaps he would rather chuse you should be there, than where you are ... Voltaire, Rousseau ... we might enjoy the benefit of their conversation. I began this purposely to let you know of my intended journey.'[18] Temple never did go, but Lord Auchinleck would not have thanked him for muddying the waters of his son's mind with such harebrained ideas.

That Boswell impressed Temple was probably due to his *gravitas* and introspection when they first met. But he was changing rapidly: 'Don't be surprized', he cautioned Temple in September 1758, 'if your grave, sedate, philosophick friend, who used to carry it so high, and talk with such composed indifference of the beauteous sex, and whom you used to admonish not to turn an Old Man too soon', should fall for an 'adorable Dulcinea'. Literature, not women, however, was the most comfortable subject for the meeting of their minds. While Boswell and Grange visited taverns and the theatre, he and Temple spent hours discussing books and poetry. Their early letters are full of precocious literary chat. Temple told Boswell in October 1756 that he had spent the summer reading the classics and mathematics, but that he had also dipped into the best English poets for fun:

> I see you have studied pretty hard, I assure you I [have] done so too ...
> There's nothing in my opinion, can give a man so much real joy & satisfaction,
> as upon reflection to find, that he has spent his youthful days, in doing all
> he cou'd, to make himself a useful member of society, & that he can look
> into futurity with a pleasant countenance. This is the reason why I study ...[19]

Temple sorely missed all this once he began his dreary legal studies at Cambridge and it was quickly evident that he needed Boswell more than Boswell needed him. At Trinity Hall, he pined for their devoted friendship, almost like a forlorn lover: 'Give me retirement, give me books, give me a friend, & I shall be happy ... O Boswell! when shall we together turn over the volumes of antient wisdom, when shall we, in a philosophick retirement, amid rocks and falling waters, in the grove sacred to friendship and to love, converse with a Socrates, a Plato or a Tully!' Cambridge had its attractions, like Thomas Gray and William

Mason, two of England's popular new poets – Temple and the dandyish Gray had even become friendly – but they were not enough:

> Do not imagine my dear Boswell, that absense can diminish my love for you; my friendship is as warm, as sincere as ever. Absence had endeared you more to me, it has given me leisure more thoroughly to contemplate your virtues, it has occasioned my reflecting how happy we have been when together; how agreable, and in a manner how worthy of our selves we have entertained each other ... You have been the subject of my thoughts when awake, when in bed, even when I lay dissolv'd in soft slumbers. None of my present acquaintance are to my taste ... After my studies are over (which is commonly by nine) what pleasure would it give me to have you to withdraw to, to spend the remainder of the night with you, to talk over my studies with you, and to impart to you my most secret thoughts. Oh Boswell! I never knew 'till now that I could not live without you.

In his reply a couple of weeks later, Boswell was not to be outdone; his letter embarrasses with its intense sentimentality:

> The warm professions you make of the continuance of your friendship for me, made me almost weep with joy, as I know them to be the genuine sentiments of your heart ... It would be needless for me to describe what I have felt in absence from my better part [Temple]. Your beautifull and moving letter speaks my inmost thoughts ... may the sacred flame still increase, till at the last we reach the glorious world above, when we shall never be separated, but enjoy an everlasting society of bliss.

But he was extremely busy with his studies and social life, not at all as empty as Temple among his profligate companions at Cambridge. He was now, in his sixth year at the College, studying law, astronomy, and 'Roman antiquities'; he had Johnston; he had Auchinleck; and he had the Edinburgh theatre.[20]

3

Boswell experienced an acute depression in the summer of 1757, brought on by his exposure in Stevenson's class to metaphysics and readings on God's foreknowledge and man's free will and their implications for salvation. He could not make up his mind whether he had free will or not, an especially urgent question for a boy who was becoming aware of his sexuality and its attendant sense of guilt. Worried, he turned to Methodism, which 'shook my passions'[21] – a variant of Presbyterianism in which his mother had taken an interest as early as 1741. He may even have attended lectures on it in May by the crowd-pleasing evangelist George Whitfield. Methodism provided him with the emotional reassurance of faith and feeling as a route to salvation, to counter the rationalism of determinism. Ultimately, it failed, however, not least because it had to contend with the gloomy undertow of Boswell's hypochondria. He fell prey to a nervous breakdown and was sent again to Moffat. There he remained into the autumn, failing to matriculate for the new College term, sorely missed by Grange and Temple.

This second stretch at Moffat impressed Boswell even more deeply than the first. He went there deeply troubled, overwhelmed with a teenage misanthropy, unable to see the good in anything. Writing about this 'severe illness' in his journal in December 1762, he still was pained by the memory of it: 'I gave myself up as devoted to misery. I entertained a most gloomy and odd way of thinking. I was much hurt at being good for nothing in life.' Off the patriarchal Edinburgh leash at Moffat, he indulged in an odd behaviour to match his 'odd way of thinking', attaching himself to an 'old Pythagorean' from whom he adopted an eccentric vegetarianism and equally eccentric notions of the afterlife. With this asceticism he resolved 'to suffer everything as a martyr to humanity. I looked upon the whole human race with horror.'[22]

His misanthropy gradually dissolved at Moffat, pushed out of his mind both by the physical regimen of sulphurous baths and 'received opinions' about religion and the afterlife. Now, at almost seventeen, he must have engaged in the more genteel amusements of the spa, limited though they were, and undoubtedly flirted with the women there. Above all, he managed an excursion to Carlisle, his momentous first steps on English soil, and his spirits soared. When in Carlisle thirty years later, in much sadder times, he 'took great pleasure in recalling vividly the time that I was first at *Carlisle in Cumberland,* low-spirited and marvelling at everything English'. He made a point of attending his first Anglican cathedral service, following on Temple's taking him to his first English service in Edinburgh several months earlier; it appealed to his taste for ritual, the visual, and church music: 'here for the first time my soul was raised to heaven by the solemn devotion of a cathedral'.[23]

4

After he returned from Moffat in the autumn, Boswell felt less oppressed by domestic and religious constraints and displayed a new social confidence. In the next two years, he had a freer rein at home and out in the town, liberally indulged in his passion for companionship, experimented with Anglicanism, became intoxicated with the Edinburgh theatre, fell in love with an actress and one or two other women, became something of a histrionic exhibitionist and a mimic, and took to singing in society. He began to show a repugnance for what he saw as Scottish insularity and crudeness of expression, warmed to all things English, and started to write verses. It also sank in that hypochondria would be the 'black dog' constantly at his heels, shaping and colouring much of his experience. He came back from Moffat apparently convinced that he was out of the ordinary, destined for greatness. He could not see what he was going to be great *at*, but he soon began to hope it would not be the law. The shy, timid, sickly youth was gone. Replacing him was a robust and plump young man, with a dark complexion and thick, wavy hair, only about five-and-a-half-feet tall. He fancied that his darker complexion suggested virility.

There were hints of rebelliousness, too. He became a likable and agreeable character, dynamic, but essentially at odds with an authoritarian and highly reserved father, Presbyterianism, the law, and an assortment of 'narrow' Scottish institutions. He was born again as a bundle of contradictions and paradoxes, subject to abrupt and restless shifts of mood and temper. Many have explained this sudden turmoil as rooted in a love–hate relationship with Scotland, a fantastic (even manic) version of Caledonian 'antisyzygy' or union of opposites, with his father at the centre of much of his resentment towards his native country. His turbulent opposites are seen as an 'adolescent peripety' accounting for both his brilliance and despair, in rapid alternation.[24]

The remarkable thing is that he survived such oscillations of mind and spirit as well as he did. 'I am a composition of an infinite variety of ingredients,' he wrote vainly. In his commonplace book, he said of himself in his late teens:

Boswell, who had a good deal of whim, used not only to form wild projects in his imagination, but would sometimes reduce them to practice. In his calm hours, he said, with great good humour, 'There have been many people who built castles in the air, but I believe I am the first that ever attempted to live in them.'

In 1766, after a sexual encounter with the gardener's daughter at Auchinleck, which he tantalizingly narrated for Temple, he conceded, 'There are few people who could give credit to it. But you, who have traced me since ever I fairly entered on the stage, will not doubt of it ... It was the effect of great force and great weakness of mind. I am certainly a most various composition.' By the new 'stage' he meant after his second visit to Moffat. His frenzied 'soul' at this time was largely at the mercy of his hyperactive body, fondly characterized as a machine in another commonplace book entry:

> Our frame and temper of mind depends much on the state of our bodies ... The soul sits in the machine. As one who in a chaise when driving hard cannot hear or give attention, I have been conscious of the corporeal machine running on with such rapidity that I felt to apply seriously to anything was in vain for me while that continued.[25]

It was not, as he acknowledged, a mind-set conducive to study, especially of the law. But it was one good way to keep at bay the 'dim-ey'd fiend' of 'Sour Melancholy'.[26]

5

Boswell's final year at the College, 1757–8, was spent studying civil law. He looked elsewhere for stimulation and found it in the Edinburgh theatre scene and in the literary encouragement of two noblemen, his first substitute father-figures: Sir David Dalrymple, fourteen years his senior and in 1766, as Lord Hailes, appointed a Lord of Session; and James Somerville, the twelfth Baron Somerville, who at near sixty when Boswell got to know him was older even than his father. These were the first of a string of older men of eminence whose literary companionship he cultivated. Nothing could accelerate his heartbeat more, for example, than Somerville's telling him he had dined and drunk burgundy with the 'little man', Alexander Pope – one of the literary gods in his personal pantheon.

While his father had not a spark of appreciation and understanding of Boswell's early 'propensity to distinguish himself in literary composition', as he put it, these two noblemen nourished it. They filled him with badly needed confidence and he began to versify – and publish. In the autumn of 1757 he dedicated his earliest-known poem, 'October', an imitation of James Thomson's *Seasons*, to Somerville, his 'indulgent Patron who at first with gracious look, smil'd on my (early) tender year'. Like most of Boswell's verse, the poem is forgettable, but Somerville's influence was not. Almost thirty-five years later, he called Somerville 'the first person of high rank that took particular notice of me in the way most flattering to a young man, fondly ambitious of being distinguished for his literary talents'. His lordship made him think better of himself, in stark contrast to his father: 'Never shall I forget the hours which I enjoyed with him at his apartments in the Royal Palace of Holy-Rood House,' or at his elegant country house near Edinburgh.[27]

In the autumn of 1758, instead of allowing his son to visit Temple at Berwick, Lord Auchinleck lugged him along on the Northern Circuit for an apprenticeship on the fieldwork in criminal cases at Perth, Inverness, and Aberdeen. Nothing could be bleaker for the boy – until he heard that Dalrymple, his 'worthy Maecenas', was coming too. Suddenly, he was impatient to 'enjoy the happiness of his agreable and improving conversation, and see the country with a double relish, in such refined company'. Dalrymple was an accomplished author, better known for his diverse literary, historical, and antiquarian talents than as a jurist. Ecstatic to be in the same chaise with him for the entire Circuit, Boswell assaulted Dalrymple, then thirty-two, with a barrage of literary questions. And he kept a journal on the trip, his first (now lost), which he sent back to his new actor friend James Dance (alias Love), the manager of the Edinburgh Theatre, who had suggested that he write it in the first place. His father sat back, one supposes fairly content at the journal-keeping, but undoubtedly ignorant of the alarming thespian 'vagrant' to whom his son was sending his journal by every post.[28]

6

Lord Somerville, among his other virtues, was a patron of the fledgling Edinburgh stage, then much in need of patronage since the Church and strong, even violent, public opinion were determined to purge all traces of it from the town's cultural life. It was against the law to stage plays in unlicensed playhouses, and there was no legal theatre in the town until one was formally licensed as the Theatre Royal in 1767. Such dramatic

performances as surfaced had to be tacked on to concerts in a hall in the
Canongate and performed by a reasonably good collection of actors who
continued, against odds, to be 'in residence' in town. This is where
Somerville played his part, endearing himself to Boswell in the process:
by hiring the entire company nominally as domestic servants, he freed
them from the law's strictures against vagrancy to which actors were
particularly vulnerable. It was a deft move, enabling the stage to remain
alive in an unsympathetic environment. For Boswell, whose lifelong
passion for the theatre began at this time, it was crucial. Over the next
two years he frequently attended plays, formed friendships among the
actors, and even wrote prologues for productions. There is no mistaking
the streak of protest here against his father – who disliked actors – and
the Church, but his Presbyterian conscience was none the less dogged
by guilt. His mother regarded any theatre as the house of the Devil.
Visiting the actor John Lee in London in 1762, who had been the manager
of the Edinburgh Theatre, Boswell reflected fondly on how his theatrical
intoxication had fairly taken over his life:

> I ... called on Mr Lee, who is a good, agreeable, honest man, and with whom
> I associate fine gay ideas of the Edinburgh theatre in my boyish days, when
> I used to walk down the Canongate and think of players with a mixture of
> narrow-minded horror and lively-minded pleasure; and used to wonder at
> painted equipages and painted ladies, and sing 'The bonny bush aboon
> Traquair' ...

That popular Scots song was the epitome for Boswell of the amorousness
waiting in an Edinburgh he had never known before. Edinburgh gloom
was passing momentarily into Edinburgh glory.[29]

The theatre at this point was merely a source of amusement – later it
would cohere for Boswell into a more complex metaphor for studying
and measuring himself. Still, there were signs even this early of his
realization that the life of a player was admirable and much abused,
especially in Edinburgh. The sting in his three essays, 'On the Profession
of a Player', which he wrote in 1770, derived form the guilt he was made
to feel and his rebellious urge to make actors into his friends and heroes –
and mistresses. The acting profession, Boswell protests, 'ought to be
ranked amongst the learned professions: for the truth is, that in order to
be a good player, there is required a greater share of genius, knowledge,
and accomplishments, than for any one profession whatever; for this
reason, that the profession of a player comprehends the whole system of

human life.' As for the moral strictures against the theatre he grew up hearing, 'I cannot see any reason why the profession of a player should corrupt the morals more than any other. If it is the dissimulation necessary to assume a feigned character, that is thought so hurtful, I flatter myself that I have shewn that the art of a player is not dissimulation, but a mysterious power of being to a certain degree the character which he represents.' Acting is very hard work. Actors do not have time for 'vicious pursuits': 'may we hope to see our players treated with a just decency and politeness, and secured against affronts from sport or malevolence...'[30]

The step from a feeling of respect for the 'dissimulation' of an actor to a histrionic talent for 'feigning' characters was not a big one for Boswell. Part of his adolescent peripety of this period was his passion for chameleon-like role-playing. He sought out models he wanted to emulate, then imagined himself as them. He found he was excellent both at mimicry and the imaginative entering into another's character.

In the spring of 1758, Boswell experienced his first period of full independence in Edinburgh. When his parents and younger brothers went off to Auchinleck for April and May, he stayed behind alone in Edinburgh. He may have insisted on it. There probably were arguments. His parents shut up the house, so he took lodgings and for two months the world of Edinburgh was his oyster. He cultivated actors, scribbled verses, and attended numerous plays, such as *Othello*, *The Beggar's Opera*, and *The Conscious Lovers*.

One actor in particular, West Digges, fascinated him. Handsome and charming, Digges was a gentleman and soldier of fine taste and good education who turned to acting after he resigned his commission in the army, arriving in Edinburgh in 1756, soon to become manager of the theatre. He held the job until he was herded out of town in 1758 largely because of debts and attacks from the hostile Church. Boswell later wrote, 'He was the first actor I ever saw ... It was He who threw open to me the portals of theatrical Enchantment.' They knew each other by April 1757 when Boswell (then only sixteen) sent him a prologue he had written, probably for John Home's highly controversial *Douglas*, and which Digges found too hot to handle because he was sure it would make the Church even more angry about the performance. As Home was a Presbyterian minister, the Church not unreasonably thought he should be denouncing the theatre, not writing plays for it. Boswell's prologue, which is lost, very likely defended the play and the theatre. None the less, Digges thought it contained poetry, given the age of its writer, 'very pleasing, and deserving of Commendation'.[31]

Apart from his glamour as an actor, what made Digges attractive to Boswell was his elegant and dashing figure, rather like Macheath in Boswell's favourite, *The Beggar's Opera*, one of the three or so roles that made the actor famous. For years, Boswell treasured Digges as a model of manners and elegance: 'I must say Digges has more or as much of the deportment of a man of fashion as anybody I ever saw; and he keeps up this so well that he never once lessened upon me even on an intimate acquaintance, although he is now and then somewhat melancholy.' More than twenty years later, he was still fond of Digges, as he told the actor-manager David Garrick: 'He and Pleasure are inseparably associated in my mind.'[32]

Another actor friend was the Irishman Francis Gentleman who began performing at the Edinburgh Theatre in 1758 and served some time as temporary manager there; he was also a critic and playwright. Of a literary turn, he and Boswell became friends and may even have collaborated on some play reviews in the *Edinburgh Review*. James Love, on the other hand, sixteen years Boswell's senior but more like a comrade-in-arms than a father-figure, played a crucial part in his early education. Among other things, Love helped him enormously by teaching him English pronunciation. The brother of the famous portrait painter, Nathaniel Dance, he proved something of a disappointment when Boswell saw him later in London, 'vulgar, stupid, and malevolent', but at first the actor (who had joined the Drury Lane company in 1762) became his 'second best friend', second to Temple, that is. Why he took Boswell on as an 'intimate' is not so clear, although he could not have been impervious to the flattery of having the son of a Lord of the Justiciary lionize him so completely, as both actor and poet. His young friend also eagerly lent him money. 'He is really a man,' Boswell told Temple, all excited, with 'not only taste, genius, and learning but a good heart'.[33]

The heady excitement and glamour in the spring and summer of 1758, centred chiefly on the theatre, set Boswell's poetic juices flowing. 'Trifles', 'the production of a leisure hour', came fast and furious, it seems, at least three finding their way into the *Scots Magazine* for August, November, and December 1758. 'An Evening-Walk in the Abbey-church of Holy-roodhouse', which begins with, 'Such is the present time, now Sober Eve', is pleasantly meditative, though not memorably lyrical; but with the others his poetic muse, as it almost always would, failed to launch him even into a middle flight. His love poems are strictly conventional, with tired phrases and images. He had no interest in vernacular Scots, clearly preferring the more genteel sounds of English. One poem starts out, ''Twas hard indeed, 'twas wondrous hard'. Another, 'Epigram on a Marriage between a beautiful young Lady, and a coarse hulk of a Gentleman', is a whimsical and satirical trot of verses lamenting the violation of a lovely young Scottish nymph by her boorish and undeserving husband – a theme that interested Boswell, for he frequently wondered how men of inferior parts to himself were able to win certain women where he had failed. In any case, he clearly fancied himself a poet at this point and, until about 1762, continued to write poetry largely for his own enjoyment.[34]

At about this time Boswell fell deeply in love with Martha Whyte, a lovely eighteen-year-old heiress of £30,000. He even thought of marrying her. He told Temple all about her in a flush of hope, warning him that his old studious, retiring friend, formerly in danger of turning into an 'Old Man', might suddenly spring into a Don Quixote over this 'adorable Dulcinea'. Martha Whyte was the first of many girls he hoped might become his wife. No sooner did an attractive and rich one, who returned his attentions, come into view than she became a candidate. In the sentimental passage that follows, he portrays himself self-consciously as Martha's soulful lover who, in honour of his communion-friendship with Temple, sees, or tries to see, more to her than her physical attributes:

> I at first fell violently in love with her, and thought I should be quite miserable if I did not obtain her; but now it is changed to a rational esteem of her good qualities, so that I should be extremely happy to pass my life with her ... She is indeed extremely pretty and possessed of every amiable qualification. She dances, sings, and plays upon several instruments equally well, draws with a great deal of taste, and reads the best authors; at the same time she has a just regard to true piety and religion, and behaves in the most easy, affable way. She is just such a young lady as I could wish for the partner of my soul, and you know that is not every one, for you and I have often talked how nice we would be in such a choice.

Finding him attractive, Martha invited Boswell to tea, 'kindly entertained' him, and told him to come again. 'A youth of my turn', he concluded, might just win her, by which he meant that he was lively, romantic, affable, and cultured. Temple must keep this under his hat: 'Oh, Willie! how happy should I be if she consented, some years after this, to make me blest! How transporting to think of such a lady to entertain you at Auchinleck!' It all came to naught, of course. Martha married an earl the following year. 'How did you bear it?' Temple asked after the marriage. In 'A Crambo Song: On Losing my Mistress', written in a sprawling hand that suggests he was a little drunk at the time, he put an epigrammatical twist on his disappointment:

> Although I be an honest Laird
> In person rather strong and brawney
> For me the Heiress never cared
> For she would have the Knight Sir Sawney
>
> *
>
> She told me with a scornful look
> I was as ugly as a Tawney
> For she a better fish could hook,
> The rich and gallant Knight Sir Sawney.

The episode is instructive: there is little trace left of the morbid young adolescent in the whimsical, capricious, and fantastic suitor.[35]

7

On his own in Edinburgh during the summer of 1757, Boswell plucked up courage to call on the great philosopher and historian David Hume at his house in Riddle's Close, off the High Street. Somerville and Dalyrymple were eminent, but Hume was a literary lion, famous throughout Europe, an icon of the Enlightenment. Boswell did not have to travel very far to meet him, but it nevertheless took a good deal of courage and audacity to knock on his door. What made Hume additionally tantalizing, a type of forbidden fruit to be tasted but not digested, was his atheism and refusal to accept any notion of an afterlife. When they met, Hume was writing his *History of Great Britain*, the first volume of which had already appeared in 1754. He is 'a most discreet, affable man as ever I met with' with enormous learning and 'a choice collection of books', truly 'extraordinary'. They spoke of genius, fine language, and prose style, the ancients, and history, all of which was entertaining as well as instructive. Hume, he decided, was 'a very proper person for a young man to cultivate an acquaintance with', except that his taste was not entirely 'delicate'.[36]

8

The new term was suddenly upon him and Boswell spent most of the year studying law, an increasingly onerous task. Temple went off to Cambridge, the family was in residence again at Blair's Land, and the visionary gleam had fled. Staring him in the face until the spring was the following dull regime: 'From 9 to 10, I attend the law class; from 10 to 11, the Astronomy; from 11 to 1, study at home; and from 1 to 2, attend a college upon Roman Antiquities. The afternoon and evening I likewise spend in study.' To make matters worse, 'I never walk except on Saturdays' – Saturdays, we recall, had been his boyhood days of fancy and romantic dreaming. Temple put it to his 'dear Jimmy' that an absence from books should have sharpened his appetite for study, but that was not the effect at all.[37] Somehow he got through the oppressiveness of the academic year under his father's watchful eye, apparently without any serious hypochondria, and in April was again looking forward to the prospect of a couple of months alone in Edinburgh.

While his father was assuming that he was studying law, Boswell was in fact studying actresses. He began to flirt with Mrs Love and at the same time had his first full-fledged affair with another married actress, Mrs Cowper, a devout Catholic about ten years his senior. In Edinburgh this sort of thing was hard to keep quiet, especially as the affair appears to have lasted several months. By September, even Temple in Berwick had heard of his 'affection' for 'Sylvia', Boswell's name for Mrs Cowper probably taken from her leading role that season in Farquhar's *The Recruiting Officer*. Temple, whose notions of 'gallantry' or adultery were not as liberal as his friend's, was hurt at having heard this on the grapevine. 'I heard an odd story here, of you and one Mrs Cooper. I scarce imagined my grave friend wou'd have turned a gallant so soon.'[38]

An uncharacteristically mellifluous quatrain which Boswell wrote about her some time that summer, with echoes of Andrew Marvell, hints at how smitten he was:

> When from the Harpsichord she drew
> Tunes sweet and delicately true
> He'd twist his body round and round,
> And languish at the silver sound.

Mrs Cowper was a good actress and musician, as well as very beautiful, and she played successfully at Bath, Drury Lane and Dublin over the next ten years, but Temple was not impressed when she performed in

Newcastle later in the year. How could this thirty-year-old woman, married to her music master of all things, appeal to his College chum? 'She is a pretty good actress', he grumbled, 'but I cannot say I was much taken with her. Both her manner of acting and her voice were far from transporting me. Her person is tolerable. You are the best judge of the charms of her conversation.' What Temple could not, or would not, appreciate was that Mrs Cowper was not only Boswell's initiation in gallantry, but also a conquest, a victory for his new gregarious and loquacious self.[39]

Temple continued to disapprove. Boswell at last decided that a playful, unapologetic poem might serve to soothe his ruffled feelings. He dashed off his 'Epistle to Temple' and sent it down to Cambridge in the spring of 1761. It is hard to imagine that Temple was either satisfied with it as a whimsical explanation of Boswell's sexual life or pleased by its jogtrot verse; the infectious humour and geniality of the piece, though, must surely have amused him:

> You tell me (and I thank you for it)
> That you have heard an odd report
> That your old friend, strange alteration,
> Is now at deeds of fornication
> Just as expert as formerly
> At grave sedate philosophy.
> An actress too (you know her name)
> Is said to be his favourite flame;
> Great honour sure to soar so high
> In the bright sphere of Gallantry.
> But don't you laugh tho' serious I
> My honour quit for Chastity
> And by relating downright truth
> Convince you that I'm still the youth
> You knew me when at Edin College
> We generous rivals were in knowledge.

He goes on to poeticize Mrs Cowper's ('Lavinia's') misfortunes, how she fell foul of a bad marriage and was driven to the stage, leaving the 'poor dejected wife / To wander thro' the maze of life ...' Temple must understand that he was now spreading his net more widely. Dalrymple 'still shall have / Due honour from his faithful slave', but a new Boswell was in play, for 'when the dear Ladies come in Play / Indeed he cannot be say'd nay'.[40]

Not only was Boswell attending plays regularly, but he had also become something of an appendage to the company, lingering around the theatre in the Canongate and fraternizing with the actors and actresses. And there are good reasons to think that he wrote four anonymous reviews of plays he saw during the summer for the *Edinburgh Chronicle*. If so, their exaggerated praise of his mistress and elegant friend Digges cannot exactly be described as unbiased. Boswell was annoyed that Digges, while he was away acting in Ireland, had recently been passed over as a partner in the theatre and hence Digges's rivals, including Love and his wife, fared far from well in these reviews. The Edinburgh Theatre needed Digges back badly, Boswell wrote in his *Epistle to Mr Digges*:

> Come then, delight our wond'ring eyes,
> Come and illume our northern skies,
> Come, please an ever-grateful age, .
> And yet restore our sinking stage.

The main point, though, is that if the reviews were, with the occasional poems, Boswell's first published writings, they provide evidence of the 'propensity' for early literary distinction he mentioned in his 'Memoir'. Jaunty, opinionated, and ostensibly 'moral' and instructive, they were written simply to get himself into print. In February 1760, the four reviews were brought together and published, still anonymously, as a pamphlet in London under the title, *A View of the Edinburgh Theatre During the Summer Season, 1759*. It is dedicated to Digges.[41]

In the vortex of all this activity, Boswell managed to keep melancholy at bay. 'I hope you have ... been troubled with no ... gloomy thoughts, but have been blessed with a temperament of mind calm and serene,' wrote Temple.[42] This period, though, was the storm before the calm – Boswell's exile to Glasgow.

9

As soon as he returned to Edinburgh with his family at the end of the summer, or perhaps even earlier, Lord Auchinleck's keen antennae picked up some disturbing intelligence about his son: of very little studying and something about players, an affair with an actress, and (perhaps worse) rumours about publishing in the press. If he had any interest at all in his son's writing, it was to criticize. Not a spark of appreciation for Boswell's efforts as a writer, much less his imaginative skills, ever escaped his lips.

Sexual escapades Lord Auchinleck could understand – he could still remember his own. Indeed, as Boswell's commonplace book occasionally reveals, he was not without a rough, ironic (and sometimes bawdy) sense of humour, often at his son's expense, but he saw nothing funny about his volatility and increasing unconventionality. Plans for a final year at the College were scrapped. In November, almost before he realised what had happened, Boswell was on his way to study at Glasgow University, ripped away from Grange and other College chums and, especially, from his theatrical friends. There was no theatre in Glasgow.

It is important to remember that Boswell's attitude towards his father was unfailingly respectful. They sorely tried each other's patience and love, but whereas his father in time developed an antipathy towards him and his younger brothers, David and John, Boswell struggled to preserve his love for his father and admiration of his solid character as laird, judge, and even parent. On this occasion, after what must have been a furious disagreement, he tried to put a brave face on his Glasgow exile. Having 'resolved to bring my mind to be contented with the Situation which was thought proper for me', he confided to Grange, he found that Glasgow, although a pale cultural shadow of Edinburgh in the late eighteenth century, was not quite as depressing as he had expected.[43]

At least it contained Francis Gentleman, his stage friend who had been eking out an existence there since his dismissal from the Edinburgh Theatre. The two must have seen each other regularly for several weeks because in February Gentleman published an adaptation of Aphra Behn's novel *Oroonoko* which he dedicated to, of all people, Boswell, who doubtless paid him for the distinction. Lord Auchinleck, hoping that by exiling his son to Glasgow he had cut him off cleanly from theatres and actors, cannot have been pleased. Glasgow also contained Adam Smith, and it was he, not Gentleman, who left the deepest impression.

Smith's monumental *Wealth of Nations* would not appear until 1776, but his *Theory of Moral Sentiments* had just been published (1759) and as Professor of Moral Philosophy at the university his lectures on rhetoric and belles lettres were famous. Here was a genuine humanist whose philosophy was central to the Enlightenment: not derived from formal religion or social convention and 'method', but speaking to the human condition of individual man. The lectures were 'truly excellent', Boswell reported to Grange, with 'Sentiments [that] are striking, profound and beautifull', a method of delivery 'clear, accurate and orderly', and a language 'correct perspicuous and elegantly phrased'. What also went a long way with him was Smith's ease of manner and amiability, so unlike 'that formal stiffness and Pedantry which is too often found in Professors' at Edinburgh. Best of all, Smith was 'extremely fond of having his Students with him', treating them with 'all the easiness and affability imaginable'. All in all, he answered perfectly to Boswell's ideal of the intellectual hero: learned, highly intelligent, expressive, morally sensitive, friendly, and very human. For his part, Smith warmed to Boswell's liveliness and quickness; he praised him for his 'happy facility of manners', a remark that stuck to Boswell like wallpaper for many years. At first Boswell luxuriated in the 'academical life' of Glasgow, stuck to his lodgings, rarely visited Auchinleck although it was not far away and, with the exception of Gentleman, saw only his teachers and studious friends. It seems possible he may even have boarded with Smith for a while.[44] But as the days stretched on, he grew desperately unhappy. Neither Smith nor Gentleman was enough to compensate him for the loss of his Edinburgh circle. His vivaciousness and robust drive for companionship had no outlet. An unrelieved concentration on academic work flattened his spirits. There was no gentleness around – a requisite, he believed, for someone of his sensitive temperament – to help him cope with these problems. He was lonely and felt irreparably cut off from his family, with which in any case he tended to associate bleakness. In spite of the company of Adam Smith, he was bored and vulnerable. Something began to simmer in his consciousness: Catholicism, engendered by his love for Mrs Cowper.

One morning in March he bolted to Moffat and then to Carlisle, where he mounted a fresh horse and rode all the way to London in two-and-a-half days, a furious pace by any standard. His object: to submit himself to the Roman Catholic Church.

THREE

Escape to London

I

In Edinburgh Mrs Cowper had introduced Boswell to her 'little Mr Duchat, the popish priest', a Jesuit, who supplied him with Catholic books. The promised visual spectacle, ritual, and drama of the Catholic liturgy aroused his imagination, and once in Glasgow, his discontent conspired with these books to push him towards conversion. His irresponsible flight to London suggests the unhappy state of his relations with his parents, in spite of what he might say on the subject, and also the depth of this unhappiness in Glasgow. Before he fled he wrote to inform his father that he intended to become a monk or priest but keeping his destination a secret for the time being. His friendships with Temple and Johnston were also pushed into the background. Temple was beside himself with worry when he heard that Boswell had bolted: 'Was it kind of you to take this journey without letting me know your motives for so doing? . . . I am concerned for you, my dear Boswell, very much. For God's sake let me see you immediately.'[1] Moreover, the stakes were extremely high. As a Catholic, Boswell would be unable to achieve most of his goals and ambitions. He could neither inherit Auchinleck nor receive its income. Nor could he practise law, enter the army, or serve in Parliament. He would also be denied the best society in Edinburgh and London.

One of Boswell's first letters from London was to Dalrymple on 22 March. He dared not write to his father but he needed to confide in one of his mentors about what had happened. His flight was not as irresponsible and impulsive as it seemed, he assured Sir David:

My leaving Glasgow in the abrupt manner I have done could not fail to appear extremely unaccountable. It certainly must carry the face of a very romantic and inconsiderate step. But don't blame me too much: for I can assure you that motives of the highest importance influenced my conduct; and although my elopement (as it may be justly stiled) is imagined to be the effect of a rash and hasty resolution, I give you my word that I had thought of it, for a long time; and that during the last winter, it was generally the subject of consideration, in my most serious hours.[2]

'What indeed gives me the most sensible pain', he continued to Dalrymple, 'is the uneasiness which my worthy Father must feel from it. Nobody knows of how much goodness of heart he is posest, so well as I do. His strictness was nothing but what Prudence would dictate, and he has allways treated me with affection and indulgence.' He makes no mention of his mother.

He went on to tell of his romantic 'adventures' since leaving Glasgow on 1 March. He had set out early in the morning, having slept little the night before, 'when all the House where I lodged were gone to bed and I was walking solitary & pensive through my moon-enlightened chambers, ruminating with as Tragic a countenance, as that of Mr Digges, on *Tomorrow! tomorrow and tomorrow* and uttering or rather groaning forth these deep-ton'd lines in [Addison's] *Cato* –

> O! think what anxious moments pass between
> The birth of plots and their last fatal Periods.'

He had travelled in the dark first to Moffat and then to Carlisle, a total of one hundred miles, on 'a couple of Glasgow Hacks'. He galloped on from Carlisle with fresh horses, arriving in London two days later where he took an assumed name and – 'now pray don't laugh at me' – adopted a 'parsimonious course' in the event, as he feared, of being disinherited by his father.

For a couple of weeks he remained incognito in London, living under a false name in the grubby lodgings of a Catholic wigmaker to which somebody had referred him, possibly Mrs Cowper or her priest. He sought out a few Roman Catholic contacts, especially a bookseller in Drury Lane who facilitated a type of underground Catholic lifeline for new converts and directed him for instruction to a priest at the Bavarian Chapel where he enthusiastically heard his first Mass and took communion. He even mulled over the idea of retiring to a monastery in France.

What he did not tell Dalrymple was that his excitement had as much to do with finding himself in the great metropolis as with the religious life. London was the perfect antidote to Glasgow. It did not seem to occur to Boswell that the pleasures of London and the life of a monk were not exactly compatible.

2

Having been informed of his son's whereabouts, Lord Auchinleck promptly asked his Ayrshire neighbour the Earl of Eglinton (then in London), a sportsman and rakish man-about-town who claimed as friends the scapegrace Duke of York and the Earl of Bute, to track him down. Eglinton's men had little trouble finding the fugitive. Boswell hesitated briefly when he was sent for, but at last he 'took courage [and] waited upon them', explaining his situation. 'They took it in good part: and made me at once, emerge from my obscurity. I then took handsome lodgings at a Guinea a week, and became, in short, a Gentleman.' So much for religious fervour. On the same day that he wrote to Dalrymple and heard from Temple, Boswell moved to Eglinton's house in Mayfair.

Eglinton rescued him from the snares and 'giddy fervour' of two extremes, one spiritual and the other animal and epicurean. Boswell was already in the middle of Catholic instruction, as he recalled in his journal in March 1768: 'Romish clergy filled me with solemn ideas, and, although their statues and many movable ornaments are gone, yet they drew some pictures upon my [mental] walls with such deep strokes that they still remain.' In an attempt to divert him from this, Dalrymple urged him to seek out Horace Walpole, but Boswell decided that the writer inhabited 'too high a sphere'. He also appealed to Dr John Jortin, a respected Anglican divine in London, hoping that Jortin could at least steer him towards the Church of England. Jortin succeeded for a while but then heard no more of the young fugitive: 'He began, I suppose, to suspect some design upon him,' he reported back to Dalrymple, 'and his new [Catholic] friends and fathers may have represented me to him as an heretic and an infidel.'[3]

Boswell now took up with the itinerant Irish actor and Grub Street writer, Samuel Derrick, a friend of Francis Gentleman. Derrick introduced him to Thomas Davies, at whose bookshop Boswell would later meet Samuel Johnson, and to the pleasures of David Garrick and Colley Cibber on the stage. Boswell must have seen Garrick, whom as a boy he 'used to adore and look upon as a heathen god', on stage numerous times. But not content, as in the Edinburgh Theatre, to worship performers from a distance, he managed to get Derrick to introduce him to this greatest actor of the century. Derrick also introduced his eager protégé to the shabbier 'sportive' world of London. This period of initiation lasted only for a couple of weeks, but it included Boswell's memorable visit to his first prostitute, Sally Forrester, 'the Paphian Queen', 'my first Lady of Venus's Bedchamber', where he partook of the 'melting and transporting rites of Love' at an inn, the Blue Periwig, in Southampton Street. Although there were no immediate ill consequences, it did not take him long to regret his connection with 'this creature' Derrick. Two years later he still recoiled from any approach by him, recalling, 'after I found him out to be a little blackguard pimping dog, I did not know how to get rid of him'.[4]

The Earl of Eglinton's antidote for the boy's curious and obscure diet of the holy and the unholy was to bring him into proper society and give him a lesson in libertinism that would make his undesirable Catholic friends appear pale and ineffectual. Three years later, Boswell reminded Eglinton of his rescue: 'You pulled me out of the mire, washed me and cleaned me and made me fit to be seen.'[5] Eglinton's world revealed to him a dazzling vision of conversation, wit, and humour that made Scottish society seem more unpolished than ever; fashionable houses, furniture, and clothes; the finest food; excellent music and theatre; varied recreation that included a visit to the races at Newmarket and enjoyment of the prestigious Jockey Club; sparkling nights at the Ranelagh and Vauxhall assemblies; varied sexual activity conducted in erotic good taste; and even the extraordinary luck of occasionally finding himself in the company of, among others, the Earl of Bute and the Duke of York, then only eighteen, the presumptive heir to the British throne. This was unimaginable good fortune for the nineteen-year-old Boswell. He had finally discovered his calling, the real meaning of life.

In a letter to Eglinton that he published anonymously (though indiscreetly) a year later in the *Scots Magazine*, Boswell titillates the reader with gossipy allusions to the Duke of York, at the same time speciously claiming the lifestyle to which Eglinton had introduced him as the only fitting one for a young man of finely tuned sensibilities and genius like himself. Having hobnobbed with English royalty and aristocracy, he pictures himself as a liberated, even libertine, model for those of his disadvantaged Scottish brethren who do not have 'the eyes of a mole, or the perceptions of a burgomaster':

you and I have run through ... agreeable scenes together, when I had the

honour of living under your Lordship's roof and patronage, at London. I say
living, for at that time, by enjoying, I really knew the value of life. Your
Lordship convinced me, that this same existence of ours, – bad as some
philosophers and divines may call it, – is yet worth the having ... if we will
but make the most of it.

He luxuriates in memories of returning with Eglinton from Ranelagh
evenings, sitting together in his dining room with 'an enlivening bottle
of Old Hock', and 'with all imaginable gaiety' reliving the adventures of
the day and 'indeed the former night too'. He thanks his mentor for his
tutelage – 'Did you not find me an excellent scholar?' – but he craves 'a
regular course of lectures' when his guiding stars, Venus and Mars, land
him back in 'the delightful BRITISH METROPOLIS'.[6]

Three years later when Boswell was fancying himself less wild and
studying to be 'a real philosopher', he saw the publication of this letter
as foolish but understandable:

It was a great matter of pride for a Scot when he returned to his own country
to speak of the conversations which he had had with his Royal Highness.
And indeed the thing was well known in Scotland ... but ... greatly exaggerated. The solicitors of Edinburgh, as they drank their punch, said that I
was quite the companion of the Duke of York, that we ran together through
the streets of London at all hours of the night, and that we made no ceremony
with each other: it was just 'James' and 'Ned'.

The fact was, he added, 'I knew him only very little and he never did me
the least service.'[7]

3

One of the more memorable meetings under Eglinton's wing was with
Laurence Sterne, whose novel *Tristram Shandy* had just taken London
by storm and made its author the talk of the town. They met at Sterne's
lodgings in the Mall, and Boswell decided to worship him, partly because
Sterne was the literary man of the hour, partly because the writer's
personal and literary style perfectly suited his own ascendant capricious,
light, fanciful temperament.[8] Here was a parson who had emerged from
obscurity in Yorkshire to literary fame in London. Was he not a model
of how Boswell's own genius could carry him to fame? Even more

encouraging was the fact that Sterne could play the part of the fool and get away with it in respectable London society. He actually thrived by impersonating the oddities of his own hero, Tristram Shandy, which in turn sold copies of his book. There was more to life than conventional and halting respectability. Here was a literary sensation which proved that laughter and merriment were cathartic, central to the good life, as Sterne explains in his novel:

> If 'tis wrote against any thing, – 'tis wrote, an' please your worships, against the spleen, in order, by a more frequent and more convulsive elevation and depression of the diaphragm, and the succussations of the intercostal muscles in laughter, to drive the *gall* and other *bitter juices* from the gall bladder, liver, and sweet-bread of his majesty's subjects, with all their inimicitious passions which belong to them, down into their duodenums.[9]

As Sterne soon discovered, however, society would tolerate buffoonery only for so long. That, too, was an object lesson for Boswell, but would he heed it?

Sterne's influence on Boswell as a role model, which was out of all proportion with the degree of their acquaintance – so far as we know, they met only once – explains much of his feverish literary and social activity in Edinburgh over the following two years. When he returned to his boring legal studies in Edinburgh in the late summer of 1761, imagining himself a straitjacketed genius, he pined for those exhilarating moments in Sterne's company. In his 'Poetical Epistle to Doctor Sterne', written at this time, his sketch of the writer and the poem's auto-biographical glimpses are both infected with Shandyism. Like a chameleon, he seems to have become Shandy himself.[10]

In a similar vein, before going home, Boswell also composed *The Cub at New-Market*, a pamphlet-length autobiographical poem in the Shandean style, inspired at the races and put on paper in the Jockey Club coffee room. He read it to Sterne, who predictably 'caper'd at my Cub', and to the Duke of York, who was amused by it, but that was in private. When Boswell published the poem in 1762, he recklessly dedicated it to the Duke. To have his name publicly associated with such frivolous nonsense infuriated the Duke and, in turn, Eglinton, who was astonished at Boswell's indiscretion and told him so.[11]

4

This London jaunt brought home to Boswell that he wanted nothing whatever to do with a legal career. For some time he had been entertaining the idea of a commission in the Guards, and now Eglinton persuaded him that he would be wasting his talents either as a Catholic or an advocate, that he was cut out to be a soldier in a red coat. Boswell seized on the idea and wrote to his father about it. For the next two years, except for a brief flirtation with the idea of studying law at the Inner Temple in London, an army commission was his steady theme. Even his friends grew tired of hearing about it. Later, defending his proposal when Boswell accused him of not helping him enough to get the commission, Eglinton reminded his young friend why he had made the suggestion in the first place:

> Now, Jamie ... when you was first in London, I found that you had been much hurt by being forced to studies contrary to the natural bent of your genius, and been obliged to live with your parents, who, though very good people, had a strictness and confined way of thing which a man of your strength of imagination and natural freedom of sentiment could not put up with. I pointed out the Guards to you, as I thought the gaiety of a military life was the best thing in the world to keep off that melancholy to which you was a little subject.[12]

'Strength of imagination and natural freedom of sentiment' – these were encouraging additions to Boswell's growing assortment of self-images. But commissions in the Guards cost money and depended upon the influence of the great. And the timing was poor. The Seven Years' War was drawing to a close and the demand for soldiers was about to fall dramatically. In any case, Boswell's father, who had just exerted himself to see his younger son John into the army, had little inclination to do the same for his eldest son.

Lord Auchinleck came down to London in May to take stock of matters. He was a poor father but not an unfeeling man, and here was his lost sheep rescued from Papist clutches and almost back in the fold. After a warm reunion he took his son to talk to the distinguished Duke of Argyll about joining the Guards. Argyll was not encouraging. Hardly anybody was. Boswell reluctantly agreed to return with his father to Edinburgh and they left London at the end of the month.

Once home, Lord Auchinleck extracted an agreement from his son: if he would settle down to a couple of years of private legal tuition at home, and pass the examinations to become an advocate, then he would provide the funds for him to return to London to see if he could obtain a commission in the Guards. If further attempts failed, as his father was convinced they would, he could return to Edinburgh and begin his legal career. Boswell agreed to the bargain because he was convinced that once back in London he would never again have to subject his genius to the deadening rigours of the law.

Returning to Edinburgh with a sexual infection contracted from some prostitute, Boswell was not the conquering hero of his imagination. For several weeks he had floated in the ether of 'grand ideas of London' and had come to believe he was a 'superior animal'. Back once more among the 'hamely' Scots, he succumbed to the first attack of low spirits, or hypochondria, for over a year. When he got around to describing his return to Temple he was very bitter about his present lot:

> I grant you, that my behaviour has not been entirely what it ought to be. But consider my particular situation. A young fellow whose happiness was allways centred in London, who had at last got there, and had begun to taste its delights – who had got his mind filled with the most gay ideas – getting into the Guards, being about Court, enjoying the happiness of the *beau monde* and the company of men of Genius; in short, every thing that he could wish – consider this poor fellow hauled away to the town of Edinburgh – obliged to conform to every Scotch custom, or be laughed at, – '*will you hae some jeel?' O fie! O fie!* His flighty imagination quite cramped, and he obliged to study *Corpus Juris Civilis*, and live in his father's strict family: is there any wonder, Sir, that the unlucky dog should be somewhat fretfull? Yoke a Newmarket courser to a dung-cart, and I'll lay my life on't, he'll either caper and kick most confoundedly, or be as stupid and restive as an old, battered post-horse. Not one in a hundred can understand this. You do.[13]

There were deep wounds there, festering.

5

For the next three years Boswell's dependence on his father, chiefly financial but also emotional, inhibited him, clouded his imagination. He suspected that his ultimate destiny was to lead an urbane and controlled Addisonian life of letters, tempered by sobriety and good taste, but first he aspired to make his mark in a more jaunty vein, to establish a personal style by which he could be known and talked about. His two springs and summers of independence in Edinburgh had given him a handful of theatrical friends, a smattering of literary activity, and opportunities for sexual dalliance and flirtation. But London life had quickly brought home to him that he was an awkward 'cub' and taught him that Scottish insularity would never do if he meant to cut a figure in the world.

How was he to show his Scottish friends and acquaintances that he was a provincial no longer? He decided that he could best do this by adopting a Shandean persona, or so he said in an illuminating self-analysis in his journal two-and-a-half years later. 'After my wild expedition to London in the year 1760,' he wrote, 'after I got rid of the load of serious reflection [Catholicism] which then burthened me, by being always in Lord Eglinton's company, very fond of him, and much caressed by him, I became dissipated and thoughtless.' Low-spirited but determined to keep up the appearance of gaiety, which hurt him in the effort, 'like a man who takes to drinking to banish care, I threw myself loose as a heedless, dissipated, rattling fellow who might say or do every ridiculous thing'. While this earned him popularity 'for the present hour', it reduced him in own estimation to a 'very inferior being'. Accordingly, people treated him as a lightweight companion, which 'gave me much pain'. This was not what he had had in mind: 'I was, in short, a character very different from what GOD intended me and I myself chose.' He had fallen so much into the habit of laughing at everything that it took him some time to 'render my imagination solid' and attain 'some degree of propriety': 'Mr Addison's character in sentiment, mixed with a little gaiety of Sir Richard Steele and the manners of Mr Digges, were the ideas which I aimed to realize.' The problem was that he was trying to remodel himself to an abstract pattern based on self-conscious 'ideas' of personality. This self-orchestration of temper was a strain. It was bound to weigh him down, with distinctly unhappy effects.[14]

FOUR

Early Scribblings

I

Boswell's convalescence from his first gonorrhoeal infection took some ten weeks. Apart from the discomfort of the ailment, having to recuperate under the same roof with his mother, father, and brothers was humiliating. He and his father had made their way directly to Auchinleck to join the family, which was eagerly watching the building of the new Palladian house up the hill. They all returned to Edinburgh in the first week of June, where the prodigal son began his tutorials with his father in civil law. 'I was hurried down to Scotland,' he informed Eglinton, 'confined to live in my father's family, and pressed to study law, so that my situation was very unhappy.'[1] From this point on, the father kept the son on a short rein.

The triple affliction of gonorrhoea, confinement, and intense law study with his unrelenting father was not Boswell's idea of a homecoming after a seven-month absence. By mid-August, he was well again but immediately caught another venereal infection. 'Hurried on by the heat of youth', he had gone to 'a house or recreation' in the city and 'catch'd a Tartar, too, with a vengeance'. Vengeance, indeed, for he suffered four more months of debilitating confinement and law study at home. Back at Auchinleck on 22 September, he was again 'taking a regular course of Medicines, and keeping within doors, with spare diet, in order to get effectually rid of my indisposition, that troublesome companion and bar to my innocent pleasures'. Confinement under his father's watchful eye brought on more low spirits – 'I have been sometimes *sixty* since you left me,' he told Grange, deploying the image of age as their shorthand for depression. He was now socially out of commission until late December. At Auchinleck or in Edinburgh, there was little to do except study law, read, and write. Writing was his lifeline. It could keep up his spirits and remind him who he really was, although the 'foul fiend' of hypochondria kept robbing him of 'juvenility' and the disposition to 'rove about', for him a prerequisite for creativity.[2]

2

The obvious subject to write about was himself. Few things at this point interested Boswell more. He began with a ballad opera, *Give Your Son His Will*, that afforded him secret and sweet revenge against his father's domination. He completed only half of it, a discussion between Sir Solomon Positive (solemn Lord Auchinleck) and his friend Sagely (perhaps Eglinton), who pleads on behalf of Sir Solomon's son Charles to let him join the army instead of entering his father's business. Sagely's argument is of course Boswell's. He urges that choosing a profession is like choosing a wife: inclination, 'which we strongly feel, and cannot explain ... must be allowed to have great weight'. Charles wants to join 'out of honour and a desire for glory'. In Sir Solomon's speeches, he imitates his father's mannerisms: 'Come, do resolve upon it. You'll find trade [substitute the law] much more agreeable than you imagine. Consider too how advantageous and respectful it is.' Boswell paraphrased its major theme in a letter to George Lewis Scott, tutor to the Prince of Wales and Commissioner of Excise, a sympathetic friend of the family and thirty years his senior. Hoping that Scott would prevail on his father to see things from his point of view, he maintained that someone as wild as himself must not, could not, be tamed and forced into a particular profession:

> A young fellow of an impetuosity of temper must be allowed some head, lest he should be driven to disagreeable shifts. When a big – swoln River comes rapidly tumbling from the Mountains we must not expect that its courses will be entirely according to what we could wish. We ought to be content if we can make it run in a *tollerable channel.*[3]

The 'Newmarket courser' has become a romantic swollen river which must be allowed to spill over its banks if it is not going to prove destructive.

He sent Scott several 'Juvenile Verses'. 'Boswell the Poet', as he called himself, was born during this period of submission to his father. These and others written between 1760 and 1762 comprise most of his poetic output. He came close to publishing them as 'a neat pocket Volume' of about one hundred-and-fifty pages, but in the end was content to let them take 'an eternal nap', as he put it to Lady Northumberland. Their diversity, if not their quality, is striking. Modern editors have found places for them in the following categories: jovial, amorous, melancholy, epigrammatic, satirical, 'boozy', open-hearted, spiritual, whimsical, epistolary, lamentable, and literary. About thirty turned out to be just what Alexander Donaldson was looking for to fill out the second volume of his Edinburgh anthology, *A Collection of Original Poems by Scotch Gentlemen*, published in 1762.[4]

3

A new figure of influence now entered Boswell's life. Andrew Erskine was the same age and also a hypochondriac, but a better poet, whose work had been included in Donaldson's first volume of *Original Poems* published in 1760. Erskine was a lieutenant in the army when they met in May 1761 at Fort George, north of Inverness. In Boswell's eyes, this swarthy young man was blessed with three advantages: a little success as a poet, a military career, and a colourful family history. Never mind that Erskine's poetry was unmistakably minor and that his career in the 71st Regiment of Foot was soon to end with the conclusion of the Seven Years' War. His father, the fifth Earl of Kellie, brother of Thomas, sixth Earl, the well-known Edinburgh composer, appealed to Boswell because he had fought in 1745 as a colonel in the Jacobite army and was imprisoned in Edinburgh Castle for three years. Erskine was spirited and fun-loving when he was not depressed and indolent. Ready for literary adventures, with an instinct for the irreverent and impudent, he was the sort of sparkling, companionable, unconventional, 'blackguard' friend Boswell needed. A couple of years later when they met up again in London, Boswell summed up his attraction: 'Erskine drank tea with me. We were in a luscious flow of spirits and vastly merry. "How we do chase a thought", said Erskine, "when once it is started. Let it run as it pleases over hill and dale and take numberless windings, still we are at it. It has a greyhound at its heels every turn." '[5]

Boswell met Erskine through George Dempster, an advocate and the Provost of St Andrews who, at great personal expense, had recently been elected MP for Perth Burghs. He was an extrovert bachelor and like Erskine a scribbler of verse. As Boswell later described his friendship with

Dempster and Erskine: 'It is only fancy that cements us. It is only because we are entertaining to one another that we are so much together.'[6] On 10 May, after they had talked for hours 'quite in the Genius style', Dempster gave Boswell a letter of introduction to Erskine. Boswell was about to depart for the north with his father on the Northern Circuit and Dempster saw this both as a chance for two kindred spirits to meet and a means to lessen the tedium of the legal business of the trip for his young friend.

Boswell attempted to minimize the boredom he feared on the journey by again keeping a journal. Although this first surviving journal is low on introspection because he may have felt imaginatively cramped by his father's presence, it does describe the huge amount of socializing he managed to fit in during the three-week trip. Only a few days turned out to be unbearably boring, such as 8 May when he was 'in court all forenoon'. Otherwise the progress north unfolded as a succession of recorded visits to castles and country seats, walks through exquisite gardens, tea parties, dances, and girls. At Moncrieff House in Perthshire, he met a pretty young heiress, Miss Balneves, who was too cold and composed for his taste. Miss Dallas, however, a third cousin, was another matter. He breakfasted with her at Inverness on 16 May: 'a charming creature indeed – excessively pretty – a most engaging manner – Great good sense – surprising propriety of language and facility of Expression. We were very merry.' They went for a walk: 'We fell behind – Upon my soul a delightfull Girl . . . Was in raptures to myself with her – Witty and good natured at the same time . . . Went home and sat with her till 9.' At Inverness, he danced with the celebrated and married Lady Anne Mackintosh, fifteen years his senior, who played a big part in the Jacobite Rebellion by raising a regiment on behalf of Bonnie Prince Charlie and, as the story goes, saving him from capture at her estate, Moyhall. Charming one of the most famous of Scotswomen was a new feather in Boswell's cap. Later he corresponded and exchanged poetry with her.[7]

On arriving in Inverness with Dempster's letter, Boswell lost little time in riding the eleven miles north up to Fort George. Their meeting lasted a day or two, after which Erskine said he was in 'awe' of Boswell. They watched regimental manoeuvres and Boswell learned of the second volume of Donaldson's *Original Poems* then struggling towards publication, for which Erskine (and Dempster, to a lesser extent) had already sent Donaldson a quantity of verse. Erskine doubtless told his energetic new acquaintance that Donaldson was having trouble finding enough poetry to fill the volume, for Boswell left Fort George with his head full of this promising conduit for his literary genius and fame.

On 28 July he mustered enough courage to send Donaldson two poems in imitation of Thomas Gray. Donaldson forwarded them, as he did most poems submitted to him, to Erskine, his poetaster, for a verdict. The next thing we know, on 10 August 1761, Donaldson unexpectedly published a sixpenny pamphlet, *An Elegy on the Death of an Amiable Young Lady. With An Epistle from Lycidas to Manalcas*, together with three 'Recommendatory' letters by 'G.D., A.F., and J.B.'. Although Erskine did not much like the poems, he recognized them as Boswell's and, rather than hurt his feelings, he hatched a plan: they could be published as burlesques with (except for their initials) anonymous puffs by himself and Dempster, who was brought in on the scheme. Boswell warmed to the idea and decided that he would make a merry trio of it with his own anonymous letter extravagantly praising his own poems. Donaldson went along with the plan. The recommendatory letters, of more interest than the poems, mark the start of Boswell's and Erskine's literary correspondence.[8]

4

The 'gay sociality' that characterized Boswell's verse after he returned from London was epitomized by his founding a 'jovial society' in Edinburgh in late 1760 which he dubbed the Soaping Club. It numbered only four or five who met to 'rattle' away every Tuesday evening at Thom's and took its name from Boswell's motto, 'Let every man soap his own beard' or, to paraphrase it in his words, 'Let every man indulge his own humour'. As the 'King' of the club, he was in his element. His limping lines in 'B—, A Song' catch the spirit of these Tuesday evening rollicks and the prominent part his 'soaping' self played in them:

> Boswell, of Soapers the King
> > On Tuesdays at Thom's does appear,
> And when he does talk or does sing,
> > To him ne'er a one can come near.
> For he talks with such ease and such grace,
> > That all charm'd to attention we sit,
> And he sings with so comic a face
> > That our sides are just ready to split.

Boswell was not only the founder but also the life and soul of the club.

At the meetings he played the mimic, exercised his good singing voice, recited poetry, recounted his amorous adventures, and doubtless regaled his friends with tales of his London jaunt and dreams of a commission in the Guards:

> B— is pleasant and gay,
>   For frolic by nature design'd
> And heedlessly rattles away
>   When the company is to his mind.
>   *
>
> B— does women adore,
>   And never once means to deceive,
> He's in love with at least half a score –
>   If they're serious he smiles in his sleeve.
> He has all the bright fancy of youth,
>   With the judgement of forty and five;
> In short, to declare the plain truth,
>   There is no better fellow alive.[9]

Erskine was game for all this. When Boswell missed a meeting one Tuesday, he sent him these lines from Thom's, 'Just before supper':

> The Soapers are met
> The lather is rais'd
> What! Boswell forget!
> Oh! how we're amaz'd!

The Rev. Edward Colquitt, another of Boswell's amusing new friends and a fellow founding member of the club was incorrectly blamed for the young 'soaper's' social excesses during this period. Lord Auchinleck and Dalrymple also blamed Colquitt for nourishing Boswell's taste for Anglicanism. Dalrymple, in fact, would not let Boswell forget how frivolous he thought the Soaping Club was and how inimical both it and Colquitt were to his Presbyterianism. As late as October 1764, long after the club had ceased to meet, Dalrymple wrote to Boswell in far-off Germany scolding him for his determination to attend only Church of England services when he returned to Edinburgh: 'The world is a per-petual puppet shew in our eyes . . . if you like the Puppet shew I suppose your father will have no objection to your being of the Church of England, for "Ned C— the Priest" is not in this country . . . You will pardon me for thinking that your Soaping Club is at the bottom of this unphilosophical esteem for the English ceremonys.'[10]

The Church of England had three prime attractions for Boswell that had nothing to do with the club: it was English, its services possessed a liturgical and ceremonial drama (though not so highly pitched as in the Catholic Church), and it had priests like Colquitt, who was full of the joy Boswell found lacking in Presbyterian clerics and was not beyond joining in the fun at the local tavern.

5

At the other end of the literary spectrum, towards the end of 1761 Boswell became a member of the Select Society of Edinburgh, the city's most distinguished society of men of letters in the golden period of the Scottish Enlightenment, founded in 1754 by Allan Ramsay. In his 1791 *Memoirs* Boswell proudly mentions it:

> Having no uncommon desire for the company of men distinguished for talents and literature, he was fortunate enough to get himself received into that of those who were considerably his superiors in age; such as Lord Elibank, Lord Kames [Henry Home], Sir David Dalrymple, Dr [William] Robertson, Dr [Hugh] Blair, Mr David Hume; Dr [Alexander] Carlyle, Mr Andrew Stuart, and others; and was admitted a member of the *Select Society* of Edinburgh.[11]

That he could feel at ease both in the roistering Soaping Club and in the elegant company of scholars, writers, and philosophers in the Select Society was not unique in Edinburgh. When Burns came to Edinburgh in 1786–7, he commonly attended formal evening parties with the literati and then afterwards sought out the taverns for more raucous sport, as did Ramsay and Robert Fergusson. Social lines were not as clearly drawn in Edinburgh as in London: this was one of the factors that engendered cross-fertilization between the popular and intellectual traditions and continued to feed the richness of Scottish literature, even after 1707 and the decline of native Scots vernacular verse. Even Boswell's early verse shows the effects of a lifestyle that had him constantly on the move, studying law, fraternizing at Select Society meetings with famous writers in the more genteel European tradition, and frolicking at his own Soaping Club with his legal, clerical, and poetic friends. His poetry, for all its banality, represents a spectrum of popular, epigrammatic, classical and sentimental styles.[12]

Still, the Select Society did draw the line between social and professional conduct. Its members could drink every bit as hard as tradesmen,
innkeepers, and poets, but not at the society's meetings; they met each
week to discuss literary and philosophical topics, not to carouse. They
did not meet to generate a sense of native community, but instead looked
out from Scotland to England and Europe. David Daiches has made this
point with a Scots flourish: 'Fergusson's convivial evenings at Walter
Scott's tavern in Geddes Close with fellow members of the Cape Club
or taking oysters and gin at Lucky Middlemass's or his dish of rizzard
haddock and bicker of tippeny at some other Edinburgh howff – these
were different from the more formal meetings of the Select Society.'[13]

It is surprising therefore that a twenty-one-year-old scribbler of verse
and a gadabout, albeit of engaging manners and very clubbable, should
be admitted to such august company. Undoubtedly Dalrymple, Hume,
and Kames helped Boswell to gain entry. Of equal importance perhaps,
was that he held the sorts of attitudes toward Scottish culture and
language that the Society found compatible. It stood for religious moderation and a desire to promote English-style gentility; and it dedicated
itself to encouraging 'correct' Scottish use of the English language and
discouraging native solecisms and vernacular usage that handicapped the
reception of Scottish literature in England. David Hume even went so
far as to draw up a private list of Scottish idioms (later published) to be
avoided by cultured men and women. Boswell's motivation for purging
Scotticisms from his own speech and writing was mainly emotional at
this point: he wanted to feel like an Englishman. He had come to feel
very nervous about his accent, perhaps taking to heart the English
politician Charles Townshend's anti-Scottish remark, 'Why can't you
learn to speak the English language as you have already learned to write
it?' Later, when he began to write seriously for publication, he knew it
was crucial to write in 'correct' English in order to be understood and
respected south of the border. He was by no means alone in this. Dr
William Robertson, to be elected Principal of Edinburgh University in
1762, had advertised the importance of this process of refinement in 1759
when he published his acclaimed *History of Scotland.* He explained that
because of the Union of Parliaments in 1707 Scotland could not sustain
two languages or comparable dialects: 'by the accession the English
naturally became the sole judges and lawgivers in Language, and rejected,
as solecisms, every form of speech to which their ear was not accu-
stomed.'[14] Acclaimed though he was, and although they agreed on the
matter of language, Robertson never became one of Boswell's heroes.

There was nothing for it but for Edinburgh folk to try to speak more like the English. An Irishman from Dublin, Thomas Sheridan, heard the Select Society's call and in the summer of 1761 marched triumphantly into Edinburgh to teach elocution and the subtleties of the English tongue. Sheridan, the fanatical elocutionist, actor, and father of the celebrated dramatist Richard Brinsley Sheridan, set himself up to lecture to three hundred gentlemen, Boswell, Erskine, and Dempster among them, on how to speak with the cadence of the English. One of Sheridan's principal theories was that the spoken word is a gift of God and hence infinitely superior to the written word. But God's gift was English, not Scots. Apparently the majority of his audiences agreed. In spite of his strong Irish brogue, the irony of which surely could not have been lost on many of his listeners, Sheridan was such a success that he made bold to offer another series of lectures just for women, which were equally successful. While there were those who mocked this campaign, large numbers in genteel and not so genteel Edinburgh society wanted to speak like the English, it seems. Most of the literati in the Select Society attended the lectures.[15]

6

Boswell soon fell under Sheridan's influence, writing to him: 'You are My Socrates. You have said so yourself. With unfeigned Joy do I thank Heaven for it.' They talked for hours at the Star and Garter in the Writers' Court, a gathering place of the city's lawyers, about Boswell's plans for the Guards, his desire to live in London, his legal studies, his literary interests, his father, his hypochondria, and so on. Sheridan told Boswell about London life and the theatre and, especially, about Samuel Johnson. Boswell hoped that the Irishman could 'save' him, a tender plant, 'from perishing in the Flower, and before its Fruit came to Perfection'. 'Am not I then a "hopeful Plant?",' he cried, amazed at his impudence.[16] When Sheridan left for London and Boswell retreated to Auchinleck for the holidays, a friendship had been cemented between the vain young man and the equally vain and flattered older man, who now thought of himself as 'dear Boswell's' 'godfather'.

Boswell impressed on Sheridan that he needed to flower poetically and that this was not as likely to happen in Edinburgh as in London. Unless he got to London, his poetic self might, like Milton's Lycidas, die before it bore fruit. He knew the poems he was writing, rapidly now, for

Donaldson's collection were not soaring in the Miltonic vein, but surely he was not a middling person: poetry and 'Genius' were restive in him. Sheridan considered the problem and decided that neither the study of Scottish law in Edinburgh nor the Guards scheme was likely to bring Boswell back to London and keep him there: Scottish law would strand him in Scotland if indeed he ever became an advocate. The best idea would be for him to study English law at the Inner Temple and qualify for the English Bar. Boswell still cherished the hope of joining the Guards but he was prepared to agree to the Inner Temple as a compromise with his father's insistence on a legal career. Besides, should he later decide that he wanted to live in Edinburgh after all, as an English barrister he could in theory practise law and be appointed a judge in the Court of the Exchequer in his native city.

In London, Sheridan promptly put Boswell's name down at the Inner Temple; he also indulged the latter's taste for role-playing by addressing his next letter to Boswell as 'Student of the Inner Temple'. The formal note of admission was in Boswell's hands towards the end of November. Apparently under the impression that his father was in agreement with the plan, that in his eyes it was better to study law in London than take up a commission in the Guards, Boswell hoped to take up his studies there in the New Year. By 25 November, however, the plan had unravelled. Lord Auchinleck had 'forgot our Agreement', Boswell moaned: 'I am certain he must really have forgot it; for he is a worthy, honest man.' They argued and he refused to go near his father for several days – 'I scarcely know how to behave to him. In sober sadness, I am much afraid that we shall never agree.' Yet two weeks later, all was well again, for Lord Auchinleck had come round, though to what is still unclear: 'He is an excellent man. You know I always said so, even when he and I were upon the worst terms together ... Every thing will now go smoothly on; and I flatter myself that we shall see a completion of your great design – to make Boswell a *Man*.'[17]

But it still was not to be. The Guards scheme revived and the English barrister scheme faded away. The prospect of intense legal study, even in London, may have put Boswell off. His father's rigorous tuition at home had been bad enough. Many years later, when he tried to practise law in London and virtually drowned in his ignorance of English law, he was to rue the collapse of Sheridan's dreamy scenario.

7

His father's legal instruction became even more irrelevant in the autumn and winter of 1761–2. There was so much else on Boswell's plate, of which Lord Auchinleck had only the merest inkling. Hypochondria was in arrest. The 'Fire of his Genius' was being kindled. Alone at Auchinleck in late August, 'a good deal pensive' without 'THE FAMILY', he studied 'inveterately', to be sure, but he was also reading Shenstone's poetry, pining for new friends like Erskine and old friends like Grange, and writing verse. He refused to go on the Western Circuit with his father in September, irrespective of the consequences. There was also Donaldson's *Collection* to think about.[18]

Lord Kames, one of his father's colleagues on the bench but far more exuberant and appreciative of Boswell's volatility and spirit than his father, good-naturedly compared him to Fielding's wandering, well-meaning, amorous hero, Tom Jones. The idea charmed Boswell, although Kames knew confusion and dissipation when he saw it. Boswell was engaged in more than one clandestine affair at the time, with Mrs Love and Peggy Doig, for example, even as he openly courted the respectable Kitty Colquhoun, the eligible eighteen-year-old daughter of the distinguished Highlander Sir James Colquhoun of Luss.

For several months he had been pursuing this 'angel of light' intensely enough to launch rumours that he was about to marry her. She was certainly worthy of Boswell and Tom Jones, 'a beautiful young lady ... the idol of every public place, the toast of every private company', and she also wrote verses. As a Highlander, however, she probably did not measure up to Lord Auchinleck's hopes for his son as much as an Ayrshire girl with an estate near Auchinleck would have done. She threw Boswell into raptures in December by sending him a lock of her hair tied with a pink ribbon: 'Ye Gods! She condescends to bid me wear it!' he wrote back; 'Yes, Peerless Maid! suspended by that lovely Pink Ribbon, thy divine, Golden lock shall hang upon the Breast of Boswell. If it does not, may I have a Soul the reverse of Tom Jones.' For good measure, he composed a long poem to her that eventually found its way into Donaldson's collection. The poem, which identifies her only as 'Kitty', pleased her, but he lost her suddenly when he published his letter to Eglinton in which he insulted her and her family with an ill-judged parade of his wit. Erskine refers on 2 March 1762 to her 'last kiss'. Three years later she married, ironically, a captain in the Guards.[19]

Boswell published that letter because he was genuinely taken with his own witty prose, and it is true that his literary talent first showed itself in letters. His highly allusive correspondence with Erskine, for example, sparkles with wit and inventiveness. He thought it good enough to publish. Erskine had no objection : 'You hate flattery ... but in spite of your teeth I must tell you, that you are the best poet, and the most humourous letter-writer I know; and that you have a finer complexion, and dance better than any man of my acquaintance.' Dempster chimed in, too (as relayed by Erskine): 'there is a great deal of humility in your vanity, a great deal of tallness in your shortness, and a great deal of whiteness in your black complexion ... a great deal of poetry in your prose, and a great deal of prose in your poetry ... a great deal of liveliness in your stupidity, and a great deal of stupidity in your liveliness.'[20]

For the moment, though, Boswell's poetic muse took priority, stirred by Donaldson's need for more poems to complete his volume. Verses on all sorts of subjects continued to pour from his pen with embarrassing ease. It was not long before his contribution to the collection was equal to Erskine's. One of these poems, 'The Ode to Tragedy', sixteen dull stanzas, signed with one of Boswell's favourite pseudonyms, 'A Gentleman of Scotland', Donaldson published for him in a sixpenny pamphlet early in December. As a joke, and the probable reason for its separate publication, he dedicated the ode to himself: 'James Boswell, Esq ... for your particular kindness to me, and chiefly for the profound respect with which you have always treated me.' Erskine was not in on the joke, but Boswell soon revealed himself with a portrait – self-portrait – of the poet, playing on private jokes:

> a most excellent man ... of an ancient family in the west of Scotland, upon which he values himself, not a little. His Education has been good; though carried on in various modes. He has travelled in Post-Chaises, miles without number. He eats of every good dish. He drinks Old Hock. He wears tolerable Pumps. How his Mother brought him forth we dont know. But at his nativity, there appeared omens of his future glory ... He has a very fine temper. He is somewhat of an humourist, and a little tinctured with pride. He has a good manly countenance, and he owns himself to be amorous. He has infinite vivacity, yet is observed at times to have a melancholy cast ... He is rather fat than lean; rather short than tall. He never wears spectacles.[21]

Apropos of his tendency to plumpness, Boswell also wrote an 'Ode to Gluttony' for Donaldson. His chubbiness amused Erskine and other friends, especially in light of his vain amorousness. When on one occasion he complimented Erskine's poems and expressed his surprise that a thin person could be so passionate, Erskine replied gleefully that it was the 'spindle-shanked lover' like himself who made the most headway with women: 'In vain does Cupid shoot his arrows at the plump existence, who is entrenched in a solid wall of fat: they are buried like shrimps in melted butter; as eggs are preserved by mutton-tallow, from rottenness and putrefaction, so he, by his grease, is preserved from love.'[22]

On the banks of Loch Lomond, Erskine felt removed from the nerve centre of this outpouring: 'why am I not in Edinburgh? why am I not chain'd to Donaldson's shop?' Boswell rubbed it in with accounts of delicious meals at Donaldson's home, the fat fowls, oysters, apple pie with raisins, and mutton with cauliflower. He even became Donaldson's proof-reader for the collection, which was Erskine's job for the first volume. After an eleventh-hour scramble for more poems, two hundred lines of which Boswell supplied in late January, the project raced to completion. It was published in early February. His and Erskine's poems made up the lion's share, ninety-five out of 232 pages. He had thirty-two poems in the volume, almost all of them unremarkable. James Beattie (author of *The Minstrel*) and James Macpherson (author of the *Ossian* poems), among a host of others, were also represented. There was plenty of nonsense and unevenness in the poems. The critics on the whole neglected the collection, though one reviewer in the *Critical Review* delighted Boswell by speaking of 'the agreeable light pieces by J.B. Esq.' 'I puff about it,' he told Erskine, who was not so happy when the reviewer said his poem 'Cloaciniad' had all Swift's 'stench without his spirit'.[23]

Donaldson's *Collection* was all in all a worthwhile literary project for Boswell who, if nothing else, throughout its preparation, kept up his spirits and beat down depression in a flood of breezy letters exchanged with Erskine. Looking back on it all a few months later, he was pleased with himself: 'You and I Erskine are, to be sure, somewhat vain. We have some reason too. The Reviewers gave great applause to your Odes to Indolence and Impudence; and they called my poems "agreeable light pieces", which was the very character I wished for. Had they said less, I should not have been satisfied; and had they said more, I should have thought it a burlesque.'[24]

8

The merry letters with Erskine continued throughout the following year, which began with a good deal of dissipation and 'giddy Volatility', a sure sign of increasing hypochondria. Boswell's fondness for dressing up was revealed at a January ball at the Palace of Holyrood, attended by over six hundred guests in honour of Queen Charlotte's birthday. He described himself to Erskine: 'I exhibited my existence in a minuet, and as I was drest in a full chocolate suit, and wore my most solemn countenance, I looked as you used to tell me, like the fifth act of a deep Tragedy.' His solemn countenance did not appear to put off Peggy Stewart, daughter of a baronet, with whom he danced several times and imagined himself in love.[25]

Somehow he continued to study through all this, but he hated it. With hopes of studying law in London now dead, his great escape route remained the Guards. On 24 March, he and his father formally agreed to what hitherto had been only an understanding. He could go to London as soon as he passed his law exams. Now that the dream had almost become a reality, Erskine tried to dissuade him, in verse as well as prose:

> Then coolly, Sir, I say repent,
> And in derision hold a tent;
> Leave not the sweet poetic band,
> To scold recruits . . .
> Trust me, 'twill be a foolish sight
> To see you facing to the right;
> And then, of all your sense bereft,
> Returning back unto the left.

Boswell replied that 'For military operation / I have a wondrous inclination', but admitted that the real reason he wanted a commission was 'a city called London, for which I have as violent an affection, as the most romantic lover ever had for his mistress'.[26]

He lost no time writing to Eglinton to cash in on his promised help. But he was asking for the virtually impossible: a London battalion, not a marching regiment that would take him away from the great metropolis. Eglinton replied swiftly and firmly that this was a request requiring more influence than he possessed. After all, beggars could not be choosers, and Boswell unquestionably was begging. It was a stiff rebuke, unlooked for from his London saviour. As Eglinton saw it, Boswell had been guilty of 'genteel evasion' by saying he was 'willing to go abroad' but intending to shun doing so at all costs. Boswell later recorded in his journal how he defended himself to Eglinton: 'Well, I assure you, my Lord, that my meaning was this: that my great plan in getting into the Guards was not so much to be a soldier as to be in the genteel character of a gentleman; and therefore I would have rather chose that my commission should have been in one of the battalions at home. But I should certainly have rather gone abroad than not get in.' Devastated by Eglinton's apparent rebuff, he turned to his father for help, who (according to their agreement) wrote to the Duke of Queensberry and received a vague promise of help. There the matter rested until Boswell could go to London to do something about it himself.[27]

Part of his agreement with his father was that in April he would return to Auchinleck with the rest of the family for the holidays and study for his exams until June. It was a souring prospect with which to return to the paternal acres, even though his father had also agreed to give him an unconditional allowance of £100 per year. His father, however, gave with one hand and took away with the other. He forced Boswell to agree to place himself under the control of trustees should he unexpectedly succeed to the estate in the near future. So much for parental confidence. Lord Auchinleck's disapproval of his son went as far as threatening to disinherit him and sell the estate – or at least the additional lands he had himself purchased – which would have been in violation of his marriage contract that entailed the estate on his heirs male exclusively. Boswell knew about that contract, of course, but was frightened by the threat, especially coming from a learned legal authority like his father.

9

The hypochondria that had only nipped at his heels since his return from London now suddenly rose up against him menacingly. Erskine was his confidant: 'I have never at any time, been so insipid so muddy and so standing-water, as I have been of late ... I really have a very uncommon distaste of a rural life.' He tried to reason it out. This melancholy had come on him either because rural life did not measure up to his pastoral dream, nurtured in his Auchinleck youth; or because there was a want of good society in the Auchinleck neighbourhood and he felt on the margin of life there; or because the air was 'moist and heavy', made heavier by the study of civil law. The melancholy core of this realization explains his chronic restlessness and inability to live there in years to come.[28]

His moods swung like a pendulum. On 9 May, for example, the sun was shining and Auchinleck was again dear to him: he was 'fond of the Country', enlivened 'prodigiously', 'chearfull and happy'. It was Sunday, but instead of attending church he wandered 'placid and serene up and down the sweetest Place in the world . . . I am indulging the most agreable reveries imaginable.' He felt up to anything: shining in the Guards; 'feasting on the delicious Prospects of France and Italy' and writing noble poetry 'on the banks of the Tiber'; settling down after a progression of amours 'suited to my romantic Disposition' to married life with a young woman of 'sense, delicacy and softness'; breeding children that would prove a credit to their family and themselves; and living comfortably and graciously in both London and Auchinleck. A month later, however, even on a lovely day, he was again 'the Dungeon Slave of black Melancholy', staring with aversion at the delicious shades of Auchinleck that mocked his mind's 'cloudy darkness'. He came up with another despairing explanation: perhaps he had been too 'speculative', thinking too much about the 'eternal fitness of Things', the doctrine of Necessity, predestination. The sinister thread of his own early experiences with religion embroidered his anxiety.[29]

The black dregs of melancholy finally evaporated in mid-June when he left Auchinleck for Edinburgh. After more than a month of cramming with William Wallace, Advocate and Professor of History at the university, he at last took his exams at the end of the month and passed with flying colours. 'I was very happy at its being over indeed,' he wrote in his journal with heartfelt relief.[30] He was out of his cage.

FIVE

Harvest Jaunt

I

At last Lord Auchinleck had what he wanted: his son was qualified to practise law as a Scottish advocate, even if that was the last thing he intended to do. Instead, London lay ahead – and the Guards. It was too early to go right away, though. Fashionable society would not return to the city until the winter season began in November. Moreover, the Edinburgh theatre was in full swing, Boswell had friends like Grange and Erskine with whom to spend some carefree time, and (not least) he was still busy sexually with Mrs Love, a mysterious 'A', and the servant-girl Peggy Doig. The big surprise, or shock rather, was that Peggy was already five to six months' pregnant with his child. Needless to say, this was not something he told his family. He needed to make arrangements for the child, whom to his credit he was willing to support and educate, but he had to do it quietly.

By mid-August, he was back in Auchinleck, where this time there was the great bustle and excitement of moving into the new classical mansion. Boswell proudly took up residence in his room, 'a neat elegant Apartment which contributes to render me chearfull and well'. Not cheerful enough, though. He soon felt oppressed again and 'heated'. As soon as he got there, he impulsively shaved his head to relieve the pressure on his brain and ward off another attack of melancholy. It 'was agreeable at first by letting the heat of my brain evaporate', he explained to Grange, 'but as it requires a long time to grow, I am quite confined can see no Company, and am obliged to wear my Nightcap. I shall take care of playing such a trick in time coming.' It was a race against time, for it had to grow out enough before he could set out in three weeks on an extended farewell 'jaunt' to the homes of several family friends in the Lowlands. While he waited, he arranged for Dr John Cairnie to meet with Grange and 'concert a plan about my little affair', the details of caring for Peggy Doig. There was no need to do anything until November, Cairnie reassured him, at which time the three of them could meet secretly to plan for the birth.[1]

The prospect of his September 'jaunt' sustained Boswell through a month of 'the deepest dungeon of age' at Auchinleck. When he was ready to leave, as was always the case with him, he had a return of 'good health and a moderate flow of lively spirits'.[2]

2

Boswell's peregrinations throughout the Lowlands are well documented in his first full journal, 'Journal of My Jaunt, Harvest 1762': 'I intend to keep a journal in order to acquire a method, for doing it, when I launch into the Ocean of high life.' His preliminary remarks suggest that he saw it as a risky literary venture but he wrote it for his 'true friends' Grange and William McQuhae, to whom he could 'unbosom my anxious mind'. McQuhae, then twenty-five, was the young, jocular clergyman who had served as domestic tutor to Boswell's younger brothers at Auchinleck. Boswell thought him a 'good-natured, indolent, honest man', not at all preachy. With his two friends sympathetically reading the journal, Boswell decided to try for literary effect as well as self-revelation in conveying the life and richness of a moment or setting, conversation, characterization, dramatic texture, a unique blend of the observer and the observed, and wit and humour. Not too modestly, he had high hopes for the 'brilliancy of its thoughts and the elegant ease of its language'. Moreover, 'now and then it will surprise with an oddity and peculiar turn of humour or a vivacious wildness of fancy'.[3]

He started nervously and self-consciously: 'As I am *seriously afraid* that my journal will rather be bad than otherwise, I would not choose to have it considered with a microscopic eye.' He was also defensive because this journal would be more intimate than anything he had yet written. His poetry and the letters to Erskine impart relatively little about him: their display of rollicking wit and pretentious prattle conceals rather than reveals. This journal would expose his complexity, for better or for worse:

> a man who is found out to be changeable in his opinions, and especially in his schemes of life is looked upon by the generality of mankind as a weak and often a silly fellow. For with the multitude, obstinate perseverance, even

in dulness, meets with more quarter than the most sprightly fickleness.

There was the rub, for the 'character of my journal is a very mixed one':

> As it is written for amusement and in a careless, dissipated way, it cannot fail
> to be very incorrect both in the arrangement of the subjects and in the
> expression. It must therefore meet with much indulgence; and, although
> it should appear sometimes trifling and insipid and sometimes stupidly
> sententious, it must not be allowed to disgrace its writer.[4]

3

There is more bathos than heroism in Boswell's record of the first hours
of the jaunt, as if he were consciously impersonating both Don Quixote
and Tom Jones. Riding off on 14 September, his horse promptly threw
him into a mire; and the boredom at his first destination, Berboth, the
seat of the Laird of Craigengillan, almost killed him, 'having exhausted
all my little stock of country conversation, I mean of tilling the ground
and feeding cattle'. He made a quick exit, preferring to be lashed by the
rain on horseback to the 'stagnation' of more such talk and the prospect
of 'raw rooms and damp beds'. He arrived that evening at Lagwine, the
seat of James McAdam, whose son (then six) grew up to be the famous
road builder. Here he liked what he found and was soon singing and
acting pantomimes with the children by a cosy fire, taking genteel meals
with ample wine, and playing on the German flute, lessons on which he
had begun in Edinburgh. He felt clever, facetious, and admired at dinner.
The children adored him.[5]

   At his next stop, Lord Kenmure's seat at Kenmure, he began 'grave and
constrained' because the family was too formal. He also had nightmares
because he slept close to a portrait of the Lord Kenmure executed for
high treason on Tower Hill in 1716. A delightful surprise, though, was
Lady Kenmure, who flirted with him. At tea, she sang 'little pretty
chansons' and danced around the room, then 'wrapped her capuchin
round me and lisped such little expressions of tenderness as are used to
children of whom one is fond'. He captured a charming moment:
noticing that he had no sugar in his tea, ' "What," says she, "I suppose
there is so much sweetness *there* (carelessly stirring the tea, but with her
eyes, beaming full upon mine) that there is no need of sugar." ' Had she
been English, he would have suspected she wanted an intrigue, but it

was all sportive gallantry, even her playful suggestion that they meet in Paris when he became an officer in the Guards.[6]

On the 18th, he left for Kirroughtrie (near Newton Stewart), the home of Lord Kames's eighteen-year-old daughter Jean and her husband Patrick Heron, where he stayed for over two weeks – long enough to have a delicious affair. Jean's husband was away. He told Rousseau about it in 1764:

> I was in love with the daughter of a man of the first distinction in Scotland. She married a gentleman of great wealth. She let me see that she loved me more than she did her husband. She made no difficulty of granting me all. She was a subtle philosopher. She said, 'I love my husband as a husband, and you as a lover, each in his own sphere. I perform for him all the duties of a good wife. With you I give myself up to delicious pleasures. We keep our secret. Nature has made me that I shall never bear children. No one suffers because of our loves. My conscience does not reproach me, and I am sure that God cannot be offended by them.'

He had visited Jean frequently at her father's estate in 1761 when she was sixteen, before her marriage, and had more or less fallen in love with her in the process. 'Often have your fingers fair / Pick'd for my mouth the choicest Pear,' he wrote in a poem to her before she married. It is likely that they had made love almost a year earlier, just after her marriage, though it beggars belief that they would have waited until then before doing so. Their affection for each other could not have gone unnoticed by Lord and Lady Kames who were exceedingly fond of him; but Boswell was not a big enough catch and nobody appears seriously to have considered the prospect of their marriage.[7]

This present adultery was a dangerous game because, had Lord Kames discovered it, that would have been the end of a friendship with a great man of letters whom Boswell genuinely liked. But Jean was lovely (though 'not a flaming beauty'), genteel, sensible, sweet, very lively, and funny, qualities in a woman that Boswell always found difficult to resist; she was also not a little wanton. There is not a whisper of their affair in the journal because Grange and McQuhae would read it, but he allowed himself the whimsical remark, 'She promises to make a good wife, and a very complete woman.' She did not, in fact, make a good wife. Caught in another adulterous relationship in 1772 with a young army officer, her husband promptly divorced her, much to her parents' dismay.[8]

During the two weeks at Kirroughtrie, Boswell see-sawed between

gloominess and exuberance. Even Jeany's company could not keep off
hypochondria, which now began to creep up on him. His journal entries
are flecked with it. He was one of 'the finer souls' on the planet, whose
mind needed to be 'gently soothed and tenderly indulged' if it was to be
controlled. A Presbyterian service, like bad weather, could have the
reverse effect, so he avoided church on Sunday and wrote poetry instead.
Bad weather easily knocked him off balance: '[I] lost relish for everything,
despised myself for being so weak and so easily affected, have not been
able to do anything and so felt a load of time, which, of all burthens that
poor mortals are doomed to bear, is the heaviest.'[9]

At Kirroughtrie he also launched what he egocentrically called his
'Boswelliana', 'in which I intend from time to time to treasure up wit
and humour'[10] – his own as well as others'. And he took to reading and
talking about Dr Johnson's famous essays in the *Rambler*, which became
a Bible to him in the next few years as he struggled against the fiendish
vapours of hypochondria. He rounded out his stay by riding to hounds,
only to end up in a watery ditch, walking for hours in the garden with
Jeany, and talking with Lady Kames about her family – ' a strong sign of
my being very amiable'. Lord Murray of Broughton and his beautiful
wife Lady Katie arrived for a couple of days, after whose departure Jeany
told him that Lady Katie thought him 'the finest creature she had ever
seen'.[11]

His and Jeany's parting was emotional. They had a long and serious
talk, knowing they would not meet again for a long time: 'I was somewhat
dejected, comparing my present situation of ease and distinction with
the disagreeable state of dependence and anxiety that I have to endure
in London before I get my commission ... Mrs Heron said some things
which affected me a good deal.'[12] Jeany never again played a part in his
life.

4

As he headed for the eastern Lowlands, Boswell was on the whole happy
with his journal. He had gone through a dry patch, 'like a horse whose
legs are stocked', but by 8 October he was thoroughly warmed up
and writing with ease and pleasure,[13] discovering in himself the most
interesting and inexhaustible of subjects.

He knew that in order to write a vivid journal he had to be able to
portray character tightly and engagingly, revealing in a few short 'strokes'

the defining elements of personality. To this end, he tried his hand at thumbnail sketches or 'characters'. It cost him a good deal of effort. At one point, he decided enough was enough: 'I am now weary of the custom of drawing characters wherever I go, and therefore from this time that must not be expected in this my journal. I shall just take down one now and then when I choose it, and sometimes give only a stroke or two.' But he persisted and improved, with a growing facility for recording conversation: 'I have got into an excellent method of taking down conversations, and thus am able to furnish out a tolerable day, on which, being confined to the house, I must necessarily have a barrenness of incident.' He was waking up to his genius of seizing in a few words the kernel of a personality and vitality of a scene. There are a number of good ones: Lord and Lady Kames, Mrs Love, James Macpherson, Erskine, Hume, his uncle Dr John Boswell, Dempster, Donaldson, a few Edinburgh chums, and his father. 'I find myself strongly impelled to give a sketch of the characters that I meet with,' he admits cautiously, 'notwithstanding my former declaration. I shall therefore beg leave to indulge this as I find it agreeable. Indeed my figures are but very naked. They are but rude unfinished draughts and must not be taken as complete images.'[14]

There are also memorable scenes in this journal that seem effortlessly written, most of them having to do with women. At Springkell, Sir William Maxwell's seat in Dumfriesshire, Boswell met a kindred spirit, Kitty Gilpin, with whom he sang and acted to the delight of the assembled company. He was not, for once, interested in her sexually but because she was vivacious, bright, and satiric – and a poetess. The charm of his evening with her was matched by the charm of the way he brought it to life on the page:

> I contrived to make our personages talk together, which was a most ludicrous scene. She learnt me a method of quarrelling to 'Prince Eugene's March', by alternately singing bars and half bars of it and varying our tones and countenances till we gradually rose to the highest pitch of rage. This had a most wonderful effect upon the company, who were quite distressed with laughing. We likewise took off the Italian opera, and although we neither knew a word of the language nor a single tune, we thrilled away the most pathetic expression set to the tenderest music, which we succeeded in to a degree that was surprising. While we sat at table we agreed to humbug the company, and accordingly I whispered something to her with great earnestness, at which she seemed to be much shocked, started from me and

said, 'I don't understand, sir – such usage, sir, and I am sure you must mean to affront me – ' This and two three more little exclamations of the same kind delivered with the proper emphasis, joined with the disconcerted shee-piness of look which I nicely affected, fairly took in the whole company, who were really concerned, and could scarcely be persuaded that we were in joke.

A few qualities of his best prose are already evident: eagerness, sen-suousness, evocation, and unassuming and pleasing cadences. The rhythm and modulation are perfect, carried by such words and phrases as 'distressed with laughing', 'thrilled away', 'humbug', and 'disconcerted sheepiness of look'. What is striking is that he wrote at great speed and yet his manuscript is virtually free of corrections.[15]

The next day he bought a good strong grey horse at Springkell and rode down into Cumberland and Northumberland, ecstatic to be back in England. He attended a puppet show in Brampton, dressed fit to kill: 'As I had my Bath greatcoat with a gold binding, my gold-laced hat smartly set upon my head, and twirled my cane switch with a good deal of gentility, I looked exceedingly like an officer of the Army.' There the Boswellian magic played on a girl who sat behind him. The Punch itself was not memorable but his piquant recollections of it are:

Little did I think when I entered this scene of rude amusement that the gentle Goddess of Love was laying snares for me. However, that was the case. On the bench behind me sat a young lady in a red cloak and black hat ... I instantly addressed myself to her in the most engaging manner that I could, and found her tender enough; and during the hubbub, I obtained from her the sweetest kiss that virgin ever gave. She told me that she was maid to an innkeeper in the town, and that she could not have an opportunity of seeing me. However, she agreed that she would go to London with me if I would take her. Dear little creature! How fond was I of her.

He created another vivid scene with yet another female protagonist that night at his inn. He set the stage, pictured the girl, struck an erotic note, and ended with a comic footnote, all with an engaging innocence of manner:

At supper I fell much in love with the chambermaid who served us who was a handsome girl with an insinuating wantonness of look. I made her light me to my room, and when I had her there, she indulged me in many endearments, but would by no means consent to the main object of my ardent desires, and seemed afraid of the people in the house hearing us make noise. So I was obliged to sleep by myself. However, I discovered that sleep has prevented me from felicity, for Lord Kames's servant joked me next morning and told me seriously that he saw her go into my room and shut the door after I was gone to bed. This was going pretty far; but I suppose she had not assurance enough to wake me.[16]

5

Boswell made his way back north to Kames on 16 October, by which time Jeany had returned to her husband's estate at Kirroughtrie. Lord Kames was not, of course, oblivious to his roving eye. 'Boswell,' he declared fondly and with some exasperation, 'how many qualitys good and bad does that name bundle up together.' Boswell recorded his avuncular (and welcome) advice in a sincere spirit of self-improvement typical of all the journals that were to come: he 'told me that my greatest disadvantage was a too great avidity of pleasure, by which he understood elevation of spirits and high relish of company, which rendered me idle and made me unhappy in a calm situation ... "Now," said he, "Boswell, take care of splitting upon the same rock. You are going to London. You are very agreeable; your company will be much sought after. Be upon your guard in time. Be your own master. Keep the reins in your own hand. Resolve to be able to live at times by yourself." '[17]

It flattered Boswell to be appreciated by this colleague of his father's, one of the leading contemporary writers in English, a representative figure of the Scottish Enlightenment, who was then basking in the afterglow from the publication of his influential *Elements of Criticism* (1762). He featured him in one of his 'characters' in the journal: a diverse scholar, 'a good companion, cheerful and lively', though also 'now and then a little whimsical and impatient of contradiction'. Lady Kames does not fare quite as well: very handsome, a woman of good understanding and well bred, well endowed with humour, and a great family organiser, but now and then a little marred with lowness of spirits, 'which renders her more apt to be disturbed and offended than one could wish, and makes her say pretty severe things'.[18]

It did not take him long, however, to get bored at Kames. There was good literary conversation – Kames encouraged him to be a writer and he travelled over to see the ancient Lord Marchmont at Marchmont House, expressly for anecdotal tidbits about the latter's great friend

Alexander Pope – but his spirits sank with little to do. He played the German flute. He drifted to the races at nearby Kelso and lost some money he had borrowed from the Earl of Kellie. Several days of gloom and greyness descended on him:

> I despised learning, taste, and everything else, especially myself. I got a large packet of letters. I read them without pleasure ... I had no prospect of ever being well. I was weary of my present state, and wanted to fly somewhere else, yet had no expectation of relief. Good heaven! how comes this about? What can thus distemper the mind, and render it useless and fretful?

He left abruptly and rudely, and made straight for Edinburgh. 'It is difficult to let a man know that you are wearied of his company. I did not stay breakfast, so did not see my Lady', who was wounded by his sudden departure.[19]

6

At the end of a hard day's thirty-mile gallop through wild country and roads deep in stiff clay, worse than anything in Ayrshire, he revived when his eyes fell on the 'prospect of the Firth of Forth, the Lomonds hills, Arthur Seat, and the ancient city of Edina'. His family were still at Auchinleck, so he stopped with an overjoyed Mrs Love at Bristo Port (on the Firth of Forth) where after a mock-heroic hunt for a bed for him to sleep on – worthy of 'a good comic tale' – they continued their liaison for a few days. His 'speculative indifference' vanished and his confidence returned as this 'smart, clever, good-humoured creature' read him her husband's letters from London full of theatre news and sat, supped, and slept with him.[20]

Before setting off to join Erskine at Kellie on the 30th, he found time to talk to Dr Cairnie to make sure Peggy Doig was in good health. From his uncle Dr John Boswell, he also heard worrying news about his brother John at Plymouth, who was showing the first signs of the mental illness that would soon end his military career and sentence him to years of confinement in Newcastle. It was imperative that this news remain secret, not least because it would reflect on Boswell and hurt his marriage prospects. On 8 February 1763, not wanting to admit the problem even to Grange, he pretended that John's disorder was caused by an accident: 'If you hear the story of his illness mentioned, pray let the fall be known.'[21]

He was greeted at Kellie with 'roars of applause' by Erskine and his three sisters – one of whom, Lady Betty, he thought he loved – and stayed until 3 November. He then returned with Erskine to Edinburgh where they met up with Dempster and his sister Jeanie at Paxton's New Inn, 'a fine woman, very well-looked indeed, elegant and remarkably witty', worth keeping in mind for a wife: 'I this night felt myself much in love with Miss Dempster. My passion for Lady Betty, which I should have remarked as possessing me at Kellie, was now gone. I thought Miss Dempster the most engaging of her sex. I professed the highest admiration and I groaned in despair. I have indeed the most veering amorous affections that I ever knew anybody have.'[22]

He and Erskine also called on David Hume at his newly renovated house in St James's Court. They found the great sceptic philosopher reading Homer. With his talent for getting people to talk, Boswell easily started Hume off on literature, chiefly about Macpherson and Dr Johnson. Then he made an audacious suggestion:

> I asked Mr Hume to write more. He said he had done enough and was almost ashamed to see his own bulk on a shelf. We paid him a few compliments in pleasant mirth. Thus did an hour and a half of our existence move along. We were very happy. I showed away, started subjects, and now and then spoke tolerably, much better than my knowledge entitles me to do. I have remembered the heads and the very words of a great part of Mr Hume's conversation with us.

Hume also roused Boswell's talent for mimicry: 'I had not only his external address, but his sentiments and mode of expression.' But he made up his mind to leave off the habit once in the Guards, 'as a mimic is but an inferior person in company'.[23]

As the day approached for his abandonment of Scotland, Boswell's friends worried about how he would make out in London. He might fall among the thorns, 'blackguard geniuses ... bucks and choice spirits, under-players and fellows who write droll songs, who would admire my humour, make me king of the company, and allow me to pay the bill'. His friend William Nairne (an advocate and later a judge) could not decipher what made him tick: he 'declared that there was no character like mine in this country, and that I was certainly the native of a more southern climate' – his friends always joked about his dark complexion. But they were outgrowing the antics of the Soaping Club, whereas Boswell was still going strong. Dempster, Grange, Erskine, and Nairne were as ready as anyone to laugh through the night with him, but even with them he took his 'shaving' too far, so that 'they were kept in continual apprehension and never knew whether to take me in earnest or not'. It was time to lay aside childish things. He agreed that people would not talk to him openly and seriously if they thought they were only making themselves ridiculous in his eyes. After he got into the Guards and was in 'real life', he would desist.[24]

7

Since his family was still not back from Auchinleck, he moved into a room in Mrs Mackenna's lodging 'in our own stair' in Blair's Land, Parliament Close, brimming with youthful associations. It was not a good idea. When he got up the next morning, he was trembling: 'I had the room where Mr Fergusson and Davy [now fourteen] used to sleep. Greasy, black, Seceder mystical books were lying on a cabinet-head. All the dreary ideas of my youth recurred upon me. I thought myself a boy and an unhappy discontented being.'[25] To shake off depression, he went out immediately and breakfasted with another, younger, progressive, and very different Fergusson, Patrick, later the inventor of the first breech-loading rifle used in the British Army. All his momentum was forward, into the future, towards London. It was almost as if these phantoms of the past had conspired to arrest him on the threshold of freedom.

When his mother, father, and Davy returned a couple of days later, he enjoyed their company lounging around the house, 'easy and content' in 'a careless nightgown way'. They agreed to his leaving in just under a week. Oddly, in his journal he wrote nothing of a personal nature about his mother, who was surely distraught at the prospect of his departure, except that he had a long and serious conversation with her and his father and that he felt 'a very warm filial regard for them'. He also gave Davy a few words of big-brother advice before he left: to be diligent in his chosen profession as a banker, make money, and be happy. He took in a few last plays and *The Beggar's Opera*, again with Digges as Macheath. He called on Commissioner Cochrane who told him his father would give him an annual allowance of two hundred pounds, that he should keep an exact list of debts, and that 'if I did not do well, I should only have myself to blame'. He paid off his creditors, packed, and said his final goodbyes. Thus he concluded his journal, happy enough about it on the whole to want to start a new one: 'I shall continue the method of keeping a journal, which will amuse me at the time and lay up a store of entertainment for me afterwards.'[26]

SIX

London: The Promised Land

I

Boswell left Edinburgh on 15 November trailing 'a golden train of ideas', although busy Edinburgh teemed all around him, oblivious to the event. As he rattled his way down the High Street in his post-chaise, smiling at passing acquaintances, only in his fancy did the caddies and chairmen bow reverentially and say, 'GOD prosper long our noble Boswell'. Edinburgh and the glory of ancient Scotland also demanded some homage, so at the foot of the Canongate he stopped the chaise and, while his fellow passenger waited patiently, dashed to the Palace and Abbey of Holyrood with the dark crags of his beloved Arthur's Seat towering in the background. There in the quadrangle he silently performed his own personal ritual of farewell – 'I am a man whom nature has endowed with a love of forms and Ceremonies,' he told Grange – bowing three times, once to the Palace, once to the Scottish Crown above the front gate, and once to the 'venerable old Chapel'. Then from the court he bowed three times to Arthur's Seat, 'that lofty romantic mountain on which I have so often strayed in my days of youth, ingulged meditation and felt the raptures of a soul filled with ideas of the magnificence of GOD and his creation.' Thus nostalgically and spiritually in tune with his home and homeland, and immensely pleased with himself, he rushed back to the chaise and turned his course south.[1]

The 'triumphal' journey to London was neither 'heroic' nor easy. Halfway to Berwick a wheel on the chaise broke. The driver expected his two passengers to ride the rest of the way, but Boswell refused. He demanded that a new chaise be sent to the 'dirty little village' of Ayton to pick them up, where for three dismal hours they cooled their heels in a cold alehouse, dining on 'beefsteak ill-dressed' with nothing to drink but muddy beer. Roasted on one side by the fire and shivering on the other, they got headaches and no sleep. The chaise at long last arrived and they reached Berwick at midnight. The next two days were uneventful, but the day after that between Stamford and Stilton an unruly horse overturned their chaise, giving them a 'pretty severe rap' and injuring Boswell's arm. Turning the vehicle back on to its wheels, the distraught passengers rumbled on into the night, terrified by the real threat of robbers and tightly clutching their loaded pistols in the unrelieved darkness. The next day the cold air blowing through the broken windows virtually froze them. The misery of the journey suddenly vanished, however, when around midday, from Highgate Hill, their first view of London suddenly unfolded before them. Boswell was beside himself with 'life and joy': he broke into song and shouted three huzzas as they drove 'briskly' down into his Promised Land.

2

The Prime Minister in November 1762 was John Stuart, third Earl of Bute, a Scot. In gaining power by royal favour that May, Bute had alienated countless English politicians, including the popular William Pitt, and through his ineptitude exposed himself to comprehensive English mockery. He made derision of the Scots a fresh national pastime. 'No Scots! No Scots!' shouted the gallery mob at the Covent Garden Theatre when two officers of a Highland regiment fresh from a successful campaign in the West Indies arrived; they were bombarded with apples. To succeed in London society and get his commission, Boswell concluded he must play down his Scottishness. He could attend the English church, for one thing, and ration out his socializing with Scottish friends in the city, but there was not much he could do about his accent.

However, there was a larger obstacle to his social ambitions. Commissions in the Guards, especially ones based in London for which he hungered, had dried up. With the end of the Seven Years' War (or French and Indian War), regiments were being disbanded, not formed. The only real chance of obtaining the sort of 'gentlemanly' commission he wanted was to buy one, but his father refused to lay out any money. Lord Auchinleck made a few feeble efforts to pull strings on his son's behalf, but almost everyone except Boswell knew that without money nothing was going to happen. He spent his first few months in London currying favour with the likes of the Duchess of Northumberland, the Dukes of

Grafton and Queensberry, and Lord Eglinton, in a cause that had virtually no chance of succeeding.

3

The London that Boswell hoped would launch his career was deliciously enticing. There was movement and energy everywhere. It was a relatively new city, most of the medieval buildings having burned down in the Great Fire of 1666. The rate of demolition and building throughout the century was astonishing, especially in the newer and more 'polite' end of town, St James's, so different from the older city with its dark and winding lanes. London was progressive, the pride of Europe. 'He that is tired of London is tired of life, for there is in London all that life can afford,' Samuel Johnson remarked, and there certainly was a multiplicity of amusements and a richness of history, intellect, culture, and politics there to bear him out.

For a hypochondriac, as long as he was an active pleasure-seeker and made a point of doing the rounds, London was the great antidote to depression. As London historian Roy Porter recently described, Georgian London had a well-mapped topography of pleasure:

> A culture of sociability – hedonism even – was emerging, increasingly secular in form and content, contributing to what has been called the commercialization of leisure ... The precincts around Fleet Street, the Strand, Covent Garden and Charing Cross – once very superior – were being taken over by inns and taverns, shops, shows and street performers ... The main corridor connecting Westminster and the City, Fleet Street and the Strand were perfect for watching the world go by.

A century earlier the French moralist La Rochefoucauld had expressed amazement at the lifestyle of the London gentleman to which Boswell now aspired: 'The conduct of an Englishman's day in London leaves little time for work. He gets up at ten or eleven and has breakfast (always with tea). He then makes a tour of the town for about four hours until 5 o'clock, which is the dinner hour; at 9 o'clock in the evening he meets his friends in a tavern or a club and there the night is passed in play and drink.'[2]

There was also plenty in London to frighten both resident and visitor. Vice abounded. The glamorous and the lurid rubbed shoulders. William

Cowper summed it up in these lines from his poem *The Task*:

> Such London is, by taste and wealth proclaim'd
> The fairest capital of all the world,
> By riot and incontinence the worst.

On the one hand, here was a luminous city of the Enlightenment. The most famous men and women in Europe dined at each others' homes with lavish regularity. There were societies and clubs of every description, Ranelagh and Vauxhall pleasure gardens, the Pantheon, the House of Commons, the Inns of Court, the two major theatres at Drury Lane and Covent Garden, art galleries, coffee-houses, taverns, chop-houses, elegant private houses and mansions, small residential squares, public parks, spacious streets, and handsome parades. On the darker side there were prisons and places of execution (by hanging mostly) at Tyburn and Newgate, prostitution, gambling, and violence of many kinds from barbaric sports to theft and murder. At the Temple Bar, the pikes were still adorned with the heads of traitors, though the practice was abandoned during Boswell's lifetime. Ironically, the last heads to be displayed were the skulls of Jacobite officers from the rebellion of 1745.

Boswell threw himself into this vortex of beauty and ugliness with unparalleled exuberance. Moreover, while multitudes experienced what Dr Johnson referred to as London's 'full tide of human existence', nobody even came close to recording it with his animation and open-eyed detail. That is why Boswell remains by far the best source of information on London life of that era.

Boswell could scarcely believe his luck. Here he was at last, an independent young man with the promise of a regular stipend from his father and all of London before him. His 'genius' was surely now transplanted to fertile soil. He could pursue his Guards scheme at leisure and in the meantime with Eglinton's help try to establish literary contacts, move among great people, indulge his inexhaustible taste for the theatre, and also find time for a few dangerous liaisons in addition to those less savoury encounters with strumpets that were fairly expected of young men of means on their own in the city. 'I am all in a flutter of joy,' he wrote to Grange on the day after his arrival, 'full of fine wild romantic feeling to find myself really in LONDON.' He was more 'wildly struck' than on his first visit by 'the noise, the crowd, the glare of shops and signs'. London's 'amazing bundle of existence' was bound to open all sorts of doors for him, literary as well as military. He fantasized to Erskine: 'It is not impossible but I may catch a little true poetic inspiration, and have my works splendidly printed at Strawberry-hill, under the benign influence of the Honourable Horace Walpole.'[3]

On his first night he saw *Every Man in His Humour* at Covent Garden, then moved in temporarily with his friend Andrew Douglas, a surgeon in Pall Mall, who quickly brought him down to earth. Lady Louisa Stuart once remarked that 'Fifteen or sixteen hundred a year would not do much for two people who must live in London and appear in fine clothes at St James's twice a week.' Quick calculations with Douglas's help revealed that, given London's costs and his meagre £200 per year, Boswell would have to tighten his belt dramatically in order to live anything like a 'gentleman'.

The next day he visited the Mayfair Chapel and made a round of visits to Scottish friends like the Erskines (in London for the season with Lady Betty Macfarlane, Andrew's newly married sister) and his fellow countryman Dr John Pringle, the well-known physician and scientist who would become a great friend and confidante. Then he made for the Blue Periwig to find Sally Forrester, his 'first love' from his earlier London escapade. She was long gone and nobody knew anything of her, so he sought out Jeany Wells of Soho, but she too had fled on the heels of some sort of ruinous 'extravagance'. What sort of homecoming was this for the heroic and romantic Boswell?[4]

He 'melted' in the refuge of Eglinton's company the next evening, though he was now determined to think of the Earl as an equal, a companion, not mainly as a patron by whom he might again be disappointed. A pressing need was to find his own lodgings for he was having to endure a bit too much of Mrs Douglas's tedious and witless garrulousness. He needed his own space for the emergence of his London persona. He also needed women. He felt the downward grey pressure of inertia when all should be motion and progress. 'I lay abed very gloomy. I thought London did me no good. I rather disliked it; and I thought of going back to Edinburgh immediately. In short, I was most miserable.' As would often be the case when he felt colourless, he resorted to whores though he had resolved to keep away from them because he could not risk another infection. 'I was really unhappy for want of women,' he complains in his journal, so he picked up a girl in the Strand, but as neither he nor she had 'armour' (a condom) he merely toyed with her. She was amazed at his 'size' and told him that if he ever took a girl's maidenhead, he would make her 'squeak'. Afterwards, he 'trembled' at the danger he had run. He would have to wait for some 'safe girl' to appear, or more exciting, a 'woman of fashion'.[5]

He found lodgings at last in Downing Street – the house has since been demolished – up two flights of stairs with the morning use of the parlour for forty guineas per year. Included was the privilege of dining with Mr and Mrs Terrie, the landlords, any time he wished for the additional cost of one shilling. It was a genteel setting, near the House of Commons and 'healthful'. The rooms were a godsend. The Terrie family, obviously fond of the genial young Scot, became an extended family for him: 'They do everything to serve me ... Mrs Terrie gets all things I want bought for me, and Miss sews the laced ruffles on my shirts, and does anything of that kind. They have always a good plain dinner.' To round out the new independence of these lodgings, he sped to his banker William Cochrane to pick up his six-week allowance of £25. This was more like it.[6]

Eglinton swept him up and did his best to check his depression, chiefly through festive evenings at his lordship's house. The following year, during his travels, Boswell thought back on his diversions with Eglinton, especially at the famous London musical society, the Catch Club, writing appreciatively:

> Lord Eglinton is one of the most famous members of this society. He sings in charming taste. He had the goodness to teach me some songs ... My Lord did me the honour to say that there were not three better ears in the whole society than mine. How many happy evenings have I passed at his house, singing! But he is not merely a singer. He is truly a man of distinguished mind.[7]

His 'dullness' lingered on, however. Curiously, Eglinton was at the centre of it. He would not acknowledge that Boswell had matured: 'He imagined me much in the style that I was three years ago: raw, curious, volatile, credulous. He little knew the experience I had got and the notions and the composure that I had obtained by reflection.' 'My Lord,' Boswell insisted, 'I am now a little wiser.' 'Not so much as you think,' Eglinton replied, 'for, as a boy who has just learned the alphabet when he begins to make out words thinks himself a great master of reading, so the little advance you have made in prudence appears very great, as it is so much before what you was formerly.' Boswell grudgingly allowed that he might still need a little more 'diffidence', but after three years of studying law, publishing, loving, and circulating in the highest Scottish literary and social circles – after all, he could claim both Kames and Hume as friends – it was not a little irritating to return to London and find himself still treated as a green Scottish youth. He retaliated (in his journal) by judging that while Eglinton was sparkling, good-natured, and humorous, he was also dilettantish, flighty, 'downright trifling', and selfish. Theirs would always remain an uneasy friendship. He suspected Eglinton of siding with Lord Auchinleck against him, as in the case of the Guards, for example. The truth is that Eglinton knew Boswell better than Boswell thought; he also knew that the Guards, even a commission based in London, would not suit his young friend's temperament.[8]

A meeting with Sheridan on 28 November also led to disillusionment. There were signs of pedantry: 'he is rather too much of an enthusiast in favour of his darling study.' Sheridan 'sinned', too, by criticizing Samuel Johnson for duplicity in accepting a royal pension and then continuing to attack both the King and Bute's ministry. Another piece of Sheridan's jealousy and 'malevolence' was his denigration of Garrick's acting. The final straw came in January concerning a prologue Mrs Sheridan asked Boswell to write for her new play, *The Discovery*, a thrilling request since Garrick was going to read it on the Drury Lane stage. When Boswell called in to hear what the Sheridans thought of his verses, Sheridan pounced on them 'with an insolent bitterness and a clumsy ridicule that hurt me much, and when I answered them, bore down my words with a boisterous vociferation'. How 'puerile and stupid' of him, Boswell scoffed; Erskine and Dempster agreed. To compound the offence, Mrs Sheridan then plagiarized his verses in composing her own 'inferior' prologue.[9]

He wrote in his journal: 'I was sorry that I had been so much with him, and I resolved to take an opportunity of breaking off acquaintance and then lashing him for a presumptuous dunce.' When Mrs Sheridan's play was presented at Drury Lane in February, Boswell sat in the pit with Dempster and Erskine and 'damned' it to his heart's content. The play 'jogged' through heavily, even without their intervention.[10]

The problem was that he was no longer a boy and resented being treated like one. As if to underline that, in November Peggy Doig presented him with a son, Charles. He was delighted. 'By all means let the Nurse give my child the sirname of Boswell immediately,' he wrote to Grange; 'I am not ashamed of him. And I am not afraid of it's being known.' Later, he wrote, 'I wish from my heart that I may be able to make myself a Man, and to become steady and sensible in my Conduct ... What I want to do is to bring myself to that equality of behaviour that whether my spirits are high or low, people may see little odds upon me. I am persuaded that when I can restrain my flightiness and keep an even external tenor, that my mind will attain a settled serenity.'[11]

It is not difficult to see he had got this the wrong way round. His melancholia, as he recorded it in his journal, often arose from his failure to succeed in the struggle to adopt, or at least sustain, a new character. As a dinner guest, he must not laugh too much, talk too much, drink too much; or he must not be too quiet and sullen, too dull. He must act out a part, and unlike his mimicry and singing, he must sustain it. Over a long stretch, this was impossible. It would damage him simply to attempt it. Guilt and remorse over how he behaved in society now crop up regularly in his journal.

A persistent aggravation was that while he was trying to put on a show of reserve and moderation, he was seeing too much of people who knew him in Scotland – Erskine, for example, and the Macfarlanes. He felt they held him back with their good-natured but coarse conviviality and 'intemperate mirth', their too familiar conversation. Even Erskine's behaviour embarrassed him. This is not to say he ignored his friends at home. He wrote faithfully to McQuhae, Lord and Lady Kames, Digges, Grange, Commissioner Cochrane, and others. But when Erskine, Lady Betty Macfarlane, Lady Anne Erskine, and Miss Dempster, all the dearest of Scottish friends, suddenly arrived in London, he was obliged to go to them although he would have preferred not to see them:

> To tell the plain truth, I was vexed at their coming. For to see just the plain *hamely* Fife family hurt my grand ideas of London. Besides, I was now upon a plan of studying polite reserved behaviour, which is the only way to keep up dignity of character. And as I have a good share of pride, which I think is very proper and even noble, I am hurt with the taunts of ridicule and am unsatisfied if I do not feel myself something of a superior animal.

The only solution might be to go abroad. In the meantime, he had no choice but to wait for them to leave: 'Summer will come when all Scots will be gone. Then you'll grow more English & fine.'[12]

4

Boswell's first London journal displays an earnestness and artistic focus that make his previous efforts in the genre seem amateurish. He did not know it, but at twenty-two he was embarking on a major literary work. Since its publication in 1950, the world has come to see it as a literary masterpiece, regarded by many as the high point in more than thirty years of journal-keeping. It sold over one million copies. The journal was not simply a record of events and thoughts; it was a way of living, of self-realization and fulfilment. It was life itself. Boswell observed that he would not like to live any more of life than he could record.

A day or two before leaving Edinburgh, he wrote an 'Introduction' to the journal. His fundamental premiss is that to 'know thyself' is the most valuable knowledge a person can have. There is no better way to acquire that knowledge than by attending to 'the feelings of his heart and to his external actions, from which he may with tolerable certainty judge "what manner of person he is." '[13] Moreover, if the writer knows he is going to write about himself, he will make a point of trying to behave better. So the journal can be 'useful' as a kind of conscience or reckoning, with the virtue that it cannot talk back like a disgruntled father or a disapproving society. The author can watch himself. He will be both the participant and the spectator.

The fascinating result is that there are two identities in the journals. The Boswell who watches himself is more complex than Boswell the doer. The vitality of the journals derives from the former, the identity that constantly searches for meaning in the experience of the latter. As the first editor of the journals, Geoffrey Scott, observed: because of this introspection the journals *are* Boswell's life more than the events he reflects on. It is in the spectator, not the actor, that we find his continuous (though not consistent) identity, a seemingly endless stream of meditation. In his *Life of Johnson*, after hearing Dr Johnson say that the use of a diary or journal is for a man to review his own mind, Boswell adds, 'As a lady adjusts her dress before a mirror, a man adjusts his character by looking at his journal.' 'Adjusts' here does not mean to distort, as authors often have done with autobiographical works; it means regard, appreciate, and evaluate. It is impossible to sum up properly such a 'creature', as Bertrand Bronson once explained:

One could not reconstruct such an existence by a set of principles, presumptively; one could only follow it . . . with unremitting attention, careful to trace every slightest movement on to the page. Moreover, one need not be too much dismayed by the odd and disreputable conduct of such a being: one could at any rate do nothing about it at the time, one could not tax oneself with responsibility for these vagaries, which one had neither forseen nor yet professed to understand. One need not therefore be troubled unduly by a sense of personal shame, nor refrain from putting down what actually happened.[14]

There were many different sides to Boswell's character, all competing for supremacy. His talent for mimicry hinted at this. He could be many things to many people. These various aspects of his character were often incompatible and contradictory – shamefully so if one is in the mood for censure, wonderfully so if one recognizes his sincerity and genuine talent for making himself a pleasing and exuberant companion, and tragically so if the intricate mix of roles for him never adds up to an essential constructive self. Temple, whom Boswell finally ran into in St Paul's Churchyard after their separation for more than four years, worried about the journal. He felt that Boswell's unsteady and unreserved behaviour could be traced to the journal because, in Boswell's words, 'it made me hunt about for adventures to adorn it with, whereas I should endeavour to be calm and studious and regular in my conduct'. But while accepting that consistency of behaviour was of the 'utmost importance', Boswell refused to find fault with the journal,

> which is far from wishing for extravagant adventures, and is as willing to receive my silent and serious meditations as my loud and boisterous rhodomantades [boasting]. Indeed, I do think the keeping of a journal a very excellent scheme if judiciously executed. To be sure, it may take up too much time from more serious concerns. But I shall endeavour to keep it with as much conciseness as possible.

For us, his complexity and openness, as expressed in the journal, is his essence. We must thank the literary muses who watched over him that he did not succeed, against his better artistic judgement, in being concise.[15]

Often he simply enjoyed portraying himself in terms of fanciful self-images, in which he relished all kinds of experiences, dissipated as well as ennobling. He was frequently awed by himself: 'I shall here put down my thoughts on different subjects at different times, the whims that may seize me and the sallies of my luxuriant imagination.'[16] He was fascinated by his imagination, how his mind worked, but he never presumed, as did Wordsworth, that they were inexorably leading him to some heightened state of consciousness and achievement. He was always full of doubts and insecurities. Self-analysis does not necessarily lead to self-discovery, nor did he think it must. That was his peculiar strength. Still, Boswell believed that even if the journal's check on his behaviour was not enough, it could 'assist me in resolutions of doing better'. This journal and all those that follow are littered with resolutions, minute or sweeping, to improve his behaviour.

Boswell often stated that one of the functions of his journals was to beat back melancholia, his mind-usurping mania: 'I shall find daily employment for myself, which will save me from indolence and help to keep off the spleen ...' He failed. If he had succeeded, it is conceivable we would have fewer journals than we do, just as if he had been either on better or much worse terms with his father he might have lifted himself out of that middle ground of dispiriting dependency and spared himself much of the misery that flowed into the journals. What is more to the point is the second half of his statement: 'I shall lay up a store of entertainment for my after life. Very often we have more pleasure in reflecting on agreeable scenes that we have been in than we had from the scenes themselves.'[17] The journal would serve as a memory and 'a reservoir of ideas' by assuring him, in his hours of gloom and self-doubt, that he was capable of higher thought and behaviour, that he was a worthwhile person.

For the sake of economy in the journal, he insists, 'I shall not study much correctness.' This raises the question of the quality and level of art in the writing. It is true that the manuscripts of the journals, written in his characteristically large handwriting, for which Erskine and others teased him, are strikingly free of revision. But are they simply an outpouring of unconsidered and untempered thoughts – uncorrected and therefore unrefined?

To begin with, in spite of having very little to do in London Boswell could not keep up to date with his journal and was repeatedly in the position of having to set aside a large slice of a day, sometimes an entire night and morning, for this purpose. On 21 March 1763, for example, he complains of 'running about so much' that 'near a whole week had elapsed without my writing a single page of it. By way therefore of penance for my idleness, and by way of making up for the time lost and bringing up my business, I determined to sit up all night; which I accordingly did, and wrote a great deal.' But not without some adversity, for at two in the morning his candle went out. After prowling around the house trying to find the means to relight it and fearing his landlord might at any moment shoot him as a burglar, he sat quietly in the dark until the watchman came around at three and he could 'relume' his candle 'without danger': 'Thus was I relieved and continued busy till eight next day.'[18] Since at times he fell as much as three weeks behind, he had to rely on a system of memoranda to trigger his recollections. Despite the fact that whenever he wrote up several days, even weeks, in a single sitting, he did so knowing what lay ahead, Boswell succeeded in presenting events as a dramatist would. His vocabulary and imagery lend an immediacy to each scene as it arises while pointing towards an eventual climax. It was a creative game, involving the endless variety of human faces and personalities he encountered. What he added was the texture of a plot, or at least an unfolding drama, with himself as the chief protagonist.

The particularity of Boswell's record is also striking. Whether in the telling or living of events, even when suffering from attacks of hypochondria his prose is highly allusive and associative, anchored to physical images. He was ever on the alert to fill in the scene with words and imagery that would root the experience, seldom lapsing into abstraction. Abstractions, in fact, depressed him. Even so, he was not often satisfied: 'I observe continually how imperfectly, upon most occasions, words preserve our ideas ... in description we omit insensibly many little touches which give life to objects. With how small a speck does a painter give life to an eye! ... I find myself ready to write unintelligibly when I attempt to give any kind of idea of such subjects.' Having just seen David Garrick on stage, he says he is at a loss for words, but this is not true: 'The vivid glances of Garrick's features, which cannot be copied in words, will illuminate an extent of sensation, if that term may be used, as a spark from a flint will throw a lustre in a dark night for a considerable space around it.' Garrick's glances aside, Boswell here has illuminated his living space. Even as he says he cannot do it, he does so. He also enriches a scene by measuring it against his previous experiences and emotions so that a recorded event seldom appears unadorned by association.'[19]

The London journal was written for Grange to read, in regular instalments, to impress, entertain and cheer him, to help him over his patches of melancholia: 'You must stay at home on Sunday forenoon[;] never open the Packet till then so as that you may read it when warm and comfortable in bed, which will make you enjoy it more fully and with a more cordial satisfaction.'[20] Several of the other journals, or parts of them, were written for Temple and Dempster as well. Despite the strong confessional strain, which is honest and sincere, Boswell wanted the journal to entertain. It can still be trusted, though, as an autobiographical record. His imagination adapts and transforms, but it does not lie or misrepresent. The truth is in his sincerity, his fidelity to his own feelings. As Dr Johnson once said, 'moral truth' is when you tell a thing sincerely and precisely as it *appears* to you. It is physical truth to say that someone has walked across the street if he has actually done so; it is moral truth to say he walked across if you think he did, even if he did not. Boswell may occasionally 'lie' by omission, to conceal. But in a journal which astonishes with its generosity of detail, its fullness, its extraordinary frankness, it seems ungenerous to fault it for occasionally holding back. As it is, he suffered great anxiety over the danger he courted in exposing himself as much as he did. Grange had to reassure him repeatedly that he placed his journal and letters, as he received them, in a strongbox.

5

Boswell's sudden brilliance as a journalist is nowhere more evident than in his beautifully contrived account of his first major sexual campaign in London. By 14 December he had been in London for over three weeks 'without ever enjoying the delightful sex, although I am surrounded with numbers of free-hearted ladies of all kinds: from the splendid Madam at fifty guineas a night, down to the civil nymph with white-thread stockings who tramps along the Strand and will resign her engaging person to your honour for a pint of wine and shilling'. There were three reasons for this: economy, which ruled out 'first-rate dames'; a shuddering fear of again catching the clap; and his past record in Scotland of 'delicious intrigues' with women of 'beauty, sentiment, and spirit'. After his taste of 'paradisial scenes of gallantry', he could not think of 'stooping so far as to make a most intimate companion of a groveling-minded, ill-bred, worthless creature, nor can my delicacy be pleased with the gross voluptuousness of the stews'. Only a woman 'worthy of my love' would do. One month after he arrived, he found one in a beautiful, twenty-four-year-old actress whom he discreetly calls Louisa. Born of good parents, she had married much too early a disagreeable man from whom she was eventually separated. She was then forced to become an actress to make a living, and when Boswell found her she was performing at Covent Garden as the Queen in *Hamlet* and Mrs Ford in *Merry Wives*. Once he decided to pursue her, she filled the void he had settled into during his first few weeks in London owing to the failure of obtaining a commission.[21]

The journal during the five or six weeks of their relationship reads like a crafted short story, complete with animated and plausible dialogue, subplots, and some stage direction. It was written to engage the reader (Grange) in a drama, not simply to record what happened. The florid manner of Boswell's erotic frankness reflects pleasure in documenting his life in London.

In the opening scene on the 14th Boswell visits Louisa, is admitted, and finds her in a 'pleasing undress' and looking very pretty. At first, there is a little awkwardness and they are too shy to look at each other, but he asks if he may visit again; she invites him for tea a couple of days later. He leaves 'very well satisfied'. The reader then is left in suspense for two days. On his next visit, they talk freely about the different ways in which Frenchmen and Englishmen court women. They joke; she is coy and appealing, making 'a fine artful pretty speech'. After three or four hours, he leaves, having 'made no visible progress in my amour' but actually achieving much, for 'I was informing her by my looks of my passion for her.' Yet he was not prepared for what happened, for though he began this gallantry only for 'convenient pleasure', he suddenly felt 'the fine delirium of love'. He rushes back the next day, finds her alone, 'soft and beautiful', and declares his 'affection' for her. Just to have an 'agreeable female companion, where I can be at home and have tea and genteel conversation', he tells her, is his great desire. Pleased, she invites him to come 'every evening, if you please'. 'This is just what I wanted,' Boswell whispers to his journal.[22]

He returns the next day, cutting a figure like Digges, 'a young fellow of spirit and fashion, heir to a good fortune, enjoying the pleasures of London, and now making his addresses in order to have an intrigue with that delicious subject of gallantry, an actress'. Two short visits follow over the next two days as he builds up his capital with her, though he is thrown a bit off balance when she raises the matter of a debt and he is drawn into lending her a couple of guineas – which he could ill afford as his first allowance had virtually run out and the next was not due for another two weeks. He also rashly promises her up to ten guineas should she need it, rationalizing that this was 'a moderate expense for women during the winter'. When in gratitude she begins to sing to him, he suddenly rises in rapture and kisses her 'with great warmth'. They arrange to meet a couple of evenings later, not for tea but for what he hopes will be the climax. When the magical night arrives, however, he does not measure up.[23]

For all his talk, one of Boswell's recurring problems was a fear of performing unsatisfactorily when with a woman of some social stature and dignity. He worried that he would not be passionate enough, that he would be discovered less of a man than his self-image advertised. This is what happened on 21 December when he went to Louisa's expecting 'consummate bliss'. He was ravished at the prospect, yet 'I had such an anxiety upon me that I was afraid that my powers would be enervated.'

He sits down next to her 'in a most melancholy plight'. She patiently hears him speak 'with the distance of a new acquaintance'. He is about to give it up and leave when at the last minute he finds his 'powers' excited and declares his love. The perfect tactician, she withdraws, asking for two days to consider. Content, he retreats to the solitude of his lodgings to sup on bread, cheese, apples, and water – a diet he is forced into by having parted with his two guineas, though he finds waiting for him at home thirteen magical shillings of royalties from Robert Dodsley, his first major London publisher, for *The Cub at New-Market*. 'I comforted myself by thinking that I suffered in the service of my Mistress; and I was romantically amused to think that I was now obliged to my wits, and living on the profit of my works ...' When they next meet, she is cold, fearing discovery, but agrees to his idea of a week's separation for reflection. If after that they are still for it, 'she would then make me blessed'.[24]

In the meantime, he sought out Thomas Davies, Johnson's publisher, at his bookshop in Russell Street, and told him he wished to meet his most famous author. Then come for Christmas dinner, Davies replied, and you shall. The promise of a hot meal would alone have been worth going for, as no warm food had passed his lips for four days. Johnson did not appear, as it happened, a sore disappointment, but Boswell contented himself with the two other guests, Robert Dodsley and Oliver Goldsmith. Even without Johnson, this was unquestionably an entertaining dinner. 'We talked entirely in the way of Geniuses.' Dodsley had not only printed his *Cub at New-Market* in London but was the famous bookseller and publisher of many of the leading authors of the early eighteenth century, including Pope, Gray and Shenstone (and Goldsmith, too). Goldsmith was on the verge of literary fame. Boswell later described him as one of the brightest ornaments of Johnson's school. His novel *The Vicar of Wakefield* (published in 1764) would take its place as one of the most popular works of fiction in the language. In 1763, he became one of the nine original members of Johnson's famous 'Club', (later known as the Literary Club) and in 1764 his poem 'The Traveller' made him a celebrity overnight.

But all that lay in the future and at their first meeting Boswell thought Goldsmith 'a curious, odd, pedantic fellow with some genius'. Goldsmith did not like Thomas Gray, one of Boswell's favourite poets, he would not allow Shakespeare great merit, and he thought the verse of the

Restoration and early eighteenth century vastly superior to that of the present. Boswell agreed with none of this: 'I said nothing, but thought him a most impudent puppy.' A few weeks later, they met again at Drury Lane for Mrs Sheridan's play, when Goldsmith decided to sit in the row behind Boswell in the pit. Goldsmith's conversation still struck him as eccentric, though this time with his imaginative dexterity at getting caught up in the 'idea' of something Boswell found himself revived 'with the true ideas of London authors, which are to me something curious, and, as it were, mystical'. By the time of their next meeting, at the Mitre tavern in July, Boswell had at last met Johnson and was even more in raptures over keeping company with literary geniuses. Far from being intimidated by Goldsmith, he even suggested that he should publish a volume of poetry. Like almost everyone who met him, Goldsmith took an instant liking to Boswell. When Goldsmith told him he had 'a method of making people speak', Boswell replied, 'Sir, that is next best to speaking myself.' 'Nay,' Goldsmith replied, 'but you do both.' Boswell was convinced this was an elemental streak in his own genius, which some day would make him famous: 'I must say indeed that if I excel in anything, it is in address and making myself easily agreeable.'[25]

The week passed and on the appointed day, 2 January, after dining at his lodgings on roast beef and a warm apple pie, Boswell hastened to his 'charmer'. Sexual anxiety and a return of hypochondria went along with him:

> here I was, a young man full of vigour and vivacity, the favourite lover of a handsome actress and going to enjoy the full possession of my warmest wishes. And yet melancholy threw a cloud over my mind. I could relish nothing. I felt dispirited and languid. I approached Louisa with a kind of an uneasy tremor. I sat down. I toyed with her. Yet I was not inspired by Venus. I felt rather a delicate sensation of love than a violent amorous inclination for her. I was very miserable. I thought myself feeble as a gallant, although I had experienced the reverse many a time. Louisa knew not my powers. She might imagine me impotent. I sweated almost with anxiety, which made me worse.

She gives him time to recover. He presses her alabaster breasts and kisses her delicious lips, but just on the verge of his triumph he turns himself into a Tom Jones, the hero of a comedy of errors. He leads her 'all fluttering' from the dining room into her bedchamber, and as he is about to make a 'triumphal entry', the landlady comes up the stairs. 'O Fortune why did it happen thus?' he cries. Louisa rushes out of the bedchamber to stop the landlady, then returns to the dining room and they again fall into each other's arms, 'sighing and panting'. Her ubiquitous brother then comes in. With a typical touch of the incongruous, Boswell suddenly remembers he has not been to church and rushes out to the five o'clock service, after which he returns for another charge. Annoyingly, the brother is still there and the three of them have to talk for an hour. He leaves frustrated.[26]

Clearly, their consummation would have to occur elsewhere, so he chooses the Black Lion in Water Lane, off Fleet Street. How easy to arrange something clandestine like this in England, he thinks, while in Scotland 'we should have been married with a vengeance'. After more than a week's delay, they meet in Covent Garden and drive off in a hackney coach to the 'destined scene of delight'. With not a little cheek, he checks them in as Mr and Mrs Digges.

He has now reached the climax in the affair, and the journal entry for 12 January, some three printed pages, records its ecstasy in detail. First they eat and drink in the privacy of their room, so that 'Ceres and Bacchus might in moderation lend their assistance to Venus'; then they talk. He describes her with his natural capacity for appreciating a woman: 'Now I contemplated my fair prize. Louisa is just twenty-four, of a tall rather than short figure, finely made in person, with a handsome face and an enchanting languish in her eyes. She dresses with taste. She has sense, good humour, and vivacity, and looks quite a woman in genteel life.' He cannot believe his good fortune, 'to think that so fine a woman was at this moment in my possession, that without any motives of interest she had come with me to an inn, agreed to be my intimate companion, as to be my bedfellow all night, and to permit me the full enjoyment of her person.' Without brothers and landladies around, the road ahead is all clear; and this time he has no doubts about his ability to perform. His account of their love-making is erotic but not pornographic: its voluptuousness is literary, conveyed through suggestion, with words and passages such as 'I came softly into the room', 'sweet delirium', 'clasped in her snowy arms and pressed to her milk-white bosom', 'blushes', 'amorous dalliance', 'friendly curtain of darkness', 'animated with the strongest powers of love', 'most luscious feast', and 'voluptuous night'. We imagine the act rather than 'see' it, but we visualize the place: the room; the bowl of negus next to the bed as a 'reviving cordial'; Louisa being undressed by the maid, too modest to do so in front of Boswell who with candle in hand paces impatiently outside in the dark and cold courtyard; the bells of St Bride's ringing merrily in the January night, no match for 'the bells in Cupid's court [that] would be this night set a-ringing for joy at our union'; her 'mixture of delicacy and wantonness'. The scene is seductive because it is so vivid. Needless to say, he has his way with her.[27]

The most distinctive theme in the account is Boswell's amazement at his sexual powers. To deploy an image he loved to use whenever he was thoroughly pleased with himself, he 'hugged' himself: proud of his 'godlike vigour' in the 'full glow of health' without any trace of 'effeminacy and weakness'. Louisa was 'madly fond of me' and astonished that five times he was 'lost in supreme rapture'. Could this be normal? she asked. Would not twice have sufficed? Was it not animal-like? No, he boasted, because it was refined by sentiment. He did not tell her this, but it was also heightened by his wanton imagination: 'I could not help roving in fancy to the embraces of some other ladies which my lively imagination strongly pictured.' Admitting that this was not altogether fair, he still gives Louisa 'all the advantage'. He can now style himself 'a Man of Pleasure'. She has been his London initiation. In the name of Digges, he has performed like Digges.[28]

The next morning he 'patrols' up and down Fleet Street imagining himself one of the wits in the reign of Charles II, his 'conquest' complete. 'I really conducted this affair', he croons, 'with a manliness and prudence that pleased me very much', adding that he did it with only eighteen shillings. When he next attends one of Lady Northumberland's assemblies at Northumberland House, instead of awkwardly standing by when others gamble at cards and drifting clumsily in and out of conversations, trying to appear a man of spirit and culture, he now 'strutted up and down, considering myself as a valiant man who could gratify a lady's loving desires five times a night'. If all the ladies in the rooms knew this and his other 'great' qualities, they would all want to make love to him. 'You must know, Madam,' he says to one of the ladies, 'I run up and down this town just like a wild colt.' Her reply confirms his new persona: 'Why, Sir, then, don't you stray into my stable, amongst others?'[29]

His conquest spent itself sooner than he expected, to be followed by the bleakest period of his London visit. He kept up with Louisa for a few days, half-heartedly 'plunging' into 'the fount of love'. He wanted to be loyal, but it was no good. Her conversation was insipid and she was too fond of him. The bloom was off the rose. Worse, he had contracted another gonorrhoeal infection. Dempster and Erskine teased him about it when he first told them, so certain had he been that his Louisa was his 'ideal lady'. 'Can corruption lodge beneath so fair a form?' 'Am I, who have had safe and elegant intrigues with fine women, become the dupe of a strumpet?'[30]

His first thought, when the diagnosis was confirmed, was of all the pain he knew he would suffer; his second was how his confinement would deprive him of the spectacle of London, his walks around St James's Park, the brilliant Guards on parade, and so on; his third was to go to Louisa and confront her. Tense and suspenseful, his record of their exchange is probably one of the best renderings of such a scene in English literature. It even has a few stage directions, Boswell representing himself like a character in a play. He hammers away at her. She had an infection, she admits, but it has long since been healed. Then, when he assures her it would be beneath him to blacken her name around town, she seems to confess: 'Sir, this is being more generous than I could expect.' Satisfied with his brisk performance, he leaves abruptly, muttering to himself that the odds favour her being 'a most consummate dissembling whore'.[31]

As soon as he returned to his lodgings, he wrote her a priggish and harsh letter saying it was all over and asking for his two guineas back. He wrote angrily that he 'neither *paid* [the money] for prostitution nor *gave* it in charity'. She sent the money, but the prospect of a winter of 'safe copulation' had vanished; instead, long, frustrating weeks of confinement and recuperation lay ahead. Boswell never saw her alone again.

6

The biggest danger posed by 'Signor Gonorrhoea' was to his mind, not his body. Enforced immobility, as in Glasgow in 1760, unquestionably would bring on a severe case of hypochondria unless enough people came to visit him and he could keep busy reading and writing: 'A distemper of this kind is more dreadful to me than most people. I am of a warm constitution: a complexion, as physicians say, exceedingly amorous, and therefore suck in the poison more deeply.'[32] The length of his two previous attacks, the first lasting ten weeks, the second twelve, worried him, but perhaps this would be a mild case.

Before laying aside his hat and sword, on 20 January he sought out David Garrick at Drury Lane. Garrick was nonplussed by his forwardness: 'Sir, you will be a very great man,' he told Boswell, 'and when you are so, remember the year 1763.' Unawed by this icon of the theatre,

Boswell agreed: 'I think there is a blossom about me of something more distinguished than the generality of mankind. But I am much afraid that this blossom will never swell into fruit.' His melancholy and 'imbecility of mind' (inconsistency), he feared, would threaten it. Garrick wanted to do his part towards 'saving' him: if Boswell would come for breakfast, 'the cups shall dance and the saucers skip'. This was generous indeed, 'to find him paying me so much respect!'. Great men like Garrick were not used to having young worshippers take their hands in the manner Boswell now did and blurt out, 'Thou greatest of men, I cannot express how happy you make me.' After breakfast at Garrick's the next morning, he felt he had found a friend and the perfect place to meet all the geniuses of the age. However, he met Garrick privately only once more that season, for breakfast again after watching him as Lear on 12 May, a performance that made him shed 'an abundance of tears'.[33]

Garrick temporarily took Boswell's mind off his 'distemper', but once his confinement began his mood swung between hope and gloom. Week after week, he had only his journal and occasional guests to keep him company, including his brother John whose mental problems had abated enough to allow him to come to London. The most pleasant surprise was his journal. It could easily have lapsed into a 'dreary vacancy', but words came 'skipping to me like lambs upon Moffat Hill'. He was like a 'skilful wheelwright turning tops in a turning-loom'. Having his hair dressed regularly also gave him a feeling of well-being. There was plenty of time to read and keep up with his correspondence, too. Hume's six-volume *History of England* kept him busy, giving him the luxury of 'great ideas' to write about to his father. He practised the violin. He even had the entertainment of a publishing venture with Erskine and Dempster under pseudonyms, a pamphlet attack on David Mallet's *Elvira*, which they had seen as a lark a few days before Boswell shut himself up in his rooms. Mallet, Alexander Pope's friend, was unpopular in England for his toadyism and even more so in Scotland since anglicizing his name from Malloch – 'the only Scot whom Scotchmen did not commend'. They had hissed the play and could hardly wait to abuse it in print. Too scurrilous at first, they toned down their comments and published the pamphlet on or near 27 January under the title *Critical Strictures on the New Tragedy of Elvira*. It was damned almost as much as its authors damned the play, the *Critical Review* dismissing it as envious, petulant, and self-conceited. They amused themselves deciding which of these sins belonged to whom.[34]

At times, all this activity was enough to keep up his spirits. Often it was not. He feared his father would learn of his venereal 'distemper'. He tired of Erskine and Dempster's unrelieved strain of fancy and ludicrousness, impatient as well with his own readiness to 'laugh everything off' in their company. Erskine's levity was more palatable in Scotland than London. If only Grange, Temple, and McQuhae could drop in on him. They would better match his present mood. More mature conversation, that was what he needed, though what he was beginning to feel was a deepening need for more maturity, more serious reflection with his friends, more sober contemplation of religion. The important thing was to behave with more reserve, with more '*retenu*', as he put it.

He persevered with the medicines and on Sunday morning, 27 February, Douglas gave him a clean bill of health, only a small 'gleet' remaining of the infection. Lured by the drums of a battalion of the German Guards on parade in St James's Park, Boswell wrapped himself up in his overcoat and, for the first time in more than five weeks, stepped outside into the fresh air of a sunny day, 'from obscurity and confinement, to light and to life'.[35]

SEVEN

'The Johnsonian Æther'

I

The day after Boswell met Goldsmith he heard from the Duke of Queensberry that a commission in the Guards was a 'fruitless pursuit'. Queensberry's reasons were that Boswell was too old and that the army was contracting, not expanding. His advice was to forget about it and think instead of a civil occupation. He did not even refer the matter to higher powers. Boswell was enraged and suspected that his father was at the bottom of it. His mind ignited with rebellious alternatives, such as enlisting for five years as a soldier in India. Lady Northumberland was his next best hope, he decided.[1]

'I want to be something,' he wrote to her the following day, 'and I like nothing but the Army.' In his first full interview with her on the subject three days later, he set about selling himself, somewhat brazenly but also ingenuously and charmingly. When she offered, through family connections, to help him into the Royal Horse Life-Guards – not quite as good as the Guards because it was based outside London, but good enough – he was delighted: 'I left her, in high glee at my success. This day may show on what a good footing I have the honour to be with this noble countess and excellent woman . . .'[2]

Weeks went by, however, and in spite of Lady Northumberland's invitations to her large evening assemblies he began to suspect that she was avoiding him. Then Lord Bute assured Eglinton, who had also seemed neglectful, that a commission for the likes of Boswell was impossible: plenty of people with powerful parliamentary leverage were 'pushing to purchase them', and money of that order Boswell did not have. Predictably, Boswell's hypochondria revived. He considered returning to Scotland and the drudgery of an advocate, pleasing his father and gaining prudence and earning money. Reports of his ambitious and extravagant conversation around town, probably from Eglinton, had reached Lord Auchinleck in Edinburgh. 'Don't let such silly expressions drop from your Pen that you would rather be a Seargent in the Guards than have five hundred pounds in any other part of the World,' Commissioner Cochrane warned him. 'Play the Politician. Don't speak out every thing you think. Number of Folks that you converse with are going their game with you pumping every thing they can get out of you purposely either to repeat to your father or to those that will.' Nevertheless, Scotland might well be the easiest place for him to moderate his behaviour and become a man of 'consequence', where he could coast along with his family connections:

> I considered that the law seemed to be pointed out by fate for me. That the family of Auchinleck had been raised by it. I would soon be made Advocate Depute on the circuits and in all probability be made a Baron of Exchequer, and by this means have respect and yet an easy life ... I considered that my notions of an advocate were false. That I connected with that character low breeding and Presbyterian stiffness, whereas many of them were very genteel people. That I might have the wit and humour of Sir David Dalrymple, the show of Baron Maule, and the elegant taste of Baron Grant. I thought I might write books like Lord Kames and be a buck like Mr James Erskine. That I might keep a handsome machine. Have a good agreeable wife and fine children and keep an excellent house. That I might show all the dull, vulgar, plodding young lawyers how easily superior parts can outstrip them.[3]

But his mood could swing the other way and this plan would suddenly strike him as impetuous; he feared that his 'relish for pleasure' had been temporarily 'tamed' as a result of stagnation and too much medicine. The boredom of the law would paralyze his imagination, while 'the hurry and bustle of life' and a variety of 'brilliant scenes' would energize his spirits. He told himself that his dread of returning home with his tail between his legs for the second time was the Devil's talk, 'the unripe fruit of vexatious thought': 'It pained me to the heart to think that all the gay schemes which I had planned were to prove abortive, and that all my intentions of seeing the world should be frustrated.'[4]

Thus did his mind run back and forth between the Guards and the law. Black days passed; he thought himself ill used by his father, Eglinton, Queensberry – by everyone, in fact, who had anything to do with his military plans. Perhaps travel would be a better alternative than either the army or Scotland. Suddenly Lord Bute offered him a commission in a marching regiment, exactly what Boswell did not want. It is an indication of his desperation that he considered accepting it only if it was a regiment about to be 'broke' or disbanded, affording him the opportunity of exchanging it with a retiring officer for one at half-pay with virtually no responsibilities. That way he would have a foot in the door with a salary that at least would give him some independence from his father, who 'still imagines he is to have me under his eye'. Grange did not like the 'queer' opportunistic ring to this idea, however, and persuaded him to reject Bute's offer. Then Boswell received a rare letter from his mother telling him of their unhappiness with him and his father's threat to cut off his allowance when the year in London ended:

> I suppose you have no expectations new of a commission in the Guards and as you are following no other business I believe nobody would think it reasonable or advise your father after your year is out to continue your allowance to live idly at London. I know no young gentleman of this country that lives there in that way; your poor father is still in great distress about you. Your showing a dislike at this country is a thing very disagreeable to him. However, I hope you will come to see that it is both your duty and interest to settle here before the end of this year.[5]

Finally, in May, the mists of Boswell's military fantasies had dispersed and he realized the die was cast for a legal career. It had at last sunk in that the goodwill of the great, if based only on personal liking, was relatively useless, especially if his influential father was not lending his support. 'I am disgusted with the neglect and hollowness of these great People from whom I expected great cordiality,' he told Grange bitterly. Ironically, a 'kind' and reasoned letter from his father on 30 May sealed the fate of his Guards scheme. It said, 'if I would pursue the law, though moderately, and be in the style of his eldest son, that he would give me all encouragement. It was a most sensible and indulgent letter.'[6]

2

In spite of his conciliatory letter, which he wrote at his wife's urging, Lord Auchinleck's fury reached new heights when George Reid, minister of Ochiltree, near Auchinleck, 'repeated many things' he had read in Boswell's 'Harvest Journal' – unbelievably, McQuhae, to whom Boswell sent the journal, had shown it to Reid. Lord Auchinleck was still fuming when he wrote his letter, still threatening to disinherit his son: 'I by your strange conduct had come [to] the resolution of selling all off from the principle that it is better to snuff a candle out than leave it to stink in a socket.' This mode of writing perplexed Lord Auchinleck, who regarded journalizing as a distasteful kind of exhibitionism: it was simply 'childish' to keep 'a register of . . . follies and communicate it to others as if proud of them'. If it were known that Boswell wrote this sort of thing, nobody would want to risk keeping company with him, 'for who would incline to have his character traduced in so strange a manner, and this frequently after your receiving the greatest civilities and marks of friendship?' Auchinleck had also heard that his son was going around mimicking eminent people, a shameful tactlessness that gave him 'vast pain' and created enemies; besides, it had always been 'justly considered as the lowest and meanest kind of wit'. Was this humiliation the way he should be repaid for all his 'tenderness', expense, and labour?

> What I have said will account for my not having wrote you these three months. Indeed, finding that I could be of no use to you, I had determined to abandon you, to free myself as much as possible from sharing your ignominy, and to take the strongest and most public steps for declaring to the world that I was come to this resolution.

He was writing now only because in his reply to his mother Boswell had shown a hint of remorse.[7]

There was another reason for the anger in this letter. Lord Auchinleck had apparently opened the sealed letter packets which Boswell (in an attempt to keep his personal papers from his father's prying eyes) had asked his brother David, about to be apprenticed to the Edinburgh bankers John Coutts & Co., to forward to Grange for safekeeping. When they eventually arrived, Grange noticed that the seals on the packets were broken. Boswell wrote to Grange: 'This was so very ungenteel and really so very hard that it pains me exceedingly. It was doing what no Parent has a right to do, in the case of a Son who is a Man, and therefore an independent Individual.'[8]

When an octavo edition of correspondence between Boswell and Erskine was published in mid-April 1763, it was a 'fresh mortification' to his father. At Jedburgh on the Circuit, Lord Auchinleck's eyes fell on one of the letters quoted in a newspaper review. He could scarcely believe that the rage to publish could make such a fool of his boy: 'though it might pass between two intimate young lads in the same way that people over a bottle will be vastly entertained with one another's rant, it was extremely odd to send such a piece to the press to be perused by all and sundry.'[9]

Boswell had hatched the scheme to publish his and Erskine's lively letters near the start of his venereal confinement, partly because he wanted literary labour to keep up his spirits, partly because he believed the letters were wonderfully witty, and partly because he ached to see his name in print. The letters required extensive editing and additions. 'Let your Letters be lively & whimsical & have no real names & serious sentences & c,' he wrote in a memorandum to himself on 15 February. On 3 March: 'At night copy letters. Sharpen them & throw in fine sallies & write some new ones.' As a result, the published letters are more polished and even more lively than the originals, but not notably less personal and intimate or more discreet. Covering the fifteen months before he left for London, they are impudent, irreverent, facetious, and youthfully egocentric. For all these reasons, they make good reading.[10]

When the letters were published on 12 April Boswell's and Erskine's names appeared on the title page. It was the only time Boswell brought himself to publish under his own name – until his first major publication in 1768 – hence his father's incredulity and dismay. Dalrymple, his current guide, philosopher, and friend, wrote to him on 21 April: 'In Mr Boswell's letters there is much good humoured levity, some wit & attempts at wit, a moderate degree of egotism and of that which can be expressed in no language but English, Oddity.' Dalrymple later grew heated over what he felt were his young friend's monumental indiscretions, sneering especially at the Soaping Club: 'the *soaping Club* has confounded your ideas. I know no maxim more absurd and at the same time more dull than that implied in the phrase *every man soap his own beard*.' The newspapers were, on the whole, critical and condescending, with two singular exceptions: the *Public Advertiser* and the *Monthly Review* which gratifyingly compared the letters of Boswell and Erskine to *Tristram Shandy*: 'two juvenile Wits ... full of blood, full of spirits, and full of *fun* ... away they scribble, away they publish; freely abandoning their names ... to the mercy of the wide world!' Boswell did his bit to help the book's reception by writing his own enthusiastic review of it in the *London Chronicle*, comparing Erskine and himself to Rabelais.[11]

3

Boswell was no longer enjoying life in London. Pressure and threats from his father; the infection from Louisa; his disappointment over the Guards and deep indecision about what to do with his life; a degree of abstinence from women, wine, and gaming, which always put him on edge; and beneath the surface of his hectic round of diners, assemblies, theatre-going, and social calls, a pervasive feeling of loneliness all contributed to his unhappiness. He sorely missed Grange and McQuhae, despite their letters of encouragement. Desperate, he decided in February to write to Dalrymple every other Saturday for advice and pleasure: 'I wanted to be rationally happy, yet easy and gay, and hoped he would take a charge of me; would let me know what books to read, and what company to keep, and how to conduct myself.' Dalrymple went along with the idea but insisted on weekly letters, thinking that way he could keep track of the prodigal son and act as intermediary between him and his father, whom he saw regularly on the bench. He wrote on 16 June:

> I think I may promise you from a conversation I had with your father that all disgusts will be forgotten, & that it is you alone who can make them remembered. He is a firm man, but he is not inflexible, & wishes, perhaps too eagerly, to see you add honour to an old & respected family. Let me tell you that you have a fair prospect of doing so, unless you think it worth your pains to pursue every butterfly and pluck every bryar, that comes in your road.

Craving to preserve every aspect of his self-portraiture, Boswell implored his mentor to keep his letters, but Dalrymple refused and begged Boswell to destroy his, too. Dalrymple was a worthy and respected historian, but history for him did not extend to the preservation and possible publication of awkward family secrets.[12]

4

Correspondence with Dalrymple failed to beat down the 'foul fiend'. Boswell's journal and his letters to Grange and Temple are sprinkled with references to this unwanted guest and the pervasive 'spirit of dissipation' that lingered on even when the oppressive gloom subsided. Neither Eglinton nor Erskine's cheerful company could make a dent in it. His brother John's presence did not help either: 'He brought many low old Sunday ideas when we were boys into my memory. I wanted to indulge my gloom in solitude.' Coldness and rain made matters worse. 'All was dark' on 29 March. People could not fathom the depths of his problem – Mrs Douglas 'joked ... about that disease, and said it was people's own fault'. A brief excursion to Oxford in late April only depressed him more, its medieval spires reminding him of Edinburgh's oppressive university quarters: 'I had a kind of horror upon me from thinking of confinement and other gloomy circumstances.' From Oxford, he told Grange: 'I am really an instrument very easily put out of tune ... I require the nicest and most delicate management.'[13]

He began to search for relief in the macabre novelty of attending executions. On 3 May he visited several condemned criminals in the 'dark mansions' of Newgate prison, regretting it afterwards when he felt even more melancholy, 'Newgate being upon my mind like a black cloud'. With a compulsive and 'horrid eagerness' to see criminals actually hung at Tyburn, a terrible place about which he had read as a youth, the next morning he perched himself on a scaffold near the 'fatal tree' so he could clearly see the dismal scene. Permanent gallows had been built at Tyburn (now Marble Arch) in 1571 and by the eighteenth century executions had assumed a type of holiday atmosphere. Boswell does not say whether he joined the procession of the condemned men from Newgate to Tyburn, which would last about two hours, but by taking up his place so close to the gallows he was guaranteed to hear and see the full proceedings: 'I was most terribly shocked, and thrown into a very deep melancholy.' Gloomy terrors mingled with 'heavy, confused, and splenetic' weariness – 'Every morning this is the case with me.' He took to dancing around his room, which momentarily 'expelled the phlegm from my heart, gave my blood a free circulation, and my spirits a brisk flow', but by night-time he was again 'haunted with frightful imaginations' and fled to Erskine's lodgings to sleep with him.[14]

Boswell called this state of mind 'dissipation' not only because he suffered mental weakness and irresolution but also because it generated a sexual promiscuity the like of which he had not experienced before. The pattern from now on was that when he was at his most melancholy he became dissolute and unhealthily sexual, taking prostitutes wherever he could get them, with total abandon and even some violence. It was a sickness. On 25 March, for example, coming home at night feeling out of sorts, he felt 'carnal inclinations raging through my frame' and determined to gratify them. With no trouble at all in St James's Park, a favourite haunt for streetwalkers, he picked up a whore from Shropshire, this time protected by 'armour'. A week later he strolled into the Park again, feeling 'lowish', and 'took the first whore I met, whom I without many words copulated with free from danger, being safely sheathed. She was ugly and lean and her breath smelt of spirits.' Significantly, he never asked her name, which he usually did. This was the moral low point of his London adventure. A few days later, again in search of the bizarre and incongruous, he grabbed a 'strong, jolly young damsel' on 10 May at the bottom of the Haymarket and escorted her to the middle of Westminster Bridge where, suitably armed, he had his way with her. 'The whim of doing it there with the Thames rolling below us amused me much.' Here was Boswell watching himself again. He returned home so late that the chambermaid had already locked up and gone to bed, so he took refuge at Eglinton's, in the 'old little chamber' of his first London visit: 'But when I compared my ideas then with those I had now, the present seemed very dim and very tasteless.'[15]

He now saw himself as a 'libertine', vastly different from the studious and morbid youth Temple had known when they parted five years earlier in Edinburgh. Guilt and depression assaulted him as he reflected on his 'brutish appetite' and despised himself for it. His felicitous phrase for this fierce desire for whores is 'foul fiend of the genitals'[16] – a fiend that continued to torment him or sometimes thrill him with pleasure, according to the women involved, for the rest of his stay in London.

5

Such was his confused emotional and physical state when on 16 May, while he was taking tea with Thomas Davies in the parlour behind his bookshop, the most important event in his life took place. Samuel Johnson unexpectedly walked in. He was a large and growling sort of man who never suffered fools gladly, slovenly and nearsighted with a compulsive tic, scarred by scrofula, and ugly – a man who had suffered considerable adversity and had had to work heroically to survive in the London he loved. Boswell's heart heaved into his throat. Here at last in the flesh was the man whose *Rambler* essays he had revered so much for years, the greatest literary figure of the age. 'Don't tell where I come from,' he whispered urgently to Davies, knowing Johnson's 'mortal antipathy' towards the Scots. He had barely got the words out when Davies 'roguishly' introduced him as 'from Scotland'. Covering himself with 'I cannot help it,' Boswell elicited from this 'very big man' with 'uncouth' voice one of the most famous ripostes ever recorded: 'Sir, that, I find, is what a very great many of your countrymen cannot help.' Boswell committed another gaffe by presuming to tell Johnson about Garrick, for which Johnson struck at him again: 'Sir (said he, with a stern look) I have known David Garrick longer than you have done: and I know no right you have to talk to me on the subject.' A less resilient young man would have withdrawn, but Boswell 'remained upon the field not wholly discomfited' to hear Johnson talk. He even managed a few words which Johnson received 'civilly'. As he left, he thought he had bungled the meeting, but Davies reassured him, 'Don't be uneasy. I can see he likes you very well.' Thus began the most famous friendship in English literary history.[17]

When Johnson met Boswell he was fifty-four and a legend in his own time. In addition to his fame as the author of universally admired moral essays in the *Rambler* and *Idler*, he had published his monumental and astonishing *Dictionary of the English Language* in 1755, the first comprehensive work of its kind in the language. Poetry, a successful play, the didactic romance *Rasselas*, and various other writings rounded out his literary output, and he would go on to write more, including his celebrated *Lives of the Poets*. But Johnson was infinitely more than the sum total of his authorship. He was the Great Cham, a huge personality, the brilliant conversationalist whose rough, blunt, and opinionated manner of talking concealed a profound religiosity and humanity.

A week later, on 24 May – one is surprised that he waited so long – Boswell was on his way to Johnson's chambers at No. 1 Inner Temple Lane (where he lived from 1760 to 1765) when, by chance, he met the notorious politician John Wilkes whose demagoguery and heroic populism secretly fascinated and 'enlivened' him. Were it not for his meeting with Johnson, this encounter with Wilkes might well have been the climax of his London visit. Unfortunately, but prudently, Boswell did not record this and later conversations with Wilkes because the politician was being watched by government spies and Boswell feared that if he were seen too often in his company, his journal and letters might be intercepted in the post and read.[18]

Johnson received him courteously, and as he was at that moment in the full flight of conversation Boswell had time to take in this 'Giant in his den': the 'sloven particularities' of his rough brown suit, loose-fitting shirt and breeches, 'old shrivelled unpowdered wig', stockings 'ill drawn up', and unbuckled shoes that served as slippers. After a while, when

Boswell rose to leave with the other guests, Johnson surprised him by saying, 'Nay, don't go.' They talked for some time alone, about madness and the 'mad' poet Christopher Smart, sensitive subjects for Johnson who always feared his own tendencies to melancholia and 'madness'. When Boswell rose again to leave, 'the great oracle' again stopped him. Boswell then began to talk openly, innocently asking Johnson whether he thought that by the late hours he kept, and the indolence they implied, he was misusing his talents. Johnson agreed. Years later, Boswell was amazed that he had spoken so freely, but Johnson read his naïvety and sincerity correctly: 'Before we parted, he was so good as to promise to favour me with his company one evening at my lodgings; and, as I took my leave, shook me cordially by the hand.' Boswell left walking on air. 'Upon my word, I am very fortunate. I shall cultivate this acquaintance.'[19]

Cultivate it he did, though Johnson was surprised that he waited three weeks before their next meeting. Boswell admitted in his journal that it was his 'dissipation' that prevented it – he had been picking up prostitutes right and left. They met again on 25 June at the Mitre Tavern, Johnson's favourite venue. Johnson luxuriated in the English tavern – the French had nothing like it, he scoffed – where one could dine and converse freely without having to please a host. A tavern chair is 'the throne of human felicity', he once remarked. Boswell was sure he would be in a talkative vein there. He was.[20]

In their progress through a fine meal and a bottle of port, they touched on a multitude of subjects, among them religion, Lord Auchinleck and, most important of all, Boswell's favourite subject, himself. 'I then told my history to Mr Johnson, which he listened to with attention,' especially his account of how he had turned from strict Christianity to 'infidelity' and then back to Christianity. Struck by his appealing openness, Johnson sprang from his chair and cried, 'Give me your hand. I have taken a liking to you.' Boswell must have spoken about his father with equal candour for Johnson astutely observed, 'Your father has been wanting to make the man of you at twenty which you will be at thirty'; then Johnson went on to praise the dignity and responsibility of inheriting a Scottish paternal estate. Lay aside 'idle connections' he urged Boswell, and go abroad, perhaps to Spain, from which he could return to publish his observations. When Boswell lamented that he had little knowledge of books, Johnson offered to map out a study plan for him. 'Will you really take a charge of me?' Boswell replied. Johnson was stirred to hear him speak so 'from the heart': 'Sir, I am glad we have met. I hope we shall

pass many evenings and mornings too together.' They lingered in the
Mitre until one or two in the morning.²¹

From this night on, Boswell was with Johnson at every available
opportunity: at the Mitre and the Turk's Head, in Temple's chambers at
the Middle Temple to which he moved in July, in Johnson's chambers,
and so on. After one conversation at the Turk's Head on 28 July, Boswell
had to pinch himself to make sure these meetings were not a dream: 'It
must be something curious for the people in the Turk's Head Coffee-
house to see this great man and poor Me so often together by ourselves.
My vanity is much flattered.' Boldly, he invited Johnson and Goldsmith
to dine with him one night at his own lodgings, though he had to move
the venue to the Mitre because of a quarrel with his landlord: 'I sat with
much secret pride, thinking of my having such a company with me. I
behaved with ease and propriety, and did not attempt at all to show
away; but gently assisted conversation by those little arts which serve to
make people throw out their sentiments with ease and freedom.'²²

Johnson's friendship, he felt, was the crowning justification of his
journal. It was a challenge, though, to keep the 'lagging journal' from
drowning in this tidal wave of talk: 'In recollecting Mr Johnson's conversation, I labour under much difficulty. It requires more parts than I
am master of even to retain that strength of sentiment and perspicuity
of expression ... I shall just do my best and relate as much as I can.' His
best was excellent, full of the energy and wisdom of his idol, often
composed with a dramatic power – a movable feast of conversation
vividly depicted, in different London settings: 'In progress of time, when
my mind was, as it were, *strongly impregnated with the Johnsonian æther,*
I could, with much more facility and exactness, carry in my memory and
commit to paper the exuberant variety of his wisdom and wit.' Johnson
did not discover that Boswell kept a journal until one day he urged him
to keep one, 'fair and undisguised': 'there is nothing too little for so little
a creature as man.' Boswell took this as the endorsement he needed but
which had been denied him by his father and Dalrymple:

And now O my journal! art thou not highly dignified? Shalt thou not flourish
tenfold? No former solicitations or censures could tempt me to lay thee aside;
and now is there any argument which can outweigh the sanction of Mr
Samuel Johnson? ... I have at present such an affection for this my journal
that it shocks me to think of burning it. I rather encourage the idea of having
it carefully laid up among the archives of Auchinleck.

He could not resist a smug smile when he told Dalrymple that Johnson 'desired me to keep just the journal that I do' and that he 'was glad I was upon so good a plan with it'. 'Would you believe', he boasted,

> that we sat from half an hour after eight till between two and three? He took me cordially by the hand; and said, 'My dear Boswell, I love you very much.' Can I help being somewhat vain? But I assure you real solid satisfaction fills my mind more than vanity. I look upon my obtaining the friendship of this great and good man as one of the most important events in my life. I think better of myself when in his company than at any other time.

Dalrymple, of course, greatly approved – 'I envy you the free and undisguised converse with such a man' – though no hint of approval came from his father, who disapproved of living authors in general. Temple was highly impressed: 'Whatever you may think of yourself you may depend upon it you have merit, otherwise you never could have recommended yourself to so many men of learning and virtue. I question whether there is one young man in Britain, who can boast of so good an acquaintance ... Mr Johnson will at all times be your guardian angel.'[23]

Taking Boswell by the hand at the Mitre one night, Johnson exclaimed, 'My dear Boswell! I do love you very much.' Johnson's moral and religious influence flowed into him. He wanted to be better and this most admired of men would help him be so. Spending time with him was a bit like going to church, except that Johnson made a deeper moral impression on Boswell, inspiring him to consider more seriously 'the duties of morality and religion and the dignity of human nature', especially in relation to his voracious appetite for 'concubinage' – a favourite term of his:

> I have considered that promiscuous concubinage is certainly wrong. It is contributing one's share towards bringing confusion and misery into society; and it is a transgression of the laws of the Almighty Creator, who has ordained marriage for the mutual comfort of the sexes and the procreation and right educating of children.

Out of respect for Johnson, he told himself, he must try. It was easier said than done. Coming up the Strand very late one July night, he was 'tapped on the shoulder by a fine fresh lass'. He went to her home with her, unable to resist 'indulging myself with the enjoyment of her'. He struggled with his conscience, but not for long: 'Surely, in such a situation, when the woman is already abandoned, the crime must be alleviated, though in strict morality, illicit love is always wrong.' Johnson was not always with him, that was the problem.[24]

Boswell soon became a regular visitor at No. 1 Inner Temple Lane and on friendly terms with Johnson's unconventional 'household'. There was Dr Robert Levett the indigent physician whom Johnson had taken off the street and on whose death he wrote one of his most moving poems. One day Dr Levett sneaked Boswell up 'four pairs of stairs' to Johnson's library. This was hallowed ground. There was also the peevish Anna Williams, whom Johnson's late wife 'Tetty' had brought into their house as a resident companion, soon after which the servant went 'stone-blind'. After his wife's death, in memory of her and out of pity for Miss Williams, Johnson had kept her on as his housekeeper. Since 1760, when he moved to Inner Temple Lane, she had been living on her own not far away, and Boswell tells us that never a night passed, however late, when Johnson did not call on her to drink tea. On one occasion Johnson took him to visit Miss Williams, 'who has a snug lodging in Bolt Court, Fleet Street', where Johnson himself later lived. 'I had now made good my title to be a privileged man,' he purred.[25]

6

Through Dalrymple's intercession, Boswell and his father began to reach a compromise near the end of June. In exchange for Boswell giving up the idea of the Guards, his father agreed to let him study law at the University of Utrecht for a year. Holland was the customary choice of young Scots wanting to study law on the Continent, for its legal system, like the Scots system, was based on Roman law. Lord Auchinleck himself, and his father before him, had studied in Leyden. Utrecht was about as exotic a destination as Boswell's father would allow him. Southern Europe with its dangerous allurements was definitely prohibited. Then it would be back to Edinburgh to take up the duties of an advocate. This was far better than having to return to Edinburgh right away and endure the inevitable ridicule for his 'inconsistent desultory conduct'.

Boswell had his doubts about Utrecht. Dr Johnson, he told Dalrymple, was 'not very fond of the notion of spending a whole winter in a Dutch town. He thinks I may do much more by private study, than by attending lectures. He would have me to *perambulate* ... Spain ... He advises me in general to move about a good deal.' This good advice shows that

Johnson understood Boswell's hypochondria. Dalrymple, who himself had studied law in Utrecht and had fond memories of it, tried to cheer up his young correspondent by telling him he had lots of female friends in Utrecht; and that if they were too old for him, they had daughters who were doubtless as agreeable. Boswell had it in the back of his mind to endure Utrecht as best he could so that afterwards he could go to Germany and Italy in an attenuated form of the classical Grand Tour. Some compromise over this, it seems, had yet to be reached.[26]

Meanwhile, mixed reports of Utrecht as both a 'dull stiff starched place' with little in the way of fashionable entertainments and a beautiful city with cheerful and polite people 'in the French taste' confused Boswell and darkened his mood. 'I am afraid of growing melancholy there,' he told Grange. It worried him that his father had thrived in Utrecht. They were different plants and needed different soils. He at last agreed to go when his father, at Dalrymple's prodding, allowed to let him travel for a few months afterwards to the Low Countries and Germany. Though he continued to worry about the strict and incompatible regimen of study to which he would be subjected in Utrecht, the arrangement brightened him up: 'I hope to return from abroad a settled decent Man ... I shall study steadiness: and I don't despair of attaining it. Habit is all in all. When I am abroad, I will not have such temptations to foolish extravagant conduct; as I will be among Strangers, and so may take what character I chuse, and persist in it.' There is a disconcerting ring of tidiness in this plan, as if all he needed to do was con a new part, dress up in new clothes, and then simply step out of character and mimic the part he wanted to play.[27]

Lord Auchinleck wanted his son to be in Utrecht by mid-July – to get him away from London's dissipation as soon as possible – but Boswell was in less of a hurry. There were too many loose ends in London, principally Johnson. The growing love between himself and Johnson was the dominant theme of the last month. Everything else paled in comparison, though he now began to correspond regularly with Temple again. Boswell's infant son Charles, born in November, also occupied his mind with genuine affection. He arranged for an annuity of ten pounds for the child, and when Peggy Doig came to London in July he enjoyed hearing all about him. Grange went to see the baby in Edinburgh that month and gave Boswell a full account of him, which overjoyed the father: 'Poor little creature! I wish from my heart, that I had seen him, before I left England. His resembling me is a most agreeable thing. I am positive that he is my own. He shall allways find me an affectionate

Father.' When he returned from the Continent, he would send the child to some school in a small English village 'where his parentage shall not be known; as the scoffing of his companions might break his spirit'.[28]

7

Suddenly there was not much time left with Johnson. Why not, Johnson suggested, 'make a day of it' and 'go down to Greenwich and dine?' On 30 July then, they took a sculler from Temple-stairs down 'the silver Thames', talking constantly to the rhythm of the boy who rowed them, taking over the oars themselves after the Swan at Billingsgate. It was a perfect clear day, with the sun shining on 'beautiful fields on each side of the river'. Boswell had had the prescience to bring with him a copy of Johnson's famous poem 'London'. With his instinct for personal ritual and the dramatic moment, he read aloud the passage on the banks of the Thames and then, falling to his knees like the speaker in the poem, 'literally "kissed the consecrated earth" ' – one of several of such kisses in his journals. As they walked through Greenwich Park, Johnson sketched out a course of reading for him. They stayed so long in the evening air that Boswell shivered for all of the return sail up the river. The more robust Johnson wondered at his 'paltry effeminacy'.[29]

Back in the city, they deposited themselves in the Turk's Head, where Boswell, lapsing into a reflective and intimate mood, started in with a reverie about Auchinleck and his ancient family. Johnson was as urban a creature as could be conceived in the eighteenth century, but something about Boswell's description of 'the romantick seat of my ancestors' in the remote north stirred him to say, 'I must be there, and we will live in the Old Castle; and if there is no room remaining, we will build one.' Boswell almost fell out of his seat: 'This was the most pleasing idea that I could possibly have: to think of seeing this great man at the venerable seat of my ancestor.' The idea was not totally whimsical, for a few days earlier Johnson had planted the first seed in a scheme that ten years later germinated in an astonishing journey. 'He says he will probably go to Scotland with me when I return from abroad, and in the mean time he is to correspond with me. He told me, with an affection that almost made me cry, "My dear Boswell! it would give me great pain to part with you, if I thought that we were not to meet again." '[30]

To delay their separation, Johnson insisted, 'I must see thee go; I will go down with you to Harwich.' 'This prodigious mark of his affection,'

Boswell wrote in his journal, 'filled me with gratitude and vanity.' And well it might. The greatest writer of the age wanted to travel with him to a port several hours up the Essex coast just to see him off. In the meantime, there were lots of goodbyes to say, letters to write, and the journal to bring up to date, which kept Boswell up two entire nights in the final days. He put off his packing until the last minute – as he always did – so he was up all of the last night as well. He felt 'strangely agitated' and melancholic, and his mind shrank from leaving. He took stock:

> Let me recollect my life since this journal began. Has it not passed like a dream? Yes, but I have been attaining a knowledge of the world. I came to town to go into the Guards. How different is my scheme now! I am now upon a less pleasurable but a more rational and lasting plan.

He sent Grange the last section of his journal, which now amounted to 734 manuscript pages, with the demand that after he had read them he should put them away and not read them, or his letters, again until he returned. This was a symbolic 'embargo', an attention to 'form', Boswell's way of sealing up his personal history to this point, putting it behind him. The future, he hoped, would make him a new man with new experiences in a wider world. Without any sleep he met Johnson bright and early on the morning of 5 August to set off in the coach for Harwich.[31]

There is no record of their journey in the journal, only the account in the *Life of Johnson* that dwells mainly on the older man's conversation. At Colchester, however, where they stayed the night, Boswell allowed himself an autobiographical moment:

> I teased him with fanciful apprehensions of unhappiness. A moth having fluttered round the candle, and burnt itself, he laid hold of this little incident to admonish me; saying, with a sly look, and in a solemn but quiet tone, 'That creature was its own tormentor, and I believe its name was BOSWELL.'

They arrived in Harwich the next day. Boswell booked his passage to Helvoetsluys on the packet-boat *Prince of Wales*, put his bags on board, dined with Johnson at their inn, and then visited the church where Johnson admonished him to pray about his journey. Afterwards, they walked down to the beach together where they warmly embraced, the young and obscure but abundantly affable Scot and the greatest man of letters of the second half of the century:

I said, 'I hope, Sir, you will not forget me in my absence.' JOHNSON: 'Nay, Sir, it is more likely you should forget me, than that I should forget you.' As the vessel put out to sea, I kept my eyes upon him for a considerable time, while he remained rolling his majestick frame in his usual manner; and at last I perceived him walk back into the town, and he disappeared.[32]

PART II

Travel and Marriage

1763–1769

EIGHT

Utrecht: Acquiring a Noble Character

I

One of the great tragedies of Boswell's time in Utrecht is that his journal for that period, beginning with the journey to Harwich with Johnson, was lost. When he left the city for good in May 1764, he deposited all but the last three weeks of it (536 manuscript pages) with his friend, the Rev. Robert Brown, to be forwarded to Scotland with all his other papers. When the parcel arrived at Auchinleck on 28 April 1767, the journal was missing. 'I was much vexed,' he wrote; 'I figured its being exposed to a hundred enemies.'[1] It has not been heard of since. The Dutch journal is his only major manuscript not to have come to light this century.

What we know about his stay in Utrecht is pieced together from letters, memoranda, a sequence of ten-line poems, thirty-one French and six Dutch Themes averaging about five hundred words each, a handful of dialogues, and the last three weeks of the journal which, because he was behind, he completed after he had left the city. The record that has survived, not to mention the missing journal, suggests that he applied himself to a large amount of writing during the ten months he was in Utrecht. There were three reasons for this: he was turning over a new leaf, determined to study and learn, not to show off; he aspired to develop further his art as a writer, particularly the essay form in the manner of Johnson's *Rambler*; and he needed to write in French regularly, in addition to his academic writing, in order to become fluent in the language. The lost journal is especially lamentable because it denies us the chance to gauge Boswell's development as a writer in this purposeful period of his life.

2

Anticipating Utrecht, several days before he left London Boswell began the large enterprise of changing his temperament. In a memorandum for 1 August, he implores himself to be reserved and calm in Holland, to keep his melancholy to himself, 'to sustain a consistent character', and to have the 'manly' resolution 'to improve' – all this for the honour and dignity of the Boswells of Auchinleck. He must cut a dignified figure. He must not set himself up as buffoon or 'jolly dog'. Premonitions of the disastrous effects this self-imposed strait-jacketing of his personality might have in Utrecht had already worn him out by the time he boarded the boat at Harwich. As the vessel set sail and Johnson disappeared from view, he immediately turned his gaze painfully upon himself: 'I was sick and filled with a crowd of different ideas.' His heavy heart told him that if only he had been allowed to travel first to 'the gay regions of Italy and France', he would be arriving in Utrecht with fewer 'dismal imaginations'. As it was, after an uneventful crossing, several unremarkable days in Leyden and Rotterdam, and nine hours of sluggish jolting (which he always hated) along the roads from Leyden to Utrecht, without anyone to talk to, he was a mental wreck. 'A deep melancholy seized upon me,' he groaned in a letter to Grange. He checked into a dreary room on a remote upper floor of the Castle of Antwerp, where he had to eat by himself. Worst of all, every hour on the hour he had to endure the tolling of a 'dreary Psalm tune' from the surviving lofty tower of the medieval cathedral on the other side of the square. He fell asleep feeling desperately lonely, trapped in that room by an assortment of sensations, any one of which in other circumstances would have been enough to depress him.[2]

In the rhythms of the carillon bells, the 'foul fiend' was clapping its hands in anticipation of the sunrise. The next morning confirmed the worst. The 'dreadful bell' still tolled dolefully, only now it was Sunday, and the Presbyterian service he attended made him go almost 'mad'. He felt his spirit being crushed and he wept bitterly: 'Poor Boswell! is it come to this? Miserable wretch that I am.' Dissipation of the worst kind was better than this blackest species of hypochondria. 'I can now feel how my poor brother was afflicted,' he wrote to Temple on 16 August. His sense of a huge vacuum in his life was aggravated by the fact of his coming to Utrecht one whole month before the university term began. The following day, the 15th, he bolted, escaping back to Rotterdam where he stayed with Archibald Stewart whose sister Margaret he had once hoped to make his wife. So much for the 'prudent plan' to which he and his father had agreed. Should he fly off to Berlin? Geneva? What he really wanted to do was double back to Temple's 'calm retreat' in the Inner Temple. He sent a cry for help to Dempster, who was in Paris, asking him to meet him in Brussels right away, then wrote again telling Dempster to write before leaving. In the meantime, he went off with an American medical student, John Morgan, later to become physician-in-chief in the American army, to tour several Dutch cities. They stopped in Utrecht for a couple of days, but it still appeared 'terrible'. Back in Rotterdam several days later, he discovered to his chagrin that Dempster, rushing off before receiving his second letter, had covered '62 leagues in 30 hours' to Brussels to minister to him in his hour of need, only to find he had never come.[3]

Johnson was not with him, but his *Rambler* essays were. Boswell read essays on fortitude and patience, man's control over his destiny, keeping the mind and body busy enough to ward off 'little evils', and not indulging in 'gloomy fancy'. Encouraged by them, he returned in a wagon to Utrecht on 5 September clutching the *Rambler* in his hands as if it were the Bible, like a man fearful of sliding into oblivion. His profound gratitude to Johnson, his 'mental physician', and to God, was exceeded only by his realization that by an act of will he had actually won that round against hypochondria; surely he could prevail again in the future. Buy the *Rambler* for twelve shillings and devour it, he admonished Grange:

> I had always yielded to spleen as to an invincible foe. He at last pushed the oppression of a Conqueror so hard that I turned upon him and fairly obtained a victory. Observe my friend that I never before attempted to oppose the foul fiend so never before enjoyed happiness on any sure foundation. I told you that my honoured friend Mr Samuel Johnson had supplied me with the weapons of philosophy. It was in the *Rambler* that I found the causes of my woe described, and cures pointed out . . . It is the best book that England has produced for such people as you and me.

It remained to be seen how long his Johnsonian 'mental cure' would last. For the moment he took lodgings in a 'neat house', began to decorate his rooms, bought himself 'a Leyden suit of green and silver' to supplement his 'scarlet and gold' – sartorial enthusiasm always meant he was in a positive mood – started a course of lectures at the university on civil law, and found a servant, François Mazerac.[4]

Since he was not shy about telling a number of his old friends about his first weeks in Holland, he received advice from all directions. The waggish Stewart suggested fifteen minutes of deep breathing with his mouth open at the window first thing in the morning, dancing around his room for twenty-five minutes, almost half a gallon of porridge for breakfast, and yelling at his servant to exercise his tongue. Such cheering nonsense had a better chance of rousing him than the heavy opinion he received from Grange and Temple. Dempster, unperturbed by his fruit-less dash to Brussels, encouraged him with an account of his own success against hypochondria: 'Spleen is like a bullying boy at school: insupportable till he is once heartily thrashed, and for ever after your humble servant. It is but six years since I drubbed the dog to his contentment, and he has never disturbed me since.' As for Dalrymple, 'I *foretold* that your fund of patience and affection was too small to bear living among a set of Dutch professors in tartan nightgowns, long pipes . . . who set a real value on a library of musty books, who consider mirth as a shame and rampaging as a sin, who neither care how they spend their time nor what kind of weather it is, provided their sundials, their barometers, and thermometers indicate properly.' It was enough 'to turn the head of a marble statue and to affect the serenity of a Lord Auch-inleck'. Dalrymple's advice was very practical, but about as sensitive to the real problem as an officious schoolmaster: 'When the weather is bad, get into a wagon or chaise of some kind, and jolt off your listlessness. As soon as the weather sets in for frost, learn to skate. You will find a master for that exercise where you are. Skate in company and you will run no danger of drowning, nor much of ducking.'⁵

3

Once Boswell emerged from his first weeks of gloom, he waged a mighty war against hypochondria. His method was, for him, a repugnantly rigid regimen of study, monitored and cultivated by what he called *retenu* or calm and evenly paced reserve. The word *retenu* tolls like another kind of bell throughout his memoranda and letters. He measured his success or failure by how closely he adhered to it, censuring himself when he was too loud and lively, patting himself on the back when he was steady, 'upon your guard'.

He had the best chance of winning if he could keep himself busy. On 16 September, the routine was already under way: 'Latin till breakfast, something till eleven, then dress and at twelve French, then walk and dine. Afternoon, journal &c. But next week you go to lectures, which will employ two hours and one in writing notes, about which you need not be exact.' All this was in addition to the French Themes on any subject that might come to mind – his favourite, as always, himself – and the ten lines of verse every day. His diligent study and practice of French paid off, for he came close to fluency in the language by the end of the year, and in Dutch by the following summer. By 5 October, he was forcing himself into an even more feverish pitch of study, rising at 6.30 a.m.: 'seven to eight, Ovid; eight to nine, French version; ten to eleven, Tacitus; three to four, French; four to five, Greek; six to seven, Civil Law; seven to eight, Scots; eight to ten, Voltaire. Then journal, letters, and other books. Learn by all means *retenu* and being easy without talking of yourself, and guard against ridicule; so don't encourage viewing objects in ridiculous lights.' And so it went.[6]

Knowing that this intense application to study warred with his natural self, a battle which he was always in danger of losing, in October Boswell composed what he called an 'Inviolable Plan', an ambitious and portentous document 'to be read over frequently', spelling out what he expected to make of himself and why. It was a personal manifesto or creed to see him through Utrecht, into the rest of his travels, and back home for a productive and honourable life as advocate or judge and, eventually, Laird of Auchinleck. Its main theme was that he was a good seed with noble prospects, that he must prevent himself from going to the bad. It is interesting that at the beginning of the 'Plan', knowing well the dangers he was running, he cautions himself not to become 'stiff and unnatural', affected, and out of character. That was what worried Dempster, and Johnson too, about his going to Utrecht: that he would be miserable trying to manipulate himself into a respectability that was alien to his temperament. There was no problem with the first few imperatives: avoid idleness; remember religion and morality, keeping clear of 'gloomy [Presbyterian] notions which have nothing to do with the mild and elegant religion of Jesus'; avoid profanity. It was the rest of the 'Plan' that was more testing: keeping 'firm', in 'constant command of yourself'; restraining 'ludicrous talents' like mimicry and singing in public; deflecting 'uneasy trifles' – i.e., idle entertainments like billiards and gaming; shunning 'antipathies' to people and places. Throughout the London months Boswell had commented how much he preferred people who were exuberant, spontaneous, and forceful to those who were political and programmed. However many times he instructed himself to the contrary, he knew that this kind of 'dignity' was not his natural character. His father, of course, welcomed these resolutions, which Boswell willingly shared with him, and during the few months in Utrecht, while Boswell was busy trying not to be himself, they were closer in spirit and sentiment than they had ever been before or would be again. His father actually began his letters with, 'My Dear Son'.[7]

The 'Plan' does not specifically mention it, but 'sauntering' and sex were most definitely banned. He resolved to abstain not only from whoring but also from talking about whoring. A 'trifle', for example, a bawdy conversational lapse on 23 October, repelled him:

> Yesterday you was still too jocular and talked of yourself, particularly of your whoring, which was shameful ... Try firmly this week never once to speak of yourself. It will be great ... If you can once be silent and have habits of study and manly thought and conduct, you will do well and may marry a woman of the best family in England. Bravo!

The fact that he kept to this resolution for so many months is one reason why he was so unhappy in Utrecht.[8]

Throughout October and November the monotony and routine 'of a life almost solitary' deflated him. Then, in early December, he relaxed somewhat, changing the Plan to include three hours every evening for 'amusement', telling himself that he had come abroad to see foreign manners as well as to study. In preparation for the Christmas season the town had filled with the *noblesse* and come alive with ladies' smiling faces, card assemblies, balls, and private parties. He was complimented by a Dutch wit, 'It's not every Englishman who is well received.' He was befriended by the Countess of Nassau, the thirty-year-old sister-in-law of the Grand Bailiff of Utrecht, 'the finest woman upon earth', whose husband (to whom Boswell had an introduction from Sir David Dalrymple) was seventy and whose indiscretions were becoming notorious. In this new 'vortex of pleasure', the old spontaneous Boswell sometimes intruded: he could kick himself for 'giving a kind of jump when you heard she was to be at your two next parties'. In October he allowed himself the lapse of one splendid sartorial outing to the Count of Nassau's for dinner, where he doubtless made a sensational impression as a young man of fashion: 'Dress in scarlet and gold, fine swiss, white silk stockings, handsome pumps, and have silver-and-silk sword knot, Barcelona handkerchief, and elegant toothpick-case which you had in a present from a lady. Be quite the man of fashion and keep up your dignity.' Now, on 8 December, he was walking around the town with the Countess, being introduced to the best Utrecht society, talking 'charming French' all the way. 'How delicious!' he wrote in a memorandum.[9]

But alarm bells rang. He scented danger from the Countess as well as within himself: 'Be very *retenu* . . . Have a care. Don't alter.' He could admire her, but he must not allow himself to be 'vicious', for although it would 'inflame' him, it would also 'fever your heart and ruin your *Plan*'. This higher life, which included much more eating and drinking, began to disagree with him, as he told himself on 9 December: 'You are not quite right at present. Your health is not perfect. That disorder of the stomach distresses you. Be more regular to go to bed. Eat a lighter dinner; drink less wine and a good deal of water to give a clear digestion.' He must take more physical exercise in the Mall every day, a beautiful tree-lined avenue in Utrecht where he could play the croquet-like game of 'pall-mall'. Above all, 'withstand pleasure or you will be dissolved'.[10]

As Boswell travelled to Leyden for the Christmas holidays on 19 December, with his 'Inviolable Plan' tucked reassuringly in his trunk, he believed he had turned his life round: 'Formerly you made your general plan yield to the present moment. Now you make the present moment yield to the general plan, as it soon passes.' To please his father, he was about to spend Christmas with his Dutch relations, the Sommelsdyck family, and he was determined to have a pleasing time – if he could only remember some basic rules of *retenu*: 'Never aim at being too brilliant. Be rather an amiable, pretty man. Have no affectation. Cure vanity. Be quite temperate and have self-command amid all the pleasures. Think of Epictetus and Johnson. You have acquired a noble character at Utrecht. Maintain it.'[11]

The Sommelsdycks received him with 'all the affection of kindred' and things went well from the start. He was introduced to a wide social set at parties, dinners, card assemblies and a variety of other elegant occasions. In a more erudite vein, he called on Abraham Gronovius, classical scholar and Librarian of the University of Leyden, on a scholarly mission for his father. Then, on the 21st, a barge carried him peaceably along a canal to The Hague for more of the same, though the society there was a degree more elegant. Archibald Stewart wrote to him there that he need not have worried about his reception: 'you are full of wit and good humour, besides being remarkably handsome.' He was welcomed with open arms. The conversation was lively and full of 'novelty', and as Boswell figured impressively in it with his performance as the dignified and *retenu* son of a Scottish baron, he decided to show himself off by recording it at length, in French, in his 'Dialogues at The

Hague'. Baron von Spaen invited him to attend a morning society of people of the highest fashion 'where one chats or plays or makes the acquaintance of everybody'. Sir Joseph Yorke, Ambassador to The Hague, took him under his wing, entertained him and, as something of a climax, introduced him to William V, the Prince of Orange, then only fifteen. He was presented to other princes as well, and to all the foreign ambassadors – 'in short, to everybody'. He was positively ecstatic about the 'brilliant gaiety' at The Hague, 'much in the manner of Paris', he supposed. He could not wait to get back to Utrecht on the 9th to write it all up in his journal, which by 20 January had reached 310 pages.[12]

It had been a whirlwind vacation full of 'brilliant dissipation' – social, not sexual, but he returned to Utrecht, 'the seat of the dutch muses', with his mind and resolution 'weakened', after which he lacked his former vigour in resisting the spleen: 'Lethargic gloom is now attempting you, but by exercise till you sweat, drive him off.' A streak of restlessness was beginning to appear: 'Perhaps, I am too much an enthusiast in rectitude . . . I am not quite content: for I do not enjoy enough, I am afraid to resign myself to pleasing sensations lest I should be too susceptible of uneasy ones.' He also felt too fat and sluggish. He liked the image an English officer had used to sum up this 'extraordinary constitution' that was the mystery of Boswell: 'He said that I was like a great stone couched on the slope of a mountain, and while I stayed there, I was lumpish and heavy; but when I was once set in motion, I went with amazing velocity, so that it was impossible to stop me until the projectile force being exhausted, I came again to rest.' It was not yet clear what would set the stone moving, so his mood and actions were unpredictable. Indolence, which made him wretched, alternated erratically with industriousness.[13]

His spirits sank further with a severe cold and then he received the cruellest blow. Grange wrote in February 1764 that his son Charles was dead. He had never seen the baby, but 'I mourn for an idea', he told Temple, for the loss of all the plans 'which must now be dashed from my mind'. He made himself out to be another Job in his ten-line poem for 8 March:

> I weep for him whom I have never seen.
> For in my heart the warm affection dwelt,
> For I a father's tender fondness felt.

The death of Charles affected him so deeply not because he mourned the loss of a child but because the 'ideas' he had been cherishing of parental affection were now destroyed. It was his persona, or at least one of his self-images, that suffered a blow.[14]

As time crept by and he became more desperate, he confided in a few of his new friends and in academics like the affable Professor Christian Heinrich Trotz of Utrecht, with whom he studied civil law, and Hieronymus David Gaubius of Leyden, physician and Professor of Chemistry. As late as May he consulted Gaubius, who had written about hypochondria from a physiological point of view; he found the consultation 'curious' and quite amusing. Gaubius missed the point and was annoyingly facile: 'You will be cured by thirty.'[15]

One of the reasons why Gaubius's medical diagnosis was useless was that much of Boswell's anxiety was religious in origin, precipitated by excessive metaphysical speculation and a 'disordered fancy'. He was perplexed with doubts about Christianity. The 'meanest and most frightful Presbyterian notions' still haunted him: 'I think of death, and I shudder.' A few weeks later, he told Temple:

> While I have been crushed with a load of gloom, I have strove with severe intenseness of thought to find out the 'Spirit of Man'. But all my thinking has been in vain. It has increased my disorder and turned my speculations inwards upon my own mind, concerning which distempered imagination has formed the most wild and dreary conjectures.

He feared the extinction of 'the last spark of celestial fire'. With his fondness for turning his phantasms of annihilation into imagery, he pictured his mind's fragility:

> I have thought, if my mind is a collection of springs, these springs are all unhinged, and the Machine is all destroyed; or if my mind is a waxen table, the wax is melted by the furnace of sorrow, and all my ideas and all my principles are dissolved, are run into one dead mass. Good GOD, my friend, what horrid chimaeras!'[16]

4

Boswell's mainstays during the bleak Utrecht winter were two Scottish male friends, the Reverend Brown and James Rose, and two beautiful females whom he courted at the same time and who (like Mistresses Ford and Page in *The Merry Wives of Windsor*) were very good friends

with one another: Catherina Elizabeth van Geelvinck ('La Veuve') and
Isabella van Tuyll, Belle de Zuylen (or Zélide). Brown, with whom he dined
regularly, together with his sister and sister-in-law, had literary proclivities,
taught him Dutch, geography, and Greek and generally acted as a substitute for Temple. Rose, who was more in the mould of Grange, was a
good companion and wit, as well as a mild hypochondriac. Neither of
them appreciated Boswell's profound mental problems. They illustrated
the lack of sympathy for 'hypochondriacal melancholy' often met with in
society at that time, to which John Moore made reference in his *Medical
Sketches* of 1786: 'As this disease is in reality more distressing than dangerous, and as his looks are not impaired in a degree that corresponds with
the account he gives of his distress, [the sufferer] seldom meets with that
sympathy which his sensibility requires and his sufferings deserve.'[17]

　　With Madame Geelvinck and, especially, Zélide, there was much
fuller emotional interplay. Although Boswell carried on his courtships in
French, in the company of these women he shone, vivaciously and
excitingly. He fell in love with them both, more or less simultaneously,
while they were charmed by his transparency and innocent frankness,
his naïvety and absurdity. They teased him and laughed at him, perhaps
even loved him. Either woman could have dramatically changed his life
and fortunes, had he been up to the change or open to the challenge. As
he confided to Temple, his perennial sounding-board on marital matters:

> There are two Ladies here, a young, handsome, amiable Widow with £4,000
> a year & Mademoiselle de Zuyl[en] who has only a fortune of £20,000. She
> is a charming creature. But she is a *savante* & a *Bel esprit* & has published
> some things. She is much my superior. One does not like that. One does not
> like a widow neither. You won't allow me to yoke myself here? You *will* have
> me married to an English Woman.

He sounds more certain than he was. Temple did not know how close
he came to a painful subject when he asked, 'Have you been chaste since
you left us, or do Dutch women feel it all o'er as ours do, and is human
nature in that respect every where the same? Strange questions these,
Boswell, but not unnatural ones.'[18]

　　The beautiful, rich, and soft 'La Veuve', as he called Madame Geelvinck, was only twenty-five but she had a son of six or seven and had
already been a widow for six years. She was a glittering prize. Looking
'brilliant' in sea-green and silver at an assembly in February, he fancied
himself falling deliciously in love with her: 'O *la belle Veuve*! She talked

low to you and close, perhaps to feel breath . . . You took her hand to the coach, and your frame thrilled.' An affectionate 'portrait' of her by Zélide, which Boswell gallantly promised her he would read, describes her beauty as 'more fetching' than any of her individual features. In a two-page dialogue between himself and 'La Veuve' on 8 February, Boswell told her she had introduced him to true love. She asked if he was good-natured, to which he replied, 'I am a very honest man with a very generous heart. But I am a little capricious, though I shall cure that. It was only a year ago that I was the slave of imagination and talked like Mademoiselle de Zuylen [imprudently].' Over the next few weeks, he repeatedly declared his love for her. She remained cautious and testing, full of questions.[19]

In another long dialogue on 19 February, just before she left for a visit to The Hague, 'La Veuve' urged him to cure himself of his passion and insisted she would never fall in love. He implored her to give him some encouragement, but she declined until the end of their conversation when she whispered seductively, 'I leave my heart with you.' Boswell commented on the interview: 'This was truly an adventure, and you did an immense deal. She is delicious but impregnable.' On the 21st, he rose before seven and convinced a carbineer at St Catherine's Gate to allow him to hide in his sentry-box so that he could catch a glimpse of her as she passed by on the way to The Hague. He stood on the ramparts and, 'quite torn with love', watched her disappear from view. For the rest of the day and for several days afterwards, he was flat and stale. The passion 'tore and hurt my mind', he told Grange. Thus far the courtship had lasted for three weeks. They wrote to each other, but by the time she returned to Utrecht, he had realised the madness of marrying her, as he told her with inimitable directness: 'I could not bring myself to confess the truth, and here it is. I adore you, but I would not marry you for anything in the world. My feelings have changed.' Her bemused comment was simply, 'You are very frank,' and they continued to see each other cordially and politely, often in the company of Zélide who may well have been the reason why Boswell changed his mind about marrying 'La Veuve'.[20]

5

Zélide was unfinished business he would need to attend to before leaving Utrecht. Otherwise he had exhausted the pleasures of the city and was thoroughly fed up with studying. He had never before applied himself so much to his books. In addition to his journal and learning French and Dutch, he had embarked on two erudite literary projects, a Scots dictionary and a translation into Latin of John Erskine's *Principles of the Laws of Scotland.* He had also made a good impression on Professors Trotz and Gronovius, though admittedly more for his congeniality than his academic prowess – he gave Gronovius forty-five bottles of port.[21]

Another round of visits to Leyden and The Hague, a long overdue visit to Amsterdam in late May, and plans for his Grand Tour did more than anything else to raise his spirits during his final weeks in Holland.

'If you whore, all ideas change,' he reminded himself in April after a near capitulation to his sexual urges, even as he courted Zélide. Throughout April and May he strove heroically to control his sexual drive, a moral struggle he recorded in the only surviving part of his journal. He almost succumbed at The Hague but resisted temptation by telling himself that Amsterdam would be safer and that he would end his sexual fast, if at all, only with a 'fine' girl. 'Concubinage is no dire sin,' he rationalized, 'but never do it unless some very extraordinary opportunity of fresh girl that can do no harm' – 'irregular coition was not commendable but . . . no dreadful crime.' He held out until, on a short visit to Amsterdam in late May, he walked into a brothel and was shown upstairs to a room where a girl was waiting. He had no 'armour' and, in any case, found the girl so repulsive that he made a hasty exit, 'hurt' none the less to find himself in 'the sinks of gross debauchery'. Later he strolled up and down the dangerous Amsterdam streets, entered a *speelhuis* and danced a 'blackguard minuet' with a woman in laced ridingclothes. Still he had no 'armour' and again he escaped. The next day, Sunday, after a gloomy sermon that depressed him with 'old Scots gloomy ideas', he drifted in and out of 'mean brothels in dirty lanes', but his spleen caught up with him and he did nothing. He returned immediately to Zélide in Utrecht, still able to hold his head up with *retenu* and a clear conscience in her company.[22]

NINE

Zélide

Boswell was fascinated by Zélide.[1] At first, he did not seek her out so much as her noble father, Monsieur de Tuyll, and his six-hundred-year-old family, one of the oldest in Holland. He was a governor of the Province, a man of extreme integrity. The family owned a town house in Utrecht, and a moated castle in the village of Zuilen, about an hour's pleasant walk from the city along the River Vecht. A description of the Castle of Zuylen by Philippe Godet in 1906 suggests its opulence and scale:

> Flanked by turrets at the four corners, it is, in the fashion of the country, surrounded on three sides by water. You cross a wide moat on a bridge of three arches, after having passed under a postern gate which must be of very ancient construction, where are carved, beside the arms of Utrecht and of Zuylen, those of the families of Tuyll and Weede. Not far from the main building are grouped its dependencies; its farms, barns, and carriage-houses. Through the curtain of century-old trees which frame the Castle, the eye embraces the vast perspectives of the plain of Holland.[2]

This family was the ideal social connection for Boswell to balance against his drab and rigorous academic study.

Monsieur de Tuyll promptly welcomed Boswell into his home in Utrecht. Boswell met the sons and then the daughter, Zélide, who was exactly his age. Attractive but not as beautiful as 'La Veuve', she dazzled him immediately with her brilliance and irreverence, though he made Herculean efforts to maintain his *retenu*. He must have been impressed that this girl, his contemporary, had just published a novel, *Le Noble*, that scandalized her respectable and provincial world of rank and privilege. It is a measure of her liveliness, her mocking and satiric unconventionality, that the heroine of the story, the daughter of a distinguished though dull baron, against the wishes of her family falls in love with the young son of a recently created nobleman. As she escapes through the window of her room, she throws down several portraits of her ancestors to cushion her fall. Zélide writes, 'She had never believed that one could get so much support from one's grandfathers.'

Soon after meeting Belle de Zuylen, the name she preferred, towards the end of October, Boswell scribbled a ten-line poem about this remarkable woman who had nothing Dutch about her but her name and had made his 'gay bosom beat with love's alarms'. He decided he would call her Zélide, a name she later adopted for literary purposes. At first, he was 'absurdly bashful' in her company, but by the end of November he was seeing her regularly.[3]

Boswell's deep respect for Zélide's intellect mingled with a sometimes priggish pique at her imprudence. The apparently frivolous way in which she spoke of her family offended his sacred feelings about his own equally ancient one. In awe of her intellectual powers and shocked by her religious unorthodoxy, he thought she talked far too much for one of her sex, too fast and tactlessly, though obviously she had the manners and decorum to behave herself when she wanted to. He had the feeling she was teasing him much of the time, finding his circumspection and moral pretentiousness absurd. He may not have known such a woman could exist.

It disturbed him to be put constantly on the defensive by a very clever woman with no scruples about speaking her mind. When he told Zélide, for example, about his ambitious plan to prepare a Scots dictionary – which would be Scotland's answer to Johnson's English dictionary, a way of saving the Scottish language from someday becoming unintelligible and thereby rescuing Scottish literature from oblivion[4] – she 'roasted' him about its being trifling, saying that it would be less useful than the turf burning in the stove. He was all for frankness – having just made a 'pact of frankness' with her for the whole winter – but she was beginning to wear on his nerves: 'was really hurt with her imprudent rattling and constant grin. You was angry for having thought of putting any confidence in her, for she blabbed, "It is your continual study to check your imagination." She is really foolish and *raised*.'[5]

After 'La Veuve' vanished to The Hague and Boswell's passion for her cooled, Zélide was still there with her enigmatic charm, pulling him in all sorts of directions at once. She was fascinating enough to write a play about, he thought, and sketched out the plot for *Female Scribbler*, which he never wrote. She gave a harpsichord concert: 'fine, really charmed and soothed; she, sweet and mild.' In March 1764, he saw her almost every day. He devoured a 'Portrait' of herself that she had written for her dear friend 'La Veuve'. A few passages of Zélide's sparkling prose best convey the charm that was ensnaring him:

> You will ask me perhaps if Zélide is beautiful, or pretty, or merely passable. I do not know. It all depends on your loving her or her wishing to make herself beloved. She has a beautiful neck; she knows it, and displays a little more of it than modesty allows...
>
> Affectionate in the extreme and even more fastidious, she cannot be happy either with love or without it. But where did Friendship ever find a temple more hallowed, more worthy of his presence, than Zélide's heart?...
>
> Too lively and too powerful feelings; too much inner activity with no satisfactory outlet: there is the source of all her misfortunes...
>
> Aware of the futility of planning and the uncertainty of the future, she seeks above all to make the passing moment happy. Can you not guess her secret? Zélide is something of a sensualist...
>
> It is her lack of concern for the future that has caused Zélide to commit a thousand imprudences... Fortunately the blame of a thousand fools and of a hundred thousand prudes is not worth a moment of regret.[6]

Could the beauty and spirit of this woman be enough to tame Boswell? Could she cure his dissipation, banish the 'foul fiend', and harness his divergent impulses into a constant productive focus? Would her literary instincts help him to realize his? It was too early to tell, but in any case Boswell was thinking more of taming Zélide. If she was indeed like a 'badly drilled battalion of troops', as she was described by the Baroness von Spaen, another of her Utrecht friends, could he not be happy as its colonel? She could be 'remedied'. She deserved 'a great deal more fame and love than she gets', he told Madame de Spaen; 'she has quite superior parts and the best heart in the world'. Madame de Spaen, whom Zélide described as 'an immense collection of pretensions, of which her talk is the catalogue', was a little confused: she approved of his friendship with her, but where did that leave 'La Veuve'? Could either one persuade him to stay longer in Holland? He wrote to his father, it seems, asking if he could continue his wooing, to which his father replied with the names of eligible Scottish girls, recently snapped up. 'Your Dutch wit and Dutch widow,' he wrote, 'are not so easily catched as our Scots lasses.'[7]

Boswell did not think he was missing much at home, even if he felt twinges of regret that Stewart's sister had just been betrothed, or that his Edinburgh classmates were according to his father moving ahead lucratively as advocates. He had too many plans. His father, on amicable terms with him at present, told him travel was 'a useless thing' except for 'rubbing off bashfulness, which is not your case', and that he would be better off returning to get on with his profession. Perhaps a brief tour of the German courts until the end of the year would be 'amusing', but no more. Boswell had grander ideas – a Grand Tour, in fact, lasting for at least a couple of years, taking in not only the German courts but also Switzerland where he might visit, of all people, Voltaire and Rousseau; then across the Alps into Italy, followed by Spain, ending up in Paris. 'Upon this Plan,' he announced to Temple, 'I cannot expect to be in Britain before the autumn of 1765.' He was not sure how he was going to pay for it all. Never mind – for the moment Zélide was still paramount in his mind.[8]

From Boswell's descriptions, Temple himself fell in love with her. You take the widow, he wrote, I'll take the 'savante et bel esprit'. A nervous conversation with her on 25 May brought Boswell's frustrations out in the open dramatically in front of the whole Zuylen family. She was too iconoclastic and railed against the 'system' and common sense: 'You must show a little decorum. You are among rational beings, who boast of their reason, and who do not like to hear it flouted.' Delighted with the rebuke, Zélide's father and others in the room almost applauded. Here at last was a young, attractive Scot of some dignity who might be able to put sense into her head. Later he took up the theme again:

> I talked to her seriously and bid her marry a *bon baron* of good sense and amiable manners who would be her superior in common life, while he admired her fine genius and all that. She said she would marry such a man if she saw him. But still she would fain have something finer ... I said she should never have a man of much sensibility. For instance, 'I would not marry you if you would make me King of the Seven Provinces.'

He did not record her reply.[9]

As his departure drew nigh, Boswell still had not come to any understanding with her. On 30 May he was invited to the Castle of Zuylen for the first time, where he resolved to 'talk to her sweet'. Again, in these opulent surroundings, he found her too vivacious: 'I was discontented.'

Still, there was magic about her, and it had cast a spell on him. He confessed it to Madame de Spaen:

Perhaps you ask me, Madame, if I am leaving Utrecht with perfect indiffer-ence, if I feel no tender regrets ... O Baroness! do not ask me. Yes, yes. I feel regrets indeed. Charming Zélide! May heaven grant her the happiness she deserves. To hear that Zélide is happy will rejoice my soul.[10]

When they met for the last time, on 17 June, over tea in the open air before the castle gate, he was in no doubt that she loved him – agitated, with many tender looks, her hand in his, and 'the tender tear' standing 'crystal in her eye'. 'Be assured,' he wrote to Temple, 'I could have this angelic creature for my wife, but she has such an imagination, that I pity the man who puts his head in her power. For my part, I choose to be safe.' He left Utrecht the following day with thoughts of marrying Zélide tumbling over themselves in his mind. His plan was to come back to her on his way back to Britain after his travels, and they would correspond in the meantime. He would postpone the decision until then.[11]

2

Boswell's affection for Zélide grew in proportion to the distance he travelled away from her. For the next year-and-a-half, he conducted a courtship through correspondence, largely through her father, signing himself 'Boswell D'Auchinleck'. The letters are bizarre and erratic. He cast himself as Zélide's avuncular and objective mentor, mixing telltale words of praise and admiration for her with cautious gestures of 'delicacy' and respectability. Eventually, he talked of love. Monsieur de Tuyll was nonplussed. His daughter, to whom he showed most of the letters, thought them 'the most tactful in the world'. Boswell hinted, probed, retreated, prevaricated, and disclaimed. He reasoned himself in and out of love, in and out of marriage to her. One of his strong suits was that de Tuyll liked him – 'I felt an inclination to treat you as a friend when I saw your good sense, your gaiety, and your cordiality.' There were other suitors, though, especially Bellegarde who had proposed, about whom Zélide's father was perfectly candid. A further complication was de Tuyll's hope, almost insistence, that her marriage would not take her away from Holland.[12]

Nothing fires the heart of a lover more than his love's silence, and silent she was for months, until 27 January 1765. 'And must I then marry a Dutchwoman?' he complained to Temple in exasperation on 28 December, 'must the proud Boswell yield to a tender inclination? Must he in the strength and vigour of his youth resign his liberty for life to one woman?' On the other hand, would she not be a great catch, even (as it turned out) with only £400 a year? In a remarkably vain Christmas Day letter, imploring Zélide to write, he teased her by repeating the affectionate things she had once said to him. He told her how disappointed he was with her; in the next breath he hoped to tempt her to declare her passion for him:

Mademoiselle, I am proud, and I shall be proud always. You ought to be flattered by my attachment. I know not if I ought to have been equally flattered by yours. A man who has a mind and a heart like mine is rare. A woman with many talents is not so rare. Perhaps I blame you unreasonably ... O Zélide! I believed you to be without the weaknesses of your sex. I had almost come to count upon your heart ... My friend, have I been mistaken? Tell me the simple truth without reserve.

This was too much. She sprang to the attack: 'I find this a very strange whim in a man who does not love me and thinks it incumbent on him (from motives of delicacy) to tell me so in the most express and vigorous terms.' He was acting with 'the puerile vanity of a fatuous fool, coupled with the arrogant rigidity of an old Cato'. Burn her letters, she implored him, except for what did credit to her, if he expected to receive new ones. What he needed to treasure were their many serious and lighthearted talks, when they were drawn to each other as kindred spirits. 'I am not inconstant. I dissimulate nothing, I have not ceased to be your friend, and I shall be your friend always.' In his long reply, Boswell came close to proposing to her, backing off only at the last moment. Family, father, Auchinleck, Scotland, and ideas about the ideal wife kept him from the brink.[13]

'I have indeed much feeling for you, and now that you exempt me from saying or believing that I am in love with you, all will go well between us,' she replied in late May. The shoe was now on the other foot: it was Zélide who was disclaiming love. She told him she would probably marry Bellegarde early the following year, but he was a Roman Catholic and it would have to depend on what her parents decided. It was clear by now that she and Boswell thought they loved each other, that he was struggling to overcome his reservations so that he could propose, and that she was patiently waiting and hoping for that to happen. They were convinced that they knew each other profoundly well, though not how the other would respond to the various social pressures under which they lived.[14]

Then, in Paris, in January 1766, Boswell persuaded himself that it would not be 'madness' to marry her. A tête-à-tête with Zélide's eldest brother, who happened to be there, decided it. He dashed off a letter to his father proposing the match, asking for permission to return home via Utrecht; and on the 16th, fearing that after all this time she would have changed her mind about him, he locked himself in his room to write what he called a 'magnificent' (and interminable) letter, announcing his desire to marry her.[15]

Boswell argued his case not with liveliness and love but with what he felt would win him success in the eyes of a venerable and wealthy Dutch family. It was Zélide's heart, not her mind, that he wanted, he explained, though he would never have sustained his interest in her if it had not been for her intellect and wit – and money. 'I am singular and romantic, and such a character is made to give her infinite pleasure.' He would marry her only on the condition that she took an oath, to be witnessed by her family, that she would remain faithful, never have a liaison, never publish any of her writings, and never speak against established religion. These stipulations were presumably not that objectionable to the reserved de Tuyll who found his daughter something of a handful. More so was Boswell's intention of keeping Zélide in Scotland except for a visit home every two or three years. He admitted that he had faults, in addition to his hypochondria: 'My knowledge is very restricted. I have an excess of self-esteem. I cannot apply myself to study. I can nevertheless maintain my energy where my attention is interested. I have no sufficient zest for life. I have the greatest imaginable difficulty in overcoming avarice.' All he needed was two days with her to reach a 'satisfactory decision'. He was ready to set off at any time.[16]

De Zuylen's reply was noncommittal and restrained. 'A difficult decision,' he volunteered. In any case, there was Bellegarde's proposal still pending. As for Lord Auchinleck, he was implacably hostile to Boswell's marriage to any foreigner: 'a scheme which you in your unstayed state are absolutely unfit for at present, and ... ruinous – a foreigner, a *bel esprit* and one who even in your own opinion has not solidity enough for this country.' Boswell received neither of these letters before events conspired most cruelly to force his return to Scotland. Zélide was silent, so we can only imagine her disappointment at the turn of events. A golden opportunity was lost. Boswell was unable to return to Utrecht. His father saw to that. He and Zélide never saw each other again.[17]

TEN

'Let Me Be Boswell':
Touring Germany and Switzerland

I

When the university term ended, Dempster advised Boswell to 'leave Utrecht as fast as possible'.¹ By touring the German courts and venturing into Switzerland, Boswell hoped to meet great men and thinkers who would help him realize his own native 'genius', test his own embryonic ideas about religion and literature, rouse his stifled imagination, energize his literary instincts. He had his eyes on lofty targets: Frederick the Great of Prussia, Rousseau, and Voltaire, all of whose writings he read along the way in anticipation of meeting them. He also resolved to meet as many German princes and princesses as he could and he had his heart set on Italy, too, if he could only secure his father's co-operation.

Boswell in travel mode was a happier man – 'My Mercury is again put in motion.' His hypochondria, while definitely a travelling companion, took a back seat. He was able to detach himself from it somewhat and analyse it in others. 'I study hypochondria as a science,' he announced to Grange in September. That fact alone helps to explain much of his success on his Grand Tour.²

2

Temple was mystified as to why Boswell should want to flit about in Germany:

What can possess you, that you are so fond of visiting Courts one never heard of? Who but yourself would think of going to the of Baldon Dourlach to see mankind and learn politeness? I dare say you saw more of both here in England at Lady Northumberland's, and Carlisle-House, than you will see in all the courts of Germany, except that of Berlin.

However, Lord Auchinleck favoured the idea as a reward for his son's hard work, on the mistaken assumption that Germany (as a northern region) held few temptations to undo the allegedly beneficial effects of Utrecht. And as luck would have it, George Keith, tenth Earl Marischal of Scotland, a Jacobite nobleman, one of Frederick the Great's most trusted counsellors who was just then returning to Berlin from a visit to Scotland, was prevailed on by Lord Auchinleck to allow his son to accompany him there. A more distinguished escort Boswell could not have hoped for. On the same day that he heard about this, he also received notice that his father would let him have credit of thirty pounds per month for this trip. Here was cause for rejoicing: 'Never was man happier than I this morning. I was now to travel with a venerable Scots nobleman who had passed all his life abroad, had known intimately kings and great men of all kinds, and could introduce me with the greatest advantage at courts.' His spirit 'glowed' and his imagination filled with 'rich ideas' of success and fame. He even felt new faith in the immortality of the soul, the truth of Christianity, 'for I see how a man can be quite extinguished and yet can revive'.[3]

Marischal, who was in his seventies and one of the more colourful political and military figures in Europe, arrived in Utrecht on 13 June. His romantic career as an old warrior in the Jacobite cause and his colourful and noble service to Frederick and Prussia during the Seven Years' War made him a coveted guest wherever he went in Germany. To travel privately with him and his adopted Turkish daughter in a chaise for a month, hearing his reminiscences along the way, would be something for Boswell to tell his grandchildren about.[4]

Marischal had expected to stay one night, but his travelling companion was not ready and they lingered on in Utrecht for several days. There were goodbyes to say, especially to Zélide, and perhaps Boswell had not yet bought the new clothes Marischal recommended, 'now you are going to courts. A suit of summer clothes, fine camlet with a gold thread button but no lace; and against winter a complete suit of worked flowered velvet, the buttons of velvet; four pairs of laced ruffles.' At the last minute Boswell hired a new servant, a Swiss named Jacob Hanni, and finally on the 18th they were ready to leave.[5]

3

In their chaise, Madame de Froment, Marischal's Turkish daughter, said practically nothing; and Marischal himself was tight-lipped while they rumbled east through Kleve, Wesel, Haltern, Herford, Minden, and Hanover, arriving in Brunswick on the 26th. Not even a famous travelling companion could guarantee comfortable lodgings in Germany's rural hinterland. One night Boswell slept on a table covered with straw, another on straw spread on the floor, literally flanked by horses and cows and overlooked by a shrill cock that put him in mind of 'the wisdom of the Sybarites, who slew all those noisy birds'. Near his head was an 'immense mastiff' that growled horribly and rattled its chain. He boasted of eating nothing but eggs and 'black and sour' bread for dinner.[6]

Yet he discovered he had a taste for living rough. 'I do not have an exquisite sensibility,' he wrote to Monsieur de Zuylen; 'I was very well satisfied. I enjoyed the fine season. I enjoyed the pretty countryside.' 'A good Scot born in a romantic land', Boswell also relished the mountains after almost a year of Holland's flatness. Much has been made of his inattention to open landscape in his journal – and indeed he did virtually ignore the spectacular beauty of the European landscape that enraptured people like Thomas Gray on his Grand Tour – but he had a deep appreciation of the wilder beauties of nature, instilled in him by his homeland.[7] For his journals he preferred to adopt Alexander Pope's dictum, 'The proper study of Mankind is Man'. He still had to free himself of 'the clouds which hung upon me', and fiendish hypochondria struck at him several times on the way to Berlin, though not seriously enough to mar the journey. At Minden it was significant to him that he heard Mass at a Roman Catholic church and 'had not one Scots Sunday idea'; there was nothing of the kirk here.[8]

4

Boswell's journal while travelling through Germany and Switzerland is, like his London journal, one of English literature's most brilliant fusions of people and their conversation with self-imaging, self-assessment, and self-dramatization. He continued to be his own most interesting subject: 'I am one of the most engaging men that ever lived ... Amidst the innumerable multitude of existences that have past thro' this world I believe upon my honour that very few have been blest with more agreable talents.'⁹ 'Notwithstanding of all the objects around me,' he told Grange, 'I cannot help reflecting on myself. O Johnston forgive me for harping upon this string which one would think must e'er now have been thrummed to pieces.'⁹

But now Boswell was on a larger stage and his journal became more expansive, teeming with extraordinarily beautiful places; fascinating people from princes and princesses to professors, authors and philosophers; and a diversity of social experience. He worked at it with impressive regularity and discipline:

> At night indolence made me think, why give myself so much labour to write this journal, in which I really do not insert much that can be called useful? Beg your pardon. Does it contain a faithful register of my variations of mind? Does it contain many ingenious observations and pleasing strokes which can afterwards be enlarged? Well, but I may die. True, but I may live; and what a rich treasure for my after days will be this my journal.

And later: 'I must observe that my journal serves me not so much as a history as it serves me merely as a reservoir of ideas', a source book on himself. It is not necessarily more introspective than the London journal, but it is more reflective. The elements of anxiety in it are therefore more portentous. He worried about his future; about religion, revelation, and salvation – the 'sickly theory' of metaphysical speculation; about fornication; and about his deportment. Because hypochondria was not casting shadows everywhere, we can see more clearly and for longer periods how his character could flourish given the chance.¹⁰

Since he could not always find the time to keep the journal up to date, he kept memoranda (as in Holland) of what he had done and seen the previous day – at times writing these late into the night of the day he was recording, dating them the following morning – with the idea of fleshing them out later: 'Sometimes I am three, four, five days without journalizing. When I have time and spirits, I bring up this my journal as well as I can in the hasty manner in which I write it. Some years hence I shall perhaps abridge it.' The idea was to read the whole thing to Grange when he returned home.¹¹

5

In the eighteenth century Germany was an empire nation made up of a loose federation of many independent principalities, some of them very small. This empire stretched across much of northern Europe and also included Austria and Czechoslovakia as they existed until 1935. It was a huge area, ruled in theory by an Emperor (Frederick William II of Prussia) elected by nine so-called Electors or princes of the larger principalities. One of these, the Elector of Hanover, George Lewis, had become King George I of England in 1714. As the princes governed and financed their own principalities without political or civil interference from the Emperor, to whom they expressed their loyalty and who engendered a strong German national consciousness, they all had their own courts; and splendidly luxurious many of them were, too.[12] For the genteel Boswell, who enjoyed nothing more than meeting and talking to princes and their families and attendants in opulent settings, these courts were ideal targets. 'In dress most elegant', he could skip between them easily, like a stone skimming the water. Doubtless helped by Marischal's introductions but also on account of his claim to a Scottish lairdship and his natural vivacity and likability, Boswell was a success at all the courts he visited. He was eager and ambitious, thirsty to discuss philosophical and religious ideas with the Enlightenment personalities he was meeting. His willingness to listen and absorb without necessarily agreeing with what he heard made him a welcome guest.[13]

With a letter of introduction from Count Bentinck de Varel at The Hague, he was welcomed in Brunswick, and 'struck to find myself at table' that afternoon with the Duke and Duchess, sister of Frederick the Great. After 'plenty of burgundy and other wines', he was introduced to Karl Wilhelm Ferdinand, the Duke's son and heir or Hereditary Prince, who was renowned as a brilliant general in the Seven Years' War and became Duke in 1780, and his princess (Augusta), sister of George III, 'a free English lass', whose hand he kissed. A few weeks later, at her invitation, he actually danced a minuet 'with the grand-daughter of King George whose birthday I have so often helped to celebrate at Old Edinburgh; with the daughter of the Prince of Wales, who patronised [James] Thomson and other votaries of science and the music'. He danced with all the princesses, in fact. The next day he dined with them and chatted away effortlessly with the nostalgic Augusta about such London topics as Lord Eglinton and the Catch Club that Boswell had so enjoyed. The Prince received him in his bedchamber, an interview

Boswell vividly recreated in his journal: 'It was splendid. The canopy was sumptuous. He had a number of pretty pictures and an elegant collection of books. He talked a good time to me. It was luxury. I stood with a mind full of the ideas of the last glorious war. I was talking to a distinguished hero.'[14]

It did not end there. At night he returned to the 'Reigning Court' and talked on and on with the Duke who appeared genuinely to like him:

> Here now do I find myself in the very sphere of magnificence. I live with princes, and a court is my home. I took leave of the Duke, and a cordial adieu of all the courtiers. I found myself already liked by them with affection. They asked me to return to Brunswick in August, when I would see the Fair.

What a long way he had come from the gloom of Utrecht. Indeed, what a long way from Scottish provinciality, coarseness, and excessive familiarity. Was this not liberation and fulfilment? Had he not always suspected that he was different? At the end of August, bidding farewell to the Duke for the last time, he confidently said, 'Sire, you have had people at your Court more brilliant than I, but never a better man.'[15]

Off went the trio in their chaise the following morning, with Boswell unexpectedly suffering from a touch of depression contracted from too much speculation the previous day regarding Christian revelation and salvation – 'my thoughts were horrid, yet my manners were cheerful.' As they bumped along, Marischal laughed at his 'religious gloom' and whet his appetite to go to Spain with stories of his military exploits there. At Potsdam, after meeting King Frederick's son, they visited the great palace, but Boswell was too gloomy to enjoy it. The 'foul fiend' fled, however, when he left for Berlin.[16]

6

From the moment he set foot in Berlin, with its spacious streets, river, and well-built houses spread over a beautiful plain, Boswell launched himself into a dizzying social campaign. 'Am I indeed the dull dog of Utrecht?' he asked. 'If ever man underwent an alteration, it is the man who writeth this journal.' Meeting up with a Scots Highlander, Lauchlan Macpherson, he donned his genteel wardrobe and went out on the town, dining, playing billiards, taking a hearty walk through the Tiergarten, snoozing in the afternoon after a big meal. Parties, concerts, audiences with royalty, dinners, riding lessons, visits to museums and sundry 'cabinets of curiosities' – all this kept him constantly on the move for the next two months. Melancholia made an occasional appearance, but on the whole he kept it at bay. Along with his new wardrobe, he was putting on the 'new man'.[17]

He moved into a perfect apartment in the oldest part of Berlin with 'a pretty silk bed' – 'small elegancies' like that always raised his spirits. 'Never was a fellow so kindly used as I am here,' he scribbled in his journal. His landlord, Monsieur Kircheisen, President of the City Council, told him, 'Your being sent to my house was an act of Providence.' Kircheisen's pretty seventeen-year-old daughter Caroline, 'fresh, good-humoured, and gay' with 'an ease of behaviour', particularly put him in a 'pleasing frame'. The moment he laid eyes on her he thought of marrying her: 'I must observe of myself that from my early years I have never seen an agreeable lady but my warm imagination has fancied as how I might marry her and has suggested a crowd of ideas ... very true, but very, very absurd.' She played the harpsichord for him, gave him 'rural' presents of cherries, went riding with him, and wrote to him when he was away for a day or two. She was his principal female interest in Berlin, although he never took liberties with her.[18]

Ever since leaving Holland, Boswell wrote to Zélide, he had been 'as chaste as an Anchorite', and he swore to remain that way in case he should have the opportunity of meeting Rousseau, on whom he was anxious to make a good impression. He 'toyed' with several girls but kept his resolve except once, with the pregnant wife of a soldier: 'Oho! a safe piece. Into my closet ... To be directly. In a minute – over. I rose cool and astonished, half angry, half laughing. I sent her off.' This lapse confused him. Should he torment himself with 'speculations on sin, and on losing in one morning the merit of a year's chastity?' (He seemed to forget he had succumbed once in Holland.) No, he answered himself, but he was sorry it had happened – 'Divine Being! Pardon the errors of a weak mortal. Give me more steadiness.' In Dresden, in October, he flirted with 'easy street girls' and went on the prowl for the 'ugliest woman I could find', but restrained himself.[19]

7

Within a few days of arriving in Berlin he had been presented to the Queen and 'all the Princes and Princesses', but not yet to Frederick, the warrior-king, who came to Berlin from Potsdam too seldom, at least as far as Boswell was concerned. On the advice of Sir Andrew Mitchell, a Scot from Aberdeenshire and British Ambassador to Prussia who was a close personal friend of Frederick, one day he and Macpherson went off to Potsdam to catch sight of the mighty King. With the exception of Britain, all the major European powers had fought against Frederick, the defender of Protestantism, in the Seven Years' War, from which he and Prussia had emerged relatively unscathed. Now he was styled 'the Great', an evocative image of military power and genius. To Boswell he must have seemed like a god on parade, a 'glorious sight', dressed in 'a suit of plain blue, with a star and a plain hat with a white feather'. Another 'crowd of ideas' of fame and glory danced around Boswell, transporting him with visions, or delusions, of grandeur; but they also made him feel petty and small, unfulfilled, with a long way to go in his programme of self-improvement.[20]

Now here was a tempting prize for the young Scots monarchist, another scalp to add to his growing list of the famous and mighty: he must meet with Frederick and talk to him. He felt it in his bones that he could make this great man like him. Had he not been received by the Duke of Brunswick in his very bedchamber? He asked both Mitchell and Marischal to help procure him an introduction to the King, but neither was encouraging and nothing happened. Others not so worthy as he, so Boswell thought, were gaining interviews. He decided a frontal attack was best. On 31 July he wrote to Henri de Catt, the King's reader, suggesting he was no common petitioner: 'You Sir, whose blood does not circulate so rapidly as mine, may laugh at a stranger. No doubt I seem to you like a child who gazes open-mouthed at a picture of Alexander or Julius Caesar. Well and good. I am willing to keep something of the spirit of childhood.' He had seen the King several times, but 'I am not satisfied.' He confessed that one evening at Charlottenburg he was near Frederick in the palace garden and had 'a powerful impulse to throw myself at his feet and risk telling him how much I had wished to see his Majesty'. De Catt's reply was cordial but negative. Boswell lingered on in Berlin well into September, hoping for a summons to Court which never came. It was a memorable failure in his triumphal march through Europe.[21]

*

Unknown to him, Boswell's Scottish egotism may have undermined his efforts to obtain an interview with Frederick. Alexander Burnet, the British Ambassador's secretary, wrote to Mitchell on 8 September expressing annoyance at Boswell's inflated Scottish pride, his 'absurd distinction betwixt Englishmen and Scotchmen'.[22] As both Burnet and Mitchell were Scotsmen, they may well have been worried that Boswell would say something 'very ridiculous' in an audience with the King and disgrace them all, Marischal included: 'He has told me that he must be presented as a Scotchman and that if H.P.M. [His Prussian Majesty] should ask him such trifling questions as he generally does strangers, he would fairly desire him to speak to him as a Scotchman and not as an Englishman ... You may easily judge after this if it would be prudent to have him presented.' That this young Scottish 'baron' was indeed a liability became clear on 21 September when, in a last-ditch effort, Boswell staked out a spot close to where the King was to pass on parade, adorned with a blue Ayrshire bonnet to appear 'quite a Scots gentleman'. This is as close as the King ever came to noticing him. 'What is that little cap which that gentleman is wearing?' Frederick asked an attendant. Alas he did not like it.[23]

8

When Boswell left Berlin on 23 September, heading for Geneva, he was still arguing with his father over the extent and duration of his travels. From Geneva, he wanted to proceed to Italy and spend at least four months there. Conceding another year on the Continent, his father urged him to go back to Utrecht for further study, or to head for Paris for several months, or to spend the year in Geneva where he could also attend the university. But not Italy: 'my father is averse to my going to that intoxicating region.' Everyone else agreed with Boswell that Italy was not to be missed. Both Marischal and Mitchell, at his request, wrote to his father to persuade him to let him go. No word had come by the time Boswell set out for Geneva.[24]

In the meantime, there were plenty of German courts to visit on the journey. This now became serious work, essential to his education as a gentleman, a 'baron', a 'prince' at Auchinleck. 'A Scots baron cannot do better than travel in Germany,' he wrote to Lord Kames (his first letter to him since leaving London):

When he goes to Italy and France, he lives with artificial men cooped up in towns and formed in such a manner that Nature is quite destroyed ... Let him then go and visit the German courts, where he can acquire French and polite manners, and at the same time be with people who live much in the same style that he must do at home. He may thus learn to support his character with dignity, and upon his paternal estate may have the felicity of a prince.

Styling himself a 'baron' suited him, especially in Germany, Boswell noted, 'as I have just the same right to it as the good gentry whom I see around me'. Indeed, his status in Scotland was at least equal to that of several of the German barons he was to meet at the smaller courts en route to Switzerland. The rank he brandished opened many doors for him, though occasionally he had trouble reconciling it with the plebeian, jolting carts and *Postwagens* in which he was forced to travel, 'transported like a sack', eating with servants and dirty soldiers, and sleeping on wet hay in shared rooms with stale air. Instead of grumbling, he took to rhyming:

> the roughly rumbling wagon wild
> Is just to me as cradle to a child.
> As on the rugged roads I bouncing reel,
> My firm corporeal strength with pride I feel,
> And while my back upon the boards is knock'd,
> I think, 'twas thus great Hercules was rock'd.[25]

Of the seventeen or more major towns and cities through which he passed over the next two months, twelve of them had courts. In scarlet and gold or 'flowered velvet of five colours', he dined with princes and princesses; attended balls, musical events, and plays; inspected libraries and museums, cabinets of medals, coin collections and art collections; and visited splendidly ornamental gardens. He also enjoyed some riding on princely horses and took part in several princely stag and duck hunts.

After some grudging hospitality at Mannheim by the Elector and Electress Palatine, he was received in style at the court of Karl Friedrich, the Margrave of Baden-Durlach in Karlsruhe where beauty mingled with grace and dignity.[26] After dinner, the Margrave, who had visited England twice, talked to him in English about a number of mutual Scottish friends, the Select Society, Hume and Robertson, and Scottish literature, which he knew well. Boswell was amazed. 'I found that I was truly agreeable to him.' He was discovering that the Margrave was one of the most intelligent of all German princes, a friend of Voltaire, and an extremely successful ruler of Baden – in short, the epitome of the German Enlightenment. He would later become an Elector and then Grand Duke. That night Boswell's elation may easily be imagined when, at dinner with court officials, he was asked to sit at the head of the table.

While looking over the Margrave's first-rate library the following day, he was told that His Highness had said, 'This gentleman pleases me greatly. He is a true philosopher.' Instead of staying three days, he decided to skip Stuttgart and stay seven or eight. Over the next few days he spent long periods with the Margrave discussing Scottish Presbyterianism, religion, fate, free will, and the human soul: 'I maintained the religion of Jesus as displayed in the four Gospels ... I talked with vehemence against David Hume and other infidels who destroyed our principles and put nothing firm in their place.' The Margrave listened to him attentively. 'I was quite a genteel *literatus*,' he wrote in his journal.

He had won the Margrave's regard, so why not his favour, too? His Highness could create Knights of the Order of Fidelity who wore 'a star and ribbon hanging from their necks':

I was determined if possible to obtain it ... I asked him once *en passant* if only counts could have it. He said, 'It is enough to be a good gentleman' ... I then took courage and said, 'Sir, I have a favour to ask of you, a very great favour. I don't know whether I should mention it.' I was quite the courtier, for I appeared modest and embarrassed, when in reality I was perfectly unconcerned. He said, 'What, Sir?' I replied ... 'Sir, might I presume to ask you that, if I bring you proof of my being a very good gentleman, I may obtain the order?' He paused. I looked at him steadily. He answered, 'I shall think of it.' I said, 'Sir, you have already been so good to me that I flatter myself that I have the merit for obtaining such a favour. As to my rank, I can assure you that I am a very old gentleman ... I can count kindred with my sovereign from my being related to the family of Lennox and the royal family of Stuart. Sir, I am one of your old proud Scots' ... He seemed pleased ... He said, 'Let me have your genealogy attested, and when you return, we shall see.' Oh, I shall have it.

The Margrave kept his word by writing at least one letter to Boswell in Geneva, and Boswell himself wrote at least three times in the next few months of his travel, 'without ceremony' (at the Margrave's urging). An enticing mystery and hint of foul play followed. As Boswell never heard from him again, he concluded that the Margrave had lost interest in him and the hope of the Order of Felicity had died by the time he returned to Scotland. Preserved in the Grand-Ducal family archives at Karlsruhe, however, is a formal transcript of a letter the Margrave wrote to Boswell on 24 May 1768 expressing puzzlement and genuine regret that Boswell had failed to reply to his first letter: 'After having enjoyed your agreeable and instructive conversation, I am now deprived of, I should be too much at a loss if you did not make me amends for by writing. In this sweet expectation, I am with all my heart, Sir, your affectionate . . .' Yet Boswell never mentioned this letter to anybody or noted receiving it; nor has there been any trace of it among his papers.[27]

Could the letters have been lost in the post? Or did an overly protective aide intervene, embarrassed or envious at the Margrave's familiarity with this ambitious young Scot? Whatever the reason for the breakdown in communication, it is sad that they never knew of their continued affection for each other. The Margrave lost a warm friend. For Boswell, whose self-worth turned largely on his genius for friendship and its fruits, it was a demoralizing postscript to his German experience.

ELEVEN

'Above the Vulgar Crowd':
Meeting Rousseau and Voltaire

I

Reading Rousseau's sensational novels *Nouvelle Héloïse* and *Émile*, Boswell entered Switzerland via Strasbourg, to spend three days in Bâle, two in Soleure, and two more in Berne. Then he veered to the west towards Neuchâtel and Rousseau. 'Voltaire, Rousseau, immortal names!' he and Temple had declared to each other when students in Edinburgh. Now his dream of meeting them seemed about to come true.

He carried with him a feeble letter of introduction to Rousseau from Marischal which he was sure would have the desired effect, but the landlord's pretty and chatty daughter at the inn in Brot, three miles short of Môtiers, the small mountain village near which Rousscau lived in a 'wild valley', was not too encouraging: 'he doesn't like to have people come and stare at him as if he were a man with two heads. Heavens! the curiosity of people is incredible. Many, many people come to see him; and often he will not receive them. He is ill, and doesn't wish to be disturbed.' Boswell pushed on to Môtiers 'with a kind of pleasing trepidation':

> I wished that I might not see Rousseau till the moment that I had permission to wait upon him. I perceived a white house with green window-boards. He mentions such a one in *Émile*. I imagined it might perhaps be his, and turned away my eyes from it. I rode calmly down the street, and put up at the Maison de Village.[1]

Rousseau, then fifty-two, was living in seclusion at Môtiers because he had been hounded out of Paris in the spring of 1762 for his revolutionary social and religious views, chiefly in *Émile*. Threatened with arrest, he fled first to Berne, but as the Genevan authorities closed in on him there, he retreated to Môtiers, befriended by Marischal and under the protection of Frederick the Great. When Boswell arrived, Rousseau was at the height of his fame, one of the most powerful and controversial literary personalities in Europe: temperamental and eccentric; a genuine ascetic with a reputation as the 'savage philosopher' whose primitivism confounded rigid social attitudes to education, sex, religion, and government; suffering from urethritis; dressed most of the time in an Armenian caftan; and living with his mistress of twenty years, Thérèse Le Vasseur, with whom he had secretly had five children, all farmed out to the Foundling Hospital in Paris. Boswell knew nothing of Rousseau's personal life (which would have shocked him), but the notoriety and intellectual stature of the man made him a delectable target for his celebrity-hunting.

As a Scots 'baron' with conventional ideas of social behaviour, Boswell was naturally drawn to a man iconoclastically at odds with society, much as he was attracted to the firebrand John Wilkes and (in spite of himself) to Zélide and her flaunting of public decorum. Where others shied away or were ushered out by Rousseau, he would rush in aggressively and contrive to remain. This new note of forcefulness was one of the effects of Boswell's exposure to so many independent thinkers in Germany, people who believed in reason, religious tolerance, and self-development as opposed to dogmatism. He fancied that much of the neoclassical in his temper and values was in the process of being overtaken by certain Romantic elements of counter-culture. He felt a compatibility of spirit with Rousseau that he was convinced would lead him to ask the right questions in the right way.

He decided not to lean on the crutch of Marischal's letter. His 'romantic genius, which will never be extinguished', really left him no choice: he must put his merit 'to the severest trial' by composing a direct appeal to Rousseau. In the privacy of his room at the inn, he laboured over three drafts of a letter, trying to strike the right balance between what he said about himself, 'the heart and soul' of his letter, and what he understood of Rousseau's ideas on education, religion, sex, and family life. The final draft could 'neither be abridged nor transposed', he exulted, 'for it is really a masterpiece, I shall ever preserve it as a proof that my soul can be sublime'. He sent it off immediately, hoping for a reply that evening. In the meantime, he worried, 'Is not this romantic madness? Was I not sure of admittance by my recommendations? Could I not see him as any other gentleman would do? No: I am above the vulgar crowd ... I must have things in my own way.'[2]

The letter, written in French, is a study in calculated ingenuousness. Boswell was young and ignorant, not too fluent in French but travelling to improve himself. He was encouraged that Rousseau scarcely spoke to anyone; were it any other way, he would not be 'striving so eagerly to be received' into his house. He was special, with little to recommend him but his 'singular merit . . . a feeling heart, a lively but melancholy spirit'. It was enough for him to put himself before the sage philosopher, for in 'the silence and the solitude of your sacred retreat . . . you shall judge of me'. May he come and be put to the 'severest test'? 'Believe me, you will be glad to have seen me . . . I cannot restrain myself . . . Enlightened Mentor! Eloquent and amiable Rousseau! I have a presentiment that a truly noble friendship will be born today.' He also made out that, young though he was, he had had a 'variety of existence' that would 'amaze' Rousseau. He needed counsel from the author of *Nouvelle Héloïse*: 'Open your door, then, Sir, to a man who dares to tell you that he deserves to enter it.' But this first meeting would be a sacred trust; he must see Rousseau alone, or it would be spoiled.[3]

2

The reply came quickly: 'I am ill, in pain, really in no state to receive visits. Yet I cannot deprive myself of Mr Boswell's, provided that out of consideration for the state of my health, he is willing to make it short.' Ecstatic, though worried about the 'short', Boswell rushed off immediately to see the 'wild philosopher'. He took no notes, prompts or prepared script. Mademoiselle Le Vasseur was waiting for him outside the house. She was forty-three, though he describes her as a 'little, lively, neat French girl'. She took him upstairs to the kitchen, where he waited. In a few moments, the door opened and in walked Rousseau, 'a genteel black man in the dress of an Armenian'. 'Many, many thanks,' the young pilgrim blurted. Instead of sitting down, they walked around the room, talking.[4]

The severe test had begun, but Boswell thought less of accounting for himself than of the magic of the place and the moment, revelling in (and astonished by) the wonder of what his ego had engineered. He was not only a performer in this mini-drama but also the director. He wanted to be stirred by feelings in a Romantic vein, and he wanted to stir Rousseau's compassion for him.

His record of the conversation in the journal was not as 'exact' as he wanted, nor as polished and objective as his later journal conversations with Johnson, but its beauty is Boswellian: spontaneously and freshly revealing more about himself than Rousseau, though his account of Rousseau's speech is accepted as the most vivid known to exist. Boswell asked him of his books, and they spoke of Marischal (whom Rousseau loved) and Scotland, the 'cursed Union' – 'you undid yourselves' there, Rousseau pronounced. But in his journal account, Boswell instinctively manoeuvred the focus on to himself: his resplendent clothing, unpremeditated manner, and what Rousseau thought of his unique tactics for winning an interview.

> I was dressed in a coat and waistcoat, scarlet with gold lace, buckskin breeches, and boots. Above all I wore a greatcoat of green camlet lined with fox-skin fur, with the collar and cuffs of the same fur. I had a free air and spoke well, and when Monsieur Rousseau said what touched me more than ordinary, I seized his hand, I thumped him on the shoulder. I was without restraint.

Rousseau had acknowledged the 'merit' of Boswell's letter; Marischal's introduction would have succeeded, too, he said, but a perfunctory appointment merely out of respect for an old friend was not the sort of event Boswell had in mind.

Rousseau reassured Boswell he was not 'the bear' the world held him to be, though he 'cannot tolerate the world as it is . . . Mankind disgusts me. And my housekeeper tells me that I am in far better humour on the days when I have been alone than on those when I have been in company.' If that was a hint for Boswell to leave, he deftly turned it around: 'Tell me, Sir, do you not find that I answer to the description I gave you of myself?' It was too early to judge, Rousseau replied, but 'all appearances are in your favour.' But when Boswell announced, 'I shall take the honour of returning tomorrow,' Rousseau demurred, 'Oh, as to that, I can't tell . . . I am overwhelmed with visits from idle people.' As Boswell headed for the door, Rousseau appeared to come with him. 'What, you are coming further?' 'I am not coming with you. I am going for a walk in the passage. Goodbye.' Thus ended the interview.

It had lasted an hour-and-a-half. Two weeks later in a letter to his friend Alexander Deleyre, a French *philosophe* then living in Parma, Rousseau described why he had succumbed to this strange young man:

> Although I have never courted any man, I have responded so readily to the overtures of a thousand people who have courted me that I have, so to speak,

thrown myself at their heads. They have all fallen off at the first rub, and, behold, almost the only one of the lot I was difficult with, stays with me, consoles me in my misfortunes and pardons me the wrongs I did him ... In the first letter he wrote me, he told me that he was a man 'of singular merit'. I was curious to see a man who spoke of himself in such a fashion, and I found that he had told me the truth.

He might have added that his visitor helped him take his mind off himself. They agreed that Boswell should stay in the village for a few days and Rousseau would see him again if his health permitted it. Boswell was confident and ready to wait. 'I am here in a beautiful wild valley surrounded by immense mountains,' he jubilantly wrote to Dempster, 'I am supremely happy.'⁵

Nobody answered when Boswell knocked on the door the next morning but in the street he met Mademoiselle Le Vasseur who offered some hope for the afternoon. At five, he returned and was let in. Rousseau was 'more gay than he had been yesterday. We joked on Mademoiselle Le Vasseur for keeping him under lock and key.' Rousseau spoke of the Abbé de Saint-Pierre, one of his heroes from the reign of Louis XIV, a man of total honesty and principle, the kind who should be in modern government but was not. 'If you become a Member of Parliament,' he told his visitor, 'you must resemble the Abbé de Saint-Pierre.' A Member of Parliament who is strictly honest, Boswell replied, is seen as 'a crazy fool'. So be it, then, 'you must be a crazy fool of a Member; and believe me, such a man will be respected.' Boswell was taken aback, though, when after praising the Scots, Rousseau said, '*you* are irksome to me. It's my nature. I cannot help it.' This threw him off-balance, but he rallied, 'Do not stand on ceremony with me.' 'Go away,' Rousseau shot back, half petulantly, half teasingly. Even that injunction seemed to hold the promise of yet another interview. Thérèse saw him out.⁶

Boswell returned early the next morning. In pain, Rousseau did not want to talk, but that was a minor obstacle to his petitioner: 'I took care to waive such excuses, and immediately set conversation a-going.' Walking around the room, Boswell tried to talk about himself, to coax this great philosopher into offering him advice. To his confession that he had experimented with Catholicism and planned to hide himself in a 'convent' in France, Rousseau replied not very encouragingly, 'What folly!' Then: 'I stopped him in the middle of the room and I said to him, "But tell me sincerely, are you a Christian?" ' They paused, Rousseau suspicious. 'I looked at him with a searching eye. His countenance was no less animated. Each stood steady and watched the other's looks. He struck his breast, and replied, "Yes. I pique myself upon being one." ' He added that he too believed in the Gospels and the Trinity and that Boswell should not allow himself to be buffeted 'to and fro' by men's judgements. Compared to the Gospels, ecclesiastic rituals were nothing but 'mummeries' invented by men.[7]

In a final effort to get on a more intimate footing, Boswell introduced the subject of hypochondria. Was Rousseau melancholic? Not naturally, only through his misfortunes. Boswell teasingly confessed he had done so much 'evil' that he doubted he could ever be happy again. Not wanting to know about it, Rousseau suggested, 'Begin your life anew. God is good, for he is just. Do good. You will cancel all the debt of evil.' That was not enough:

BOSWELL: 'Will you, Sir, assume direction of me?' ROUSSEAU: 'I cannot. I can be responsible only for myself.' BOSWELL: 'But I shall come back.' ROUSSEAU: 'I don't promise to see you. I am in pain. I need a chamber-pot every minute.' BOSWELL: 'Yes you will see me.' ROUSSEAU: 'Be off; and a good journey to you'.[8]

If Rousseau thought he had seen the last of his visitor, he was mistaken. One way Boswell could relate the story of his troubled and 'sinful' life was to give Thérèse a 'Sketch' of it to pass on to him. Then, when they spoke next, Rousseau could not help but be more intimately involved with him and they could talk on a more personal and sympathetic level. Boswell wrote the 'Sketch' (in French), several drafts of it, in a few short hours in Môtiers before leaving on an excursion to Neuchâtel to pick up his post. It is a remarkably candid autobiography, as we have already seen, meant for Rousseau's eyes alone, touching on his wretched religious education, hypochondria, and adulterous affair with Lord Kames's daughter. In a covering letter, he implored Rousseau's help to sort out the opposing sides of his tormented mind and body: 'Oh, vouchsafe to preserve a true Scot! . . . You love that ancient country. Preserve a sapling from it.'[9]

3

Fourteen letters awaited Boswell in Neuchâtel. One of them was a mocking sermon from Dalrymple, a cold blast of Scottish reality intruding on the euphoria of his travels, written in October in reply to Boswell's breezy description of the conditions under which he would pick up his life in Scotland. Dalrymple derided him for his self-importance and wayward, Soaping Club manner, and he outlined several flaws in his character and goals: (1) The way Boswell was going, he would end up not a 'true Young laird' but an idle and dissipated one. (2) If Boswell wanted to worship in the Church of England, that was fine, but 'you are captivated with shew. The world is a perpetual puppet-shew in your eyes, and what is remarkable, still retaining the graces of novelty. However if you like the puppet-shew, I suppose your father will have no objection to your being of the Church of England.' (3) As for Boswell's idea of making an annual journey to London, it was madness: 'If you were my son I would never consent to such a journey. You mean to wind up the watch backwards, and thus undo what had been done, and break the spring.' If he had legal or political business, fine, but otherwise he may as well go to Sodom and Gomorrah. (4) Finally, these extensive travels of Boswell's were burning up good time. Italy, perhaps, but why go to Spain just to see 'idle & ignorant gentlemen'?[10]

The 'humorous severity' of the letter was a 'scourge'; it made Boswell 'almost angry'. It was of course written to the raw boy who had left Edinburgh in 1762; it was read by the more sophisticated man who had travelled and communed with the great. Dalrymple was hopelessly out of touch, Boswell thought. But that letter paled into insignificance beside one from his father with the spectacular news that he was prepared to agree to the trip to Italy, though only for four months. Boswell was warmed by it: 'he wrote to me as to a man'. Marischal's influence had prevailed. The glories of the classical and Renaissance world suddenly opened up before him. Dalrymple, Edinburgh, Scottish wives, the law – they all receded further into the mists of the forgettable.

4

After a few social calls in Neuchâtel, Boswell mounted his horse and galloped back through the spectacular mountain scenery to Môtiers and Rousseau. He was eager to learn what Rousseau thought of his 'Sketch'.

To prepare himself, this time he scribbled out a memorandum of topics to discuss, ranging from hypochondria and family madness to marriage, sexual appetites, life prospects, his father, and his personal cowardice.

He dismounted in front of Rousseau's house to find that the philosopher was ill and in much pain. Still, he was invited in. Rousseau's first comment on the 'Sketch' pertained to his flirtation with Roman Catholicism: 'You have been gulled. You ought never to see a priest.' Boswell's biggest problem, he added, was that he was too introspective. 'Come back in the afternoon. But put your watch on the table.' Boswell took that as cue to negotiate: 'BOSWELL: 'For how long?' ROUSSEAU: 'A quarter of an hour, and no longer.' BOSWELL: 'Twenty minutes.' ROUSSEAU: 'Be off with you! – Ha! Ha!' Notwithstanding the pain he was in, he was touched with my singular sally and laughed most really. He had a gay look immediately.'[11]

He was back again at four and this time it was evident that the 'Sketch' gambit had paid off.[12] With Thérèse sitting beside them, Rousseau happily entered into personal talk. Boswell began with the remark that morals were to him 'uncertain', even with his Christian faith, and he would like to have thirty women. Could he not satisfy that desire?

ROUSSEAU: 'No!' BOSWELL: 'Why?' ROUSSEAU: 'Ha! Ha! If Mademoiselle were not here, I would give you a most ample reason why.' BOSWELL: 'But consider: if I am rich, I can take a number of girls; I get them with child; propagation is thus increased. I give them dowries, and I marry them off to good peasants who are very happy to have them. Thus they become wives at the same age as would have been the case if they had remained virgins, and I, on my side, have had the benefit of enjoying a great variety of women.'

This talk must have been titillating for Thérèse, who sat quietly by but doubtless was forming her own impressions of Boswell. The patriarchal practice of concubinage and its moral implications had long perplexed him. Rousseau was practical: 'Oh, you will be landed in jealousies, betrayals, and treachery ... You must not pick and choose one law here and another law there.' As for Jean Heron, Lord Kames's married daughter, he must go back and tell her there would be no more deception – 'there is no expiation for evil except good'.

Might he not indulge in gallantries, then, when he gets to Italy, where 'the husbands do not resent your making love to their wives'? Only if he wants to become a 'corpse', was the reply. At this point, Thérèse withdrew. 'See now, you are driving Mademoiselle out of the room.' She returned when Boswell turned to his life prospects and the subject of his father. He should try to share some 'amusement' with his father, Rousseau volunteered, like shooting, which would put them on an equal footing. And, once he started, he should stick to the law rather than scatter his fire. Boswell was greedy for more advice and invited himself to a meal the following day. 'Come then at noon; it will give us time to talk.'

5

He rose at seven the next morning. Wanting to feel the sublime immanence of wild mountain scenery before his fifth and last interview with the great proponent of Primitivism, he rode to the source of the River Reuse. 'Full of fine spirits', he returned to Rousseau early enough for some good talk before lunch.[13] To be invited for a meal was heady stuff, proof that Rousseau liked him; it was a vindication of his 'genius', something to brag about back home: 'I supposed myself in the rude world. I supposed a parcel of young fellows saying, "Come, Boswell, you'll dine with us today?" "No, gentlemen, excuse me; I'm engaged. I dine today with Rousseau" ... Temple! You would have given half a guinea to see me at that moment.'

Before dinner, they talked of Johnson, of whose character Rousseau was ignorant: 'I should like that man ... I would not disturb his principles if I could. I should like to see him, but from a distance, for fear he might maul me.' They dined in the kitchen, Rousseau 'in all his simplicity', nothing formal, feasting on a generous meal of soup, cold pork, pickled trout, and so on, followed by a dessert of stoned (cored) pears and chestnuts – all with red and white wines:

> I sometimes forgot myself and became ceremonious. 'May I help you to some of this dish?' ROUSSEAU: 'No, Sir. I can help myself to it.' Or, 'May I help myself to some more of that?' ROUSSEAU: 'Is your arm long enough? ... Let each one ask for what he wants; if it is there to give, let him be given it ... Here you see true hospitality.'

Boswell found Rousseau's 'simplicity' liberating compared with the stiff dignity of the English and the thistle-pricks of rude Scottish familiarity. He was surprised not to find the 'Great Rousseau' 'enthroned' as a grave authority. Rousseau was amused. 'Uttering oracles? Ha! Ha! Ha!' In Scotland, however, even he would feel the barbs of 'sarcastical vivacity':

they would begin at the very start by calling you Rousseau; they would say, 'Jean Jacques, how goes it?' with the utmost familiarity ... they would say, 'Poh! Jean Jacques, why do you allow yourself all these fantasies? You're a pretty man to put forward such claims. Come, come, settle down in society like other people.'

To Rousseau's 'Ah, that's bad', Boswell observed, 'There he felt the thistle, when it was applied to himself on the tender part. It was just as if I had said, "Hoot, Johnnie Rousseau man, what for hae ye sae mony figmagairies. Ye're a bonny man indeed to mauk siccan a wark; set ye up." ' Even in a remote Swiss village, recollections of home obviously still stung him. How could his free spirit thrive in Scotland? Or in England? To flourish, it needed the intellectual and religious tolerance of Europe.

At this point in the final interview, Boswell mentions for the first time in his journal the current struggle for liberty of the Corsican people against the Genoese and French. He had just read Rousseau's *Social Contract* in which he had proposed Corsica, with its famous and attractive General Pasquale Paoli, as an ideal model of social and political liberty in a Europe that, as he saw it, had politically corrupted itself many times over. In one of those odd historical coincidences, Rousseau had only a few days before receiving a letter from Matteo Buttafoco, a Corsican officer, inviting him to draw up a constitution for the island. Rousseau worked on this, but the fruits of his efforts were not published until 1861 and Paoli had no intention of allowing any foreigner draw up his island's laws. He did however want Rousseau to come to Corsica to aid in the propaganda war against France.[14] Boswell confessed that he had 'leanings' towards social despotism, a feudal insistence that an 'ancient laird', for example, must have respect from his tenants, and that society's hierarchies had to be preserved. Political freedom was different: he was taken immediately with the Romantic 'idea' of Corsica's struggle as the underdog. Rousseau's mention of drawing up a set of laws for an island that, in its political primitiveness or innocence, was a type of political *tabula rasa* caught his imagination. The idea would ferment there quietly for eight months or so until he decided to do something about it.

Another skirmish followed about how much more of Rousseau's time Boswell could have. 'Now go away,' he implored. Boswell maintained he still had twenty-five minutes left. He appealed to his 'excellent friend' Thérèse, who said she would count out the remaining minutes.

When Boswell did leave, he extracted from Rousseau a promise to write:

> He kissed me several times, and held me in his arms with elegant cordiality. Oh, I shall never forget that I have been thus. ROUSSEAU: 'Good-bye. You are a fine fellow.' BOSWELL: 'You have shown me great goodness. But I deserved it.' ROUSSEAU: 'Yes, You are malicious; but 'tis pleasant malice, a malice I don't dislike. Write and tell me how you are.' BOSWELL: 'And you will write to me?' ROUSSEAU: 'I know not how to reach you.' BOSWELL: 'Yes, you shall write to me in Scotland.' ROUSSEAU: 'certainly, and even at Paris.' BOSWELL: 'Bravo! If I live twenty years, you will write to me for twenty years?' ROUSSEAU: 'Yes.'

With his flair for the dramatic, he then plucked out a hair from his head: 'Can I feel sure that I am held to you by a thread, even if of the finest? By a hair?' Their souls were bound together, Rousseau assured him. No words since he parted from Johnson had been sweeter to Boswell: 'I, with my melancholy, I, who often look on myself as a despicable being, as a good-for-nothing creature who should make his exit from life – I shall be upheld for ever by the thought that I am bound to Monsieur Rousseau.'

At the door, he took his leave of Thérèse, not for the last time as it turned out. She asked him if he would send her a garnet necklace, which he did at the end of the month. Back at the inn to gather his belongings, his landlady thought he had been crying – 'a true eulogium of my humanity,' he observed. As he rode past the house, Thérèse was still at the door, waving, '*Bon voyage*, write to us.' A bright spirit was galloping out of her and Rousseau's lives.

Rousseau was deeply impressed by his young confessor. He was also alarmed by his vulnerability. In his recommendatory letter to Deleyre in Parma, which as an act of trust Rousseau asked Boswell to read before slipping it into his bag for the trip to Italy, he presented him as burdened with the legacy of harsh Calvinist theology, with hypochondria, a 'soul' trailing clouds of 'gloomy notions'. The light and beauty of the fine arts in Italy, not sermonizing, might effect a cure, as well as 'consoling and tender' encouragement: 'He is a convalescent whom the least relapse will infallibly destroy. I should have been interested in him even if he had not been recommended to me by Lord Marischal.' Johnson had discovered the same thing. Boswell's father, for all his virtues, never did.

6

Boswell's next target was Voltaire, the universal genius of the Enlightenment, then seventy-one, who since 1758 had been living in philosophical retreat in a chateau at Ferney, in France, four miles from Geneva. 'Shall you, Sir, see Monsieur de Voltaire?' asked Thérèse in the final moments of that last visit. 'Most certainly,' Boswell answered confidently, knowing that Rousseau had learned to hate Voltaire's ruthless machinations and mocking scepticism. Boswell was lucky to have timed his visit to Rousseau during a period of relative peace and well-being at Môtiers. The philosopher's personal life and health suffered greatly not long after they met, largely as a result of Voltaire's stirring up ecclesiastical bigotry against him. Boswell could not wait to get to ask Voltaire what he thought of Rousseau. Perhaps he could even work a miracle by arranging for the two men to meet, with himself listening in. It could be one of the great literary meetings in western history.[15]

He reached Geneva on 22 December, where he received his first letter from Rousseau. On the morning of the 24th, he made his way to Ferney, attired in his 'sea-green and silver', arriving unannounced but with a letter of introduction from Zélide's secret correspondent, Constant d'Hermenches, Voltaire's good friend from The Hague. Two or three footmen greeted him at the handsome chateau and showed him into an elegant room to wait with several others while his letter was taken to Voltaire. 'Monsieur de Voltaire is very much annoyed at being disturbed. He is abed,' the message came back, but Boswell lingered on until the infidel philosopher finally appeared in his blue dressing-gown.

Neither of them was in the best of spirits and Boswell did not shine, but during their conversation Voltaire with his sarcastic smile made good use of his famous raillery and wit. After half an hour, Voltaire retired and left Boswell to dine with seven members of his family and a dozen others, not exactly the intimate sort of occasion he had hoped for. He sat by the hostess, Madame Denis, Voltaire's niece, who was 'remarkably good to me', helping him to a double portion of a sweet tart. Obliged to return to Geneva before the city gates closed at five, he left early, though not before hearing ugly bigotry and calumny at Rousseau's expense. It was not, except for Madame Denis, a memorable introduction to the 'Monarch of French Literature'.[16]

On Christmas morning, while listening to one of his favourite organ voluntaries in the formerly Catholic Eglise de St Pierre, Boswell decided he would write to Madame Denis 'begging' to be allowed to spend a night under the same roof with Voltaire. The 'absurd' Geneva curfew had interfered with his efforts to engage Voltaire, 'before the illustrious landlord has had time to shine upon his guests ... I greatly wish to behold him in full blaze.' It would be a feather in his cap, another victory, to write about and take home with him. 'I am a hardy and vigorous Scot. You may mount me to the highest and coldest garret. I shall not even refuse to sleep upon two chairs in the bedchamber of your maid,' he quipped, in a witty letter somewhat in the Soaping Club vein that he hoped would appeal to Voltaire. A joke or two more about Voltaire's nightcap completed the letter. Voltaire's niece replied quickly, inviting him to stay the night: 'We have few beds, but you will not sleep on two chairs. My uncle, tho very sick, hath guess'd at your merit. I know it more, because I have seen you longer.' Boswell's charm had prevailed again.[17]

He chose the 27th for his second visit to 'the enchanted castle'. Again, Voltaire did not dine with the assembled company, and Boswell was unexpectedly struck with a 'heavy ennui' to find himself in a French chateau, like any Scottish country house, one of several guests sitting idly by the fire, chatting, singing, playing the guitar, and playing shuttle-cock. The 'Magician' at last appeared around seven, just before supper, to play chess. Boswell vividly recreated the ensuing scene for Temple in one of the very best letters in all his correspondence.

Voltaire was brilliant. The sparks of wit, recitations and discussion of English poetry, racy English oaths, and nonsensical banter were almost unbelievable in a Frenchman. He 'touched the keys in unison with his Imagination'. Here was a unique blend of brilliant intellect and imagination with an extravagant earthiness of humour. With his probing questions, Boswell soon drew attention to himself. Stanislas Jean, the charismatic Chevalier de Boufflers, wrote to his mother about this atten-tive young man 'who never wearies of hearing [Voltaire] talk English and recite all the poems of Dryden'.[19]

When the other guests rose for supper, Boswell did not budge and for an hour-and-a-half had Voltaire to himself:

M. de Voltaire and I remained in the drawing room with a great Bible before us; and if ever two mortal men disputed with vehemence we did. Yes – upon that occasion He was one Individual and I another. For a certain portion of time there was a fair opposition between Voltaire and Boswell. The daring bursts of his Ridicule confounded my understanding; He stood like an Orator of ancient Rome ... He went too far. His aged form trembled beneath him. He cried 'O I am very sick; my head turns round' and he let himself gently fall upon an easy chair.

Boswell pressed him. Did he have faith? Yes, he resigned himself to the Supreme Being, whom he loved, but he knew nothing of immortality. 'Are you sincere, are you really sincere?' Boswell hammered away. It would always remain of profound importance to him whether great thinkers like Voltaire, Rousseau, Hume, and Johnson believed in salvation. If they did, there seemed all the more hope for him.

After the other guests returned and Voltaire escaped to bed, Madame Denis, taking pity on Boswell, served him his supper in the drawing room where, the centre of interest, he 'eat and drank cheerfully with the gay company around me'. 'I am magnificence itself,' he proclaimed, 'I eat alone, like the King of England.'

Boswell stayed another day and night, but as Voltaire was 'sick and out of spirits' – too much animated talk with his young petitioner perhaps? – he fell into 'low spirits' that spoiled his 'relish of the most illustrious genius'. He was dressed in his flowered velvet, but there was nothing much to do in it. In the afternoon, tickled with the idea of writing letters under Voltaire's roof, he dashed off a few lines to his father, Temple, and Dalrymple. That evening he spoke to Voltaire for only a few minutes. Retiring to his room, he jotted down his notes of their conversations – 'eight quarto pages' – which he planned some time soon to convert into one continuous narrative in his journal, for a magazine, or as part of a larger account of his travels.[20]

7

The next morning he was still gloomy and eager to leave, but not before spending twenty or so more minutes with Voltaire. There was just enough time for Voltaire to promise to write (he did once, on 11 February 1765) and then Boswell was off. 'Thinking hard', he later reflected on what 'his variety of mind' had managed to pull off on his travels thus far, and what manner of man he was. What possible explanation could there be for his happy reception everywhere from the great and the famous? He could boast 'neither profound knowledge, strong judgement, not constant gaiety' but he had a 'noble soul' which in spite of that 'shines forth', some knowledge, 'original humour and turn of expression', and (most important of all) 'a remarkable knowledge of human nature'. 'I can tune myself so to the tone of any bearable man I am with that he is as much at freedom as with another self, and, till I am gone, cannot imagine me a stranger.' He saw in himself the child who would ever be the 'father of the man' if society were not always jarring the 'soul'. As he put it to Voltaire in a letter of 15 January, what his 'soul' had given him was 'natural'. It had 'neither spice nor perfume. It was fresh from the dairy. It was curds and cream.'[21]

TWELVE

O Italy!

I

On New Year's Day Boswell set out for Italy in a chaise or 'Alps machine' designed for crossing the mountains, a rudely fashioned contraption of two saplings joined by twisted cords on which he sat, with boards for his back, arms and feet. It tipped up so far in front that he said he was 'thrown back like a bishop in his studying-chair'. On this he was carried by six men, on a track flanked by six-foot snowdrifts, over the 'horridly grand' mountains on the Mount Cenis route. Rousseau, not the sublime scenery through which he passed, filled his mind. He felt like a new man, the philosopher's disciple, strengthened by the gentle and pious deism of his 'Creed of a Savoyard Vicar' from the fourth book of *Émile*. As Boswell wrote in an unsent letter to Rousseau that reads like the sequel to his 'Sketch': 'I carried over the Alps ideas of the most rigorous morality. I thought of myself as a penitent who must expiate the sins which he had confessed to you in your sacred retreat; I felt like a hero of austerity in a dissolute age.' He had left Britain 'idle dissipated ridiculous and regardless of reputation', he wrote to Temple, but now he was proud of his character. None the less, since Ferney and the desultory scene there he had succumbed to gloomy periods, buffeted by a 'whirlwind of agitation', innumerable balls, card parties, and dinners he had enjoyed en route. He was also rather sickly, having stayed up very late writing letters on a succession of nights, so that he had fainted at Mass at the foot of Mount Cenis. Arriving in the Piedmontese capital, Turin, on 7 January, 'dirty' and exhausted, he immediately went to the opera and promptly fell asleep from fatigue.[1]

The Italy that Boswell entered was, like Germany, a land of petty courts although here there was even less national coherence. What struck eighteenth-century British tourists seeking a once-in-a-lifetime exposure to Italy's cosmopolitanism and classical grace was the stark contrast between the artistic remnants of its former grandeur and its present social insularity, even grubbiness. The cosmopolitanism was effete, not gracious or enlightening. As the historian G. M. Trevelyan described it,

> the Italy of Piranesi's prints, was peaceful and stagnant – a land of hard-working, ragged, submissive peasants, of idle beggars, and of cultured dilettante nobles and clergy with few interests in life beyond the innocent occupation of reading to each other insipid compositions in verse, and disquisitions, learned and sentimental, on the monuments of antiquity – a land strangely different from the fierce and passionate Italy of the Middle Ages, of the later Risorgimento, or of modern Fascism.[2]

Boswell seldom described the environment of the nobles he visited, dined with, attended the opera with, and danced with, as fully as he did in Germany. Most of his illuminating descriptions of Italy are of churches and classical ruins, not palaces, villas and opulent town houses. It was religion, in fact, the spectacle of the Roman Catholic Church, that activated his imagination here. It thrilled him to see the Pope in St Peter's, as did visiting the holy shrine at Loretto, where he gave up some of his faith in 'human testimony' and the luxurious 'grandeur' of the High Mass filled him with a 'serious awe' infinitely preferable to the 'levity of mirth' he found in the homes of the nobles. His most rewarding quest was one of the imagination, driven by his schoolboy reading of Horace, Virgil, and Ovid and Christian history. He was presented at the courts of Italy's rulers and he met a few important artists, but 'golden Italy' nonetheless disappointed him, perhaps largely because there were no literary, political, or social heroes like Rousseau and Voltaire to track down. The word 'debauched' occurs frequently in his journal, used both metaphorically and literally to describe himself and what he was experiencing.

Everyone except Boswell's father was enthusiastic about his going to Italy, but most of the advice was to stay for a conventionally short period of three to four months. He must have remembered, and wished to dissociate himself from, his old mentor Adam Smith's scathing account of the effects of the Grand Tour:

> In the course of his travels a young man generally acquires some knowledge of one or two foreign languages; a knowledge, however, which is seldom sufficient to enable him either to speak or write them with propriety. In other

respects he commonly returns home more conceited, more unprincipled, more dissipated, and more incapable of any serious application, either to study or to business, than he could well have become in so short a time had he lived at home.[3]

If Smith had been able to observe Boswell on his passage through Italy, it would have confirmed his bias.

2

He stayed in Turin for more than two weeks, an oddly disproportionate length of time given the antique riches which lay ahead and their relative scarcity in this city. The reason: he had started on a sexual pilgrimage that often made him appear unattractive and ridiculous in this land of female milk and honey. As Geoffrey Scott remarked, he was 'pedantic in Holland, princely in Germany, philosophic in Switzerland, and amorous in Italy'. The Italian Boswell was also most like the Boswell of Edinburgh and London. After his almost total sexual abstinence over the past year-and-a-half, Italy's reputation for easy women, married or otherwise, was a temptation he could not resist. To be fair, there were plenty of other young British men on the 'Tour' doing the same thing, many of whom thought that gallantry in Italy was as obligatory as art and music. 'The ladies of Turin were very beautiful, and I thought that I might allow myself *one* intrigue in Italy, in order to increase my knowledge of the world and give me a contempt for shameless women. So I made myself into a gallant.' So much for his resolutions at Môtiers.[4]

On that first morning in Turin, he rose at his *auberge*, which was significantly called the Bonne Femme, shook off the creeping 'fiend', and hurried off to collect his money and post, including the first letter from his devoted mother since he had left home, which put to rest 'dreary ideas' of her death or disapproval. A letter of introduction to the Contessa di San Gillio, the middle-aged daughter-in-law of the late King of Sardinia, whom Casanova described as the organizer of all social intrigues in Turin, then gave him access to the best society the city had to offer. At a ball that evening at the Théâtre de Carignan, 'the counts and other pretty gentlemen told me whenever I admired a lady, "Sir, you can have her. It would not be difficult." ' They were jesting, he thought at first, but perhaps not, for 'the women are so debauched that they are hardly to be considered as moral agents, but as inferior beings'.[5]

The women, he soon discovered, would not thank him for that attitude. Even in Italy they required sensitive courtship, but as he would only be spending two weeks in Turin he would have to dispense with some of the preliminaries. An 'oldish lady', a countess who would be grateful for his favours, would do. The Countess di San Gillion, with whom he had already taken a coach ride, seemed a promising candidate, so, at the opera and somewhat prematurely, he sat 'vis-à-vis to her and pressed her legs with mine, which she took very graciously'. There was also a countess in another box. When Captain Billon took him to meet the beautiful countess Burgaretta, Boswell's mind was 'quite in fermentation'. After the opera, he made 'plain addresses' to Countess di San Gillion but, though she liked him, not surprisingly she refused him: 'I am not that kind of woman.' Boswell was not expecting this reply from a 'debauch'd' Italian matron but took no 'pains' about it and, the next morning, advanced instead on the Countess Burgaretta, having decide he was 'quite in love' with her. To his credit, Boswell felt like a rascal, but 'when a man gives himself up to gross gallantry he must lose much of his delicacy of principle'. The Countess refused to see him and when, later that evening, he blundered over his attentions to the French Ambassador's wife, he grew proud and sullen and retreated to his *auberge* where he quarrelled with the landlord.[6]

He almost succeeded in the Countess Burgaretta's box, at the opera the following evening. For the sake of appearances, the Countess first discouraged him but then whispered in his ear to come to her the following afternoon. In the morning a letter from her cancelled the visit because he had been so open in announcing his progress that too many people knew about it. Billon, his 'genteel pimp', told him he had failed because he went at it like a bull in a china shop: 'I saw he looked upon me as a very simple young man; for amongst the thoroughbred libertines of Turin to have sentiment is to be a child.' Boswell persevered. He wrote the Countess wild letters declaring his love; he kissed the letters she sent in return. She would have none of it. The two merry wives of Turin were leading him a dance. At last the Countess di San Gillion gave him some badly needed advice: 'I think you have studied a great deal. You ought to go back to your books. You should not follow the profession of gallant or you will be terribly taken in. Be careful of your health and your purse. For you don't know the world.' 'I have too much warmth,' he admitted to himself, 'ever to have the cunning necessary for a general commerce with the corrupted human race.'[7]

It was much simpler to have Billon procure him some 'willing girls', which he did, though not before Boswell had tried his hand with yet another countess, this one only seven years older than he. He was 'mad' enough even to consider writing to ask his father to let him spend the winter in Turin because of his attachment to her. She was encouraging, but on reading his wildly passionate letter, she dismissed him peremptorily. Thoroughly fed up, he resolved to leave Turin post haste. 'O Rousseau, how am I fallen since I was with thee!' he moaned.[8]

3

On the way out of the city Boswell saw people rushing to witness the execution of a thief. He jumped out of his chaise and found a place very close to the gallows where he could clearly see and hear the suffering victim. It was grisly: 'He was tossed over and hung with his face uncovered, which was hideous . . . The hangman put his feet on the criminal's head and neck and had him strangled in a minute.' Boswell 'stood fixed in attention to this spectacle'. He then went into a church and 'kneeled with great devotion before an altar splendidly lighted up' – luxurious images of Roman Catholicism to counter the blackness of his feelings. Garish imagery clashed in his mind: 'I felt three successive scenes: raging love – gloomy horror – grand devotion. The horror indeed I only *should* have felt.' Holland, Germany, and Switzerland had not prepared him for anything like his first three weeks in Italy. The classical and Christian Mecca of Europe had as yet provided him only with debauchery and violence. It was small wonder that his ideas were all 'mean' and he despised himself.[9]

4

He reached Milan on 25 January 1765 and spent two days visiting ancient shrines and several churches, including the cathedral and Leonardo da Vinci's *Last Supper* in the refectory of Santa Maria delle Grazie. Most important to Boswell was an introduction to the Dominican brother Padre Allegranza at a Milanese convent who gave him fresh food for thought about conversion to Roman Catholicism, but he now found himself 'too philosophical to feel the force of ecclesiastical reasoning' – he was a 'Sceptic. But a devout one.' More practically, the priest gave him an introduction to another Dominican priest, in Bologna, thus opening the way for a string of Dominican contacts as he moved 'from convent to convent' throughout the country, treated with 'great distinction'. Roman Catholicism had never before seemed so benign to him.[10]

At Parma on the 29th he looked up Deleyre, to whom Rousseau had gingerly recommended him and who provided Boswell with some much need company during the two days he stayed there. At this point he abandoned his journal in Italy, except for occasional short spurts, and took to writing memoranda instead. There is a letter from Deleyre to Rousseau on 18 February which confirms that Boswell was unhappy, lonely, and especially susceptible to the influences of Catholic sects: 'I saw him go with the more regret because he has only himself for company: his oddness, his youth, and his melancholy being likely to keep him from gathering from his tour the fruits which he promises himself and which he badly needs.' 'I hope', Deleyre added, 'that as the heat of youth subsides, the tumult of his blood will subside too … that he will form a virtuous attachment, and that as its bonds strengthen, he will acquire a taste for life.' In those two days Boswell had 'conceived for him an immediate and lasting affection'.[11]

Setting out for Rome, which he approached via Bologna, Rimini, and Ancona, Boswell resolved to keep away from girls and then to indulge in 'gallantry' only once a week; but although antiquities ('Romanising') and religion began to claim much of his attention once he arrived in Rome on 16 February, he did not keep to his resolution. In fact, the juxtaposition of religion and sex did much to stimulate his amorousness. 'Be Spaniard: girl every day,' he told himself. He felt 'brutish'. All this he combined with an energetic programme of sightseeing.[12]

From Rome, Naples took him five 'disagreeable' days to reach along the Appian Way. Arriving there in the first week of March, he followed the same pattern of 'seeing the classical places all around' and indulging in carnal pleasures while trying to fight off hypochondria. Deleyre had been right. Boswell's 'gloominess of temper', he had written to his affectionate older friend Sir Alexander Dick, 'has, to be sure, been an interruption to my enjoyment. This it is not in my power to prevent.' At least it did not interfere with his sightseeing. During his three-week stay, he visited the Royal Palace at Porticini with its porcelain-panelled room; climbed Vesuvius on a 'smoky' day; was guided personally through the antiquities of Pompeii and Herculaneum, only a small part of which had then been excavated, by Camillo Paderni; explored a number of churches; and generally tried to imbibe the spirit of Virgil's landscape.

'Is it possible', he wrote to Grange, 'to conceive a richer scene than the finest bay diversified with islands and bordered by fields where Virgil's Muses charmed the Creation, where the renowned of ancient Rome enjoyed the luxury of glorious retreat, and the true flow of Soul ...?' Whereas the beauty of the Alps reminded him of 'romantic' Scotland, Italian landscape launched him into the imaginative realm of the classical golden ages.[13]

On the other hand, the roughness of Naples was oppressive, for 'modern Naples has nothing of the ancient Parthenope except its heat and its idleness. The people are the most shocking race, eaters of garlic and catchers of vermin, an exercise which they scruple not to perform on the public streets.' In Naples, too, Boswell became the 'true libertine': 'I ran after girls without restraint. My blood was inflamed by the burning climate, and my passions were violent. I indulged them; my mind had almost nothing to do with it. I found some very pretty girls.' The heat infected him with 'a prodigious scurvy' that covered his chin and neck; irritating though this was, however, he admitted that it probably protected him from a return of gonorrhoea since momentarily he had to keep the girls at a distance.[14]

5

Back in Rome on 24 March, he enrolled in a six-day intensive course on art and antiquities recommended for tourists, for the duration of which he resumed his journal. In the company of his tutor, a resident Scottish antiquary, he saw the Pope again at Santa Maria sopra Minerva and, from dawn to dusk,[15] visited many other churches, the Capitoline Hill, the Forum, the Colosseum (where people kept animals in pens), the Palatine Hill, and the Baths of Diocletian. He was 'seized with enthusiasm' and began to speak Latin, so that 'we harangued on Roman antiquities in the language of the Romans themselves'.

Casting himself in the role of the traditional British collector and connoisseur, Boswell decided that he wanted a large historical painting to take back to Scotland. This he commissioned from Gavin Hamilton, a Scots painter who lived in Rome. For the subject he consulted Andrew Lumisden, Private Secretary to the Old Pretender, who lived with the exiled King (then in the last year of his life) at the Palazzo Muti-Papazzurri in Rome. Lumisden was at the centre of the Scots *emigrés* in Rome, many of them diehard Jacobites, so this was a somewhat risky liaison for Boswell if ever he hoped to hold political office in England. Not surprisingly, influenced by an old Jacobite with 'old-fashioned principles', the subject Boswell chose for the picture was the abdication of Mary Queen of Scots. Money was no object, he told Hamilton, for which his father would not have thanked him. Hamilton did not get around to finishing the painting until 1776, and then it was a great disappointment.[16]

While in Rome, Boswell had his portrait painted by another Scottish painter, George Willison, then aged twenty-three. He sat for it twice in May, dressed in the vivid colours of his splendid 'greatcoat of green camlet lined with fox-skin fur' over the scarlet waistcoat with gold lace – his proud attire when he visited Rousseau. Willison's picture is the first of only a handful that Boswell commissioned of himself, and the only one in his youth. It turned out to be an elegantly flattering image of young man with, in Boswell's words, 'a plain, bold, serious attitude', free and wandering through Europe, before the weight of the Scottish world of law and responsibility had begun to take its toll. Lumisden thought it was 'exceedingly like', though there is no hint in it of Boswell's swarthy complexion and thick dark hair. The painting answers well to his Roman idea of himself, or rather, the idea he was striving to maintain, of a young man totally in control, cultured, and the favoured friend of great authors: 'an amiable, pretty man' with 'a soul truly noble, a soul which in reality sets me higher in the scale of being than if I had attained to the first honours which superior talents procure and been without such a soul'.

6

Insufferably smug and complacent though Boswell may appear in Willison's portrait,[17] he was riddled with self-doubt in Rome. He wrote to Rousseau: 'I know my worth sometimes, and I think and act nobly. But then melancholy attacks me, I despise myself, and it seems to me a waste of time to try to improve so petty a thing.' Thoughts of his ancient family, parents, and friends encouraged him, but not thoughts of returning home. He was not 'steady' enough for application to 'business'; 'labour of mind' had never been his strength. Utrecht had proved that to him for ever. What was the point in tormenting himself with 'ineffectual struggles' to change his nature? It was time to scale down his aspirations and stop the grand (and idle) talk with Temple about great careers. The important thing would be to get his father to understand him as he really was.[18]

During his eleven weeks in Rome, Boswell kept visiting prostitutes. 'I sallied forth of an evening like an imperious lion.' He justified the rampage with thoughts of 'the rakish deeds of Horace and other amorous Roman poets' on that same classic soil. In any case, in Rome the prostitutes were 'licensed' by the Cardinal Vicar. On 29 April, the Old Pretender's physician informed him that he had contracted his fourth case of gonorrhoea, this time complicated by crab lice – 'discovered beasts ... ludicrous distress'. He carried the infection with him from Rome to Padua, all the time still sexually active. The 'wounds of my Roman wars were scarcely healed', he informed Rousseau with shame, before he 'received fresh ones' in July from a 'pretty dancer' in Venice.[19]

This debauchery alternated grotesquely with uplifting religious interludes at St Peter's and other churches where he relished the elaborate ritual of 'solemn services' in gorgeously ornate settings. The spectacle of the Pope's appearances thrilled him no less, as at the papal palace, Monte Cavallo, where, introduced by his Dominican contacts, he kneeled and kissed the Pope's 'toe', or, to be precise, his 'slipper rich with gold'. They spoke together, after which the Pope remarked, 'Very pleasing manners ... He begins to speak Italian.' On Easter Sunday at St Peter's, it was ecstasy to see the Pope conducting a service that promised resurrection and salvation in spite of the sins of the world, and of Boswell himself. His gratitude was unbounded:

> I was sure that the revelation given by Jesus was true; and when I saw the Christian High Priest with venerable magnificence elevate before the Eternal Justice a Sacrifice for the sins of the whole world, I fell to my knees ... I struck my breast, and with all the ardour of which my soul was capable I prostrated myself at the feet of my Father 'who is in Heaven', convinced that, by varied ways of which we know nothing clearly, he would one day lead all his creatures to happiness.

He was not in the least ashamed of his public display of religious fervour. 'Let cold beings sneer,' he wrote, with perfect sincerity. Here was light and inspiration. 'I was never more nobly happy than on that day.'[20]

7

One of Boswell's happy surprises in Italy was to meet John Wilkes in Turin. Wilkes was there in retreat from London, having fallen foul of the King and Lord Bute. As Member of Parliament for Aylesbury, he had remained unnoticed until, with the poet Charles Churchill, he started the periodical *The North Briton* and recklessly began to attack the King and Bute politically and personally. Though the London mob embraced him as their persecuted hero with their famous rallying cry of 'Wilkes and Liberty', he was imprisoned briefly in 1763; he was then impeached, hounded out of England, and in his absence convicted of seditious libel and declared an outlaw the following year. The King, Pitt, Bute, Scotland and much of Parliament hated him. He was not an ideal friend for anyone who was thinking, however vaguely, of a life in politics.[21]

As a Tory and a Scot, Boswell should have despised Wilkes, but the man's charm was irresistible. Moreover, Erskine had once hit the nail on the head when he remarked that Boswell was 'a Tory with Whig principles': a defender of lost causes, a hyperactive embodiment of ideological contradictions, a loose cannon who could live happily with both his strong monarchical principles and his distaste for royal tyranny. He was a blithe conundrum, a bundle of contradictions. Instinctively, he often felt as the mob did, attracted to the underdog.

When Boswell discovered that Wilkes was in Turin, he wrote to him right away saying that as a Scotsman he abhorred him, as a friend he valued him, and as a companion he loved him. Even though it was indiscreet to suggest it, could they share 'a feast of most excellent wine and choice conversation'? Thus developed one of the most valued friendships of his life. They often dined together in Turin, and when they met up again in Naples, where Wilkes had decided to spend some time with his Italian mistress Gertrude Corradini, they continued to see each other frequently. They may even have climbed Vesuvius together. 'He is a man who has thought much without being gloomy', Boswell confided to Rousseau, 'a man who had done much evil without being a scoundrel'. Wilkes's 'lively and energetic sallies on moral questions' convinced him 'that God could create a soul completely serene and gay notwithstanding the alarming reflection that we all must die'. Boswell told Temple that despite their disagreement on every important subject, what he liked about Wilkes was that he was an iconoclast whose 'constant felicity shakes my solid speculations on human woe. He has an elasticity of mind that nothing can crush.' On the eve of his departure from Naples on 20

March, he feared they might never meet again: 'You say you have two or three souls. May that which I have found so congenial to mine live for ever, while the spirit of the Whig goeth downwards.' Wilkes reciprocated his affection: 'You are engraved on my heart.'[22]

Boswell kept up the correspondence from Rome and then Venice, describing himself as a 'crucible' with a rare talent for finding the gold in Wilkes's character; and he even wrote a 'Heroic Epistle' to him. But he never showed the least inclination to fall in with his politics. He was at times almost brutal in telling Wilkes where they differed, calling him an 'enemy to the true old British Constitution and to the order and happiness of society'.[23]

A more promising political relationship was struck up with John, Viscount Mountstuart, Lord Bute's eldest son whom Boswell met in Rome. A charming and indolent young man of twenty also making the Grand Tour, Mountstuart took a liking to Boswell right away. 'Boswell, I will teach you how to live,' he announced. Although delighted to be 'taught' by a future star in the firmament of English society, one with almost as much sexual experience as himself, and also eager to become more sociable after weeks of loneliness in Italy, Boswell was running out of time. So, at his urging, Mountstuart wrote to Lord Auchinleck asking him to let his son stay longer in Italy. Lord Auchinleck knew what this could mean for his son's fortunes and immediately agreed. The pair left Rome on 14 June.[24]

Two others made up the party, Colonel James Edmondstone, Mountstuart's 'governor' on the trip, and Paul Henri Mallet, a Genevan historian, the young lord's 'tutor'. Boswell saw himself as Mallet's social superior, but Mallet was a distinguished intellectual with a streak of cranky arrogance. He irritated and taunted Boswell mercilessly for his pretentiousness. Mountstuart, in 'childish mood', also irritated him by calling him 'Jamie', a name he hated as beneath him and too familiar. Boswell knew he was being too sycophantic: 'What! Boswell, *the man of singular merit!* The friend of Rousseau! Is Boswell so far overcome by vile interest as to depend on the moods of a young Lord? I recollected myself. I made my Lord realise that I was proud as ever. I did it too emphatically.' He started quarrelling with them about everything, from their travel itinerary to his own education. They teamed up against him. It was open season on his personality.[25]

Mallet 'discovered how little I had studied either of science or of history, and he said to me, "If I were as ignorant as you are, I should be ashamed to show my face."' Rousseau must have laughed at Boswell behind his back, Mountstuart said. Boswell defended himself but privately acknowledged that Mallet was not far off the mark, although he knew that hypochondria was partly to blame: 'In my black moments when I judged myself by the opinions of others, I was a libertine and ignoramus. I was bashful, and distrustful of my ability to distinguish myself in my own country.' Although the troupe had its bright intervals, this unhappiness continued all the way to Venice, where he and Mountstuart one night pitched their tents in the arms of the infected dancer with fatal consequences. Mallet and the Colonel blamed Boswell for leading their ward astray, though Mountstuart may have been equally culpable.[26]

In Venice the party decided to break up as Mountstuart had to return to England. On the way to Milan, they grew 'tender' with one another, and as they parted Mountstuart said to Boswell, 'I have great esteem for you. I shall always be your friend in London. But you have a terrible disposition.' Boswell's reply, spontaneous and forgiving, was typically egocentric: ' "My Lord, if you do not have a lasting affection for me, you will never have it for anybody." I was very sorry to lose him.' Even Mallet was conciliatory. Boswell asked to correspond with him to show that he bore no malice, to which Mallet replied, 'I shall never speak ill of you, and if I am asked about you, I shall say, "But what do you expect from a lively mind?" ' As for the Colonel, he was rather less forgiving. 'You're geck [foolish], man. If you wanted to make friendship, [you should] not [have been] so familiar.' Later, he told Lord Auchinleck that he thought his son was 'a mischief-making lad, vain, and penurious'.[27]

8

One of Mountstuart's parting gifts to Boswell was an introduction to his mistress in Siena, Porzia Sansedoni, thirty-five, wife of a prominent public figure and mother of three. After two unhappy weeks in Florence, where he endured another venereal attack, he arrived in Siena in the last week of August, eager to try his luck. The closest he had come to success in Italy thus far with a woman of fashion was to see her knees.

As in Turin, he was ready to embark on an affair. The setting was perfect: a beautiful Tuscan town, gorgeous weather, and a charming nobility that thought well of him. He took flute and singing lessons, studied Italian (in its purest form, he explained to his father, hoping to persuade him to allow him more time there), and enjoyed complete

freedom. He stayed in sumptuous rooms ornamented lavishly with paintings and an assortment of mirrors, including five around his bed. He
gave himself up completely to the 'delirium of love', courting two married
women at the same time. If Mountstuart had been successful with Porzia,
surely he could too. He made the same mistakes, though. His letters to
her were in the vein of 'brave attacks'. Invoking Mountstuart, he assured
Porzia that his friend wanted him to succeed with her. If she were not
responsive, he might have to turn to another woman whom he knew was
eager to have him. 'Do not lose him. Time passes. A moment of despair
may remove me for ever. Think seriously. I adore you.' In one of the
letters, he added the postscript, 'Read this letter with care. It contains
very, very romantic sentiments,' as if she might fail to notice that his
letters were unique, full of 'the heart of your brave Scot of ancient line',
breathing with 'fire'. All in vain. Try as he might, his extraordinary letters
brimming over with extravagant love-talk, he failed to have his way with
her. Eventually, he asked for his letters back, with which she obliged
him.[28]

The other woman, Girolama Piccolimini ('Moma'), small and attractive, thirty-seven, and wife of the mayor of Siena with four children, was
more accommodating. Perhaps because Boswell courted her in a much
lower key, she fell hopelessly in love with him: 'I want to give myself up
to you, and I would lose all others for your sake.' Both women knew he
was pursuing the other – 'it required an unparalleled dexterity,' he wrote –
but Moma also knew she was not the preferred one. For him, it was mere
gallantry, at least at the beginning. 'I lied to her certainly no fewer than
a hundred times a day,' he confessed to Rousseau. All of a sudden,
however, he found himself in love with her, too, confessed to her his lies,
and gave himself up to weeks of 'delicious enjoyment' in the Italian mode
such as he and Grange used to dream of on summer afternoons in
Edinburgh.[29]

Married at sixteen to an older man whom she did not love, Moma
had had many affairs, but she had never met anyone like Boswell before.
Her letters to him are remarkably intense. Although under no illusions
about his intentions and character in love, she could still write to him
after a parting of only two days:

> O God, what shall I do when you are no longer here, if so short an absence
> is unendurable? But courage is always needed to conquer oneself; and instead
> of thinking of your good qualities I shall remind myself that you are a
> deceiver and a faithless lover, and then I shall laugh at you. But in the

meantime I see you as lovable and, I would almost dare say, tender towards me.[30]

After five intense weeks, he had to leave. Ever since his first meeting with Rousseau, he had been playing with the idea of a visit to the freedom fighters in Corsica, a reckless and dangerous notion but one that gained on him steadily as he made his way through Italy. He had in his pocket a recommendation from Rousseau to the authorities in the island – 'it will be singular if they hang me as a spy,' he joked. However, his father's patience was wearing thin, so if he wanted to visit Corsica he had better go quickly. Moma was distraught. They parted on Sunday morning, 29 September, his bags packed, the chaise waiting to take him to Lucca, Pisa, and then Leghorn where a fair wind would carry him to Centuri on the northern tip of the island. He 'took her to bed' for the last time. She pleaded with him to return to her after visiting Corsica, but he was 'reserved'. One of her last pitiful statements was, 'You go to greater and greater happiness, but you leave me her to go continually from bad to worse; for after a few years my youth will be gone ... and I am among people for whom I care nothing.' Her husband then entered the room to say goodbye, making Boswell's departure easier. When he failed to return to Siena, or to write as she thought a man in love should, Moma showered him with complaining letters and continued to do so for two years, long after he had returned to Scotland, her letters mingling rebuke with great affection.[31]

9

Boswell wrote to his father from Parma and Siena, but arranged to be gone before any letters arrived in return. He knew his father would be furious with him for not having returned to London with Mountstuart at the end of their tour. One of Lord Auchinleck's letters written on 1 October, about a week before Boswell sailed to Corsica, commanded him to come straight home, stopping for a couple of weeks at the most in Paris on the way – 'there is nothing to be learned by travelling in France.' His lordship was suffering from a 'stoppage of urine' and his wife was ill, too: filial duty at least, if not conscience and personal responsibility, should compel the traveller home.[32] Since his son did not receive these letters, he was not in the compromising position of having to disobey them. He could plead ignorance. He was also particularly careful not to write of his Corsican plan to his father, who would have thought it a wild idea to say the least.

Rousseau and Voltaire were among the few who did not think Boswell was mad to go to Corsica. With the risk of pirates, the crossing itself was perilous, even with the 'passport' or identification he had obtained in Leghorn from the Commander of the British squadron in the Mediterranean. Moreover, the island itself was brimming with bandits. 'I do run some little risk from the sea and from Barbary Corsairs and from Corsican Banditti,' he wrote to Grange on the eve of his sailing.[33] But the 'brave islanders', led by the inspired General Paoli, the Garibaldi of his day, were also in the throes of fighting for their independence from the Genoese and, increasingly, French oppression. No British gentleman, it seems, had ever ventured on to the island. Moreover, as Boswell was in quest of Paoli who was then living in the south, he would have to travel there mostly by foot over mountains and through dense forests and thick *maquis* or undergrowth.

At this point his belief in the Corsican cause, as he understood it from Rousseau, was the stuff of a romantic travel tale, though he would always take the side of the underdog. When the War of Revolution broke out in America he took the part of the revolutionaries there too.[34] The most significant thing about his Corsican adventure of 1765 – it had become more political by the time he got around to writing about it in his *Account of Corsica* (1768) – was that it was inspired less by philosophical ideas on liberty than by the stature and personalities of two men, Rousseau and Paoli. Boswell went to Corsica chasing a dream made up largely of clichés; by the time he left, the dream had solidified into a cause.[35]

10

Even before he sailed from Leghorn, Boswell discovered that he was suspected by the local authorities to be a British agent sent to negotiate a treaty with Corsica. Why else would he come to such an out-of-the-way and dangerous place? Denials did no good, so he played along with it, allowing them 'to make a minister of me till time should undeceive them'. His entering the island through the 'back door', the port of Centuri, a small and isolated harbour well away from the French garrison at Bastia, must also have given credence to the idea. It partly explains the fine treatment he often received. Nevertheless, this was going to be a rugged journey, as he soon discovered.[36]

He set sail on 11 October on a small 'merchant bark', manned by the master and six Corsican sailors and carrying two Corsican merchants and a boy in addition to Boswell and his servant Jacob. When he was not seasick on the tedious two-day crossing, he played the flute to while away the hours, or pitched in with some rowing if the wind dropped. He was obligingly warned by the Corsicans on board that if he tried to 'debauch' any of their women, he could expect 'instant death'.

They landed at Centuri at seven in the evening and immediately he and Jacob made their way by foot to Morsiglia a mile off, with prospects along the way of 'agreeable' mountains 'covered with vines and olives' and decorated with 'aromatic shrubs and flowers'. That night he heard his first 'veneration' of Paoli. The next day they strapped their baggage to a donkey and continued walking south to Pino, along a frightening path 'scrambling along the face of a rock overhanging the sea', sometimes not even a foot wide. The donkey's progress was too slow, so after a while a man carried the baggage instead; eventually he was replaced by two women. There were no inns along the wild route they took, so they bedded down wherever they could.[37]

They reached Corte on 17 October, only to discover that Paoli was twice as far south at Sollacarò, presiding over a *sindicato*. They had covered about forty miles, the last twenty on horses or mules, through rough terrain, 'wild, mountainous, rocky country, diversified with some large valleys'. After a couple of days' rest they set off on good mules over the mountains towards Sollacarò, well supplied with food and wine by the fathers of the Franciscan convent in Corte and led by expert guides.[38]

One of Boswell's themes for the rest of the journey was the happiness of these 'primitive' or 'savage' peoples whose lives combined the innocence and purity of nature with a revival, under Paoli's enlightened leadership, of the classical republicanism of the ancients. He participated vigorously in their primitivism:

> When we grew hungry, we threw stones among the thick branches of the chestnut trees which overshadowed us, and in that manner we brought down a shower of chestnuts with which we filled our pockets, and went on eating them with great relish; and when this made us thirsty, we lay down by the side of the first brook, put our mouths to the stream and drank sufficiently. It was just being for a little while one of the 'prisca gens mortalium' ['primitive race of men', Horace, *Epodes*, ii.2].

He cast himself in the role of the chronicler of the 'brave, rude men', reminding them that they needed to be patient, were still carving out their social and economic Renaissance on the island, and were much better off than the corrupt Europeans across the water: 'I bid them remember that they were much happier in their present state than in a state of refinement and vice, and that therefore they should beware of luxury.'[39]

By the time Boswell rode into Sollacarò on the 20th, Paoli had turned into 'something above humanity' in his imagination. Would he 'sink to nothing' in front of Paoli? He passed nervously through the village with his mules and guides, headed straight for Paoli's house, walked past the guards into the antechamber, and then was ushered into Paoli's sacred chamber where he found the modern Lycurgus alone. Boswell produced his recommendations, including the one from Rousseau.

At first Paoli, tall, large, and imposing with reddish-blonde hair, was reserved and suspicious, not knowing what to make of his visitor. He paced up and down the room in silence for ten minutes, stealing deep looks at his guest – he was an expert in physiognomy, said Boswell: 'with a steadfast, keen, and penetrating eye, as if he searched my very soul.' Then he invited Boswell to sit next to him at dinner where they were also joined by several nobles. Years later Fanny Burney offered a different version of this meeting, one tinged with mockery, which she said she had heard from Paoli himself.

> He came to my country, and he fetched me some letters of recommending him, but I was of the belief he might be an impostor, and I supposed in my minte he was an espy; for I look away from him, and in a moment I look to him again and I behold his tablets. Oh! he was to the work of writing down all I say! Indeed I was angry. But soon I discover he was no impostor and no espy, and I only find I was myself the monster he had come to discern.

Burney's mischievousness may have got the better of her here, for it is unlikely that at such a moment Boswell would have rudely resorted to taking notes. And he generally made notes of his conversations at night or the following morning, not in company. In any case, once Paoli discovered that Boswell's mission was simply to study him, he opened up before his worshipping guest who feasted on his every move and sentence.[40]

From the start Boswell took notes with the half-baked idea of making Paoli the hero of a book on Corsica that would serve to convince the British government to come to his aid against the French. That this idea bore fruit in a book – unlike most of Boswell's projects – testifies not only to the warmth of his reception by Paoli but also to the speed with which his commitment to Corsican liberty deepened while he was there. In the book Paoli became a study of heroic leadership, wit, culture, classical learning, and practical wisdom. He is cast as the 'illustrious chief', recalling the heroes of antiquity, a modern example of Roman nobility, a type of Henry V at Agincourt, a latter-day Solomon dispensing justice, and a Joseph-like interpreter of dreams. The book is also an autobiography in which Boswell sketches himself as the honoured and wide-eyed guest, privileged to drink from the fount of his hero's wisdom. Paoli's hospitality was almost lavish, as if Boswell were indeed an envoy. He went riding on Paoli's own horse with his personal guards wearing 'crimson velvet' and 'gold lace', and was served chocolate in the morning on a silver salver, visited by all the nobility, and nicknamed by soldiers and peasants the *ambasciatore inglese*. Indeed, he pictures himself, Gulliver-like, as the ideal ambassador: 'I did everything in my power to make them fond of the British, and bid them hope for an alliance with us. They asked me a thousand questions about my country, all which I cheerfully answered as well as I could.' He played Scottish airs on his flute – 'the pathetic simplicity and pastoral gaiety of the Scots music will always please those who have the genuine feelings of nature' – and sang Garrick's song, 'Hearts of Oak', to resounding cheers of 'Bravo Inglese!'.[41]

One day he donned Corsican dress, which he had asked to be made for him, and equipped with a brace of Paoli's own Corsican pistols walked out 'with an air of true satisfaction'. Elsewhere he spoke of himself as 'a man of spirit and education' who might make a good foreign minister – perhaps for Corsica? He even slipped in a few brief reflections on marriage, with himself as the obvious centre of attention. Licentious pleasures were 'delusive and transient', Paoli told him: 'you must go home to your own country and marry some fine woman whom you really like. I shall rejoice to hear of it.'[42]

On parting, there was a sentimental moment when Paoli shook his hand 'as a friend', about which he wrote, 'I dare not transcribe from my private notes the feelings which I had at this interview. I should perhaps appear too enthusiastic.' For the rest of his life he was 'set free from a slavish timidity in the presence of great men'. He felt he had crossed the threshold of manhood. As he remarked to Paoli in London years later, 'I had got upon a rock in Corsica, and jumped into the middle of life.' He had become 'Corsica Boswell', a tag by which he would be known to thousands in the years to come.[43]

In an unheroic anticlimax, not far out of Sollacarò on 28 October, he came down with the ague or malaria. He struggled north with a fever, more or less collapsing at Culotti after covering fifteen miles, 'wet to the skin and quite overcome by the severity of the storm'. The following day he pushed on to Corte, where the ague confined him to the convent for several days. He was a very sick man by the time he reached Bastia, his port of embarkation, on 9 November. The French commander there, the Comte de Marbeuf – 'the best man I ever met with' – kindly took him in, organized medical attention, saw that he was fed the proper foods, and restricted visitors in order to conserve his strength. Boswell deplored the French presence in Corsica, but he could not help feeling gratitude for the grace and warmth with which he was nursed. The French accepted no payment for his care and even lent him some money. He left Bastia with his health restored, almost two weeks after arriving on the island.[44]

He set sail for Genoa on 29 November, in the company of an increasingly irritable Jacob and a new companion, Paoli's dog Jachone, a large wild boar-hunting dog that occasioned some black comedy in the next few weeks. The voyage to Genoa was miserable. A storm drove them into Capraja, a tiny 'barren' Genoese island only eighteen miles from the northern tip of Corsica, where Boswell had to cool his heels for six exasperating days. He lodged comfortably enough in another Franciscan convent, but he was hardly serene. He argued with the fathers about the Corsican struggle, with Jacob who accused him of being too stingy, and with the master of a felucca who delayed their departure: 'You stupid bugger, I won't be ballocksed around any more. I want absolutely to leave this evening.' This had its effect and they finally escaped the island on 27 November, Boswell terrified by the lashing winds.[45]

He landed at Genoa in the early hours of 30 November to be greeted by a barrage of letters from his father and Moma, all of which made unpalatable demands on him. He also discovered that he had indeed been suspected as a spy and placed under surveillance by the Genoese authorities all the time he was in Corsica. The Doge of Genoa summoned him for questioning soon after he arrived back. French spies had also been sending reports of his progress to Paris, and even the King of Sardinia in Turin, who looked on Corsica with more than just a passing interest, was receiving reports on this mysterious young man. All this interest in him because of his friendship with the 'terrible enemy Paoli' frightened Boswell at the same time as it fed his vanity. At any moment he expected 'to have had a Stiletto slipped into my back', he reported to

Grange, 'or to have got me in prison and very quietly given me a little poison; but the British flag makes them tremble.' And the authorities were justified in their concern. Boswell immediately visited the British Consul in Genoa and embarked on a three-year campaign to persuade the British government to go to Corsica's aid against the French.[46]

II

Boswell stayed in Genoa for ten days, nursing a painful ingrown toenail that had developed on his walks over the Corsican mountains in ill-fitting boots and, with his father's commands ringing in his ear, embarked for France by felucca along the coast on 10 December, at which point his fully written journal resumes.[47]

On board the felucca, a love-hate relationship developed with Jachone, Paoli's dog. Noticing that the dog was sick, Boswell threw him overboard, 'thinking that when he had swum ashore he would follow the boat'. Instead of keeping pace with the boat to Vado, however, the dog ran off 'like a criminal' back to Savona. That night he was told Jachone had been seen at the butchers' stalls. Next morning the dog was returned to him, and though at first overjoyed, Boswell promptly flew into a rage over the disobedient animal: 'I resolved to punish him sufficiently, so I took him to the inn, tied him to a bedstead, and beat him without mercy' – a sentence, incidentally, that he later crossed out in his journal. His servant Jacob screamed at him for his cruelty: 'If my brother did a thing like that, I would thrash him.' Typical of Swiss peasants, Boswell thought; he continued to beat and starve the animal in order to 'humble' him.[48]

For some reason, the dog made him act like a madman; or perhaps the beast was simply a scapegoat for his general irritation – with his servant Jacob, the anticlimax of having to head for home, and the barbarity of the Genoese. He quarrelled violently with Jacob when he caught him feeding the dog on the sly. After that, at Noli, he decided to let Jacob and the baggage continue by water while he and (inexplicably) Jachone started walking. Then the abuse of the dog began in earnest. Once he 'hung him fairly up twice upon trees for half a minute, but he grasped them with his feet and saved his neck'. As he walked and rode along on what became an increasingly wild journey, with outlaws and thieves lurking all around, at least in his imagination, he let the dog run loose and, when not hugging it, was bloodying its nose. Once or twice it got lost.[49] Jacob rejoined him and they continued on through Nice, Antibes, Toulon, Marseilles, Aix, and up to Avignon, arguing much of the way. 'I believe, Sir, that you have been badly brought up. You have not the manners of a nobleman. Your heart is too open,' Jacob bravely volunteered. This was the same criticism that François Mazerac, Boswell's servant in Holland, had levelled at him: he did not sufficiently preserve the distance between master and servant; he was too 'free', always asking him questions. Boswell knew Jacob was not far off the mark. 'Sir,' Jacob added, 'I do not think you should marry. At least, if you marry you should not live in the same house with your wife; otherwise, *ma foi!* there will shortly be disputes.' As for children, he should not have them; or if he did, he should not live with them, or they would be 'as badly brought up as you'.[50]

After golden Italy, Boswell did not like France. The food and inns were unpredictable, the carriages unbearably slow, the theatre in Marseilles 'insufferable', the French men often 'impudent', and the women too often strumpet-like. He pined for Italy: 'O Italy! Land of felicity! True seat of all elegant delight! . . . Thy divine music has harmonised my soul.' He spent Christmas in Avignon, where the pageantry of the church services made a deep impression. 'You know I am half a Catholic,' he wrote to Grange, 'I love the solemn and magnificent worship of the Church of Rome.' Then, after brief visits to the Roman ruins of Nîmes and freezing Montpelier, he worked his way up to Lyons, where Jachone makes a reappearance: 'Poor Jachone had his feet swelled and sore with fatigue. I caused [to] make a bed of hay for him in the corner of my room, where he lay very snugly.' Then the dog ran away for good. Jacob also left him at last, saying nothing could prevail on him to endure Boswell's stinginess all the way to Paris.[51]

From Lyons he wrote to Rousseau, delighted to hear that the philosopher, who had been on the run from the authorities ever since they had parted in Môtiers, was going to England. 'What a wonderful prospect for me!', of introducing him to Dr Johnson and taking him up to Scotland to show him 'the venerable woods of my ancestors'. Boswell hoped to catch up with him in Paris but when he arrived there on 12 January Rousseau was gone.

Paris brought him no elevation of 'ideas', just 'old' ones. Also, he had a return of melancholia when one bright possibility turned sour.[52] He sought out Horace Walpole, who called Rousseau a 'mountebank' and told Boswell he must write something original about Corsica – ironic advice since when the *Account of Corsica* was published Walpole ridiculed him in a letter to Thomas Gray:

> The author, Boswell, is a strange being, and ... has a rage of knowing anybody that ever was talked of. He forced himself upon me at Paris in spite of my teeth and my doors ... He then took an antipathy to me on Rousseau's account, abused me in the newspapers, and exhorted Rousseau to do so too: but as he came to see me no more, I forgave all the rest.

Walpole was one literary celebrity who seemed able to resist the Boswellian charm, seeing instead meddlesome exuberance and vanity.[53]

On the 27th, while visiting Wilkes, quite by chance Boswell read in the *St James's Chronicle* that his mother had died a couple of weeks earlier. He was stunned. The following morning a letter from his grieving father, written out by his brother David, confirmed it. 'Too true; Mother gone. Was quite stupefied. In all morning. Wept in bursts; prayed to her like most solemn Catholic to saint.' The pitiful tone of his father's letter was a new experience for him. 'My dear son,' it begins, 'I am now reduced to a destitute state; I have lost my friend, I have lost my adviser in all things ... I need your assistance.' Twice he appeals to 'dear Jamie' and offers to pay all his debts if he will only come home. A wave of compassion for his father overcame Boswell, a desire to comfort him and dedicate himself to 'parental piety'. Wilkes urged him to rush home and to remember that he had at least 'avoided the pain of seeing mother dying'; now he must comfort his father. Boswell never forgot his kindness.[54]

12

His journey home was complicated by the arrival in Paris of Thérèse Le Vasseur. Rousseau had fled to London from Strasbourg and Thérèse was following him, but she was worried about the crossing. 'Mon Dieu, Monsieur, if we could only go together!' she exclaimed when Boswell visited her at the Hôtel Luxembourg. This was agreed and they left Paris together on 31 January. The idea of seducing Thérèse on the journey did not occur to Boswell before they set out, but seduce her he did, or vice versa, in one of the most bizarre episodes of his love-life. However, the full story of that seduction is obscured by one of the more fascinating mysteries of the Boswell papers.

Lieutenant-Colonel Isham maintained until his death that Lady

Talbot, the owner of the Boswell papers, had thrown into the fire twelve
pages of the journal describing Boswell and Thérèse's return to London
because they were shamefully racy. He also maintained that he had read
them first and he dictated their contents as well as he could to Geoffrey
Scott, the first editor of the journals. That account stood until, decades
later, Frederick Pottle and others began to cast doubt on it. Much in it
is now discredited as Isham's invention. But the fact remains that twelve
pages are missing from the journal and there is much in Isham's account
that rings true. It is too tempting to ignore.[55]

As Boswell was distressed about his mother and Thérèse was anxious
about the journey, they sought solace from each other. On the second
night, according to Isham, they shared the same bed at an inn but Boswell
did not rise to the challenge until Thérèse coaxed him back to his
'vigorous' self. Boswell almost never experienced impotence with a
woman of inferior social status, but in making love to the mistress of the
famous Rousseau, he was venturing into sacred terrain. The next morning
he made the mistake of boasting about it. Thérèse's reply stunned him:
'I allow that you are a hardy and vigorous lover, but you have no art.'
She offered to teach him a few things about the 'art of love'. If he felt
humiliated on the first night, it was nothing to the night that followed.
With Thérèse calling to him from the bed, Boswell paced around, drank
a bottle of wine, talked to her fitfully about Rousseau, and finally sank
into the bed, more out of exhaustion than desire. She then instructed
him: 'He must be gentle though ardent; he must not hurry. She asked
him, as a man who had travelled much, if he had not noticed how many
things were achieved by men's hands.' Afterwards, he described her
performance as 'agitated, like a bad rider galloping downhill', and admitted that her lectures bored him. He began to talk to her again of Rousseau,
hoping at least to glean a few good quotations, but she in turn found
that boring. He concluded that it was a bad idea to make love to an old
man's mistress.[56]

None the less, they appear to have made love throughout the eleven-
day journey. Boswell was satisfied, noting in Dover on 12 February,
'Yesterday morning had gone to bed very early, and had done it [at] once:
thirteen in all.' With Thérèse 'much fatigued', they made their way to
London and Boswell dropped her off at David Hume's, who had obtained
a pension for Rousseau from the British government, while he went to
visit Temple.

Whether because of this affair with Thérèse, or all the animosity
towards Rousseau he had encountered in Italy and France, or seeing him

in London 'oldish and weak', Boswell no longer found the great man so 'illustrious'. Thérèse had sworn him to secrecy about their affair, which he honoured to his dying day. Whether or not she told Rousseau is less clear. In the months to come, the friendship cooled between Boswell and the ailing and increasingly paranoid philosopher. Boswell appears to have suspected Thérèse as the reason for Rousseau's coolness, but he also knew that Rousseau was convinced that he, Hume, and Horace Walpole were at the root of a conspiracy against him. The details of the alleged conspiracy are less important than the spectacle of Rousseau's fallibility; Boswell described him on 15 October as 'a man advancing in years, and a man whose life has not been easy. He is infirm, ill, and delicate to a degree that I would never have believed had I not seen it.' He believed that Rousseau's quarrels amounted to a 'literary tragi-comedy'. He even published anonymously a brief description of a satirical scene featuring Rousseau, Hume, and Walpole that, as luck would have it, someone used as the basis for an engraved caricature entitled 'The Savage Man'.[57]

The sad postscript to their friendship is that during the ensuing months Rousseau came to distrust Boswell and Boswell was surprised to find himself increasingly disappointed in Rousseau. After Boswell left London in February 1766, they corresponded a few times during the rest of the year but never saw each other again.

THIRTEEN

'Like Embroidery upon Gauze'
Corsica, *Law*, and Propaganda

I

Once Boswell was back in London, everything – except General Paoli – paled in importance beside Johnson. Rousseau had turned into a peevish old man picking quarrels with lesser beings; Voltaire was dissipating his genius in spiteful and petty *ad hominem* squabbles; Hume was a source of fascination ('I was very hearty with him here this winter') but a sceptic; and most of his other influential acquaintances were cultivated to inflate his vanity rather than for their ideas and moral and intellectual energy.

He and Johnson had barely corresponded while he was away, but all the time Johnson remained Boswell's moral and religious anchor. From Wittenberg on 30 September 1764, with a great sense of occasion Boswell had written to Johnson while draping himself over the tomb of Melanchthon, one of the principal advocates of the Reformation in the early sixteenth century:

> My paper rests upon the grave-stone of that great and good man ... At this tomb, then, my ever dear and respected friend, I vow to thee an eternal attachment. It shall be my study to do what I can to render your life happy, and if you die before me, I shall endeavour to do honour to your memory...

'Johnsonian principles and Johnsonian force' drew him back like a magnet. All pretension vanished. When they met, he kneeled and asked for a blessing as before a sacred oracle. Johnson was even more famous now than when they had parted at Harwich, having published in 1765 his edition of Shakespeare with its celebrated Preface. Goldsmith, who was very glad to have Boswell's companionship again but a little jealous of Johnson, warned him against too much Johnsonian worship: 'Sir, no man is proof against continual adulation.'[1]

Hugging his 'dear Bozzy' 'like a sack', Johnson said, 'I hope we shall pass many years of regard.' He commended Boswell on his achievements and encouraged him to write his book on Corsica, remembering to 'give us as many anecdotes as you can' – that is where the value of any such book would lie. This was all a comfort: 'he was as great as ever ... you was fine. Home and slept sound.' But Boswell had a lingering idea of his travels as a dream, and himself as essentially insubstantial: 'my brilliant qualities are like embroidery upon gauze.'[2]

2

Urgent as it was for him to be reunited with his father after the death of his mother, it is surprising that Boswell stayed in London for three weeks before heading north. Business as well as pleasure kept him there.

There was a lot of catching up to do with Dempster and Temple. The latter, who was about to take Orders in Cambridge and travelled to London just to see Boswell, joked that he was half afraid to meet him again after his mighty conquests over 'princes and *literati*'. Boswell took Temple to meet Johnson at the Mitre – 'fine to have *Magnus Apollo* and dearest friend together' – only to find that Temple found the sage 'monstrously overbearing'. Notwithstanding, he and Temple felt 'easier' with each other and much more mature, laughing over their 'airy, youthful plans of grandeur', when Temple was to be 'a great man in the state', and he 'a great statesman and a great poet into the bargain'. They spoke of Zélide and Anne Stow, Temple's marital prospect, and decided they would not make suitable wives. Later, irresponsibly, Boswell went out of his way to seek out Anne Stow and inform her that Temple was uncertain about her, for which Temple firmly scolded him, 'Do not interfere at all in this affair, either by writing to her or in any other way.' Not surprisingly, she took an active dislike to Boswell. Temple married her the following year anyway.[3]

Boswell dropped in on Eglinton who was not as impressed as he should have been with his adventures and new 'gravity', and Mountstuart who responded to his peace overtures with a princely dismissiveness: 'I don't care sixpence about it.' Eglinton did take him to court, though, and introduced him to the Earl of Denbigh, who then introduced him to the King apparently on the grounds of his Corsican adventure. All the King could muster was, 'Lately come over?', but Boswell was 'easy and not a bit struck'. His visits to his cousins the Montgomeries of Lainshaw, near neighbours in Ayrshire, and to Dr Pringle, were more difficult to handle because of their Scottish tones and manners: 'Now enlarged and enlightened by travel, even worth could not make you often bear uncouth Scots manners.'[4]

One family in which he took a keen interest while in London, among all his other social calls, was the Yorkshire Bosvilles, not only because he good-naturedly adopted Godfrey Bosville as a sort of 'chief' of the Boswell clan but also because his daughter Elizabeth Diana was remarkably beautiful – 'vastly pretty: black hair, charming complexion, quite modest', though too quiet. His marriage-conscious mind immediately identified her as a great catch.[5]

3

One piece of business he still had to perform before leaving London was an interview with William Pitt, 'just a member of Parliament' since 1761 when he had resigned as Prime Minister. This was Boswell at his most audacious, except that on this occasion he had a purpose: to speak about the 'illustrious' Paoli. Pitt could not shut the door on a man who described him as ever 'the prime minister of the brave, the secretary of freedom and of spirit',[6] and threatened to call ten times if necessary.

Pitt had read in the foreign newspapers about Boswell's meeting with Paoli and therefore had a good idea of what he wanted to talk about. Boswell played his Rousseau and Voltaire cards first, then (when they were alone) turned the discussion to Paoli and the Corsica problem. Pitt had to be circumspect. As a member of the Privy Council, he could not listen to any representation from a foreign power without 'declaring' it to the King and Council. But if Mr Boswell wished to speak of his travels on the island, he would be happy to be entertained. Boswell emphasized the fact that Paoli severely lamented Britain's neglect. Pitt admitted it did appear strange that an island so important to navigation in the Mediterranean should be undervalued by the government. He was free with compliments for Paoli but saw 'not the least ground, at present, for this Country to interfere ...' Here the interview ended apparently without Boswell saying anything of substance regarding the Corsican cause or Paoli's policies. Still, he thought it was a 'noble conference' and. it introduced him to one of the most glittering political figures of the century.[7]

That conversation was Boswell's first effort in Britain to win government support for Paoli's cause, a noble if at times egocentric campaign he began in Marseilles and Paris and continued for two or three years after the publication of his *Account of Corsica.* Between January 1766 (more than a month before he returned to England) and November 1771 he wrote at least eighty articles or 'news paragraphs' about Corsica for the *London Chronicle,* many under his own name but most of them by fictitious people who were in one way or another connected with Corsica or Paoli.[8] There were pieces about Boswell's intimacy with Paoli, attempts to assassinate Paoli, fictitious painters sent out to Corsica to paint Paoli, a rumoured visit by Voltaire to Corsica, and so on. When his *Account of Corsica* was about to be published, he also inserted a number of anonymous articles extravagantly puffing the book; and in his Preface he wrote misleadingly that Horace Walpole first suggested the idea of the book – a fine piece of calculated self-flattery.

By late October 1766 he was writing the book. Insufficient information about the history of the island delayed him, but in the new year he received a sixteen-page letter from Paoli loaded with information, and a packet of material from Thomas Davies and Sir John Dick in Leghorn. In March he sat down to three months of hard work on it. Hume promised to arrange publication with Andrew Millar, the publisher of Dr Johnson's *Dictionary.* Dalrymple, who in March was raised to the bench as Lord Hailes, also encouraged him.[9]

The only major dissenting voice was Johnson who thought he should be getting on with his legal career and not playing about, like Wilkes, with vague ideas of 'liberty'. It was time to grow up. 'You have, somehow or other, warmed your imagination,' he wrote disapprovingly in a letter Boswell decided to include in his *Life of Johnson.* 'I wish there were some cure, like the lover's leap, for all heads of which some single idea has obtained an unreasonable and irregular possession. Mind your own affairs, and leave the Corsicans to theirs.'[10]

Boswell ignored this advice, the first sign in his literary career of a stubborn insistence on the sanctity and veracity of what he wrote. To tell him what he could and could not write was to emasculate his literary persona. When Johnson saw in the published *Corsica* that Boswell had silently appropriated a letter of his, still technically his property, he erupted, 'Who would write to men who publish the letters of their friends, without their leave?' 'Empty your head' of Corsica, he repeated, to which Boswell replied, 'But how can you bid me "empty my head of Corsica?" My noble-minded friend, do you not feel for an oppressed nation bravely struggling to be free? ... Empty my head of Corsica!

Empty it of honour, empty it of humanity, empty it of friendship, empty it of piety. No!'[11]

Nothing elevated his soul, he told Temple, like writing this book. At last he was doing something he was good at, writing about a subject on which he had become an authority. His confidence soared. By June he had written most if not all of the first section on Corsica's history and over the summer he sent parts of the manuscript to Temple, Sir Alexander Dick, who was taken by his 'fascinating manner of writing', and Lord Hailes, who seemed surprised to find himself 'entertained and instructed' and gave him no fewer than seven pages of comments on it, among which was his injunction that Boswell should 'sacrifice to modesty and leave out yourself'.[12]

In September, Boswell finished writing up his journal, the second part of the book, and sent it to Temple to read. He had more than a faint premonition that it would be this part that would prove 'most valuable'. Temple read it extremely closely and, among many suggestions, recommended the removal of Johnson's letter and an allusion to his gallantry in Siena with Moma. Sir Alexander Dick, on the contrary, an indelible youthful spirit like Boswell, loved the 'young Hercules' Boswell, a fusion of 'the soft endearments of Siena and the rude virtuous paths to Paoli at Corsica'. All the 'wise old parents of the debaucht youth of Brittain', he added, would be grateful for his delicacy in the passage. In the meantime, Millar had lost interest in publishing it, and Thomas Davies (much to his chagrin later) would not touch it because he thought it would prove 'dry and unentertaining', of interest only to antiquarians. So in August Boswell signed a contract with the talkative Edward Dilly by which he would be paid one hundred guineas for the copyright (after publication), on the understanding that the first edition would be published in Scotland, not London, by the Glasgow printers Andrew and Robert Foulis – friends of his from those weeks at Glasgow University. Given Dilly's (and his brother Charles's) weakness for liberal causes and writers such as Wilkes, Catherine Macaulay, and the North American patriots, they were natural publishers for the book.[13]

From this point, things moved crisply along. Boswell received proofs for Part I in September, an exhilarating experience for him as for any writer who has long laboured on a book in the solitude of his study. They 'amuse me finely, at breakfast', he told Temple. 'I cannot help hoping for some applause.' The book would make him more marriageable and his disposition would instantly become 'grave and reserved though cheerful and communicative'. He buried himself in corrections, especially heeding Hailes's comments on content and style. Finally, an advertisement for the London edition appeared in the *London Chronicle* on 8 October, after which it was only a matter of waiting.[14]

The book appeared on 13 February 1768. Dilly had read the market well. The first edition was for 3,500 copies at six shillings a copy, a large print run by any reckoning, and it sold out in six weeks. A new edition in April, again for 3,500 copies, sold out within a year. Ultimately *Corsica* sold more copies than anything else Boswell wrote, including the *Life of Johnson*. He sent copies to Walpole and Johnson, among others, and crossed his fingers. The news was arrestingly good. 'My book has amazing celebrity,' he announced to Temple. 'Lord Lyttelton, Mr Walpole, Mrs [Catherine] Macaulay [the author of a *History of England*], Mr Garrick have all written me noble letters about it.' Thomas Gray, whose approval he craved, was also enthusiastic: 'It has pleased and moved me strangely, all (I mean) that relates to Paoli. He is a man born two thousand years after his time!' But about Boswell personally Gray was less generous. 'The pamphlet proves what I have always maintained,' he quipped in a letter to Walpole, 'that any fool may write a most valuable book by chance, if he will only tell us what he heard and saw with veracity. Of Mr Boswell's truth I have not the least suspicion, because I am sure he could invent nothing of this kind. The true title of this part of his work is, "A Dialogue between a Green-goose and a Hero." '[15]

It is extraordinary that a poet and man of letters like Gray should think that any 'fool' could move him 'strangely' like this by 'chance', without talent playing its part. But these were uncharted literary waters. 'Your History is like other histories,' Johnson wrote, 'but your Journal is in a very high degree curious and delightful ... Your history was copied from books; your journal rose out of your own experience and observation.' Whatever Johnson thought of Boswell's imprudence, he knew good biography when he saw it. It was the little unremembered acts and remarks of common existence, especially if reflected through the biographer's personal lens, that made it so. This was a lesson that Boswell had learned well from the *Rambler* and to which here he gave fresh and dynamic expression. The journal section appealed also because of its imagery, touches of immediacy, the ability to create a living scene or catch the essence of a character. The public had not seen anything quite like this before. It was a new style of travelogue and biography, combined with an extraordinary self-portrait. Johnson drew the line, however, at reviewing the book, as Boswell wanted him to. 'No, one ass [should not] scratch [another],' he said.[16]

Within a year of publication, the *Account of Corsica* had been translated into French (twice, one version possibly by Zélide), Dutch, German, and Italian.[17] The translations made Boswell more famous on the Continent in his lifetime than even Johnson. In addition, there were three Irish editions. The reviews were enthusiastic but one constant criticism was that three-quarters of the book consisted of relatively dull Corsican history and only one-quarter was devoted to the author's personal pilgrimage to Paoli.

Boswell did not become complacent over the success of *Corsica*. He raised no less than £20,000 by subscription in Scotland for the Corsicans, much of it sent to Leghorn in the form of ammunition. He also used his instant fame to push strongly for British intervention in deciding the destiny of the island. Pitt apparently was of no use to him, but the book had embarrassed the government somewhat and Boswell was determined to 'keep up the spirit'. In December 1768, the Dilly brothers brought out a small pamphlet, *British Essays in Favour of the Brave Corsicans, Collected and Published by James Boswell* (dated 1769), a collection of twenty 'essays' or open letters culled from the various newspapers, six or so written by Boswell, for which he also wrote the Introduction.[18]

His most bizarre exhibition of Corsican zeal was at Garrick's famous Shakespeare Jubilee, held in Stratford in September 1769. The Jubilee event was supposed to be a glorious three-day celebration of the Bard with poetry, music, speeches, a ball, a horse race, fireworks, and a concluding procession in Shakespearean costumes. Soon after Boswell arrived in London on 1 September, he decided that such a public occasion was tailor-made for another instalment of Corsican publicity. He had become known as 'Corsica Boswell', a tag that stuck to him for the rest of his life, so why not play it up? He had only four days to get ready for the Jubilee, which began on 6 September, because his plan was to appear at the masquerade ball on the 7th in the authentic 'character of an armed Corsican Chief'. First, he asked an embroiderer in Bow Street to stitch the words 'Viva la Libertà' in gold thread on the front of a Corsican cap that he cut out in paper. The native Corsican costume he had brought back with him was in Edinburgh, so he and Dilly scoured London for the 'necessary accoutrements'. He stuffed what he found into a travelling bag, bought a fine 'Jubilee staff' in Cheapside with a bird carved out of the root end of a vine – 'the bird of Avon', he called it – procured a musket, and set off.[19]

His first view of Stratford, already a literary Mecca, was a sublime moment, thrilling him with 'those feelings which men of enthusiasm have on seeing remarkable places'. The festivities opened that night in Holy Trinity Church, Shakespeare's burial place next to the Avon, with a performance of Thomas Arne's oratorio *Judith* (which Arne himself conducted). But the heavens opened with a vengeance just as Boswell arrived: 'my hair hung wet about my ears; my black suit and the postilion's grey duffle above it, several inches too short every way.' Well-dressed people stared at him, wondering who this could possibly be, especially when he cordially shook hands with David Garrick, the man of the hour. But he wanted to remain incognito until he first appeared in his Corsican costume and Garrick was happy to play along, telling everyone he was a 'clergyman in disguise'. Though tired and wet, he was in high spirits to be among the great and the learned gathered within the hallowed walls of Shakespeare's church.[20]

The masquerade at which Boswell planned to reveal himself, the famous author on Corsica, impersonating a brave Corsican in arms, took place the following night. For greater effect he decided at the last minute to write some verses and penned forty-six lines honouring Britain while invoking the dream of Corsican liberty. Unfortunately, he failed to get these printed in time to 'give them about in my Corsican dress', but against all the odds he managed to recite them. 'My Corsican dress attracted everybody. I was as much a favourite as I could desire.' He lingered on, savouring the occasion, until six the next morning, entirely pleased with 'ideas' about what a unique celebrity he had been: 'It is fine to have such a character as I have. I enjoy it much.'[21]

Back in London, he wrote up his part in the spectacle under his own name and published it in several periodicals. He also asked the artist Samuel Wale to come to Dilly's in the Poultry, where he was staying, and draw him in his Corsican splendour: 'It was pleasing to think that I was at that moment getting my figure done in London, to be engraved for four thousand *London Magazines.*'[22] The full-page illustration appeared as the frontispiece of the September issue which contained his article. That was not all. Garrick staged a dramatic version of the Jubilee in which an actor played Boswell as a Corsican, with 'Corsica Boswell' written on his cap.

The ironic postscript to Boswell's Corsican mission was that the island had already fallen under French control in May of that year, Paoli escaping to Leghorn in July. A few days after the Jubilee, he was in London where he would remain in comfortable exile for several years on a government pension. The reunion on 22 September between the famous and grateful general and the now famous young Scottish literary champion of a lost cause was charged with feeling. Boswell tapped on Paoli's door in Old Bond Street and was greeted by a Corsican footman who, at his name, 'gave a jump, catched hold of my hand and kissed it, and clapped his hand several times upon my shoulders with such a natural joy and fondness as flattered me exceedingly'. They both ran upstairs to Paoli's room where he was breathlessly announced: 'I heard the General give a shout before I saw him. When I entered he was in his night-gown and nightcap. He ran to me, took me all in his arms, and held me there for some time.' He had the sensation of 'a curious imagination as if I had passed through death and was really in Elysium'.[23]

Thus began one of the most enduring intimacies in Boswell's life. Paoli was a prolific source of personal advice, a model of noble morality, and a gracious host on his many visits to London. Boswell's 'idea' of Paoli never wavered: 'I was afraid to see him in bed, lest it might lessen his dignity and diminish my grand idea of him. But it had no such effect. Though his hands and arms were under the clothes and he showed his countenance only, he appeared with superior lustre.' In his mind Paoli was more perfect than Johnson. They rarely disagreed. Boswell took delight and credit in introducing him to friends and acquaintances – the Duke of Queensberry, Sheridan, Johnson, and many others – but the climax of self-importance came on the day they went together to see the King, George III: 'The King said, "I have read Boswell's book, which is very well written ... May I depend upon it as an authentic account?" The General answered, "Your Majesty may be assured that everything in that book is true, except the compliments which Mr Boswell has been pleased to pay to his friend." ' 'Friend' of the great Paoli! That was enough.[24]

4

Boswell returned to Scotland in early March 1766, after an absence of almost three-and-a-half years. Would the death of his mother and the grief he shared with his father help to inaugurate a period of forgiveness and understanding? Could his father now accept him for what he was, even take some satisfaction from his successful Continental tour? Would his legal career reassure and satisfy him enough to make him more sympathetic towards Boswell's other interests? Would his father be able to sit down and talk sensibly, or even warmly, to his son about his need to get married and his search for a wife? Would he, in short, become a loving parent? The answer to all these questions was a resounding 'no'. If the next three years were the happiest and most successful in Boswell's life – apart from the years of the Grand Tour – it was not his father who made them that way.

Riding straight for Auchinleck, since his father was there during the court's recess, he immediately fell under a 'cloud'. The poignant loss of his mother struck him everywhere. Although he was looking forward to seeing his brother David again, who was still working for Coutts & Co. in Edinburgh and lived at home, there was also a melancholy awareness of John who was now in Newcastle in the care of the Rev. Edward Aitken, trying to recover from his mental instability. His father received him warmly, however, and he resigned himself to work, settling down to prepare a Latin thesis, the only requirement left before he could be admitted to the Bar. At first, relations between his father and himself were good: 'I have been giving sensible comfort to a most affectionate father, and been preparing myself to be of use in the world.' They walked together in the 'venerable shades' and for 'whole evenings' his father told him stories of his ancestors.[25]

Temple, who had taken Holy Orders and was about to be installed in his living in Mamhead, Devon, was warmed by the father–son reconciliation. 'Though perhaps wrong in some things,' he wrote to Boswell, 'he means well, is a good man, and you are a good son to sacrifice so much to please him ... Indeed, Jemmy, you are the best creature in the world, and believe me, I love you better than I do any body in the world.' Johnson, however, warned Boswell, 'Your resolution to obey your father I sincerely approve; but do not accustom yourself to enchain your volatility by vows: they will sometime leave a thorn in your mind, which you will, perhaps, never be able to extract or eject. Take this warning, it is of great importance.' It was spectacularly good advice but Boswell, precisely because of his volatility, found it difficult to follow. A decade later Johnson was still warning him about vows, long after the mental thorns had done their damage: 'BOSWELL: "But you would not have me to bind myself by a solemn obligation?" JOHNSON: (much agitated) "What! a vow – O, no, Sir, a vow is a horrible thing, it is a snare for sin. The man who cannot go to Heaven without a vow – may go – " '[26]

Auchinleck and its ancient heritage endowed Boswell with a significant part of his identity but his father and he had widely diverging attitudes towards the paternal acres. Lord Auchinleck was a shrewd and efficient landowner, no more sensitive to the needs of his tenants than it suited him to be, well informed in country-house ownership and agricultural management, and (in Boswell's mind especially) cold and unimaginative in his feelings about the history of the place. He was committed chiefly to making it pay and he hoped that with a good marriage his son would, among other things, accelerate this process. Boswell, on the other hand, saw his demesne as an evocative paradigm of romantic, ancient, feudal grandeur. His father tried to interest him in estate management, but Boswell hated it. He did not even want to live at Auchinleck much, feeling generally bored there and subject to black moods. He saw himself visiting the family home only briefly, during court recesses, then making his way to the excitement of London.

But Boswell stuck to his course and, much to his father's relief, on 26 July he successfully defended his thesis in Latin on the legacies of household furniture (fulsomely – and oddly – dedicated to Lord Mountstuart), and on the 29th was admitted to the Faculty of Advocates in Edinburgh.

5

At the start of his legal career, the split in Boswell's self-perception between the kind of man he knew himself to be – an almost harmless Mr Hyde, as it were, whom he had to control – and the reserved kind of advocate he felt he ought to be was nowhere better illustrated than in the two camps of older men with whom he chose to correspond and keep company. Either they praised him and reassured him that he was a unique and talented young man who simply needed a few touches of prudence and reserve to round out his personality, or they upbraided him and urged major reforms in his tastes and attitudes.

One of the latter was Lord Marischal, to whom he continued to write in Germany, seeking advice on everything from Corsica and his legal work to love and marriage. Marischal was witty, which Boswell enjoyed, but he tended to deploy his ironic turn of mind in defence of Lord Auchinleck's arguments, at times mocking Boswell's anxieties. Sir John Pringle was another, more taciturn, spokesman for his father. Pringle was the Queen's personal physician and later the President of the Royal Society. Boswell respected him deeply and always made a point of visiting him in London, for he served to keep the lines of communication open with his father, but invariably struggled to make him smile. When Pringle introduced him to the American statesman Benjamin Franklin, Boswell's comment was, 'Here is a fine contrast: acid and alkali.'[27]

Lord Hailes was Boswell's most valued confidant among the older men in Lord Auchinleck's camp. A Scottish baronet who worked diligently as a judge, with an Anglo-Scottish background and literary reputation, he was a daunting model for the young advocate and literary aspirant. In the many letters between them during the first two years of Boswell's legal career, Hailes constantly tried to hammer home the point that without decorum and temperance he could not expect to get anywhere. But they were both fond of literary talk, too. Hailes suggested that Boswell establish his professional reputation by publishing a glossary of old Scots law terms, though he did not know his man there – literature was Boswell's escape from the law, not to be used in its service. Hailes recognized and respected his young friend's literary enthusiasm and talents, but in Hailes' view that counted for little if he could not succeed in the law, be a dutiful son, marry well, and be a blessing to his family and Auchinleck. He harped on these themes endlessly.

In Sir Alexander Dick, he had one delightful elderly friend who not only charmed and praised him but also almost never lectured him. Dick was sixty-three in 1766 and had retired from the College of Physicians of Edinburgh. 'I don't believe there ever existed a man more continually amiable than Sir Alexander,' Boswell wrote in his journal. Prestonfield House, Sir Alexander's estate a mile out of Edinburgh at the southern base of Arthur's Seat, to which Boswell fell into the habit of walking on Saturdays, became an escape route and oasis for him, a place of relaxation and convivial enjoyment. No one judged him there. He idealized Sir Alexander at Prestonfield in the tradition of Virgil's old hospitable Corycian farmer, a blessed and benign figure in the Scottish landscape, puttering about at his 'classical villa' in his acres and welcoming all his friends. In December 1766, Boswell wrote to him from Auchinleck, 'I am sorry to lose a Saturday with you: but I comfort myself by reflecting that I am now a sort of established man at Prestonfield, and can come and go as if I had a claim to the place. So should all friends live. But there are very few who deserve to be called friends.' Whenever relations with his father deteriorated, 'the sweet place and amiable people soothed me'. Most interesting, the child in him matched the child in Sir Alexander. Here was comfort indeed for a son who, soon after he began to practise law, started to fall out with his father all over again.[28]

6

In his 'Boswelliana' Boswell wrote of his launch into the legal profession:

> Boswell had a great aversion to the law, but forced himself to enter upon that laborious profession in compliance with the anxious desire of his father, for whom he had the greatest regard. After putting on the gown, he said with great good humour to his brother advocates, 'Gentlemen, I am prest into the service here; but I have observed that a prest man, either by sea or land, after a little time does just as well as a volunteer.'[29]

Once he began to practise as an advocate, three days after he was admitted to the Bar, he kept it up without interruption for about twenty years. This was paying his dues indeed.

The advocate was, and still is, the Scots equivalent to the English barrister, while the Writer to the Signet corresponded to the English solicitor. The Writer's task was to prepare the cause (Scots for 'case') and brief and engage the advocate who would plead it in court. These proceedings in the Court of Session were for the most part conducted through paperwork, not by two advocates squaring off against each other, though on a few occasions when the causes were important enough Boswell did have the chance to display his eloquence and plead *viva voce*. Most of his work was in the Court of Session, the supreme court for civil cases, which sat from nine in the morning on weekdays in Parliament House for two sessions per year: 12 June to 11 August and 12 November to 11 March (with a Christmas break). At a quick glance, this does not seem too onerous a bondage: for six months of the year he was generally free to do as he wished.[30]

Never once from 1766 until 1783 did Boswell miss a Session. In his first few years he quickly earned a well-deserved reputation for his eloquence and emotional persuasiveness. It was hard work, requiring 'labour and poring ... reading long papers', not like writing 'essays for a newspaper, without reading much'. At one point in that first December he had no fewer than seven causes on his plate at once, pleading all of them, as it happened, before his father. Lord Auchinleck, in fact, carefully nursed him along in the early months of his career and occasionally notes of gratitude, touching if brief, surface in Boswell's journal, as on 25 February 1767: 'Was with Father; was hearty. Asked him, "Am I not doing well as you would wish?" HE: "Yes." Took his hand.' At about this time he wrote in his 'Boswelliana': 'My father said to me, "I am much pleased with your conduct in every respect." After all my anxiety while abroad, here is the most perfect approbation and calm of mind. I never felt such solid happiness.' Yet all was not well beneath the surface: 'I feel I am not so happy with this approbation and this calm as I expected to be. Alas! such is the condition of humanity, that we are not allowed here the perfect enjoyment of the satisfaction which arises even from worth.'[31]

By March he had earned an impressive eighty guineas. Although he was feeling justly pleased with himself: 'I already speak with so much ease and boldness, and have already the language of the bar so much at command', he seemed cocky, pretentiously talking of 'the unavoidable occupations of a laborious employment'. Grange, Temple, and others fairly roasted him. Temple was typically blunt: '*Do not, do not* think such methods necessary to raise my esteem of you.' But Boswell defended himself against the charge of 'affected importance' by observing that 'the absurdity of mankind makes nineteen out of twenty employ the son of the judge before whom their cause is heard . . . I am as yet but a very raw counsellor so that a moderate share of business is really a load to me.' He acknowledged, however, that he may now and then 'assume some airs'.[32]

One of these causes was on behalf of a fairly obscure claim to the hereditary rights of an estate through the male line. The present owner of the estate was being challenged because he had descended through the female line. Boswell lost the cause but it highlighted what was for him the profoundly important hereditary principle that the entail of family estates through the male line must never be broken. In another cause the following April, Mackenzie v. Mackenzie, he expeditiously took up the defence of a male heir whose estate was put at risk by a father who wished to break an entail in order to provide for the children of his second wife. He composed his defence of entails for this cause in the library at Auchinleck, 'to inspire you with noble ideas of antiquity of family'. He stated bluntly that entails preserve ancient families which are 'like beams in the constitution' maintaining the freedoms of the people from 'tyrannical encroachments'. They also ensure the happiness of society by perpetuating 'just subordination'. Within two years, events would painfully test his commitment to this principle when he crossed swords with his father over the entail at Auchinleck.[33]

In the meantime, he was also retained in his first criminal cause. In September, John Reid, a farmer, had been jailed in Glasgow, accused of stealing one hundred and twenty sheep from a Peebleshire farm and driving them to Glasgow to be slaughtered. A guilty verdict for this crime would almost certainly lead to hanging. Reid, a rough-and-ready sort of character, admitted to Boswell that he had stolen a few sheep in the past, but not this time. Someone had commissioned him to sell these sheep in Glasgow, he insisted. For some reason Boswell believed him and threw his heart and soul into the cause. First, he cunningly managed to delay the trial by having it moved to Edinburgh, with the argument that Reid's bad reputation in Glasgow would not permit a fair trial there. In Edinburgh, he visited the prisoner in the Tolbooth, talked to him frequently to ferret out the truth, supplied him with clothes, and even provided him with some religious solace. In November Reid himself thought he had no chance at all – a new charge that he had stolen twenty or so other sheep had been added to the original one – and tried to persuade Boswell to plead for the mercy of transportation. Boswell would have none of this. In mid-December he pleaded the cause in front of the Court of Justiciary and won a verdict of 'Not Proven', tantamount to 'Not Guilty'. It was a spectacular triumph for him in the face of seemingly incontrovertible evidence.[34]

Sir Alexander was overjoyed. 'If you go on this way you will have all the world at your knocker daily.' Even the grave Pringle applauded him: 'If you continue to give application you will soon get the start of all our young men in the Parliament House, and will give the tone for a new eloquence very different from what prevailed there in my time.' One of the factors that gave him an advantage, Pringle thought, was his 'possessing the English and the accent in a greater degree than any of your rivals, and a turn for expressing yourself in a clear and energetic manner, without those hyperbolical modes of speech that were introduced long ago, and were still kept up during my youth, and which slipped from the bar to the tea tables at Edinburgh'. Pringle also told him that, at this rate, in a year or two his father would look on him no longer as a 'boy' but 'seek to communicate to you all his most secret affairs'.[35]

In early May 1767, Boswell accompanied his father on the southern Justiciary Circuit. He was plagued at the start with the first attack of 'feverish' hypochondria in many months, induced by the tedious prospect of a couple of weeks on the road with his father, learning circuit court business. Their first stop was Dumfries, where the boredom of trivial socializing was excruciating. When they arrived in Ayr, things improved because Boswell was asked to defend several Ayrshire men who had incited the starving people of Garliestoun, Wigtown, Whithorn, Newton Stewart, and Stewarton to riot. The riots had broken out because merchants were selling inexpensive meal for higher prices in distant markets instead of offering it locally at reasonable rates. Rioters had seized the grain and sold it to the locals at fair prices. Boswell identified with the hungry tenants and the townspeople whom he felt were not shielded adequately from the vagaries of the market by landowners. He succeeded in obtaining a 'Not Proven' verdict for most of the rioters and walked away with 'a handsome fee of six guineas'.[36]

The Reid cause and his defence of the rioters illustrate two defining qualities in the young advocate: his tendency to involve himself personally in causes and an instinct to support the underdog. Both landed him in considerable trouble throughout his career. A few of the judges in the Reid cause, including his father, disapproved of his habit of 'strongly protesting' the innocence of his clients. This was precisely what Lord Hailes had warned him not to do. But Boswell continued to develop emotional ties with his clients, as in the defence of Robert Hay, a young soldier accused of assault and robbery, potentially a capital offence. Boswell pleaded for him without success, painting a pitiful picture of him as 'the favourite child of an old and distressed mother ... whose grey hairs must be brought with sorrow to the grave should her unfortunate son be condemned'. The jury unanimously found Hay guilty but recommended against hanging. Boswell knew, however, that the judges would not be inclined to show mercy since Hay had at first concealed the identity of his accomplice. So he sent a petition directly to the King, explaining the crime and begging transportation for Hay. It did no good and the judges did indeed sentence 'poor Hay' to hanging. Distraught, Boswell visited him in prison several times, unable to shut the door on the cause. For days after the execution on 25 March, which he attended, he had nightmares and recurring fears of ghosts.[37]

He was still thinking about Hay a year later when he unsuccessfully defended the forger John Raybould: 'The clanking of the iron-room door was terrible. I found him very composed. I sat by him an hour and a half by the light of a dim farthing candle.' Boswell spoke to Raybould of religion, told him not to fear, even got the condemned man to laugh heartily with him. For the execution, gloomily, he secured a place at a nearby merchant's window where he could study the criminal closely, just as in London the following month he was inexorably drawn to Tyburn for the hanging of an attorney for forgery. He wrote in his journal, 'The Abbé du Bos ingeniously shows that we have all a strong desire of having our passions moved, and the interesting scene of a man with death before his eyes cannot but move us greatly.' But the after-effects were always depressing and not infrequently drove him to prostitutes, as they did on this occasion.[38]

This capacity for fellow-feeling, for entering into the misery of his clients and the condemned, was a kind of emotional communion with the economically disadvantaged or socially rejected. It was also a mild form of rebellion. Boswell had no choice but to close ranks with, and be a spokesman for, the oppressive Scots legal establishment in order to have a career, but in this way he could play the turncoat by becoming the people's advocate. The same sort of libertarian impulse against authority had fired him on behalf of the Corsicans and tempted him into Wilkes's company. It was also a way of rebelling against his father.

7

While Boswell declined to use his literary skills in the dull service of the legal profession, it was another matter to write as a propagandist on behalf of particular clients. This was risky, of course, if it was found to be in contempt of court. A sensational opportunity to publicize a cause, one that fitted his talents like a glove, arose in February 1767 when Sir Adam Fergusson summed up the Douglas cause, that had been simmering since 1762, in a memorial or brief for the Court of Session.

The Douglas cause has been described as the most important civil trial in eighteenth-century Scotland. Its outlines are simple and dramatic. Archibald, Duke of Douglas, died in 1761 without an heir. Thirteen years earlier his sister Lady Jane Douglas had broadcast that she had given birth to twins in Paris by Colonel John Stewart whom she married in 1746. One had died, but she claimed that the other, Archibald, was the legal heir to the Douglas estates – legal, that is, if he was indeed her son. Casting aside the name Stewart in favour of Douglas, Archibald had taken possession of the Douglas estates, but guardians and lawyers for James George, the seventh Duke of Hamilton, claiming the estates for him, argued that Douglas was a fraud. They alleged that the twins were abducted French babies, the children of a glass manufacturer and rope-dancer. Whether a woman of fifty in the 1740s could plausibly give birth to twins was not the issue so much as the lack of reliable witnesses of the births. Lady Jane herself had died in 1753 and her husband was also dead. The presiding French surgeon, dead too by the time the cause came to trial, purportedly wrote four letters confirming the births, but in such poor French that the suspicion arose that they had been forged by Colonel Stewart. One important witness to the birth could not be found; another, a companion of Lady Jane's, was suspect.

Boswell entered the lists as a propagandist, not an advocate. He passionately believed that the spectacle of a great duke turned out of his estate threatened family stability, 'filiation' (to use his word), and the principles of established inheritance. Later he wrote that the cause had shaken 'the sacred security of *birth-right* in Scotland to its foundation'; had it occurred before the Union, it 'would have left the great fortress of honours and of property in ruins'. It is almost irrelevant to ask whether, on the evidence, he thought the Duke of Hamilton or the Duke of Douglas had the better claim. It was enough for him that Douglas was the Duke; it was too late and disruptive to contest this. A verdict in favour of Hamilton would send all the wrong messages. In verse and prose, he would 'touch the heart and rouse the parental and sympathetic feelings'.[39]

In February he dashed off two ballads in sprightly Scots dialect. One of them, attacking Fergusson's brief to the Court of Session on behalf of the Hamilton party, he showed to Hailes who replied, 'Very witty, but put it in the fire; you'll make yourself enemies.' This 'frightened' him momentarily, but as Hume and others liked it and saw no venom in it, he went ahead and published it in the *Scots Magazine* for March. He went further, in good voice and with the '*vivida vis* [lively force] of Wilkes' singing it in Parliament House 'with a circle around you'. He composed the other ballad, celebrating Douglas, on horseback one day in May while riding with his father to Ayr; it appeared as a two-page broadside, *The Douglas Cause.*[40]

The more colourful success was *Dorando, A Spanish Tale*, a fifty-page allegorical prose romance set in Spain with characters representing the various players in the Douglas drama. It was an audacious distortion of the facts designed to whip up public opinion in favour of Douglas. Boswell dictated it with astonishing speed to James Brown, his clerk, and a couple of weeks later it was in proof, to be printed anonymously in May by the Foulis brothers, and published on 15 June in both Scotland and London, just one month before the Justiciary Court ruled in the cause. Within a month it was into a third edition.[41]

Not many readers were fooled by the thinly disguised allegory, but it was a clever move on Boswell's part because it protected him and whoever published it (including the newspapers which carried extracts) from prosecution for blatant contempt of court. *Dorando* influenced Scottish

public opinion in favour of Douglas, especially the resounding conclusion when, after Prince Dorando proves he is the rightful heir in the
province of Andalucia, an 'illustrious grandee' (alias Boswell) stands up
in the assembly in Madrid and delivers a peroration against threats to
feudal succession within families:

> It is a question of the most public nature – in the event of which every thing
> that is dear and valuable to humanity is concerned. What is Spain? What is
> our country? It is not the valleys, though ever so gay. It is not the fields,
> though ever so rich, that attach us to our native land. No. It is our family. It
> is our wives. It is our children. And what have we before us? A daring attempt
> to render our children uncertain. If adulterers have been thought worthy of
> death, what punishment do those deserve, who would introduce what is still
> more dangerous to society?[42]

He was uninterested in concealing his authorship, dropping enough
hints here and there to put anyone paying attention in the know. On 26
June, for example, he anonymously reviewed *Dorando* in the *Edinburgh
Advertiser*, dismissing rumours of the author's identity with: 'nor, because
Dorando is the name of a noble family at Genoa, would we ascribe it to
anyone connected with CORSICA.' The Court of Session did not look
kindly on this sort of sensational interference in the process of law and
prosecuted four Edinburgh newspapers for it. Whereupon, in an act that
has been described among the most impudent in a life 'not unremarkable
for impudent actions', Boswell served as counsel for a couple of the
papers, arguing in effect in defence of his own contempt of court. The
proprietors managed to escape with a warning.[43]

When the Douglas cause came to be judged in the Court of Session
in July, after twenty-one days of pleading the judges were evenly divided,
leaving Dundas to cast the deciding vote against Douglas. 'I suppose
Boswell is still raging about it,' Andrew Erskine wrote to Grange in
August.[44] The cause was appealed immediately to the House of Lords
which delayed a decision until March 1769.

In the meantime, Boswell prepared to mount a new publication
campaign, a flood of propaganda castigating the Scottish judgement and
championing the Douglasites. Since the cause had now been removed to
the London arena, he targeted that audience. In the next twenty-one
months, he published over twenty-five pieces in eight newspapers. When
Dundas, irate by now, prosecuted the magazines in July for contempt of
court, Boswell again defended a few of them. On 24 November he went

further, publishing *The Essence of the Douglas Cause*, a distillation of the thousands of pages of court proceedings into a cogent pamphlet of eighty pages that even the casual reader could understand – all angled in Douglas's favour. Then four days later, perhaps with another editor's help, came *Letters of Lady Jane Douglas*, again a deception since Boswell selected letters, or fragments of letters, projecting the integrity and pathos of Lady Jane's character and situation.[45]

Not content with shaping public opinion, the following May on a visit to London he found his way to the nerve centre of the Douglas appeal, the Scotsman William Murray, Lord Mansfield, Lord Chief Justice of the King's Bench and the most powerful legal figure in Britain. Mansfield (along with the Lord Chancellor, Charles Camden) was one of the two law lords who might speak to the appeal when it came before the House. Boswell's purpose in calling on him was to gauge where he stood and argue on Douglas's side. He was, in effect, interfering with the legal process. Their conversation is one of the most enticing he ever recorded in the journal,[46] as we see him inching ever closer to the issue and staking out his ground – an amazing (and risky) effort for an advocate with less than two years' experience.

When he made a move to leave, Mansfield stopped him: 'Sit still, Mr Boswell.' He wanted to hear more. That was his cue, Boswell wrote, to do 'all the good I could'. The Hamilton judges, he continued, were 'obnoxious' to argue against the existence of any laws protecting 'filiation'. ' "My Lord, when you thus deny a man the great privilege of filiation, you are taking the very pavement from under his feet. You are depriving him of half his cause." MANSFIELD: "You are so." ... BOSWELL: "I asked my father where I was born. He mentioned a house. I asked an old woman who was in the house at the birth, and she said another house. My Lord, if my birth had been scrutinized, my father and this old woman would have been declared perjured, as contradicting one another." MANSFIELD: "Very true." '

When it came to the vote by the House of Lords on 27 February, both Mansfield and Camden spoke for Douglas and the Court of Session ruling was expeditiously overturned without a division. There were bonfires and riots in the streets when the news reached Edinburgh on the night of 2 December. The rioters ordered all the judges, regardless of how they had voted, to put lights in their windows; those who failed to do so were seen as anti-Douglasites and had their windows broken. The word soon spread, not least because he bragged about it everywhere he went, that Boswell, caught up in the excitement, headed the mob in an orgy of celebration. John Ramsay of Ochtertyre, on good evidence, described Boswell's actions:

> In the Douglas cause he was keen and intemperate to a degree of absurdity ... on hearing that the House of Peers had reversed the decision of the Court of Session, [he] headed the mob which broke the judges' windows, and insulted them in the most licentious manner. His behaviour on that occasion savoured so much of insanity, that it was generally imputed to his Dutch blood.

Since his father, who had voted for Douglas, showed solidarity with Dundas (who was almost mauled at his home) and the other judges by not lighting a candle, Boswell threw a rock through his window, too. Ramsay said that Lord Auchinleck pleaded with the Lord President to put his son in gaol. Dundas did not, in deference to his father, but Boswell was made to explain himself to the Sheriff. He was able to escape public censure by fudging the facts so as to conceal what plans had been hatched when he joined the rioters at the Cross Inn.[47]

Hailes, whose windows were also broken and who knew that Boswell was at the head of the mob, was furious. It was one of the greatest insults he had ever suffered, he told him. Over the next two years he wrote his protégé only three rather cold letters. Dempster, however, joked about it. And Lord Marischal for some reason told Boswell he was glad he had broken his father's windows – 'Bravo, Bravissimo!'. But Boswell had seriously diminished himself in his father's estimation.[48]

FOURTEEN

'Happy as an Unmarried Man Can Be'

I

Boswell described himself during the years between his return from the Continent and his marriage in 1769 as 'happy as an unmarried man can be'. At twenty-six he was a successful advocate and author, definitely the up-and-coming young man. But he needed an anchor. On his way to London in March 1768, thoughts of Mary, an Edinburgh prostitute he had just met, set him thinking about himself:

> How strange this is! the author of the *Account of Corsica* the sport of a frivolous passion. Shall my mind ever be all solid and rational? Yes. A room which is hung with the slightest chintz and gaudiest paper may by and by be hung with substantial velvet or even thick arras hangings with Scripture stories wrought upon them. My walls are good, so they will bear any sort of hangings. Often they have been substantially hung. But as yet I have changed my furniture as whim suggested.

When Mary began to fade two days later, 'I thought of marriage and was determined to have a good match, as I was become so agreeable and so happy a man. Miss Bosville my Yorkshire beauty, Mademoiselle de Zuylen my Utrecht *bel esprit* and friend, were both before me. Yet still I had no determined purpose.'[1]

In spite of his chronic musing over this or that woman as a potential wife, Boswell did not have that many serious candidates from which to choose. Other than Zélide there were only two; and one of these was something of a last-minute thought. However, pressure on him was building from his father and older friends to get married and be done with it. He knew his happiness depended on finding the right wife, but he did not make a determined effort to seek one until the summer of 1767.

In the meantime, he still had to feed his libido and thee was little place for love in his voracious sexual appetite. Indeed, one of the factors delaying his marriage was his inability to see sex and love as mutually enhancing. Marriage would be a way to balance the equation, to achieve love, peace, and equanimity, even to inject a badly needed infusion of capital into Auchinleck. He might be lucky enough to find a wife who could respond adequately to the demands of his sexuality, but knowing himself he thought the odds were against it. A prospective wife's finances and love were more important to him than her sexual performance, although he wanted an attractive bride.

This division between sex and love did not weigh on him too much before marriage. The moment he returned to Auchinleck in March 1766, for example, he fell in love with the gardener's daughter, a virgin, who in his absence had grown into a beautiful girl with 'the most amiable face' and 'the prettiest foot and ankle'. Because in principle he was against seducing innocent virgins – and always would be – he had the piquant idea of marrying her: 'Only think of the proud Boswell,' he wrote to Temple, 'with all that you know of him, the fervent adorer of a country girl of three and twenty. I rave about her. I was never so much in love as I am now. My fancy is quite inflamed. It riots in extravagance.' He knew that ten days after possessing her she would become 'insipid' to him, but still he dreamed of 'delightful nuptials'. What made her more attractive was her pedigree as his childhood companion, when they used to play on the sunny banks of Lugar Water. Now he kissed her hand and told her she was beautiful. They exchanged secret notes by placing them under the cloth on his table. She allowed him to cut off a lock of her hair, on which he doted. Was not this yet another strange scene in the 'play of his life'? Must some mere unromantic schoolmaster or dolt of a farmer without a 'soul' enjoy her? Could this 'dear delirium' last for a lifetime?[2]

2

Certainly not, and a visit to the Moffat waters in May quickly helped him to get the gardener's daughter out of his mind. While thinking as much as ever of Zélide, whom he yet 'may perhaps take up', he met a Mrs Dodds, a young pretty woman of his own class whose husband had left her. This was ideal: Mrs Dodds was safe from disease, not interested in marriage, and 'at full liberty'. She had raven-black hair and was 'paradisial in bed'. The perfect mistress. He seems to have fallen genuinely in love with her. When he returned to Edinburgh, she followed and took lodgings to be near him. 'Nothing so convenient as an eloped wife,' Temple remarked. 'How are you so lucky in mistresses?' he wondered.[3]

Boswell was uneasy about the affair but rationalized it on the grounds that her husband was living with another woman:

> There is a baseness in all deceit which my soul is virtuous enough ever to abhor, and therefore I look with horror upon adultery. But my amiable mistress is no longer bound to him who was her husband. He has used her shockingly ill . . . Is she not then free? She is.

The average eighteenth-century gentleman felt little compunction about taking a mistress. It would appear that Boswell did. 'You say well that I find mistresses wherever I am,' he wrote to Temple. 'But I am a sad dupe, a perfect Don Quixote'.[4]

The affair was more complicated than he thought it would be. Where, for example, could he find a secret but convenient love-nest? At first he paid for her lodgings, 'the rendezvous of our amours'. By February he decided on a separate house for her in Borthwick's Close, but perhaps thinking that was too close to the centre of things, she chose another. 'Furnishing a house and maintaining her with a maid will cost me a great deal of money,' he complained. And was he not in effect creating there 'a family' for himself with his 'sweet little mistress'? The arrangement was free of the threats of 'desperate matrimony' but somehow it also smacked too much of marriage or a 'settled plan of licentiousness'.[5]

Then when she told him about her former 'intrigues', he agonized over them:

> How am I tormented because my charmer has formerly loved others? I am disgusted to think of it. My lively imagination often represents her former lovers in actual enjoyment of her. My desire fails, I am unfit for love. Besides she is illbred, quite a rompish girl. She debases my dignity. She has no refinement. But she is very handsome, very lively and admirably formed for amorous dalliance.

Erskine, Grange, brother David, and Temple all implored him to drop her. He wanted to, but she was his Circe. When he confessed that hearing about her past lovers pained him, 'she said I should not mind her faults before I knew her, since her conduct was now most circumspect'. She confessed to him that she loved him more than she had ever loved her husband, adding that as she did not censure him for his former 'follies', they were on an equal footing. 'I embraced her with transport.' He remained her 'slave'.[6]

With his inimitable relish for incongruities, for juxtaposing the beautiful with the grotesque, Boswell describes in his journal how on the very evening of this conversation with Mrs Dodds, he succumbed to a prostitute. It was at about this time that he also began to drink too much, to dissolve the pressures of the tedious business of the law and melt away the icy rigidity of sharing a house with his father. At a supper party he gave for friends with whom he had made a wager of a guinea that he would not get the clap on his travels – a wager he admitted he had lost – he became so hopelessly drunk that on the way home he staggered into 'a low house in one of the alleys in Edinburgh where I knew a common girl lodged, and like a brute as I was I lay all night with her'. The next morning he already showed signs of his sixth infection, though the suddenness suggested not gonorrhoea but either a recrudescence of an old infection or (more likely) a mild ('nonspecific') form of urethritis aggravated by sexual contact. It was a good thing for Mrs Dodds that the symptoms did show themselves, else he 'might have polluted her sweet body'. Honest as he was about such things, he told her about his problem immediately, lying down and kissing her feet as he confessed. She forgave him readily and appealed to him to give up drink altogether.[7]

By 17 April (five painful weeks later) he was free of the infection, but in June he did exactly the same thing, with worse results, spending the night at a brothel with a whore – 'a whore worthy of Boswell if Boswell must have a whore' – after an evening of heavy drinking at a bachelor party, toasting the health of one of his marital prospects. This time the disease took a month to appear so he did not interrupt his sexual relations with Mrs Dodds. He was all gloom when he realized that he must surely have infected her. She was safe, however. Not until early October, nine painful weeks later, did he recover. 'Your libation to Bacchus is excusable enough,' Temple chided him, 'but you might have omitted the sacrifice to Venus.' These two infections opened up a new pattern of liquor and sex that would bedevil him for years.[8]

Mrs Dodds may have remained supportive to Boswell despite these lapses of drinking and whoring because, in April, she discovered she was pregnant by him. He was 'half delighted to obtain what I had wished, and half vexed to think of the expense'. 'O world, world', more exactly conveyed his dismay, but as in the case of his first illegitimate child, he behaved with humour and generosity. As both he and Mrs Dodds had dark complexions, he joked, the child must inevitably be called 'Edward, the Black Prince'.[9]

He might joke about it, but his father would not have thought this reckless indiscretion at all funny, and he must have known about it as Boswell was far from tight-lipped. He had even obtained Lord Marischal's permission to name a son after him. Marischal replied sportively that the boy should become a Spaniard since illegitimate children in that country have more status and inherit as much as legitimate ones. Thinking the baby already born, Marischal wrote again on 12 September with a streak of sarcasm flavoured with the ridiculous: 'Bonny wark, Colonel, getting the lassys wi bairns, and worse to your sel ... what's done is done; get well; take care of Keith Boswell; who in time I hope shall become a Nabob.'[10] Lord Auchinleck also knew about his son's infections. Now Boswell's relations with his father began to worsen significantly. Sex, illegitimate children, Corsica, Douglas, the drinking – it was all becoming unbearable.

A daughter, Sally, not a son, was born in December. 'My black friend has brought me the finest little girl I ever saw ... It is healthy and strong. I take the greatest care of the mother, but shall have her no more in keeping.' He paid all the expenses of the birth, but he would 'keep' Mrs Dodds no longer because, by this time, he had ceased to love her and had been seeking out prostitutes regularly in the latter stages of her pregnancy. He was also drinking more heavily and had his third gon-orrhoeal infection of the year. Judging himself healthy in late January 1768, he picked up with Mrs Dodds again but only briefly as he was now deep into the courtship of his main marital prospect and 'Princess', Catherine Blair of Adamton. The last we hear of Mrs Dodds is in June, so it may be assumed that Sally died during her first year.[11]

3

Boswell had not yet demonstrated that he was a good judge of women, but in singling out the eighteen-year-old Catherine Blair he seemed at last to be acting with circumspection. The heiress of the estate of Adamton, just a two-hour ride from Auchinleck, Catherine Blair had her own income of two to three hundred pounds a year. From the start, he called her (somewhat tongue-in-cheek) 'the Heiress' or 'the Princess'. His father, whose ward she had been, and the other elders favoured the match for that reason. She was attractive enough, though not a great beauty like Elizabeth Bosville. There is little hint of passion in his first description of her as she graced the Boswell pew in St Giles's in March 1767: 'a genteel person, an agreeable face, of a good family, sensible, good-tempered, cheerful, pious.' None the less, though rather unromantic and candid, she was prudent and she was Scottish. As soon as he got over his venereal disorder in June, he began to court her. The courtship lasted eight months.[12]

The most attractive fact about Boswell to a young woman like Catherine Blair was not his person, profession, or literary character, but his estate. He had told himself that his *Account of Corsica* would make him more impressive to a woman hunting for a husband, but it had had no such effect. Land and money were what counted and he knew it. To boost his chances, therefore, as well as to increase his family's status and influence, he purchased the small upland Dalblair estate for £2,400 at auction in April, beautifully romantic acreage in the wild vale of Glenmuir bordering the Auchinleck estates about ten miles to the east. The views from it were exquisite, of Ben Lomond and the Galloway hills, and beyond them the islands of Jura and Islay. The hitch was that to buy it Boswell incurred a debt that for years hung around his neck like an albatross.[13]

Everything seemed full of promise when one day in late May of 1767 Catherine and her mother paid a visit to Auchinleck. For four days the two were shown the sacred spots invested with Boswellian magic and folklore: castles, groves, grotto, the river up to dreamy Broomholm, caves, avenues, and 'gothic' bridge. In spite of a little return of 'gloom' and some 'free and rampageneous' lapses in his talk, everything seemed to go well. Amid the 'romantic groves' he 'adored her like a divinity', and his father was 'very desirous' that they should marry. Catherine looked 'quite at home' there. Her picture would be an ornament in the gallery. By 22 June he thought he had decided she would be his, but he did not tell her so. He wanted Temple, who was planning a visit to Auchinleck, to meet his 'bride' first.[14]

Temple came at the end of the month. They relived their old salad days as students in Edinburgh and went out to Adamton for a visit. Temple was impressed with Catherine, but during their visit they met the 'Nabob', the wealthy William Fullarton, on a visit home from India, who seemed himself to be courting the 'Heiress'. What if, Boswell mused, 'so good a bird in the hand has made the Heiress quit the uncertain prospect of catching the bird on the bush?' Temple had his own preoccupations, like his tentative marriage to Anne Stow in early August – 'Do I repent? God knows; I'll tell you a twelvemonth hence' – but he still found time to be his friend's 'principal minister in forwarding the alliance'.[15]

When no encouraging words had come from Adamton by late August, Temple saw which way the wind blew: 'the Nabob with bended knee has offered her his crown, and she is in doubt whether to accept of it.' He advised Boswell for once to be explicit: 'Tell her immediately you love her, will marry her, or be content to lose her.' This was good advice but it was not Boswell's way. He preferred paying court to a phantom of his imagination's delight than to a real woman who might actually accept him. There was nothing complicated about this woman of sense and prudence, Temple reminded him. 'We must not look for wit and humour indeed, but for simplicity and unaffected freedom.' Finally, Boswell received an encouraging letter from her six weeks after his and Temple's visit. All was well now between 'the prince of Auchinleck and his fair neighbouring princess'. But was the prince worthy? 'All my objections arise from my own faults. Tell me, can I honestly ask so fine a woman to risk her happiness with a man of my character?' Could such a woman put up with his sexual antics? Any objective witness would have to say no, and he knew it.[16]

He wrote but received no answer. He went to see her again at Adamton. There was a quarrel, apparently about his intentions. She denied any connection with the Nabob. The course of this love was not running smoothly, largely because there was no love on either side. Should the 'proud Boswell' do any more to help the courtship along? 'I have not yet found out that I was to blame.' He asked for a lock of hair, but she refused. Then on 8 November he had had enough: 'she is cunning and sees my weakness. But I now see her.' He had discovered 'the snake' before it was too late: 'I should have been ruined had I made such a woman my wife.' Luckily, he heard in Ayr that Catherine had the reputation of 'a d–ned jilt'. 'After this, I shall be upon my guard against ever indulging the least fondness for a *Scots lass*.'[17]

The next day he changed his mind – 'I love her, Temple, with my whole heart' – although she was certainly difficult to decipher, one day encouraging, the next distant and reserved. Then, in late December, Catherine's cousin told him that this was only because Boswell was so noncommittal, dishonourably keeping himself 'free' while engaging her affections. The Nabob's hand had been refused so all he had to do was to declare himself.[18]

He sought her out the next day in Edinburgh and declared his love, but he still did not propose. Now, he asked her, do you have 'any particular liking for me'? ' "I really", said she, "have no particular liking for you. I like many people as well as you." ' Writing to Temple on 24 December, he reconstructed their exchange in his best journal manner. Was it possible she could love him?

> PRINCESS: 'I don't know what is possible' ... BOSWELL: 'What would you have me do?' PRINCESS: 'I really don't know what you should do.' ... BOSWELL: 'If you should happen to love me, will you own it?' PRINCESS: 'Yes.' ... BOSWELL: 'Well, you are very good' (often squeezing and kissing her fine hand, while she looked at me with those beautiful black eyes).

Although she added, 'I wish I liked you as well as I do Auchinleck', he felt satisfied after an hour-and-a-half of that. The next day she was indifferent again and he became angry. Four hours at tea with her and her mother left him no wiser. This was the same week that he contracted another (mild) case of gonorrhoea – 'amidst all this love I have been wild as ever' – and that he became a father for the second time.[19]

Temple was unsympathetic: 'The great Baron, the friend of Rousseau and Voltaire, the companion of Paoli, the author of that immortal work the Account of Corsica, is dwindled into a whining, fawning lover, the slave of a fair hand and a pair of black eyes.' A few weeks later, Boswell ran into the Nabob, who assured him that he, too, had shivered at Catherine's coldness. Not very gallantly, they plotted to confront her one after the other. Offended by this collusion, which she had little trouble detecting, she told them both that she had accepted another man. Later, the two of them struck up a friendship and agreed that she was nothing but a coquette but that if she had loved anyone, it was Boswell – 'as much as a woman could love a man'. The real culprit, they agreed, was the 'wary mother' who spearheaded the effort to find a man with more than a thousand pounds per year, like 'salmon fishing'. The Nabob concluded: 'I am positive you are the fish, and [other suitors are] only a mock salmon to force you to jump more expeditiously at the bait.' He was wrong. She eventually married Sir William Maxwell of Monreith. Pringle was right.[20]

A postscript to Boswell's failure to win Catherine Blair was provided by her 'wary mother' who later told him that Catherine was ready to accept him but that he had made 'such a joke of *my love for the Heiress* in every company that she was piqued and did not believe that I had any serious intentions'.[21] By then he was on to a different scent.

4

Throughout his courtship of her, Catherine Blair had competition. Elizabeth Bosville's extraordinary beauty fascinated Boswell, her father Godfrey was a good friend, and the Bosvilles had a wealthy estate. But he could never see her leaving her beloved Yorkshire hills for the remoter charms of Auchinleck. She was 'too fine for this northern air'. Lord Eglinton agreed, less delicately adapting a Highland saying: 'A cow fed in fine Lowland parks was unco bonny, but turned lean and scabbed when she was turned out to the wild hills.'[22] Not surprisingly Elizabeth faded from the picture and in March 1768 accepted Sir Alexander Macdonald of Skye.

Zélide was also still haunting Boswell. What Catherine Blair lacked in imagination, Zélide possessed in abundance. Moreover, she had money. Zélide remained interested in him, but almost as a bemused spectator. In March 1767 he was astonished to hear that she had just been in London without telling him. Sir John Pringle attended her as her physician, after which he wrote to Lord Auchinleck, 'She has too much vivacity. She talks of your son without either resentment or attachment.' 'I am well rid of her,' Boswell concluded.[23]

However, out of the blue she wrote to him in October, in English, 'an old flame is easily rekindled.' Encouraged, he could not resist testing the waters once more. He replied on 10 January 1768, professing his love all over again but not going so far as to propose marriage. Unbelievably, he also confided in her his perplexing courtship of Catherine Blair and asked for her advice.[24]

Sadly, both these letters have been lost, but her response on 16 February is wonderfully feminine, intelligent, and exasperated. She showed that she understood Boswell better than any other woman he had known:

> The fact is you do not love conclusions; you love problems which can never be solved. The debate you have been conducting for so long concerning our fate if we were married is the proof of this taste of yours ... Aside from the fact that I am not clever enough to decide it, I take little pleasure in discussing so idle a question. I do not know your Scotland. On the map it appears to

me a little out of the world ... I have seen it produce decidedly despotic husbands and humble, simple wives who blushed and looked at their lords before opening their mouths ... But why should I decide ... I leave it to you for your amusement. Allow me to remark that you certainly take your time for everything. You waited to fall in love with me until you were in the island of Corsica; and to tell me so, you waited until you were in love with another woman and had spoke to her of marriage.

In spite of all this, she still loved his 'imagination' which often prompted him to say foolish things. But what harm in that? 'I read your belated endearments with pleasure, with a smile ... It seems to me that you interest me and belong to me a little more because of that than if you had always been my cold and philosophic friend.'[25]

A few days later, he composed for Zélide a truthful and beautifully written account of their spasmodic courtship since 1764. For the first time he divulged his hypochondria. He also confessed his licentiousness, that his father and Pringle opposed a match with her, that entering the law had made him too rational and forgetful of her, that he had decided the safe choice would be a 'good home-bred heiress, with health and common sense instead of genius and accomplishments', and that recently the Rev. Robert Brown had arrived in Scotland and stirred up his feelings for her all over again so that he now could kick himself for wasting so much time.[26]

She wanted him to propose but instead he asked for her advice about what they should do. As she had requested a copy of the *Account of Corsica* as well as *The Essence of Douglas* with the intention of translating them into French, he enclosed both books and settled back to wait for her next letter.

No response from her survives. All we know is that she did not give him any advice except on his book. She had a contract with a publisher for the translation but needed to make some changes and cuts. She asked for his permission, he refused point blank, and that was the end not only of the contract but also of their relationship, as she explained to D'Hermenches: 'The author, although he had at the moment *almost* made up his mind to marry me if I would have him, was not willing to sacrifice a syllable of his book to my taste. I wrote to him that I was firmly decided never to marry him, and I have abandoned the translation.' She had unknowingly trespassed into the one area in which he would brook no intrusion. From her point of view, this was an example of that Scots male despotism of which she wanted no part.[27]

It is generally agreed that Boswell was lucky not to have married Zélide, that marriage to her would have been a constant battle which he would have lost most of the time. She might not have accepted him, of course, but the letters rather suggest otherwise, that she was only waiting for him to ask. But, as with Catherine Blair, he seemed incapable of doing so. In both cases, he seems to have wanted his suit to fail. Catherine would have brought him money but little love. Zélide offered money, vitality, intellectual stimulation, love, variety, humour, respect. He opted for neither woman, saying that his prudence had saved him, but his 'salvation' was really due to his irresolution. One ironic fact is plain: his father was less pleased with the choice that he did eventually make than he would have been with Zélide.

FIFTEEN

'The Rage for Matrimony'

I

As soon as the Court of Session broke for the spring recess in March Boswell was off to London, his first visit in two years, to see Dr Johnson, Goldsmith and Garrick, and bask in the afterglow of the *Account of Corsica*. He heralded his arrival with his own notices in the *London Chronicle*, such as the one on 24 March: 'Yesterday James Boswell, Esquire, arrived from Scotland at his apartments in Half Moon Street, Piccadilly.'

Soon afterwards, 'I had a neat little lass *in armour*, at a tavern in the Strand.' After eight venereal infections, he was not going to be careless about 'armour', but condoms were hard to come by – the only place to get them, coincidentally, was at a Mrs Phillips' shop in Half Moon Street, near where he was lodging. He knew his time as a bachelor was nearing its end and he was going to make good use of it.[1]

When Boswell first arrived in London, Johnson was in Oxford staying with his good friend Robert Chambers, Principal of New Inn Hall and Vinerian Professor of Law. Boswell followed him there on the 26th. Their delayed meeting was a delicious moment for him, apprehensive as he had been about the use of his revered friend's letters in *Account of Corsica*. All was forgiven. 'He took me all in his arms and kissed me on both sides of the head.' Touched by Boswell's tracking him to New Inn Hall, Johnson was overjoyed to hear of his financial successes in the law: 'What, Bozzy? Two hundred pounds! A great deal.' They reminisced about travelling to Harwich together and the good times at the Mitre and elsewhere during that first year; and, significantly, Johnson 'renewed his promise of coming to Scotland and visiting with me some of the Western Isles'. Over the next three days their conversation ranged over a number of diverse topics: politics, the law, Scottish literature (against which Johnson 'still retained his prejudice'), and adultery, all recorded with vividness, wit and humour in his journal.[2]

Boswell was once more in his element, delighted to be free of hypochondria (even in gloomy Oxford) and holding his own not only with Johnson but also with Chambers and a number of distinguished guests. 'How different was I from what I was when I last [in February 1766] saw Mr Johnson in London, when I was still wavering and often clouded. I am now serene and steady.'

With thoughts of marriage still in his mind, Boswell brought adultery into one of their conversations. What Johnson said on the subject did not comfort him. Adultery for a man was an offence against God, Johnson proposed, but he did not thereby do a 'material' injury against his wife provided he did not insult her. 'A woman', on the other hand, 'who breaks her marriage vows is so much more criminal than a man' because she broke the peace of families and introduced 'confusion of progeny'. Boswell asked him 'if it was not hard that one deviation from chastity should so absolutely ruin a woman.' 'JOHNSON: "Why, no, Sir; the great principle which every woman is taught is to keep her legs together. When she has given up that principle, she has given up every notion of female honour and virtue, which are all included in chastity."'

After an excursion to Henley, Windsor, and Eton, which he visited reverently holding a copy of Gray's 'Ode on a Distant Prospect of Eton College' and repeating the verses aloud, Boswell left Johnson in Oxford and returned to London on the 29th where he picked up with the whores at a furious pace. Dropping off his belongings at his lodgings and not bothering to get any 'armour' from Mrs Phillips, he 'sallied' out immediately to 'rage'.

The next six pages of the journal have been torn out by some censorious hand, but Boswell's notes fill in some details: 'Wanted two [whores] like Bolingbroke. Got red-haired hussy; went to Bob Derry's, had brandy and water. She went for companion; found her not. Then once. Then home with her ... Horrid room; no fire, no curtains, dirty sheets, &c. All night; three here.' Predictably, the next morning he awoke full of shame and self-recrimination for having fallen into 'the very sink of vice'.[3] A further twenty-six pages of the journal have been ripped out, so it would appear that he remained in the 'sink of vice'.

During this London visit Boswell endured a painful operation on his ingrown toenail, a legacy of his Corsican expedition, but even more painful was his reinfection with gonorrhoea for the ninth time – it did not surprise him – one of the severest cases yet, which imprisoned him in his room in Half Moon Street for a curative period of six weeks throughout April and into May. So severe was it – from now on he was perpetually infected – that just before leaving for Edinburgh in June he made his way to St Paul's Cathedral where he vowed not to have any 'licentious connections of any kind' for six months. Pain moved him more effectively than shame. 'If there is any firmness at all in me,' he swore, 'be assured that I shall never again behave in a manner so unworthy of the friend of Paoli.'[4]

While Boswell was out of commission he was privileged to enjoy more conversations with important and famous men than in any comparable period he ever spent in London. *Corsica* had made him the man of the hour. He held court in his room to, among others, Johnson, Giuseppe Baretti (Johnson's rude friend and Club member, author of the celebrated *Account of the Manners and Customs of Italy*, whom Boswell had met in Italy), Hume (whom he now familiarly called 'David'), Garrick, the Dillys, Lord Lyttelton (who came to talk over the politics of Corsica), General James Edward Oglethorpe (the founder of the American colony of Georgia), Sir John Pringle, and Benjamin Franklin (the most famous American of them all, then living abroad, who dined with him). Franklin appeared to make little impression on him. 'I am really the *Great Man* now,' Boswell boasted to Temple. 'I give admirable dinners and good claret and the moment I go abroad again ... I set up my chariot.' This attention on his own turf was as gratifying to Boswell as any other achievement in his entire life.[5]

2

A measure of his new confidence in London, and the highlight of his last days there, was a dinner he organised at the Crown and Anchor tavern for Johnson and a galaxy of other personalities who could be relied on to provide sparkling conversation that he could later record in his journal: Johnson's friend the Rev. Dr Thomas Percy (grocer's son, scholar, Bishop of Dromore, and member of The Club) who in 1765 published his *Reliques of Ancient English Poetry*, hugely influential in establishing a taste for older English poetry; Dr John Douglas, Bishop of Carlisle; Johnson's friend Bennet Langton, an original member of the Club; William Robertson, Principal of Edinburgh University and renowned author of the *History of Scotland* (1759); Boswell's eminent literary friend Dr Hugh Blair whose *Critical Dissertation on the Poems of Ossian* Johnson held as 'cheap'; and Thomas Davies who salivated at the thought of meeting the latter two. Boswell well knew Johnson's bias against Scottish literature, so expected that the talk between them all would heat up quickly. However, the sparks flew chiefly between Johnson and the pompous Percy, not between him and Blair and Robertson who had the good sense to keep quiet. 'Well, we had good talk,' Johnson remarked the next morning, to which Boswell replied, 'Yes, Sir, you tossed and gored several persons.'[6]

The one mildly discordant note in his reunion with Johnson was the discovery that for the past two years, Johnson had been taken up by Mrs Hester Thrale, wife of a successful London brewer, Henry Thrale, whose 'charming villa' six miles out of town in Streatham he had begun to think of as his second home. According to Mrs Thrale, they had rescued Johnson from a severe attack of morbid depression, brought him to Streatham, given him his own room, and generally ministered to his needs. Boswell was more inclined to the view that Mrs Thrale was initially more interested in the cachet of having Johnson in her house. That was probably ungenerous, but it is true that Johnson held 'court' there and she, proud of her prize, liked to show him off. Boswell felt twinges of jealousy, for Mrs Thrale was in a far better position than he was to see Johnson regularly and partake of his conversation, both in Streatham and at her house in Southwark. He discovered that she was also keeping a commonplace book in which she recorded Johnson's conversation and anecdotes concerning him. Although they had not been introduced, seeing her coach waiting at Johnson's Court one day, Boswell impetuously hopped in and began talking to her – 'not I hope from impudence, but from that agreeable kind of attraction which makes one forget ceremony'. This was probably the occasion he had in mind when in the *Life of Johnson* he states that one morning in 1768 he 'had conversation enough with her to admire her talents, and to shew her that I was as Johnsonian as herself'. There is no mistaking the competitiveness in that remark.[7]

3

Boswell left London on 9 June, just three days before the Court of Session convened for the summer. Inexplicably, no journal exists between then and the following April but correspondence with Temple and Dempster supplies a few details of his marital schemes. After an unevent-

ful summer, except for a return to an adolescent vice, gambling at cards
for which he discovered 'the fever still lurking in my veins', he rode out
one day in August to see his cousins the Montgomeries fifteen miles
north at Lainshaw. His first cousin Margaret, the youngest (living)
daughter of David Montgomerie of Lainshaw, for whom he had always
cherished a soft and trusting spot in his heart, introduced him to her
beautiful Irish cousin Mary Ann Boyd who was staying for a few days.
Mary Ann was only sixteen but for her beauty Boswell dubbed her 'the
finest creature that ever was formed: *la belle Irelandaise*', 'formed like
a Grecian nymph with the sweetest countenance, full of sensibility,
accomplished, with a Dublin education'. She would make the perfect
wife, he wrote feverishly to Temple. Not insignificantly, she also would
be heiress to an estate of £1,000 per year and 'about £10,000 in ready
money'.[8]

He fell in love with Mary Ann and from morning to night spoke to
her of the magic of Auchinleck: 'I was allowed to walk a great deal with
Miss. I repeated my fervent passion to her, again and again. She was
pleased, and I could swear that her little heart beat.' He carved her initials
on a tree and cut off an ill-defended lock of her hair. He felt quite the
Sicilian swain to the youthful and unreserved Arcadian shepherdess. In
a flash she had become 'part of my very soul'. Her parents were impressed
and invited him to visit them in the spring. He promised to do so in
March. Thank goodness he had vowed celibacy at St Paul's. That would
make him more worthy of her.

When he finally made the journey to Ireland in late April he persuaded
his cousin Margaret to accompany him. The two had been companions
and friends since toddlers at Auchinleck and Lainshaw and had remained
confiding and affectionate cousins. They also shared a common bond
with the picturesque Ayrshire landscape that teemed with benign associations of youth and innocence. A favourite joke between them was to
declare their love for each other, decide to get married, and then forget
about it. 'Often have I thought of marrying her, and often told her so,'
Boswell revealed to Temple in May. 'But we talked of my wonderful
inconstancy, were merry, and perhaps in two days after the most ardent
professions to her I came and told her that I was desperately in love with
another woman.' He was her 'dear Jamie' and 'affectionate cousin'. She
was his relaxed and relaxing 'Peggie'. He was anxious and doubtful about
his mission, about whether he actually wanted to marry an Irish girl who
was scarcely a teenager, even for £10,000, and turned to Margaret for
advice. He needed her encouragement also because his father was against

the expedition, which he thought just another of his son's capers when there were plenty of eligible Scottish girls around to choose from. On the day of their departure, Lord Auchinleck walked out of the room without saying goodbye. Still, a good round sum of money might speak volumes to him, Boswell thought.[9]

As they worked their way down the south-west coast of Scotland to Portpatrick for the crossing to Donaghadee, Margaret imperceptibly took control of his mind, like sunshine moving softly across a shadowy landscape. Struggle against it as he did, almost immediately he discovered he loved her. 'I found her both by sea and land the best companion I ever saw,' he wrote to Temple the day after their five-hour sail. 'I highly value her. If ever a man had his full choice of a wife, I would have it in her.'[10] But of course he did not have a free choice. Some thought it was an impediment that she was thirty-one, two years older than him; but the real obstacle was his father, who 'would be violent against my marrying her, as she would bring neither money nor interest'. With his desire to 'aggrandize' the family, he confessed he saw it the same way. Lainshaw was a smaller and far less valuable estate than Auchinleck and financially insecure. In any case, as the youngest daughter Margaret had no fortune, nor any prospect of one except £1,000 which she had invested in an annuity. She was the proverbial poor relation.

Attractive though not beautiful, well informed though not well educated, and gracious though provincial, Margaret was worlds removed form the Yorkshire beauty Elizabeth Bosville, for example, or from Catherine Blair's brittle porcelain appeal. 'My cousin is of a fine, firm, and lively temperament, and never can be old [i.e., melancholic],' he wrote. 'She may have as many children as I wish, and from what she has already done as an aunt I am sure she would make a very good mother. Would not my children be more obliged to me for such a mother than for many thousands?' He did not fail to notice, incidentally, that although no great beauty Margaret was 'well built' – 'her person is to me the most desirable that I ever saw.' She became 'my lady'. He was tormented by his indecision. Perhaps Temple could advise him what to do.[11]

Margaret naturally read the frustration and indecision on Boswell's face but said nothing until he openly declared his love for her a couple of days after they arrived in Donaghadee. He did it, characteristically, by letting her read his joyful celebration of her in his letter to Temple. The letter was a measure of his 'soul'. She advised him not to send it. She would not get in the way; she would gently help him marry anyone who would please his father and be good for the family. This did not really help; it only 'showed me more of her excellent character'. Her perfect sincerity cannot be doubted in a situation where her conduct might easily be construed as opportunist. But she was a woman with a woman's feelings for a man she loved and who loved her. Also, less important but relevant – and it is not unkind to speculate about this – marriage to Boswell would be spectacular good fortune for her.[12]

By the time Boswell saw Mary Ann in Dublin during the second week of May, his feelings for her were stone cold, even if her money still tempted him. He later told Dempster that he was received with open arms in Dublin but could not bring himself to warm to the occasion except perhaps for some reddening of his face. The girl appeared to him as the child she was, 'the sweetest, loveliest little creature that ever was born. But so young, so childish, so much *yes* and *no*, that (between ourselves) I was ashamed of having raved so much about her.' Well he might have been. He could certainly have had her, it seems, and when he was assured of at least £500 per year he wavered, but Margaret 'hung on my *heart*'. Her mature womanhood prevailed, 'like a heathen goddess painted alfresco on the ceiling of a palace at Rome . . . compared with the delicate little Miss'. He told Sir Alexander Dick that Margaret's conversation soothed him 'like sweet milk tempers and smooths my agitated mind'; she was his 'amiable governess'.[13]

In Dublin, he was treated like a Corsican hero, wined and dined, all 'very flattering to the blood of Auchinleck'.[14] Mary Ann was neglected and although his excuse was that he must be tentative because his father had not approved of the visit, the family was offended. They would have been even more so if they had known that he visited a brothel or two in the city. After a few excursions to country houses in the region, and then a trek up to see Lough Neach and the Giant's Causeway, he and Margaret left Ireland on 7 June.

4

After seeing Margaret home to Lainshaw, Boswell returned to his father in Edinburgh. Instead of the good news of the expected wife and fortune, he was full of Margaret. A less jubilant reception cannot easily be imagined. The conversation was 'slow and rather dry' and he was shortly left alone in his room to muse on 'my lady'. He had a lot of explaining to do, not just to his father but to all manner of people at Parliament House the following day. Teasingly asked where his heiress was, he laughed them off nervously with, 'My time's not come' or 'Aha, I'm just as I was'. Erskine confronted him at the Cross Inn and suggested that the only reason he had taken his cousin with him was to compare her with Mary Ann 'and take the one I liked best'.[15]

The next three months were an unhappy return to the old routine. Living in the house with his father and brother John (who was now in residence), his spirits sank immediately. His now regular journal entries, which he resumed with the start of the summer term of the Court of Session, are frequently in images of flatness, uneasiness, and gloom.[16] The 'varnish of life' was off. One reason was news of the Corsicans' defeat by the French and Paoli's flight from the island. The loss of Corsica was more than a political disappointment for Boswell; it marked the loss of his youthful enthusiasms and ideals. Another reason for his gloom was that his legal duties seemed anticlimactic after the distractions of London and there was little business around. Thoughts of escaping from the Scottish to the English Bar began to creep in with disconcerting frequency, although it was a boost to his morale in July when the Duke of Douglas appointed him as one of his regular counsel out of gratitude for his literary efforts on behalf of the Douglas cause.

Boswell was also still agonizing about whom to marry. He had discovered that loving Margaret was unlike any feeling he had ever had for a woman. He longed to slip away from Edinburgh and be with her at Lainshaw. They wrote to each other passionately. And yet, he could not shake off the thought that by marrying her he would miss out on a life that only money could bring. 'I was quite dull', he moaned, 'thinking that I had given up all gay and brilliant schemes of marriage.' Temple added to his perplexity by insisting that his exalted family obligations and ambitions ruled out marrying just for love. Everyone else was in favour of Margaret, seeing her as the stable and noble counterpoise to his volatility – including the eccentric judge James Burnett, Lord Mondobbo, who backed her because, like an experienced horse, she did not require the patience to train. Everyone was for her, that is, except Lord Auchinleck.

Boswell had long had intimations of his father's disapproval of any woman he would choose, rich or poor. A 'jarring of tempers' divided them. He feared that when he did marry, his father would expect him and his wife to live with him in subjection – unless he took a new wife himself. Pringle warned that this was a real possibility: 'Remember that by leaving him lonely, he may be tempted to take a companion likewise. Perhaps the best for you both would be for each to have a good one.'[17]

When Lord Auchinleck heard that his son had again failed to catch a rich wife, howsoever ill-advised the last one looked to him, and had instead fallen in love with his impoverished cousin, he was disgusted. All his cajoling, patient financial help, advice about prudence (along with that of his friends Lords Hailes and Pringle), toleration of literary ventures that brought only unwelcome publicity to the Boswell name and to himself on the bench, had had little effect. As if out of spiteful revenge, to cloud (if not also to thwart) his son's happiness, he began to spend time with 'Mrs Betty', his first cousin Elizabeth Boswell, daughter of his uncle John Boswell of Balmuto. On the night of 1 July, when his father hinted at remarriage, Boswell was devastated: 'I was amazed and hurt. It threw me quite into wild melancholy.' All he could think of was to escape and let his father entail the estate on the Balmutos or whoever else he had in mind. He told himself he had never taken root at Auchinleck anyway after his escape to London in 1761. He felt like 'a tree sunk in a flowerpot'.[18]

The danger that Lord Auchinleck's remarriage posed was that his son might be disinherited, or that a large part of the estate would be denied him. It was a nightmarish possibility. Boswell also regarded it as an insult to the memory of his mother and to their ancient family. Mondobbo thought the remarriage would be a 'terrible thing – a burthen on a family', and he urged Boswell to press his father immediately for an ironclad settlement. Boswell wrote to Margaret like a madman, threatening a complete breach with his father, but she replied firmly and evenly, knowing well what was at stake: 'For God's sake do not ... take any rash resolutions. You are warm, I know, but surely you will not allow any heat of passion to get the better of your good sense.'[19]

Prodded by her, he decided to confront his father on 13 July:

> I spoke in the strongest terms, and fairly told him he should be no more troubled with me. I was really calm and determined. It is wonderful [i.e., incredible] to think how he and I have differed to such a degree for so many years. O unfeeling world! ...

He awoke on 16 July even more angry. His entry on that day is as strident as the journal ever gets:

> 'Damn him. Curse him,' sounded somehow involuntarily in my ears perpetually. I was absolutely mad. I sent for worthy Grange, and was so furious and black-minded and uttered such horrid ideas that he could not help

shedding tears, and even went so far as to say that if I talked so he would never see me again. I looked on my father's marrying again as the most ungrateful return to me for my having submitted so much to please him.

'What an infamous woman must she be who can impose on an old man worn out with business, and ruin the peace of a family!' he wrote bitterly to Margaret. Elizabeth Boswell would become 'the legal prostitute of libidinous old age' if she married his father, as well as destroying the family peace.[20]

On top of all this, on 13 July Boswell discovered to his horror that he had another serious venereal infection, his tenth. 'Mr Macdonald blooded me today,' he wrote, 'to begin the cure of a severe symptom. It is hard for one night of Irish extravagance to suffer so much.' It would take him no fewer than five months to recover from this one. His obligations at Parliament House prevented him from confining and starving himself at home. The attack could not have come at a worse time. It was so severe that by then he knew he would have to go to London for a cure in September.[21]

On 20 July Boswell finally proposed to Margaret by letter but made the proposal a test of her motives and willingness. Would she accept him not as the heir of Auchinleck but with only his expected £100 per year to add to the interest on her own £1,000? This would be enough to live somewhere in Europe. He insisted that her answer contain 'no mediocrity, no reasoning, no hesitation'. He added, 'Read this in your own room and think as long as you please.' Then he waited. If she should hedge, he would set sail for America and become 'a wild Indian'. Her answer arrived promptly: 'J.B. with £100 a year is every bit as valuable to me as if possessed of the estate of Auchinleck. I only regret the want of wealth on your account.' She was not sure he could be happy without the money. For a few gasping seconds, her acceptance made him panic: 'For a minute or two my habits of terror for marriage returned. I found myself at last fixed for ever; my heart beat and my head was giddy.' He soon recovered. His father sarcastically agreed to the marriage soon afterwards, convinced that it would not last more than six months. Temple fell in with the news good-naturedly: 'What a different turn will it give to your letters! No more venereal disasters, no more intrigues, no more Zélide, no more gardener's daughters. The volatile, the witty, the amorous Boswell will then write like any other grave, sensible man.' He prayed that it would eventually bring him and his father together again.[22]

There are two paintings of Margaret which show clearly her intelligent

good looks. One is a family portrait, now hanging in the Scottish Portrait
Gallery in Edinburgh, in which she is the artist's main interest. The other
is a portrait by Sir Gilbert Eliott of Stobs. In neither is she pert, dreamy,
or soft, but refreshingly clear-eyed and firm. She looks like a woman a
man could trust with his life and family. She has a look of unpretentious
grace, well-proportioned facial and bodily features, and thin, well-shaped
arms and hands. Indeed, if the Lainshaw estate had been more prosperous, she looks like a woman who would have commanded much
more male attention than she apparently did. Boswell, one feels, was
lucky to get her.

Margaret wanted to marry soon after the court recessed, but Boswell
had to go to London first for a cure. She was ignorant of the seriousness
of his illness, thinking it was merely the fruit of 'hard drinking and going
to the opera'. 'If your health is not in question, you could see Mr Johnson
some other time.'[23] Aware of the need for a healing of the rift with Lord
Auchinleck, she feared correctly that he would be greatly offended by
another trip to London. Hailes and Pringle tried to calm him, but he
was not in a conciliatory mood and, in any case, his son never listened
to him.

One of the last conversations Boswell had with his father before he
left for London deteriorated into a 'warm dispute' on the sensitive subject
of male and female succession, which he recorded in tense detail. The
flagship now of their mutual antipathy, this subject would divide them
for the rest of Lord Auchinleck's life. Boswell's position, which he felt
protected not only his own birthright but also the 'principle of family,
of supporting the race of Thomas Boswell of Auchinleck', was simple
but dated:

> I argued that a male alone could support a family, could represent his
> forefathers. That females, in a feudal light, were only vehicles for carrying
> down men to posterity, and that a man might as well entail his estate on his
> postchaise, and put one into it who should bear his name, as entail it upon
> his daughter and make her husband take his name.

A grandson by a daughter is not 'as near a grandson by a son'. Having
studied some botany at the university, he indulged in some horticultural
imagery to make the point another way: 'I say the *stamen* is derived from
the *man*. The woman in only like the ground where a tree is planted. A
grandson by a daughter has no connection with my original stock.' We
can only be thankful that Boswell was not born into an age of 'political

correctness'. It is a 'foolish fondness for daughters', he went on, that has led to monstrous absurdities such as entailing estates on females. His father, he realized was immovable, committed to the more progressive principle of 'heirs whatsoever'. More hurtful was the realization that he adopted that view because he did not trust his son, 'that my dissipated and profligate conduct' was what made him think of an entail. Boswell shouted that he would leave the country and spend the rest of his life in a warm climate, like brother David who had recently gone to live in Valencia. 'I was too hot for a son to a father. But I could not help it. I was like an old Roman when his country was at stake.'[24]

5

He stayed in London for more than two months. After depositing himself at Edward Dilly's in the Poultry, his first business was to consult the doctors regarding a cure for the persistent symptoms of gonorrhoea. He carried a letter of introduction from his uncle Dr John Boswell to Dr Gilbert Kennedy in Lincoln's Inn Fields, who agreed to treat him. Boswell began a regimen of Kennedy's Lisbon Diet Drink, advertised as a cure for scurvy, leprosy, and a multitude of other ailments, including one other 'certain disorder'. Kennedy turned out to be something of a quack, though the 'decoction' did seem to subdue the 'fire' of infection. By mid-October, however, it was evident that more serious treatment was needed, so Boswell submitted to the knife at the hands of Dr Duncan Forbes to deal with either a local infection or relieve a case of phimosis. 'My illness has taken various turns,' he reported to Grange on 16 October. 'At last I see a prospect of being soon perfectly well, and you may believe I am very much relieved; for I have been under sad anxiety. The knife has been absolutely necessary. And you know I am a very bad bearer of pain.' That seemed to be the turning point, after which he enjoyed the rest of his London visit in relative comfort.[25]

Temple suspected other reasons for his wandering friend's visit to London. 'As you move about so much, I fancy ill-health was only a pretence to get to London.' You thought you would not see the metropolis again for a long time. You chose to enjoy your celebrity, to indulge your humour. Marriage, business, a family will not admit of such excursions.' He was right, of course. Boswell knew Paoli would be arriving in London at any moment. Johnson, Goldsmith, Garrick, the theatre, the world of publishing – they all beckoned to him. Margaret was under no illusions and did not want him to go. 'I must have many promises of sobriety before I give my consent to your going to London,' she wrote on 11 August. 'Consider, my dear Jamie, that my happiness is entirely in your power, and I'm sure your generosity will make you deny yourself an indulgence that may be hurtful to you as well as to your friend.' He did not let her down, not once on this visit venturing into London's sexual underworld. Besides, he longed to tell everyone in London about her. Grange told Erskine, 'The rage of matrimony has taken such a firm hold of him, that he seems to feel nothing else.'[26]

Aching to speak to Johnson about Margaret and his father's threats to remarry, Boswell wrote to him in Brighton, where he was then staying, but received no reply. So he asked Mrs Thrale to write to see if Johnson would mind his coming to Brighton, as he had travelled to Oxford to see him a year earlier. That Boswell should ask her to do this reveals his grasp of how much Johnson had fallen under her influence. He reminded her that they were 'rivals for that great man. You would take him to the country, when I was anxious to keep him in town.' She did write and Johnson's reply was full of affection: 'I have always loved and valued you, and shall you and value you still more as you become more regular and useful.' His welcome advice regarding Lord Auchinleck was right to the point: 'The disputes between you and him are matters of sensation, not of judgement. So it is in vain to reason with him. He grumbles because you come to London. He cannot understand why it is very right you should from time to time enjoy London. There is no help for it. Let him grumble.' He also urged the married couple to have their own house, near enough to Lord Auchinleck to see him frequently without being under his thumb. This could deter his remarriage as effectually as actually living with him. Boswell agreed, for it would be 'mixing gall with my honey' to live under the same roof. But above all, Johnson added, Boswell must not 'give up *with everything and everybody*' if his father did remarry. That was harder advice to follow. To marry that 'infamous wretch' Elizabeth Boswell would not be an act of family love, and he forbade Margaret to speak to her. He grudgingly agreed to do nothing rash, however.[27]

When Johnson returned from Brighton, they still had five weeks together and Boswell picked up with him where he had left off the previous year, visiting him at Johnson's Court, dining with him at the Mitre, introducing him to Paoli who had just arrived, and inviting him to his own rooms in Old Bond Street (to which he moved to be near Paoli). On one occasion Johnson saw to it that Boswell was invited to the Thrales' home in Streatham Park. There on 6 October Boswell saw, with mixed feelings, how the sage was 'venerated' by both host and hostess in a comfortable genteel setting. He was also mildly confused by the way Johnson now spoke to him – a little more mocking in tone, a little readier to put him in his place, regarding Scotland and, unaccountably, Corsica. It was as if Johnson were reassuring the Thrales that he was theirs first. Or he may have been joking or impatient, even embarrassed, over Boswell's 'extravagant' reverence for him.[28]

On the whole, Boswell faithfully recorded their conversations, most of which (except for the ones about his father) found their way into his *Life of Johnson*. During these sessions, he felt he was a sort of suspended Boswell, lifted from Scotland, marriage, family, and the minutiae of personal concerns that defined him there. He stepped out of himself and became a sounding board, an actor in scenes he had created, dramatically charged with Johnson's intellectual and rational energy. It was great therapy. With a seemingly endless stream of questions, he encouraged the great moralist to full conversational flight on an array of topics: Scotland (as usual), London, marriage, Garrick, Corsica, literature, death, Roman Catholicism, the law, and a panoply of other subjects. With his generally superficial knowledge of a good many subjects, Boswell was able to keep up his mentor's interest and coax the talk along, although inevitably he strayed into areas where he was a ripe target for Johnson's wit and impatience.

It was a risk he was willing to take. One memorable instance was their conversation about death, a subject that for both psychological and religious reasons always fascinated Boswell and, according to his own gratuitous notice in the *London Chronicle* of 24 October, had lately drawn him to see six men executed at Tyburn. Again to get a good view, he sat on top of the hearse in which one of the bodies was to be carried away. None of the condemned men, he told Johnson, seemed to be afraid. Johnson scoffed at this. A few days later, knowing that Johnson was 'dismally apprehensive' of death, he suggested that this fear might be overcome. Neither the actor Samuel Foote nor Hume was afraid of it. Johnson retaliated, 'Hold a pistol to Foote's breast or to Hume's breast and threaten to kill them, and you'll see how they behave.' Boswell then found himself in deep water:

> I attempted to continue the conversation. He was so provoked, that he said, 'Give us no more of this'; and was thrown into such a state of agitation, that he expressed himself in a way that alarmed and distressed me; shewed an

impatience that I should leave him, and when I was going away, called to me
sternly, 'Don't let us meet to-morrow.'

He felt Johnson had been too severe with him: 'I seemed to myself like
the man who had put his head into the lion's mouth a great many times
with perfect safety, but at last had it bit off.' That night he agonized over
his blunder and after a sleepless night sent Johnson a note to say that he
would call on him for just five minutes: 'You are ... in my mind, since
last night, surrounded with cloud and storm. Let me have a glimpse
of sunshine ...' Fearfully he made his way to Johnson's Court for a
reconciliation. After a few minutes of talk about literature, 'I whispered
to him, "Well, Sir, you are now in good humour."' And when he
attempted to leave, Johnson (smiling) stopped him with, ' "Get you gone
in," a curious mode of inviting me to stay.'[29]

There were reunions with Goldsmith, Garrick, and Davies, too, and
new friendships with Sir Joshua Reynolds – the most famous English
painter of the age who would become an important and intimate friend –
and the popular dramatists Arthur Murphy and George Colman, all of
whom he invited to dinner with Johnson at Old Bond Street one memorable October evening. Boswell was again finding himself quite popular
in London. Goldsmith told him that at a dinner he had attended he 'was
highly spoken of, and that Mr Colman had very justly observed that my
character was simplicity: not in a sense of weakness, but of being plain
and unaffected'.[30]

Paoli, as we have seen, was a rich addition to Boswell's galaxy of
friends. Minutes after their reunion he ran into the exalted Duke of
Queensberry in St James's Street and carried him back victoriously to
meet the General. 'His Grace seemed much struck.' One of his finer
moments was introducing his two idols, Johnson and Paoli, to one
another and seeing them hit it off. Paoli had the 'loftiest port of any man
he had ever seen', said Johnson. With Paoli now in his orbit, Boswell
needed a new wardrobe as well as elegant new rooms, so he spent money
he could ill afford on a 'slate-blue frock suit' and a 'full suit of a kind of
purple cloth with rich gold buttons' for good measure. Dilly supplied
him with a silver-hilted sword. His rooms just a few doors down from
Paoli, which he secured at half-price off-season rates, comprised a large
dining room with three windows opening to the street, a bedchamber
and dressing room looking out on Burlington Gardens, and 'a large
extent of green ground and stately trees in the very centre of the court
end of the town'. He also took on a foreign servant.[31]

Paoli delighted Boswell by saying he wanted to attend his wedding, though the news petrified Margaret. 'Remember,' she wrote, 'with advantages vastly superior to mine, you yourself was uneasy in the presence of the illustrious Chief.' 'I wish you could steal out of Edinburgh,' she wrote later, 'when nobody can suspect where you are going and let the ceremony be put over as privately as possible ...' In the end, Paoli did not attend, but he did witness and sign his name to a mock-legal marriage contract drawn up by Boswell. Johnson and later the Duke of Douglas signed it, too, as did he and Margaret. A solemn pledge to be faithful and tolerant spouses, it was Boswell's idea of certifying or authorizing their marriage with the imprimatur of the imaginative, the great and the famous. Mere banns could never achieve this.[32]

Saying his goodbyes to all his friends as he prepared to leave for Edinburgh on 9 November, Boswell was again nonplussed to find that Johnson was staying with the Thrales at Streatham. He dashed off a note: would Johnson come back to see him off or should he come to Streatham? He should come out, came the reply, which he did on the following morning. They talked of his approaching marriage and then Johnson came back with him to London. That was good, but Hester Thrale was beginning to make things a bit less convenient for Boswell and his 'Oracle'.[33]

6

Instead of returning directly home, Boswell journeyed deep into the West Country to visit Temple and his new wife at their parsonage in Mamhead, Devon, a small thatched cottage, humble and cramped enough but comfortable, where Temple was scraping out an existence on eighty pounds per year preaching to a meagre congregation of about fifty. Boswell enjoyed his visit despite Temple's constant complaining, attended one of his friend's sermons, was reintroduced to his wife Anne with whom this time he seems to have got on better, and walked in the parsonage glebe with delightful views of the sea. Temple's domestic arrangements filled him with 'present contentment and future hope'. The grand schemes of their youth had gone awry for his friend, but with his own achievements and bright marital and career prospects the future looked bright.[34]

Before leaving for Scotland he received the shocking news from Margaret that Lord Eglinton had been tragically shot and killed on his estate while apprehending a poacher. Her distress mingled with fear for his own safety: 'What must I not suffer for the man I prefer to every earthly being, when I consider that he is not well, and, for aught I know, may at present be under the greatest distress.' Another shock awaited him when he arrived in Scotland: his father had decided to marry Elizabeth Boswell on 25 November. As an act of defiance, Boswell seems to have decided on the spot to match that timing perfectly, getting Margaret to agree to the 25th as the day of their own nuptials. It was not the other way round, as has often been thought. Now neither could attend the other's wedding – not that the son would ever have graced his father's with his presence anyway.[35]

The younger couple were married at Lainshaw, honoured with the presence of the Duke of Douglas. Margaret wore a silver dress Boswell had brought back with him from London. Her ring, also bought in London, was a plain gold band. At dinner that night, they both wore white. One day just before or just after his marriage, he stole over from Lainshaw to Auchinleck and 'with a piece of the Old Castle in my hand, I knelt upon the ruins and swore that if any man had the estate in exclusion of the rightful heir this stone should swim in his heart's blood'. He still had that stone in 1775. Since the court was in session, the newly-weds returned to Edinburgh after the marriage and, surprisingly, for three months moved into the apartment directly above the family home where his father and stepmother now lived with John. With his father's sour presence below, it cannot have been an ideal beginning to married life.[36]

Lord Auchinleck's ill-timed remarriage caused consternation among friends and relatives. Temple, as ever, was full of good advice: 'Do not allow your father's marriage to affect your spirits. As I said before, it cannot be attended with any ill consequence to you unless by your own fault. Keep a watch then over your conduct; humour your father, cultivate your stepmother's good opinion.' Think of the disastrous effects on Margaret and their future children, he pointed out, if his temper should provoke his father to 'leave his estate past you'.[37] It would not be easy, but a new chapter in Boswell's life had opened bright with promise. What sustained him above all else was his love for Margaret, and hers for him.

PART III

Stagnation:
The Middle Years
1769–1782

SIXTEEN

Settling Down:
'The Antechamber of His Mind'

I

Boswell stopped writing a full journal two months before his marriage in November 1769 and, except for random notes and memoranda, did not start another for two-and-a-half years. It is no coincidence that this period of journalistic silence stretched across his first two years of married life.

He was devoted to Margaret who filled the dark and restless corners of his spirit with such domestic contentment and love that it can almost be said he ceased to be himself. His painful feelings about his father and, increasingly, his stepmother, did not go away, but his peace was otherwise so complete that he was simply not compelled to write about himself. For his own and Margaret's sake, and for the sake of his legal career, the happiness and respectability he experienced was a blessing; for posterity it has created something of a literary drought. He turned his back not only on his own complexity, but also on London and his many friends there. Astonishingly, he did not write to Johnson for a year-and-a-half, nor to Goldsmith and Garrick. He kept up with Temple and Grange at a slower rate, appearing respectable and obedient, even a little dull, in his letters of this period. By May 1770 Temple, who could scarcely believe it, felt that some teasing was in order. 'Does Mrs Boswell engross you entirely? Can the gay, the volatile Boswell, whom hardly variety itself could satiate, confine himself to one object? Have you no expedition in your head, no essay in prose, no epistle in verse? Or do you begin to think it your chief merit to be a good husband and a good lawyer?'[1]

If he was to have something to write about, either the spectral forces of hypochondria and gloom needed to regain their hold or he had to extricate himself from his uxorious, sober, busy domestic cocoon and throw himself into the more complicated and thrilling literary world of London.

2

Margaret was such an enormous comfort to him that he could scarcely bear to be apart from her. 'Believe me, my dearest,' he wrote to her in February, 'the short absence which I have now suffered has convinced me still more feelingly than before how much I love you . . . how ill I can do without you.' So dependent was he on her that he let her keep watch over his thoughts for him, 'like a child that lets itself fall purposely, to have the pleasure of being tenderly raised up again, by those who are fond of it'. In Margaret's care, he did not need to fight a constant battle against gloominess. He acknowledged that he still had some 'seeds of . . . discontent' about having to live in Scotland and represent clients in civil causes that did little to rouse his imagination, but the all-important blessing was that he was secure at home and thus able to conduct his professional duties with poise and consistency.[2]

The shoe was now on the other foot. It was Boswell's turn to cheer up Temple, who was sounding doleful and self-pitying over his straitened and isolated life in Devon. He was godfather to Temple's first son and had discovered on his trip to Mamhead that he liked his wife Ann more than he had at first. He encouraged him to apply for a living in Northumberland – and to come for a visit as soon as possible. Temple stayed with them in September 1770 for ten delightful days of 'elegant friendship and classical sociability', and he was astonished at his friend's good fortune. 'It is absolute cruelty and tyranny to give that woman the least room for uneasiness . . . Continue to love her, to respect her.' He said this because he knew Boswell of old and had a dream that his friend had already been unfaithful to Margaret.[3]

Soon the newly-weds moved to a modest flat in the Cowgate, near the Excise Office. In May 1770 they moved again, this time to the new and fashionable Chessel's Buildings in the Canongate, where the apartments had much more elegant rooms complete with 'panelling, pulvinated friezes on the chimneypieces, overmantels painted with romantic scenes', and handsomely decorated doorways.[4]

After a painful and dangerous delivery lasting two days, their first child, a boy, was born there on 28 August but died within a few hours. 'Pray come to me directly,' Boswell pleaded with Grange. He took it very hard and implored Temple, too, to come to him in his hour of need. Margaret made a slow recovery, and from now on her uncertain health was a recurrent theme in Boswell's writing.[5]

When she had regained her strength sufficiently they set out for

Lainshaw and Auchinleck, their first visit to the family home since their marriage. What happened on that visit is a mystery, but it can be guessed at by Margaret's conspicuous absence when Boswell later spent four days at Auchinleck. She stayed instead with her married sister Mary at Treesbank. It was a deliberate snub but apparently Margaret could not bear to spend another night under the same roof as her father-in-law. In the late autumn Boswell was at Auchinleck again, for a more prolonged visit, and again without her. 'I have suffered much more than any body would imagine, on account of so long a separation from my wife,' he wrote to Grange. 'I have been seized with fits of impatience and my heart has fluttered like a bird confined in a cage.' And he had to suffer in silence since nobody there was much interested in his loneliness.[6]

Despite these trials, difficult for any newly married couple to bear with grace, they remained happy. In May 1771, after returning from two weeks of country air in the west where Margaret had grown 'fatter' and taken on a 'stronger look', they made a very good move to James's Court, conveniently located on the north side of the Lawnmarket between the Castle and Parliament Close, where they would remain for the rest of their time in Edinburgh. The small third-floor flat was owned and rented to them by David Hume – an association that made the place additionally attractive to Boswell. Two years later they also took a larger apartment downstairs. Unusual for Edinburgh, their home now had two floors with its own internal stair, four bedrooms and 'two genteel well-finished public rooms each above 18 feet long, with handsome marble chimneys and hearths ... and one of the rooms ornamented with a Chinese temple, Apollo and the muses'. Here was the ideal place in which to settle down, entertain the eminent, and await the children who would surely come.[7]

On another happy 'jaunt' together, in August 1771, they slipped down south of the border.[8] Margaret, who was pregnant again, seems to have loved every minute of it, not least the fine weather and the 'quick lively motion of driving post' as they took in a number of country seats, castles, and abbeys. They stopped at Newcastle for a few days hoping to visit brother John who, after an argument with his stepmother, had angrily moved back there to board under the care of Dr Andrew Wilson, but John had left for a jaunt of his own to London. While staying in Newcastle they squeezed in an excursion to Durham where they heard a 'solemn service' in the great cathedral. From there they made for Alnwick where Boswell wrote to Thomas Percy, at that moment resident in Alnwick Castle in his capacity as chaplain to the Duke of North-umberland. Could Percy join them at the White Hart that evening for some pleasant London conversation? He did and they talked for a full hour about Johnson which could not have been very interesting for Margaret. Percy managed to get them invited to a ball the following night to be given by the Duke of Northumberland in Berwick-upon-Tweed but a shortage of horses prevented them from attending and the next morning they turned north, following the Tweed up to Melrose Abbey and then making their way back to Edinburgh.

It was a travelling holiday of discovery and warm companionship such as they never again enjoyed together. The following March Margaret had another miscarriage. Meanwhile Boswell began to think increasingly of trips to London and reunions with his literary and artistic circle. Seeing Percy at Alnwick doubtless made him realize how much he missed his London friends and the stimulation of literary talk.

3

Boswell knew that he had to protect his inheritance for the sake of his wife and family. In any case, Temple pointed out, what did he have to fear from a stepmother in her forties? – 'his wife can have no children, and I suppose he will leave her a very moderate jointure.' Moreover, his father was suffering from an enlarged prostate and deserved filial affection for that reason at the very least. So Boswell made another effort to get along with him. 'My Father is come to town and never looked better in his life,' he wrote in June 1770. 'Honest Man, he really is I believe very fond of me; and we are at present on very good terms.' As for the wicked stepmother, 'I behave with prudence towards the person who has occasioned so much uneasiness. I do not as yet see any appearance of her multiplying.' Temple was delighted: 'You never had any reason to doubt of his affection for you.' About a year later he was still dwelling on the same theme: 'I rejoice to hear of no tendency to pregnancy in Lady Auchinleck, and that you conduct yourself with regard to her as you ought.'[9]

Twice in 1771 Boswell spent part of his vacation with his father. The first time was on the Western Circuit in May which took them to Inveraray and the 'wild grandeur' of the Highlands for over a week, the second at Auchinleck where he shook off some lingering illness, perhaps the malaria he had picked up in Corsica, doing an 'apprenticeship' in pruning and tree management. For the sake of his father he put a good face on this arboriculture: he hoped 'in time, to be a skillful and diligent

Guardian of the trees here', but nothing could have interested him less. His father also gave him 'a college upon the Election-Law of Scotland mixed with its antiquities' which he appreciatively wrote down for future use. Hailes told him he was a lucky young man to be able to sit at the feet of such an authority on the law. It seems to have been a bonding time between them, when they concentrated 'to good purpose' on ideas and activity instead of each focusing on the other.[10]

Lord Auchinleck could not help but have been pleased at the volume of work Boswell continued to attract. In May 1770 he became a church lawyer, practising at the Bar of the General Assembly of the Church of Scotland, the supreme ecclesiastical court that sat each May in an apartment in St Giles's Church, where he earned some additional guineas in exchange for his free time and a good deal of boredom. One year later he complained – or was it a boast? – that he had no fewer than six causes in progress in the 'Venerable Court', in which he was pleading on either side of the thorny issue of patronage – whether a curate should be appointee of the landowner of the parish or be chosen by the parish itself. His libertarian principles probably disposed him against the landlords in these causes, but generally he cared little who won the causes if they did not affect his own status. A few lines from one of the Edinburgh lawyers' repertory of professional drinking songs put this view in a nutshell:

> But let them say or let them do
> It's aw ane to me
> If I but get into my pouch
> A braw swinging fee.[11]

One of these causes, however, kindled his interest more than most. It concerned a curate whose settlement in a living was contested because five years earlier he had been accused of fornication. The degree of immorality in fornication was a matter that always fascinated Boswell, and he mentioned the cause to Johnson in April 1772. Johnson thought it was an unnecessary fuss since the man had repented: 'a man who is good enough to go to heaven is good enough to be a clergyman', even a Presbyterian one. Why should a man like this be called a 'whoremonger' just because he got 'one wench with child'? Boswell agreed in principle that fornication was not a 'heinous' sin except that this man had tried to pass off the child as someone else's. The General Assembly rejected the curate's appointment. John MacLaurin, a close professional friend who as Lord Dreghorn became a judge in the Court of Session in 1788, delighted in teasing the great Boswell about having to plead at this unspectacular court in St Giles's:

> Sure great is the folly
> In him whom Paoli
> His friendship permitted to share
>   To go for a guinea
>   (Dear Boswell, what mean ye?)
> To plead at so scurvy a bar.[12]

Most of the civil causes he pleaded were so flat and humdrum that they drove him to hyperactive socializing and drinking with his professional cronies. The drinking was a tendency that increasingly worried Margaret. What kept up his interest in the legal profession was the occasional criminal cause into which he threw both his rational and his emotional energies. One such cause involved William Harris, an Ayrshire merchant accused of forging banknotes, who after languishing in prison for fifteen months awaiting trial escaped by cutting the bars of his window, was caught and put in chains, and then unsuccessfully tried to strangle himself. In the days just before his trial in March 1770, Boswell visited him repeatedly and, according to the gaoler, even gave him a guinea. His best legal efforts proved unsuccessful and Harris was hanged. 'He suffered great pain to all appearance. I was much shocked, and am still gloomy.'[13]

The Harris cause raised fresh doubts in his mind about a matter that had perplexed him from the beginning of his professional life: the morality of a legal process which placed an advocate like himself in the tenuous position of having to plead on behalf of a client in whose innocence he did not believe. This was one of the reasons he visited condemned prisoners such as Harris on the eve of their executions to worm out of them eleventh-hour confessions. He once asked Johnson whether this sort of repeated compromise with the 'nice feeling of honesty' was not a species of 'dissimulation': 'Is there not some danger that a lawyer may put on the same mask in common life in the intercourse with his friends?' Absolutely not, Johnson replied. A lawyer is paid for 'affecting warmth' for his client: 'a man will no more carry the artifice of the bar into the common intercourse of society, than a man who is paid for tumbling upon his hands will continue to tumble upon his hands when he would walk on his feet.'[14]

4

Although in this first stretch of his marriage Boswell neglected his London literary alliances, his instincts as a public man of letters remained acute. His father, to be sure, would not have minded if he never published his work again, nor would Pringle and Hailes who were all too aware that his literary activity had interrupted his legal studies and driven a wedge between him and his father. They dismissed his writing (Pringle more emphatically than Hailes) merely as a feature of his exhibitionism and vanity. But Margaret did not want his new settled existence to snuff out his literary persona, nor did a host of others like Sir Alexander Dick, Hume, Kames, Temple, and Grange. There was no chance of it anyway. The newspapers offered too tempting an outlet, as did the world of the theatre.

Between autumn 1769 and spring 1772 Boswell sent to various periodicals close to forty assorted anonymous articles on an eclectic span of subjects, most of them frivolous 'inventions', exercises in self-puffery, and reports of gossip covering subjects such as experiments in freezing bodies for later resuscitation, his having been seen mounting a hearse at a Tyburn execution, a spate of disgraceful bankruptcies in Scotland, the constitution of the Church of Scotland, and a defence of Garrick's Shakespeare Jubilee. The *London Chronicle* and the *London Magazine* carried most of them, and several also found their way into the *Scots Magazine* and the *Edinburgh Advertiser*.[15]

Moreover, Boswell now had a vested interest in the *London Magazine* and a particular motive for writing for it because in October 1769 he bought a one-sixth interest in it – an investment of over two hundred pounds. Neither Margaret nor Temple approved of this extravagance, especially in relation to a magazine whose readership the latter described as including 'hucksters and pedlars'.[16] But Temple, out of touch as he was in remote Devon, did not seem to know that Edward Dilly, John Rivington, and Richard Baldwin, Jr., all respectable booksellers, were three of the other owners and that they hoped with their publication to rival the distinguished *Gentleman's Magazine* – a forlorn hope, as it turned out. Boswell was probably persuaded to become involved by Dilly and he did so, one feels, less as an investment than to have a ready mouthpiece for the essays he planned to write.

Occasionally Boswell wrote serious pieces. Three of the most important, which make up 'On the Profession of a Player', appeared in the *London Magazine* from August to October 1770. The first two are analyses and celebrations of Garrick's acting, but taken together they reveal more clearly than ever the psychological appeal of the stage for Boswell. The actor appeared to him to be the perfect metaphor for Everyman, who carries with him through life a split perspective: even as he acts his way through life's ever-changing moments he is aware of a kind of 'double feeling': 'The feelings and passions of the character which he represents must take full possession as it were of the antechamber of his mind, while his own character remains in the innermost recess.' He also compared the actor with the barrister or advocate 'who enters warmly into the cause of his client, while at the same time, when he examines himself coolly, he knows that he is much in the wrong, and does not even wish to prevail'. The fascinating part of the acting process, then, was the double drama being played out in the actor's own mind, unseen by others. Boswell imagined that the actor must be his own greatest source of fascination, just as he was fascinated by himself acting the roles of married man, advocate, friend, performer at dinner parties, mimic, singer. He even likened his efforts to cultivate a sober and sensitive character during these years as a type of mask or 'antechamber of the mind' sitting alongside his real consciousness.[17]

He was especially alive to the Edinburgh theatre these days having written an opening-night Prologue for the new Theatre Royal which was launched (against local opposition) in December 1767. There was more excitement than usual during the 1770–1 season when the theatre was leased by Samuel Foote, the actor and dramatist known as the 'English Aristophanes', who had built the Haymarket Theatre in London in 1767. Foote was particularly known for his sometimes savage comic mimicry. Boswell had first met him in London, and on several occasions talked to Johnson about him. Foote had never been fool enough to mimic him, Johnson told Boswell: 'fear restrained him; he knew I'd break his bones. I would have saved him the trouble of cutting off a leg; I would not have left him a leg to cut off' – an allusion to Foote's amputated leg. To have Foote up in Edinburgh for the season was a definite coup, 'the first legitimate "star" who ever ventured so far as Edinburgh'. Boswell lapped it all up: 'we have been kept laughing all this winter by Foote.'[18]

If only he could prevail on Garrick to follow Foote's example. After a year-and-a-half it was time to dust off his friendship with him, as with Johnson. 'Will you my dear Sir never favour Scotland with a visit? Often have you talk'd of it ... Come and add Caledonia to the dominions which your genius has illuminated.' Who knew, if Johnson from time to time spoke of a tour through the Highlands, why not Garrick, too? 'Your health would be the better of a jaunt to our Highlands' to see 'many scenes of wild nature'. Garrick did concede to Boswell in April 1771 that the Edinburgh theatre needed more than the 'English Aristophanes' to revive its fortunes, but he was suffering from gout and playing with the idea of 'putting into port' at last. When Boswell, visiting him at his house in London in April 1772, pointed out that he had acted in Dublin so why not in Edinburgh, Garrick replied: ' "When I went to Ireland, I went to get money. It was harvest time then with me. But when the barn's full" (stretching himself in his chair) "one grows lazy." ' Boswell was quick to retort, 'But you have not yet had the harvest of *oats*.'[19]

He had already done homage to Garrick with his essays on acting; in 1771 he went further, providing Donaldson's new Edinburgh edition of Shakespeare with a special dedication to the actor. It has long been a fact in Britain that if one thought of Garrick, one also thought of Shakespeare. By linking himself with both Shakespeare and Garrick in Donaldson's edition, Boswell associated himself in print with two national idols in his expanding literary pantheon: 'All your panegyrists have not expressed more than I feel,' he wrote confidently. He made sure Garrick knew he was the author of the three *London Magazine* essays and the dedication. For his part, Garrick was thrilled to hear of Boswell's happy marriage – 'rakes make the best husbands' – and looked forward to seeing him in London in the spring: 'I shall kiss your hands with pleasure.'[20]

This was the warmest period of their friendship, though the relationship was always one-sided: Boswell taking the initiative, Garrick responding. Garrick never did come to visit him or act in Edinburgh. He could even get ruffled over Boswell's impetuous officiousness, as he did in the autumn of 1772 when Boswell asked Garrick for Johnsoniana, assuring him that if he wrote about his and Johnson's complicated and essentially cold relationship for the public, he would do so with 'delicacy' and 'truth'. Garrick was unimpressed, even irritated. If he wanted his friendship with Johnson explained, which he did not, he would do it himself.[21]

Paoli did what Garrick failed to do, travelling up to Edinburgh just to visit the Corsican champion and his wife from 3–12 September 1771. He was accompanied by the Polish ambassador Count Tadeusz Burzynski and stayed in the elegant new apartments in James's Court. A rare honour it was, by any standard, for a young Edinburgh advocate to be visited in his native city by one of the great European heroes of the day. Boswell was vain enough to write an 'authentick account' of Paoli's visit in that month's issue of the *London Magazine*.[22] After a few days at home, where he doubtless introduced Paoli to all his friends and the elders of Edinburgh society, they made their way west to the Carron Iron Works that manufactured the 'cannon and warlike stores' Boswell was instrumental in sending to Corsica. Then they continued on to Glasgow, taking in the university, and finally to Auchinleck where they spent two days and Paoli met his father.

However, Paoli's visit also occasioned a dispute with Hailes. Edinburgh – more specifically, Hailes's brother the Lord Provost – had failed to confer on the visiting hero the freedom of the city or to entertain him officially. Boswell was irate about this and recklessly (and anonymously) attacked the Lord Provost in two ironic 'letters' to the *London Chronicle* on 25 October and 28 November. He stated that the Lord Provost was nothing more than 'a *Luckenbooths Merchant*' who kept a shop for 'retailing cloths, silks, and other materials for dress' and was not about to confer on Paoli the freedom of the city since he had no prospect of selling him anything.

Hailes had no trouble identifying the author. He was furious:

I hope that because you was dissatisfied with his conduct in one particular, *you* did not insinuate that there were other *unnamed* circumstances in his conduct which you *could* mention as blameworthy. I hope that while you *attacked* with a *charge* you did not stab with an *insinuation* – that *you* did not represent him as a servile dependant on a rich man, that *you* did not endeavour to depreciate a gentleman of his fashion and connexions by treating him in the character of a shop keeper in the retail way ... in other words, I hope *you* are *not* the author of the two articles in the London Newspapers.

Hailes called it 'illiberal abuse', a failure to separate reason and impulse. Would this talented young man ever learn to control his pen? The incident yet again damaged relations between them, this time for years. Hailes wrote a note at the bottom of a copy of his letter: 'No answer made to this: but he visited me no longer.'[23]

5

On 18 April 1771 Boswell broke his eighteen-month silence and wrote to Johnson. 'I wished for your letter a long time,' Johnson confessed in reply, delighted to hear of his steady marriage and way of life, 'and when it came, it amply recompensed the delay. I ... sincerely hope, that between publick business, improving studies, and domestick pleasures, neither melancholy nor caprice will find any place for entrance.' With his eyes on the Hebrides, he added, 'I hope the time will come when we may try our powers both with cliffs and water.' To restore some momentum to their friendship, in July Boswell wrote him a letter of introduction to James Beattie, the poet and professor of moral philosophy at Marischal College, Aberdeen, who in 1770 published an important refutation of Hume's religious scepticism, *An Essay on the Nature and Immutability of Truth*. In 1771 Beattie also published the first part of his influential 'preromantic' poem, *The Minstrel* (foreshadowing Wordsworth's *The Prelude*) on the origins of poetical genius. Just to have attacked Hume endeared Beattie to Johnson, but Boswell gave Beattie good advice on how to talk to the great man of letters: 'You must not be discouraged though he should appear reserved and wanting in some of the commonplace modes of making a stranger easy. Bring him upon something worthy of his ability as soon as you can, and I will venture to promise you conversation superior to any you have ever heard.' Boswell could take some credit for initiating a great friendship for the two hit it off famously, Johnson treating Beattie like a brother, spending entire days with him, and taking him to meet Reynolds, Davies, and many others.[24]

Margaret had not been at all well since her recent miscarriage so Boswell again felt he needed a respectable excuse for visiting London. The reason he came up with was respectable enough: to plead on behalf of a Scots schoolmaster, John Hastie, who had lost his teaching post because he was too severe in disciplining the boys. The Court of Session restored Hastie to his post but the cause was appealed to the House of Lords and Boswell was appointed to defend him there. He told Johnson he wanted to consult with him about the cause before he planned his defence, although he could honourably have delegated the work to someone else. His true reasons were summarised in his journal:

to refresh my mind by the variety and spirit of the metropolis, the conversation of my revered friend Mr Samuel Johnson and that of other men of genius and learning; to try if I could get something for myself, or be of service to any of my friends by means of the Duke of Queensberry, Lord Mountstuart, or Douglas, all of whom had given me reason to expect their assistance to be employed in Scotch appeals in the House of Lords, and also see how the land might lie for me at the English bar; and to endeavour to get my brother David well settled as a merchant in London.

Johnson replied that his many friends were looking forward to his arrival but, possibly alluding to some bias he had heard against Boswell, the letter continued: 'Whether to love you be right or wrong, I have many on my side: Mrs Thrale loves you, and Mrs Williams love you, and what would have inclined me to love you, if I had been neutral before, you are a great favourite of Dr Beattie.'[25]

Mrs Thrale apparently was less loving than Johnson thought. Years later, when Boswell published this letter in the *Life of Johnson*, she wrote in the margin, 'Not I. I never loved him.' He knew he was going to be seeing a fair amount of her on his visit, but it seems unlikely that he deluded himself into thinking that she might feel anything like love for him. It was cordiality at the most.

On this visit Boswell also hoped to persuade Johnson 'to fix our voyage to the Hebrides or at least our journey through the highlands of Scotland' for the autumn. Johnson was still interested, though worried that Boswell would pester him about it: '[I] have not given up the western voyage. But however all this may be or not, let us try to make each other happy when we meet, and not refer our pleasure to distant times or distant places.' There was no real danger of that. After a long drought, the stage was set for what Boswell hoped would be a memorable 'homecoming'.[26]

SEVENTEEN

'The Down upon a Plum'

I

Boswell was in a 'flutter' of anticipation when he left Edinburgh for the five-day journey to London on 14 March 1772, but he could not suppress his lurking sense of guilt at leaving Margaret. He would be gone for seven weeks. She was very unwell and he was 'seriously concerned' at parting from her, which rather spoiled the joy he always had in the exciting moments when the post-chaise rumbled out of town. He also had to contend with the uncertainty of his responses to the higher sexual temperature in the metropolis. He told himself that he was more emotionally stable than he had been during any of his previous visits, his 'present firmness and cheerfulness of mind' encouraging him when he thought of the 'weakness and gloominess' of 'former parts of my life'; but even on the journey south he groaned inwardly when he looked on the beautiful figure of a clergyman's daughter: 'I cannot help being instantaneously affected by the sight of beauty ... a glance from a fine eye can yet affect my assurance ... I compared myself to one of those animals who by their strong scales or tough skins are invulnerable by a bullet but may be wounded by the sharp point of a sword.'[1]

Within hours of his arrival in London, walking past 'a variety of fine girls, genteelly dressed' in the Strand, 'all wearing Venus's girdle' and beckoning him to 'amorous intercourse', his thoughts ran into 'their old channels, which were pretty deeply worn' and he found himself musing, as he had with Rousseau, on 'polygamy and the concubines of the patriarchs and the harmlessness of temporary likings unconnected with mental attachment'. Resolving then and there, earnestly but feebly, 'never again to come to London without bringing my wife along with me', he none the less kept talking to prostitutes, 'from a kind of inclination to entertain my curiosity, without deviating from my fidelity to my valuable spouse'. After a week in the city he managed to stem this inclination lest he 'fall into an infidelity which would make me very miserable'. It was a struggle, though Johnson saw some mirth in the figure of the faithful husband he was now presenting. Were it not for 'public amusements' at places like the Pantheon, where they had just been with their mutual friend General James Oglethorpe, Johnson said, turning to Boswell, 'you now would have been with a wench ... Oh, I forgot you were married.'[2]

Boswell successfully resisted temptation for his entire London visit. To lessen the pain of separation from Margaret, he wrote dozens of letters to her over the seven weeks – 'corresponding with my dear wife is a great happiness to me,' he noted in his journal, which he began again to keep in full the day he left Edinburgh. When he had been absent for a month Grange did not help by sending reports of Margaret's loneliness: 'so much alone, indeed she has not many people here at present that she can be quite easy with.' Lord and Lady Auchinleck virtually ignored her. At the end of April, his hypochondria returned a little. 'Uneasy at valuable friend's complaints. Gloomy fate, or doubts as to it, clouded me.' Once or twice he drank too much to dull his worries about her.[3]

In his longing for his wife and battle against the temptations of infidelity, he turned to her attractive and vivacious girlhood friend Margaret ('Peggie' Cunynghame) Stuart, the niece of Eglinton and wife of the Earl of Bute's second son, Lieut.-Col. James Archibald Stuart. For some reason he had originally viewed Margaret Stuart in 'black colours' and disapproved of his wife's continuing her friendship with her, but now he made Margaret his own confidante, perhaps thinking she would have a more sympathetic and knowing ear than Temple regarding his sexual frustrations. Their relationship was unique. She was one of the few beautiful and charming women he seems to have known intimately without a sexual interest, though he grew sentimentally fond of her and she was not beyond some flirtatious badinage. At her house in Mayfair, she talked candidly to him of the harmlessness of 'an occasional infidelity in her husband, as she did not think it at all connected with affection'. A special mistress or frequent infidelity was one thing, but 'a transient fancy for a girl, or being led by one's companions after drinking to an improper place, was not to be considered as inconsistent with true affection'. Such thoughts were bound to come home to roost. For the time being, though, she thought Boswell was the ideal husband: 'If all husbands here [were] like you, wives [would] not wish to go to heaven.'[4]

2

Although Boswell was lonely without Margaret, this was still the happiest and most satisfying visit to London he had yet made. He had had 'almost complete felicity' since he arrived, he told Grange on 9 May just before leaving, 'admirable health, fine spirits, the conversation of the first geniuses. I am now sitting in Mr Samuel Johnson's study' – not quite like writing from Melanchthon's tomb but close to it. The cradle of his felicity, in addition to his literary fame, was the confidence and respectability he felt he had acquired through his good marriage. He now felt complete, impervious to hypochondria, fascinated with the difference he felt to his former character in London:

> I dined very comfortably [at Dolly's beefsteak house], meditating on old times when I used to dine there frequently and was in a most dissipated and sickly state of mind ... hardly able to observe common decency of conduct ...

> now I am firm and cheerful and contented in general ... very rarely does a cloud darken my mind.[5]

Twice in his journal the phrase 'hugged myself' captures his delight in rich social and intellectual moments. He endowed such moments with dazzling imagery. One such entry was on 10 April:

> Mr Johnson and Dr Goldsmith and nobody else were the company. I felt a completion of happiness. I just sat and hugged myself in my own mind. Here I am in London, at the house of General Oglethorpe, who introduced himself to me just because I had distinguished myself [with the *Account of Corsica*]; and here is Mr Johnson, whose character is so vast; here is Dr Goldsmith, so distinguished in literature. Words cannot describe our feelings. The finer parts are lost, as the down upon a plum; the radiance of light cannot be painted.

The other was at a meeting of the *London Magazine* partners when he glowed with the idea of himself, a Scot, discussing business with distinguished London publishers. 'From my perfect art of melting myself into the general mass', as in a 'crucible filled with lead or silver', the national distinction was 'quite forgotten', he wrote, though he had the capacity to recover his Scots individuality: 'But when the heat is over, I gather myself up as firm as ever, with perhaps only a small plate or thin leaf of the other metal upon me sufficient to make me glitter, and even that I can rub off if I choose it.' The chameleon in him enabled him to be transported into a 'sensation':

> I was a man of considerable consequence. The place of our meeting, St Paul's Churchyard, the sound of St Paul's clock striking the hours, the busy and bustling countenances of the partners around me, all contributed to give me a complete sensation of the kind. I hugged myself in it. I thought how different this was from the usual objects of a Scots laird. I had a joy in indulging my own humour.

He also indulged in too much wine and Dilly had to take him back to his house for the night.[6]

3

The list of 'first geniuses', literary, artistic, theatrical, political, judicial and scientific, with whom Boswell found himself in easy conversation reads like a roll-call of the late-eighteenth-century London Enlightenment: Johnson, Reynolds, Garrick, Goldsmith, the naturalist-explorer Sir Joseph Banks, the botanist Daniel Carl Solander, Dr Joseph Priestley (who discovered oxygen and was described by Coleridge as 'Patriot, and Saint, and Sage'), Paoli, Lord Mansfield, Lord North, Wilkes, Percy, Benjamin Franklin, Dr Charles Burney (the music historian and father of the novelist Fanny Burney), and (not least) Edmund Burke. His friendship with Goldsmith, so tentative at first because of the other's vanity and ridiculously extravagant behaviour, blossomed. Goldsmith, who was just embarking on a book of natural history, and who in 1773 would become celebrated for his play *She Stoops to Conquer*, had convinced Boswell that he was capable of warm and interested friendship. It was a pleasant thought that here was a literary lion with whom to enjoy many years of London companionship.[7]

Paoli, too, was as genial and encouraging as ever. On Easter Sunday, after breakfasting on chocolate and sweet biscuits at the General's, they worshipped together at the Sardinian Chapel in Lincoln's Inn Fields where the ceremonial 'solemnity' of the Catholic High Mass, 'the music, the wax lights, and the odour of the frankincense' as always stirred his religious devotion. (The Anglican service also had that effect on him, especially at Westminster Abbey – the 'grand old building, the painted glass windows, the noble music, the excellent service of the Church and a very good sermon'.) He and Johnson together called on Paoli at least twice. Paoli in his still shaky English pressed Johnson to come often. 'I will come with my friend Boswell,' Johnson replied, 'and so I'll get a habit of coming.' Paoli also gave Boswell almost unlimited use of his fine coach. On 19 April, for example, he and Dilly rode in high style to the Lord Mayor's dinner and ball at the Mansion House, with 'the General's coachman and Swiss footman in silver-laced liveries, and Joseph my servant also, mounted behind for the sake of grandeur'. Inevitably, wrenched from his country and reduced to the life of a civilian with little to do in London, Johnson noticed that Paoli had 'lost somewhat of that grandeur in his air and manner which he had when he came first to England'.[8]

Garrick was more difficult to track down, but there was the occasional satisfying encounter. Boswell breakfasted 'by appointment' at Garrick's house on 15 April, for example, where he picked up some conversation that he used in the *Life of Johnson*, as a reporter might, to clarify for the public the misunderstandings between Garrick and Johnson that muddied the waters of their friendship. Garrick volunteered that Johnson had misrepresented him in the Preface to his Shakespeare edition (1765) by intimating that he had not freely made available his fabulous collection of early Shakespeare editions. Quite the opposite was true, the actor maintained: not only had Johnson's black servant Francis Barber fetched several crucial volumes but Garrick had instructed his servants to light a fire for Johnson if he came himself to use more of the collection. In his journal, Boswell wrote his own explanation of what happened, later transferring it almost verbatim to the *Life of Johnson*, which neither Garrick nor Johnson lived to read but for which public airing neither would have thanked him:

I was sorry to find any coldness between Mr Johnson and Mr Garrick. They had misunderstood one another. Mr Garrick had imagined that showing his old plays was a favour. I have since learnt from Mr Johnson that his idea was that Garrick wanted to be courted for them, and that on the contrary he ought rather to have courted him and sent him the plays of his own accord. He denied that his black ever got any of them. Mr Johnson may perhaps be insensibly fretted a little that *Davy Garrick*, who was his pupil and who came up to London at the same time with him [from Lichfield] to try the chance of life, should be so very general a favourite and should have fourscore thousand pounds, an immense sum, when *he* had so little. He accordingly will allow no great merit in acting. Garrick cannot but be hurt at this, and so unhappily there is not the harmony that one would wish.

Events like this vindicated Boswell's obsession to travel to London, the seat of his imagination. He was now at the centre of his only meaningful universe.[9]

On 8 May Garrick called on Boswell early in the morning, announcing himself as 'Rantum Scantum'. Together they sauntered to St James's Park and over to the Thames where Garrick thrilled him by reciting a few lines from *Macbeth*, one of his most famous roles. For a man who glorified the theatre as much as Boswell, this was magic, something to tell his children in years to come. A year later, preparing himself for another visit to London, he reminisced about that sacred riverside recitation in a letter to Garrick: 'I must beg that you will play Macbeth while I am in London. You may remember what an impression you made upon me, by repeating only a few lines of it, while we walked one morning last spring on the banks of the Thames near the Adelphi.' Garrick never did play Macbeth again.[10]

Boswell also had a reunion after six years with Wilkes. He saw his old friend at the Lord Mayor's banquet. Wilkes knew it was risky for an aspiring Scots advocate and future laird with political aspirations to be seen with him, but he amicably chided Boswell anyway for avoiding him on his previous visits to London. 'Don't sit by me or it will be in the *Public Advertiser* tomorrow,' he joked. This popular demagogue, after a gaol sentence, election to and expulsion from the House of Commons, was now Sheriff of London and a somewhat safer companion, although they would not resume their close friendship until 1775 when Wilkes became Lord Mayor. They sat down together. Wilkes, ever good-natured, teased him a bit: 'Well, Boswell, you was a pleasant fellow when I knew you. But now you're grown the gravest of grave mortals. You should have come and seen a friend in gaol.' 'I do assure you I am glad to meet with you,' Boswell replied, 'but I cannot come to see you. I am a Scotch laird and a Scotch lawyer and a Scotch married man. It would not be decent.' They then reminisced a little about their diversions on the Continent and parted hoping for a more congenial political climate soon in which to resume their friendship.[11]

4

Johnson as always commanded most of Boswell's attention. 'I do love thee, I do love thee ... I am glad to see you again, very glad to see you again,' Johnson said when they were reunited. It was on this London visit that the idea of writing a biography of the sage crystallised. After hearing Johnson pronounce on 31 March that Goldsmith's *Life of Parnell* was poorly written because 'nobody could furnish the life of a man but those who had eat and drank and lived in social intercourse with him', Boswell wrote unequivocally in his journal, 'I have a constant plan to write the life of Mr Johnson. I have not told him of it yet, nor do I know if I should tell him.' Afraid of being rebuffed outright and thereafter denied the luxury of asking so many questions, Boswell eventually broached the matter indirectly: 'I said that if it was not troublesome and presuming too much, I would beg of him to tell me all the little circumstances of his life, what schools he attended, when he came to Oxford, when he came to London, etc., etc. He did not disapprove of my curiosity as to these particulars, but said, "They'll come out by degrees."' They spoke of friends and of writing their Lives. Johnson seemed to understand what his disciple had in mind: 'I hope you'll write all their lives.'[12]

Because Boswell was now a member of Johnson's circle, he was able to represent conversations with Johnson and others more insightfully. And as an accepted satellite in the Johnsonian orbit, he could see things about Johnson and other people which he had not seen before. He could use himself to draw Johnson out – the slightly comic Scot pumping him for his pronouncements on Scotland, the spirited companion willing to stay up talking into the early hours of the morning and drinking tea with him and Mrs Williams, the sympathetic defender of those whom he knew Johnson criticized unfairly, the industrious and earnest family man and advocate, the aspiring writer, the amateur (and not very well informed) philosopher and, finally but very important, the willing target of Johnson's wit.

A good example of the last, a role that helped engender his reputation as a buffoon, was a conversation with Johnson and Bennet Langton at the Crown and Anchor on 15 April. Knowing Johnson's intolerance of Methodists, Boswell played the devil's advocate by defending six Methodist students who had been thrown out of Oxford several years earlier for preaching their doctrine. Boswell maintained they were 'good beings', to which Johnson shot back, 'But they were not fit to be in the University of Oxford. A cow is a very good animal in the field. But we turn her out of a garden.' Aware that Johnson was careful never to drink wine, he then opened another subject by defending 'convivial' drinking of wine. Here he was in perilous waters where the likes of Langton trembled to enter. 'BOSWELL: "Would not you, Sir, now, allow a man oppressed with care to drink and make himself merry?" JOHNSON: "Yes; if he sat next you." ' 'This was one of his great broadsides,' Boswell crowed. Langton understood Boswell's strategy: 'I saw that you would bring something upon yourself.' Boswell noted, 'I never was disturbed. I know Mr Johnson so well and delight in his grand explosions, even when directed against myself, so much that I am not at all hurt.'[13]

Most of Boswell's London literary friends saw what Langton had just noticed in his method. But what he needed were more regular opportunities to dip his oar into the currents of such conversation. If only he could be a member of the Club, which assembled every Friday evening at the Turk's Head, Gerard Street, Soho. However, this was not the year for it. His time was running out in London.

5

Boswell had irritated his father by unnecessarily and expensively coming to London long before the Hastie cause came before the Lords. Though he attended several appeals in the Lords during his first month in London to make himself feel at home there and see one of the Law Lords, Lord Mansfield, in action – who impressed him wonderfully with his eloquence – he and Andrew Crosbie, who was helping him, did little to prepare until the week before the appeal.[14]

Johnson rescued him at the eleventh hour. Boswell had shown the Session papers on the cause to him three weeks earlier and received some valuable advice: 'You must show some learning upon this occasion ... that a schoolmaster has a prescriptive right to beat, and that an action of assault and battery cannot be admitted against him unless there is some great excess, some barbarity. This has maimed none of his boys.' But they spoke of it little more until three days before the Lords were due to hear the cause. Then Boswell had to scramble. He asked Johnson to write out the arguments to be made, partly because such a document would be a great addition to the Auchinleck archives. However, the most 'the great man' would agree to do was dictate it – a dictation, incidentally, that Boswell printed verbatim in the *Life*.[15]

On the morning of the 14th he donned the robes of an English barrister (as was the custom for Scots advocates pleading in the Lords), gulped down a couple of large bumpers of wine (as Pringle advised) that confused him rather than 'inspiriting' him, and strode into venerable Westminster Hall with Crosbie. Thoughts of coming to the English Bar to plead every spring danced in his mind. 'The House of Lords will be a fine theatre for your talents,' Temple told him, feeding his fantasy. The ceremonious nature of the proceedings, all noted in his journal, was tailor-made to his taste for the big occasion. He drew strength from it, relishing 'the solemnity and form of making three bows', the spectacle of the gowned peers assembled in greater numbers than usual, and the public 'uncommonly numerous'. Mountstuart, Oglethorpe, Garrick, Lord Lyttelton, Edward Dilly and other friends were there to lend moral support, though not Johnson who had already done his bit.[16]

Boswell was 'all in a flutter' until it was time for him to appear. He mounted the octagonal platform in much 'palpitation' and began to speak from the text he had prepared from Johnson's dictation. It was an uphill fight since Mansfield had made it clear that he was against Hastie. But it was not just his client's future that was at stake, it was his own reputation: 'I begun with a very low voice and rose gradually; but restrained myself from appearing anyhow bold or even easy.' Speaking slowly and distinctly, he desisted from the bold theatrics he was wont to use in Edinburgh. He even managed a joke about his own unruly behaviour as a schoolboy and won 'bravos' from the Lords and a smile from Mansfield. Mansfield concluded expeditiously with a fine speech and the Court of Session verdict was overturned. It was unfortunate for Hastie but a good day's work for Boswell.

The congratulations flowed in immediately. Boswell changed his wig and sped over to the elegant Mayfair house of Elizabeth Montague, author and hostess, dubbed by Johnson 'the Queen of the Blues', who boasted she never invited idiots. Paoli had inveigled him an invitation to dinner, attended that evening by Lord Lyttelton, the Archbishop of York, Paoli himself, and two or three others. Leaning over to him, Lyttelton passed on Mansfield's remark: 'Mr Boswell is too good a counsel; for in order to assist his client he would give us a bad impression of his own character, when he tells us that when he was at school he would have done his master a mischief if he could.' Lyttelton's own ironic observation to the assembled guests was that Boswell 'has been pleading for tyranny, a thing he never did before, nor never will do again'. The Archbishop then invited him to dine. What an excellent place London was, Boswell thought. The following day, Garrick told him he could have been more animated in court, though he understood that Boswell had had to muzzle himself to some extent because his reputation as a wild card had preceded him. That night, over midnight tea with Johnson and Mrs Williams, Boswell regaled them with all the compliments. 'Well', Johnson replied, 'that was worth coming to London for.' Even Lord Auchinleck would have agreed.[17]

6

Notwithstanding Johnson's warning not to press him about the Hebridean adventure, Boswell seems to have discreetly circled around the subject. Sir Alexander Macdonald of the Isle of Skye, to whom Boswell made a point of introducing Johnson on 28 March, may well have pushed the scheme; his wife Elizabeth Bosville, Boswell's former flame, did her part by charming Johnson, who remarked after meeting her, 'I will go to Skye with this lady. I'll go anywhere under this lady's protection.' With his keen eye for incongruities, Boswell could not help observing, 'There was a fine contrast between his robust and rather dreadful figure and that of the beautiful Lady.'[18]

Some romantic talk about the remote and wild isle of St Kilda in the Outer Hebrides undoubtedly also whetted Johnson's appetite. Boswell boasted that he thought of buying it. 'Pray do,' Johnson chimed in, 'we shall go and pass a winter amid the blasts there. We shall have fine fish, and we shall take some dried tongues with us and some books. We shall have a strong-built vessel and some Orkney men to navigate her. We must build a tolerable house. But we may carry with us a wooden house ready made and nothing to do but to put it up.' If Boswell would buy the island, he would save the islanders from 'worse hands': 'We must give them a clergyman, and he shall be one of Beattie's choosing. I'll be your Lord Chancellor or what you please.' This outburst hints at the appeal to Johnson of the idea of an arduous adventure such as his friend was proposing, a Rasselas-type exploration of primitive or savage life.[19]

It remained to be seen whether Johnson would commit himself to this romantic autumn journey into the northern wilds, but in the meantime Boswell fed his own imagination on the literary possibilities of such a magical journey with the greatest Englishman of letters of the age. Except for his journal on this London visit, he had been through a dry patch in his writing and knew that at the very least the Hebridean journey would be a gold-mine both for his journal and for the biography of Johnson. As he left London on 12 May, he felt his urge to write returning. He had been adding to the 'rich collection of good things' in his 'Boswelliana', which Dempster playfully predicted would become 'the greatest treasure of this age'. He had also pushed himself to write an article on the controversial but not consummately interesting question of patronage in the Church of Scotland for the *London Magazine* on 17 April, wearing himself out by sitting up all night to do it: 'The time was when I have sitten up four nights in one week in London. But I found this night very hard upon me.' A more fascinating subject to him than the Church was melancholia, about which he could write with painful self-knowledge. He promised Dilly a significant and lengthy series on it for their magazine, to be titled, 'The Hypochondriack', which he thought might well be a major contribution to the literature on the subject.[20]

7

With little time and less energy to keep a full journal in Edinburgh, Boswell's life between 20 April 1772 and 30 March 1773 is sketchy. We do know that once he returned home he squandered what literary energy and productive writing time he had by sequestering himself in the Parliament House archives and copying out 'curious passages' from the old records of the Privy Council of Scotland with a view to publishing a book of extracts. He thought it would enhance his status as advocate and please his father. In spite of his pleasure in the hunt for 'nuggets' of Scottish legal history, the exercise, which came to nothing, had a deadening effect on his literary energy. So did an anonymous pamphlet he published in November, *Reflections on the Bankruptcies in Scotland. 1772*, on the failure of the Ayr bank, Douglas, Heron & Company, though it is more interesting than the title suggests.[21] It attacks aspects of contemporary Scottish life and manners that Boswell despised, the origins of which he traced back to the Union. Winking at his own excesses, he complained that there was 'more hard drinking in Scotland than in any other country in Europe', with men huddling boorishly together at parties to consume liquour while the ladies were relegated to drawing rooms as if to nunneries. It was his old theme of Scottish vulgarity.

After hearing in the autumn that Johnson had abandoned the idea of the Hebridean tour because of bad health, Boswell gave more thought to a biography of the great man. In London, Percy had given him an

inaccurate 'catalogue' of Johnson's publications. He now asked Garrick
to add to it: 'I know you will give me your kind assistance in collecting
everything that may be had with regard to your old preceptor ... If I
survive Mr Johnson, I shall publish a Life of him, for which I have a
store of materials.' Garrick did not respond. Not in the least discouraged,
Boswell promised to 'trouble you to give me all of him that I want' in
the spring. He also drew freely on Langton who, with his wife the
Dowager Lady Rothes, spent several weeks in Edinburgh that autumn.[22]

In another literary vein, he showed his taste for the antique in British
poetry by encouraging Beattie to complete *The Minstrel.* The work had
patriotic appeal for Boswell partly because it is full of descriptions of
Scottish scenery and traditional folklore, and partly because it resonated
with echoes of primitive Gaelic poetry of the Highlands immensely
popular in Scotland since James Macpherson's famous (and notorious)
Ossian in 1762. He also took it upon himself to encourage Percy to
publish, as a sequel to his famous *Reliques of Ancient English Poetry,* three
more volumes of 'Ancient English and Scottish Poems'. Percy told Boswell
in August that his collection would consist of poems that had 'lain hid
in old MSS' and would celebrate the ancient spirit of chivalry and the
state of manners in the Border country before the Union, both subjects
dear to Boswell's heart. Percy asked him to be on the lookout for any
Scottish poems to include. 'Were I to judge from my own feelings alone,
and indeed my own wishes,' Boswell wrote back, 'I should be for your
publishing as many volumes of the same kind ... I defy you to publish
more than I shall read with pleasure.' He acknowledged himself to be
one of those 'lovers of British antiquity' who gloried in 'the feudal spirit'.
Percy never published his collection.[23]

8

Margaret welcomed him home from London in May with open arms
and it was not long before she was pregnant again. The irritating issue
of the Auchinleck entail also awaited him, continuing to sour his relationship with his father. What nettled Boswell was his father's possession
of the deed that he had signed away in 1762 in exchange for an annual
allowance of £100. He could have stolen the deed one day at Auchinleck
when he saw it lying about – perhaps a snare laid by his father? Johnson
told him he had done a 'foolish thing' to renounce the estate but that to
steal the deed would have been criminal: 'We should have had you

hanged, ha! ha! ha! No. You would not have been hanged, but you might have been whipped, or transported, ha! ha! ha!' Johnson admonished Boswell not to 'tease' his father about it and predicted that eventually the argument would fizzle out. Pringle thought the same and was aghast when Boswell peevishly declined an invitation to Auchinleck. Correct this faux pas immediately, he urged, by apologizing and hastening to Auchinleck where he could begin to show himself the dutiful son. Temple recommended the same. Boswell followed none of this advice and the two families grew even further apart.[24]

In spite of these resentments, Lord Auchinleck could not complain about his son's legal work. He was busy and profitable, at one point in November earning twenty-three guineas in a week. In March 1773, just before escaping to London again, he represented three men accused in the December and January 'meal riots' in Dundee and Perth, enjoying almost complete success when two were freed and the third was sentenced to transportation instead of hanging. A sign of how personally involved Boswell could still become in causes, even ones in which he was not retained, was his visit that month to Alexander Murdison in prison, three days before he was due to hang for sheep-stealing. He also witnessed the execution in the Grassmarket of Murdison, his accomplice, and a burglar, observing in his brief journal notes (as he had the previous year at Tyburn) that 'the effect diminished as each went'.[25]

However, most of his legal work was plodding, and he sought relief in drinking and, increasingly, gambling at whist. The card-playing irritated Margaret, especially when it took place at home and the sessions lasted into the early hours of the morning. There was a sexual lapse, too, in October, perhaps his first instance of marital infidelity, in the Old Town after drinking too much wine. Then he dreaded another infection. He confessed all to Margaret, who was quick to forgive him and insisted that his surgeon Alexander Wood be called in. 'She is my best friend, and the most generous heart,' he wrote. Forgiveness is not always the best route to reform, however, and in January he strayed into another prostitute's arms. Again, Margaret called in Woods and patiently forgave him: 'My wife's kind attention about me wonderful.' Both times he escaped infection.[26]

Without the journal, we cannot properly gauge Boswell's response to these lapses, but the strains of the claustrophobic and intense professional and social life he was leading, and constant anxiety over the entail, were taking their toll. He must also have been nervous about Margaret's third pregnancy. The baby was due in mid-March, yet even that happy event was a source of perplexity because he had his heart set on a visit to London in the spring. Apart from London's regular attractions, there was the Hebrides scheme to keep alive in Johnson's mind. But what would his friends think of him if he left his wife for two long months so soon after the birth of their baby? How would Margaret take it? By March he had made up his mind, as he told Percy: 'My wife is to lie in this month. If it shall please GOD to grant her a good recovery, I intend being in London by the first of April, when I shall have the pleasure of meeting you.'[27]

On 15 March 1773 Margaret gave birth to a healthy daughter, Veronica. Two weeks later, at three o'clock one morning, Boswell was driven quietly out of Edinburgh leaving her not fully recovered. As usual on these occasions, he took a bad conscience with him:

> I had still the awful thought that I might never return to Scotland and meet my dearest wife. Either of us might die during our separation. This thought, when it presses strongly upon the mind, is terrible. It is enough to make one never separate from a valuable spouse ... When the fly had rumbled me a mile or two, rational and manly sensations took the place of tender and timid feebleness. I considered that I had left my wife and little daughter well. That I was going to London, whither so many Members of Parliament, lawyers, merchants, and others go and return in safety to their families. I saw nothing dangerous, nothing melancholy. I had taken leave of my wife last night, which had affected my spirits a good deal. She is of an anxious temper at all times; but being not yet fully recovered from child-birth, she was more anxious than usual.

Whatever his wife's state of mind, Boswell was surprised to find himself quite at peace in London on 5 April: 'I know not how it is, but I am less anxious in being absent from my valuable spouse this year than I was last. Perhaps her having a little daughter to amuse her makes the scene more lively to my imagination; but then ought I not to feel a double anxiety this year, when I am absent both from a wife and a child?' Perhaps he should have done, but he did not.[28]

On the day before he left for London he wrote eleven letters proudly announcing the birth of Veronica, an effort that not every father would find time to make amid the bustle of preparing for a journey. In one of these, to Goldsmith, he celebrates his infant daughter by connecting her birth with the first performance at Covent Garden of *She Stoops to Conquer*. He hopes Goldsmith's new comic spirit on the stage will reverberate in Veronica's life: 'You must know my wife was safely delivered of a daughter, the very evening that *She Stoops to Conquer* first appeared. I am fond of the coincidence.' He flatters himself that his 'little daughter' will be blest with the enlivening 'cheerfulness of your Comick Muse' and escape the weakening sentimentalism currently afflicting English comedy: 'She has nothing of that wretched whining and crying which we see children so often have; nothing of the *Comédie Larmoyante*. I hope she shall live to be an agreeable companion, and to diffuse gayety over the days of her father, which are sometimes a little cloudy.'[29]

9

After spending the first night at Dilly's, Boswell found lodgings at a milliner's opposite Melbourne House in Piccadilly for a guinea per week. It was near Paoli's new lodgings in fashionable Jermyn Street.

'I'm glad you're come,' Johnson said, embracing him. They immediately began to talk of Goldsmith's play and his skirmish with Thomas Evans, the publisher of the *London Packet*. Evans had published a scurrilous abuse of Goldsmith by one 'Anti-Gnatho', probably the scoundrel William Kenrick who had already attacked Boswell himself and Johnson in his *Letter to James Boswell* (1769), addressed 'to the Luminary of *Auchinleck*, the Pencil of Historic Excellence, the Syren Throat of Soul-moving Song, the Emerald of Masquerade, etc'. Goldsmith, 'irascible as a hornet', retaliated by marching briskly over to Evans's house and thrashing him with his cane; unfortunately, Evans hit him back so that he appeared at the Club that night with a bloody face. Goldsmith was lighthearted enough about the whole episode, calling himself London's only '*Poet militant*', even though Evans was suing him. Johnson's comment to Boswell on Goldsmith's public self-defence in the *London Chronicle* was, 'He has done it well; but 'tis a foolish thing well done.' Johnson thought it was the first time Goldsmith had beaten someone but not the first time he had been beaten – ''tis a new plume to him'.[30]

Boswell's reunion with Goldsmith on the morning of 7 April at the latter's bedside – often a symbol in Boswell's mind of intimacy and informality – is one of the most tender he ever recorded:

He was not up, and I was shown into his dining-room and library. When he heard that it was I, he roared from his bed, 'Boswell!' I ran to him. We had a cordial embrace. I sat upon the side of his bed and we talked of the success of his new comedy, which he saw that I sincerely enjoyed, and of his beating Evans the publisher.

Just how much that warmth meant to him may be judged from his comment on the starkly contrasting meeting with Lord Mansfield a few days later: 'His cold reserve and sharpness, too, were still too much for me. It was like being cut with a very, very cold instrument. I have not for a long time experienced that weakness of mind which I had formerly in a woeful degree in the company of the great or the clever . . . He chills the most generous blood.' Mansfield was too much like his father. On the 12th Boswell saw *She Stoops to Conquer*, over which he 'laughed most heartily': 'It was really a rich evening to me. I would not stay to see the farce. I would not put the taste of Goldsmith's fruit out of my mouth.'[31]

Goldsmith at times became irritated even with Boswell himself for the way he hung on to every Johnsonian word. With typical disarming self-effacement, Boswell included one instance of this in the *Life of Johnson*. One evening in 'a circle of wits', probably still smarting from Johnson's tyranny of conversation, Goldsmith 'found fault with me for talking of Johnson as entitled to the honour of unquestionable superiority. "Sir, (said he), you are for making a monarchy of what should be a republick." '[32]

Boswell's journal entries about Goldsmith in the spring of 1773, as well as his reference to him in the *Life of Johnson*, are especially poignant since he would not be seeing him again. Goldsmith died (from a kidney infection in his early forties) in April of the following year, mourned by the Club, Johnson, and not least Boswell himself. 'I have not been so much affected with any event that has happened of a long time,' Boswell wrote to Garrick on 11 April 1774. The news grieved him especially because he had decided not to visit London that spring and had to come to terms with it far away from the comforts and understanding of fellow Club members. He longed to talk about Goldsmith with his friends, to be part of dinner conversations such as the one at Reynolds's house soon after the tragedy. A number of the guests criticized Goldsmith, until Johnson, who had listened patiently, rose and growled, 'If nobody was suffered to abuse poor Goldy, but those who could write as well, he would have few censors.' There was no talk like that about Goldsmith in Edinburgh, nobody in the city who knew him well. Boswell pleaded with his friends to send him accounts of Goldsmith's last moments, but so far as we know only Oglethorpe and Johnson responded satisfyingly.

He himself wrote a moving tribute to 'Goldy' for the *London Magazine* in June.[33]

10

So eager was Boswell to talk and dine with his many friends that his London journal suffered as a result. By 20 April he had not even written the entry for 3 April. He finally gave up keeping a full journal on 14 April, reverting to his method of keeping notes which – in many cases, as long as fifteen years later – he used to jog his astonishing memory. This is a minor literary tragedy, given the fullness of his social life and the groundwork he was laying that month to win election to the Club.

Having petitioned Johnson, Reynolds, Goldsmith, and Percy to nominate and vote for him, he invited them all to his lodgings on the 24th, apparently confident that by then, if nominated on the 16th and elected on the 23rd, he could celebrate his election. Oddly, nobody nominated him, so Johnson took matters in hand on the 23rd with a note to Goldsmith who was chairman that evening: 'I beg that you will excuse my absence to the Club. I am going this evening to Oxford. I have another favour to beg. It is that I may be considered as proposing Mr Boswell for a candidate of our Society, and that he may be considered as regularly nominated.'[34]

On the memorable evening of the 30th, Johnson took Boswell for dinner at Beauclerk's – 'I do love Boswell monstrously,' Beauclerk had told Langton, liking his 'open downright manners' – to meet a few of the Club members, including Beauclerk's charming wife Lady Diana, Reynolds and the Irishman Lord Charlemont. When they all left for the Turk's Head, Boswell stayed behind with Lady Diana, awaiting word of whether or not any member had dropped an ominous black ball that would exclude him. 'I sat in a state of anxiety which even the charming conversation of Lady Di Beauclerk could not entirely dissipate.' In less than an hour, Beauclerk sent back the triumphant news that he had been elected. He hastened to the Turk's Head to be introduced to 'such a society as can seldom be found'. Johnson stood and, leaning over the back of a chair 'as on a desk or pulpit' and with a 'humorous formality', proceeded to explain the conduct expected of every 'good member'. Johnson told Boswell that he had succeeded where others failed because he had canvassed for membership like a politician in an election. Even so, he had almost been blackballed – by Burke, of all people:

'Burke told me he doubted if you were fit for it, but now you are in, none of them are sorry. Burke says that you have so much good humour naturally, it is scarce a virtue.' BOSWELL: 'They were afraid of you, sir, as it was you who proposed me.' JOHNSON: 'Sir, they knew that if they refused you, they'd probably never have got in another. I'd have kept them all out. Beauclerk was very earnest for you.'[35]

Boswell met Burke for the first time on the night of his election, but he had heard him speak a few days before in the House of Commons. It was an exhilarating experience that made him fantasize about someday becoming a Member of Parliament. He had never heard anything like the oratorical fireworks of Burke's two speeches against Lord Clive's dealings in East Indian affairs:

It was a great feast to me who had never heard him before. It was astonishing how all kinds of figures of speech crowded upon him. He was like a man in an orchard where boughs loaded with fruit hung around him, and he pulled apples as fast as he pleased and pelted the Ministry ... It seemed to me, however, that his oratory rather tended to distinguish himself than to assist his cause ... It was like the exhibition of a favourite actor. But I would have been exceedingly happy to be him.[36]

After meeting Burke at the Club, he tried several times to corner him for a tête-à-tête during his remaining two weeks in London, but Burke proved frustratingly elusive.

II

The Thrales were going through hard times. The previous autumn they had lost a child ten hours after its birth and Henry Thrale had also suffered something of a business crisis at his Southwark brewery. To make things worse, the papers had maliciously started rumours that Mrs Thrale had been Johnson's lover and that her eldest son resembled him. Now she was pregnant again and her mother was very ill at Streatham Park. Partly to economize and partly to provide her mother with the tranquillity she needed, in November, she had shifted the whole family to the Thrales' house in Southwark, thus for the time being depriving Johnson of his comfortable country retreat.[37]

Boswell was quick to take advantage of Johnson's accessibility and they met virtually every day of his six weeks in London. On Good Friday, after conversation at Johnson's house with Dr Levett over tea and hot cross buns, they prayed together at St Clement Dane's church in the Strand, after which they returned to Johnson's Court. Then Johnson invited him to supper on Easter Sunday. So, after receiving the Holy Sacrament at St Paul's and being 'struck and elevated as usual by the service' though without 'that firm conviction which I have done at different periods of my life, owing I believe to an indolence of mind', he joined Johnson for what he assumed would be a supper of simple 'pie', perhaps even served without cutlery. But to his surprise he, Johnson, Mrs Williams, and an unidentified woman not only had cutlery but also sat down to 'a very good soup, a boiled leg of lamb and spinach, a veal pie, an excellent rice pudding, pickled walnuts and onions, porter and port wine'.[38]

The conversation touched on Boswell's journal. Johnson confessed that he had tried as many as fourteen times to keep one but could never sustain it. Staring at Boswell, he stressed that 'the great thing' 'is the state of your own mind; and you ought to write down everything that you can, for you cannot judge at first what is good or bad; and write immediately while the impression is fresh, for it will not be the same a week after'. Boswell took that advice to heart. He often felt he was failing with his journal. It still vexed him to think of the lost eight hundred pages of his Dutch journal; somebody at that moment might be reading them and discovering the 'full state of my mind when in a deep melancholy'. Johnson's response must have offered him small comfort: 'Probably they had fallen into the hands of somebody who could not understand them, and would be destroyed as waste-paper.'

When Boswell pressed him for details of his early life, Johnson acknowledged for the first time that his friend was planning a biography: 'You shall have them ... all for twopence. I hope you shall know a great deal more of me before you write my Life.' He tossed him a few tidbits about his boyhood and his father, a bookseller in Lichfield. Boswell thought he would go to Oxford and seek out Johnson's tutor there, Dr William Adams of Pembroke College. ' "Sir," said he, "'tis not worth while. You know more of me than he does." '

At the Mitre on 1 May, Johnson paid him a high compliment, or at least Boswell thought so. The Irish, he argued, mixed more freely with the English than the Scots; their language was closer to English, and they were not so nationalistic as the Scots. But Boswell was different: 'I will do you, Boswell, the justice to say, that you are the most *unscottified* of your countrymen. You are almost the only instance of a Scotchman that I have known, who did not at every other sentence bring in some other Scotchman.' His fellow countrymen would not thank him for including that remark in the *Life*.[39]

Johnson's praise of Boswell as an anglicised Scot struck quite a different note from his anger with him a few days later on Mrs Thrale's less congenial turf. When he defended the charming Lady Diana Beauclerk's divorce from Viscount Bolingbroke by citing an Act of Parliament, Johnson blew up: 'Go to Scotland! Go to Scotland! I never heard you talk so foolishly.' Many years later that outburst still pained him, so much that he left it out of the *Life*, slipping in instead the milder rebuke, 'My dear Sir, never accustom your mind to mingle virtue and vice. The woman's a whore, and there's an end on't.'[40]

In spite of the rebuff, they parted affectionately on 10 May, Boswell travelling with Temple and his wife as far as Berwick on a mission to raise badly needed capital by selling some old family property. He was 'hurt a little' by their rusticated, provincial appearance but delighted to have their company. All went well until a breakfast conversation erupted into an argument between Anne Temple and Boswell who had snobbishly insisted that the Temple children could never hope to be anything more than clerks and stewards to noblemen. Anne shed bitter tears. 'I was rough to Mrs Temple ... I was wrong,' he admitted. Temple agreed: 'You certainly were indelicate ... You should not then have been so severe and rough with your friend ... I fear I cannot persuade her to pay you a visit.' She never forgave him. Temple, though, visited him and Margaret in Edinburgh in June, when Boswell made a point of introducing him to a number of his literary friends, including Hume and Kames. They also went out to Prestonfield to see Sir Alexander and to Auchinleck to see his father. It was one of the happiest visits Temple ever had with his old friend.[41]

12

By the end of the summer, Margaret was pregnant again and relations with his father and stepmother had stabilized into a cold predictability. He was in the thick of legal work in both the General Assembly and the Court of Session and had unsuccessfully defended three men accused of murder. One was a poor man unjustly sentenced to death for mistakenly stabbing a friend and the other two were thieving tinkers who were justly hanged for killing members of a family in an isolated crofter's cottage on the moors. The verdicts aside, Boswell distinguished himself in these and in other causes. On 24 June he was honoured to be elected Right Worshipful Master of St John's Lodge of Canongate Kilwinning Masonic Lodge, an office he held for the next two years. 'In short,' he told Langton, 'in most particulars I am as happy as you could wish me.'[42]

One important cause in which he triumphed, on the historic issue of literary property or copyright, deserves special mention.[43] In July he represented his publisher friend Alexander Donaldson in his fight for the right to publish in Edinburgh and London cheap reprints of English classics not protected, as he maintained, by the Copyright Act dating from the reign of Queen Anne. Ever since that Act the London publishers had argued that copyright existed in perpetuity rather than for just the fourteen years specified by the Act (plus fourteen more if the author were still alive at the end of that period). For years, Donaldson had been making handsome profits from these cheap reprints by ignoring the 'perpetual nature of copyright at common law'. In 1769 the London publishers had won a ruling in the Court of Chancery to stop what they regarded as his piracy. In 1773 they turned their attention to his Edinburgh trade and found a plaintiff in the London bookseller John Hinton. Donaldson chose Boswell with his friend John Maclaurin as counsel because of their long literary friendship. Boswell spoke eloquently: his main argument was that the London publishers' 'perpetual exclusive property' of books would create a monopoly and raise prices. Donaldson won the cause.

Emboldened by his victory in Edinburgh, Donaldson decided to make a rout of it in 1774 by appealing to the House of Lords to have the 1769 ruling overturned. Although Boswell was unable to take part in the appeal because he did not go to London that year, he was still involved in a way that paralleled the Douglas cause. Soon after the Court of Session ruling, he thought a published report of the speeches in the cause would sell, and Donaldson agreed that, as in 1769, these speeches might well influence the peers when the appeal was heard in the House of Lords in February 1774. An article in the *London Chronicle* on 3 August 1773, probably written by Boswell, put it this way: 'the attention of all the Literati of Europe' is 'naturally interested in a question so much connected with learning'. So in Edinburgh on 2 February, under his own name, Boswell published *The Decision of the Court of Session upon the Question of Literary Property*. It was, to be sure, only one of several factors in the appeal, but it had its effect and the Lords reversed the 1769 ruling in a decision that is still the basis for copyright law in England and America.

13

In May the prospects for Boswell and Johnson's Hebridean journey looked bleak. Johnson was melancholy and had developed a painfully inflamed eye. For a time Mrs Thrale looked after him, but with her own problems she was not sorry to part with him once he recovered. On 30 May she urged him to take heart and go to Scotland: 'Dissipation is to you a glorious medicine, and I believe Mr Boswell will be at last your best physician.' In July, replying to yet more of Boswell's prodding, he wrote, 'My eye is gradually growing stronger; and I hope will be able to take some delight in the survey of a Caledonian loch ... Let me know the exact time when your Courts intermit.' That was good to hear, as was the news that Sir Robert Chambers, the law professor whom they had visited in Oxford in 1768, was coming up to Newcastle and would accompany Johnson that far. But Boswell was leaving nothing to chance. He wrote to Thrale at the end of July, 'I must once more apply to you and Mrs Thrale to *launch* him from London, as I call it ... You can scarcely imagine how great joy I feel in the prospect of his coming.'[44]

And Johnson did come. In 'high spirits' Boswell wrote to Langton on 13 August that he expected 'to have him under my roof this night' and begin their 'expedition' in three or four days' time. 'What an intellectual feast is before me! I shall never murmur though he should at times treat me with more roughness than ever.'[45] He was convinced of Johnson's vigour of mind and body, but uncertain of his response to Scotland, the Scots, and the physical hardship they would certainly encounter. The stage was set for one of the most famous literary expeditions in British history.

EIGHTEEN

The Hebrides

I

On Saturday evening, 14 August, Johnson arrived at Boyd's Inn, at the head of the Canongate. Almost immediately he experienced at first hand in Boswell's words 'a bad specimen of Scottish cleanliness' and his bias against Scotland seemed to be confirmed. Waiting at the scruffy inn for Boswell to come and meet him, 'He asked to have his lemonade made sweeter, upon which the waiter with his greasy fingers lifted a lump of sugar, and put it into it.' Indignant, Johnson threw the drink out of the window and appeared to be about to assault the waiter when Boswell appeared: 'He embraced me cordially, and I exulted in the thought that I now had him actually in Caledonia.' Johnson put on a clean shirt because he was about to meet Margaret, and arm-in-arm they marched up the High Street to James's Court. On the way Johnson uttered one of his more memorable remarks, immortalized by Thomas Rowlandson's cartoon depicting the moment – one in a series that burlesqued the tour and proved to be a runaway bestseller. With the famous evening effluvia of the city wafting their not very salubrious odours all around as they walked along in the dark, Johnson leaned over to Boswell and grumbled in his ear, 'I smell you in the dark!' The lemonade and the effluvia seemed to bode ill to Boswell who was anxious that the great sage be well received in his native country and city.[1]

For all his embarrassment as a Scot in London and his distaste for what he regarded as Scottish backwardness and insularity, Boswell was fiercely proud of his country, its history and traditions, and its beauty. In the introductory pages to his *Tour* he wrote:

I am, I flatter myself, completely a citizen of the world. In my travels through Holland, Germany, Switzerland, Italy, Corsica, France, I never felt myself from home; and I sincerely love 'every kindred and tongue and people and nation'. I subscribe to what my late truly learned and philosophical friend Mr Crosbie said: that the English are better animals than the Scots; they are nearer the sun, their blood is richer and more mellow; but when I humour any of them in an outrageous contempt of Scotland, I fairly own I treat them as children. And thus I have, at some moments, found myself obliged to treat even Dr Johnson.

As one critic has recently written, Scotland was for Boswell 'the past as well as the present, a virtue to be practised, a source of feeling, with which sober rationality has little to do'. Yet here was the famed Samuel Johnson, the high priest of late-century neoclassicism and rationality, slipping into the capital city quietly at night. In the morning, he would begin to see what Scotland was really like. What would this icon of polite, literary, and political London think? What would Edinburgh think of him? How would Boswell bear up under the strain of seeing Scotland and his own Scottishness through Johnson's eyes?[2]

Margaret was awaiting their arrival at James's Court. If she had felt insecure over Paoli's visit, Johnson made her even more nervous. But her attitude to Johnson was compounded by currents of jealousy and even resentment. Here was the man who more than anyone else drew her husband away almost every year, for weeks on end. Now he was about to go off with him again, this time for heaven knew how long. Putting a brave face on the visit, however, she welcomed him in and sat up quite late talking, then she insisted on giving up her own bedchamber to him – 'one of a thousand obligations which I owe her,' Boswell remarked. Johnson was impressed with their 'very handsome and spacious rooms', as he told Mrs Thrale in the first of several letters, and he made himself at home, staying up until two in the morning talking to Boswell, long after Margaret had gone to bed.[3]

Margaret was obliged, in Boswell's words, 'to devote the greater part of the morning to the endless task of pouring out tea for my friend and his visitors'. This irked her somewhat, though not as much as Johnson's manners. Margaret did her best to conceal her exasperation, but Johnson sensed her unease, especially during the last few days in Edinburgh at the end of the tour. In a note in the *Life of Johnson*, Boswell summarized what was happening:

My wife paid him the most assiduous and respectful attention, while he was our guest; so that I wonder how he discovered her wishing for his departure.

The truth is, that his irregular hours and uncouth habits, such as turning the candles with their heads downwards, when they did not burn bright enough, and letting the wax drop upon the carpet, could not but be disagreeable to a lady. Besides, she had not that high admiration of him which was felt by most of those who knew him; and what was very natural to a female mind, she thought he had too much influence over her husband. She once in a little warmth, made, with more point that justice, this remark upon that subject [to me], 'I have seen many a bear led by a man; but I never before saw a man led by a bear.'

For his part, Johnson thought her pleasant enough though unremarkable: 'Mrs Boswell has the mien and manners of a Gentlewoman, and such a person and mind, as would not be in any place either admired or contemned. She is in a proper degree inferior to her husband; she cannot rival him, nor can he ever be ashamed of her.' That he underestimated her intelligence and strength, both physical and spiritual, cannot be wondered at, given her supporting role and shy deference during his visit. Neither had much opportunity after this to correct the other's misapprehensions.[4]

Guests streamed into the house at James's Court, notably Dr William Robertson who sent Boswell a note asking impatiently when he would be invited 'to take [Johnson] by the hand'; the banker William Forbes, a good friend of the family who later became a trusted friend of Boswell and one of his executors; Lord Hailes; Sir Alexander Dick; the Duchess of Douglas; John Maclaurin, Andrew Crosbie and William Nairne; and Dr Thomas Blacklock, the 'blind bard'. Johnson 'looked on him with reverence'. One star of the Edinburgh Enlightenment not invited was David Hume, whose atheism was anathema to Johnson. 'As to Hume,' Johnson announced in one of their conversations in James's Court, 'a man who has so much conceit as to tell all mankind that they have bubbled for ages and he is the wise man who sees better than they, a man who has so little scrupulosity as to venture to oppose those principles which have been thought necessary to human happiness – is he to be surprised if another man comes and laughs at him?'[5]

Johnson gathered a train behind him wherever he went, offering a pithy commentary as he did the rounds of all the historic sites. At the end of the third day, Boswell had reason to be relieved. His friends and acquaintances had acquitted themselves admirably. Johnson had indulged in a few 'pleasant hits' at Scotland, but nobody was offended. And Johnson liked what he saw. So far so good.

2

Boswell became impatient to leave. He was about to take this famous Londoner from the relative cosmopolitanism of Edinburgh into the misty Highlands and even more primitive western islands. There he would have Johnson all to himself. He compared himself to a dog who steals away with a delectable bone to some hidden and private place so he can enjoy it greedily without interruption.

The journey would be a study in incongruity. The fierce ruggedness of the landscape, dangerous roads (many of them little more than tracks), unpredictable weather, rough sleeping conditions, endless miles on ponies and by foot, and tempestuous seas were the stuff of Romanticism. When Mendelssohn visited the Highlands and Hebrides in 1829, he was overwhelmed: 'Few of my Switzerland reminiscences can compare to this; everything looks so stern and robust, half-enveloped in haze or smoke or fog.' This would be a journey from neoclassic lucidity to the sublime and obscure regions at the edges of the planet. Johnson, by his presence, would juxtapose the neoclassic and the Romantic. It was an opposition that Boswell felt naturally within his own character; this trip would in a sense objectify it. As for Johnson, what more fertile ground for incongruity could present itself than the spectacle of this oversized literary giant on an undersized horse in the pouring rain, or clambering bearishly over rocks on his way into a deep cave on Scotland's western shore, or bedding down damp and fully-clothed in a bedroom with pools of mud on the floor and the cold wind whistling through cracks in the wall?

Continuing his ritual of writing important letters from unique places, Boswell summed up the bizarre character of it all for Garrick when they arrived in Inverness on 29 August:

> Here I am and Mr Samuel Johnson actually with me. We were a night at Forres, in coming to which in the dusk of the evening we passed over the bleak and blasted heath where Macbeth met the witches ... I have had great romantic satisfaction in seeing Johnson upon the classical scenes of Shakespeare in Scotland, which I really looked upon as almost as improbable as that 'Birnam wood should come to Dunsinane'. Indeed as I have always been accustomed to view him as a permanent London object, it would not be much more wonderful to me to see St Paul's Church moving along where we now are.

The bleak heath of the weird sisters struck Johnson as 'classic ground', and he remarks that his and Boswell's imaginations were 'heated', but he did not catch the associations of literature and landscape there that, as at Auchinleck or on the Continent, often moved Boswell. He chose instead to parody *Macbeth* and demythologize the heath by aiming a mirthful dart at Boswell and his proud 'feudal' claims. 'All hail Dalblair!' he shouted to his companion, 'hail to thee, Laird of Auchinleck!' They travelled on, Johnson wrote, 'on the road on which Macbeth heard the fatal prediction; but we travelled on not interrupted by promises of kingdoms'.[6]

The differences in these two friends as travellers created another eccentricity in the journey. Johnson came to Scotland as an observer and moralist, a critic of society and amateur anthropologist – a 'moral explorer', as he has been called.[7] He wanted to see how the islanders lived their lives, what signs of progress, industry, and civilized culture stirred in their homes and communities: he was curious about food, education, religion, language, books, pastimes, natural economy, and architecture. Also, he had read earlier accounts of the Hebrides, notably Martin Martin's *Descriptions of the Western Islands of Scotland* (1703), a late edition of which he carried with him on the trip, and Thomas Pennant's *Tour in Scotland* (1771), based on a 1769 tour of the mainland. Pennant had visited the Highlands and Hebrides in 1772, and Johnson was stimulated by his example to discover for himself the wild and savage life of the region. As the most famous of lexicographers, he also had the urge to assimilate some vocabulary of the sublime, to know what a travel writer actually felt and saw when he used certain words to describe scenery that most of the English reading public had never seen. The watercolours of Paul Sandby evoked more of Scotland's sublimity than any artist before him, but they were not enough. The sensuous world had to be reckoned with: smells, sounds, mist, wetness, rain, rocks, mud, and space. Johnson had seen the Peak District, certainly wild, but there was nothing in Britain as remote as western Scotland.

Boswell, on the other hand, set out with his eyes firmly fixed on Johnson. If he remarked on the physical conditions in which the High-landers lived, it was in order to reveal Johnson's reactions to them. Boswell was keen to expose the extravagance in Johnson's, as well as his own, responses to Scottish primitiveness, which made his journal more personal and emotional than the relatively objective record Johnson kept and eventually turned into a book. Emotion and patriotism also lay behind Boswell's laments on the rapid decline of the clan system since

1745 and the alarming emigration from the Highlands and islands. He was interested in this disappearance of a way of life not as a social commentator but as an elegist.

Johnson mentions his fellow traveller very little in his published account, *Journey to the Western Islands of Scotland* (1774), but when he does so he alludes mostly to Boswell's personality, his emotional make-up, a mixture of good spirits, energy, and enthusiasm. Boswell's 'troublesome kindness' was the oil that calmed agitated waters along the way, the energy and spark that created opportunities; his companion not only tried to make things happen in just the right way but also created his own excitement through his resilience and urge to discover. In his very first sentence Johnson explains that he was 'induced' to visit the Hebrides 'by finding in Mr Boswell a companion, whose acuteness would help my inquiry, and whose gaiety of conversation and civility of manners are sufficient to counteract the inconveniencies of travel, in countries less hospitable than we have passed'. A couple of days out of Edinburgh, they scrambled about the ruins of he monastery of Aberbrothic, at the mouth of the Brothock Water just north of Dundee, where in order to see into a turret 'Mr Boswell, whose inquisitiveness is seconded by great activity, scrambled in at a high window, but found the stairs within broken, and could not reach the top.' The boy in Boswell could get them into places and reveal 'truth' in ways that a more sober individual could not. Near Ullinish they saw a boy fishing on a rocky point and, at Boswell's instigation, rowed out to him, where Boswell borrowed the boy's rod and, says Johnson, 'caught a cuddy'. 'Mr Boswell's frankness and gaiety made every body communicative,' he wrote.[8]

3

Boswell's manuscript journal for the Hebridean expedition, dating from 18 August to 26 October and containing 318 leaves, was one of the major documents found among his papers at Malahide Castle. Until its discovery, the details of this remarkable journey were known chiefly through the highly edited version that he published twelve years later, his manuscript journal notes, Johnson's *Journey* and his letters to Mrs Thrale en route. The journal is as much, and often more, about Boswell than it is about Johnson; the published book is a little more discreet. As Frederick Pottle put it, the journal is 'the personal Boswell-record with the Johnson-record flowing in and out'.[9] It is thoroughly Boswell: childlike, ridiculous, anxious, self-doubting, heroic, brilliantly imagistic, dramatic, fluent, penetrating about Johnson, crammed with physical details that bring people and places and conversation vividly to life. Its language is also more Scottish than that in the book. The student of Boswell's life, then, cannot be too grateful for this sensational discovery, for in the manuscript he finds nothing less than the heart and mind of Boswell in his best prose.

Once he began the full journal on 21 August, he kept it up astonishingly well, no mean feat given the rigour and inconvenience of the trip. He even worried that he was writing too much:

> Perhaps I put down too many things in this journal. I have no fanners in my head, at least no good ones, to separate wheat from chaff. Yet for as much as I put down, what is written falls greatly short of the quantity of thought. A page of my journal is like a cake of portable soup. A little may be diffused into a considerable portion.

He showed it to Johnson. At Dunvegan Castle in Skye on 19 September:

> He came to my room this morning before breakfast to read my journal, which he has done all along. He often before said, 'I take great delight in reading it.' Today he said, 'You improve. It grows better and better.' I observed there was a danger of my getting a habit of writing in a slovenly manner. 'Sir,' said he, 'it is not written in a slovenly manner. It might be printed, were the subject fit for printing.'

How odd it was, Boswell thought, that he would 'run from one end of London to another to have an hour with him', yet on the tour 'should omit to seize any spare time to be in his company when I am in the house with him. But my journal is really a task of much time and labour, and Mr Johnson forbids me to contract it.' After reading some more of it on the 27th, Johnson told him what any author needs to hear occasionally: 'The more I read of this, I think the more highly of you.' 'Are you in earnest?' Boswell asked. 'It is true, whether I am in earnest or no,' Johnson replied unhesitatingly. Plainly, Johnson knew he was seeing one of the great journals in English literary history in the making: 'He said today while reading my journal, "This will be a great treasure to us some years hence."' Boswell asked him to translate it into good English whenever he was tempted. 'Sir,' Johnson replied, 'it is very good English.' Not only that, he said it was a 'very exact' picture.[10]

4

Before they left Edinburgh on 18 August they found a servant to accompany them, a Bohemian, Joseph Ritter, 'a fine stately fellow above six feet high, who had been over a great part of Europe, and spoke many languages'. Margaret 'did not seem quite easy when we left her', but 'away we went', Boswell wrote. Heading north along the coast, they made good progress, passing through St Andrews, Montrose, Aberdeen, Banff, Forres, Cawdor, and Fort George, and arriving in Inverness on the 28th. The roads were good and they rode much of the way in a post-chaise, Johnson now and again cracking his favourite joke about the lack of trees, the 'nakedness' of Scotland.[11]

On the way to St Andrews where they stayed for two days, dining with and well received by the university professors, Boswell had a hideous dream: 'I *saw*, rather in a dream or vision, my child, dead, then her face eaten by worms, then a skeleton of her head. Was shocked and dreary . . . I was sunk.' Shaking that off, north of Montrose, after some discussion he persuaded Johnson to call in on the eccentric Lord Monboddo, author of a book that was the object of some derision, *The Origin of Language*, because of its thesis that in some places on earth humans have tails like other beasts. From a brief meeting in London, Johnson had conceived a dislike for Monboddo and his nonsensical talk about orang-outangs, humans, and the superiority of the savage state; but the manipulative Boswell was tantalized precisely by the idea of seeing Johnson in the company of someone he did not like. Monboddo greeted them at the gate of his 'wretched place, wild and naked, with a poor old house', dressed in a 'rustic suit' and wearing 'a little round hat'. Right away Johnson contradicted their host. Boswell 'was afraid there would have been a violent altercation in the very close, before we got into the house'. But Monboddo was on his best behaviour: 'I should not have forgiven Mr Boswell had he not brought you here, Dr Johnson,' and the 'farmer's dinner' he provided was a study in hospitality. 'Bravo!' thought Boswell, 'they agree like two brothers.'[12]

They moved on to Aberdeen for the night and after a long day on the road Johnson was feeling his sixty-three years, tired to the bone with the tedious drive across a wild and dreary moor in the rain. He shuddered at the thought of ever having to mount a pony. 'If we must *ride* much,' he grumbled, 'we shall not go; and there's an end on't.' The next morning, rested and game for anything, he talked spiritedly of Skye. Boswell had a gleam in his eye and a trace of a smile on his face: ' "Why, sir, you was beginning to despond yesterday. You're a delicate Londoner – you're a macaroni! You can't ride!" JOHNSON: "Sir, I shall ride better than you. I was only afraid I should not find a horse able to carry me." I hoped then there would be no fear of fulfilling our wild Tour.'[13]

They were distressed to find that the New Inn in Aberdeen where Boswell's father always stayed on Circuit was full, but then one of the staff recognized Boswell – 'I thought I knew you, by your likeness to your father' – and they were quickly given quarters. 'Mr Boswell made himself known,' Johnson noted in his *Journey*, 'his name overpowered all objection, and we found a very good house and civil treatment.' Space was still limited, though, and Boswell had to be inventive: 'I was to sleep in a little box-bed in Mr Johnson's room. I had it wheeled out into the dining-room, and there I lay very well.'[14]

In the morning, it was Johnson's name, not Boswell's, that swept them along. They met sundry professors, though disappointingly not Beattie who was still in London. Quite spontaneously, the Aberdeen magistrates honoured Johnson with 'the freedom of the city'. This roused him enough to offer a rare compliment: 'Let me pay Scotland one just praise; there was no officer gaping for a fee; this could have been said of no city on the English side of the Tweed.' He was less generous about Scottish food. Watching him devour 'platefuls of Scotch broth with pease in them', Boswell asked him if he had never eaten it before; Johnson replied, 'No, sir, but I don't care how soon I eat it again.'[15]

Off they went on the 24th up the coast, stopping to take in the famous Bullers of Buchan, Johnson's first taste of the 'horrid' Scottish sublime, where Boswell found it 'alarming to see Mr Johnson poking his way' boldly along 'tremendous' narrow rocks around a 'monstrous cauldron', on each side of which the sea was deep enough 'for a man-of-war to ride in'. Johnson scoffed at the danger but did admit: 'He that ventures to look downwards sees, that if his foot should slip, he must fall from his dreadful elevation upon stones on one side, or into the water on the other.' It may have occurred to Boswell that the world would not thank him for allowing the great Johnson to slip and drown or crack his head open on Scottish rocks.[16]

As they turned west from Bullers of Buchan and made for Inverness, their excitement grew in anticipation of the grandeur that lay ahead. Johnson became impatient with mere pastoral charm and was eager to be in the middle of Highland ruggedness, of mountains and wild waters: 'He always said that he was not come to Scotland to see fine places, of which there were enough in England, but wild objects – mountains, waterfalls, peculiar manners: in short, things which he had not seen before. I have a notion that he at no time has had much taste for rural beauties. I have very little.' But Boswell's mood had suddenly turned gloomy, which it often did when he felt the immanence of spirits and spectres – a haunting residue of his Edinburgh boyhood. Here the sombre scene was compounded by a body that had hung for two months on the gallows:

> By the road I had, from that strange curiosity which I always have about any thing dismal, stepped out of the chaise and run up close to the gallows where Kenneth Leal hangs in chains for robbing the mail. As he had not hung but about two months, the body was quite entire. It was still a *man* hanging. The sight impressed me with a degree of gloom. Mr Johnson did not know this, or, he told me afterwards, he would not have talked as he did, for he diverted himself with trying to frighten me, as if the witches would come and dance at the foot of my bed. I said he would be the most frightened of the two. But that I would rather see three witches than one of anything else. I was really a little uneasy. However, the door of my room [in Forres] opened into his. This gave me a security, and I soon fell asleep.[17]

This gloom continued to provoke him in Cawdor where they dined with the minsiter Kenneth Macaulay and his mind was still clouded when they reached Inverness the following day. There was no letter from Margaret there to allay his fears after the nightmare about his daughter, though he had instructed her to send her first letter to Skye. He despaired of being without her for many weeks more. He was now firmly in the grip of hypochondria, the last thing he had expected to happen on this tour: 'Clouds passed over my imagination, and in these clouds I saw objects somewhat dismal. She might die or I might die; and I felt a momentary impatience to be home.'[18] Johnson then came to Boswell's rescue, gave him 'firmness', just as his essays had done so many times earlier in his life, and he reminded himself that he was in the middle of a remarkable journey, 'the recollection of which would be a treasure to me for life'. Then that afternoon at 'Macbeth's Castle', wrongly identified as the one where Lady Macbeth did her sleepwalking, he had the 'romantic satisfaction' of seeing Johnson in it and hearing the croak of a raven on a chimney. To commemorate the moment, Boswell repeated the lines from *Macbeth* beginning with, 'The raven himself is hoarse', and he suddenly felt better: 'I exulted in comparing my former hypochondriac state when at Inverness [in 1758] with my present soundness and vigour of mind."[19]

Inverness marked a physical and imaginative turning point in the tour. With an itinerary that Macaulay had mapped out for them, they now headed southwest along the east bank of Loch Ness, into the Highlands. As Johnson put it, they had left the 'fertility of culture' behind them and were now 'to bid farewell to the luxury of travelling, and to enter a country upon which perhaps no wheel has ever rolled'. They procured four horses, ponies really, three for the travellers and one for their baggage; two Highlanders walked alongside as guides. Boswell thought Johnson rode well, though his generous bulk must certainly have dwarfed his mount.[20]

On their left were majestically high rocks clad in birch and fern; to the right were the crystal-blue waters of Loch Ness. Boswell found the scene 'as sequestered and agreeably wild as could be desired'. On the lookout for a 'scene for Mr Johnson', come afternoon he spotted a 'wretched little hovel' of earth, with only a hole for a window that could easily have been stopped up with a piece of turf. An 'oldish woman' stood alone outside it. 'Let's go in,' Boswell suggested. This scene is among the funniest and most vivid in Boswell's Hebrides journal, unlike Johnson's account which is objective, detailed, informative, and relatively cold. Inside, the woman was boiling goat's flesh. She sat them down to take a dram of whisky. She wanted snuff but, not having any, they each gave her a sixpence. Johnson wanted to know where she slept:

> I asked one of the guides, who asked her in Erse. She spoke with a kind of high tone. He told us she was afraid we wanted to go to bed to her. This coquetry, or whatever it may be called, of so wretched a like being was truly ludicrous. Mr Johnson and I afterwards made merry upon it. I said it was he who alarmed the poor woman's virtue. 'No, sir,' said he. 'She'll say, "There came a wicked young fellow, a wild young dog, who I believe would have ravished me had there not been with him a grave old gentleman who repressed him. But when he gets out of the sight of his tutor, I'll warrant you he'll spare no woman he meets, young or old."' 'No,' said I. 'She'll say, "There was a terrible ruffian who would have forced me, had it not been for a gentle, mild-looking youth, who, I take it, was an angel!"'[21]

Johnson was too discreet to explore, but Boswell, of 'a more ardent curiosity', lit a piece of paper, and walked into 'the place where her bed was' beyond a wicker partition. All he could see was 'a kind of bedstead of wood with heath upon it for a bed'. The woman watched. Her husband was eighty and they had five children, the oldest only thirteen.

They turned west at Fort Augustus, at the southern tip of Loch Ness, where Johnson had one of the best night's sleep in his life. Their way now lay over the mountains which, unlike Boswell, Johnson was taking in with philosophical measure: 'Regions mountainous and wild, thinly inhabited, and little cultivated, make a great part of the earth, and he that has never seen them, must live unacquainted with much of the face of nature, and with one of the great scenes of human existence.' One did not so much climb these mountains, he wrote, as traverse them, so that as they went forward 'we saw our baggage following us below in a direction exactly contrary'. It was somewhere near here that Johnson first thought of publishing an account of the expedition.[22]

At Glen Moriston they bedded down in a turf hut after a supper of eggs, mutton, chicken, sausage, and rum. At supper Boswell was reduced to tears by their host's stirring reminiscences of the tragic battle at Culloden – 'the very Highland names, or the sound of a bagpipe, will stir my blood and fill me with a mixture of melancholy'. Their beds were separated only by a woman's gown acting as a screen. Joseph spread on them the sheets Margaret had insisted they take along lest they 'catch something'. They debated whether to get into bed dressed or undressed. Heroically, Boswell shouted at last, 'I'll plunge in! I shall have less room for vermin to settle about me when I strip!' Johnson felt as if he was about to jump into a cold bath but fell asleep immediately, while Boswell tossed about, fancying himself 'bit by innumerable vermin under my clothes, and that a spider was travelling from the *wainscot* towards my mouth'. Rowlandson thought well of the comic possibilities of the scene, too, using it as the subject for another of his cartoons. When Boswell got up on the morning of the first of September, Johnson was still asleep in his 'sty' with 'a coloured handkerchief tied round his head'.[23]

All day long they wound their way slowly through scenes of desolation and lofty mountains, through Glen Shiel, scene of a bloody battle in 1719, and the village of Auchnasheal where they sat upon a green turf seat drinking 'two wooden dishes of milk' frothed like a syllabub, encircled by savage-looking men, women, and children who spoke not a word of English and may as well have been, said Johnson, 'a tribe of Indians'. One of the village girls, however, struck Boswell 'as comely as the figure of Sappho'.[24]

Having climbed with much difficulty to the steep summit of 'Rattachan', they were confronted with an even more awkward descent to

Boswell in Rome, aged 25, by George Willison, 1765.

Boswell's father
Alexander Boswell,
Lord Auchinleck,
in his gown of a
Lord of Session, by
Allan Ramsay, 1754.

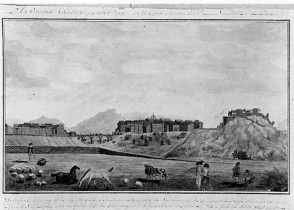

Edinburgh in 1780.
Drawing by John
Gabriel Steadman.

The Tolbooth,
Edinburgh, late
eighteenth century.

LEFT
Parliament House and
St Giles, Edinburgh,
late eighteenth century.

CENTRE
Auchinleck House was built
by Boswell's father, *c.* 1760.

BELOW
Samuel Johnson by Sir
Joshua Reynolds, 1756.

ABOVE
John Wilkes and Mrs Corradini
at her spinnet.

ABOVE RIGHT
Jean-Jacques Rousseau by Allan
Ramsay, 1766, a year after Boswell
saw him in Switzerland.

RIGHT
Boswell dressed up as an armed
Corsican chief for the Shakespeare
Jubilee in Stratford in 1769.

J. Wale del.   J. Miller sc.
JAMES BOSWELL Esq.ʳ
In the Dress of an Armed Corsican Chief, as he appear'd at
Shakespeare's Jubilee, at Stratford upon Avon September 1769.

ABOVE
Mrs Thrale by
Robert Edge Pine, 1781.

ABOVE LEFT
Boswell's wife,
Margaret, in an
oil painting attributed
to George Willison.

LEFT
Fanny Burney by
E. F. Burney.

TEA.

"My Wife had Tea ready for him which it is well known he delighted to drink at all hours, particularly when sitting up late. He shewed much complacency that the Mistress of the House was so attentive to his singular habit; and as no man could be more polite when he chose to be so, his address to her was most Courteous and engaging, and his conversation soon charmed her into a forgetfulness of his external appearance."

Vide Journal p. 44.

Publish'd May 15.ᵗʰ 1786. by E. Jackson Nº 14 Mary-le-bone Street Golden Square.

SAILING AMONG THE HEBRIDES.

"As I saw them all busy doing something, I asked Col with much earnestness what I could do. He with a happy readiness put into my hand a rope which was fixed to the top of one of the Masts, and told me to hold it till he bid me pull. If I had conceived the smallest I might have considered this could not be of the least service, but his object was to keep me out of the way of those who were busy working the Vessel, and at the same time to divert my fear by employing me, and making me think that I was of use. It rusted Island firm to my post, while the wind and rain beat upon me, always expecting a call to pull."

Vide Journal.

Publish'd May 15. 1786. by E. Jackson Nº 14 Mary-le-bone Street Golden Square.

ABOVE
Boswell and Dr Johnson at
tea with Flora Macdonald
at Dunvegan Castle, 1773.
Artist unknown.

RIGHT
Oliver Goldsmith by Sir
Joshua Reynolds, *c.* 1769.

TOP LEFT
A satirical engraving of
Boswell, his wife and
Johnson at tea in Edinburgh,
1773. Etched by Thomas
Rowlandson after a sketch
by Samuel Collings, 1786.

LEFT
A satirical engraving of a
terrified Boswell holding a
dangling rope on the sail to
Coll. Etched by Rowlandson
after Collings, 1786.

REVISING FOR THE SECOND EDITION.

"Having found on a revision of this work, that a few observations had escaped me, the publication of which might be considered as passing the bounds of a strict decorum, I immediately ordered that they should be omitted in the present edition." Vide Journal p.537. 2d Ed.

"Let Lord McDonald threat thy breech to kick."

"And o'er thy shrinking shoulders shake his stick." Vide Poetical Epistle to Jas. Boswell Esq. by Peter Pindar Esq.

Pub.d 15 June 1786 by E. Jackson N.o 14 Mary-bone Street Golden Square.

E-152.

Sir Alexander Macdonald shown threatening Boswell with violence if he did not make the necessary revisions for the second edition of the Hebrides. By Rowlandson after Collings, 1786.

Johnson appearing to Boswell as a ghost in Rowlandson's satirical print, *Thou art a Retailer of Phrases.*

TOP Boswell, his wife and three of their children by Henry Singleton, late 1780s.

ABOVE *A Literary Party* depicted at Sir Joshua Reynold's house, by W. Walker after oil by J. E. Doyle. Left to right: Boswell, Johnson, Reynolds, Garrick, Burke, Paoli, Burney, Thomas Warton and Goldsmith.

Garrick and his
wife, Eva Maria by
Sir Joshua Reynolds,
1773.

Sir Joshua Reynolds,
a self-portrait as
President of the
Royal Academy
of Arts, *c.* 1780.

Samuel Johnson,
c. 1784, the year
of his death.
Artist unknown.

Edmund Burke
by Sir Joshua
Reynolds, 1774.

lonely Glenelg, on the shore across the water from Skye. On the way down, Johnson's weight proved almost too much for his pony, which staggered and gave him his only major fright of the journey. Boswell, though, was convulsed with laughter at the sight of the guide taking the bridle and coaxing both the pony and Johnson down:

> just when Mr Johnson was uttering his displeasure, the fellow says, 'See such pretty goats.' Then *whu!* he whistled, and made them jump. Here was now a common ignorant horse-hirer imagining that he could divert, as one does a child, *Mr Samuel Johnson!* The ludicrousness, absurdity, and extraordinary contrast between what the fellow fancied and the reality, was as highly comic as anything that I ever witnessed. I laughed immoderately, and must laugh as often as I recollect it.

Johnson was far from amused. When Boswell, impatient at their snail's pace, tried to ride on alone to see if Sir Alexander Macdonald of Armadale had sent his boat to Glenelg to take them across to his home, Johnson called him back with 'a tremendous shout'. He remained very angry for the rest of the day and night.[25]

A bleaker 'inn' could not be imagined than the one they found at Glenelg. There was little sign of food and the accommodation was filthy: 'bare walls, a variety of bad smells, a coarse black fir greasy table ... and from a wretched bed started a fellow from his sleep like Edgar in *King Lear*. "Poor Tom's a-cold" '. 'Boswell blustered but nothing could he get,' Johnson wrote to Mrs Thrale. To make things worse, Johnson's anger still smouldered. 'Sir, had you gone on,' he scolded him, 'I was thinking that I should have returned with you to Edinburgh and then parted, and never spoke to you more.' Boswell spread hay on the floor, laid out the sheets on top of it, stripped, and had Joseph spread his clothes over him as blankets. Less fussy, Johnson just lay down 'buttoned up in his greatcoat'. As he put it in his *Journey* a bit fretfully, 'Mr Boswell being more delicate, laid himself sheets with hay over and under him, and lay in linen like a gentleman.'[26]

5

Parting company with their Highlander guides in the morning, they were rowed down the Sound of Slate, passing by the point where Bonnie Prince Charlie first landed – 'that stirred my mind' – and disembarking twelve tedious rainy miles later at Armadale, near the southern tip of Skye, the first Hebridean soil of their tour. Although it was quite a distance out of their way, Macdonald had issued the invitation when he and Boswell had met in London. Now, dressed in his tartan, he greeted them down by the water, while his beautiful wife Elizabeth, Boswell's cousin and old flame, 'stood at the top of the bank and made a kind of jumping for joy'.

The four days there ought to have been a civilized delight. However, Boswell's account of their stay is an angry attack on the miserable hospitality they received. Even Johnson was critical. Their first dinner was 'ill-dressed' and there was no claret, no 'ringing of glasses', no conviviality. Sir Alexander's behaviour was a nightmare of boorishness and rudeness. He kept his guests standing while he stuck his fork into the liver pudding. He drank punch 'without souring and with little spirits in it', serving it with the same pewter spoon he had used for the broth. Boswell, whose Scottish pride was injured, was 'quite hurt with the meanness and unsuitable appearance of everything' and wanted to leave in the morning, but out of politeness Johnson resolved they should 'weather it out' until the 6th.[27]

Things did not improve and the next day Boswell did not shrink from telling Sir Alexander exactly what he thought. The man also seemed to be mistreating his wife. Nowhere in his journals thus far had he shown such anger: 'I fell upon him with perhaps too great violence upon his behaviour to his people; on the meanness of his appearance here; upon my lady's neither having a maid, nor being dressed better than one. In short, I gave him a volley.' Sir Alexander 'was thrown into a violent passion; said he could not bear it; called in my lady and complained to her, at the same time defending himself with considerable plausibility.' Not even Johnson could rouse him into any intelligent discussion. 'Sir, we shall make nothing of him,' he complained to Boswell. He had no 'ideas of chief' – 'all is wrong'. Boswell was also disappointed with Elizabeth. The years on the island had made her half-dead: 'Indeed I was quite disgusted with her nothingness and insipidity.' 'Mr Johnson said, "This woman would sink a ninety-gun ship. She is so dull – so heavy." ' She seemed 'cut out of a cabbage'.[28]

Before they left on Monday, the 6th, 'this mean mansion' brought on a mild return of Boswell's spleen. He escaped just in time, with the help of Johnson's firmness. As the word spread quickly throughout the island that they were there, they received an invitation to visit the MacLeods on the island of Raasay just off the eastern coast of Skye. So they headed

northwest via Coirechatachan,[29] near Broadford, to a farmhouse tenanted
by Lachlan Mackinnon, to whose clan all these lands had once belonged.
There they were entertained with all the grace and politeness they had
been denied at Armadale, and Boswell made a point of emphasizing the
glorious difference. It was like a table opened in the wilderness. There
were eleven or twelve guests that first night for dinner.

They stayed two nights instead of one because of heavy rains and,
although the good food continued, tediousness set in – 'my mind changed
today into a prison', Boswell moaned. To alleviate boredom, Johnson
entertained them for a few minutes by mimicking Lady Macdonald,
'leaning forward with a hand on each cheek and her mouth open – quite
insipidity on a monument grinning at sense and spirit'. Boswell thought
it was a masterpiece. 'To see a beauty represented by Mr Johnson was
excessively high.'

On the morning of 8 September, led by old Malcolm MacLeod of
Raasay, who in 1745 helped the Young Pretender to escape from the
pursuing King's troops, they crossed on Macdonald's horses (much to
Johnson's displeasure) to Broadford and then boarded a boat for the ten-
mile row to Raasay, with Johnson sitting 'high on the stern like a
magnificent Triton'. The wind whipped up the seas as they rowed out of
Broadford Bay and made along the coast through Caolas Scalpay and up
into the Narrows of Raasay. Boswell disliked the rough waters but
Johnson came alive: 'This now is the Atlantic. If I should tell at a tea-
table in London that I have crossed the Atlantic in an open boat, how
they'd shudder and what a fool they'd think me . . .'[30] There was a good
deal of singing of Erse songs and some talk about the authenticity of
Macpherson's *Ossian*. The hours sped by.

Fifteen miles long by two miles wide, Raasay is an island that not even
Boswell could fail to respond to as they sailed into the bay before Raasay
House on a lovely afternoon: 'We saw before us a beautiful bay, well
defended with a rocky coast; a good gentleman's house, a fine verdure
about it, a considerable number of trees, and beyond it hills and mountains in gradation of wildness.'[31] The songs of the rowers merged with
the songs of the reapers along the shore. Looking back towards Skye,
they took in the breathtaking panorama of the choppy blue waters
framed by purple, misty mountains, with the Cuillin Hills dominating
in the background.

As they touched land, Boswell could see in front of them a host of
MacLeods filing out of the house excitedly to greet them, and inside
there were yet more women, ten daughters and three sons. They found

there 'all the marks of improved life' and the whole place was permeated by an air of festivity. That first night the carpets were rolled up, a fiddler appeared, and everybody was invited to dance. Boswell observed that Johnson, who did not dance, was none the less in his element. 'They sing, and dance,' Johnson wrote to Mrs Thrale, 'and without expence, have upon their table most of what sea, air, or earth can afford.' It all 'struck the imagination with a delightful surprise, analogous to that which is felt at an unexpected emersion from darkness into light'. Boswell was satisfied at last that he had landed Johnson in a comfortable house with 'eleven fine rooms', amid the lively and cultured company of the MacLeods and the rugged and pastoral beauty of the Hebrides. The great man was all gratitude. 'Mr Johnson was in fine spirits. He said, "This is truly the patriarchal life. This is what we came to find." Minute things mark civilized life. We had here variety of preserves, and two parrots in cages were set out before the door to bask in the sun.'[32]

Bright and early on the 10th, leaving Johnson comfortable in his bed, Boswell, Malcolm, Joseph, and one or two others spent the day trekking twenty-four twisting rugged miles up and down the length of the island, magnificent views all the way, taking in the ruins of Broachel Castle dramatically poised on the northeast coast. The beauty of his sur-roundings moved him, untypically, to devote fifteen pages of his journal purely to descriptions of the island. It is curious that in the middle of this he wrote, 'I find a wretched deficiency in expressing visible objects', for his portrait of the island is particular and accurate, if not inspiring. The hike at least put him in the right Highland spirit, for that night, 'I exerted myself in an extraordinary degree in dancing . . . drinking porter heartily at intervals, and thinking that I was fit to lead on Highlanders.' For the first time on the tour, the landscape had put him in emotional rapport and communion with the locals.

After three days Johnson was ready to move on, not finding in the midst of all this youthful merrymaking much space for what Boswell called 'majestic conversation'. Boswell was again feeling guilty over having left Margaret and Veronica for so long: 'The thought of my being absent from them damped my happiness.' Their destination now was Dunvegan Castle on the west coast of Skye, the seat of the Laird of MacLeod. For Johnson's benefit, to avoid having to ride up the coast to Portree, they had Macdonald's horses sent up to the town while they launched them-selves on the water again in Raasay's four-sculler. It was a beautiful autumn Sunday morning, the water sparkled, and Johnson discoursed with 'manly eloquence' on death as they rowed the five or six miles to Portree.

They spent the night by Portree's pretty harbour, where Boswell gratefully received a reassuring letter from Margaret. In the morning, they were obliged to resort to horses for the six rainy miles northwest to Kingsburgh to meet the celebrated Flora Macdonald, famed for courageously and cunningly conducting Bonnie Prince Charlie, dressed up as her maid, from the island of Lewis to Skye.[33] Not surprisingly, the ride put Johnson in a bad mood and he muttered something about wanting to get back to civilization, by which he meant not Edinburgh but London. He also caught a cold which made him somewhat deaf. 'I apprehended his giving up Mull and Icolmkill [Iona],' Boswell worried, 'for he said something of his fears of being detained by bad weather.' It was nothing, however, that a 'dish' of tea, good food, and a warm bed could not cure. Kingsburgh, Flora's husband from the same clan, warmly received them and 'supported' Johnson into the house.

Their meeting with Flora Macdonald was a colourful climax for Boswell. To see Johnson kissing this 'little woman, of a mild and genteel appearance, mighty soft and well-bred' was 'a wonderful romantic scene to me'. They hung on to every word as she told them how she had daringly engineered the Prince's escape. Johnson had the honour of sleeping in the Prince's bed. Both travellers were filled with Jacobite ideas, though Boswell used this moment on the trip to express in his journal contentment with the Hanoverians and their claim to the throne now that they had been on it for so long. It was a delicate subject that required some careful editing when he got around to publishing his journal. There was also an air of melancholy about their stay, at least for Boswell, for Kingsburgh confirmed that their debts were such that they would have to emigrate to North Carolina the following year. Emigration was a malaise the travellers noticed everywhere they went in Scotland. Johnson said they had come too late to see the Highland culture intact. Flora returned to Skye after the Americans captured her husband in the War of Revolution. He did not return until 1783. She died in 1790.

Sparing themselves eight rugged miles by horse, on 13 September they sailed across Lochs Snizort Beag and Greshornish, two of the 'arms of the sea, which flow in upon all the coasts of Skye' making travel by horseback lengthy and arduous. The horses met them on the other side. From Greshornish they still had a long ride through bleak moorland, not unlike 'the wilds of America', to Dunvegan Castle on the shore of the loch. Several times on this stretch Johnson had to walk, which was hard on him, and once he fell from his horse trying to dismount. While he was careful not to mention this incident in his *Journey*, Boswell was careful to include it in the *Tour*.[34]

'This is feudal indeed,' Boswell remarked as in the late afternoon they climbed the twenty-two steps to the castle, perched on a rock overlooking Loch Dunvegan and surrounded (more austerely than today) only by barren and craggy rock and moor.[35] It was a beautiful spot. Lady MacLeod greeted them, they had tea with the ladies ('bred in England'), and at dinner they were joined by the Laird and Colonel John MacLeod ('Talisker'). Johnson 'became quite joyous' with the company and 'civilized order' of everything. ' "Sir," said I, "it was best to keep this for the last." He answered, "I'd have it both first and last." ' Boswell recorded his conversation at great length during the eight days they remained at the castle, detained by rain, on subjects such as female chastity, wives and women, honesty and natural goodness, emigration, language and literature, Burke, Highland customs, clothing, the Erse language, Pennant, the Hebrides economy, the martial arts, the bodily superiority of the English over the French, and Macpherson. Boswell was vexed he could not 'take down his full strain of eloquence'. They were 'feasting upon him undisturbed at Dunvegan'.

Boswell shifted into autobiographical gear at Dunvegan. His renowned 'forwardness' came up in the conversation, which produced this valuable self-assessment in his journal – toned down in the published version:

> Let me value my forwardness. It has procured me much happiness. I do not think it is impudence. It is an eagerness to share the best society, and a diligence to attain what I desire. If a man is praised for seeking knowledge though mountains and seas are in his way, is it not laudable in me to seek it at the risk of mortification from repulses? I have never yet exerted ambition in rising in the state. But sure I am, no man has made his way better to the best of company. Were my *places* to be ranged after my name, as 'Member of the Club at the Turk's Head,' etc., I should make as great a figure as most peers.

After the ladies left the room one night after dinner, however, he got into trouble with Johnson. When he laughed at the ridiculousness of his friend's speculations on how he would have his harem dress if he kept a seraglio, Johnson retaliated by expatiating at length on what a wonderful eunuch Boswell would make in his harem. Though he was of 'a firmer metal than Langton and can stand a rub better', this time Boswell was 'hurt': 'Though he treats his friends with uncommon freedom, he does not like a return. He seemed to me to be a little angry ... He made me quite contemptible for the moment.' Many years later, when Boswell was revising this passage for publication, it still hurt him to think about it.

His feudal enthusiasm also landed him in a quarrel with Lady MacLeod who remarked that the castle was so inconvenient sitting on a rock that she wanted to build a house on some gentler land five miles off where she could have a garden and generally an easier life. Build what you want, he and Johnson admonished her, but do not move the residence of the Laird of MacLeod away from the castle. When she differed, Boswell became quite upset:

> I was very keen. I was vexed to find the alloy of modern refinement in a lady who had so much old family spirit. 'Madam,' said I, 'if once you quit this rock, this centre of gravity, there is no knowing where you may settle ... No, no; keep to the rock. It is the very jewel of the estate. It looks as if it had been let down from heaven by the four corners, to be the residence of a chief.'

It was easy for him to talk like this, she replied, who had life so easy at Auchinleck. 'Madam,' Johnson chimed in, mocking Boswell's feudal hobby-horse, 'rather than quit the old rock, Boswell would live in the pit. He'd make his bedchamber in the dungeon.' But essentially Johnson agreed with him.

Finally, on the 21st they left Dunvegan with MacLeod and Talisker, staying two nights with another MacLeod at Ullinish, a lonely place close to the Cuillin Hills, and two further nights at Talisker, an even more isolated house at the head of Talisker Bay on the west coast. It was at Ullinish that Johnson delivered his most ringing denunciation of Macpherson's *Ossian*. Frequently on their travels he had heard people playing with the idea that Macpherson's poem was a translation of an authentic Erse epic. He had had enough. Boswell captured his indignation: 'I look upon Macpherson's *Fingal* to be as gross an imposition as ever the world was troubled with. Had it been really an ancient work, a true specimen how men thought at that time, it would have been a curiosity of the first rate. As a modern production, it is nothing.'[36]

At Talisker they met 'Young Coll' (Donald Maclean), Talisker's nephew and the younger brother of the Laird of Coll, whose other uncle, Professor Maclean, they had met in Aberdeen. They took to him right away, 'a little brisk young man' who had studied farming in England and was determined to improve his father's lands without sacrificing Highland traditions.[37] He promised to be their guide to the islands of Mull, Eigg, Muck, Coll and Tyree. They left Talisker with him on 25 September, riding back across the island to rejoin their merry friends the Mackinnons at Coirechatachan.

Rain 'imprisoned' them for three days at Coirechatachan.[38] On their first night, after Johnson had gone to bed, Boswell got drunk on punch and did not find his own bed until five o'clock in the morning. Johnson found him still there, with a severe headache, early the following afternoon: 'What, drunk yet?' 'They kept me up,' he replied. 'No, you kept them up, you drunken dog.' Boswell then described the charming scene that followed when Johnson, Coll and others gathered around his bed and he was offered a dram. ' "Ay," said Dr Johnson, "fill him drunk again. Do it in the morning, that we may laugh at him all day. It is a poor thing for a fellow to get drunk at night, and skulk to bed, and let his friends have no sport." ' Laughing, Johnson allowed him to take the dram which cured his headache. Boswell then opened the Prayer Book apparently at random and read, 'And be not drunk with wine, wherein there is excess.' He insisted on including this scene in his published version and not surprisingly was roasted for it, but he defended it as an autobiographical interlude on the grounds that it revealed yet more of Johnson's 'indulgence and good humour'. To that end, he was happy to sacrifice himself.

A couple of nights later in bed he had premonitions of his hypochondria returning: 'all the gloomy chances that imagination can figure disturbed me. I had the utmost impatience to get home. I was tormented for some time ...' The weather was not helping. Suddenly, the tables had turned. Johnson was for seeing as many islands as possible, while Boswell wanted to make straight for Mull, reach the mainland quickly, and return to Margaret and Veronica. 'I have more the spirit of adventure than you,' Johnson gloated.

Boswell had now been in Johnson's constant company for six weeks and gleaned a rich harvest of his talk in many highly unusual, grotesque, comic, and serious moments. And it was largely his doing, as Johnson acknowledged; Boswell's energy, facility for leading conversation, and untiring enthusiasm had helped to bring these moments about. It was time to give himself another comprehensive pat on the back: 'I must take some merit from my assiduous attention to him, and the happy art which I have of contriving that he shall be easy wherever he goes.' He included that in his published work, as he did this more resounding paragraph of self-praise in which he placed himself boldly at centre-stage:

> I have also an admirable talent of leading the conversation; I do not mean
> leading as in an orchestra, by playing the first fiddle, but leading as one does
> in examining a witness: starting topics, and making the company pursue
> them. Mr Johnson appeared to me like a great mill, into which a subject is
> thrown to be ground. That is the test of a subject. But indeed it requires
> fertile minds to furnish materials for this mill. It vexes me when I see it
> unemployed, but sometimes I feel myself quite barren, and have nothing to
> throw in.

It was a 'co-partnery' between himself and Johnson. 'The fountain was
locked up till I interfered.'[39]

6

On 3 October the weather broke. With 'Young Coll' as their guide, they
sailed from Skye in a twelve-ton vessel that had a little 'den' in the
forecastle with two beds and a fire in it. They hoped to make Iona
or, failing that, the Sound of Mull and the picturesque harbour of
Tobermory.[40] The winds were brisk and this time it was Johnson who
became sick ('in a state of annihilation') and ducked down below deck
while Boswell braved the fresh air above, eating and feeling quite 'the
stout seaman'. Pride goeth before a fall. After a meal below he, too, fell
sick. They passed Eigg and Muck, and just as they approached the Sound
the wind changed violently against them, blowing them out to sea. By
then, it was almost perfectly dark. Coll and the mariners could not decide
where to aim the boat in the darkness and for a time confusion reigned
as the winds shrieked more violently. Boswell was horrified by the
'prodigious sea with immense billows coming upon a vessel, so that it
seemed hardly possible to escape'. He might never live to see Margaret
again. It was time to pray and promise God that, if saved, he would
behave 'ten times better'. Johnson below was quiet and unconcerned,
'lying in philosophic tranquillity, with a greyhound of Coll's at his back
keeping him warm'. He never realized the danger they were in and in his
Journey made light of the night's work except for saying it might have
made a 'pathetick' tale.

   At eleven thirty, it was decided they should try to 'hit' one of the
harbours on the island of Coll. ' "Then," said the skipper, "let us run for

it, in GOD'S name."' They feared the sails would be torn to shreds. Everyone on deck was frantically busy except for Boswell who was close to panicking, so Coll told him to grab hold of a rope hanging uselessly from the top of the mast until he was commanded to pull. He stayed that way, quaking in his boots, until they were safe. He could not resist making himself the butt of another joke in the *Tour*: 'There did I stand firm to my post while the wind and rain beat upon me, always expecting a call to pull my rope.' Rowlandson could not resist it either, using the scene for another of his wicked cartoons.

In the dark, Coll made out the harbour of Loch Eatharna and they sailed safely in. But it was too rough even in the harbour for them to disembark for the night, so they were compelled to sleep aboard, cold, sick, and wet. Boswell had a miserable night in his soaked clothes: 'My head was very cold, as having only my wig for a night-cap. In the morning I fell upon the expedient of wrapping my coat around it, which made me warm enough.'

There was relatively little to see in Coll, a low-lying island abut four by twelve miles, but exasperatingly they had to stay there ten days longer than anywhere else on the journey. The storm blew and it rained 'prodigiously' day after day. There was no chance of leaving. Though for much of the time they were sick with boredom, Boswell used it to good purpose to write about fifty pages in his journal. They stayed the first night with a farmer Captain Lauchlan Maclean, in a house so small they had no option but to share bedrooms. Boswell had to share even his bed with Coll, not a prospect he enjoyed: 'I have a mortal aversion at sleeping in the same bed with a man; and a young Highlander was always somewhat suspicious as to scorbutic symptoms.' He contemplated sleeping on chairs but thought this would offend his good friend. In any case, 'upon inspection ... he seemed to be quite clean, and the bed was very broad'. The house was stone, without mortar, 'as cold as a stable'.

The following day Coll took them to his unoccupied, spacious three-storey house with two wings or pavilions, where his family had always lived, about six miles to the west, on Breachacha Bay. That was better except that the rain blew in through the rotting window frames. They remained there comfortably for the next six nights, visiting sundry sites like the ruins of the old castle and exploring the rocky coast. Coll went with them everywhere. Boswell kept himself as busy as he could by riding horseback on the beach, feeling quite Arabian galloping over sandy hills, shooting some starlings and eating them, rummaging around in the Maclean archives for some local and family history, learning about the ecology and topography of the island, and taking to drinking a dram of whisky every morning until Johnson intervened, 'For shame!' And of course there was the journal to which he devoted hours, cheered on by Johnson. He wrote so much that he finished a notebook Johnson had given him and had to scrounge loose sheets of paper from a little shop.

Johnson became restless: 'I want to be on the mainland, and go on with my existence.' For Boswell, some gloom and spleen set in. He worried that he would run out of time and be late back for the sitting of the Session, would not be able to take Johnson to Auchinleck to meet his father, or to see 'my own land of Dalblair'. 'I found the enamel of philosophy which I had upon my mind, broke, worn off, or worn very thin, and fretfulness corroding it.' The brilliant sun the next morning repaired his spirits – the enamel 'had not been broke, I take it, for it is not easily repaired'; but his restless 'bustling and walking quickly up and down' continued, for which Johnson reproved him, 'All boys do it and you are longer a boy than others.'

After a few abortive attempts, Boswell, Johnson, and Coll finally escaped on the 14th and sailed to Tobermory on the northeast coast of Mull. Johnson teased Boswell for his jubilation: 'Boswell is now all alive. He is like Antaeus; he gets new vigour whenever he touches land.' At Tobermory, Boswell rededicated himself to 'lay up authentic materials for THE LIFE OF SAMUEL JOHNSON, LL.D.'.[41]

He and Johnson fell out again that evening, however, at Dr Hector Maclean's house in Erray about one mile out of the village. The source of the quarrel seems to have been Boswell's mounting impatience at seeing Johnson write so many letters to Mrs Thrale. Letters to her reminded him that he did not exclusively 'own' Johnson on this trip. Now that Johnson was in Mull and close to the mainland, his thoughts were with the Thrales even more. They promised warmth, comfort, and civilization. Dr Maclean had written the history of the Macleans, but Johnson wanted nothing of it: 'I have no great patience to stay to hear the history of the Macleans. I'd rather hear the history of the Thrales.' He even denigrated their journey. When Boswell boasted that this was their fourth island, he answered with a childish spite: 'Nay, we cannot boast of the number we have seen. We thought we should see many more. We thought of sailing about easily from island to island; and so we should, had we come at a better season; but we, being wise men, thought it should be summer all the year where we were.' Mrs Thrale had all but travelled with them, as a sort of saint about whom no levity was allowed, and there was nothing that Boswell could do about it.

When they did get to the mainland, Boswell proposed a good-natured toast to Mrs Thrale in whisky, but Johnson refused: 'He would not have *her* drank in whisky, but rather some insular lady.'[42]

They had only seven days left on the islands, one of which was wasted at Maclean's house when rain again delayed them. On the 16th they made heir way across 'dolorous country' to the northwest coast of the island. Young Coll was leading them to Sir Allan Maclean's cottage on the island of Inchkenneth, just off the coast next to the island of Ulva at the mouth of Loch Na Keal. When they arrived at the Sound of Ulva, it was late in the evening and the wind blew against them for the sail to Inchkenneth, so Coll decided they should spend the night on Ulva instead. It was in crossing the narrow channel here in a longboat like the one that now ferried them over that young Coll in September of the following year was tragically drowned. Johnson was deeply depressed by the news; Margaret wept. They had by now developed great affection for this little, amicable, purposeful clansman.

The next morning, Sunday the 17th, fifteen minutes of rowing took them to Inchkenneth where, unexpectedly, they stayed for two very pleasant nights.[43] Inchkenneth is the sparsest of islands, a mile or so long by half-a-mile wide, unusually green and verdant for a rocky outcrop but without trees. Sir Allan, the chief of his clan who knew Boswell's father and was a great companion of the Earl of Eglinton, lived in a simple cottage with tiny bedrooms in the loft – Johnson described it as 'a thatched hut with no chambers'.[44] But the cottage seemed 'commodious' and was crammed with good things, not least a good library. It is difficult today to imagine the touches of civilization that Sir Allan achieved in this forlorn and desolate place. Sir Walter Scott, when he visited the island many years later and saw the ruins of the cottages, could not imagine how Johnson could have been pleased to stay here. But Johnson and Boswell were indeed charmed by the surprise of such a cultured paradise existing in the wild. They were also moved by the piety of the family. Instead of finding in Sir Allan a riotous 'bottle companion' as he half-expected of a former officer in a Highland regiment, Boswell discovered a man of feeling and grace. They held a little service that evening, Sir Allan's daughters reading prayers and singing hymns, and Boswell tells us that Johnson thought it 'the most agreeable Sunday evening that he had ever passed in his life'.

That night Boswell walked in the dark to the ruins of a little chapel, knelt before the cross outside, 'and holding it with both my hands, I prayed with strong devotion'. He was working himself into a pious spirit as he came closer to the shrine of St Columba at Iona. His imagination, always active in 'sacred' places, was filling with the aura of Christian sanctity. 'I felt a kind of pleasing awful confusion.' He wanted to walk into the chapel but 'a tremor seized me for ghosts, and I hastened back to the house', in his 'timorous hurry' stepping into a hole in the ground and pulling a muscle in his foot. Before breakfast next morning, however, he did go into the chapel, knelt at the ruined altar, and prayed fervently that he never again would be 'vicious' – immoral and dissipated – and that his mind would always be at peace. Later, he returned to the chapel with Johnson. Digging a hole, he gathered up some human bones that were littering the floor of the chapel and buried them. 'I said I hoped somebody would do as much for me. JOHNSON: "Well said." He praised me for what I had done, though he said he would not do it. He showed, in the chapel at Raasay, his horror at dead men's bones.'

They both felt the lure of Inchkenneth and Boswell daydreamed about owning it and the tiny island next to it called Samalan as a family retreat. 'This shall be your island,' Johnson called to Boswell, 'and it shall be called Inch Boswell.' They spent their time exploring the beaches and caves, gathering pebbles, and rowing around the island. On their last evening, one of Maclean's daughters played the harpsichord while Boswell danced with the other daughter, though he confessed that his dancing in various Hebridean homes was 'forced by a reflex desire to promote lively good humour', not because he enjoyed it.

In Maclean's boat with 'four stout rowers', they launched themselves towards Iona on the 19th, stopping along the coast to explore a huge and deep cavern called Mackinnon's Cave. With only a single candle to light their way, they walked bravely in for several hundred feet. They rowed near Staffa, described by Sir Joseph Banks the previous year as one of the world's greatest natural curiosities, but unfortunately the rough seas did not allow them to see the famed Fingal's Cave there, immortalized in 1830 by Mendelssohn in his *Hebrides Overture*. They rowed on by moonlight, sailing between gloomy rocks in swelling seas. 'This is roving among the Hebrides, or nothing is,' Johnson exclaimed. Boswell trembled with fear again and prayed mightily. Very late, after no fewer than forty miles of rowing, they arrived at Iona. Here they were at last, at 'the venerable seat of ancient sanctity', where St Columba in 563 had founded a monastery, a base for the eventual conversion to Christianity of all of Scotland. For Boswell, the thrill was in seeing 'the Rambler upon the spot!' He shook hands with him as if to sanctify the moment for ever.

For want of any house on the island to stay in, they bedded down for the night on straw in a farmer's barn.[45]

They stayed only one night but saw all the religious sites, which disappointed Boswell in their look of insignificant smallness. None the less, he enacted his 'pleasing serious exercises of piety' in the ruins of the 'cathedral', warming his soul with 'religious resolutions'. He hoped that from this point on he would live with 'exemplary conduct'. He read aloud from the Bible and Ogden's *Sermons*, relishing the sound of his voice 'resounding in the ancient cathedral of Icolmkill'. He performed several little ceremonial acts, like putting a stone in a wall in the cathedral precinct by way of symbolically linking himself to the spot. While he did that, Johnson measured the ruins.

Two days later on 23 October, after Boswell violated his 'holy resolutions' on Iona by getting drunk on 'poonch', as Johnson put it, they arrived back on the mainland at Oban and struck out on horseback for the Duke of Argyll's seat at Inveraray. The full journal ends at this point and is replaced by rough notes, a source of persistent regret to Boswell nine years later when he came to write up the rest of the journey.[46]

Inveraray posed a delicate problem for him dating from the Douglas cause.[47] The famously beautiful Duchess of Argyll, Elizabeth, formerly the Duchess of Hamilton, had been the moving spirit behind the suit against Archibald Stewart Douglas on behalf of the Duke of Hamilton's claim to the Douglas estates. Since Boswell had spearheaded the publicity campaign against the Hamiltons, the Duchess remained implacably hostile towards him. Should he and Johnson call on the Duke and Duchess or not? Johnson encouraged him to ride over from their inn to pay their respects. If the Duke should invite them to dinner the next day, all well and good. Around teatime Boswell galloped off to Inveraray Castle and was graciously received by the Duke, who did invite them to dinner the following day, but the beautiful Duchess was as cold as the icy waters of nearby Loch Fyne. She did not even look at Boswell when the Duke brought him into the drawing room.

They duly arrived for dinner and the Duke was all attentiveness. Boswell was seated in the middle of the table and had to pass the soup, all the time aware of the Duchess's 'peevish resentment'. He acted unconcerned and even had the cheek to rise and offer her a toast so that he 'might have the satisfaction for once to look the Duchess in the face, with a glass in my hand ... But she had set me at defiance.' However, she hung on every word of Johnson's. When he explained that they had taken their tour late because Boswell had to finish at the Court of Session,

she spat out, 'I know *nothing* of Mr Boswell.' Boswell felt as if he had
been 'strangled by a silken cord'.

From Inveraray they slowly worked their way down to Auchinleck
where they arrived on 2 November to find Lord Auchinleck waiting for
them. In his published version of his journal, Boswell wrote that since
his father and Johnson differed profoundly in matters of religion and
politics – his father, who had not read much, if anything, by Johnson,
often referred to him as 'a *Jacobite fellow*' – he would never have brought
them together unless his father had desired it. He might have added that
he had long dreamed of showing Johnson where he had grown up. When
Johnson had visited Auchinleck, Boswell felt he would know him more
completely. As they walked in the groves, Boswell went so far as to say
that if he outlived Johnson, he would erect a monument to him there, a
piece of iconography that would invest the landscape with more associations. They clambered together amid the 'sullen dignity' of the old
castle ruins. They must both have recalled Johnson's enthusiastic remark
years earlier in London when their talk turned to Auchinleck, 'I must be
there, and we will live in the Old Castle; and if there is no room
remaining, we will build one.'[48]

In the great meeting between Boswell's father and his revered father-
figure, there were countless minefields to be avoided. Boswell told
Johnson of just three: Whiggism, Presbyterianism, and Sir John Pringle
(loved by Lord Auchinleck and loathed by Johnson). At first everything
went well. Both men were classical scholars and Johnson spent hours
looking over the excellent library of manuscripts and rare editions up on
the first floor of the mansion. Then, suddenly, on the fourth or fifth day
the two men collided. Rowlandson honoured the scene that followed
with another caricature. Lord Auchinleck was showing Johnson his fine
collection of medals when a mischievous coin of Cromwell unexpectedly
introduced Charles I and Toryism into their talk. These subjects were
dynamite and for several heated minutes Boswell looked on helplessly
while these two 'intellectual gladiators', whom he revered, were locked
in verbal combat. He declined to titillate the public with an account of
their argument out of respect for both men, but he did say that Whiggism
and Presbyterianism, and Toryism and Episcopacy, were 'terribly buffeted'. A day or two later, they parted cordially but with little good feeling.
In Edinburgh a few days later, Lord Auchinleck under his breath called
Johnson 'Ursa Major', the great bear.[49]

On 9 November, to Margaret's immense relief, eight-three days after
they had left Edinburgh and just three days before the sitting of the

Court of Session, the travellers returned. Again, she was the selfless hostess, pouring tea and suffering a 'constant levee of various persons' to parade in and out of her house. She could barely conceal her irritation. How much longer would Johnson stay? Finally on 20 November he left, with Boswell accompanying him as far as Blackshiels. After a last night together at an inn, Johnson boarded a coach to return again to 'the great theatre of life and animated exertion'. Boswell turned, not a little disconsolately, towards Edinburgh. When Johnson was back in London, he wrote to Boswell, 'I know Mrs Boswell wished me well to go,' but he cherished no resentment; 'tell her that I do not love her the less for wishing me away. I gave her trouble enough, and shall be glad, in recompence, to give her any pleasure.' For years afterwards, he tried to make it up to her.[50]

Johnson often told Boswell this tour was 'the pleasantest part of his life'. Boswell knew he had done a great service to England's literary heritage: 'Had it not been for me, I am persuaded Dr Johnson never would have undertaken such a journey and I must be allowed to assume some merit from having been the cause that our language has been enriched with such a book as that which he published on his return.'[51] The great journey was now over. Would anything ever seem so fine again?

NINETEEN

Post-Hebrides: Ominous Edinburgh Flatness

I

When Boswell drove back into Edinburgh, passed through his front door, and picked up his life again at home and work, his spirits slumped. Johnson had intellectually and emotionally exhausted him:

> I was long in a state of languor. My mind had been kept upon its utmost stretch in his company. I had exhausted all my powers to entertain him. While he was with me, his noble exuberance of genius excited my spirits to a high degree, so that I did not feel at the time how much I was weakened. I was like a man who drinks hard and is kept in a high glee by what is wasting his constitution, but perceives its enfeebling effects as soon as he lives without it. I was not, however, in a state of despondency. I waited patiently till my force should be restored.

He had a long wait. Despondency did set in, mostly as dissatisfaction and frustration. As he complained to Erskine in June 1774,

> we never have a long continuation of agreeable life. It is frequently interrupted. A company who have been very happy together must have the pain of parting. After every enjoyment comes weariness or disgust. We never have a large lawn of agreeable life. It is cut to pieces with sunk fences, ha-has, even where it is smoothest.

Boredom now was the main cross he had to bear. He fought against it with some courage but failed alarmingly. His image of the enfeebling effect of alcohol was apt, for when he failed, he drank; and when he drank, he drank far too much.[1]

His doldrums were aggravated by a dramatic falling-off of legal business in the Court of Session during the summer due to a minor recession. This suited his 'indolent and listless state', he wrote – he rarely rose in the morning before eight – and he still made a good annual income of 150 guineas from the work he did get, but there was precious little in it to compensate for the monotony of Edinburgh's limited social and intellectual life. His world contracted. He fretted in 'this provincial corner where I find nothing to engage me warmly', feeling particularly trapped when Johnson talked him out of his annual spring jaunt to London that year. He must stay with Margaret, Johnson urged, 'Life cannot subsist in society but by reciprocal concessions. She permitted you to ramble last year, you must permit her now to keep you at home.' There would be no shaking off the dust of Edinburgh this year.[2]

In short, he was embarking on the unhappiest and most ominous period since well before his marriage.

2

In spite of Johnson's warm encouragement that Boswell continue to keep his journal once he returned to Edinburgh, until June 1774 he was too 'flat' apparently to bother. Nor has much of his personal correspondence survived for that period. Little is therefore known of 'the state of my mind' during the winter of 1773–4 beyond the languor of which he complained. But the general outlines of his life are clear.

In addition to a quantity of minor legal business, he appeared as advocate in three criminal trials between January and March that could not have lifted his spirits much, though his appointment as advocate in these causes bears witness to his growing reputation as a talented lawyer. In January he defended two young sisters accused of murder, Margaret and Agnes Adam, twenty-two and sixteen respectively, against the prosecutor for the Crown, the Solicitor-General Henry Dundas, Boswell's college classmate and *bête noire*.[3] Dundas would go on to become MP for Midlothian and eventually one of the most successful Scottish politicians of the century, the 'uncrowned King of Scotland', an immensely powerful man. He was the Hotspur in Boswell's life, the successful and pragmatic man of business and influence that his father had always hoped Boswell would become. Boswell pleaded eloquently for the girls, but they were both sentenced to hang in the Grassmarket, with their bodies to be offered to the university for dissection by the Professor of Anatomy, Alexander Monro. The younger sister was later granted a reprieve and transported, but Boswell attended the shocking hanging of Margaret. In February he lost a cause on behalf of a horse thief, though this time he managed to win the defendant a sentence of transportation; and in March, with his friend Crosbie, he won a 'Not Proven' verdict in the Justiciary Court for three men accused of arson.

Temple could not reconcile the 'languor and indolence' of which Boswell complained with all the preparations he had to make for these and other causes, but there were other contributory factors. His father's pressure on him to agree to an entail on the estate still flew in the face of his 'feudal' commitment to entirely male succession. And the ranks were joining against him. Pringle commented, 'I was sorry to find that you should so obstinately continue Goth and Vandal with regard to your feudal system.' Surely by now 'English manners and parental affection' should have made him see his father's side of the matter. Temple was amazed and angry that for the sake of such an irrational principle he would jeopardize his family's inheritance: 'I am persuaded that nothing but your own conduct can prevent your succession to the estate and influence of your family.'[4]

Lord Auchinleck ended up seriously provoking Boswell in the general election of 1774, the first time the latter involved himself in Ayrshire politics.[5] Knowing that his father had played no part in local affairs for at least twenty years, and apparently without consulting him, Boswell decided to take it upon himself to represent the Auchinleck 'interest' by backing a candidate for MP who was supported by a coalition of powerful landowners in the county, the 'old and established interest' (which included the Earl of Eglinton). Supporting what he called the 'aristocratic influence' was perfectly in character with his 'feudal' Tory soul and he assumed his father would stand by him, even applaud his immersion in local affairs. He was wrong. Robert Dundas, the Lord President of the Court of Session and elder half-brother of Henry, a great political manager in league with several independent gentlemen of the county and a couple of peers, persuaded the Whiggish Lord Auchinleck to throw his weight behind their rival candidate, Sir Adam Fergusson.

Fergusson, whom Johnson called 'a vile Whig', was a politically ambitious Scottish country gentleman and fellow advocate of Boswell who had recently earned his disdain by reneging on his pledge to pay a subscription to the Corsican cause. Boswell and Crosbie had advanced the money for him at the time and now saw no chance of being repaid. 'Let the ancient respectable families have the lead,' Boswell wrote, rather than this 'upstart', this 'spawn of a messenger'.[6] There was another purely

political issue that also fired his indignation against Fergusson: his distaste
for the practice of creating 'nominal or fictitious' voters – an eighteenth-
century method of stuffing the ballot box. In order to get Fergusson
elected, the Dundases, his father, and other 'independent gentlemen'
blatantly subscribed to this procedure. The upshot was that Fergusson
won. It was bad enough to witness this erosion of the power of the old
families in the county without knowing that his father had contributed
to it.

One fantasy that sustained Boswell was of someday living in London
and being called to the English Bar. He did not think it would make any
difference to the amount of time he spent at Auchinleck, so he would
not be abandoning or neglecting his beloved heritage. Margaret would
eventually get used to London and it would be much better to educate
the children there. Johnson was all in favour of his living in 'the fountain
of intelligence and pleasure' if he could afford it. Pringle was not,
believing that people would be unwilling to employ someone whose
head was 'turned upon other subjects' if word of Boswell's plans got
around. In any case, without his father's support he would never bring
it off; with it, 'you would have the world on your side'. The scheme from
now on would never let him alone.[7]

3

In April came the dismal news of Goldsmith's death, but there were
several bright literary spots in 1774. Donaldson won the appeal in the
House of Lords over literary property, 'great news' that Boswell gloated
over by taking tea with Lord Monboddo, the only judge who had voted
against him in the cause the previous July, in order to 'triumph over him'.
He provided Johnson with all manner of Hebridean information and
'curiosities' for his intended book on the tour – 'pick up what you can
that may be useful,' Johnson requested in February. In June, Johnson
sent to press the first sheets of his *Journey to the Western Islands of Scotland*
and forwarded to Boswell the highly gratifying opening sentence: 'I . . .
was in the autumn of the year 1773 induced to undertake the journey, by
finding in Mr Boswell a companion whose acuteness would help my
inquiry, and whose gaity of conversation and civility of manners are
sufficient to counteract the inconveniencies of travel, in countries less
hospitable than we have passed.' The pleasure was attenuated somewhat
in July when Johnson, with his manuscript incomplete, set off with the

Thrales on a journey through Wales. This was obviously (Boswell thought) Mrs Thrale's effort to compete with the Hebrides. 'You will have become quite a mountaineer, by visiting Scotland one year and Wales another,' he wrote. The trip no doubt was good for Johnson's health, he wrote smugly in the *Life*, but it failed to stimulate 'a discursive exercise of his mind as our tour to the Hebrides'.[8]

However, the literary activity that engaged Boswell most in 1774 was some legwork to help Lord Hailes in his research for the *Annals of Scotland*, a rigorous compendium of Scottish history from 1034 to 1270. The project appealed to Boswell because of its antiquarian evocation of old and brave Scotland. His job was to acquire whatever facts he could from archives in the Signet Library and later in London – ironic given Hailes's opposition to his London visits in the 1760s – and to liaise with him and Johnson chiefly on matters of style. 'I am shy of writing to Dr Johnson,' Hailes wrote; 'I do not well know in what key to take him; I am not acquainted with the stops of the instrument.'[9] Boswell was the perfect go-between. So in May he began sending Johnson specimens of Hailes's manuscript for stylistic revision. Hailes was still cold towards Boswell but was happy to avail himself of his help in obtaining assistance from Johnson. Right up to publication in 1776, with a lot of prodding from Boswell, Johnson did Hailes yeoman service, filling his manuscript with red marks.

4

The full journal Boswell again began writing in June makes clear how far his family, personal, and working life had deteriorated. Although Veronica had got over a bout of smallpox and on 20 May his second child Euphemia (named after his mother) was born, all was not well at St James's Court. The tempo in the Court of Session picked up and he was very busy during the summer session, writing fifty law papers and earning the excellent sum of 120 guineas, but without a recent London jaunt to look back on, this Session (except for one sensational criminal cause) seemed more colourless than most: it 'came on quite simple. It was just the Summer Session 1774 without any other perceptible mark. I began to receive my fees this session, as I begin to eat my two eggs on any night, with a pure sameness.' Then when the court rose in August, he had little to do until November except to attend law college, as was customary among the more ambitious advocates. Alcohol became a major problem. There were stretches when he got drunk every day. If he dined out, with or without Margaret, a recurring theme was his struggle to control how much wine, port and madeira he allowed himself.[10]

The face he presented to society was respectable and positive: in addition to two successful months of work, he had been much in company, and good company at that, and had reason 'to be satisfied, having enjoyed, withal, good health and spirits'. But keeping up appearances took its toll: 'I had been much intoxicated – I may say *drunk* six times, and still oftener heated with liquor to feverishness. I had read hardly anything but mere law; I had paid very little attention to the duties of piety, though I had almost every day, morning and evening, addressed a short prayer to GOD.' Briefly taking up his old exercise of composing ten lines of jogtrot verse a day, he described himself as a 'virtuous man who is inclined to drink; / Who feels an inward suction in his breast, / A raging vortex'. He did not need 'jovial fellows' to drink with, for the 'fire ... burns spontaneous in my vital parts'. He recognized, for all the good it did, that 'no man is more easily hurt with wine than I am' and that he had nothing to gain from being a good 'bottle companion'. On Johnson's advice, he read occasionally from Izaak Walton's gentle and admiring *Lives* – 'the simplicity and pious spirit of Walton was ... transfused into my soul' – but it soothed rather than reformed him.[11]

Heavy drinking was almost always followed by sickness, severe headaches and coldness, late rising, and ennui. The journal abounds with such passages: 'outrageously intoxicated ... After I got home, I was very ill; not sick, but like to suffocate'; 'a complete riot, which lasted until near twelve at night'; 'I drank three bottles of hock, and then staggered away'; 'I swallowed about a bottle of port, which inflamed me much, the weather being hot'; 'I grew monstrously drunk ... mingled frenzy and stupefaction'. To this debilitating sequence of drinking he added gambling, usually at whist, which now became another addiction and cost him a good deal of money, as well as taking its toll on his marriage.[12]

For almost five years this union had been ideal, except for the pressure Boswell had put on it with his long periods of absence in London and the Hebrides. Margaret had been tolerant about these because she understood their profound importance to him and how depressed he threatened to become without them. He certainly was the doting father to Veronica, with whom they took pleasant little walks in Heriot's Gardens and the Meadows. He recorded lovingly the day she began to walk and was able to say 'Papa'. But his drinking and gambling, and the first signs of his whoring in Edinburgh since their marriage, began to prove too much for Margaret. A coarse sensuality and anger crept into his behaviour in society and at home. There was at times a fury about him, almost entirely the wages of alcohol. He began to lose his temper with Margaret who not unnaturally complained about his regular pattern of returning home at two or three in the morning after hours of drinking and gambling while she fretted and worried about him. There was a particularly bad clash on 17 September when he cursed her and threw a candlestick with a lighted candle at her. On another occasion he threw a chair into the fire, followed by a walking cane broken into small pieces. She began to harp on about his obsessive 'feudal' opposition to his father's insistence on the Auchinleck entail which, she reckoned, threatened a settlement on their family. He himself worried in case he should die leaving her 'in a miserable state of dependence', but he stuck to 'those principles which are interwoven with my very heart'.[13] It was a sad, relentless cycle, for Margaret's complaints were the sparks that often ignited his explosions.

His remorse in the cold light of the morning after was always wrenching, and with a forgiveness surely rarely matched in the chronicles of the matrimonial state Margaret did her best to tend to his needs. On 9 July, after a 'riot' with Erskine, Grange and others at home, she ministered to him with 'a bowl of admirable soup'. The following morning, sick with a headache from 'last night's debauch', he was torn apart, 'vexed to think of having given my valuable spouse so much uneasiness; for she had scarcely slept any the whole night watching me. The reflection, too, of my having this summer so frequently been intoxicated galled me.' Margaret threatened to send back a letter that had just arrived from Johnson because he did not deserve it in his state: 'She thus made me think how shocking it was that a letter from Mr Samuel Johnson should find me drunk.' Although after reading it he determined to reform, on 22 July he arrived home at three in the morning to find her waiting up, 'drowsy and anxious'. 'What a price does such an evening's, or rather night's, riot cost me!' he groaned.[14]

5

Another strain on their marriage was the second trial of his old client John Reid who was charged yet again for sheep-stealing, in autumn 1773. The cause, for which Boswell was principal advocate, took over his life

for several weeks in the summer session of 1774. Reid had been caught
in possession of nineteen sheep that were not his, and was brought before
a number of angry judges who were determined to send him to the
gallows. Crosbie had helped Boswell to save Reid's life in 1766, but this
time he wisely declined to become involved.

Boswell resolved not to drink any wine for the duration of the trial,
which began on 1 August.[15] He was nervous as he stood alone in defence
against four 'procurators' or prosecutors, Henry Dundas being one of
them, but he was eloquent. He pleaded that Reid had taken the sheep
from a William Gardener in order to sell them and without knowing they
were stolen, and that the evidence against him was merely circumstantial.

His main argument was an emotional one that endangered his own
reputation: that notwithstanding the earlier acquittal the judges had been
convinced of Reid's guilt and told a number of people as much after the
first trial; and that there was thus a prejudice against him on the bench.
A few months later, while disinterestedly watching another cause in
progress, Boswell considered how vain it was to argue in front of the
Lords once a trial began: 'While the pleading lasts, the bench is like a
ship in the harbour. You may direct it or have a chance to direct it. But
when the Lords are met to decide, you may as well call to a ship fairly
sailed to return.' To tell the judges they were biased against Reid was
courageous but reckless. Lords Auchinleck and Kames were two of the
judges in the Justiciary Court on the day of Reid's trial, along with the
Lord Justice-Clerk Thomas Miller and the Lord Advocate James William
Montgomery. The accusation of prejudice was, however, true and shook
Boswell's faith in the Scottish legal system. In his 'Charge', the Lord
Advocate described Boswell as one 'who always does great justice to his
clients, especially in this court, but is sometimes righteous overmuch'.
In his reply, Boswell observed audaciously that the Lord Advocate was
'warmer' than usual owing to his connection with sheep country. The
Edinburgh Advertiser next day described Boswell's presentation of the
evidence as 'masterful and pathetic ... which did him great honour both
as a lawyer and as one who wished for a free and impartial trial by jury'.
It did not prevent the jury from finding Reid guilty, however. Boswell
could be forgiven if he was reminded of Alexander Pope's line: 'And
wretches hang that jurymen may dine'.[16]

After hearing the verdict, he went straight to Walker's Tavern to hear
people sing his praises. He imagined himself an Edmund Burke, 'a man
who united pleasantry in conversation with abilities in business and
powers as an orator'. Later, he strolled in the streets for a good while – 'a

very bad habit which I have when intoxicated'. He found no prostitutes, however, and eventually stumbled home to his wife. The next day at court he 'received great applause' for his spirited defence, though he could also sense 'Scottish envy' lurking in the halls. His friend Michael Nasmith wrote, 'Boswell was great. There never was a charge made with greater dignity and judgment. Had Corsica been at stake, he could not have stood forth with greater firmness.'[17]

After the verdict was read, Boswell pleaded unsuccessfully for a delay in sentencing so that he could mount a case against it. Only Kames took his side. John Reid was sentenced to hang on 7 September at the Grassmarket.

Two themes emerge in the journal over the next few weeks. The first is Boswell's frantic, naïve, all-consuming effort to win Reid a change of sentence to transportation. The other is his study of a condemned man. How was Reid behaving under the threat of death? Could he get him to admit guilt since he was going to his Maker? He talked often to Reid and his wife in the Tolbooth and implored him to tell the truth. He tried to convince Reid that by dying in this way he would save his soul instead of continuing as a thief and being damned to hell unrepentant. Unfortunately, Reid's behaviour was complicated by the vain hope of transportation which Boswell had inadvertently instilled into him. It was not in the circumstances a kindness to Reid, who became a victim of his lawyer's childlike gusto and thrill at a spectacle of horror.

Boswell then turned to the King, petitioning him for transportation for Reid and asking several noblemen to intercede on his behalf. The Earl of Errol refused but Boswell had a new friend, the Earl of Pembroke, Lord of the Bedchamber and a Lieutenant-General in the army, to whom he had once given a letter of introduction to Paoli. Pembroke was visiting Edinburgh and they dined together several times, once in Boswell's home. It became the talk about town that Boswell was hobnobbing with one of England's great lords, 'the master of *Wilton*'. The dinner in James's Court was a grand affair and everything went off like clockwork. Margaret, Boswell thought, conducted herself like a London woman of fashion. Veronica was brought in after dinner and shook hands with Pembroke – one of those little moments that Boswell reverentially liked to record for the family archives.[18]

While waiting for a response to his petition, he came up with the bizarre idea of an experiment to resuscitate Reid's dead body if he should be hanged. There was widespread fascination at this time with the idea of reviving the dead and Boswell discussed the notion with Crosbie and a local physician Dr William Cullen. At dinner one night he engaged Dr Monro at the university in a discussion about recovering a hanged person. Monro, Boswell wrote, thought 'it was more difficult to recover a hanged person than a drowned, because hanging forces the blood up to the brain with more violence, there being a local compression at the neck; but that he thought the thing might be done by heat and rubbing to put the blood in motion, and by blowing air into the lungs; and he said the best way was to cut a hole in the throat, in the trachea, and introduce a pipe.' If Monro believed this, it surely was food for thought. 'I laid up all this for service in case it should be necessary.'[19]

Reid was no more remarkable than a multitude of other sheep-stealers, but in his journal Boswell had idealized him into a dark persecuted hero with overtones of Macheath, a tender family man at the centre of a nightmare, a victim of the gross miscarriage of justice. He commissioned a young painter to come with him to the Tolbooth to paint Reid while, with a 'lay teacher' called Ritchie, he watched and talked with the condemned man,[20] later describing the scene and conversation like the detached narrator of a sentimental novel. In the dark room, seated with one of his legs chained to a round bar of iron, Reid told him his life story. He had stolen other sheep, he said, but not these nineteen. His wife would come to see him hang but not his son, who 'would not readily forget it if he saw it'. Boswell was amazed: 'To hear a man talk of his own execution gave me a strange kind of feeling.'

The finished painting stimulated a fresh flow of dark and nightmarish thoughts:

> As the painter advanced in doing it, I felt as if he had been raising a spectre. It was a strange thought. Here is a man sitting for his picture who is to be hanged this day eight days ... When it was finished and hung upon a nail to dry, it swung, which looked ominous, and made an impression on my fancy. I gave John a dram of whisky today again. When I got home I found several vermin upon me which I had attracted while in the gaol. It was shocking. I changed all my clothes.

He was grateful that no reprieve had come while the picture was being painted. For maximum emotional accuracy and effect, it had to be the study of a man 'while under sentence of death'.

The delusory two-week reprieve came on 2 September. During that time, despite exhaustive efforts, Boswell could not prevail on the King or anyone else to change the sentence to transportation. All he succeeded in doing was to upset Reid and Margaret, and render himself *persona non grata* with certain judges. 'The battle is betwixt Boswell and the Court,' Nasmith wrote. 'He is opposing all his interest. He is all humanity.' In a 'memorial' to the Earl of Rochford, a Secretary of State, he argued the 'illiberality' and prejudice of the court. He even went so far as to publish in the *London Chronicle* for 17–20 September – too late to have any effect even if the King had wanted to spare Reid – a letter attacking the brutality of Britain's penal laws and especially the bias of Lord Justice-Clerk Miller, who insisted in his final report that no royal mercy should be shown. 'This is a striking specimen of what goes on in this narrow country,' Boswell wrote. It was a wildly indiscreet statement to make in public.

None of this, of course, did any good and Reid was hanged on 21 September. Boswell harangued him to admit his guilt, if guilty he was, but Reid maintained his innocence to the end. There was some last-minute scrambling with Hay and Nasmith to find a suitable place near the Grassmarket to attempt Reid's resuscitation. Margaret was shocked and disgusted by the plan, and Nasmith at the eleventh hour persuaded him that it would only encourage condemned criminals to think 'that there may be a Boswell at hand the moment they are cut down'. On the morning of the execution, Boswell paid Reid a last visit in the Tolbooth. He vividly recreates this scene in his journal, Reid dressed in white pathetically praying and meeting the hangman, his wife saying goodbye and telling him she would not witness her husband being hanged. From a window he and Nasmith watched him leave the Tolbooth in a gloomy procession. Then they worked their way down to the Grassmarket and took up their places near the scaffold. Just before the fatal moment, Reid shouted, 'Take warning. Mine is an unjust sentence,' which alarmed Boswell momentarily as he thought he had said, 'just sentence'. But the executioner confirmed it was 'unjust'. 'He was effectually hanged, the rope having fixed upon his neck very firmly, and he was allowed to hang near three quarters of an hour; so that any attempt to recover him would have been in vain.' They waited until he was cut down and, no cart having appeared to take the body off for burial, paid for its removal to Greyfriars Churchyard. Alone, Boswell waited a long time for Reid's family to appear and insisted, according to the will, that his body be taken to his own burying-place, for which he also paid. When he arrived home, his wife was no comfort, 'as she thought I had carried my zeal for John too far' and 'hurt my own character and interest by it . . . as she thought him guilty'.

She was right. Boswell's capacity for detachment and objectivity in his causes was hereafter doubted, but any modern court would have sided unhesitatingly with him in rejecting any implications about Reid's character drawn from his earlier trial. Moreover, on the evidence, probably no modern court would have convicted him.

The Reid episode illustrated Boswell's uneasiness in a profession that did not allow his innate sympathies for character to count for much. In the words of one of his more insightful interpreters, he was trying to conform to the image of the 'Whig, Lowland, Presbyterian Scotland embodied most notably, in this context, by his father', but he failed to do so. John Reid was a turning point. Henceforth Boswell would swerve away from the Edinburgh judicial establishment, 'in which language had the capacity to incarcerate and destroy',[21] towards the more sympathetic instincts and calling of the biographer, in which language would confirm and immortalize humanity, not destroy it. Boswell was 'feudal', Tory monarchist, orthodox in so many ways, but at the core of his being he was a rebel, instinctively drawn to psychology, the complex mystery of the human drama – his own as well as others'. The legal profession was the crucible in which he discovered he could never be at peace hiding his true character. Although he continued to practise, he had lost heart for being a lawyer, and began to think more actively of moving to London.

6

Boswell's efforts to save Reid strengthened his credentials as a local hero and general reputation as champion for the underprivileged and oppressed. At Dumferline on 31 October, having cast his vote as a delegate for Lieut.-Col. Archibald Campbell in the election for Parliament against the powerful political interests of Sir Lawrence Dundas (MP for Edinburgh) – at the recent election meeting Campbell had chosen him as his formal counsel and delegate from the burgh of Culross – he, Campbell, the two other delegates and a number of hangers-on celebrated victory fairly riotously. At the Cross Inn, 'the mob became so fond of me that the cry changed from "Campbell for ever" to "Paoli for ever". There were echoes of the mob scene in Edinburgh following the Douglas victory in 1769: 'Most of the windows were illuminated. The mob broke several which were not. I threw my glass at one and made it crash one pane of it . . . my popular mobbish spirit still broke forth in a smaller degree.' He struggled back to his room thoroughly drunk.[22]

However, the Reid trial continued to take its toll on Boswell and his wife in the weeks that followed. He complained of depressed spirits, of feeling 'wild and timorous', 'in a sort of wild state of mind, metaphysical and fanciful, looking on the various operations of human life as machinery ... not in the plain steady view which I have had in the midst of a busy session". Before his marriage, this sort of volatility had been the portent of hypochondria. Now dark clouds gathered again as other worries and irritations conspired to confuse him. There seemed to be reasons for anxiety all around him, or at least he thought so. Metaphysical speculations about human liberty and God's foreknowledge made him melancholy, as they almost always did. And as a delegate in the election of a Member of Parliament, he agonized over whether to swear to the compulsory 'Formula' renouncing certain tenets of the Roman Catholic Church. As he believed in purgatory and the invocation of saints and angels, he could not do it in good conscience; yet, if he failed to do so, it might someday injure his chances of political office. When nobody asked him to swear, he felt 'like a man relieved from hanging over a precipice by a slight rope'. He seemed too easily to find things to worry about and then allowed them to gnaw away at him. He might profitably have thought of Macbeth's cry of despair, 'Present fears are less than horrible imaginings'. In his clearer moments, he could see that: 'Full light shows us that there is nothing to fear; and fear is the great cause of our misery. How little is there of positive present evil. It is the imagination which torments us.' In his darker moments, however, such insight was useless.[23]

Horrible imaginings apart, there were plenty of present fears to torment him, one in particular an epilogue to the Reid trial. On 6 October, he received a letter from nineteen-year-old William Miller demanding to know whether Boswell was the author of the 'letter' in the *London Chronicle* attacking his father Thomas Miller, the Lord Justice-Clerk, whose 'violent report' destroyed any hopes of getting Reid transported.[24] If so, Miller insisted on a public apology and admission that his charges were scandalous and false or else they would have to settle their differences with pistols. Boswell was amazed: 'it vexed me to think that I had a boy for my antagonist.' He proposed to ignore it, but Margaret cried bitterly: 'What! And make me and your poor children quite miserable?' She made him promise to deny having written the offending 'letter' and frantically suggested that he ride swiftly to London to check if the printer still had his manuscript as incriminating evidence. She was also for fleeing to a foreign country. They went to bed and lay awake all night 'in a sort of burning fever'.

Boswell had never seen Margaret in such a state: 'she viewed herself as on the brink of the deepest affliction.' He even found the 'faintness in her countenance' rather endearing. In the morning, they drove out to take advice from Commissioner Cochrane who approved Boswell's drafted letter to young Miller admitting authorship but denying any intended injury – which of course was not strictly true, for he had meant the piece as nothing less than a frontal attack on the Lord Justice-Clerk. In the meantime, in case it did come to a duel, Boswell asked his good friend Captain George Preston to be his second. Preston was the son of Sir George Preston of Valleyfield, where Boswell's mother had spent much of her youth and where he, too, had been 'very healthy and very happy' as a boy. Since their marriage, he and Margaret were in the habit of going to Valleyfield when they felt in need of some of the love and solace denied them by Lord Auchinleck and his wife. Preston offered a few tips on how best to kill an opponent and, in his journal, Boswell sounds deceptively bold and ready to defend his honour. But he was annoyed at the prospect of having to fight a 'serious duel with one that would make it really ludicrous, being not only young, but a little, effeminate-looking creature'. He turned over in his mind all the possible ways out of this pickle of his own indiscreet making without having to fire a shot.

Things came to a head on 17 October when young Miller checked into Paxton's Inn in Edinburgh. At eight the next morning, with Preston and Grange both in attendance at St James's Court, Miller's expected note arrived requesting an immediate meeting with Boswell and a friend. While he and Grange paced up and down the dining room, Boswell sent Preston to speak to Miller. The upshot of the meeting was that Preston skilfully settled all by sending for his friend Peter Miller, the young man's uncle, and talking sense to the hot-tempered youth. Margaret was 'like one who had been upon the rack, so that she felt a most pleasing relief'.

Then they all met up and Boswell assured the youth he had mis-interpreted his 'letter', that he had been more patient towards him than he deserved because he respected his protectiveness towards his father, and that he would explain the misunderstanding to him. He also asked young Miller not to let it be known that he was the author of the offending piece. He did not get around to seeing Lord Miller until 17 November, who it turned out knew nothing of his son's challenge. The air was thus cleared, but the judge could not allow him to leave without some advice 'as a father':

> not to go beyond the line of my profession for any client; that he imputed his success in life much to his adhering to that rule. That he had often wondered that I did not think more of myself . . . But a man of my rank and fortune and standing as a lawyer had a higher character to support. He said the less I wrote in newspapers the better, as my being known to do it gave people an opportunity of ascribing to me every abusive thing that appeared.

Boswell left with a positive sense of the Lord Justice-Clerk's humanity and admitting to himself that he was indeed often impulsive and in need of more 'decorum'. It was not a lesson, however, that stayed with him long once the scare had faded away. If anything, his urge to publish intensified. In February 1775, in one of those instances when he lost all patience with Boswell, Johnson wrote severely, 'Your love of publication is offensive and disgusting, and will end, if it be not reformed, in a general distrust among all your friends.'[25] It might also end with a bullet. There would be more such threats, quite a few more, from which Boswell escaped, usually through the efforts of friends who understood how frantic Margaret could become and were familiar with his lack of courage when it came to duels.

7

He avoided alcohol during the Reid trial, but as soon as it was over he again started to drink heavily. In Edinburgh on 4 November, he and a friend drank four or five bottles of claret, after which 'much intoxicated' he found himself running so fast down Advocates' Close that he nearly killed himself when he came upon an almost perpendicular flight of stairs: 'I could not stop, but when I came to the bottom of it, fell with a good deal of violence, which sobered me much. It was amazing that I was not killed or very much hurt.' He escaped with a severely bruised heel.[26]

In the Boswellian mode of aberrant contradiction, in the next two days he attended the Presbyterian kirk with Margaret, which depressed him as much as ever, and also the Synod, joining in a drinking bout later with ten ministers whose 'coarse merriment' at the expense of passages in the sermons offended him. To turn the wine of the sacrament into a drunken orgy which insulted religion, any religion, was an obscenity to him. In disgust Margaret told him 'it was inexcusable to be riotous in such low company'. He thought he should begin an 'era' of 'proper conduct' – perhaps this very moment so he could later say in a commemorative and triumphant spirit, 'I had not been drunk since I supped with the Synod of Lothian and Tweeddale in November 1774.' After a return of the 'symptoms of gaming' which always 'fevered' him, he also promised his wife he would never play whist again for more than a shilling per game and two shillings per rubber.[27]

His frights and excesses during these months made Margaret an unhappy woman. Loving, tolerant, faithful, and enduring though she was, she gradually became more critical of Boswell, less able to put up with him in silence. His persistent opposition to the entail continued to weigh heavily on them both and made any semblance of normal relations with Lord and Lady Auchinleck impossible. He tried to please his father, who was not well and seemed to have passed beyond any warmth for his sons: 'I told him that I was now doing all that could be wished. I was sober [only since Christmas]. I was diligent in business. I was successful in business; and if he would tell me anything with which he found fault, I would amend it ... But still he was cold and indifferent.'[28] Margaret wept over the misery of such an unloving father-in-law. In the New Year of 1775 she found she was pregnant yet again – and for much of January she was ill and disinclined to satisfy Boswell's desire for sex.

She could see, too, that although he loved her deeply he was growing bored – with the law, with Edinburgh, with society, with her. On the morning of 10 January, he woke up severely melancholic:

> I indulged hypochondria, which I had not felt of a long time. I called up into my fancy ideas of being confined all winter to an old house in the north of Scotland, and being burthened with tedium and gnawed with fretfulness. It is humiliating for me to consider that my mind is such that I can at any time be made thus wretched, merely by being placed in such a situation. But let me comfort myself that I can keep out of it. My body would be tormented were it put into a fire, as my mind would be tormented in such a situation. But as the one thought gives me no uneasiness, neither should the other. As I would not wish to have my body of stone, so I would not wish to have my mind insensible.

What worried him now more than ever before was the suddenness with which the mood and aspect of a scene could affect his feelings, taking him completely by surprise.[29]

He found himself criticizing others indiscriminately. Alexander Murray, fellow advocate and later Solicitor-General, warned him about his crankiness in Parliament House one day:

> that I should check expressing my disapprobation of characters, as people were getting a notion that I was an ill-natured man, which he knew was not my character. That it was of consequence to me to have a general good-will, with the view of representing Ayrshire in Parliament. I took his admonition kind, and considered that I really did express myself against many people in strong terms; that I had made several enemies, and might add to the number till I should be thought by the *world* a malevolent being.

Ironically, it was Murray who in December 1780 challenged him to a duel because of an ill-judged joke. Angrily, they set the date, time, and place, but Boswell avoided it by running after Murray a few minutes later. Maclaurin told him in January 1776 that speaking ill of people was a symptom of youth and 'cured by age', but Boswell was never cured. In November 1775 he took stock:

> For some time past I have indulged coarse raillery and abuse by far too much. There is hardly any character that one may not attack, either with violent accusation or lessening ridicule. I know there is a kind of mischievous gratification in such indulgence; but it is an unworthy gratification, and makes enemies to him 'that uses it'.

He resolved again to be on guard against 'evil speaking of every kind, and to cultivate a benevolent disposition, at least an external mildness'.[30]

Also worrying to Margaret were growing signs of his sexual restiveness, a 'depraved wandering'. On Christmas Eve, hopelessly drunk, he 'roved' in the streets and 'stayed above an hour with two whores at their lodging in a narrow dirty stair in the Bow'. 'Luckily I had seen enough to prevent me from running any risk with them,' he writes, and he escaped without a 'distemper'. He stumbled home at midnight, on the way falling and injuring his left hand.[31]

The root of the problem between husband and wife, however, was more complex than Boswell's drinking and gaming and the reawakening of his hypochondria and illicit sexual appetites. Margaret was ill and not at her best. She felt left out of his greatest enthusiasms, social and intellectual. Constant pregnancies and the drudgery of her own life had robbed her of some of her liveliness. She began to appear dull to him. She complained that all he spoke at home was trivial and light 'childish' nonsense; that they never had 'rational' conversation except about money and the family. In his effort to explain this to himself, he acknowledged for the first time a falling off in their relationship:

> It is not easy to give a distinct specimen of that puerile jocularity in which alone I exert myself at home. The reason of it may be partly indolence, to avoid thought; partly because my wife, though she has excellent sense and a cheerful temper, has not sentiments congenial with mine. She has no superstition, no enthusiasm, no vanity; so that to be free of a disagreeable contrariety, I may be glad to keep good humour in my mind by foolish sport.

Tantalized by a chambermaid at an inn on his way to London in March, he confessed (and boasted) to Temple, 'I am *too many*...for one woman.' He was very 'attached' to his wife, 'though *some* of my qualifications are not valued by her, as they have been by other women, ay and well educated women too'. By 'qualifications' he meant his exuberant and playful charm in general and sexual prowess in particular.[32]

Given Margaret's situation and condition, a decreasing interest in sex was not surprising, but Boswell was disappointed. 'I was quite in love with her tonight,' he wrote on 8 March 1775. 'She was sensible, amiable, and all that I could wish, except being averse to hymeneal rites.' 'I told her I must have a concubine. She said I might go to whom I pleased. She has often said so.' Concubinage was almost universal, he believed, and why should it be thought immoral if even the Old Testament patriarchs practised it? He had not insisted on his conjugal rights all month, so if he was sure she meant it he would seek one out, provided he did not injure his health or endanger his affection for her. The annoying wrinkle was that the New Testament 'seems to be against it' and the Church was very much so. Still, 'my passion, or appetite rather, was so strong that I was inclined to a laxity of interpretation.' This line of reasoning, growing out of his changed relationship with Margaret, was a preparation for his imminent visit to London, where in the spirit of a patriarch he might enjoy a few of his 'former female acquaintances'. 'No man was ever more attached to his wife than I was,' he kept arguing as he neared London; his 'exuberance of amorous faculties' was purely sensual and had nothing to do with his regard for her – in any case, she was 'moderate and averse to much dalliance'.[33]

8

Boswell left for London, his first visit in two years, on 15 March. He was careful to arrange some insignificant legal business there to strengthen his hand, but there was little opposition this time. His father probably did not care much any more, and Margaret knew it would do no good to make a fuss. She certainly understood that Boswell's long absence from London had not been beneficial to their relationship. She may even have thought that some time apart was just what they needed.

On the way, he made an important stop to see his brother John whom, the previous December, the family had committed to St Luke's House, a home for the mentally disturbed kept by Dr John Hall in Newcastle. Boswell movingly described their reunion. John recognized him at once and asked for his father, crying a little. He looked so feeble and dejected that his brother shed some tears, too. Sitting on his bed with his nightcap on and a hat on top of it, John 'waved a poker in his hand, singing some strange inarticulate sounds like Portuguese or some foreign language to the tune of "Nancy Dawson", and ending always with "Damn my heart"'! Seized at first with a 'tremor', Boswell moved close to him and held his hand, feeling 'tender affection' for his brother. There but for the grace of God was he. 'I reflected with deep seriousness on the melancholy in our family, and how I myself had been afflicted with it.' His father was no help. He had wanted to commit John to the brutal Campbell's madhouse in Musselburgh; his chief emotion was disgrace over the 'reproach' John's illness meant for the family. Boswell, whose highly compassionate nature is nowhere more evident than in his relationship with John, had objected to the plan and with the help of the Commissioner of Customs, Basil Cochrane, his mother's uncle, had managed to get John back to Newcastle for more sensitive care. He gave John three shillings and some oranges and left, encouraged that his youngest brother was in such caring hands as Dr Hall's.[34]

As he made for London, he again mulled over the scheme of moving there permanently. To help it along, he would continue eating the prescribed dinners at the Inner Temple by way of fulfilling the requirement for admission to the English Bar. As for money, he needed more of it. His annual income, less the interest on money he owed for the purchase of Dalblair, amounted to £500, from which he could spare less than £70 for his annual London visit and incidentals. Perhaps through the favours of powerful friends like Pembroke and Mountstuart he could acquire some 'independency' that would lessen his father's influence over him. Or he might be able to obtain some public appointment financed by the government. With some writing, a translation perhaps, or as a reviewer, he could pull in a few more guineas. Even good employment abroad, perhaps in India, crossed his mind, though the snag there was that he would have to give up his annual meetings with Johnson. It would also mean a breach with Auchinleck which might encourage his father to sell the estate. Auchinleck, in fact, still acted as a check on Boswell's keenness for the English Bar and a move to the metropolis: 'the Old Castle, the romantic rocks and woods of Auchinleck, must never be forsaken; and if the family is destroyed, it shall be by a fatality which no means that I can use can avert.'[35]

After some boiled milk and toast that put his stomach 'in a good frame' for the approach to London, he descended into the city on a hazy morning, on 21 March, curiously with less 'novelty and agitation' than ever before in spite of his two-years' absence. He entered the capital as 'one well acquainted with it', almost as if he were already a resident.[36]

TWENTY

Picking Up Fragments

I

Changed and breakfasted, Boswell immediately launched himself into a frenzied social life as if he had been released from a box on a coiled spring. Paoli invited him to stay in one of his apartments for the entire time but he declined, thinking the newspapers might pick up on it and suggest that a 'hungry Scotsman had got him a pension that he might live gratis with him'. That was one reason. Another was that his secret life in London could not flourish under the watchful eye of Paoli. He had to be free to come and go. Instead he found rooms in Gerard Street, Soho.

In the space of three or four days, he had managed to dine with Beauclerk and Langton, joined by Garrick; take tea with the Thrales; drop in on Lord Mansfield who greeted him with, 'we have all been reading your travels [in Johnson's *Journey*], Mr Boswell'; drop in on Pringle who surprised him by describing his coming up to London every year as 'rational'; visit Wilkes, now risen to Lord Mayor at the Mansion House; attend the Club; look in on Percy at Northumberland House, who told him that Johnson spoke of him 'with more affection' than almost anyone else; and call on Lords Mountstuart and Pembroke. Pembroke excited him by inviting him to Wilton for a few days. He was in perpetual motion. He did not let up on this pace for his entire visit.

The journal reflects his buoyant mood. It is rich with animated and varied conversation, as good as fine dialogue in a novel. He was far more successful than this remark in his journal suggests any writer could be:

I doubt much if it be possible to preserve in words the peculiar features of mind which distinguish individuals as certainly as the features of different countenances. The art of portrait painting fixes the last, and musical sounds with all their nice gradations can also be fixed. Perhaps language may be improved to such a degree as to picture the varieties of mind as minutely.[1]

The scenes in the journal which he slid into his *Life of Johnson*, and which have therefore become famous in English social and literary history, are like cameos created with small quiet flicks of the verbal brush, not the ambitious results of a high style. To have achieved this, in the midst of his hectic schedule, is astonishing. He again complained that he was falling behind, that a detailed approach took too much time and he would try to escape into the more general. But he rarely did. He was intoxicated by sensuous minutiae. We can picture him alone in his Soho room late at night after an exhausting day, or early in the morning after a night of drink and sex, scratching it all down on paper in his large sprawling handwriting. It is an artistic achievement of the first order.

2

Boswell was spending countless hours keeping his journal, but too little reading was damaging his self-image. He knew he had less knowledge from books than most people thought he did. 'You know nothing,' Pringle had once told him. He confessed to Johnson, 'I don't talk much from books; but there is a very good reason for it. I have not read many books.' Johnson was mildly disappointed to hear that: 'I wish you had read more books. The foundation must be laid by reading. General principles must be had from books. But they must be brought to the test of real life. In conversation you never get a system.' Boswell became severe with himself about this, especially as time wore on and he realised that his 'impotence of study' stunted his knowledge of law:

> There is an imperfection, a superficialness, in all my notions. I understand nothing clearly, nothing to the bottom. I pick up fragments, but never have in my memory a mass of any size. I wonder really if it be possible for me to acquire any one part of knowledge fully. I am a lawyer. I have no system of law. I write verses. I know nothing of the art of poetry. In short I could go through everything in the same way.

In a letter to Temple he resorted again to a metaphor to describe his strength within a weakness: 'I am a quick fire', 'a taper, which can light up a great and lasting fire though itself is soon extinguished'.[2]

But his friends did not look to him for expertise. They valued him for his brightness of temperament, Pringle's dour comment notwithstanding. His 'forwardness in making myself known to people' was his unique way of acquiring information. When he told Johnson he felt he was 'lessening' himself by becoming a good companion and the life of the party, Johnson was quick to reassure him: 'Sir, you are growing in reality greater as you increase your knowledge.' 'This encouraged me.' Johnson knew exactly where his strengths lay.[3]

The problem as Boswell saw it, however, was that this kind of originality was not a quality people rewarded with patronage. It did not endow one with the aura of competency. Quite the contrary, in fact, since in his case it was often accompanied by a lack of *retenu*. Since social and economic progress was the *summum bonum* of his existence, he fretted that for all his good humour and acceptance into the best social circles people did not take him seriously enough to reward him with appointments that would win him respect and secure him extra money. He had already shown the world that such originality could produce a book like *Corsica*, and Johnson and other members of his inner circle recognized his talents in the portions they had read of the Hebrides journal. But he was not much the richer for any of his writing, nor did it increase his stature as a lawyer. Many interpreted the fame he won as merely a product of his appetite for exhibitionism since highly personal and egocentric journal-writing such as he excelled in was widely thought, if published, to pose a threat to decorum.

Since Boswell wanted to learn more, Johnson decided to do what he could to help. 'He is to buy for me a chest of books of his choosing off stalls, and I am to read more and drink less. That was his counsel.' Temple was encouraged: 'You must keep your promise to Mr Johnson with regard to reading.' Johnson did send him books, but for the most part they lay neglected on his shelves.[4]

3

He did drink less on this London visit, much less, only three or four times to the point of drunkenness and never alone, sulking. One such occasion was at Beauclerk's, where Garrick dropped in unexpectedly and called him 'drunk as *muck*'. He did not waste his time gaming. There were too many interesting people to talk to, people of 'high fashion, who, though no doubt of the same clay of which we are all made, have had it refined, and are like figures of Indian earth'. His harmless fancy and nonsense flourished instead, which rescued him from depression and fear. 'I own I love nonsense,' he wrote on his second day in London:

> I deluge my mind with it at times, as Egypt is overflowed by the Nile, and I think I produce better crops. To be perpetually talking sense runs out the mind, as perpetually ploughing and taking crops runs out land. The mind must be manured, and nonsense is very good for the purpose.

As long as he did not destroy his crops with his nonsense he would be fine:

> I am a being very much consisting of feelings. I have some fixed principles. But my existence is chiefly conducted by the powers of fancy and sensation. It is my business to navigate my soul amidst the gales as steadily and smoothly as I can.[5]

Within hours of arriving, however, he was acting out his theory of concubinage. But he kept himself out of danger. He had not been infected since his marriage; he must not succumb now. On 24 March after a ball at the Bosvilles followed by the Club supper with Johnson, the great Whig statesman Charles Fox, the Shakespearean George Steevens, Beauclerk, Langton, and Percy, among others, he sauntered out:

> This night, as well as some former ones, I had wandered about with women of the town pretty late, but had not proceeded to completion. I was alarmed at finding myself approaching to viciousness, and resolved to shun such temptations; for my arguments in favour of concubinage had, either from their own weakness or by being met by prejudice from long habit, ceased to appear even plausible to me now. Besides, concubinage was something settled. This was approaching to *vaga Venus.*

Concubinage had lost none of its appeal, as a principle or as an act. Again after the Club on 31 March, he 'got into the streets and wandered among the women of the town, first with one, then with another; but had reason enough left to prevent me from proceeding to the last risk'. Walking down the Mall with Percy, female beauties all around, he drew this picture of his sensuality: 'I said when there were many of them I was kept on gay fancy. There were feathers enough to make me hover and bear me up. But when there was but one, I fell down plump on sensuality.'

On 10 April he ran into a 'beautiful Devonshire wench' in the Strand, shaped 'like a marble statue of antiquity' but not as cold, and dallied with her, stopping himself just in time. The next day, with his blood 'on fire', he went to her lodgings and 'toyed' with her for a while.[6]

Unable to find her again a couple of mornings later for a little 'dalliance', he made his way to Margaret Stuart's for some tea. Tea, in fact, becomes a symbol in these journals for penitence and control, a recovery of peace and rightness of mind. The 'great lace-woman' Mrs Elizabeth Chancellor was there plying her wares. Within an hour of hunting for the Devonshire wench, he was overtaken by an extravagant desire to buy his wife 'a suit of laces':

> My valuable spouse never yet would allow me to buy her a suit of laces. I determined to do it now, while her friend should approve of my choice. I mounted up gradually from sixteen guineas to thirty. I wished to have a suit not merely genteel but rich. I was *flattered* by the speeches which the old beldame made to me, who even called me a *handsome* gentleman. I was quite a fine fellow this morning. I was all levity and did not care how much money I spent ... I wanted to have a suit for the lady of a *baron*.

Thirty guineas' worth of lace might well neutralize his guilt.[7]

4

He was in truth relieved to be away from Margaret for a while. He did not doubt he had married a woman with a 'composition of qualities' that suited him perfectly, but there were infants in their house, she was unwell and no longer as interested in sex as she had been. He had to suppress his 'contagion of fancy' at home. In London, he gave free play to it and was appreciated and loved for it by a phalanx of wits.

Margaret Stuart emerged now as a major figure in Boswell's life, offering the combination of cosmopolitan charm and playfulness he lacked at St James's Court. For years, she would remain his principal female confidante in London. She was just the sort of woman he liked, attractive, intelligent and fun-loving, warm-hearted, somewhat unconventional in the forwardness of her opinions, but also decorous and discreet. Her husband, Lieut.-Col. James Archibald Stuart, was a good friend and although there was nothing adulterous about Boswell's friendship with her, so far as we know, it was none the less a gallant flirtation that they both enjoyed.

On his first day in London, he went to Margaret's new house in Hertford Street to dine with her 'tête-à-tête'.[8] Immediately they fell to talking of polygamy. She was all for it as it would give more women something to do who might otherwise be overlooked. Boswell agreed but asked her how she would like it if her husband had several wives. She would not mind, she replied, as long as she was the chief sultana. The difference between men and women, she explained, is that men could have affairs without involving their hearts, but women could not. The important thing was for the man not to give pain to his wife.

On 30 March he opened a discussion with her about gallantry.[9] Citing the Italian example, which he knew at first hand, half-seriously he painted a picture of 'more immediate happiness' in the constant 'delirium of love': 'If I grow indifferent to one lady, I catch a warmth for another, and my former *flame* beams kindly on some man who has grown cold to some other, and thus it goes round.' She dismissed his assertion that women were 'great cheats' because they were not a fraction as amorous as men told each other they were: 'She said she had often laughed at the men on that account; and she really believed that very few women ever thought of it [sex] when young girls ... she used to have an aversion to the very idea of it.' They would appear to have gone on to speak of much more intimate things because someone, after 1912, removed the next five pages in the journal.[10]

Boswell described their farewell tête-à-tête on 21 May for Temple, who was at a loss what to make of it:

> We dined in all the elegance of two courses and desert, with dumb waiters, except when the second course and the desert were served. We talked with unreserved freedom as we had nothing to fear. We were *philosophical* upon honour not deep but feeling. We were pious. We drank tea, and bid each other adieu as finely as romance paints. She is my wife's dearest friend. So you see how beautiful our intimacy is.

Did this 'excite no wandering, no soft, no amorous desires', Temple wrote back. Was there not more earthly than spiritual 'sympathy' at work here? 'The boundary that separates love and devotion is very slender.' Could not these tender emotions easily intoxicate him and end in 'little Stuarts'? But as Boswell explained a year later, 'My intimacy with Mrs Stuart is friendship, sister indeed to love but such as that I can never look foolish when her husband comes in who perfectly understands us and is happy that she is agreeably entertained, when he is at his Clubs.'[11]

5

While he was in London, Boswell and Johnson were seen everywhere together, at Johnson's Court, the homes of friends, the Thrales', taverns, the Club, and the theatre. After the anxieties of the past two years, it was a godsend to have 'The Rambler' to help him think things through. And for his part, Boswell was a breath of fresh air for Johnson, who could almost catch a scent of the Hebrides on him. They were nostalgic together and thoroughly enjoyed each other's company, much of it in quiet private moments when there was no pretence, no image to maintain, no fear of giving offence. The Hebrides tour had cemented their friendship. 'My regard for you is so radicated [rooted] and fixed that it is become part of my mind,' Johnson reassured him later that year.[12] This did not mean, however, that Johnson was not frequently upset and exasperated with him. There were disagreements, irritations, snubs, and anxieties to season their conviviality.

Boswell was never more careful about his recording. His mission to write Johnson's biography now motivated him with fresh energy and purpose. 'Every trifle must be authentic,' he wrote. 'I draw him in the style of a Flemish painter. I am not satisfied with hitting the large features. I must be exact as to every hair, or even every spot on his countenance.' He did not bother much about chronology. 'I am glad to collect the gold dust, as I get by degrees as much as will be an ingot.' Writing in his journal one morning at Dilly's, he said to Thomas Davies who happened to drop in, 'I am quite full of Mr Johnson's sayings. I am tapping myself.' 'Well,' Davies replied, 'it will be good wine to draw off for the public.'[13]

6

On this visit to London, the Ossian controversy was the talk of the town. Johnson had revived it in his *Journey to the Western Islands* by attacking Macpherson as a forger of the purportedly ancient Gaelic epic poem *Fingal* from Ossian's manuscripts. Macpherson was furious and spread it about that he had offered Johnson a sight of the manuscripts before the *Journey* was published – an offer which he said Johnson ignored. In

February Boswell had heard of Macpherson's fury and wanted Johnson to reassure him that this story was untrue so he could counter the calumny against him that he was hearing all over Edinburgh. Even Hailes, whom Boswell was anxious to win over to 'our side', thought the subject too hot to be drawn on it. 'As to Fingal,' Hailes wrote to Boswell, 'I see a controversy arising, and purpose to keep out of its way.'[14]

Johnson's reply to Boswell was a predictably impatient dig at Scottish patriotic literary fervour: 'I am surprised that, knowing as you do the disposition of your countrymen to tell lies in favour of each other, you can be at all affected by any reports that circulate among them.' He flatly denied that the 'ruffian' Macpherson had ever offered to show him any manuscripts, 'but thought only of intimidating me by noise and threats'. This was just another proof of 'Scotch conspiracy in national falsehood'. When Boswell in his next letter, of 18 February, was so bold as to suggest that he had actually seen an old Erse manuscript with 'the duskiness of antiquity' and suggested that a few of Macpherson's mysterious manuscripts might exist, Johnson gave him a verbal rap on the knuckles: 'You then are going wild about Ossian ... Do not be credulous; you know how little a Highlander can be trusted.' Johnson was not about to believe in Ossian even if half of Scotland did. 'You know,' he added, 'that all Scotsmen to a man – nay, not at all, but *droves* of 'em – would come and attest anything which they think for the honour of Scotland.'[15]

The conflict with the American colonies was another topic Boswell was careful to avoid with Johnson. Johnson had just published *Taxation No Tyranny,* warmly supporting the policy of American taxation. Johnson, let us not forget, offended by their adoption of slavery, once said of the Americans that they were 'a race of convicts' who ought to be thankful for anything 'short of hanging'. At first, when Johnson wrote to him that he was writing the pamphlet – 'mum, it is a secret' – Boswell was tentative, claiming he knew too little about the subject to have clear opinions. But treading lightly, he could not resist replying, 'Well do you know that I have no kindness for that race. But nations, or bodies of men, should, as well as individuals, have a fair trial, and not be condemned on character at all.' On the one hand, Boswell told Temple, 'I am a Tory, a lover of power in Monarchy, and a discourager of much liberty in the people I avow.' On the other hand, 'It is not clear to me that our colonies are completely our subjects ... At any rate, the measures of Administration seem to have been ill digested and violent.' He saw an analogy with fathers and their sons, that the latter like himself and the colonies may be oppressed if the father (Britain) does not eschew 'narrowness of comprehension' and encourage 'mutual allowances' and 'a kindness for each other' towards a common interest.[16]

By the time Boswell arrived in London, he was firmly on the side of the oppressed Americans. At summer's end, he could say to Temple, 'I am growing more and more an American. I see the unreasonableness of taxing them without the consent of their assemblies. I think our ministry are mad in undertaking this desperate war.'[17] He became progressively more strident in his support of the Americans and quite angry with Hugh Blair for the anti-American polemics he was always slipping into in his Edinburgh sermons.

7

America and Macpherson apart, Boswell and Johnson found plenty to agree on. They covered all the favourite themes: Lord Auchinleck; the Auchinleck entail; concubinage; the scheme to practise at the English Bar; the education of Boswell's children and Margaret's displeasure with Johnson; Burke and Goldsmith; religion; and literature. Much of their discourse was late at night. For example, as usual, they spent all of Good Friday together, attending services, receiving visitors, and eating quietly with Mrs Williams. After the evening service at St Clement Danes church in the Strand, as Boswell was about to walk back to his lodgings, Johnson did what he did for very few others: 'Mr Johnson then said, "Come, you shall go home with me and sit just an hour, and no longer." He however was much better than his word, for after we had drank tea with Mrs Williams, he asked me to go upstairs with him, and we sat a long time in a sort of languid, grave state, like men watching a corpse; or nearly like that.' An hour or two like this, late at night with the great Johnson up in his study, the sanctum sanctorum of literary London, Boswell took as the highest of compliments – 'the immediate enjoyment of the contemplation of greatness'. Johnson held out the tantalizing picture of what it would be like if he moved to London: 'We will have one day in the week on which we will meet by ourselves. That is the happiest conversation when there is no competition, no vanity, but a calm interchange of sentiments.' This fuelled his London scheme if anything did.[18]

On 16 April they took their one excursion together to visit the essayist and poet Richard Owen Cambridge at his pleasant villa in Twickenham. As they rumbled out in Sir Joshua's coach, Johnson was in a bright mood. 'Shaking his head and stretching himself at his ease in the coach, and smiling with much complacency, he turned to me and said, "I look upon *myself* as a good-humoured fellow." ' That was too much for Boswell:

> The epithet *fellow* applied to the great lexicographer, the stately moralist, the masterly critic, as if he had been *Sam* Johnson, a mere pleasant companion, was highly diverting; and this light notion of himself struck me with wonder. I answered, also smiling, 'No, no, Sir; that will *not* do. You are good-natured, but not good-humoured. You are irascible. You have not patience with folly and absurdity. I believe you would pardon them if there were time to deprecate your vengeance; but punishment follows so quick after sentence that they cannot escape.'

For most of the way, Boswell entertained him by reading hostile criticism of the *Journey* in the papers that he had been able to lay his hands on. Johnson had a field day with it. 'I wish the writers of them had been present,' Boswell wrote. 'They would have been sufficiently mortified.'[19]

In the drawing room of Cambridge's villa after dinner, Johnson teased Boswell in front of the assembled company: 'People soon return to their original mode: Boswell soon reverts to oatmeal.' Some time later, 'he clapped me on the shoulder kindly. I said, smiling, "Well, you gave me my oatmeal." JOHNSON (imagining I was vexed): "Digest it; digest it. I would not have given it you if I thought it would have stuck in your throat." ' It rarely did. Boswell would take lots of banter from Johnson, and even barbs, if it meant fodder for his journal.[20]

8

It was crucial on this visit that he get along well with the Thrales and be invited frequently to their London home in Southwark and perhaps, too, Streatham. There was bound to be good Johnsonian conversation there to record. Henry Thrale was indeed particularly kind to him, extending 'a general invitation to dine when not otherwise engaged as [Johnson] was to be much there'. On 1 April, he even dined with them at Southwark alone since Johnson had that day been awarded the Doctor of Laws diploma from Oxford.

Thrale's warmth, however, was not matched in his wife. The coolness between Mrs Thrale and Boswell, which was not yet out in the open, was the result of rivalry in addition to a personality clash. Thrale panicked him one day by innocently telling him of his wife's book of Johnsoniana, a 'table book' of Johnson sayings and anecdotes. Boswell also discovered she had been to Birmingham to speak to Dr Edmund Hector, a schoolfellow of Johnson's, who had given her facts about his youth and promised much more. This was competition, though at first he seems to have been more excited than worried. 'I must try to get this *Thralian* miscellany, to assist me in writing Mr Johnson's life, if Mrs Thrale does not intend to do it herself. I suppose there will be many written.' The following year he tried to see some of her material: 'It would be very kind if you would take the trouble to transmit to me sometimes a few of the admirable sayings which you collect. May I beg you to mark them down as soon as you can? . . . You and I shall make a great treasure between us.' She ignored that and all other such requests.[21]

The idea, slow to dawn on Boswell, that Mrs Thrale was herself, in fact, planning some sort of biography of Johnson helps explain some of Johnson's behaviour that puzzled Boswell at this time. On 16 May, just a few days before leaving for Edinburgh, he took his Hebrides journal with him to Streatham, from which to read to the assembled company, including Johnson. Reynolds heard a few passages and thought it was 'more entertaining' than Johnson's. But when Boswell told Johnson that someone had suggested he publish his journal as a supplement to the *Journey,* Johnson's response confused him:

> he advised me not to show my journal to anybody, but bid me draw out of it what I thought might be published, and he would look it over. This he did upon my telling him that I was asked to publish; but he did not seem desirous that my little bark should 'pursue the triumph and partake the gale'. He will assist a friend, when desired. I doubt if he spontaneously sets one forward. Perhaps he thinks that no man deserves his assistance who does not so far set forward himself.

'Between ourselves,' Boswell wrote to Temple, 'he is not apt to encourage one to *share* reputation with himself.' As a book, the journal would be a sustained biographical study, as well as competition with Johnson's own *Journey,* as a manuscript, only portions of which might be printed, it posed no threat either to the *Journey* or to any projected work of Mrs Thrale's. But Johnson was beginning to find himself in an awkward position between two dear friends and would-be biographers.[22]

This discouragement was unfortunate at the time and became even more so in the years to come. Because Boswell found his legal practice decreasingly stimulating, his prospects of a public appointment dimming, life in Edinburgh ever more tormenting, and his natural talents as a writer unfocused, he needed a major writing project. Once when Johnson told him, as he frequently did, to read more deeply and systematically, he replied that he wished instead he had a book to write. The Hebrides journal was the obvious choice, a sequel to *Corsica* in the vein of autobiographical travel and also an early foray into Johnsonian biography. It could have raised his spirits and arrested, or at least delayed, his lapse into despondency in the late 1770s. As it was, he did not get around to doing anything with his journal for ten years, until after Johnson's death. By then it was nearly too late to make much difference to his feelings about himself or to his prospects.

As he left Streatham on that last visit, he did an odd thing, given the stirrings of rivalry between himself and Mrs Thrale: he left his Hebrides journal behind so that she could read it for herself before he took to the road for Edinburgh. Was he trying to stake out his own ground, demonstrate to her that she stood little chance against him in any biographical sweepstakes? He ran a great risk of its being lost or misplaced. Perhaps Johnson encouraged him to leave it.

The journal notebooks, as anyone knows who tries to read them, are often crammed with writing squeezed into small pages. Struggling to finish them before he left London, Mrs Thrale reached only the island of Coll. She then returned the notebooks to Boswell with a surprisingly unenergetic note saying the journal was 'entertaining' and that his crammed pages had almost blinded her. She did not answer either of Johnson's enquiries as to what she thought of them.[23]

Johnson loved Boswell and knew that he had talent for a certain kind of personal, anecdotal biography, a genius for recording and presenting conversation, and a knack for lively and metaphoric narrative. But he also loved, and what is more telling, needed Hester Thrale. An impartial observer might have judged that he was more intimate and confidential with her than with Boswell. Events in the following months surely suggested as much to Boswell.

Hard on the heels of his Hebridean adventure, Johnson had toured Wales with the Thrales. Now there was active talk of a journey with them to Italy. His friends would have preferred him to go to the classical world with Boswell, from whom they could expect another brilliant journal. Langton felt he had 'the best claim surely of any one to have escorted him, and profited by his remarks as they arose'. But everyone, including Boswell who could not get away for such a trip anyway, applauded the idea of Johnson in Italy. Then suddenly in September

Johnson wrote, 'I shall not very soon write again, for I am to set out to-morrow on another journey.' Instead of Italy, he left for France with the Thrales and was gone for two months, during which he did not once write to his friend. Expecting him back almost a month before he did return, on 24 October, Boswell put the best face on it he could: 'Shall we have *A Journey to Paris* from you in the winter? You will, I hope, at any rate be kind enough to give me some account of your French travels very soon.' 'What a different scene have you viewed this autumn', he added, 'from that which you viewed in autumn 1773!' Boswell was closer to the truth than perhaps he knew, for travelling with him was worlds different from travelling with the Thrales. Johnson wrote to Robert Levett that there was 'no very great pleasure' in seeing one church, palace, and private house after another. He did not say so, but what he needed was Boswell to animate the scenes.[24]

Two days after returning home, Johnson finally wrote. Paris was 'not so fertile of novelty' as the Hebrides, 'nor affords so many opportunities of remark'. When they saw each other again in the spring of 1776, he said nothing of the Thrales, but did offer a rare compliment to Scotland, at France's expense: 'France is worse than Scotland in everything but climate. Nature has done more for the French; but they have done less for themselves than the Scotch have done.' That was about all. With no letters, the *Life of Johnson* could only draw its material on the French trip from Johnson's skimpy journal. There was nothing about Hester Thrale in it.[25]

9

Before returning to Edinburgh in late May, Boswell fulfilled his promise of visiting Pembroke at his country seat, Wilton. Paoli set out with him for the long drive to Wiltshire on 19 April. It meant leaving Johnson, but some vague hope of Pembroke's patronage impelled him. He also planned to continue west afterwards to see Temple at Mamhead for a few days.[26]

Wilton and its gardens were magnificent, but country seats, even grand ones like Wilton, were dangerous places for Boswell. It was the old story. He had nothing to do; he was not in his element; he seemed to dry up, 'darkened by temporary clouds'. Even Paoli began to bore him there: 'My spirits flagged. I was even hypochondriac ... In vain did I recollect that I was now at Wilton, that I was with the Earl of Pembroke,

that here was the very walk where Sir Philip Sidney composed his *Arcadia*.
I was sunk and nonchalant.' Excursions to Salisbury Cathedral and
Stonehenge helped, but his indolence was such that he could 'hardly
articulate'. After the night's company at dinner, they had 'a long, long
evening'. The library roused him a little. There was no sign of patronage
on the horizon, however, and (parting from Paoli) he was relieved to
leave for Mamhead on the 22nd.[27]

He stayed with Temple and his family for a week: 'It was the next
comfort to being at my own house.' He read his Hebrides journal to his
friend and swore an oath under a venerable yew not to drink more than
six glasses of wine at a time. Other than that, nothing is known of his
visit.

Back in London by 2 May, he found that his rooms had been let in
his absence so he moved in with Paoli for the final three weeks and 'had
command of his coach'. He picked up where he had left off, 'like a skiff
on the sea, driven about by a multiplicity of waves' in a 'dissipated state
of mind'. He was in a '*tourbillon* of conversations'. He was also overtaken
by another wave of indolence, as a result of which he did not write in
his journal. Wilkes invited him to dine at the Mansion House, 'classical
and gay, as when at Rome and Naples'. He promised to toast Boswell's
health with some 'friends of Wilkes and Liberty' he was expecting
for dinner: 'Mr Boswell in a bumper, huzza! huzza! huzza!'. Boswell
encouraged this former scourge of the government to start writing to
him again, 'lively sallies from a *Lord Mayor of London*' to preserve in his
'cabinet' at Auchinleck. There was, finally, some legal business to attend
to in the Lords on 17 May for which he was paid a good sum. He slept
a night with Johnson, attended two or three Club dinners, and on 22
October he left for home.[28]

10

The next ten months were unhappy and despondent, 'dissipated', and
occasionally violent. Edinburgh irritations forgotten in London assaulted
him on his return. 'The unpleasing tone, the rude familiarity, the barren
conversation of those whom I found here, in comparison with what I
had left, really hurt my feelings.' He had another attack of hypochondria,
especially during the summer, so listless about everything except his work
that he could not even bring himself to keep a journal. He did manage

to write a 'Review of my Life' up to 12 August, the end of the summer session – a bleak self-portrait if ever there was one:

> I do not remember any portion of my existence flatter than these two months. I was indolent in body and in mind; and the scenes of most lively enjoyment that I had were two dinners in the Castle with the mess of the 66 Regiment. Dr Samuel Johnson being on a jaunt in different parts of England, I had not a single letter from him during this Session; so that my mind wanted its great SUN ... My father's coldness to me, the unsettled state of our family affairs, and the poor opinion which I had of the profession of a lawyer in Scotland ... sunk my spirits woefully; and for some of the last weeks of the Session I was depressed with black melancholy. Gloomy doubts of a future existence harassed me. I thought myself disordered in mind.

He was also plagued with nightmares. 'While affected with melancholy, all the doubts which have ever disturbed thinking men, come upon me. I awake in the night dreading annihilation, or being thrown into some horrible state of being.' If only Johnson would write. 'I have need of your warming and vivifying rays,' Boswell wrote to him darkly in August.[29]

He unloaded his bitter anger at his father and mother-in-law in his letters to Temple. When he and Margaret dined with them in June, his father ignored her, although she was pregnant and he had not seen her for three months. Lord Auchinleck harped on about Boswell's loutishness in having travelled all over Scotland with 'a Brute' and 'wandering' to London at the drop of a hat instead of saving his hard-earned money. Never mind that he had earned forty-two guineas in London and ended up only twenty pounds out of pocket. 'How hard it is that I am totally excluded from parental comfort.' Nevertheless, he decided to try to please his father in September by basing himself at Auchinleck for a time 'in a kind of mixed stupidity of attention to country objects'. If that failed, the problem was too deep for tears.[30]

He was as good as his word and September found him there, 'sauntering' around the estate with his father. The place did look 'really princely'. Boswell even felt some 'dawnings of taste for the country'. But there were no signs of fatherly love. In misery, missing his family, he wrote to Temple:

> he has a method of treating me, which makes me *feel* myself like a *timid boy* ... His wife too, whom in my conscience I cannot condemn for any capital

bad quality, is so narrow minded, and I don't know how, so set upon keeping
him totally under her own management, and so suspicious, and so sourishly
tempered, that it requires the utmost exertion of practical philosophy to keep
myself quiet.[31]

When his first son Alexander (nicknamed 'Sandy') was born on 9
October 1775 in St James's Court, Boswell was elated that here at last
was the child who could fulfil his 'feudal' determination for Auchinleck
without complications of inheritance. Everyone thought this would be
the bond to bring father and son together. 'You know my dearest
friend,' he confided to Temple, 'of what importance this is to me –
of what importance it is to the Family of Auchinleck – which you
may be well convinced is my supreme object in this world.' His father
sent him congratulations on 19 October, 'though he said little', and
on 10 November paid him and Margaret a visit to see the baby. But
he was 'guarded ... against expressing joy on the birth of my son,
and today when he saw him he said very little'. There were a few
faint signs of satisfaction, but he was saddened to see 'such a
niggardliness of fondness'.[32]

Three days later, when Lord Auchinleck came again for dinner, visibly
ill and tired, he offered a small gesture of love, like an oasis in the desert,
that warmed him to the core. 'As he was going down the stair, he took
my wife kindly by the hand, as if by stealth, and said, "God bless you
all."' And a few days after that he agreed to settle Boswell's debt of
about £1,000 on the Dalblair estate that still plagued him and was now
being called in. They took the occasion to talk out their differences
regarding the last Ayrshire election in which Dundas had driven a wedge
between them. They also squared off again on the thorny issue of the
entail.[33]

However, his agony on this subject was suddenly, one might almost
say miraculously, dispelled on Sunday, 31 December, while his wife was
at church, as he read over old family papers. It came to him like 'a blaze
of light' that he had always been in error 'as to an obligation in *justice* to
give the succession all along to heirs male, seeing that we had not received
it as a sacred trust with that view'. As the 'principle' therefore was now
removed, so was his 'inclination', and he was free to agree with his father.
Margaret rejoiced. She helped him compose a six-page letter to Johnson
asking whether he was on the right track. Wonderfully relieved, Boswell
could scarcely wait to tell his father, which he did on 6 March after
Johnson had written to confirm that he was doing the right thing. This

'seemed to please him. He asked me to stay and dine.' His father never was a very demonstrative man.[34]

Although Henry Dundas had been the source of a further rift between Lord Auchinleck and his son, in March 1776 he inadvertently caused Boswell recklessly to defend his father's honour at considerable physical risk to himself. Since the Ayrshire election Boswell and Henry Dundas had not been on speaking terms, and Dundas's subsequent meteoric political rise had only made things worse between them. When in May 1775 Dundas was appointed Lord Advocate, at the age of thirty-three, Boswell could scarcely control his jealousy. It spilled out in a letter to Temple. 'I cannot help being angry and even somewhat fretful at this. He has to be sure strong parts. But he is a coarse, unlettered, unfanciful dog. Why is he so lucky? Is not such an office degraded by his getting it? ... Tell me, is it wrong to feel thus at his success?'[35]

Matters came to a head in the Fife by-election of 1776 when Lord Auchinleck voted in the Court of Session to support the validity of a vote that lost the election for one of Dundas's men, Sir John Henderson. Dundas promptly filed a petition in the House of Commons attacking Lord Auchinleck for having voted on one side of the question and spoken for the other. The audacity of this infuriated Boswell. Grange told him it was 'laughable' to get worked up over it, for his father's honour and principles were well known and nobody would be deceived by the petty politicking of a disappointed party. He also advised him to stay clear of Dundas when he got to London in March in case emotions should flare. 'The petition however roused my spirit, and I meditated challenging the Advocate if he did not make an apology.' In the middle of this came word from Johnson that he would shortly be leaving for Italy with the Thrales – vexing, to say the least, since it looked as though Boswell would miss him completely. Afraid to tell his father that he was about to leave for London again, Boswell decided to consult, of all people, Lady Auchinleck.[36]

It was the first time that he and his stepmother were on 'a confidential footing'. He confronted her with his suspicion that she did not think he was sincere.

I assured her that she was wrong. That indeed I had once hated her; but that I now thought very differently, and she *must* have no longer any suspicion of me; that I had great faults, but was upon the whole one of the best men that ever lived; that it gave me uneasiness to be at enmity with anybody. She said, 'You cannot be a better man than I wish you, on many accounts.'

She said his father was thinking of giving up his robes, provided some fairly lucrative appointment could be won for his son, but that he 'doubted of my prudence'. As if on cue, against everyone's advice Boswell resolved that when he returned to London he would challenge this 'liar and scoundrel' Dundas if he did not retract his slur. One wonders whether the irony of this challenge occurred to him. Here he was defending his father's honour just as in 1774 young Miller had defended his father's against him.[37]

Margaret knew nothing of these plans for a duel. She was aware only that he was worried and more than usually depressed. For five months Boswell had kept the oath not to drink that Temple had wrung from him, but on 10 November, the night after his father had shown such little interest in his grandson, he had broken it with a vengeance, passing around the bottles of port and claret at a friend's house in a 'Highland humour'. At home later Margaret's remonstrances angered him so much that again he fell to tearing apart the furniture. Margaret told him the next day that she had felt 'in great danger, for it seems I had aimed at her both with chairs and stick. What a monstrous account of a man!'[38]

He gambled, too. At dinner one night, when she did not back down during an argument about it, he exploded, throwing an egg and some beer into the fireplace. He felt like breaking everything in sight. After they made up, he 'begged of her to be more attentive again'.[39]

A further strain on her were several amorous episodes, one with their baby's nurse who allowed Boswell plenty of 'dalliances of much familiarity' right in their own home. Because he left his journal lying around so freely, he now began to use obscure symbols and spell out in Greek certain incriminating words he did not want Margaret to read. It was a childish and transparent ruse, of course, that merely alerted her. 'I found that my wife had been reading this journal, and, though I had used Greek letters, had understood my visits to ———. She spoke to me of it with so much reason and spirit that, as I candidly owned my folly, so I was impressed with proper feelings.' He promised to 'keep clear'. It was lucky she had read the journal as 'it gave an opportunity to check in the beginning what might have produced much mischief ... I valued and loved my wife with renewed fervour.' Even so, he carried on a couple of affairs.[40]

The darkest 'black fumes' of hypochondria engulfed him in February 1776. On the 27th, in 'a fit of gloomy passion', he threw a guinea note into the fire, rescuing it with tongs just in time to redeem its value at the bank later that day. He felt he had no future. That night his mind sank, pulled down by an inescapable freight of worries and sense of futility:

> At night I was in an inanimate, sullen frame, and sat poring over the fire in
> heavy uneasiness. My dear wife was at pains to console me, and relieved me
> somewhat; but I had a dismal apprehension of becoming as melancholy as
> my poor brother John ... I wondered when I recollected how much of my
> life since my marriage had been free from hypochondria ... I was anxious to
> be with Dr Johnson; but the confused state of my affairs, and my tender
> concern at being absent from my wife and children, distressed me. I was
> exceedingly unhappy ... Futurity was dark, and my soul had no vigour of
> piety ...

There was a frightening regularity to his hypochondria now. Was he on
the threshold of an era of melancholic misery? Was he following in the
footsteps of his brother John? 'Could I extract the hypochondria from
my mind,' he wrote, 'and deposit it in my journal, writing down would
be very valuable.' He had some legal business to attend to in London,
but his gloom became his best excuse for flying there. 'If you will come
to me,' Johnson wrote urgently on 5 March, 'you must come very quickly,'
for he was on the verge of leaving for Italy with the Thrales.

The night before his departure Boswell saw a vision of a death's head.
As he left the house on the morning of 11 March,[41] full of foreboding that he might this time catch a bullet and never return, he
said to Margaret, 'GOD grant we may meet in a better world!' He
travelled 'like a criminal, or rather a condemned man not a criminal,
in a coach to the place of execution'. He feared he would lose his
nerve. 'That timorousness was a fault in my constitution; but ... I had
a noble principle of fortitude ... What misery does a man of sensibility
suffer!'[42]

II

'I am kept a prisoner here,' John whispered to him in Newcastle where
he stopped overnight for another tender reunion. His brother was in a
sort of stupor. Boswell covered his face and shed tears. Even then,
however, he was worrying less about John than about the impending
duel and the foul fiend. 'I thought of my duel at the time; and that it
was well to have fought in a good cause before sinking into the state in
which I saw my brother and which I feared might be my fate one day.'[43]

He fled the next morning, arriving in London on the 15th, after a breakdown of the coach and a couple of thefts on the road that had him in a state of terror much of the way. After changing his clothes at the Dillys', he called on Pringle for advice about the duel. Pringle immediately pricked his balloon of self-inflated torment by telling him it was an absurd 'quixotism' to be personally affronted by what happened in a court of justice. So much for that. He still was under the weight of his depression, though. 'London struck me less now than ever. It was more a home.'

The main difference about London on this Easter pilgrimage was that Johnson had moved to No. 7 Bolt Court. The new house was more spacious, with a little garden at the back where the 'great man' was fond of watering his plants. Boswell went straight there but, as all too often, found that Johnson was with the Thrales in Southwark. He greeted Robert Levett and Francis Barber and then with scarcely a catch of the breath sailed across the river in pursuit. His reception was 'truly flattering'. With some hot chocolate before him, he settled into a chair to hear Johnson in 'the full glow of conversation'. 'I was elevated as if brought into another state of being.' He and Hester Thrale looked at each other across the table in joint admiration and love of the man.

Johnson asked him to accompany him on an excursion to Oxford, Birmingham, Lichfield, and his old friend Dr John Taylor at Ashbourne in Derbyshire the following week. This was more like it. 'I was now in that glow of good spirits which I enjoy on a fine day, walking the streets of London.' Paoli invited him to stay with him when he returned and this time he accepted – 'he said that his house and servants and coach were all at my service.' The next day he had his hair cut. 'I had ever since May last let my hair grow, thinking to wear it again to look younger to please my wife. But it was very troublesome, as I was obliged to wear a wig at the bar, and I thought my health and spirits a little hurt by the heat of my thick hair ... Such a small change has not a small influence upon my existence.' Heat always bothered him, the heat of sex, of alcohol, of gambling, of gonorrhoea, of his overactive imagination. Steadiness he linked with coolness. The imagery of hypochondria was for him heat and darkness; cutting his hair objectified a sense of release from the oppressiveness of Edinburgh.[44]

He told himself that during this London visit he would be more composed than on the last one. 'Every time I have been in London, even last year, I have insensibly overheated my mind by the rapidity of amusement. I must grease the wheels with sober attention lest they flame and be consumed.' He failed. At the end of the stay Johnson wrote to Margaret that she would be glad to have him back as he had lived a 'wild life' for two months.

When not indulging in prostitutes and also the sexual favours of Mrs Love, now over fifty and whom he identified by '36', the number of her address, he did the rounds of several individuals – Queensberry, Mountstuart, Mansfield, Douglas – whom he thought might be able to help him gain an 'independency', but all except Mountstuart were stiff and cold. His first attendance at the Club dinner at the Turk's Head was not entirely pleasing either. As Johnson said, there were too many disagreeable members now, indiscriminately chosen, although his old friends, Langton, Beauclerk, Sir Joshua and Garrick were as delightful as ever. When he called on the 'theatrical sovereign' one night between ten and eleven, he found him and Mrs Garrick with Hannah More, the Blue-Stocking poetess who this year took up residence with the Garricks and was fast becoming a favourite of Johnson, Burke, Reynolds, and other leading wits. Boswell may have first met her on 27 March 1775, again at Garrick's, when in her own words she was made 'the umpire in a trial between Garrick and Boswell, which could most nearly imitate Dr Johnson's manner. I remember I gave it for Boswell in familiar conversation, and for Garrick in reciting poetry.' Now, meeting him again, she quite liked him for his cheerfulness. 'Mr Boswell (Corsican Boswell) was here last night; he is a very agreeable and good-natured man; he perfectly adores Johnson.' She was one of the few celebrated female wits he knew who did not actually mock his 'mad' high spirits, as Mrs Stuart put it.[45]

12

Boswell set off with Johnson for their journey north on 19 March.[46] The last time he had been in Oxford was in 1763 when the Gothic gloom of the architecture had brought on another attack of depression. As if preparing himself for a recurrence, he and Johnson now spoke of melancholia. Johnson, for whom similarly the 'control' of his mind and suppression of hypochondria was a lifelong battle, told him that 'thinking down' the malady was the worst thing he could do. It was unnatural and might damage his sensibility or emotions, like forcing open a flower bud before it opened in its right time. It was better to keep a lamp burning in his bedchamber and read himself to sleep at night: 'to have the management of one's mind was a great art, and that it might be attained in a considerable degree by experience and habitual exercise.' He recommended that when Boswell succeeded to the Lairdship of Auchinleck, he should fit out a room as a chemistry laboratory and, like Mr Sober in his autobiographical *Rambler* essay on 'idleness', while away the darker hours there. ' "Sir," said he, "take a course of chemistry, or a course of rope-dancing, or a course of anything." ' Boswell's idea of a suitable distraction was not in the same spirit. 'I *thought* of a course of concubinage, but was afraid to mention it.'

Oxford this time, he was delighted to discover, held no terrors. On the contrary, he viewed it with 'high relish'. He decided that in future every time he came to London he would squeeze in an excursion there. Walking with Johnson in the cloisters of one of the colleges, he was 'elevated in spirit . . . in the stillness of moonlight'. 'This is the road to a better world,' he exulted. He made up his mind on the spot that his son should be an Oxford man, after a good education at an English school. At Pembroke College, Johnson's college for his one year at the university, they spoke to the Master, Dr William Adams, who had been his old tutor. Then they were off to Stratford-upon-Avon and Lichfield. As they passed by Blenheim Palace, Johnson remarked, 'You and I, Sir, have seen the extremes of what is to be seen: the rough, wild Mull, and now Blenheim Park.'

In Birmingham they met Edmund Hector, Johnson's old schoolmate, whom Mrs Thrale had already questioned. In his company was the Quaker Sampson Lloyd, the founder (with his father) of Lloyds Bank. Hector took Boswell two miles out of town to see the factory where Matthew Boulton, 'a sort of iron chieftain' and James Watt had just begun to manufacture steam engines. 'I sell, Sir,' Boulton said to Boswell, 'what all the world desires to have – power.' It was an interesting conjunction of the past and present. Boswell was harvesting from Hector anecdotes of Johnson's early life for a book that would celebrate much of the century's literary history and tradition even as Johnson was talking with the founder of a great bank and he himself was seeing the dawning industrial age. If only Johnson had come with them to see the factory, for 'the vastness and the contrivance of some of the machinery would have "matched his mighty mind".'

Boswell wanted to linger in Birmingham to glean more from Hector, but after a day they pushed on to Lichfield, putting up at the Three Crowns, a stone's throw from Johnson's birthplace, where Boswell stole a kiss from the 'beautiful, gentle, sweet maid' who showed him round.

They met Peter Garrick, David's brother – 'the same instrument, but not so loud or sharp' – Lucy Porter, Johnson's wealthy stepdaughter who told Boswell much about him, and Anna Seward, 'the swan of Lichfield', one of the celebrated English poets in the 1780s and 90s. Her grandfather, John Hunter, headmaster of Lichfield School, had taught Johnson. 'Miss Seward was rather a pretty woman. She had bright eyes but I thought a bad mouth. I thought one might make an epigram in the old style of conceit, and compare her eyes and mouth to lights placed at the mouth of a coal-pit.' Bad mouth notwithstanding, on subsequent visits to Lichfield in pursuit of Johnsonian anecdotes, Boswell pursued her ardently. Her father was most hospitable: 'Mr Seward said to me, "Whenever you return to Lichfield, my doors shall be oiled to receive you, and I hope you'll take a bed at my house,"' to which Johnson replied, 'Sir ... there is no house which he enters into which they will not gladly receive him again.' It was one of the finest compliments he ever received from the sage.

But Johnson was losing patience with Boswell's ceaseless questions about his early life. When Boswell pulled out a volume of recently published spurious anecdotes about Johnson and showed the dinner guests his head on the frontispiece with the comment that it was poorly drawn, Johnson snapped that he 'should never speak of a man in his own presence'. Another day, on the road back to London, Boswell complained that the rattling of the chaise was so loud he could not hear Johnson, on whose every word he hung, at which Johnson lashed out, 'Then you may go hang yourself.' Johnson could be forgiven for thinking that if this is what having his biography written was all about, perhaps it was not worth it. 'You have but two topics,' he complained to his friend on another occasion, 'yourself and me, and I'm sick of both.'

They had planned several days in Ashbourne with John Taylor, but in Lichfield Johnson received news that abruptly shortened their trip. 'One of the most dreadful things that has happened in my time,' he exclaimed: the Thrales's only son Harry, aged nine, had died. There was no help for it: they had to return swiftly to London. Arriving back on 29 March, Johnson sped over to Southwark, only to find Mrs Thrale that very moment leaving with her daughter for Bath. Dejected, he dragged his steps back home, feeling spurned. Boswell's anger at this treatment mingled with jealousy: 'After all, though his intimacy in Thrale's family has done him much good, I could wish that he had been independent of it. He would have had more dignity.' He himself spent a good deal of time and effort composing a letter of sympathy to the Thrales.

13

While Johnson brooded at home, 'in a brutal fever' Boswell roared out
to St James's Park to seek relief in some 'dalliance'. He lay with a strumpet
encountered in St James's Street, then next morning feared he may have
caught a 'venereal disorder'. This did not deter him from taking up with
another who passed herself off as a servant-girl, Nanny Smith, at the
One Tun, 'a house of lewd entertainment' in Chelsea. The day after that
'the whoring rage' came over him comprehensively. 'I thought I would
devote a night to it.' He could not himself account for this wallowing in
sensuality. He got drunk first, then with the 'bouncing wench' Nanny
Cooms on his arm walked to Charing Cross Bagnio, stripped, and went
to bed with her. Afterwards he felt dirty and choked with remorse. Again
worried about infection, the following morning he sought her out and
convinced himself she was not infected. He also saw Nanny Smith again
and was horrified to learn that she was not a servant but a whore. Nanny
referred him to a pretty girl on call whom he sent for and enjoyed in a
manner so debauched that he could not bring himself to describe it in
his journal without a code. His nerves were 'like crackers going off'. His
guilt is evident in his scratching out of much of his own prose.[47]

   Inevitably, the result of this round of 'brutal' whoring was that a
couple of days later he saw 'moderate' signs of his eleventh infection.
His friend Andrew Douglas, who had already treated him twice for
gonorrhoea but whom he had not seen since the Louisa episode in 1763,
prescribed urethral irrigation with some new kind of medication. The
attack lasted four to six weeks but did not incapacitate him. From
breakfast and chocolate to dinner, tea, and supper, with a coffee-house
sandwiched in at the end of the day, and perhaps a tavern too, he rushed
around – 'quite wrapped up in the London humour' – dining with all
his friends several times over, 'in *perfect* London spirits'.[48]

   On 2 April at Pringle's for dinner he met the celebrated Captain James
Cook, the circumnavigator whose voyage around the world from 1768–
71 had caused such a sensation when his journals and those of the botanist
Joseph Banks who accompanied him were published in 1773. Boswell
seemed now to have a passing interest in science, and from time to time
attended meetings of the Royal Society. He made a point of talking with
Cook at length, finding himself drawn to the romance of the explorer's
life. Cook was to embark in July on his final voyage, to Hawaii, an
enticing prospect to Boswell who dreamed of going with him. It is not
unlikely that Cook would have allowed him to come along. 'Take care,'

said Pringle when Boswell told him his wild idea, 'your old spirit (or some such word) is reviving.'[49]

Continuing in this exotic vein, on 18 April Boswell met the Chief of the Mohawks, Theandenaigen, better known as Joseph Brant, a very well educated Native American from Connecticut who had risen to prominence in Indian affairs in the colonies. The government had brought him to England to convince him to lead an Indian rebellion against the colonists. They succeeded, for after he returned in May he managed to whip up an Indian terror throughout the Mohawk Valley, ending in the Cherry Valley massacre. Boswell talked to him at length at a Subscription City Ball at Haberdashers' Hall, on the basis of which he published an essay on him in the *London Magazine* in July 1776; this appeared with an engraved portrait of the Chief in the 'dress of his nation' from a drawing apparently also by Boswell.

14

Johnson's Italian trip with the Thrales was still going ahead as of 5 April. In spite of his jealousy of Hester Thrale, Boswell selflessly encouraged it because he thought there was a good chance, despite his disclaimers, that it might induce Johnson to publish something about that classic ground so fertile to the eighteenth-century English imagination. But Henry Thrale was wavering. Afraid that the whole plan might collapse, Boswell tried to speed things up, but suddenly the trip was cancelled. 'This disappointed me much,' he wrote. Like many others he had hoped to see Italy through Johnson's 'noble intellectual glass'.[50]

By mid-April, Boswell was writing his journal entries forty-four days late. He finally gave up on 19 April and kept notes instead, quite obscure ones at that, for his remaining month in London. Because he did not keep his full journal, not much is known of his pursuit of Johnson and the Thrales to Bath on 26 April – something of a let-down for Johnson compared to Italy, but a diversion nevertheless. Johnson had written encouraging him to come. Boswell fell in love with the town immediately. 'It is the finest place on earth for you,' he wrote Temple from his inn, 'for you may enjoy its society and its walks without effort or fatigue.' He was 'quite in Bath spirits [with] not a grain of melancholy or of timidity'. The Thrales, grieving for their last son, welcomed him generously, introducing him to various people in the Pump Room. During the visit, he and Johnson made a pilgrimage to Bristol to see the scene of another controversial literary forgery, poems purportedly the work of an imaginary fifteenth-century Bristol poet and monk, Thomas Rowley, but actually the fabrications of the boy-wonder Thomas Chatterton. Chatterton claimed he had discovered the poems in manuscript in a chest in St Mary Redcliffe. Johnson and Boswell sought out and viewed the chest, which had already become something of a shrine of poetic fantasy. 'I was entertained with seeing him enquire upon the spot, into the authenticity of "*Rowley's* Poetry", as I had seen him enquire upon the spot into the authenticity of "*Ossian's* Poetry" ', Boswell wrote.[51]

After five days in Bath, Boswell returned to London. Johnson followed him a few days later. Boswell had, he wrote in the *Life*, 'conceived an irresistible wish, if possible, to bring Dr Johnson and Mr Wilkes together. How to manage it, was a nice and difficult matter.' Wilkes had always been anathema to Johnson. His populist 'firebrand' political career and writings had deeply offended Johnson's political principles and reverence for Britain's institutions as much as Hume's scepticism had offended his religious beliefs. Johnson called him 'a criminal from a gaol'. Wilkes, pointing to Johnson's government pension, had described him as 'a slave of the state'.[52]

Boswell's plan was to exploit Johnson's 'spirit of contradiction'. He talked over his scheme with Dilly first and they agreed that both Wilkes and Johnson would be invited to dinner. In conveying Dilly's invitation, Boswell suggested to Johnson that he might not want to attend as people he did not like might be there, maybe even Wilkes. 'JOHNSON: "And if Jack Wilkes *should* be there, what is that to *me*, Sir? . . . I am sorry to be angry with you; but really it is treating me strangely to talk to me as if I could not meet any company whatever, occasionally." ' 'Thus I secured him,' Boswell wrote.

There was a moment of panic when on 15 May he appeared at Johnson's house to accompany him to Dilly's. Covered with dust from 'battling his books', Johnson had forgotten the engagement and asked Mrs Williams to prepare dinner at home. Boswell ran downstairs to the 'blind lady's room' and with entreaties 'as earnest as most entreaties to ladies upon any occasion' prevailed on her to tell Johnson that 'all things considered, she thought he should certainly go'. He ran back upstairs and breathlessly announced this. 'Frank, a clean shirt,' Johnson ordered. He dressed quickly and off they went.

Boswell's narration of what transpired at the dinner exhibits a style of masterful immediacy and vividness, a perfectly timed dramatic rhythm. When Johnson discovered that Wilkes was indeed there, he sulked over

by the window with a book and 'kept his eyes upon it intensely for some
time till he composed himself. His situation, I dare say, was awkward
enough. But he no doubt recollected his having rated me for supposing
that he could be at all disconcerted by any company, and he therefore
tuned himself up to appear quite as an easy man of the world.' When
'the cheering sound of dinner' sounded, Wilkes made a point of sitting
beside him,

> and behaved to him with so much attention and politeness that he gained
> upon him insensibly. No man eat more heartily than Johnson, or loved better
> what was nice and tasty. Mr Wilkes was at great pains in helping him with
> some fine veal. 'Pray give me leave, Sir – it is better here – A little of the
> brown – Some fat, Sir – A bit of the stuffing – Some gravy – Let me have
> the pleasure of giving you some butter – Allow me to recommend a squeeze
> of an orange – or the lemon perhaps may have more zest.' 'Sir, Sir, I am
> obliged to you, Sir,' cried Johnson, bowing and turning his head to him with
> a look for some time of 'surly virtue', but in a short time of complacency.

The conversation quickly gathered momentum, with both Johnson
and Wilkes contributing genially, though Boswell occasionally had to
interject a comment to keep it in tune. Then when the subject turned
to Scotland, the two principal players rounded good-naturedly on
Boswell, who was delighted to be the cause of any felicity between them,
'Here was a bond of union between them.' Johnson leaned over to
Wilkes:

> 'You must know, Sir, I lately took my friend Boswell to see genuine civilized
> life in an English provincial town. I turned him loose at Lichfield, my native
> city, that he might for once see real civility. For you know he lives among
> savages at home, and among rakes in London.' WILKES: 'Except when he is
> with grave, sober, decent people like you and me.' JOHNSON: 'And we
> ashamed of him.' WILKES: 'Boswell, you have kept a great deal of bad
> company.'

When they got home, Johnson wasted no time telling Mrs Williams
how pleased he had been with Wilkes and the whole evening. Boswell
inwardly savoured his triumph, which epitomized his talent as an archi-
tect of conviviality. He had brought together two of his dearest friends
who had in common 'classical learning, political knowledge, modern
literature, wit and humour and ready repartee', and who otherwise

would have continued to hate each other. When Burke found out about Boswell's coup, he remarked, 'There was nothing to equal it in the whole history of the *Corps Diplomatique*' – a comment that Boswell was mindful to include in the *Life*.

15

Even to students of the eighteenth century, the name Mrs Margaret Caroline Rudd is not well known. Yet her name in late 1775 and early 1776 hung on people's lips. Men could not resist her and Boswell wanted to know for himself the nature of her appeal, and whether he would himself be attracted to her. He was fascinated by her, not merely because she was an enticing twenty-nine-year-old seductress and adventuress of great charm and some beauty, but because she had narrowly managed to defeat the gallows in one of the most sensational trials of the day.

In March 1775 she had been caught forging bonds and promissory notes with the two Perreau brothers, Daniel and Robert. Their fate was quickly sealed when, to defend herself from their treachery, she offered to give evidence against them in court. While they were found guilty and sentenced to hang, the court could not decide her fate. As she languished in prison for six months waiting to hear whether Lord Mansfield and the other judges would make her stand trial, rumours flew around that she was this or that lord's mistress, even Wilkes's, and her fame spread.

Married at seventeen, Mrs Rudd had left her husband, a lieutenant, not long after, passing herself off as a foreign countess, a schoolteacher and a governess, among other roles, all of which she used to extort money from wealthy men with whom she had sexual relationships. Her greatest triumph, however, was in successfully defending herself at her trial. As it concluded, she turned to the judges and said, 'I have no reliance but on you. You are honest men, and I am safe in your hands.' They returned their verdict of 'Not Guilty' in half an hour. Soon afterwards, the Perreau brothers were hanged. One of them, Daniel, was the father of three of her children.

Boswell was interested in the fact of Mrs Rudd's notoriety. It should by now be evident that for all his experience with women and despite Margaret Stuart's tutelage, he did not understand them very well. He wanted them to be modest in public and passionate in private. Nor did he value women for their intelligence and ideas. As we know, he had shied away from Zélide for that as much as for any other reason. Mrs Rudd, however, engaged his curiosity because, while brilliant, she was also an enigma.

On the afternoon of 22 April, after a few unsuccessful efforts, he was shown into her rooms in Queen Street. Mrs Rudd was out, so he waited nervously upstairs in the dining room for half an hour. He then heard her steps coming up the stairs and she appeared, 'rather a little woman, delicately made, not at all a beauty, but with a very pleasing appearance and much younger than I imagined'. He was thrown off balance. She spoke of herself, her trials and anxieties, how her imprisonment had shaken her health. She was 'so pleasing and insinuating' that he believed what he had heard about her as a sorceress. She denied she could enchant anybody. 'I told her I was convinced she could enchant, but I begged she would not enchant me too much, not change me into any other creature, but allow me to continue to be a man with some degree of reason.' It was her 'delicate imperceptible power', perfectly concealed, with 'no meretricious air, no direct attempt upon the heart. It was like hearing the music of the spheres which poets feign, and which produces its effect without the intervention of any instrument, so that the very soul of harmony immediately affects our souls.' She said she had given up hopes of happiness. Before he knew it, he was on his feet and had seized 'her silken hand, and afterwards, upon the argument being renewed a little, kissed it'. Keeping up the charade of self-control, he told himself this was just an 'experiment', but he had already fallen helplessly into her velvet net.

Her 'pretty turns of countenance' and apparent helplessness kept him transfixed. Her conversation was effortless and thoughtful. A gentleman had told her, she said, that before he met her he imagined her old and ugly. That was because enchantresses are often confused with witches, Boswell replied. 'You are, however, much *younger* than I supposed.' 'I am not a young woman. I am nine-and-twenty, and I do not think that young.' Then she showed 'a pretty little foot', which made him jump up again and declare, 'I cannot believe that you have gone through all this. Are you really Mrs Rudd?' 'I *am* Mrs Rudd.' 'I was quite calm and possessed myself fully,' he wrote, stirring the fire, moving the candles, feeling no 'confusion' when their eyes met, making himself at home. But who was pulling the strings? As he left, she told him she was always at home. 'I wished her good night with a kiss which she received without affectation of any kind. I was *then* a little confused.' He never hinted at an intrigue. 'I wondered what she thought of me. I imagined I was very agreeable.'

That night at Paoli's house he began to write his narration of the interview, intending to send it to his wife. After finishing it the following day, he thought better of that, for obvious reasons, and sent it to Temple instead. 'You know my curiosity and love of adventure,' he wrote on 28 April. 'I have got acquainted with the celebrated Mrs Rudd.'[53]

He saw her again the day before he left London. She showed him a miniature of herself painted when she was in prison. She hinted that she would have killed herself before allowing herself to be marched to the gallows. She pressed him to stay longer. 'You could make me commit murder . . . For the first time delirium seized me.'

> I: 'Is a pretty ankle one of your perfections?' SHE: 'Yes.' I: 'Your eyes – ' SHE: 'Poets and painters have told me enough of them.' When I took a kiss, she said, 'I have heard I had a fine mouth.' Snatched several, with passion. Twice I said 'Adieu'; at last, 'God bless you.'

Subsequently, she may have fallen on hard times, for in April 1778 Lord Pembroke told Boswell he had run into her at 'a certain house', probably an elegant brothel for gentlemen, and that she had spoken much of him.[54] In 1785, if not before, their paths crossed again and they embarked on a brief but passionate affair.

TWENTY-ONE

'Inexplicable Dilatory Disease'

I

As before, life seemed to go out of Boswell when he returned to Edinburgh in May 1776. He had been through a bad patch during the past
two to three years: drinking, gaming, and whoring; quarrels with his
wife, several of them violent; filial coldness; the return of his old foul
adversary, hypochondria; an inescapable realization that the law was only
a dull routine to be, at best, endured; disappointments from 'great'
friends and acquaintances regarding his prospects; and a burst of frenetic
social life in London almost every spring. For years, he had not written
much of anything except his journal and the uninspiring documents
connected with his work. Now the vista was darkened by indolence and
debility, a grey inertia, that slipped in and out of hypochondria with an
immobilizing regularity, threatening to suffocate him.

His journal, among other things, suffered in that he could scarcely
find the resolve to keep it up regularly, although paradoxically now it
was often more dramatic than ever, a fable of misery punctuated with
unprepared, sudden, and irrational moments of joy. He felt, in Hamlet's
words, stale, flat, profitless, and weary, but at any moment he might
erupt into brilliant high spirits.

The indolence was brought on chiefly by his rising suspicion that, in
spite of years of enormous effort, he was not going to achieve any of
the hopes he had cherished – as advocate, husband, son, politician or
landowner. Nor even simply as a responsible, prudent, sober, and
respected member of society. He knew that while many loved him, many
also dismissed him as unreliable and indiscreet, thought he was ludicrous,
and (with his habit of recording conversations) even an embarrassment
and threat. His spirit was tired. He knew he had a genius for pleasing,
but where exactly did that leave him? Who knew what his future as a

writer might bring, whether there would be opportunities like the Corsican struggle for independence which could engage his natural talents and again catapult him to fame. He hoped someday to write about Johnson, of course, with whom in many people's minds he was now linked as future biographer. But could he ever muster the time and sustained energy to do so? He could have turned the Hebrides journal into a book right away, but as we have seen, Johnson, who did not like being publicly exhibited, had effectively buried that idea.

Boswell was not even sure he was succeeding with his journal. Many of the entries now are full of doubt. Was he writing in too much detail? Why could he not make himself go in for broad instead of fine strokes? Why could he not keep up with it? What purpose did it serve anyway? It certainly would not make him famous. 'I really think that this dull, uninteresting journal is not worth the trouble of writing. But it is a register of my life, such as it has passed,' he wrote on 8 May 1777. At times he thought the journal was a substitute for real life, the only real substance of himself. 'I had lately a thought that appeared new to me,' he wrote on 3 February, 'that by burning all my journal and all my written traces of former life, I should be like a new being; and how soon may this be done.' It would be like changing one's address when one was tired of the old one, like rubbing the slate clean. But, of course, destroying his journal was the last thing in the world he could bring himself to do. His only option was to soldier on and see what turned up to bring him to life again.[1]

This listlessness even prevented him from looking at the selection of books Johnson had chosen for him. 'To hear that you have not opened your boxes of books is very offensive,' Johnson wrote on 2 July 1766. 'The examination and arrangement of so many volumes might have afforded you an amusement very seasonable at present, and useful for the whole of life. I am, I confess, very angry that you manage yourself so ill.' Boswell was 'averse to labour' of any kind, though he performed his legal duties respectably enough, 'all my affairs in a sort of hurried irregularity, all my exertions being occasional and forced'. This 'inexplicable dilatory disease' prevented him even from writing letters to his London friends, including Johnson. Over the next year-and-a-half, until he left for Ashbourne in September 1777 to rendezvous with Johnson, the drama of his personal life is the drama of his patternless introspection. The main ingredients may be quickly summarized: sex, illness, death, Auchinleck, and his father.[2]

2

Soon after Boswell's return home in May 1776, Margaret became pregnant again. This time her confinement was bedevilled with illness.
Coughing, pains in her breast, and sweating were symptoms of her
family's disease, consumption. When her sister died of it the following
March, she was beside herself with apprehension: 'It was gloomy to her
to be now the last of her father's children, and to dread that she would
be carried off by the lingering distemper, a consumption, as the rest had
been.' She started spitting blood in July 1777. By January 1778 she began
to talk about imminent death, advising Boswell to be ready to be 'both
father and mother to my children'. At midnight, on the 5th, his attempt
to be 'voluptuous' with her resulted only in the coughing up of yet more
blood. 'O direful! [she] thought herself gone,' he wrote. By now they
both knew the blood was her death warrant. They hoped for a miracle,
but her death seemed to them only a matter of time.[3]

Boswell would now, one would think, devote himself to Margaret,
tend to her needs, and keep aloof from the gaming, drinking, and
whoring that had pained her so much. Sadly, he was too much in the
grip of hypochondria to behave as he knew any decent husband should.
He stayed out late and drank too much, shaming himself in his own eyes
by breaking his promise to Paoli. During the rest of 1776 he became
more reckless and coarse than he had ever been before in Edinburgh as
he 'ranged the streets and followed whores'. Repeatedly, he risked infection. He could cry in some despair over Margaret's illness and yet, in
almost the next breath, be prowling around Edinburgh, driven by that
despair to wallow in sin. The pages of his journal are crammed with
illicit nocturnal escapades, and many in broad daylight, too, in open
places like 'the north brae of the Castle Hill', a frozen field behind the
Register Office, or in Barefoots Parks. 'I was shocked that the father of
a family should go amongst strumpets,' he wrote, but there was 'an
insensibility about me to virtue, I was so sensual'. He added, 'perhaps I
should not write all this.' But why not? He did not seek to hide it from
Margaret. He would return home, in wretched remorse, and confess
everything to her immediately. On several riotous occasions, he fell and
hurt himself, returning in a sorry state to her who, in her illness, could
still minister to his needs. On one touching occasion when he felt the
compulsion to stir, they went out into the night together. In her frail
condition, though, she could not keep up and had to return home,
worried and sick, while he went on wrapped in darkness.[4]

Even Margaret's tolerance could be stretched too far. When, on 3 October 1777, she read in his journal how he had recently been fondling the maids at inns, she was disgusted. But she was not as angry as when she read of his infatuation with Annie Cunninghame, her niece, who had lived with them through her teenage years and into maturity. In the autumn of 1776, 'I very foolishly indulged such a fondness for Annie Cunningham as was truly a kind of love, which made me uneasy; and I cherished licentious schemes, and was fretted, for sooth, when she made any opposition. I was truly Asiatic.' It was a sickness, he admitted; it pained him that it should interrupt his love for his wife and family. Yet he could not suppress his urges to 'romp' with her, and she seems not always to have rejected his advances. As his attentions to her increased, Margaret became more and more uneasy. Even his daughter Veronica noticed. 'Cousin's papa's dautie [pet] now,' he heard her say.[5]

As with any married couple in distress, misunderstandings and impatience were rife between them, most of it produced by Boswell's depression and drunkenness. He was infuriated by her badgering. When she complained about his getting up late one morning, he threw his tea into the fire and stalked out without breakfast. His manner, roughened by his late-night bouts with fellow lawyers – Digges described them as 'a parcel of schoolboys broke loose' – was becoming anathema to her:

> My wife, with too much keenness but with a good deal of justice, gave me this morning literally a *curtain lecture* upon the coarse, ill-bred, and abusive style of conversation which I now habitually practised. She said that it was so disagreeable and provoking that my company could not be liked, and that I had not the tenth part of the invitations now that I had before I was married.

He knew she was right. At least once he even risked his life by walking across a narrow wooden bridge without rails over the River Doon just to prove he was sober. 'I shudder to think of it,' he wrote. 'What an unhappy wife and helpless children might I in this drunken delirium have made.'[6]

One bone of contention between them, the Auchinleck entail, was finally settled in August 1776. Lord Auchinleck's health was not good and he alternated between weak states in which he behaved affectionately towards his son and periods when he was well and reverted to his normal severity and coldness. Taking heart during his father's gentler moods, Boswell still hoped to arrange a compromise whereby his daughters could be called in the entail after heirs male of his father's body. But in more lucid intervals his father slammed the door on any negotiation and conveyed a message to him through John Stobie, his dour clerk whose impudence over the years deeply offended Boswell, that 'if I did not now sign the entail, he never again would ask me, and would withhold from me my allowance'. Take it or leave it: the estate would be settled on the heirs male of Boswell's great-grandfather, and after that on heirs whatsoever. He prudently signed on 7 August, thus immediately lifting the burden off both him and Margaret.[7]

Throughout all this adversity his and Margaret's love for each other remained essentially strong. He was also an extremely doting and affectionate father. There is a lovely image at Prestonfield when under a cheering sun in August 1776 he held Veronica up to a tree 'and let her pull apricots herself'. Margaret understood him but was powerless to dispel his gloom. The support and help the couple needed, unforthcoming from his father and stepmother, was instead provided by Sir George and Lady Preston of Valleyfield who continued to act as surrogate parents to them. Sir Alexander Dick also frequently offered them sanctuary at Prestonfield, and Sir William Forbes invited them to come and live with him in his spacious and elegant new house in the New Town where the air was better and might help Margaret to recover. From London, Johnson recognized that he had been too harsh with Boswell and tried to make up for it: 'Now, my dear Bozzy, let us have done with quarrels and with censure ... Make use of youth and health while you have them.' Johnson's earlier letter was 'harsh medicine', Boswell wrote, but this one was 'balsam'.[8]

In 1777 they thought of moving from James's Court to acquire more space, fresh air, and a garden. Lord Auchinleck had just sold his house in Blair's Land, where Boswell had grown up; Boswell was unaffected by this, for 'a town property is not the subject of family attachment' – but it did set him thinking that moving house was just what they all needed. He considered one of the painter Allan Ramsay's airy houses on the north side of Castle Hill, but early in February 1777 decided in favour of leasing for a year the house his uncle had vacated on the south side of the Meadows, a park to the south of the city, where there was a garden and the children could play happily. They moved there in May. Delighted, Boswell wrote to Johnson:

We have a garden of three quarters of an acre, well stocked with fruit-trees and flowers and gooseberries and currants and peas and beans and cabbages, etc. etc., and my children are quite happy. I now write to you in a little study, from the window of which I see around me a verdant grove, and beyond it the lofty mountain called Arthur's Seat.

Johnson urged him to capitalize on the change: 'I wish I could gather currants in your garden. Now fit up a little study, and have your books ready at hand; do not spare a little money, to make your habitation pleasing to yourself.' One of the virtues of the move was its rural setting removed from the city's night-time temptations. By November, however, they were back at James's Court since the 'hut' by the Meadows inexplicably was thought to be too remote for proper attention to Margaret's health.[9]

3

Boswell was becoming obsessed with death, annihilation, and futurity – the delicate metaphysical preoccupations that more than anything else, ever since his boyhood, had troubled and depressed him. He seemed unable to leave the theme alone. Little Veronica bore some of the brunt of it. Lying on the bed one morning next to her, he 'engaged her attention with telling her how pretty angels would come and carry her from *the kirk hole* [the grave] to Heaven, where she would be with GOD and see fine things'.[10] Understandably, Veronica was frightened out of her wits and preferred the thought that her nurse would carry her straight off to heaven, without an obligatory stop at the grave. That Boswell should introduce such a subject to his little girl reveals how much he wanted to believe, Presbyterian doctrine aside, that all of God's children would go to heaven.

Hume was the most famous sceptic in England. Boswell, as we know, had discussed the afterlife with him on several occasions and found him adamant that there was only oblivion after death. This was not what Boswell wanted to hear. Johnson, for whom Hume was a dangerous infidel and a threat to order and society, was consulted repeatedly, as was Temple. And so it went on until July 1776 when Hume lay dying in his bed in the New Town. Here was an opportunity. Confronted by salvation or damnation, surely Hume would reconsider. Boswell profoundly needed him to.

He visited Hume's house on Sunday 7 July and found him reclining in the drawing room. Looking thin and drawn, Hume weakly but pleasantly welcomed his old friend. Boswell, with a forwardness that few people could match, lost little time in bringing the conversation around to immortality. He afterwards made notes of the exchange and the following March composed his brilliant and dramatic 'Account of my Last Interview with David Hume, Esq.'.[11]

First Boswell asked him whether he had ever been religious. As a boy, yes, Hume replied, but he had studied himself out of religion. He added earnestly that now 'when he heard a man was religious, he concluded he was a rascal, though he had known some instances of very good men being religious'. Boswell had trouble believing that Hume was not being 'jocular' here, but apparently he was not. Then he asked the over-whelming question: 'I had a strong curiosity to be satisfied if he persisted in disbelieving a future state even when he had death before his eyes.' Hume replied clearly that his imminent death did not make a jot of difference to his beliefs – it was 'a most unreasonable fancy that we should live forever', he stated flatly. At first, Boswell was lighthearted. ' "Well," said I, "Mr Hume, I hope to triumph over you when I meet you in a future state; and remember you are not to pretend that you was joking with all this infidelity." "No, no," said he. "But I shall have been so long there before you come that it will be nothing new." In this style of good humour and levity did I conduct the conversation.' But very quickly he succumbed to a dreadful fear:

> I however felt a degree of horror, mixed with a sort of wild, strange hurrying recollection of my excellent mother's pious instruction, of Dr Johnson's noble lessons, and of my religious sentiments and affections during the course of my life. I was like a man in sudden danger eagerly seeking his defensive arms; and I could not but be assailed by momentary doubts while I had actually before me a man of such strong abilities and extensive inquiry dying in the persuasion of being annihilated. But I maintained my faith.

He pressed Hume further but got nowhere. It was crushing. Hume's insistence would burrow away in his mind like a mole and induce hypochondria almost every time Boswell thought of their last meeting. Hume died on 26 August. Boswell and Grange attended the burial on Calton Hill, 'concealed behind a wall'; then they walked over to the Advocates' Library and spent a few hours reading Hume's work.

4

Margaret gave birth to their fourth child, David, on 15 November 1776 after a difficult delivery. 'I had now the four seasons: Veronica born in spring, Euphame [sic] in summer, Alexander in autumn, and David in winter.' But the baby was sickly and given that one-third of all infants died within fourteen days of birth, the prospects for his survival looked bleak. Whether it was the after-effects of the Hume interview, his wife's illness, or the sensation of being about to lose a child, Boswell brooded more than ever on the subject of death. Hume's scepticism was extreme, but the general decline of religious enthusiasm in society during his lifetime made death more fearful and traumatic because it was increasingly difficult to accept it as God's will. Moreover, in more tightly affectionate and private families than had existed a century earlier, the consolations of religion compensated less for the loss of a loved one. Deaths of infants or young children could no longer be shrugged off as common events. Boswell struggled to understand and accept God's heavenly direction after death, but scepticism was creeping into modern thought and he was not exempt from it:

> My affliction was a kind of *faintness of mind*, a total indifference as to all objects of whatever kind, united with a melancholy dejection. I saw death so staringly waiting for all the human race, and had such a cloudy and dark prospect beyond it, that I was miserable as far as I had animation ... I loved my wife with extraordinary affection, but I had distinctly before me the time which *must* come when we shall be separated by death. I was fond of my children. But I unhappily saw beyond them; saw the time when they too shall be dead...

When he received word that the Rev. Robert Brown, his host and friend in Utrecht, had died, his mind was 'sadly afflicted with melancholy'. And at the interment of Margaret's sister, he was struck Hamlet-like when two skulls of other family members were dug out of the grave and then 'tumbled into the earth again, with other lumps of clay'.[12]

The harshest blow to him in this morbid state of mind, however, came in late March after he had spent several days alone at Auchinleck with his ailing father. It was one of those rare and poignant times when they hit it off well, and one of Boswell's achievements had been to obtain his father's blessings for another spring visit to London. But a few days after he returned to Edinburgh, the infant David died. He immediately called off his plans for London. With a manly plea for perspective, Johnson wrote to him that the survival of three out of four (it was actually three out of five) was 'more than your share'; look at Mrs Thrale, who had only four out of eleven. At first, Boswell was calm 'and resigned to the dispensations of GOD', though Margaret was overcome with grief.

I carried the little corpse on my arms up to the drawing-room and laid it on a table covered with a table-cloth, parts of which again I spread over my child. There was something of dreariness in the blank in our nursery. Yet the gentle death of the sweet innocent, and his appearance like waxwork and at peace after his sufferings, affected us pleasingly.[13]

The next day they concluded a kind of wake among themselves in the privacy of their home:

This morning Veronica and Effie would see their little brother. Veronica calmly kissed him. But Effie was violently affected, kissed him over and over again, cried bitterly, 'O my poor billy Davie', and run to his nurse, who had also been hers, and clung about her, blubbering and calling to her, 'O come and take him off the table. Waken him, waken him, and put him in his cradle.' With much difficulty we got her pacified ... I was tenderer today than I imagined, for I cried over my little son and shed many tears. At the same time I had really a pious delight in praying with the room locked, and leaning my hands on his alabaster frame as I knelt.

His eccentric behaviour continued the following day at the interment. An upholsterer brought in a coffin, but Boswell did everything else, putting the baby in it and screwing down the lid. 'I locked myself in the drawing-room with the little *dead*, and read the funeral service over him.' Crosbie and Grange then accompanied him and Margaret as they took the coffin to Duddingston, outside Edinburgh, where with the permission of Sir Alexander Dick they interred the body in his family vaults, next to the coffin of the baby's eldest brother. 'I saw the coffin of my eldest son quite entire, except that the varnishing was a little worn off.'[14]

Almost as if the death and burial had a cathartic effect, Boswell's spirits soared in the next few weeks, as did his carnal desires. He flirted with a couple of women, one of them the sixteen-year-old 'natural' daughter of Lord Eglinton who, after allowing him 'luscious liberties', agreed to meet him some evening in the Meadows. None the less, his heart overflowed with gratitude and affection for Margaret with whom one night he 'lay down in naked bed' and enjoyed 'excellently'. Such were the extremes of his emotions and behaviour.[15]

5

In late April, he left Margaret and the children for another visit to Auchinleck, taking with him Annie Cunninghame whom he escorted to Lainshaw for a period of rest and fresh country air. Margaret seems not to have worried about what her husband might get up to with her cousin en route. He and Annie sang as they journeyed along and he felt like Hermippus, who inhaled strength and longevity from the breath of young women. He admitted he was 'too fond' of her but he 'observed decorum'. He stayed at Auchinleck for almost two weeks. Lord Auchinleck was more 'failed' than in March, but it was one of the best periods they had ever spent together. They strolled and rode around the grounds and the estate, and his father even showed some interest in seeing Alexander and Veronica at Auchinleck. 'This was the only hint that ever fell from him of a wish to see any of his grandchildren here. It was very pleasing to me. How hard is it that my warm affections are so much chilled by his coldness.' His stepmother, however, was becoming hostile and suspicious. It is at this time that he begins to use the denigrating phrase 'the *noverca*' (Italian and Latin for the cruel stepmother) to refer to her. He was convinced that she was trying to drive a wedge between him and his father:

> As a specimen of the selfish peevishness of the *noverca*, she seemed quite fretful when I kindly asked him to put on dry stockings and shoes, and, as if I had no title to interfere, said hastily, 'I'll take care of him.' I with difficulty kept my temper, and answered briskly, 'We'll all take care of him, I hope.'[16]

His legal work was routine and unremarkable during the next few months, with the exception of his appearance in a criminal cause on behalf of the prosecution – which was unusual since Boswell normally preferred to represent the underdog. In this cause, however, the prosecution's efforts were on behalf of a seventy-year-old, illiterate farmer Alexander Rule whose son allegedly had been killed by the police in a raid on his farm to confiscate property towards payment of debts owed to George Smith, a merchant. Five years after the event, pitted against Henry Dundas (Solicitor-General) and James Montgomery (Lord Advocate), he tried unsuccessfully but eloquently on numerous instances to win the farmer a murder trial. Boswell's 'Information' on Rule V. Smith, which he submitted on 16 December, is beautifully clear and convincing, as his presentations of evidence usually were. But he was greatly handicapped in that it was the police who were really on trial and the public prosecutors were hesitant to prosecute them since there was evidence of resistance on the part of the victim. A new trial was denied, but the cause nevertheless illustrated Boswell's instinct to take a stand against the Establishment.[17]

Without his annual trip to London in the spring, by the time September came round Boswell was in dire need of seeing Johnson. His hypochondria had effectively vanquished him as a correspondent for more than a year and he was feeling alarmingly out of touch. Johnson was concerned, too. 'My dear Boswell,' he wrote on 18 February, 'do not neglect to write to me; for your kindness is one of the pleasures of my life, which I should be sorry to lose.' 'I do not suppose the lady [Margaret] is yet reconciled to me,' he added. Elated, Boswell replied, 'I do not believe that a more perfect attachment ever existed in the history of mankind.' As for Margaret, she had long ago forgiven him and was about to send him 'some marmalade of oranges of her own making'.[18]

Over the spring and summer, they corresponded a little more. Boswell was worried about Veronica's strong Scots accent and wondered what could be done to soften it. Not much, replied Johnson; but was this something to worry about? After all, 'her Mamma has not much Scotch, and you have yourself very little'. There were more important things to think about. In the *Public Advertiser* in April, Boswell read an advertisement for a new edition of the English poets for which Johnson was contracted to write individual biographies. The project grew on him and he ended up writing his monumental *Lives of the English Poets*, which in his *Life* Boswell described as 'the richest, most beautiful, and indeed most perfect production of Johnson's pen'. Johnson, who disliked research, asked Boswell if he could turn up any information for him about James Thomson, the Scottish author of *The Seasons*. Boswell wondered at Johnson's wanting to write a biography of Thomson – 'it appears to me we have a pretty full account of this poet' – but as luck would have it he was just then on his way to Lanark and would actually be seeing Thomson's sister-in-law; he would try to pick up some tidbits about Thomson's youth, as well as a few of the poet's letters. They would speak more about it when next they met.[19]

Boswell proposed this should be in Carlisle in the autumn, since he had legal business there and Johnson was contemplating another visit to Taylor at Ashbourne. Carlisle was too far to travel, Johnson replied, even to see the only English cathedral he had never visited, but perhaps Manchester. Besides, his health was poor. He was having trouble breathing. Finally, in July, Johnson said he would ask Taylor to invite Boswell to Ashbourne; they would both stay in Taylor's house and have plenty of conversation. Boswell jumped at this.

He arrived at Ashbourne on 14 September, having travelled dejectedly in a cold post-chaise, unsure if he should have left Margaret, ill and opposed to the trip as she was. But it pleased him to think how different he now was from the young lad who had madly taken this route seventeen years earlier in his 'escape' from Glasgow to London. He managed to fondle a few chambermaids at the inns en route – 'how inconsistent', he thought, 'is it for me to be making a pilgrimage to meet Dr Johnson, and licentiously loving wenches by the way'.[20] Once his chaise pulled up at Taylor's door and Johnson rushed out to greet him, he put the weeks and months of anxiety and depression behind him. Here was a new, if temporary, lease on life. He stayed ten days, including one day spent on an excursion to Derby via Kedleston Hall.[21]

Boswell kept an extensive journal over these ten days, though he was almost a week behind even before he began it. 'Till I come up with time, and write each day's journal immediately, I shall not attend to the chronology of Dr Johnson's sayings. It is enough to know that he said this or that at Ashbourne in autumn 1777.' That was the main point of starting to write the journal again, for the days passed without any singular event to write about. There was no physical excitement to record. Johnson told him that if Taylor placed a pebble on his mantelpiece, you would find it there the following year. Even the chambermaids were ugly, so there were no 'incitements to amorous desires' there. Nevertheless, this journal was the first serious writing Boswell had done for over a year-and-a-half, except for the Hume interview and a series of essays he had just begun for the *London Magazine*. He was in his element, temporarily suspended from his legion of worries.

Except for a few stiff disagreements, they got on famously and talked into the early hours – 'I don't care if I sit up *all night* with you,' Johnson told him – about Hume and death, Johnson's enthusiasm for the Stuarts, Garrick and the acting profession, poetry, music, biography, the American 'controversy', and the scandalous execution of the author and clergyman Dr William Dodd for forgery, whom Johnson and many others had worked mightily to save.

Dodd had been a popular preacher and respected celebrity, but in 1777 when he ran out of enough money to maintain his high lifestyle, he forged a bond for £4,200, using the name of his former pupil, the fifth Earl of Chesterfield, to whose godfather Johnson had addressed his famous letter proudly rejecting the unwanted favours of a needless and encumbering 'patron'. Chesterfield did not come to Dodd's aid, but when called on by Dodd in his Newgate cell, Johnson did. Johnson even wrote a famous letter to the King appealing for mercy, and a letter to the judge for Dodd, but it did no good and the clergyman was publicly hanged in the face of a huge public outcry. Dodd's gratitude to Johnson was unbounded. Johnson let Boswell read all of the condemned man's letters to him. The case fascinated Boswell because it illustrated Johnson's compassionate heart and his behaviour in a very human drama. It also provided another glimpse of Johnson's attitude toward death. 'I said Dr Dodd seemed to be willing to die, and full of hopes of happiness,' Boswell observed; to which Johnson swiftly replied, 'Sir, Dr Dodd would have given both his hands and both his legs to have lived.'[22]

Their conversations also often turned on Boswell himself – his drinking, for example, a perennial favourite between them. Johnson told him that Paoli was worried about it, 'that it would make me go mad, for madness was in my family'. It was a pleasure he was unwilling to give up entirely, Boswell replied. To be sure, Johnson answered, 'not to drink wine is a great deduction from life', but we all may have to give up things that are not good for us. Boswell kept his own counsel on the matter.

Music, like wine, was another appetite he suggested Boswell should suppress if he could not control it. Like Orsino in *Twelfth Night*, music had an intoxicating influence on Boswell. It had always had this effect on him, in his Edinburgh youth, in the salons and large churches on the Grand Tour, at the playhouse, in the Anglican service, and in the concert halls. But he acknowledged that for someone with his personality music could be dangerous:

> On me it has an effect so keen as to distress my nerves and make me melancholy and ready to weep and to run any risk, such as rushing into the thickest part of a battle. I told Dr Johnson that it affected me in an extreme degree. He said I should never hear it if it made me such a fool. There is much of the effect owing to association of ideas. For Scotch reels make me melancholy, though they be brisk. But I have heard them at the time of life when I was very low-spirited and used to think of Highlanders going abroad as soldiers and never returning. The airs in *The Beggar's Opera* make me gay, I suppose from an association of them with busy, warm-spirited London ideas.

Their most serious topic was melancholia and madness, a subject Boswell decided courageously to address in his essays for the *London Magazine*. Johnson suspected that at times Boswell found it pleasurable both to indulge in hypochondria and to complain about it. He had rebuked him for this in the past. 'A man indulges his imagination while it is pleasing, till at length it overpowers his reason,' said Johnson. Boswell admitted this was not far off the mark: 'This I have experienced frequently in a certain degree. He said, "A madman loves to be with people whom he fears; not as a dog fears the lash, but of whom he stands in awe." This I almost ever experience, for I really feel myself happier in the company of those of whom I stand in awe than in any other company.' It was satisfying to hear Johnson giving a philosophical twist to something he had always strongly felt. Johnson added, ' "Madmen" are all sensual when the attacks are mild, but when they are ill their weakness makes them seek pain.' Exactly, thought Boswell. 'Often in my dismal fits of hypochondria have I wished to have some acute disease. When I had a sprained ankle my mind was a good deal relieved from misery' – 'employment and hardships prevented madness'. He told Johnson he was no longer afraid of him, but that his awe of him for years had kept away 'indolence, folly, nay, melancholy from me'. He still felt he could go into any battle while Johnson's talk and the image of his 'steady, vigorous mind' were fresh in his mind. On Sunday at the Ashbourne church, sitting next to him, listening to the uplifting peals of the organ which never failed to move him, 'my imagination filled with all the circumstances of learning, genius, worth, and literary distinction which [Johnson's] name conveys . . . I was as serenely and steadily happy as I suppose man can be.'

They also spoke of Boswell's future, of his growing plans for moving to London. If his father lived ten more years, Johnson stated, there would be no point in trying at the English Bar. It would be too late. But if he should become Laird of Auchinleck relatively soon and have the benefit of additional income, it might be worth the attempt. He must be absolutely sure of employment, however, before he moved south, or else London would become a new hell for him. Indolence and melancholy would devour him. In the meantime, he must very soon bring Margaret and the children down to London to see if they could thrive there as a family.

In encouraging discussion of Boswell's London ideas, Johnson was promoting thoughts that were not necessarily in his best interests. The London Bar was at best a long shot, and who knew when his father would die? Johnson encouraged Boswell to think he could successfully divide his time between London and Auchinleck, but he also disturbed him by suggesting that 'the Laird of Auchinleck now is not near so great a man as the Laird of Auchinleck a hundred years ago' since landowners no longer enjoyed the power and influence they once had. Even so, Boswell's feudal spirit was alive and well. 'It was an ease to my mind to be convinced that I might indulge my love of London without a violation or neglect of any duty. Yet I wished to maintain, as much as I could, the ancient feudal residence at Auchinleck.'

Dreams merged with reality and a personal mythology as images of the Auchinleck paradise as his own personal demesne flooded in on him:

> I hope to enjoy many days of comfortable satisfaction there, as its romantic scenes revive in my mind the pleasing gay hopes of my youth while I was first reading the classics and fancied nymphs and genii in the woods; and some particular scenes fill me with solemn thoughts of my grandfather, like Enoch 'walking with GOD', of death as a passage to a better world, of the calm piety of my dear mother.

He would be entirely his own master and 'have sometimes my brother David with me, sometimes my friend Temple, sometimes worthy Grange; and perhaps visits from distinguished men in England ... I know my own happiness.' Not even the 'noverca' could touch him then.

The Ashbourne visit was a great success. Boswell's notebook swelled with Johnsoniana. Johnson also let him copy out pieces he had written on the Dodd controversy, and on one occasion when Johnson was not looking he even slyly took a little 'paper-book' from his desk and copied out a prayer Johnson had composed on his last birthday. He felt guilty, but 'my veneration and love of him are such that I could not resist'.

There were stiff disagreements, however, the first when he mentioned Johnson's birthday. 'This morning at breakfast I was disappointed of my hope that during this interview Dr Johnson should not say a single harsh thing to me or of me ... I was pretty sure that mentioning his birthday would offend him, and yet did it.' Another time he let himself say that he wished he could see a 'contest' between Johnson and his adversary, Mrs Montagu, if they could be brought together in the same room. Johnson had been cross with him before over his sort of manipulating, but never before with so much vehemence. In spite of the successful dinner with Wilkes, Johnson had been harbouring a mild resentment at having been used in this way and he was not about to let it happen again:

> He grew very angry, and after a pause, while a cloud gathered on his brow, he burst out, 'No, Sir. You would not see us quarrel to make you sport. Don't you see that it is very uncivil to pit two people against one another?' Then, taking himself, and wishing to be more gentle, he added, 'I do not say you should be hanged or drowned for this, but it is very uncivil ... I would

sooner keep company with a man from whom I must guard my pockets than with a man who contrives to bring me into a dispute with somebody, that he may hear it.'

The third and worst dispute was about America on their last night at Ashbourne, and this one seems to have changed their relationship.

Boswell wrote that he said goodbye to Johnson, 'without any extraordinary emotion'. That sentence hinted at the alteration, though he was not fully aware of it at the time. It was related to his earlier remark to him that he was no longer afraid of him. When Boswell came to writing up the Ashbourne conversations for the *Life of Johnson*, with the perspective of time he was able to suggest that the difference in their relationship had something to do with Johnson's violent outburst on the 'American controversy'.

> The violent agitation into which he was thrown, while answering, or rather reprimanding me, alarmed me so, that I heartily repented of my having unthinkingly introduced the subject. I myself, however, grew warm, and the change was great, from the calm state of philosopohical discussion in which we had a little before been pleasingly employed.

Never before in their relationship had Boswell grown 'warm' in opposing Johnson. This was a new note. In the greater privacy of his journal he wrote, 'I dreaded offending him by even the gentlest doubts in favour of our fellow subjects on the other side of the Atlantic.' The fright Boswell took at this explosion started him thinking that a more mature manner was called for. Johnson's anger in this instance was akin to his anger over Boswell's manipulating him socially. He had had enough. A few months later, after a relaxing time with Johnson in London, Boswell felt the change was bittersweet: 'We were quite easy, quite as companions tonight ... I had a sort of regret that we were so easy. I missed that awful reverence with which I used to contemplate *Mr Samuel Johnson* in the complex magnitude of his literary, moral, and religious character.' He looked on him now with a 'steadier and clearer eye', adopting a new mode of 'intellectual collaboration'.[23]

Boswell stopped to see his brother John in Newcastle on the way home, whom he found worse than ever, 'quite insane and raving incoherently'. He prayed for him and came away shattered, rejoining Margaret and the children at his house behind the Meadows 'in good temper', more sanguine about the future than he had been for a long time.[24]

6

In no time his spirits plummeted. During the following months,[25] until his next spring journey to London, he was regularly melancholic, arguing with Margaret when she took him to task about his fondling of maids, of which she had read in his journal, attending to his business in a desultory and lacklustre way, ill much of the time, alarmed by his wife's illnesses, demoralized and angered by the 'noverca' and his father's coldness and hostility, stung by a rebuke from Johnson for his 'cowardly caution' regarding some misunderstanding with Beauclerk, and succumbing again to a sexual infection after a couple of nights of wild wenching in late January. It made him feel no better to sit down with Forbes one day in early March and hear that he never suffered from indolence because he always kept himself so busy at his bank – 'a room which is frequently swept never gathers much dust.' Forbes also panicked Boswell by talking of a newspaper report that Johnson had just died. He doubted the report, but he trembled in anxiety and suspense for several hours until the *London Chronicle* arrived with the news that Johnson merely had a cold.

There were several positive developments amid this general gloom, however. One was that Margaret became pregnant again in late December and her health improved strikingly as the symptoms of consumption subsided. In late January, after his infection, Boswell forswore wine completely, and (except for one lapse) continued to drink only water until he left for London. On 1 December he allowed himself to be elected Deputy Grand Master of the Grand Lodge of Freemasons in Scotland, to please Forbes who was re-elected Grand Master. He had mixed feelings about it. As he looked around the table at the several 'brethren', he 'could not perceive the least ray of jocularity in any of their countenances'. At the same time, it pricked his social conscience to see so many earnest men engaged in something 'attended neither with *gain* nor with *power*'. Perhaps he could learn a lesson from them: 'I considered that it was really *honourable* to be highly distinguished in a society of very universal extent over the globe, and of which the *principles* are excellent.'[26] Neither that thought, however, nor his 'parade' with members afterwards to the Assembly Hall to celebrate, did much to raise his spirits.

In March 1778 Boswell initiated a correspondence with Burke, warning him from Edinburgh that if a bill in Parliament abolishing certain penal statutes against Scottish Catholics were passed, it would almost certainly outrage Presbyterian bigotry and ignite riots in the city. He turned out to be right, but Burke was dismissive. He had little time for Boswell's political opinions – in April he thought it was so much nonsense when Boswell again advised him against excessive 'Whiggery' and told him he was a 'Tory and an American upon my own principles'.[27] Their friendship, in fact, was unmistakably lukewarm on Burke's side, though on Boswell's it was reverential. He had adopted Burke as a model; now he wanted him as an intimate friend. He would work at it.

The most important development for his self-respect was that in the late summer of 1777 Boswell agreed with his fellow proprietors of the *London Magazine* to write monthly essays on a wide variety of subjects under the name, 'The Hypochondriack'. For a man whose keenness for self-expression is so abundantly evident in his journals, and whose identity was largely forged and given reality by words, to squander his writing talents in the ephemera and dullness of legal business was soul-destroying. An entry in his journal on the way home from Ashbourne suggests how frustrated he was that his authorial pride was starving to death: 'I have had little food for my vanity as a *celebrated man* upon this jaunt.' Nobody had once mentioned his *Account of Corsica*. 'Nor had I any kind of allusion made to my being an author, except by the Fellow of the College of Manchester, who said I might find several things in the place to put into a history.'[28] He had recently published the occasional poem and article – one on his pro-American position, for example, and another on Hume's character and religious principles, soon after his death, for the *London Chronicle* and *London Magazine*. For years he had been casting about for a sustainable subject for a book, something more immediate than the biography of Johnson, which after all had to wait on the great man's death. He had thought of a Scots dictionary; a history of Scotland since the Union; lives of Kames, Hume, Pringle, Dick, and a number of others; several projects dealing with Scottish law; histories of Ayrshire and the Isle of Man; and the list went on. None of these ever came to anything, though he amassed quite a collection of materials for a life of Kames.

In a general introduction to the series in the October issue of the *London Magazine*, written before meeting Johnson at Ashbourne, Boswell announced openly that he was a hypochondriac addressing other hypochondriacs in England, 'where the malady known by the denomination of melancholy, hypochondria, spleen, or vapours, has been long supposed almost universal'. His former sufferings had uniquely qualified him, he said, to write about the subject. 'My general purpose will be to divert Hypochondriacks of every degree, from dwelling on their uneasiness, by presenting to them such essays on various subjects as I can furnish from my own intellectual store.' He would be totally honest in this because he had now 'attained to tranquillity and cheerfulness in the general tenor of my existence'. That at least was not honest. He was very depressed when he began the series, and for most of its duration he was plagued with hypochondria, but once started he did not miss an issue for nearly six years. He hoped that this was a form of therapy that would heal him permanently as well as helping others.[29]

His earliest essays were on fear, war, and excess. Then, in February and March 1778, he published two vivid essays on the nature and effects of hypochondria itself.[30] These are among his finest. He asserts immediately that it is virtually an insurmountable problem. We may be able to 'dissipate the dreary clouds' with cheerful companionship, but 'there are excessive degrees of melancholy, which defy all our endeavours to remedy them'. None the less, we should not give in, especially if the malady 'vents itself in immoral acts'. Too often people blame melancholy for what is simply vice. He isolated one shade of the sickness that also particularly applied to him – 'languorous hypochondria', the inability to get down to anything: 'He is tantalized with a thousand ineffectual wishes which he cannot realize.' Irritation and sensitivity, however, are the worst manifestations – 'when the mind is so tender and sore that everything frets it'. The only help for it is a very accommodating and understanding companion and a good book, especially biography. He did not return to the theme of hypochondria again until December 1780.

In all, Boswell wrote no fewer than seventy 'Hypochondriack' essays on subjects that had engaged, agitated, or perplexed him for many years: love, marriage, death, reserve, authorship, drinking, criticism, country life, religion, executions, diaries, and parentage. Many, such as the ones on hypochondria, death, and marriage, are heroic in confronting the problems that plagued him. Others demonstrate a brand of intellectual curiosity that confutes suspicions that he was squeamish or dandyish. Writing them exorcized many personal devils for him.

The essays were too short and swiftly written to be often profound, but one does not read them for originality of ideas so much as for their autobiographical content. Boswell was totally honest with his readers. He knew he was in danger of exposing too much of himself in public and that he might be criticized for it. In his last essay, he wrote: 'Perhaps, indeed, I have poured out myself with more freedom than prudence will approve, and I am aware of being too much an egotist. But I trust that my readers will be generous enough not to take advantage of my openness and confidence, but rather treat me with a liberal indulgence.'[31] Still, the essays lack the personal detail in which his journals abound, that vivid particularity or 'personal transcript of the mind' which in the essay 'On Diaries' (no. 66, March 1783) he identified as his genius:

> it has been my good fortune to live in a multiplicity of instructive and enter-taining scenes, and I have thought my no.es like portable soup, of which a little bit by being dissolved in water will make a good large dish; for their substance by being expanded in words would fill a volume . . . I have regretted that there is no invention for getting an immediate and exact transcript of the mind, like that instrument by which a copy of a letter is at once taken off.[32]

Another problem with the essays is that they are often inaccurate. Boswell wrote so fast that he frequently got facts and literary allusions wrong. What is missing in accuracy, however, is made up for by his creative energy.

The essays reveal that Boswell's knowledge of literature was not to be scoffed at, even though he complained that he did very little reading. He drew heavily on his own library, as well as on the Advocates' Library, chiefly a library for lawyers but well stocked with works of English and foreign literature, ancient and modern. He probably even wrote many of his essays in the library itself, where he could dip into any book he wanted. The essays contain innumerable references to authors like Shakespeare, Milton, Pope, Young, and Thomson; the philosophy of Berkeley and Locke; modern histories by Robertson, Gibbon, and Hume; Continental works by Mon-taigne, Rousseau, and Voltaire; and the ancients.[33]

7

With the 'Hypochondriack' series in progress, Margaret healthily pregnant once more, and his affairs at home in order, Boswell was again ready for London. He wanted to take Margaret with him, but as he told Langton, she 'dislikes travelling; and prefers going to some country place in Scotland, where she can have her children along with her'. Weeping, Veronica went with him to Auchinleck to bid his father goodbye. She was now fast becom-ing Boswell's little companion and friend, even a crutch to lean on in the presence of his father, who still made him feel like a small boy, 'void of understanding'. 'Having a child of my own before me elevates me to the rank of a father and counteracts the depressing imagination to a certain degree. It is like having a little footstool to raise me.'[34]

He set out for London on 13 March 1778. The family farewell was more 'tender' than usual. Margaret was tearful and Veronica clasped him around the neck and would not let go, crying 'O Pap-a!' Alexander ('Sandy') cried, too, which particularly pleased him. Only Euphemia ('Effie'), normally the most affectionate, maintained her composure.[35]

TWENTY-TWO

Later Thirties: 'The Author and the Gentleman United'

I

When Boswell arrived in London on 17 March, he was surprised to find that Johnson had added to the inmates and pensioners of his household. Now, in addition to Francis Barber, Mrs Williams and Dr Levett, he had taken in the penniless widow Mrs Elizabeth Desmoulins, the daughter of his godfather. Johnson himself was at Streatham Park, where he remained for nearly two weeks, leaving Boswell to acknowledge the annoying truth of the printer William Strahan's remark that Johnson 'was in a great measure absorbed from the society of his old friends' by the Thrales. On the 27th he finally wrote to Johnson saying that 'a separation from him for a week, when we were so near, was equal to a separation for a year, when we were at four hundred miles distance'.[1]

From Edinburgh Boswell had done his best to accommodate the Thrales with his attentions to two of their friends whom they had asked him to welcome on recent visits to the city. Henry Thrale was genuinely grateful, but Hester Thrale sent no word of thanks. On 30 August Boswell finally wrote to her, trying to make up for his recent silence and lack of appreciation for her hospitality in Bath: 'Though I have not expressed my gratitude, I have very constantly, and very warmly felt it. A clock may go very well, though it does not strike.' What he was really after, however, was information about Johnson. She had promised him a copy of an ode Johnson had written to her from Raasay; he asked for it now. She could not have been terribly impressed with his request for any 'admirable sayings' of Johnson's she had 'collected', or with his admonition that she write them down immediately lest they be lost or misremembered, or with his sentiment that between them they would make up a 'Great Treasure' of Johnsoniana. She ignored his letter. A year later she sent him the ode, but there was no sign of any 'admirable sayings'. They were her own treasure. She was not about to share them with her chief rival.[2]

It should be said in favour of Mrs Thrale that when, in August 1777, Johnson hesitated about continuing up to Ashbourne from Oxford for his meeting with Boswell, she wrote to him, 'I shall be sorry for Mr Boswell if you don't see him. Mr Boswell will make Ashbourne alive better than three hautboys and the harpsichord' – though she also reminded him, 'you have friends at Streatham who love you more than many a man is loved by his wife and children'. 'Bozzy you know makes a huge bustle about all his own motions, and all mine,' Johnson replied good-humouredly as he waited for his friend.[3]

But all this was mere cordiality. There were signs in the spring of 1778 that Boswell was becoming irritated with Mrs Thrale's tendency to be careless over facts. This was no small matter to him, or to Johnson, since she had taken it on herself to record anecdotes about Johnson with the apparent purpose of someday publishing them. He is more strident in his criticisms of her on this point in the *Life of Johnson*, which he wrote long after he and Mrs Thrale had begun warring against each other, than he is in his journal, but the roots of the criticism are already evident there.

On 30–1 March, at Streatham, Boswell caught her out twice on inaccuracies, which she would have laughed off had not Johnson agreed: 'It is more from carelessness about truth than from intentional lying, that there is so much falsehood in the world ' – a rebuke which must have been music to Boswell's ears. A few days later while riding pleasantly in a coach in London with Johnson, Boswell returned to this theme:

> We talked of Mrs Thrale's laxity of narrative, inattention to truth, and he said, 'I'm as much vexed at the ease with which she hears it mentioned to her as the thing itself. I told her, 'Madam, you are contented to hear every day said to you what the highest of mankind have died rather than bear.'

On another occasion, Boswell noted that Mrs Thrale was eager to pick a quarrel with him, ' "As curs mouth a bone," now glad of bone to pick'. But the most gratifying development was when in confidence Johnson told him, 'Mrs Thrale sneered when I talked of my having asked you and your lady to live at my house. I was obliged to tell her you'd have as much respect in my house as in hers. Sir, the insolence of wealth will creep out.' Boswell agreed: 'She is a good woman. But she has a little both of the insolence of wealth and of the conceit of parts.'[4]

In this light, Mrs Thrale's view of Boswell's devotion to accuracy in his journal is not surprising: 'Mr Boswell keeps a regular Literary Journal I believe of everything worth remarking; 'tis a good way, but life is scarce long enough to talk, and to write, and to live to rejoice in what one has written – at least I feel that I have begun too late.' At another time she acknowledged she was no match for him in the anecdotal sweepstakes: 'Mr Boswell however is the man for a Johnsoniana: he really knows ten times more anecdotes of his life than I do who see so much more of him.' Boswell, of course, knew this, too, but sometimes lost sight of it.[5]

In spite of these competitive pressures, Boswell enjoyed dining with Johnson three times at Streatham on this London visit. After a dinner on 7 April, Johnson said to him, 'You make yourself agreeable wherever you go. Whoever has seen you once wishes to see you again.' That summer, in a chart idiosyncratically evaluating her friends according to various criteria on a scale from zero to twenty, Mrs Thrale ranked Boswell's good humour or affability with nineteen points – the highest she gave to any male friend, an almost perfect score; Johnson she gave zero for that quality. For religion, however, she gave Boswell only five to Johnson's twenty; for morality, five to Johnson's twenty; for scholarship, five to Johnson's nineteen; and for humour, only three to Johnson's sixteen.[6]

2

Good humour or not, and notwithstanding his Ashbourne resolution to be 'easy with Johnson from then on, several times Boswell was on the receiving end of some stiff rebukes. At Dilly's one day, when he implied Johnson's bias against the Americans, he 'roared again, till he was absolutely hoarse. I sat in great uneasiness ... the noise was grating and shocking.' Then on 30 March at Streatham Boswell began to speak again of giving up wine and of his regimen of drinking only water, a subject he raised as often as he could for moral support. Johnson blurted out, 'Pooh! pooh! I won't sit to hear such nonsense.'[7]

But the biggest tiff at Streatham concerned the *Lives of the Poets* that Johnson was in the middle of writing. Boswell in his bustling way had made an appointment for Johnson to speak about Alexander Pope to the Earl of Marchmont, Pope's friend, with whom he had just had a brilliant interview that he recorded at length in his journal. Boswell took pleasure in the thought that his efforts might result in Johnson's writing an especially factual 'Life of Pope'. He even ingratiatingly proposed to Marchmont that after Johnson had finished, he should 'revise' it for him. Marchmont shuddered at the thought: 'You would put me in a dangerous situation – to be a critic of Dr Johnson. Osborne the bookseller was knocked down by him.' After dinner at Streatham on 12 May, when Johnson was in a good mood, Boswell 'called' out to him with the news of what he had arranged and was smartly slapped down for his pains:

'I have been at work for you. Been with Lord Marchmont. He bid me tell you he has great respect for you, and will call on you tomorrow at one and communicate all he knows of Pope.' I was pleasing myself with making Dr Johnson happy and having active merit. But mark! JOHNSON: 'I shall not be in town tomorrow. I don't care to know about Pope.' BOSWELL: 'No, Sir? There was no means of guessing this beforehand.' MRS THRALE (surprised): 'I suppose, Sir, he thought that as you are to write Pope's life, you'd wish to know about him.' JOHNSON: 'Why, wish. If it rained knowledge, I'd hold out my hand. But I would not trouble myself to go for it.' This was really a mortifying disappointment.[8]

A year later, with Boswell in tow, Johnson did call on the aged Marchmont[9] and was treated to a feast of Popean anecdotes. Boswell listened excitedly as the two men spoke, taking careful notes that Johnson never used.

Boswell was taking his role as Johnson's biographer very seriously indeed now. Johnson was no longer just his friend and mentor; he was also his subject, his study. In Boswell's presence, not only Johnson but many of their mutual friends felt targeted, which put pressure on everyone and tended to make many social occasions unnatural. Johnson tolerated a huge amount of it, but his patience was wearing increasingly thin. Going at him with a barrage of questions on 10 April, for example, Boswell was suddenly blasted: 'The Doctor grew enraged and said, "Don't you consider, Sir, these are not the manners of a gentleman? What man of elegant manners teases one with questions so? I will not be baited with *what*: what is this? what is that? why is a cow's tail long? why is a fox's tail bushy?' BOSWELL: 'Why, Sir, you are so good.' JOHNSON: 'My being so good is no reason why you should be so ill."' A month later at Streatham Boswell began probing him to say something quotable about melancholia, his own perhaps. 'Nay, Sir, what stuff is this!' he shouted ('horribly angry'), 'I know nothing more offensive ... than to say what one knows to be foolish things by way of continuing a dispute, or to see what one will answer. To make one your butt ... Nay, if you're to bring in gabble, I'm done. I will talk no more, upon my honour.'[10] It was like having a pesky fly buzzing overhead.

After almost all such explosions, Johnson promptly forgave and comforted him. 'Will you go home with me?' Johnson asked him after one dispute. Boswell replied, 'I said I should be late, but I'd go for three minutes.' 'Or four,' Johnson answered warmly. If there was a rebuke among their good friends, Boswell recovered quickly. At the Thrales's, or at Reynolds's celebrated dinner parties, where they were virtually ensured of sympathetic company, nothing could long untune his string. After an evening there with Garrick, Reynolds, Johnson, Percy, Burney, Hannah More, Owen Cambridge, Allan Ramsay, Langton, and Gibbon (the only one he disliked – 'he is an ugly, affected, disgusting fellow and poisons our literary club to me,' he told Temple), he wrote, 'This is a great day. Cannot have it anywhere else. This is the place ... I sat a little quiet and enjoyed the scene, the *lustre* in the *light* and in *genius*.' In more mixed company, however, he took longer to recover from verbal drubbings. One such flare-up took place at Sir Joshua's on 2 May:

> upon some imaginary offence from me he attacked me with such rudeness that I was vexed and angry, because it gave those persons an opportunity of saying how ferocious he was, and how shockingly he treated his best friends ... I was so much hurt and had my pride so much roused that I kept away from him for a week, and perhaps might have kept away much longer – nay, gone to Scotland without seeing him again – had not we fortunately met and been reconciled.[11]

Boswell brooded for six days until they met again at Langton's. Johnson came straight up to him: 'Well, how have you done?' Boswell answered:

> 'Why treat me so before people who neither love you nor me?' JOHNSON: 'Well, I am sorry for it. I'll make it up to you twenty different ways, as you please.' BOSWELL: 'I said today to Sir Joshua, when he observed that you *tossed* me sometimes, "I don't care how often or how high he tosses me when it is amongst friends, when I fall upon soft ground. But I do not like falling among stones, which is the case when enemies are present."'

Johnson agreed. After all, a few days earlier he had told Boswell, 'Were you to die, it would be a limb lopped off. And remember, I tell you this that you may not always be wishing for kind words.' Kind words, though, were balm for Boswell's anxious soul. He needed constant reassurance.[12]

3

Boswell came to London in March 1778 hoping Archibald Douglas would appoint him as one of his counsel in the House of Lords relating to a new claim to the Douglas estates filed by the Duke of Hamilton. Douglas was still grateful for his earlier efforts in the cause and did take him on, but whether or not Boswell spoke for him in the Lords is not clear. He did speak for the first time at the bar of the House of Commons, however. His friend John Spottiswoode, the solicitor, who was also looking out for some work for him, chose him over an Englishman as counsel representing James Erskine in a road dispute in Stirlingshire. It was worth ten guineas. 'This was a pleasant beginning in London,' he noted, although the preliminary consultations at Spottiswoode's house made him feel inadequate: 'his advantage in having the English accent and tone struck me much, so that it was some time before I could get the better of a depressing idea of my own inferiority. But my animal spirits and vivacity of fancy bore me up.'[13]

Before speaking in the Commons on the 24th, Boswell looked in on Wilkes who volunteered some advice on how to succeed there: 'Be as impudent as you can, as merry, and say whatever comes uppermost. Jack Lee is the best heard there of any counsel, and he is the most impudent dog, and always abusing them.' Good advice for himself perhaps, but not for Boswell who doubtless exercised more discretion than that when he rose to speak. Boswell was very fond of Wilkes. Life seemed more cheerful in his company. 'I was in excellent spirits and a pretty good match for him, better than I remember myself.' It was a pity, Wilkes said, that Boswell was friends with two 'impostures', Johnson and Paoli. He added, 'Boswell, you're the most dangerous man to keep company with, as you write all down. It restrains one.' 'I don't think it restrains you,' Boswell answered.[14]

Club dinners (which he recorded in animated detail); memorable conversations with Garrick and Burke, both of whom were warmer to him than usual; an interview with General John Burgoyne about a disastrous American campaign that ended in his surrender to General Horatio Gates at Saratoga in October; and a seemingly endless round of dinners and visits with Paoli, Pembroke, Mountstuart, Oglethorpe, Percy, Langton, Beauclerk, and a host of others kept Boswell constantly on the move, displaying good nature and high spirits wherever he went. He was well received everywhere. And for the whole of his stay he remained sober. His days had a peace and control very evident to others. In fact, as he constantly made people talk about his sobriety, they advised him in several ways, not always with a straight face, as to whether total abstinence was in the best interests of his personality. At a Club dinner he reminded Garrick that two years earlier it was he who had teased him out of his promise to Paoli not to drink for a year. Garrick eagerly took this as a cue to tease him yet again for his present water-drinking:

> GARRICK: 'It gave all the company a better opinion of you that you yielded.'
> (To Johnson:) 'Sir, there was he drinking water, with his book to take down
> our conversation ... Let it be a law of The Club, either drink or we'll search
> him, that he mayn't have book. If he won't let wine search him, we will.'

Boswell scoffed at the thought that he needed to have his journal with him to record conversations immediately, as if he could not carry them in his head. But Garrick touched a raw nerve among some members of the Club. Boswell had got into the habit of carrying portions of his journal around with him and reading it in company – a rather disconcerting habit to Garrick, and especially to Percy, who did not relish the prospect of having their words, or what Johnson said about them, made public. A sober Boswell was particularly dangerous. But this time Garrick accepted defeat and people presumably watched what they said more carefully.[15]

His harvest of recorded conversations on this trip was alive with cadences of life and friendship that animate scene after scene. He was closer than ever to the art of the verbal portrait painter. On the eve of his departure, he said to Johnson, 'This is the best London I ever had, owing to no wine.' He even had equanimity enough to write two 'Hypochondriack' essays on 'Conscience' and 'Luxury' that appeared in the *London Magazine* for April and May. 'Was the author and the gentleman united, as I could wish,' he wrote.[16]

In this essentially male world, he still found time for women. Frances Reynolds, Sir Joshua's sister, chose him to entertain Elizabeth Montagu through the tedious minutes while she painted Montagu's picture. He managed to flatter her appropriately. He still harboured a little 'melancholy passion' for the enchanting Mrs Stuart who he thought might make a stirring *femme gallante*. And he found time and energy to resume his old affair with Mrs Love, now an elderly widow. He was 'vastly snug' with her. 'What harm, in your situation?' he asked her; 'to be sure,' she replied, 'or in yours, provided it does not weaken affection at home. (What a slut! To be thus merely corporeal!) *Twice.*' One woman he found it difficult to endure was Anna Seward, with whom he impatiently fell into a brief literary scuffle. He was not alone in finding her literary talk tedious – 'I was wearied with this female criticism.'[17]

On 19 May, he ate mutton on the last dining day of the term at the Inner Temple. He had to 'keep his terms', or dine on the last day of twelve terms in order to be admitted to the Bar, and thus far he had done so only twice. There were four terms in the year but he was in London only for one of them, and in the past few years he had even missed several of those. For the moment he luxuriated in the atmosphere – 'Loved to be of the Society. Was as much so as anyone. Good thought this, that *non nascimur sed fimus* ['That we are not born but are made...'].'[18]

Later the same day he bid goodbye to the household at Bolt Court, squeezing in one more brief chat with Johnson about wine. The image of Johnson that his journal gives us in this scene must have stayed with him in the turbulent months ahead in Edinburgh:

> BOSWELL: 'But if a physician prescribes it, I may take it?' JOHNSON: 'To be sure.' BOSWELL: 'So, I'm not to bind myself strictly down?' JOHNSON: 'What! a vow? Oh no, Sir. A vow is a horrible thing. 'Tis a snare for sin. No, Sir. If you can't get to Heaven without a vow, you may go – ' Here, standing erect in the middle of his library and rolling grand, his pause was truly a curious compound of the solemn and ludicrous. He whistled as *he* does and smiled, yet was checked by awe. He *would* have added 'to Hell', but was restrained.

The slight physical touches of Johnson's large bulk in the room, rocking on his feet and releasing that expressive whistle, are the perfect stage-setting for the scene's comedy. 'How attentive and accurate am I!' Boswell added, wondering at himself.[19]

He then embraced his dear friend, mounted the box, and drove off. On the way north there was a pleasing postscript to his two months' traffic among the great. The rector in Beverley, who showed him the church, asked him his name. ' "Boswell, Sir." PARSON: "There was a most famous Boswell who went to Corsica." I in a hurry said, "I am the *gentleman*." He took me by the hand: "Sir, I'm glad to see you. You're an honour to your country." ' Sweet words for a proud author whose self-image as a writer for years had been fading.[20]

4

The anticlimax of returning to Edinburgh killed Boswell's taste for journal-writing until late August when he set off for a week at Carlisle – his first English Assizes. Movement of limb always stirred his pen. Carlisle, the pageantry of the occasion, and his own purposefulness also raised his spirits. 'England and dignity of office and real affairs had full effect upon my mind.' He loved the anonymity of it all, the processions and ceremonies. 'I felt myself very happy in the midst of the hurry and crowd and noise and dust, rousing always up in my mind ideas of Old England.' 'I find myself always easiest among strangers,' he wrote, 'unless indeed among my very intimate acquaintance.' He attended a service in Carlisle Cathedral, 'a good decent *show*', and recalled again that it was there almost two decades earlier that he had first heard cathedral worship. He also continued to avoid wine. One ominous note was meeting the powerful and wealthy Sir James Lowther, later Earl of Lonsdale, the maker and breaker of political fortunes, who bowled him over with his 'Turk-like', imperious manner, just as he was wont to bowl over his so-called 'ninepins', the nine seats in Parliament he controlled. Some say, Boswell quietly wrote, 'he is capricious and proud and disobliging, and does not choose to have interest by making himself agreeable, but by compulsion'. In a few years his own fortunes would drift into Lowther's shadow and he would find out for himself whether that was true.[21]

After the Assizes were over, he declined a tour to the Lake District because he was anxious to return to Margaret, who 'might be seized with her pains in my absence' and be in danger. In any case, he took 'little or no pleasure from seeing beautiful natural scenes'. A loving family awaited him. Veronica was now six, Euphemia four, and 'Sandy' almost three, and Margaret was about to give birth to a fourth child. There were endearing moments, as when Veronica awakened Boswell one night by asking 'to be allowed to help me on with my clothes, that she might learn to do it when I was old'. Or when she slipped on the ice in the Grassmarket, hit her head against a stair, and cried, 'What will my papa say?'[22]

Boswell commemorated the birth of his second son, James Jr., on 15 September 1779, by starting his journal again after a lapse of three weeks. A big, stout boy, obviously healthy, the baby none the less caused his mother so much pain that she declared she wanted no more children. He was inclined to agree. He also celebrated James's birth by returning to wine, port, whisky, and cider. It was really for a toothache, he told himself, but it was a bad lapse, a betrayal of Paoli. He drank himself into a stupor and 'irritability of blood' several times, and he became depressed. 'My mind was in a state of unpleasing indifference, and I was fretted to think that I had neither solid science nor steady conduct, and that my two daughters were under no awe of me ... How insignificant is my existence.' He might have counselled himself with the thought that he was more friend to the girls than rigid and austere father, but at that moment he saw only failure. Two days after he started to sleep with his wife again, he began to scout the streets. He accosted 'a wanton-looking wench', not intending to 'transgress'. 'She endeavoured to hold me, and named me, "*Mr Boswell*". This was a proof to me that I must not suppose I am not known by such creatures in Edinburgh.' He resolved to restrain himself, for fear of discovery if for no other reason.[23]

He relieved his depression somewhat by writing the 'Hypochondriack' articles. A set of three on love (nos. 11–13), at times strongly auto-biographical, preoccupied him at the moment. Take this passage, for example, which with its imagery of violence and food attempts to distinguish between love and sex:

> a man, who is actuated only by sensual desire, will indulge it with any female whom he may meet; and like a glutton, who ravenously devours many dishes, will indiscriminately embrace a plurality of wenches ... But a man who *is in love* feels himself fixed to one object which appears to his imagination to be peculiarly delightful; and as it absorbs all his fondness, he is quite indifferent about every other woman.

He warns his readers to guard against succumbing to the 'torrent of softness' – a phrase that encapsulates the ambivalence of image and word in his perception of women. In the third article, he links the violence of passion to hypochondria. Marriage for the hypochondriac can be a safe mooring in a storm. It is more about 'mutual complacency and kind attachment' than about passion. That was certainly true of Boswell's own marriage.[24]

His mood momentarily soared in late September – 'such is the effect of agitation upon me'[25] – when a hundred Highlanders mutinied against their officers, setting up camp on Arthur's Seat and refusing to come down until they were assured of better pay, treatment, and living conditions. Excited by the spectacle, he and Grange joined the crowds in King's Park to gaze at them, thrilled by the 'picturesque' scene of the Highlanders 'in arms upon that lofty mountain'. 'Wonderfully animated', he hurried home and wrote up an account of the mutiny for the *Public Advertiser*, which appeared on 29 September and 1 October. After the mutineers came down, he and Maclaurin tried to persuade a sergeant to allow a few of the men to join them for a bowl of punch at a tavern. It would have been a 'curious interview' for the newspapers, but the Highlanders were prevented from coming.

Apart from his own family, not much else gave Boswell the lift he craved. Excursions to Valleyfield and Prestonfield helped, as they always did. As his father was ill, he did his best to be patient with him, but that was difficult with the '*novercā*' lurking about. On 23 October he rode over to Auchinleck (again without his family) for a two-week visit and was surprised to have 'a pretty good reception' from his father, though 'his indifference about my wife and children hurt me'.[26] He spent much of his time reading and listening to his father's old stories. For the first time, his father was even willing to let him look through old family papers where, with the dour Stobie's help, he came across his mother's marriage contract. From it he made the disconcerting discovery that his father never did have the power to entail that part of the estate he had inherited from his own father because he himself had received it already entailed on heirs male of his grandfather. He felt a fool as he reflected on the agony he had been made to endure for so many years.

The most pleasant part of his stay was becoming reacquainted with James Bruce, his father's agent, who suspected it would not be long before there was a new Laird of Auchinleck and was eager to establish a productive friendship with him. Together they walked up to the top of the Old Castle and over much of the estate. Boswell passed several days appearing to take an interest in it, with Bruce taking him on a tour of the conifers he had planted in his youth and encouraging him to help with pruning and transplanting. 'It is not impossible,' he wrote, 'but I may grow very fond of the country.'

Lord Auchinleck's health continued to deteriorate. When Boswell took the three older children to visit him in Edinburgh in February, his coldness seemed more spiteful than usual. The children were unfeelingly, even cruelly, ordered to walk home in the pouring rain while the son had to linger on to humour his father. It is easy for us to overlook the fact that the son's love for his father somehow survived these years of family insults. He worried about Lord Auchinleck's illness, became gloomy at the thought of his death, and forced himself not to feel superior that his own 'warmth of enjoyment', even if not as steady and prudent, had brought him a richer life. A false report of his father's death later that month devastated him. When he saw him alive and well the next day, he 'got him by the hand with great affection, and was truly comforted'.[27]

On 2 March Boswell was deeply grieved to hear that one of his dearest father-figures, Sir George Preston, had died. He attended the 'dreary coffining' at Valleyfield a few days later. As if that were not enough, Lady Preston followed her husband to the grave eight months later. With two people so dear to him gone, he lost a warm link with his past. The mortality of a number of his older friends, as well as of his wife's and father's, chimed in with the thoughts on death he had just finished putting on paper in another set of three 'Hypochondriack' essays (nos. 14–16) between November and January 1779. In the first, he wrote,

> A Hypochondriack fancies himself at different times suffering death in all the various ways in which it has been observed; and thus he dies many times before his death. I myself have been frequently terrified and dismally afflicted in this way nor can I yet secure my mind against it at gloomy seasons of dejection.[28]

At least he still had his other Edinburgh father-figure, Sir Alexander Dick, whose biography he was now very eager to write. He had been thinking of doing this as an act of love for a couple of years. Since Sir Alexander was ill, Boswell urged him to jot down all he could about his life before it was too late. In January 1777, Sir Alexander had written in his diary: 'Last week Mr James Boswell, my friend, expressed a desire to make a biographical account of my life to my 74th year ... I looked over many jottings ... of past times and we had some droll interviews, and it becomes, he says, very interesting.' Like most of Boswell's ideas for books, as the months passed this one imperceptibly faded.[29]

5

In January, he received another blow when David Garrick died at the age of sixty-two. It galled him not to have ridden in the elaborate funeral procession from the actor's house to Westminster Abbey, consisting of thirty-three mourning coaches in addition to thirty-four others, five of which were reserved for 'Gentlemen of the Literary Club'. He wrote to Johnson, 'I am sure you will be tenderly affected with his departure; and I would wish to hear from you upon the subject.' Johnson did take it badly, but disappointingly Boswell heard nothing from him. 'I wish he had more of a kindly tenderness for weaker minds than his own,' Boswell grumbled to Langton. What may have disappointed him most was that there was nothing Johnsonian to add to the Auchinleck archives arising from the death of Johnson's old friend. As for himself, although Boswell told Langton he was 'greatly affected' by Garrick's death, there is little suggestion of grief in his known remarks about it. The initiative in their friendship had always been taken by Boswell. There were moments of intimacy between them, but not much sustained warmth.[30]

He ached to be in London, but even before he left Edinburgh he irritated Johnson again by writing to Henry Thrale for news about him and to Francis Barber asking him to preserve whatever manuscripts and proof sheets of the *Lives* he might see lying around the house after the first volume was published. 'Why should you take such delight to make a bustle,' Johnson wrote, 'to write to Mr Thrale that I am negligent, and to Francis to do what is so very unnecessary ... I shall spare Francis the trouble by ordering a set both of the Lives and Poets to dear Mrs Boswell, in acknowledgement of her marmalade.' Half-seriously, Johnson added that if he thought she would receive them 'scornfully', he would send them instead to Veronica, 'who, I hope, has yet none of her mamma's ill-will to me'. Johnson rather missed the point. What Boswell wanted was the 'scrapings', the manuscript evidence, with omissions, deletions, and so on – anything, in fact, that would help him sketch out Johnson's labours as an author. There is no evidence he ever received such papers.[31]

6

Boswell arrived in London on 15 March. As was now his custom, he stayed with Paoli, whose conversation seemed mostly devoted to urging his friend to give up drinking again. But he recorded little conversation with anyone on this trip. In the *Life* he admits he was 'unaccountably negligent' in recording Johnson's, 'more so than at any time when I was happy enough to have an opportunity of hearing his wisdom and wit'. It was a good crop and he was 'ashamed and vexed to think how much has been lost'.[32]

One of the factors that conspired against his journal was a recurrence of the ingrown toenail that had plagued him since his Corsican exped-ition: 'Left foot swelled and inflamed so that I could not stir without pain ... Was quite apprehensive of gout or mortification,' he wrote on

26 April. He had to sleep on top of the bedclothes because he could not bear the slightest pressure on his foot. Confined to bed with his spirits 'sadly sunk', he was warmed by a visit from Johnson and Reynolds and eager to 'infuse every drop of genuine sweetness into my biographical cup', as he recalled in the *Life*. They sat on his bed and their conversation was 'the most pleasing opiate to pain that could have been administered'. Johnson, however, did not allow the visit to end without rebuking Boswell for his 'affectation of *sentiment*' that was making him feel worse than he was. The festering toe continued to bother him, even through the summer in Edinburgh, but there were compensations. In the fly on the way home, as he told Temple, 'an agreeable young widow nursed me and supported my lame foot on her knee. Am I not fortunate in having something about me that interests people at first sight in my favour?'[33]

When he dropped in on Johnson on 31 March, after not having seen him for two days, Johnson replied to his greeting, 'How could I be well when you have not seen me for a day and two nights.' One evening at Sir Joshua's, Johnson was especially eloquent on the subject of wines, and Boswell could not resist reminding him of how 'jollily' they used to drink wine together and how he would get headaches afterwards from the late nights. Johnson retaliated with a 'witty stroke'; 'Nay, Sir; it was not the *wine* that made your head ache but the *sense* that I put into it.' How could anyone with 'a true relish of pleasantry' be offended by this, Boswell observed. At Beauclerk's on 24 April, Johnson remarked to him that although the Scots had no gaiety, '*you* are an exception; and let us candidly admit that there is one Scotchman who is cheerful'. Beauclerk then chimed in, 'But he's a very unnatural Scotchman.' Boswell's good nature luxuriated in this banter at his own expense. People did wonder at his setting himself up so often for Johnson's 'executions'. Burke's comment to him on this was, 'he'd rather see your execution than none'. 'But he recovers me,' Boswell answered. 'Yes,' Burke added, 'he takes you to the Humane Society afterwards. He has it in his breast.'[34]

There was a rousing argument between Beauclerk and Johnson at the Literary Club one night that Boswell did record in detail. Beauclerk, who felt that Johnson was getting surlier by the day – 'at his age he should be thinking of better things than to abuse people' – did not flinch from the confrontation. It is one of Boswell's best portrayals, conveying both men's anger with an intensity and rhythm again worthy of a fine novelist. They were arguing about pistols and the recent murder of Martha Ray, the notorious mistress of Lord Sandwich, First Lord of the Admiralty, by her insanely jealous suitor the Rev. James Hackman at

Covent Garden Theatre. When Johnson appeared to get the better of Beauclerk with a 'triumphant' remark, Beauclerk declared, 'This is what you don't know, and I know.'

> There was then a cessation of the dispute; and some minutes intervened, during which dinner and the glass went on cheerfully. When all at once, Dr Johnson abruptly said, 'Mr Beauclerk, how come you to talk so petulantly to me as, "This is what you don't know and I know"? One thing I know which you don't know: that you are very uncivil.' Mr Beauclerk said, 'Because you began by being uncivil (which you always are).' The words in parenthesis were, I believe, not heard by Dr Johnson.

There was another 'cessation of arms' while Johnson brooded over whether or not to be offended. He decided he would be:

> A little while after this, the conversation turned on the violence of Hackman's temper. Dr Johnson then said, 'It was his business to *command* his temper, as my friend Mr Beauclerk should have done a little ago.' 'I should learn of you,' said Mr Beauclerk. Dr Johnson answered, 'You have given *me* opportunities enough of learning, when I have been in your company. No man loves to be treated with contempt.' Beauclerk (with a polite inclination towards the Doctor) said, 'You have known me twenty years and however I may have treated others, you may be sure I could never mean to treat *you* with contempt.' 'Sir,' said the Doctor, 'you have said more than was necessary.'

Boswell recalls that they stayed behind afterwards licking their wounds and consoling each other. When he told Burke about the quarrel, Burke said it was between 'Fury and Malevolence'.[35]

The Hackman case, which became the talk of the town, provided Boswell with some literary activity in April when he began writing an article for the *London Post* (8–10 April) sensationally describing the murder. He then attended the trial and wrote a long account of it for the *St James's Chronicle* (15–17 April), wringing the emotional juice out of Hackman's moving confession and how his virtuous character had been betrayed by the passion of love. He felt, 'an unusual depression of spirits' at the thought of what he himself might do if such passion acted on his own 'lively sensations and warm temper'. He even included in the article a long passage plucked out of his 'Hypochondriack' article on the violence of love (no. 13). On the 19th he talked to Hackman in Newgate, then made his way to Tyburn to watch the execution. However, he was horrified by an account in *Lloyd's Evening Post* (16–19 April) erroneously claiming that he had actually climbed into the cart and accompanied Hackman to Tyburn, and that when they got there Hackman bade him an 'affectionate farewell'. Should he deny it? Burke thought that would make matters worse:

> BURKE: 'Was not you in Newgate?' BOSWELL: 'Yes.' BURKE: 'Was not you at Tyburn?' BOSWELL: 'Yes.' BURKE: 'Why, then, they only sent you in a coach. Besides, why be angry at their making you perform one of the most amiable Christian duties: to visit those in prison?'

He did deny it, though, with Johnson's approval, in the *Public Advertiser* on 21 April.[36]

The major literary event of this London visit was the publication in April of the first four volumes of Johnson's *Lives of the Poets*, containing twenty-two biographies. Boswell was beside himself with admiration: 'I serve him on the knee: present him the golden cup ... O wonderful man!' He could scarcely credit how a man of seventy could write like this. For the first time in literary history Johnson had revealed what psychological and moral insight could be achieved in biographies of thinkers and writers.[37]

At the end of April a letter arrived from Margaret with the news that Lord Auchinleck was very ill. Boswell just had time to squeeze in that memorable Pope interview at Marchmont's, complete another term at the Temple, and persuade Johnson to join him for dinner at Dilly's, his London 'literary head quarters' in the Poultry. On 4 May, two weeks earlier than planned, he left with Dilly for his family residence, Southhill, in Bedfordshire, to say goodbye to John's brother, Edward, his first publisher and for eleven years the warmest of friends, who was 'adying' and 'cried with affection' when he saw Boswell. He died soon afterwards.

The night before Boswell left London he renewed his correspondence with Temple with a letter to which he kept adding as he travelled north and which serves as something of a substitute journal.[38] Temple had moved with his family to St Gluvias in Penryn, Cornwall, where in May 1777 he had taken up a more prosperous living. He was still in debt but with much happier prospects. He had also just published a book on his Whiggish political theories, *Moral and Political Memoirs*, which was calculated to provoke Boswell's ire. 'I must candidly tell you,' he wrote on 8 May, 'that I think you should not puzzle yourself with political speculations more than I do. Neither of us is fit for that sort of mental labour.' 'Your letters to me and your cursory remarks on authours ... are, in my opinion, so much better than the college-like sentences your book contains ... You are an agreeable companion in a post chaise; but by no means fit to be a driver.' He did not spare himself either in his letter to Temple of 4 January 1780: 'I really think my *Hypochondriack* goes on wonderfully well. But how inconsiderable are both you and I in comparison with what we used to hope we should be ... we both want solidity and force of mind, such as we observe in those who rise in active life.'[39] He was perfectly right. Neither of them was cut out for public life and, in the case of Boswell, this would become abundantly clear in the new decade.

TWENTY-THREE

No Considerable Figure:
Politics, Family, and Hypochondria

I

Lord Auchinleck was now chronically ill and required the daily attendance of his doctor. Boswell did not reach Auchinleck until 29 May. Finding his father out of any danger, in a flush of reckless gratitude he promised that from now on he would go to London only if they agreed there was a particular reason to do so. After galloping around the estate with James Bruce, he rode over to visit young Annie Cunninghame who was dangerously ill with consumption. In her sickness she railed against Lady Auchinleck with all the resentment she could muster on behalf of her aunt Margaret and her family:

> she wished only she could live to see her obliged to quit Auchinleck, which, though she might have pride enough to conceal it from me, would vex or gall her ... She said *how* could she set herself up in the corner of the seat at church, and pretend to be religious, when nothing could be more wicked than to estrange a father from his children? She might well be said to make religion a cloak for maliciousness.[1]

Annie did not live to see the expulsion of the matron. She died in August, deeply lamented by Margaret.

What made Margaret's unhappiness particularly acute at this time was that Lainshaw, her last link with her youth, had to be sold. Coming home from the sale on 15 July, she fled to her room and wept. Boswell wished he could buy it but he knew he would be facing 'distress and a gaol' if he attempted it – although he seriously considered buying Crawfordston, an Ayrshire estate near Auchinleck: 'I have really a rage for buying land in the shire of Ayr.' It went for two hundred pounds more than he was prepared to offer. Rage or not, it was madness for him to think of acquiring more land. He felt his own impotence and berated himself for having let Margaret down over Lainshaw, 'stunned by some dismal, wonderful casualty'.[2]

It was not a good summer in several other ways. Without his father's regular presence in Edinburgh during the Session to enhance his status Boswell obtained less business and his income plummeted. And his drinking and sexual antics continued unabated. He had the scare of a possible 'taint' after a visit to a brothel called 'Pleasance'. It disgusted Margaret that he chose to traffic there in the full light of day, perfectly sober. She was also 'justly hurt' by his illicit visit to a widow whose doors were open to him. But to his infinite relief, on the same day that Lainshaw was sold, when she felt bereft of family roots and the old family hearth, she forgave him all. He vowed fidelity and resolved to devote his 'utmost attention to make her easy and as happy as possible, and now that her own family was quite extinguished, to make up to her for the want to the utmost of my power'.[3] Except for one near miss, he kept his promise until the autumn.

His morale was low. His toe was inflamed and at times excruciatingly painful. Although he read Goldsmith's *History of the Earth* and Burke's *A Philosophical Enquiry into the Sublime and Beautiful* – and wrote three 'Hypochondriack' essays during the summer, he felt ineffectual, insignificant and deficient in 'vigour of mind'. Even his journal worried him. He feared it was evidence against himself, like 'filling a mine which may be sprung by accident or intention'. Hypochondria, 'the black dog', came on. There was nothing 'elevated' around him 'either of my present or future state' as in 'warmer and younger days'.[4]

A real aggravation was the '*noverca*', who was becoming increasingly hostile and argumentative. It was as if she was trying to make Auchinleck into a fortress, with herself as the sentinel to keep at bay anyone who might exercise influence over her husband. The Rev. John Dun, minister of Auchinleck, also noticed this: 'He said he had observed Lady Auchinleck keeping at a distance from my father all who had a real regard for him.' She viewed any effort on Boswell's part to be friendly as a subtle way of ingratiating himself in his father's favour. When Lord Auchinleck came to Edinburgh in late July to attend the court, they spent part of almost every evening together for a couple of weeks, though not apparently alone. It was a 'sad business', he wrote.[5]

2

When Boswell returned from London he decided on an experiment: he would delay writing to Johnson just to see if Johnson would write to him first. It would be a test of friendship. On 13 July Johnson duly wrote, anxiously enquiring whether anything drastic had happened, though he knew his man and suspected foul play: 'If ill should happen, why should it be concealed from him who loves you? Is it a fit of humour, that has disposed you to try who can hold out longest without writing? If it be, you have the victory.' Boswell was delighted and wrote back immediately of his 'high satisfaction' at this proof of intimacy. He promised he would never 'test' him again. But on 9 September Johnson wrote again, angry: 'Are you playing the same trick again, and trying who can keep silence longest? Remember that all tricks are either knavish or childish; and it is as foolish to make experiments upon the constancy of a friend, as upon the chastity of a wife.'[6]

Their correspondence at this time of the year was usually carried on with the knowledge that they would not be seeing each other again at least until the following spring. This year, however, a rare opportunity presented itself when Lord Bute's son, Colonel James Stuart, who was recruiting in Scotland for a militia, invited Boswell to come with him to Leeds, its headquarters, then to London, and afterwards to other places where the regiment might be ordered. Boswell later told Johnson that his record of the trip, 'Journal of My Jaunt with the Honourable Colonel James Stuart', was 'truly a log-book of felicity' – an enticing description – but it has never been found. Apart from the lost Dutch journal, it is the only major journal that has never been accounted for. Fortunately, he incorporated much of it into his first draft of the *Life* so we have a good record of his conversations with Johnson – the only 'second crop in one year' of their entire friendship.[7]

Boswell surprised and delighted Johnson by knocking on his door on 4 October, finding him still in bed, nursing his own bad toe and a weakness in the ankles. It took Johnson's breath away to see him so unexpectedly. 'Frank, go and get coffee and let us breakfast in splendour,' he shouted. Boswell arrived during a period of relative strain in Johnson's friendship with Hester Thrale, which may explain the special warmth of his reception. Henry Thrale had suffered an apoplectic stroke in June, and in August Hester Thrale had had a miscarriage. Apparently she felt she had enough on her plate at Streatham without Johnson's cumbersome company. He felt the slight. Soon after Boswell arrived, the family set off to convalesce in Brighton. Boswell had Johnson all to himself.

His stay was so short that he saw none of his friends and apparently had no time even for a Literary Club meeting. With his promise to his wife still fresh in memory, neither did he taste of London's underworld. His six pages or so of conversation for this period are devoted almost entirely to Johnson. Among other subjects, they spoke of guardians for Boswell's children, the London poor, Pope, Lord Hailes's *Annals of Scotland* which Johnson found accurate but dull, the House of Commons, marital fidelity, and Ireland. He tempted Johnson by suggesting another tour, this time to Ireland, but Johnson did not bite. He was too old. In any case, he did not fancy Ireland: 'JOHNSON: "It is the last place where I should wish to travel." BOSWELL: "Is not the Giant's Causeway worth seeing?" JOHNSON: "Worth seeing, yes; but not worth going to see."'

Boswell left for Chester with Stuart on the 18th, stopping en route at Lichfield where he ordered a post-chaise and 'sallied forth to make a round of visits' among Johnson's friends, gathering material for the *Life* wherever he went. In Chester, 'I am daily obtaining an extension of agreeable acquaintance, so that I am kept in animated variety,' he reported to Johnson, who immediately wrote back approvingly, 'the oftener you are seen, the more you will be liked'. 'Animated variety', was the perfect recipe against hypochondria. No period of his life had been more sound and cheerful, he told Langton. He stayed for a fortnight. Johnson admonished him urgently to preserve that animation and keep away 'the black dog' when he returned home. The key was to keep busy with writing and research projects like ancient Scottish history. Above all, he added, '*Be not solitary; be not idle.* which I would thus modify; – If you are idle, be not solitary; if you are solitary, be not idle.'[8]

Boswell's 'stock of fine spirits' carried him back to Edinburgh and lasted him through the Session in spite of an attack of scurvy on his thighs and legs and persistent pain in his toe. He wrote twice the number of legal papers he had written the previous winter, did everything with 'ability and ease', felt no hint of hypochondria, and 'relished life much'. He almost never got drunk. Only once did he resort to a 'Dulcinea', but she was 'perfectly safe'. His mind had a 'firm bottom'. He sustained himself also with the thought that Carlisle was less than one hundred miles from Auchinleck, that he could set out on any Saturday morning, arrive comfortably by evening, get a good night's sleep at a good inn, and then attend the 'solemn service of a High Festival in the cathedral'. The sublimity of a great English cathedral was his for the taking any time he needed to escape from Edinburgh 'lowness'.[9]

He also rejoiced in his children. His turbulent emotional life did not make him the ideal husband, but his fatherhood was never in any doubt. There was a level on which the 'boy' in Boswell naturally related to and took refuge in their loving openness, and vice versa. He would do anything for them, as he assured Wilkes on 14 March: 'I have now two sons and two daughters, and some of them are beginning to cost me pretty handsomely. But as they are a multiplication of myself, I consider that I am dancing and playing on the harpsichord, and cheerfully amused in their little persons.' Veronica's playing on the harpsichord particularly soothed and delighted him – she was like some 'fine spirit' touching the keys. The children, even the toddler Jamie, a 'fine, big, strong boy' who first called him 'papa' on 3 May 1780, were the harmonious chord answering the discordant notes sounding from his father and the 'noverca'. It was a constant dagger in his heart that his old and sick father would not allow his children to visit Auchinleck – 'What the plague would you bring bairns of their age?' – and only grudgingly allowed them to visit him in Edinburgh. He was worried enough about a settlement on his children that in January he wrote out a document appointing his wife as guardian and Forbes as 'curator' for them, specifying 'that all my children may be partly educated in England, and any of my sons who have a disposition for learning may be kept some years at the University of Oxford'.[10]

Veronica and Effie were six and seven respectively in 1780, and he talked to them with increasing frequency of God, the fall of man, Christ's redemption, and heaven – subjects that continued to be crucial to his own mental health and which he was determined to present correctly, without fear, to his children. Inadvertently, though, as we have seen, he did pass on to them some of his own metaphysical paranoia. Sandy, his heir, who was now five, he tried to interest more in the family history, in spite of Margaret's impatience with patriarchal self-importance, her feeling 'that our pride and high estimation of ourselves as if German princes (my phrase) was ridiculous in the eyes of other people, who looked upon us not only as no better than any other gentleman's family, but as a stiff and inhospitable family'. He admitted she had a point, but he wanted to encourage 'sacred reverence and attachment of his ancestors'. He 'catechized' Sandy with it:

'What is your duty?' 'My duty to GOD.' 'What is your second duty?' 'My duty to the family of Auchinleck.' 'Who was the first laird of Auchinleck?' 'Thomas Boswell.' 'From whom did he get the estate?' 'From his king.' 'Who was his king?' 'King James the IV of Scotland.' 'What became of Thomas Boswell?' 'He was killed at Flodden Field fighting with his king against the English, for Scotland and England were then two kingdoms.'

More fun were the girls' dancing lessons with Signora Marcucci and outings to the family's rural sanctuary at Prestonfield where they could go riding – Sandy had been given a Shetland sheltie – and romp with a freedom they did not have at home.[11]

3

Margaret was pregnant again and after months of relief began to cough badly in November. His brother John had by now left Newcastle, apparently sufficiently 'cured', and taken lodgings in Edinburgh, a risky move. Whenever he came to dinner, he was silent, sour, and sneering, though Veronica liked him. 'I told him in plain terms that I could not admit him to my house if he behaved in such a manner. He did not mind me, but went to tea, and sat all the time with his hat on, and frowned horribly.' In front of the fire, he made noises as if he were going to spit. There was even some fear he might lose his temper: 'Once he called me a scoundrel; and as he held a staff in his hand, and even lifted the tongs, I was in some apprehension of his doing violence.'[12]

Boswell sought his father's help, but as usual could not speak to him alone.

> When his lady came into the room, I mentioned my dilemma as to poor John. She treated my concern with abominable unfeeling ill-nature, as if I had only an affectation of humanity, and said she had borne more from John than I had.

He was shocked by her 'infernal harshness' and told her 'she was fit to be captain of a man-of-war'. At the end of that unruly session, his father showed some signs of warmth, 'Now that you can walk, let us see you often,' but it was a mere shaft of light breaking through the darkest of clouds. He rarely showed compassion for any of his sons and remained unrepentant, even in the last days of his life. As Boswell wrote: 'I went to my father's at night. He spoke of poor John with contemptuous disgust. I was shocked and said, "He's your son, and GOD made him." He answered very harshy, "If my sons are idiots, can I help it?" ' Surely it is a testimony of filial patience that Boswell did not at such times give up on his father, or shout at him, or denounce him. 'I had still such an affection for him as affected me tenderly. Yet I suffered much.' Or perhaps he had too much at stake as his heir to turn his back.[13]

4

The new year began dismally as the weather turned bitterly cold, and his toenail tormented him. Part of it was growing deeply into the flesh. Near the end of January 1780, Boswell began to cut the nail out but as he could not stand the pain he 'desisted humanely'.[14] A few days later he gritted his teeth and saw through what must have been a horrendously painful operation. After that it improved and on 14 February he was able to wash his foot for the first time that winter.

It was not so easy to eliminate his hypochondria. A cloud of 'very bad spirits' passed over him, lingering on month after month, spoiling his 'coarse labour of law' which continued to decline dramatically. He sometimes sat moping by the fire without a single thought in his head. 'How sad is it that I am subject to such dreary fits, which absolutely deprive me, while they last, not only of happiness but even of the very imagination of happiness!' Forbes's advice was not to think of London as some sort of residential ideal and Edinburgh as a 'cold unimportant place'. But he preferred Sir John Pringle's view that he was born for England – 'and I am so much happier in London – nay, anywhere in England – than in Edinburgh that it is hard I should be confined to this place'. He felt as colourless as the relentless grey days. 'What an insipid and often what an uneasy life do I lead in Scotland! The cold was very severe today.' He thought only of arguing his causes and getting back to bed. Margaret was as loving and kind a wife as any husband could hope for, so much so in fact that he felt even more undeserving. '*I exist in misery,*' he cried in his journal. One morning in March he woke up with the inspiration of the biblical words, 'Howbeit this kind goeth not out but by prayer and fasting', and he resolved to dedicate himself to fervent devotion. But that did little for him. The cloud still hung overhead.[15]

In late March he began to experience a few 'intermissions' in the gloom, during one of which he poured out his misery again to Johnson. His strong reply on 8 April must have rocked Boswell momentarily – the remarkable thing was that, because the advice was so characteristic of

Johnson, Boswell decided to include it in the *Life* although it meant exposing himself as a public spectacle:

> You are always complaining of melancholy, and I conclude from those complaints that you are fond of it. No man talks of that which he is desirous to conceal, and every man desires to conceal that of which he is ashamed. Do not pretend to deny it ... make it an invariable and obligatory law to yourself, never to mention your own mental diseases; if you are never to speak of them, you will think of them but little, and if you think little of them, they will molest you rarely. When you talk of them, it is plain that you want either praise or pity.

Boswell's response was, 'his advice may perhaps be good. I shall try to follow it.' Anything was worth trying. His journal and letters are less miserable afterwards even though the heavy clouds persisted at least until midsummer, but it struck him that because Johnson himself suffered from a milder type of melancholia he was not able to understand its severer forms. John Moore's 1786 analysis in *Medical Sketches* diagnosed percipiently the hypochondriac's problem of communication:

> as this disease is in reality more distressing than dangerous, and as his looks are not impaired in a degree that corresponds with the account he gives of his distress, he seldom meets with that sympathy which his sensibility requires and his sufferings deserve.

The effect of Johnson's sharp jerk back to reality was to make Boswell keep his problems tightly in check and repress his true character.[16]

His real, as distinct from imaginary, perplexities were legion, though two stood out: lack of money and Margaret's health. Unknown to his father, he had borrowed £800 which he lent to Margaret's nephews, the sons of James Campbell of Treesbank, after the death of both of their parents several years earlier, and in February £200 interest on the loan was due. Boswell did not have it and his father was the last person he would ask for it since he disapproved of Margaret's family anyway. He tried Temple, who owed him some money, but Temple himself pleaded poverty, not yet having recovered from the expense of moving to Cornwall. Lord Eglinton turned him down, too, and Forbes could only let him have a few pounds, but loyal Dilly came through with the whole amount. Erskine also appeared with a repayment of an old debt of £50 that started Boswell thinking – 'It is strange how he and I, who once were so much together, live now quite apart. I told him I had not felt poverty till this winter,' though they agreed that paled next to the hypochondria that plagued them both just then.[17]

The bleakest prospect of all was not to visit London once the Session rose. Langton sent word that Boswell's friends were demoralized by the news, especially Reynolds. Their mutual friend Frances Boscawen, whose manners were the most 'agreeable' and conversation 'best' of any woman he had ever met, wished some fictitious criminal charge could be brought against him so that he would be brought to trial in London at public expense. Desperate ends required desperate means. Then Beauclerk died at the beginning of March, mourned by Johnson and Langton especially. What was life for if not to be with Club friends at such times? He also heard from Langton that he would miss a special Club meeting on 9 May when the members would be voting on a new candidate for membership, Edmond Malone, the Irish Shakespearean scholar of whom Boswell now heard for the first time. Malone was blackballed however (probably by his rival Shakespearean George Steevens) and had to wait until 1782 for another chance. The members also voted to increase their membership to thirty-five, not at all a pleasing decision in Boswell's eyes as it made them a much less exclusive society.

5

The rest of the year sputtered itself out with as little happiness as he could ever remember. He took some pleasure in keeping up the 'Hypochondriack' articles every month, writing a series on drinking and living in the country, and one on 'pity' that strongly reflected his state of mind for most of the year:

> A sickly man goes about to everyone who pretends to skill in physick, or who he thinks has been ill like himself, hoping to obtain a cure or palliative. So a Hypochondriack whose mind is sickly, and who suspects that others are not well, his distemper having in common with the jaundice an imaginary transference of communication of itself, is perpetually trying to obtain hints for relief, and while his spirits are sunk in despondency, lays open all his weakness.[18]

His life became a chequerboard of hypochondria: Margaret's illness – she kept spitting blood, Edinburgh and professional boredom, parental coldness, 'gross desire' and alcoholic dissipation, and a return to gambling at whist (a game he acknowledged he never became good at). In February he carried on a gross affair with a landlady in Liberton's Wynd. On 10 April, drunk, he 'ranged an hour in the street and dallied with ten strumpets'. When he got home he told Margaret all about it. On this occasion she was 'good-humoured' and ministered to him with beef soup. At other times she was furious. She safely gave birth to their fifth child, Elizabeth, on 15 June 1780, after which, repeating old patterns, he went after strumpets again, alternating his roving with confessions to his wife. He ran more risk than he thought. On 14 July he contracted his fourteenth infection, lasting ten weeks, and was unable to resume conjugal relations until 28 December. The number of deletions and missing pages in the journal suggest that he may have been far more dissipated even than this.[19]

Summer was enlivened by the permanent return of his brother David from Valencia on 12 June.[20] After almost thirteen years, he had had enough of Spain and decided to see if he could make a go of it in London as a merchant and banker. It was a tender reunion, for the brothers had not seen each other since David was nineteen. Tears flowed. At his father's house, David ran to him, embraced him, kissed his hand, and shed tears again. His father seems to have contained his response. The brothers said they would not have known each other on the street. Immediately, Boswell noticed a correctness and gravity in David that put him ill at ease. But for the moment that did not matter. Here was his brother, a member of his own family with whom he could talk candidly and lovingly.

When, on 16 August, the brothers rode out together to Auchinleck for a month Boswell brightened up considerably.[21] Their reception by Lord and Lady Auchinleck was typically indifferent, but in David's company he was 'comforted and elated by seeing the seat of our ancestors ... It was truly a feast to my mind to see all the scenes of my youth, and David here again after so long an absence.' On the crumbling walls of the Old Castle, coerced by his brother, David submitted to the charade of reading out the juvenile oath of allegiance to Auchinleck they had pledged all those years ago, witnessed by the several members of James Bruce's confused family who were rounded up for the occasion. At the end of their stay on the paternal acres, Boswell actually thought that he could live there in 'independent tranquillity' after his father's death.

He returned to Edinburgh and wrote his next three 'Hypochondriack' essays on the pleasures and snares of country living (nos. 36–38), trying to reason himself into the right frame of mind to be the next Laird of Auchinleck: 'A man of vivacity unless his views are kept steady, by a constant golden prospect of gain, cannot long be pleased in looking at the operations of ploughing, dunging, harrowing, reaping, or threshing.' A hypochondriac landowner would get 'sick and sick again and again with *ennui*, and [be] tempted with wild wishes to hang himself on one of his own trees long before they are able to bear his weight'.[22]

Soon enough, David began to get on his nerves. He was too friendly with the '*novercd*, too eager to please her. His controlled manner, 'I suppose from long habits of living in restraint among the Spaniards', was also annoying. David's Spanish air began to evaporate, reducing him to his 'original clay'. He turned down convivial toasts with pompous abstemiousness. Boswell was shocked: 'His rigid uncompliance has the advantage of my easiness in keeping him free from intoxication, but on the other hand he cannot be agreeable to most people. I felt really painfully upon this occasion. He might have declined the bumper with complaisant good-humour.' David also presumed to lecture him on his high spirits: 'He said I should associate with strong-headed people, and that he had found out that those who philosophized and did not mind real life were laughed at, however ingenious ... He talked *rationally* of my *flights*, but was in the extreme opposite to imagination and gay frankness.'

The lowest ebb in their brotherly love was after Boswell had seen him off in the fly to London on 19 September:

> his rigid uncomplying manners, except by force of studied complaisance, and his want of generosity in every respect (a strong instance of which was his not feeling with the least indignation what I, his kind brother, am obliged to suffer from the incessant ill-will of a *noverca* who governs my father as if he were a child), made me not love him.[23]

From his point of view, David saw many of the family problems as being of his brother's own making and he told him so. In the world of trade and commerce, such behaviour was a recipe for failure. It was proving so, too, in those areas of politics and the law where his elder brother hoped to succeed. Brotherly love was one thing, brotherly concern was quite another.

Very likely, it was David's sober example and advice that fed his brother's shame over a few recollected 'scenes' of his youth at Auchinleck. Boswell walked briskly down to Bruce's and recovered a bundle of letters he had written to him between the ages of twenty-one and twenty-three, 'at the most foolish time of my life'. Reading them that night, he was 'sunk by viewing myself with contempt, though then a *genius* in my own eyes'. He burned all but two or three of them. It was like exorcizing a wild spirit, at least for a moment: 'Was consoled to think that I was now so much more solid.' He had always said his life did not seem real to him unless he recorded it; now he eradicated part of it by burning some of the record. A 'cloud of hypochondria' quickly engulfed him, however. It was a literary crime of the first order against himself, a loss of faith.[24]

6

Boswell decided in April 1780, as a general election seemed imminent, to take advantage of the old connections between his family and the Dundases of Arniston. It was time to start cultivating his *bête noire* Henry Dundas the Lord Advocate in the hope of a more amicable relationship leading to some political appointment or, better yet, Dundas's support if he should contest a seat in the House of Commons. He had made a start on this by fraternizing with young Robert Dundas, son of the Lord President and nephew of the Lord Advocate: 'Young Arniston seemed to take much to me, which was agreeable, as there had been a friendship between his grandfather and mine and my father and his father; in short, an hereditary kindness, which, though interrupted by his father's bad conduct to our family at [the] last Ayrshire election, was not to be lost. He supped with me very cheerfully one night.'[25]

He had not visited the elder Robert Dundas for seven years. Now a meeting was arranged through Boswell's friend Dr Webster, on condition that no mention should be made of the past or the future, and on 24 April Boswell donned his Chester coat and waistcoat and they rode out to the Dundas country estate. He 'prayed to GOD to bless a reconciliation this day with an old friend of our family'. Margaret warned him not to drink for 'that would spoil all'.[26]

The dinner was all he hoped it would be. The Lord President's 'coarseness' had always disturbed him, but on this occasion he was a model of hospitality and affability. He knew Boswell was making an effort and he responded. At one point he toasted him as the future Lord Auchinleck, nudging him and saying with a wink, 'It won't do [be] long now.' As he left, Dundas took his hand warmly and said, 'My dear James, nobody wishes you better than I do.' They had not spoken of the future, but Boswell felt he had tilled the soil:

> Thus was a reconciliation at length brought about between the President of the Court of Session, the hereditary friend of our family, and me. It was sincere on my part. For I had forgiven him for some time. What a blessed precept is that of our SAVIOUR to forgive those who have injured us!

A little complacent and self-righteous perhaps, but positive at least.

As heir to an old and honourable family, Boswell saw himself as entirely deserving of the Ayrshire seat. Moreover, it would be a perfect means to launch himself in London. The dismal state of his finances soon disqualified him, however, and instead he threw such influence as he had behind an aristocratic candidate, Major Hugh Montgomerie, heir to his friend the Earl of Eglinton, against Henry Dundas's man Adam Fergusson. In the autumn election Montgomerie won, much to the delight of Boswell and his 'aristocratic' friends.

In the flush of victory, on 21 October he and Maclaurin (a kindred radical spirit) accepted Henry Dundas's invitation to Melville, his magnificent country house near Edinburgh. Dundas feigned surprise that Boswell had never been there before. A good dinner, champagne and claret put the guests at ease and in his impetuous way Boswell wondered how he could ever have doubted that his 'prejudices against Lord Advocate were imaginary'. As they ambled through the gardens laid out along the River Esk, 'he seemed to me the frankest and best-humoured politician that could be'. It seemed to him quite natural that a friendship would blossom between himself and this political wizard who was destined to achieve the highest reaches of power in the kingdom. Together they could revive 'the old connexions of my father with both his father, and grandfather by the mother's side'.[27]

As the greatest power broker in Scottish politics in the 1780s, Henry Dundas had not yet made up his mind how to deal with Boswell.[28] He knew he would be asked for political favours, but whether he would grant any remained to be seen. He thought the future Laird of Auchinleck might well settle down into some sort of consistent personal and political behaviour, but for now two reasons why he was a risky political appointee had become abundantly clear to him.

First, while Boswell was seeking an appointment or office that would provide him with the money to live in London, he also insisted on his political independence. He wanted to have his cake and eat it too. No

428   NO CONSIDERABLE FIGURE: POLITICS, FAMILY, HYPOCHONDRIA

prominent politician would allow an appointee the freedom publicly to disagree with him if it suited him. The second reason, which was related, was that Boswell was unreliable, a loose cannon, as likely to embarrass an ally as to oppose an adversary if his pride or principles were roused. His impulse to publish in the newspapers and other publications was dangerous. However, the act of writing was sacred to Boswell, the one area of his creative life not subject to negotiation; in his mind, it must be exempt or protected from the machinations of politicians. He expected others to understand, but others did not. Politicians were not happy to have themselves sacrificed on the altar of his private literary code, Dundas least of all. If Boswell wanted help, he would have to play by a few of the rules.

A good illustration of the difficulty was Boswell's *Letter to Robert Macqueen, Lord Braxfield,* published on 8 May 1780. His father's retirement in February as a Lord of the Justiciary left open a seat on the bench that Boswell and others thought Lord Alexander Lockhart Covington should fill. Henry Dundas thought Covington was too old and infirm and pushed Lord Robert Macqueen Braxfield instead, which upset both Boswell and his father who worried about Braxfield's reputation for uncouthness and brutality. With good reason, too, for by the 1790s he became known as the hanging judge. Boswell deeply admired Covington and even thought of writing his biography. He failed to persuade Dundas to change his mind in favour of Covington. So the next best thing was to write an anonymous pamphlet in the form of a 'Letter' giving Braxfield public advice on how to do his job and declaiming against current abuses of the dignity of a judgeship by present judges.[29]

The pamphlet was a touching tribute to his father's example and conduct on the bench, which Boswell held up as a model to Braxfield. Writing it provided him with an interlude of happiness and reminded him, as he said to William Nairne, 'if I had a pamphlet to write every day, I should be happy'. He sent Johnson a copy to show him 'my mind was not languid', and in the days following publication played a game of literary hide-and-seek with friends and foes alike. Forbes, who liked the pamphlet, asked him several times if he was the author. 'I denied it even to him, though I scrupled a little, considering my confidential regard for him.' William Robertson praised it highly. 'I had some scruple as to all this disguise. Yet I thought it allowable, and it was very entertaining.' Boswell gradually let it emerge that he was the author.[30]

It is unknown what the Dundases thought of the pamphlet, but it was not long before Boswell's fancied special relationship with them was put

to the test.[31] After Major Montgomerie's victory in the Ayrshire election
of 1780, Fergusson with the Lord Advocate's support immediately
appealed to the Court of Session for a review of the freeholders' votes. It
was decided that the appeal would also go before a Select Committee of
the House of Commons, the appeals to be tried in both places in March.
Much to his delight, Boswell was chosen as one of the three or more
counsel to represent Montgomerie. By the time the case was brought to
the Court of Session on 6 March, he was very keen and 'warm'.

He announced to the Lords, 'Major Montgomerie is my friend, my
social friend. I love him as a brother. I only wish your Lordships knew
him as well as I do.' This typically Boswellian pitch seemed to irritate
the Lord President, who mockingly replied that there was not a 'gentleman' left in Ayrshire independent of political leverage. Boswell, whose
natural political sympathies were most at home with the 'independent
country gentlemen', took this as an insult from the man he had once
called 'a hollow dog':

'No, my Lord?' 'No,' said he, 'nor yourself neither.' I replied warmly, 'I beg
your Lordship's pardon,' and I think I added, 'Not so!' – and then said, 'I
crave the protection of the Court.' Some of the Lords shook their heads to
make me quiet, and some about me also composed me.

Through the intervention of Lord Braxfield, Dundas apologized privately
three days later, but Boswell still smarted from the man's arrogance. On
the 10th he demanded and received a public apology, but Dundas
attached to it some private advice regarding his pleading in London in
the days ahead: 'Keep your temper before the Committee. You have done
very well in this business. Only you have now and then been heated.'
'My Lord,' Boswell replied, 'your Lordship certainly does not dislike a
man for having a little heat of temper. I am obliged to you for your
advice, and shall be upon my guard.'

This confrontation was another nail in the coffin of his political hopes.
As it happened, he did keep his temper in London and argued well,
though to little effect as the Select Committee ruled in favour of Fergusson, upholding the Court of Session's earlier ruling to let him keep the
seat. He even fooled himself into thinking that the personal truce in
Dundas's chambers had somehow won over Dundas. 'I was active and
animated and full of hope. How very different from the dreary metaphysical wretch that I had been!' He would have done better to reflect
on how often he could go on resenting slights, imagined or real, and

striking back, while still thinking of the Dundases as the fountain of favours. Several months later, again at Melville, the Lord Advocate said to him ominously, 'It never does to go against old connections. It never succeeds.' Boswell could not resist a return volley, 'Why, My Lord ... I will not say that. You have been very fortunate. But it never *should* succeed.' It was a nervous, edgy relationship at best; at worst, on Boswell's side, it was full of growing distrust and even hatred.[32]

7

In August of 1780 Johnson was hard at work finishing his *Lives*. He was feeling better than he had for some time and told Boswell they might yet show themselves together 'on some part of Europe, Asia, or Africa' – though not America which he detested. Boswell did not much care where they went; just the sooner the better. He implored Johnson meanwhile to meet him in late October either at York or Carlisle. Johnson, however, could not afford the time and, in any case, the Thrales had a stronger claim on him at the moment. During the summer their brewery had narrowly escaped damage in the anti-Catholic Gordon riots, the most savage uprising in the eighteenth century, in which Lord Mansfield's house was burned to the ground and all his papers destroyed. In September, when Parliament was dissolved, Henry Thrale's ill-health was significantly worsened by his insistence on standing again. The voters, who saw him as a dying man, avoided him. At the same time that Boswell was clamouring for Johnson to come north, Thrale was begging him to come to Brighton where he was licking his wounds. Johnson did not like Brighton, nor did he think he would be much welcomed by the rest of the family, but duty called. He told Boswell on 17 October that their love for each other would survive a year without meeting. 'Perhaps it may please GOD to give us some time together before we are parted.'[33]

It was a bad year to miss. Johnson's good health, his current work on the *Lives*, and his active social life would have been a mine of richly recorded conversation. Boswell pleaded with Langton to send him any anecdotes he could, which his friend faithfully did. Boswell likened his growing storehouse of Johnsonian anecdotes to a 'Herculaneum'.

Without the anticipated Johnsonian fillip, he sank into another period of hypochondria in November and December. Under its full weight, he strove to see the brightness behind the cloud:

How insignificant is my life at present! How little do I read! I am making no considerable figure in any way, and I am now forty years of age. But let me not despond. I am a man better known in the world than most of my countrymen. I am very well at the bar for my standing. I lead a regular, sober life. I have a variety of knowledge and excellent talents for conversation. I have a good wife and promising children.

He was right about his family, but it probably occurred to him even as he wrote these words that his 'considerable figure' was the result of achievements now more than a decade old – that he had done little since to enhance his reputation and quite a bit to diminish it. The hypochondria was compounded when he read Lord Monboddo's treatise, *Ancient Metaphysics*, at Bothwell Castle where he was the guest of a still grateful Archibald Douglas in what was becoming a standing invitation for January. Monboddo urged absolute 'Necessity', that nothing we can do makes any difference to our destiny after death in the eternity of God's universe: 'I was shocked by such a notion and sunk into dreadful melancholy, so that I went out to the wood and groaned.'[34]

TWENTY-FOUR

The Road to Ulubrae–Auchinleck

I

It would have taken spirits 'from the vasty deep' to keep him from London in the spring of 1781. 'Come to me, my dear Bozzy,' Johnson wrote on 14 March, 'and let us be as happy as we can. We will go again to the Mitre, and talk old times over.' He arrived in London on 19 March and ran into Johnson on the 20th in Fleet Street. 'I love you better than ever I did,' Johnson blurted out. He had just finished his final thirty *Lives*; within a couple of months they were published in six volumes, a triumph of biography that raised the art to a remarkable new level in English literature. He bowled Boswell over a few days later by giving him a large portion of the original manuscript; in August he sent even more manuscript. It was a supremely flattering gift, a prize for the Auchinleck archives. When Boswell got around to writing this part of the *Life*, he used these manuscripts to compose some thirty pages of 'observations'.[1]

In the next ten weeks they met some twenty times. It would have been more often if Boswell had not been drunk so much of the time. As he told Lord Bute on 13 May, since coming to London he had damaged his health, for he had been 'living two lives ... living with people who sat up late and people who rose early'. 'And drinking hard?' asked Bute. 'Yes, my Lord,' he confessed. His excessive drinking one night at Paoli's, of all places, alarmed even Johnson – 'I hope you don't intend to get drunk tomorrow as you did at Paoli's,' he barked at him on 7 May. After that display Paoli lectured him sternly on why he would never get ahead as long as he indiscriminately drank in all sorts of company. If the King were to ask him to take Boswell with him on a mission to Corsica, said Paoli, he would invite someone else instead. Boswell again promised Paoli that he would take himself in hand, though by this time none of his friends, least of all Paoli, put much stock in such promises.[2]

Two of his outings with Johnson were particularly memorable: their reunion with Wilkes at Dilly's and another with Mrs Garrick in the Adelphi, 'one of the happiest days that I remember to have enjoyed in the whole course of my life' because of the gallery of guests assembled. He and Johnson left together, pausing by the rails of the Adelphi, gazing out on the Thames and thinking tenderly of their loss of Garrick and Beauclerk. There was an air of nostalgia in the night, as if the best of times had passed. How long would Johnson himself last? He also attended several meetings of the Club and was introduced to Edmond Malone.

A different sort of welcome was waiting for him at Lord Bute's house.[3] He had come to London partly to hunt for signs of political favour that would help him get into Parliament and move to London. He did not have many prospects. Dundas was evasive, Mountstuart had been in Turin since 1779, and Burke was not well placed in opposition to the North ministry. The unpopular former Prime Minister, Lord Bute, was in London, however, and it occurred to Boswell that through the unvarnished force of his personality he might be able to forge a useful personal link with him, as he had with two of his sons and his daughter-in-law Margaret.

So, on 3 May, with characteristic audacity he wrote to the retired statesman asking for an interview, promising (surely ingenuously) not to talk of personal favours and preferment. There was more point to his letter than politics, though. Here was one of the great figures of the second half of the century, and a Scot at that; it would be a *coup* if Boswell could meet him. Bute replied the same day with an invitation and on 5 May Boswell called: ' "My Lord," said I, "I'm very obliged to you. This has been a siege of Troy: ten years to get into your Lordship's house." ' Bute welcomed him warmly and they spoke of past politics, Corsica, family, Boswell's law practice, and Dr Johnson's pension – Boswell praised him for granting it to his friend. On 13 May Boswell brazenly called on Lord Bute again, and again he was welcomed. They spoke privately in an inner room for half an hour. 'Are you an Ayrshire man?' Bute asked. 'Yes, my Lord. I have the honour to see the island of Bute every day from the windows of my father's library.' Boswell kept his word in not asking for patronage. Even if Bute had wanted to help him, however, it is uncertain that he could have done – without a good deal of money changing hands. They never met again.

His next objective was to be presented to the King, George III, perhaps by playing his Corsica card. The obliging Paoli put in a few good words for him, and on 16 May Boswell dressed up expensively 'in scarlet with rich buttons' and rode to St James's. After kissing the King's hand, he kept close to the door hoping to exchange a few words with him. As the King passed by, he turned to Boswell, having been briefed who he was and that they had met before in 1766, and said, 'You are come to make some stay?' That was about it. Riding home with Paoli in his coach, he hugged himself, enjoying 'what my own ardent curiosity in going to Corsica and assiduity in writing an account of it had procured me'.[4]

On 24 May he was presented at court, this time to both the King and Queen, and again on the 27th when he had a longer exchange with them about his family and reluctant professional life, hinting that he hoped his days in Edinburgh were numbered. On the 30th he attended at court a fourth time and was rewarded with a long dialogue with the King, mostly about Paoli and the Corsicans who had made Boswell's reputation. One observer remarked on his way out, 'You've had a long conversation with the King.' 'Yes,' he replied, 'he is a very sensible man. I wish to be acquainted with him.' He could aim no higher, but nothing came of all his efforts. 'How shall I contrive to get £600 from government?' he whined to Burke the following March.[5]

2

Boswell's charm was undiminished. He was a different creature in London, he told Reynolds, than in the 'dull northern town' he called home, where 'I have not that jocund complacency, that eager gayety which you have frequently cherished'. And in the company of a young, attractive, and intelligent female with a sense of fun equal to his own, he was at his best. Dr Burney's younger daughter, Charlotte Ann, who was prettier and five years younger than Fanny, experienced his charm at a dinner she attended on 7 April where she met both him and Johnson. She was twenty then, a vivacious, witty girl who was ripe for Boswell's brand of playful intelligence. Her description of him at the dinner provides a rare objective glimpse of him at the age of forty. For her, he was the 'flower of the [male] flock' in the company,

the famous Mr Boswell, who is a sweet creature. I admire and like him beyond measure. He is a fine, lively, sensible, unaffected, honest, manly, good-humoured character. I never saw him before. He idolizes Dr Johnson,

and struts about, and puts himself into such ridiculous postures that he is as
good as a comedy. He seems between forty and fifty, a good-looking man
enough. N.B. He has a wife in Scotland, so there is no *scandal* in being in
raptures about him . . .

Mr Boswell said he had an engagement at General Paoli's, and turned to
Miss Mudge and me and cried *he was sorry for it*, at which I shook my head
at Dr Johnson, as much as to say he must wish to stay to be in his company;
at which Mr Boswell put himself in one of his ridiculous postures and cried,
'Nay, shake not your gory looks *that* way!'

They say Mr Boswell has such a passion for seeing *executions* that he never
misses one if he can help it; and he *seemed* as if he had all their terms
[ceremonial executions] by heart, for just after he had been complaining of
being obliged to go, the maid came and told him the *coach was at the door*,
he turned to his friend and cried, 'Here, the sheriff's officers are at the door!'

He is a charming creature. He told me he would call here, but I'm afraid
he won't.[6]

He would have been less flattered by another sketch, apparently written
by Charlotte's elder sister Fanny after a morning visit to Streatham
back in the spring of 1779.[7] It is critical and somewhat cruel, without
Charlotte's sense of humour. According to Fanny, Boswell had an 'odd,
mock solemnity of tone and manner' that he had picked up from
constantly thinking about and imitating Johnson. There was also something 'slouching in the gait and dress of Mr Boswell that wore an air,
ridiculously enough, of purporting to personify the same model'. His
clothes were too large, his wig was neglected, and he never sat still in his
chair. On this particular morning, when Boswell was denied the seat
next to Johnson which he seemed to think was his by 'prescription', he
'stared, amazed'. After a couple of minutes of confusion, he resentfully
took another chair just behind Johnson's shoulder. Fanny, 'the unheard-
of rival', 'shrunk from the explanation that she feared might ensue, as
she saw a smile stealing over every countenance, that of Dr Johnson
himself not excepted, at the discomfiture and surprise of Mr Boswell'.
The rest of the sketch depicts Boswell as going from bad to worse, the
buffoon at whose expense the company, including Johnson, can scarcely
prevent breaking into laughter. Whenever Johnson spoke, 'the attention
which it excited in Mr Boswell amounted almost to pain. His eyes
goggled with eagerness; he leant his ear almost on the shoulder of the
Doctor; and his mouth dropped open to catch every syllable that might
be uttered.' When Johnson noticed him behind him, he demanded,

'What do you do there, Sir? Go to the table, Sir!' All obsequiousness, Boswell obeyed.

Horace Walpole, defiantly anti-Johnson, was another who found Boswell easy to ridicule and remained untouched by his genial exuberance. Thinking he might still be able to conquer Walpole, Boswell called on him. Walpole complained to William Mason of the unwanted visit from this 'quintessence of busybodies', a nuisance visit if there ever was one, which he would have ducked if his footman had told him who it was knocking. He remained unmoved in front of the assault: 'After tapping many topics to which I made as dry answers as an unbribed oracle he vented his errand – "had I seen Dr Johnson's *Lives of the Poets*?" I said slightly, no, not yet, and so overlaid his whole impertinence.' Other efforts at conversation failed equally. Boswell thought the call was such a fiasco that he did not even record it in his journal. He tried at least twice more to win over Walpole, again with little success. In the spring, 1788, possibly his last attempt, he found Walpole 'the same as ever: genteel, fastidious, priggish'.[8]

3

Suddenly, Henry Thrale died on 4 April, with Johnson at his bedside feeling frantically for his pulse. Mrs Thrale, vexed, grieved, and exhausted, immediately fled to Brighton with her daughter Queeney, leaving Johnson to his own grief. Their relationship would steadily deteriorate from this point as she sought comfort and solace elsewhere, chiefly from the Italian music master Gabriel Piozzi, and tried to distance herself from the encumbrances of her husband's friends and business. Johnson's dependency she felt especially burdensome. She wanted freedom from having to care for ailing men, freedom from her husband's business interests, freedom to enjoy the life of a lady of fashion, not a brewer's widow. By May 1782, she had sold the brewery, and later that summer financial constraints forced her not only to give up the house in Southwark but to let Streatham Park for three years. At a time when he was lonely and suffering from 'repelled gout', Johnson found himself deprived of his refuge away from home. The easy intimacy between them had disappeared.

The moment Thrale died, people began to gossip about whether his widow would marry again. Did Johnson himself love her and want to wed her? He would never have admitted it, but many thought it likely. The papers were full of it even as late as the autumn of 1782. Boswell

himself wrote in his journal for 15 April that Mrs Thrale might marry
Dr Johnson and that he wished it. It is extraordinary that he should have
entertained such an idea. But, as her biographer wrote, 'Mrs Thrale never
even remotely considered such a marriage . . . She reverenced Johnson as
a father and confidant, but as a lover – the idea was absurd!'⁹

In this climate of gossip, Boswell saw the opportunity to have some
fun. He wrote a ribald burlesque 'song', an imaginary 'Ode by Dr Samuel
Johnson to Mrs Thrale upon Their Supposed Approaching Nuptials'.
That he wrote it the day after Thrale's funeral struck many as an example
of consummate bad taste, grossly insensitive to Mrs Thrale's grief and
Johnson's feelings for her. But none of the friends to whom Boswell
passed it – and he even recited it at one of Reynolds's dinners in mixed
company – seems to have been offended. In the eighteenth-century spirit
of lampoons and burlesques, it is neither malicious nor prurient. It has
a kinship, in fact, with folk verse in the native Scottish tradition, which
frequently combined lyricism with bawdy ideas and language.

A few specimens drawn from the fourteen quatrains will serve to
convey the flavour of this *jeu d'esprit*:

> If e'er my fingers touch'd the lyre
>   In satire fierce, in pleasure gay,
> Shall not my THRALIA'S smiles inspire?
>   Shall SAM refuse the sportive lay?

> To rich felicity thus rais'd
> My bosom glows with amorous fire;
>   Porter [Johnson's deceased wife] no longer shall be prais'd;
> 'Tis I MYSELF am *Thrale's Entire*.

> Ascetick now thy lover lives,
> Nor dares to touch, nor dares to kiss;
> Yet prurient fancy sometimes gives
> A prelibation of our bliss.

> Convuls'd in love's tumultuous throws,
> We feel the aphrodisian spasm,
> Tir'd nature must, at last, repose,
>   Then Wit and Wisdom fill the chasm.

Greater than Atlas was of yore,
   A nobler charge to me is given;
The sphere he on his shoulders bore,
   I, with my arms, encircle Heaven!

Determined to preserve this piece of gaiety, he published it anonymously
in 1788 with a Horatian motto, 'To bear in copulation the weight of a
ramping bull'. Apparently the first Mrs Thrale knew of it was when she
read three stanzas that Boswell squeezed into a note in the second edition
of the *Life of Johnson*. The worsening relations between them as from
this point are the subject of a later chapter.[10]

4

Then it was back to Edinburgh via Dilly's home at Southill and the poet
Edward Young's house at Welwyn. Once Boswell reached St James's
Court, his spirits, true to form, sank almost overnight. He felt ill with a
severe case of influenza and he felt fatter than usual, which served him
as a metaphor for his obtuse and coarse inadequacies: 'My belly is more
swelled than I ever remember it; and perhaps my humours are gross. I
have a torpidity of mind that I have not often experienced . . . At present
it seems to me that I am not of celestial fire. I am quite sensual, and that,
too, not exquisitely but rather swinishly.'[11]

   He did not keep a very detailed journal on his return, but the entry
for 26 February 1782 leaves little doubt as to the new depths to which he
had sunk: 'I feel my dull insignificance in this provincial situation. I have
even little employment as a lawyer, and my mind is vacant and listless
till quickened by drinking.' He even horrified himself with the sudden
thought of suicide, but banished it quickly by reflecting on how much
comfort that would afford his enemies or 'enviers'. In the 'Hypochondriack' essay on suicide for December 1781 he had written, 'Every
melancholy man who has groaned under the temptation to destroy
himself, has afterwards had such enjoyments as to make him fully sensible
that he would have acted very absurdly.' It was never clearer that only a
move to London would bring him happiness. And if he was happy,
perhaps Margaret, too, would be happier. Pringle, whose death in January
1782 deprived him of one of his most trusted mentors, had told him, 'I
know not if you will be at rest in London. But you will never be at rest
out of it.' Reynolds, who did not like to write letters, made things even

harder in October with an evocative picture of all his Club friends clamouring to have Boswell among them:

> Mr Burke dined with me yesterday. He talked much of you and with great affection. He says you are the pleasantest man he ever saw and sincerely wishes you would come and live amongst us. All your friends here I believe will subscribe to that wish. Suppose we send you a round Robin ... to invite you, will that be an inducement[?][12]

The siren song of London was at its sweetest.

5

Life was made more bearable by his family and close friends, as he took refuge in their affections and homes. Auchinleck would have been a crucial help to him had it been available to his family, but it was not. Instead, Sir Alexander Dick and Lady Colville were old friends who were particularly comforting. In his absence, Lady Colville, the one member of the Erskine family whose friendship never wore thin, apparently arranged with Margaret to have his whole family move out to her home in the country, Drumsheugh House, northwest of the city, while she went elsewhere for the summer. This provision was a godsend. It gave them a rural escape for the warm months, a place with lovely gardens in which to frolic, ideal for the children. Boswell refers gratefully several times to escaping from his 'town-house' and grinding legal work, to his 'country-house' and walking from it with Margaret back and forth into town in the peaceful countrified environment. After a cold dinner with his father one Sunday in July, he could not wait 'to go home to my country-house and be calm with my children ... When I got home I found that she [Margaret] and Veronica and Phemie were gone to church in town. I had my two sons to walk with me and eat gooseberries in the garden ... I was in a quiet, placid frame. When all the family was assembled, we had tea most agreeably.' Also beckoning was Sir Alexander's Prestonfield, just out of town to the southeast, where the family was always welcome. Rural pursuits in the warm sunshine roused his spirits with 'ideas and feelings' that were 'as immediate as the tastes of different substances'. They put him in 'a comfortable Auchinleck frame' as he dreamed one day of freely embracing his own paternal acres in the company of his own family. Further out from town to the northwest there were also the Prestons at Valleyfield who, in the face of Lord Auchinleck's coldness, were always prepared to tend to Boswell's wounded feelings and nurture his family.[13]

Not for the first time, as a form of confession, when he arrived home in June he left his recent journal around for Margaret to read. One can imagine her irritation at reading his entry for 9 April when, in a lively mood in a coach, he kissed and was gay with a plump servant-maid and then a few hours later had done the same with a widow, the mother of three children, whom he fondled on his knee for part of the journey. More palpable, however, was the venereal infection he returned home with, which lasted about nine weeks. By mid-July Margaret had forgiven him.[14]

A few nights later he had a nightmare about her. He dreamed she was married to someone else, that 'she looked smart and engaging as Miss Peggie Montgomerie'. 'Vexed' at the thought of having lost her, he awoke determined to be more attentive and loving. But in early October, during her final pregnancy, she had a miscarriage. Now his womanizing increased, with the same attendant guilt which again impelled him to leave his journal lying around the dining room. When she read the entry for 18 February, one that has since been ripped out of the journal:

> She was shocked, and declared that all connection between her and me was now at an end, and that she would continue to live with me only for decency and the sake of her children. I was miserably vexed and in a sort of stupor. But could say nothing for myself. I indulged some glimmering of hope, and just acquiesced in my fate for the present.

It was not long before she relented, but at about that time he embarked on the affair with the landlady in Liberton's Wynd. He had another mild infection to show for it.[15]

That marriage, family, and morality had been on his mind for months is borne out by the subjects of his 'Hypochondriack' articles. Numbers 41–43 (February to April) explore the theme of connubiality, and the subject in May was 'prudence'. Full of thinly disguised autobiographical reflections, they hint strongly that Boswell's feelings about his marriage were changing. He loved Margaret not less but in a different way.

There is nothing wrong, he wrote in the March essay, when a husband and wife who have been married several years become 'habituated to each other' and instead of feeling the 'livelier sensations of pleasure' grow into comfortable friendship. There must be 'a certain easy management which adapts itself to the variations of life'. But some men cannot control their sexual appetite: 'men of good characters upon the whole, nay, men who esteem and even love their wives above all other women, are apt, from exuberance of appetite and capricious fondness of variety, to indulge themselves in it.'[16]

The essays are confessional, but they do not touch on three problems within Boswell's own marriage. The first was his old contention that Margaret lacked the imagination and vivacity to make his life interesting. He would have done well to ponder how much imagination and brightness of disposition a wife can maintain when she is almost constantly pregnant for a decade. Instead, his journal entry for 4 July 1782 declared:

> She has nothing of that English juiciness of mind of which I have a great deal, which makes me delight in humour. But what hurts me more, she has nothing of that warmth of imagination which produces the pleasures of vanity and many others, and which is even a considerable cause of religious fervour. *Family*, which is a high *principle* in my mind, and genealogy, which is to me an interesting amusement, have no effect upon her.

But of course that was not true. Margaret did cherish his 'genius', even if she thought his patriarchal fervour absurd. And that he recognized she was the more prudent and sensible of the two of them is indisputable from the tender and accurate description of her fitness to be his wife that followed the above passage:

> I consider her excellent sense, her penetration, her knowledge of real life, her activity, her genuine affection, her generous conduct to me during my distracted love for her and when she married me, and her total disinterestedness and freedom from every species of selfishness during all the time she has been my wife.[17]

Another strain on their marriage was Margaret's tuberculosis. Her condition deteriorated so rapidly between 22 June and 11 November 1782 that he kept a separate journal[18] of her illness. Oddly, he derived a sort of melancholic exhilaration from the crisis, and entertained 'flights of fancy' about life as a widower that shocked him afterwards. There were also moments when she sprang back to life with a flushed exuberance that made her look more beautiful than ever, as when they went riding together at Valleyfield and she was so 'enlivened' that he was 'as much in love with her as a man could be'.[19]

6

With Margaret in this condition and debts that had risen to between two and three thousand pounds – depending on what kind of bookkeeping he used[20] – it was clear to everyone except Boswell that he should abandon all ideas of a London visit in the spring of 1782. 'Shall we ever have another frolick like our journey to the Hebrides?' a very sick Johnson wrote wistfully in January, but Johnson also cautioned him, 'in losing her you would lose your anchor, and be tost, without stability, by the waves of life'. On 28 March Johnson wrote again, this time commanding him to stay at home, if not for the sake of his wife at least in the name of financial prudence. If he persisted in borrowing money, he would end up inheriting 'the empty name of a great estate': 'Live on what you have; live if you can on less; do not borrow either for vanity or pleasure; the vanity will end in shame, and the pleasure in regret: stay therefore at home, till you have saved money for your journey hither.' Boswell remained at home that spring.[21]

The months crept by. If Margaret still doubted Johnson's sincere regard for her, she was converted when she read these words in his letter to her husband in September: 'Let nothing be omitted that can preserve Mrs Boswell . . . She is the prop and stay of your life.' Her heart went out to him, and in her relief at being well again she wrote inviting him to Scotland. Johnson lost no time in replying: 'If my health were fully recovered, I would suffer no little heat and cold, nor a wet or a rough road to keep me from you. I am, indeed, not without hope of seeing Auchinleck again; but to make it a pleasant place I must see its lady well, and brisk, and airy.' At last, after nine years, their estrangement was healed.[22]

7

When the North ministry fell in March 1782, a casualty of the lost American war, Boswell stepped up his efforts to win some sort of political patronage. This time he targeted Burke, the darling of the Rockingham Whigs whose brand of Whiggism was a unique combination of liberal reform (especially of the Royal Household to stop it from corrupting politicians) and a deeply-rooted allegiance to the constitution. 'May I not now assure myself that you are near your Apotheosis,' Boswell asked him in March 1782, expecting Burke to be promoted in some way in the new government.[23] He pined for a position of more consequence 'than drudging at the bar in Scotland; and I think I should be very happy in exerting what talents I have, under your auspices'.

One month passed and Burke failed to reply. 'Saw all my ambitious views in London all madness. Vexed at being neglected by Burke,' Boswell scribbled in his journal on 14 April. Why not forget the whole business and just keep his 'proud distance' as an 'old Scottish baron and Tory'? But on 18 April, after Burke had become Paymaster-General of the Forces under the new Rockingham–Shelburne ministry, he wrote again to ask for his help in obtaining the vacant post of Judge-Advocate in the Scottish military which was worth about £180 a year. It was essentially a sinecure with minimal attendance required at court martials. Boswell thought he deserved it because, as he said, he was the only member of the Faculty of Advocates who had consistently spoken out against the American war. He also wrote to Dempster, Lord Pembroke, and Charles James Fox about it. Dempster remained non-committal, Pembroke helped a little, and Fox never answered his letter. Burke replied that Boswell vastly overrated his capacity to serve his friends. The idea of having him in London, though, was enough of a 'bribe' to induce him to mention the matter to Fox and General Conway, the Commander-in-Chief. He sent Boswell a copy of his letter to Conway and one passage in particular thrilled him: 'Mr Boswell ... is a lawyer of ability and general erudition, and the pleasantest and best tempered man in the world.' It was all he would glean from this effort, for a week later he was disappointed, though not crushed, to hear that the prize had gone to Pringle's grand-nephew through the influence of Henry Dundas.[24]

Burke resigned as Paymaster-General, some thought too precipitously, in July when Rockingham died and Shelburne, whom he despised, succeeded as Prime Minister. He advised Boswell to cultivate Dundas instead, whom Boswell described as having 'Fortunatus's cap' because with the agility of a Swiftian Flimnap he walked a tightrope amid the chaos of these successive ministries and was always able to land on his feet. Shelburne, in fact, had just set Dundas on the threshold of becoming one of the great politicians of the day by offering to make him Treasurer of the Navy and Keeper of the Scottish Signet for life. 'It will answer I tell you,' Burke urged Boswell; he must try to drink at that trough.[25]

Boswell still felt he could lecture Dundas at the same time as he asked for favours. Dundas was patient, said he 'never felt a moment's resentment from the estrangement of your friendship from me', and that ever since Boswell's fresh overtures of friendship he had been more than ready to return to their old rapport; but he conspicuously, ominously, neglected to offer any help. Unsatisfied, a couple of days after the offer from Shelburne reached Dundas in Edinburgh Boswell cornered him in the Court of Session. They sat down together for ten minutes on a bench in the outer House, in full sight of the crowd which, Boswell wrote, 'wondered and conjectured while we talked seriously and confidentially'. He longed for something better than an Edinburgh law practice, he declared. 'Something in the other end of the island?' Dundas asked. 'Yes.' Perfectly reasonable, Dundas volunteered. He would see if he could help when he was next in London in September. Dundas added that he knew Burke wanted to help him. All in all, this was an encouraging exchange: 'I was pleased in thinking I had now another string, and that a strong string, to my bow.'[26]

8

It occurred to Boswell that publication could endow him with further independence from his father and the small world of justices, advocates, and 'writers' that he inhabited, so he began to copy out his Hebridean journal with a vague idea of turning it into a book; he also consulted with Forbes and Lord Kames about editing his 'Hypochondriack' essays as a volume. A couple of years later Johnson read over the essays and gave him the supreme accolade: 'Sir, these are very fine things; the language is excellent, the reasoning good, and there is great application of learning ... I would have you publish them in a volume and put your name to them.' Excessive praise, no doubt, though Boswell himself thought some of the sentences were as good as those of the *Rambler*. Johnson was to have revised them but he died before he could begin and nothing ever came of the project.

In any case, literary labours would not make Boswell rich, and wealth was what his family and descendants needed. Wealth could command great pleasures, he wrote in the 'Hypochondriack' for May 1782: 'the patronage of arts and sciences and learning; the relief of the indigent and being blest by every eye, like Job in his prosperity; the immediate distinction of one's own children, and the grandeur of posterity.' Wealth was power and power filled the imagination. That was the sort of Laird of Auchinleck *he* wanted to be. Both his ego and his income, however, were cramped as long as his father lived, yet he dreaded his death and was moved with compassion for him in his illness even as he flinched from his coldness.[27]

For the 'devilishness' of the '*novercá*', he felt only hatred. They became locked in combat, silent or vocal, virtually every time he called on his father. It had become a scandal among their friends that his family was never invited to Auchinleck, and that when he went there, as he was careful to do regularly, he was not made welcome. All he could do was dream 'of being *laird* myself, and ruling over such a fine Place and such an extent of country'.[28]

Finally, on the road to Dunfermline early on the morning of 29 August, he was overtaken by a caddie on horseback carrying an express letter with the news that his father was at death's door. He galloped back to his bedside in Edinburgh to be greeted by Lady Auchinleck's chilling words: ' "Don't torture him in his last moments." I was benumbed and stood off. Wept; for, alas! there was not affection between us.' In the early hours of the next morning he was amazed that his father still breathed: 'Still alive, still here! Cannot he be stopped? Breathing [grew] high, gradually ceased. Doctor closed eyes.' Suddenly, he was Laird of Auchinleck. Up all that night writing letters 'in a giddy state' – one of the first was to Johnson – he took one of his father's favourite books off the shelf and 'from affection and nervousness cried and sobbed'.[29]

In a highly emotional state, during the next two days he talked over affairs with his stepmother, Stobie, Commissioner Cochrane, and a number of others. He put himself in complete charge of the funeral arrangements, on which he did not skimp, spending about three hundred pounds, one-fifth of the annual rental of the entire estate. On 2 September the funeral cortège with Boswell and his brother John (who behaved well) but without David who was in London, left Edinburgh, spent the night at an inn, and arrived at Auchinleck House by noon the next day. The '*novercá*' remained in Edinburgh, not wanting any part in the family proceedings. That day and the following morning Boswell received visits from the Ayrshire gentry – Margaret was there but too ill to act the part of the hostess. He also went to the barn and drank the health of the tenants as the new Laird. During the funeral service at the Boswell Mausoleum in the Auchinleck village churchyard, with the rooks screeching overhead, he was in a daze in which past and future seemed to merge in the nightmarish present:

[When I was] carrying [father] to vault, was *carried* myself. Wandered; was in the state which I suppose a man going to execution is. Hardly was sensible of what was around me. Saw mother's coffin. Helped to deposit father. Then into our loft. Was affected much . . .'[30]

Writing to him the moment he heard the news, Johnson tried both to lay to rest the phantom of the father and sound the keynote of rural prudence that had to prevail in the future. Never mind now about his father's lack of love, for 'kindness, at least actual, is in our power, but fondness is not'. The important thing was to begin his lairdship with 'timorous parsimony', to get out of debt and stay out of debt. He must also cultivate the role of the classical *beatus vir*. 'Be kind to the old servants, and secure the kindness of the agents and factors; do not disgust them by asperity, or unwelcome gaiety, or apparent suspicion. From them you must learn the real state of your affairs, the characters of your tenants, and the value of your lands.'[31]

Boswell's father had denigrated and humiliated him, stunted his growth and damaged his confidence, in the process stirring a rebellious and often unruly passion for independence. But this treatment had paradoxically also made him incurably dependent on his father. Could he find the poise and contentment to which the inscription over the front door of the new mansion alluded? – 'What thou seekest is here, it is in Ulubrae, unless equanimity is lacking'. Would he be happy and successful as the new 'Master of Ulubrae'? Would that inscription be a constant rebuke to him, his father's ghost mocking him every time he passed through the door?

PART IV

Biographer and Laird of Auchinleck:
Triumph and Despair
1782–95

TWENTY-FIVE

The Cracked Enamel

I

Boswell took possession of the seat of his ancestors with Margaret and the children on 18 September 1782, coincidentally Johnson's birthday. The family had never before spent any time there all together. There was much to be done. 'I find that my presence here is essentially necessary,' Boswell wrote to Johnson on 1 October, 'there being several farms to let. But as I am very ignorant myself of country concerns and have very different opinions given me, I am perplexed how to act. I must do as well as I can at first and get more knowledge gradually.'[1]

He was not as badly off as he made out. He had James Bruce to help him, with whom he had developed his own affectionate intimacy and who now with his father gone became another (rural) mentor. In recent years he had walked and galloped with Bruce over the 27,000 acres of rolling, fertile Ayrshire countryside, planting, surveying walls, tending to fences and hedges, visiting tenants, and taking agricultural instruction. He often complained of the isolation of Auchinleck, but he was also immensely proud of the place and once he became its laird was eager to have his friends visit him there. With an increased income, he intended to be the welcoming host, a generous landlord, and an enlightened improver of his acres.

From the start he was thwarted financially by the '*novercā*'. His fears regarding the settlement his father might make on her behalf proved to be well founded. In 1776 his father had signed over to her the life-rent of twenty-four of the best farms on the estate which Boswell had regarded as a rightful part of his patrimony, adding up to £500 per annum in 1795. Boswell's own income from the estate, after running expenses and the cost of improvements, amounted to not much more than that. In addition to these life-rents, she inherited the past rents on the farms (about £500), the life-rent of his father's new house in St Andrew's Square (nearly £100 per year) and all its furnishings (worth £1,000), and even the coach and carriage horses. For an heir who at the time had a bank overdraft of over £1,300 this was an outrageous diminution of his inheritance.[2]

'Is not this an exorbitant plunder?' Boswell moaned to Johnson. He considered contesting the settlement on the grounds that his stepmother had prevailed on his father while his mind was impaired, but soon resigned himself to it. What disturbed him more was the way she had estranged himself, Margaret, and the children from his father. Unlike land, that was now irredeemable. She had gone even further:

> I find a large collection of family letters, particularly a most affectionate and pious correspondence between my grandfather and grandmother for many years, has been destroyed, though carefully bound up by my father for preservation. I suppose she has either destroyed it herself or persuaded my father that his son was unworthy to have it. She was cutting a valuable wood before it was ripe. She was letting leases at low rents, for what we call *grassums* or entry-money. In short, she was doing all she possibly could to hurt my interest so that if my father had lived a few years longer, I should have had but the skeleton of an estate.[3]

Henry Dundas told him he thought she might have got away with even more, so completely under her influence was his father. It was as if Auchinleck came to him violated.

2

None the less, his family were finally 'at home' in the demesne from which they had been exiled for so many years. Margaret coughed and spat blood, and her alarming condition made him withdraw from an impulsive autumn jaunt to London in his new status as Laird, but she recovered in October. 'I was quite happy to find my dear wife now so well and in so respectable a situation,' he wrote. 'It was as much as I suppose humanity has ever enjoyed.'[4] As for the children, they were convinced they had entered paradise, where they could clamber over the ruins of the Old Castle, explore down by the river, and ride horses to their hearts' content.

Auchinleck was an estate of which to be proud, in a county where Boswell rubbed elbows with wealth and power. Six earls had country seats there with incomes in the region of £10,000 per year. There were also the estates of thirty commoners earning annual incomes of between £1,000 and £2,000. He boasted he 'could ride ten miles forward upon his own territories', which was probably a modest estimate.[5]

Nobody was more surprised than he by his appetite for agriculture and estate management in those early months. He delighted in his control of an estate spreading into four parishes and affecting almost one thousand people. He persuaded himself that he had discovered a strong taste for agrarianism, now untrammelled by a jeering father. He told Lord Kames that he now 'looked upon a dunghill with as much pleasure as upon Lady Wallace'. Beware, replied Kames, 'lest, like a fit of enthusiasm in religion, it go off and leave you as you were'. But Boswell was convinced he had 'acquired a new sense' that was bound to last.[6]

Bruce could not have been more delighted to have the new Laird taking an interest in the estate. Boswell insisted on being consulted over all major and much minor work, and for years they worked closely together. When Bruce died in 1790, Boswell felt as if he had lost not only a member of his family but also a remnant of his youth, 'an old servant to whom I had been habituated from my infancy, or rather indeed a kind of friend and tutor with whom I had in my early years confidentially associated, who was born at Auchinleck, a most knowing and ingenious man [who] seemed in imagination to be an inseparable circumstance about the Place'.[7]

After Bruce, he took on the young Andrew Gibb as overseer, insisting still that everything at Auchinleck be kept in good repair 'and not suffer by my absence', and sending him full instructions on livestock, tenancies, bills, collection of rent, tree-cutting, planting, ploughing, and endless minutiae that not even intense work on his *Life of Johnson* could make him neglect. His attention to detail, even from London, comes across in this instruction to Gibb in 1790:

> You must therefore be particularly careful to stop all persons who attempt to pass through my parks or plantations, especially near to the old house, or the new house, or from the Whirr towards Mauchline, but see that they keep to the patent publick roads. If any persons insist to pass and accordingly do so, let me have a list of their names and I will order them to be prosecuted.[8]

Boswell's lairdship gave expression to his feudal paternalism. Half of his eighty tenancies were large enough farms to earn comfortable incomes, but the rest had fewer than two hundred acres – half a dozen were less than ten – and at times, the tenants were hard pressed to pay their rents and feed their families. Then his well-established instincts on behalf of the oppressed and the needy manifested themselves. Of one tenant who could not make ends meet, he wrote to Gibb, 'Neither he nor any one else upon my estate has reason to fear that I will be a hard master.' He also won the acquittal of four Stewarton rioters in the wake of the disastrous harvest of 1782 and made a point of storing up enough meal for his parishioners in 1783 when it was in very short supply.[9]

However, he also needed to be firm. He would not allow his tenants, for example, in their desperate need for more food to plough up more of their holdings than Bruce had told him was good for the land. 'I wish not to be a hard landlord,' he explained to Gibb, but 'I am clear that allowing them to run in arrear is ruinous to them'. The unhappy economic fact was that he had no choice but to remove many of his tenants, often taking away their possessions in the process. More than half of the farms on the estate changed hands during the years of his lairdship. On occasion, he even had to discipline Gibb himself. 'I desire to have from you', he told his overseer angrily in March 1795, 'once a fortnight a daily short note how you have been employed, such as James Bruce kept. Any reasonable jaunt shall be allowed you when you ask it.'[10]

In other ways, he was a typical late-eighteenth-century laird, maintaining and insisting on the prerogatives of privilege and place, not especially committed to the social and cultural betterment of his tenants. He failed to encourage the parish school and took no interest in the literary and academic ambitions of his tenants. Himself enthusiastic about the English and Scottish folksong tradition, he was curiously indifferent to local versifiers who showed promise. One such was the young Robert Burns who was eking out an existence farming in the neighbouring village of Mauchline. Burns was by then no obscure poet, the Kilmarnock edition of his poems in 1786 having made him famous overnight. He understandably wished to meet Ayrshire's other famous author and, to this end, wrote to Boswell's second cousin, Bruce Campbell, asking him to forward a selection of his poems to the Laird of Auchinleck:

I enclose you, for Mr Boswell, the ballad you mentioned, and as I hate sending wastepaper or mutilating a sheet, I have filled it up with one or two of my fugitive pieces that occurred. Should they procure me the honour of being introduced to Mr Boswell, I shall think they have great merit. There are few pleasures my late will-o'-wisp character has given me equal to that of having seen many of the extraordinary men, the heroes of wit and literature, in my country; and as I had the honour of drawing my first breath almost in the same parish with Mr Boswell, my pride plumes itself on the connection. To crouch in the train of mere stupid wealth and greatness, except where the commercial interests of worldly prudence find their accounts in it, I hold to be prostitution in anyone that is not born a slave; but to have been acquainted with such a man as Mr Boswell I would hand down to my posterity as one of the honours of their ancestor.[11]

His deep love for popular folksong apart, Boswell felt that literary distinction was the privilege of the educated and aristocratic. Burns did not qualify; nor did he appeal to Boswell's ambitions to cultivate the great. On the ploughman-poet's letter he simply wrote, 'Mr Robert Burns the Poet expressing very high sentiments of me.' Other lairds did encourage Burns, however, including Boswell's good friend John McAdam, Laird of Craigengillan, who was rewarded when Burns immortalized him and his three children in a verse epistle.

3

For several months after becoming Laird – until he escaped to London in the spring, in fact – Boswell 'experienced constitutional sobriety. What a happy change to be free of the rage of drinking!' He was less successful at keeping up his spirits once he returned to Edinburgh in November following his father's death. The drudgery of his work depressed him, especially now that he was a landowner and felt more than ever the slavery of a profession he had to maintain if he was to meet his expenses. Thomas Barnard (Bishop of Killaloe), fellow member of the Club with whom he had struck up a close friendship by 1781, wrote to 'offer you my congratulations on your accession to the Throne of your ancestors, no longer to be stiled Esqr. but a Baron; no longer James Boswell; but Aughinleck [sic] Himself'. In his reply Boswell revealed that his longing to live in London was as strong as ever: 'I am an ancient baron, and I would by no means estrange myself from Auchinleck the romantic seat of my ancestors, but I am very desirous that when I am absent from it I should be in London rather than in Edinburgh.' By the end of February 1783, his mind was 'miserable', 'insipid and uneasy'; he yearned for 'London, Parliament, or any state of animated exertion'.[12]

A series of remarkable interviews with Lord and Lady Kames in

Edinburgh during the closing weeks of 1782 succeeded in raising his spirits for a while.[13] Now eighty-six, Kames was one of his potential subjects for biography but, more to the point, he was dying. Still fascinated by death and how people prepare themselves for it, Boswell wanted to spend as much time with him as he could. In their sessions he tried different tactics, shifting deftly in and out of the subject of death and the afterlife, teasing, joking, testing, and flattering – and later recording it all. The trio supped, drank tea, read, laughed, argued, and reminisced whenever Boswell could find the time to drop in and when Kames had the strength to receive him. The old couple were touched that he chose to spend so much time with them. 'She said of me tonight at supper, "This is a good man. He's very good to us."'

Boswell found Kames undisturbed by the prospect of death. When he mentioned his father's 'easy death', Kames agreed that 'some men die very easily'. With an eye turned on himself Boswell noted, 'It was agreeable to see a man who had been tortured by Liberty and Necessity and other metaphysical difficulties sitting at his ease by the fireside.' Other subjects were more productive, such as the adultery of Kames's daughter, Jean. Since Boswell had committed adultery with her himself, when he was twenty-one, 'This was a strange subject. I kept myself steady, and expatiated on that unfortunate lady's many engaging qualities.'

Another time, Kames looked so 'low' that Boswell decided he would stay only six minutes. 'If you'll let me draw my breath sometimes,' Kames remarked, 'you may stay the evening.' They discussed sex in the afterlife. Kames leaned over to him and whispered, 'Why not have the pleasure of women' there? Boswell, who was terrified by the idea of predestination, jumped at the idea: '"Why not," cried I, with animation. "There is nothing in reason or revelation against our having all enjoyments sensual and intellectual."' They talked late into the night. Boswell's description of the scene is like a Rembrandt painting, shadowed and glowing as the two men huddled together in the flickering candlelight:

> I was so intent on his conversation tonight I left the candles be long without snuffing. So there was a dim, solemn light, which increased my feelings as sitting with a dying man. Yet he was as much Mr Henry Home, as much Lord Kames as ever. Sometimes death is like a fire going out gradually. Sometimes like a gun going off, when the moment before the explosion all is as entire as ever.

On the last occasion Boswell saw him, 'He put out his cold right hand

and chucked me under the chin, as if he had said, "You're a wag." ' But then he fell silent. 'He twice put out his hand and took mine cordially. I regretted that he did not say one word as a dying man.' Boswell came away with a quantity of biographical gems but, as in the Hume interview, with nothing to bring him any closer to a reconciliation with death and a firmer idea of the afterlife. Kames died five days later. Lady Kames came to him in January anxious that he should write her husband's life as soon as possible, but he never did.

4

It is surprising that so soon after his splendid entries on Kames, Boswell could write in his journal for 18 January: 'To what purpose waste time in writing a journal of so insipid a life?'[4] Fresh and alarming correlations occurred to him between the uselessness of his life, the idleness of his journal, and a consciousness of his identity. Who *was* James Boswell if he had no appointment or position of responsibility that brought prestige and money, if Auchinleck could not satisfy him fully or deeply enough, if he had to live four hundred miles north of the only world that meant anything to him, and if what he wrote or thought was consequently of little value to himself or others? He feared that the 'enamel of my sound mind' was cracking.

In a 'Hypochondriack' essay, 'On Change', that he published in January he wrote:

> Nothing is more disagreeable than for a man to find himself unstable and changeful. An Hypochondriack is very liable to this uneasy imperfection, in so much that sometimes there remains only a mere consciousness of identity. His inclinations, his tastes, his friendships, even his principles, he with regret feels, or imagines he feels, are all shifted, he knows not how.

He had no 'firmness of mind'. His 'intellectual abilities' were not developed enough to 'fix' him. In another essay, 'On Diaries', he confronted the dilemma of whether his journal was doing more harm than good. The value of diaries was that they helped focus on 'a *fair* and distinct view of our character'. But there was the lurking snare of too much introspection, for journalizing 'might weaken and relax his powers, as taking it often to pieces will hurt the machinery of a watch'. Another problem was that the watch may not be worth taking apart. It may be too simple. Even that had to be weighed against the knowledge that when he failed to keep the journal, 'the day seems to be lost'. The journal epitomized a constant struggle both to recover and be free from his self.[15]

5

Boswell arrived in London on 20 March brandishing a new 'steadiness as laird of Auchinleck' and with a firm resolve to set up a residence there as soon as possible. He cut quite an imposing figure in a new suit of mourning clothes: 'a dark raven-grey frock, black cassimere vest and breeches for common wear, and silk for genteeler occasions.' After two years, his reception was as warm as he could wish from his old 'regulars', Paoli with whom he stayed as usual, Langton, Burney, Reynolds, Wilkes, and Dempster, and also from a new player on his London stage, the agreeable Mary Palmer, 'the fair Palmeria', Sir Joshua's niece. She was happy to take tea with him and talk as much as he wished. The Club also offered him the sensation of coming home. There were five new members, notably Thomas Warton the historian of English poetry who would become Poet Laureate in 1785, Burke's son Richard, and Edmond Malone.[16]

He called on Johnson at Mrs Thrale's winter quarters in Argyll Street, where for the sake of economy she had moved after her husband's death. He did this with some trepidation since his friends had written to him about Johnson's worsening health – but not Mrs Thrale who seemed reluctant to provide him with any sort of information about Johnson except what could be conveyed in a cursory line or two. 'Anecdotes of our literary or gay friends, but particularly of our illustrious Imlac,' he had written from Edinburgh the previous July, 'would delight me'. But nothing had come. He found Johnson pale, breathing with difficulty, and querulous. 'I am glad you are come. I am very ill,' he grumbled. After some conversation, he brightened up: 'You must be as much with me as you can. You have done me good. You cannot think how much better I am since you came in.' Life had not been kind to Johnson in other ways than ill-health. 'His old attendant' Dr Levett had recently died and Mrs Thrale had been a source of unhappiness. By this time she had fallen deeply in love with Piozzi and had been forced by family and friends to give him up. In the process she had provided London with all manner of gossip and been attacked maliciously in the newspapers. Her reckless retaliations in the press were becoming notorious. Boswell had sense enough not to mention the subject to Johnson, but Johnson alluded to it:

> He sent to Mrs Thrale that I was there. She came, and I saluted her with gladness. I had not seen her since Mr Thrale's death till now ... She asked me to stay to dinner ... She said she was very glad I was come, for she was going to Bath and should have been uneasy to leave Dr Johnson till I came. He had told me of her going to Bath, and said they had driven her out of London by attacks upon her which she had provoked by attacking everybody.

In a memorandum, Boswell scribbled, 'Dr Johnson said of Mrs Thrale, "I am glad she is gone [i.e., going] to Bath, to some place where her head may cool."' He did not gloat but her extremity was certainly his opportunity. For her part, Mrs Thrale was so glad he had come to take Johnson off her hands that she even mustered a compliment when he sighed for shorthand skills to take down all Johnson was saying: 'You'll carry it all in your head. A long head is as good as shorthand.'

That Boswell was a breath of fresh air for Johnson did not stop the latter from flying into a passion at him the following day when provoked by Boswell and Mrs Desmoulins with talk of how little financial reward he had had for his literary labours. When Boswell spoke of building a house on the site of the old castle at Auchinleck, Johnson 'raged' against it: 'Talk no more in this way. People will only laugh at you, or be vexed, as I am.' In more measured tones a few days later, Johnson tried to put him off the idea of dragging his family to London to live:

> I am unwilling to repress your ambition. But it appears to me that as you would be obliged to maintain your family in some dignity here, you would find yourself embarrassed. When you come to London now and leave it because you cannot afford the expense of living in it constantly, people applaud your wisdom. Were you to settle here, they'd despise you as a man ruining himself.

If he wished to live according to his rank and maintain his family in dignity, he could not live there for under £1,000 per year, Johnson told Boswell bluntly.[17]

One of the most curious conversations that Boswell ever recorded about Johnson occurred at Bolt Court one night in April.[18] Johnson and Mrs Williams had retired early, leaving Boswell with Mrs Desmoulins and the painter Mauritius Lowe. They promptly fell to talking about

Johnson's sex life, which Boswell encouraged and recorded in detail though not even he could justify including it in the *Life*. The pages remained secret until Irma Lustig published them in 1981 in her edition of the journal.

To provoke Mrs Desmoulins to reveal what she knew on the subject, Lowe stated that he did not think that Johnson had ever had sex with any woman, not even his wife. On the contrary, there was never a man who had 'stronger amorous inclinations', Mrs Desmoulins answered forcefully; he may even have had a relationship with Mrs Williams. Boswell commented, 'I have heard people joke about it, and talk of Dr Johnson's seraglio, which included you as well as her, Madam. But nobody had a serious belief of anything for a moment.' He wanted to know if Johnson had ever consummated his marriage. She replied in the affirmative; in fact, Garrick knew as much since he once peeped through the keyhole: 'he made the Doctor ridiculous all over the country by describing him running round the bed after [his wife] had lain down, and crying, "I'm coming, my Tetsie, I'm coming, my Tetsie! ph! ph! (blowing in his manner."' Nobody had a stronger passion, Mrs Desmoulins added. Though he knew he could never publish such material, Boswell pressed her for something more personal: 'You'll forgive me, Madam. But from what you have said, I beg leave to ask you if the Doctor ever made any attempt upon you?' He had reason to since his wife most often kept him from her bed, Mrs Desmoulins replied, but he always controlled his passion with her; she used to sit up with him 'many an hour in the night and had my head upon his pillow'.

BOSWELL: 'And he showed strong signs of that passion?' MRS DESMOULINS: 'Yes, Sir. But I always respected him as a father.' BOSWELL: 'What would he do? Come now' (Lowe like to jump out of his skin), 'would he fondle you? Would he kiss you?' MRS DESMOULINS: 'Yes, Sir.' BOSWELL: 'And it was something different from a father's kiss?' MRS DESMOULINS: 'Yes, indeed.' LOWE: (approaching his hand to her bosom). 'But would he? eh?' MRS DESMOULINS: 'Sir, he never did anything that was beyond the limits of decency.' LOWE: 'And could you say, Madam, upon your oath, that you were certain he was capable?' MRS DESMOULINS: 'Y-yes, Sir.' BOSWELL: 'But he conquered his violent inclination?' MRS DESMOULINS: 'Yes, Sir. He'd push me from him and cry, "Get you gone." Oh, one can see.' BOSWELL: 'So you saw the struggle and the conquest.' MRS DESMOULINS: 'I did.'

She added that if he had ever attempted to seduce her, she could not have resisted him – such was his mind and her awe of him.

As for his own sex life, Boswell did stray on this visit, generally when he became drunk or was 'hyped'. There were 'Little Polly Bond', 'Mrs C', Mrs Love again although he found her 'disgusting' at her age, and various strumpets in St James's Park. These encounters were mixed with fruitless vows to abstain, either after he received a letter from Margaret or had attended church. On Sunday, 18 May, for example, at the Portuguese Chapel, he 'vowed before the altar no more *filles* while in London. A memorable moment.' Not so memorable, really, since five days later he was having his gold watch pinched by a whore with whom he was dallying.[19]

His social life was rounded out by as intense a schedule of visits with fashionable men and women as he had ever put himself through – old friends and new acquaintances, people from many walks of life. What with the courting of men for political favour, like Lord Mountstuart who was about as affable and warm as a slippery fish, there was very little time for edifying recreation. He did manage a couple of walks to and from Richmond Park to see the Stuarts, a few visits to the theatre, and an evening at Ranelagh Gardens as well as some executions. Burke made a joke of these extremes: 'You have seen more life and more death than any man.' 'Well,' Boswell replied, 'and I hope I shall see immortality.'[20]

6

Lord Shelburne had finally been forced to resign as head of the government on 24 February due, among other reasons, to withering opposition to his terms of peace with the United States. From then until 2 April there was in effect no government because while the King wanted the Tory Lord North to form a ministry again, he was less enthusiastic about North's coalition partner, the liberal Whig Charles James Fox, the so-called 'Man of the People'. On 2 April the King was forced to accept the Fox–North coalition. Burke accepted the office of Paymaster-General.

Dundas lost political ground during the nine months in which the coalition held power. He remained Lord Advocate but was removed as Treasurer of the Navy; he then threw his support behind Pitt in opposition and waited. Boswell lost no time looking him up in London after the new ministry was formed. Calling on 3 April, he was treated to a display of 'lofty vanity' as Dundas, 'open, frank, and hearty', read to him his correspondence with Shelburne and Pitt about whether he and Pitt would join Shelburne in power. It was flattering to have Dundas share these 'animated State papers' with him, but Boswell's obvious reason for coming was to discuss his own future. More than ever, he was a political irrelevance and nuisance to Dundas, who brushed him off with vague and tantalizing possibilities that he knew perfectly well would never come to pass. Certainly do not spend £3,000 in buying a seat in the Commons, Dundas told him. In Boswell's sanguine words:

> He was for my continuing assiduously at my profession, and said that this, and being a man of family, would give me a claim to a judge's place. That this was a time quite improper for coming into Parliament upon purchase, everything being in uncertainty. But that I might dash into Parliament afterwards if a good opportunity should offer. He engaged to be friendly to me, should I apply some time hence for a judge's place in Scotland.

Boswell still failed to realize that as long as Dundas had anything to do with it, he would not be 'dashing' into either Parliament or a judgeship.[21]

With his friendship with Burke as close as it ever would be, Boswell was invited to Burke's country house, Gregories, at Beaconsfield, on Easter Monday, 21 April. 'You're going to enjoy as much as can be had on earth perhaps,' he jotted down in an anticipatory memorandum. He was as impressed as he expected. The hall was full of classical busts and paintings, several Poussin landscapes and a Titian among them. The day's climax was a walk around almost the entire park alone with Burke, who offered him farming advice in the fashion of a latter-day Cincinnatus. 'He said I would find the occupations of a country-place very comfortable in old age.'

Then, a month later, Burke invited him to the annual dinner of Chelsea Hospital for army pensioners, of which he was Treasurer by virtue of his office as Paymaster-General. After a haircut and shave, Boswell joined him at his official residence in Whitehall, next to the Horse Guards. From there they took a hackney-coach to the Hospital where in his element at dinner, seated next to Burke, he 'drank liberally and was in high spirits'. Delighted with him, the Governor of the Hospital offered him a standing invitation to the annual dinner. Another conquest. On the way home Boswell finally brought the conversation around to his own political prospects, hoping his great friend would encourage him. After all, just a few months earlier Reynolds had written to him that Burke wanted him living 'amongst us'. Burke's reply jolted him much more than the rough road on which they were travelling. 'He counselled me to fix my mind on an employment in Scotland, and to come only for a visit to London.'[22]

Both Johnson and Burke had spoken: Boswell had a patriarchal duty to stay at Auchinleck where he could enjoy country pleasures and his family afford to live with elegance and ease. Two hundred pounds in Scotland would bring a better life than five times as much in London. There he would be a man of consequence, whereas in London all he could hope for was to eke out an existence with a great deal of labour. He could still visit London, Paris, The Hague, or wherever else, 'to enlarge and enliven'. On the evening of 30 May, the day Boswell left London, he felt he had no choice but to accept his destiny in Scotland.

7

Temple thought his friend was mad to want to live in London. It was an awful place to try to bring up a family – 'the constant noise, bustle and dissipation of it would be worse than the deadness and uniformity of the country'. Temple did not even like coming to London to see Boswell, but he did so at the beginning of May when Boswell refused to travel to Cornwall, the idea being that they would journey north together towards the end of the month as Temple had family business to attend to in Berwick.

Boswell was not entirely looking forward to the arrival of Temple. 'I wish his feeble spirits and contracted sphere of acquaintance may not produce some suspicion of my neglecting him,' he confided to Grange, 'while I am hurried round a large circle of company and amusement. I must frankly caution him.' Boswell did his best, introducing Temple to Burke, taking him to meet Johnson and Paoli, accompanying him to the Rotonda at Ranelagh, arranging for them to see Mrs Siddons perform at Drury Lane. But he did inevitably neglect him. Irritated, Temple remained unimpressed with both London and Boswell's friends, who kept delaying their departure north. 'Nothing but noise and madness. O for my wife and quiet parsonage!' he brooded. His diary entry for 25 May was shockingly severe:

> Boswell irregular in his conduct and manners, selfish, indelicate, thoughtless, no sensibility or feeling for others who have not his coarse and rustic strength and spirits. Sorry I came to town to meet him. Detaining me here to no purpose. Seems often absurd and almost mad, I think. No composure or

rational view of things. Years do not improve him. Why should I mortify myself to stay for him?

The previous night Boswell had come to his lodgings drunk, having had another gold watch filched from his pocket. The following evening he stumbled in drunk again with 'his usual ranting way and stayed till twelve, drinking wine and water glass after glass'. If his most intimate friend was disgusted, what were others thinking? To Temple he seemed more reckless than ever, more insolent and impatient, less careful about pleasing others except those from whom he craved patronage and favour.[23]

On 30 May, the night before they left London, he had an emotional parting from Johnson. Boswell invited him to Auchinleck. Not this year, Johnson said, but when stronger, 'I should like to totter about your Place, and live mostly on milk, and be taken care of by Mrs Boswell'. He added, 'If I were in distress, there is no man I would come to so soon as you. I should come to you and have a cottage in your park.' With obvious feeling, Boswell wrote, 'I got up to part from him. He took me in his arms, and said with solemn fervour, "GOD bless you for Jesus Christ's sake" ... I walked away from Dr Johnson's door with agitation and a kind of fearful apprehension of what might happen before I returned.'[24]

8

Now one of the worst attacks of hypochondria in his whole life descended on him. He kept no journal until August, but from then on, in Edinburgh and through the autumn at Auchinleck, his entries make gloomy reading. Phrases like 'dreary dulness', 'bad spirits', 'miserable spirits', 'low spirits', 'dreadful gloom', 'callous stupor', 'my mental life was often too dim or confused' and 'a life of wretched insignificance' are alarmingly frequent. He now had little relish for the country pursuits that had excited him a year earlier. 'My ignorance in the management of ground vexed me, and I was fretted at the cunning of the country people and the little regard which appeared to me to be felt for my prosperity.' To make things worse, Stobie turned up to collect farm rents for the 'noverca', money that Boswell felt ought rightly to have been his. He could not forgive the officious little man, whose 'ungrateful conduct to me when he owed so much to my mother, and his vile partiality for the woman who took advantage of my father in his old age, revived most disagreeable feelings'.[25]

There was discord with Margaret, too, as he 'burst into a paroxysm of horrible passion' at something she said. 'I put some shirts in my greatcoat pocket, got upon my horse, and rode out in a hurried dubiety which way I should go to be from home.' He was back in a few hours, remorseful over his harsh treatment of 'the most valuable of wives'. He wished only that she had 'more acquaintance with the various workings of my mind', by which he meant his hypochondria. In short – and this is an ominous and revealing remark – 'I *must* submit to life losing its vividness'.[26]

Back in Edinburgh in November, repelled by the 'vulgarity and bustle' of the Sessions, he confined himself to his legal duties. Society was 'disgusting, or at least insipid', and he could do well without it. Catching his fifteenth gonorrhoeal infection, from 13 December to early February he kept to his house, which made him 'happier upon the whole than when in a state of more fermentation'. His mind now had 'ease and elbow-room'. He saw his reclusion as a type of virtue: 'I must here remark a curious circumstance in my own character at present, which is a consciousness of having, if I choose to indulge it, a total insensibility to what others may think of me in point of decorum. I am indifferent as to all censure of my mode of living.'[27]

Finances were a great weight on his mind. Forbes informed him that his credit at the bank was exhausted, so he and Margaret resolved on 'strict frugality' until they could reduce their debt of some £1,300. On 25 November, his fourteenth wedding anniversary, there was another clash at home, very likely brought on by his amorous overtures to the children's pretty governess, Miss Young, whom he was teaching Italian. Ironically, when Margaret was being painted by Donaldson for a miniature (which has been lost) Miss Young remarked, 'Mrs Boswell has at times the pleasantest look I ever saw. Her eye glistens.' 'I would give a great deal could I have but the look described by Miss Young preserved by painting,' Boswell observed ruefully.[28]

With so much unhappiness at home, and himself as the cause of most of it, it must have seemed to him as if Temple was writing about a different human being – one left behind somewhere near London – when he told him in December of Mary Palmer's praise of him. She had spent the summer in Cornwall, visiting her sister (a Mrs Gwatkin) just two miles from the Temples. 'As you may naturally suppose,' Temple wrote, 'our conversation turned greatly upon you; so much so, that when we met[,] Miss Gwatkin (Mr Gwatkin's sister, a charming girl) used to say, well now, I do insist upon it that you do not talk about Boswell. Yes, but we will, replied Miss Palmer, and you will talk about him too when you know him, which you shall as soon as he comes to town.'[29]

9

In August, when Fox pushed Dundas out as Lord Advocate, Boswell's political hopes and London aspirations rose with equal suddenness, like a phoenix from the ashes of his resignation and despair. He immediately wrote to Burke, pleading for his help to win some office in the vacuum. Anything would do. If not Lord Advocate, he would settle for Solicitor-General, even if held jointly with someone else. It would be 'exceedingly hard' if he were to be entirely overlooked when he was an obvious choice. He appealed to Burke's 'generous friendship' to save him from languishing in 'provincial obscurity' and a state of 'dulness and discontent'.[30]

That he thought he might have a chance to become Lord Advocate, or even Solicitor-General, suggests Boswell's remoteness from political reality or unawareness of his own reputation. Burke's reply was patient but dismissive. He would put Boswell's letter forward, but he lacked influence, he was besieged by a legion of old friends, and he was ill. 'My dear Boswell, whether you believe this or not I cannot tell. But it is true.' Boswell's dismay and anger were unbounded when his old friend and fellow advocate, Henry Erskine, was appointed Lord Advocate instead. He got nothing. 'All my lively ambition was mortified. I had no object, and indolence seemed to overwhelm me.'[31]

Fox, however, fell foul of the King when he introduced his East India Bill to transfer control of the company to the government or, to be precise, to himself. It passed the Commons but on 17 December the Lords, instigated by the King, threw it out, and that was the end of Fox. The brilliant twenty-four-year old Pitt became Prime Minister and Boswell rejoiced. Fox's opposition to the King had been anathema to his monarchical and Tory soul. He now saw an opportunity to support the King and defend the constitution, flatter Pitt, and prove himself a friend to the new government ahead of a general election that was bound to be called.

In the last week of the year Boswell dashed off his *Letter to the People of Scotland, On the Present State of the Nation*.[32] The forty-eight-page pamphlet was published in Edinburgh in the first week of 1784, and Dilly brought it out in London later in January with Boswell's name in bold print on the title-page. Leaving nothing to chance, he sent copies to at least twelve people, including Pitt, Dundas, Burke, Wilkes, Johnson, and Dempster. As political pamphlets went, it was uniquely Boswellian, brimming with biographical and autobiographical reflections that still make it a good read today.

The pamphlet was a resounding success. Its declared purpose was to urge the Scottish people to address the King, while celebrating the defeat of Fox's bill and praising the King as a pillar of the constitution.[33] The *Letter* was favourably reviewed in the *Critical Review* and *Monthly Review*, the former describing Boswell as having 'always distinguished himself by an attachment to public liberty'. Both Dundas and Pitt were highly pleased by it, Dundas actually quoting part of it, by 'his friend Mr Boswell', in the House of Commons. And Pitt did no less than write to Boswell directly, praising 'the zealous and able support given to the CAUSE OF THE PUBLICK in the work you were so good to transmit to me'. Surely he would reap some harvest from the pamphlet in the general election, though Johnson had his doubts – it would certainly 'raise your character, though perhaps it may not make you a Minister of State'.[34]

Had he burned too many Whig bridges with the pamphlet's strong partisan Tory flavour? Burke's silence especially worried Boswell. 'I wish he may have philosophy enough or liberality enough,' he wrote to Barnard in March, 'to forgive me for my honest opposition to his Party.' As it turned out, he soon had a chance to find out. By mid-March he should already have been in London, but when Parliament was dissolved he had to remain at home to campaign as a candidate for Ayr in the general election. Hearing that Burke had just arrived in Glasgow for his installation as Lord Rector of the university, on 10 April he mounted a horse and rode flat out to the city, on the way almost killing himself when his horse threw him as he was overtaking a cart loaded with heavy sacks of meal. The cart's wheel ran over his hat but missed his head by inches. The carter told him he had never seen a man escape death so narrowly. Dusting himself off, he galloped into Glasgow where at Burke's inn he wrote a letter explaining his anxiety over the pamphlet, telling him he loved him, and inviting him to Auchinleck. If, he said, there was an irreparable breach, in spite of his famous liberal spirit and this being Passion Week, could Burke just quietly send his servant down to the parlour with the bitter news and be done with it? Within minutes, Burke bounded into the room 'with all the good humour he ever showed at our meeting'. They embraced. 'What has made you go so mad of late?' he asked, referring to the pamphlet. 'As to quarrelling with you, that cannot happen . . .'[35]

Burke apart, the pamphlet had already failed in one of its wildly unrealistic objectives: to win Boswell the Ayrshire seat in Parliament. Dundas, who in the new Pitt ministry had been restored as Treasurer of the Navy and was more powerful than ever, chose Montgomerie for Ayrshire and later saw to it that his henchman Fergusson obtained the Edinburgh seat. Clutching at straws, Boswell then asked Dundas to make him a judge, but again to no avail.[36]

IO

Finally, at the end of April he set off for London via Carlisle and Lichfield. He stopped in Lichfield long enough to flirt with, of all people, Anna Seward, whose fine eyes, 'bad mouth', and tedious literary talk had impressed him in 1776. This time he seemed especially taken with her, even with her mouth. From London on 18 May he wrote to her that he had been in 'a flutter' ever since seeing her; he asked her to send him a lock of the auburn hair that he had admired on that 'delicious morning' with her. It would be a talisman against all temptations until he saw her again on his way north. He was in raptures over her verse-novel, *Louisa*, which he reviewed extravagantly in the *Public Advertiser* of 3 June. Although she rejected his advances, which could 'only produce *grief* to *me* and *disappointment* to *yourself*', remarkably she seems to have sent him a lock of her hair, which one hundred and fifty years later was found tied with a pink ribbon in a letter she wrote to him in June, along with her verses,

> With spotless lilies, cull'd from friendship's bowers,
> That hide no thorns beneath their snowy flowers,
> By Boswell's hand be this light lock enwove,
> But never with the dangerous rose of love!

On the way home in July, he stopped to see Anna and her father again. He described his visit for Temple:

> Though not now a *girl*, she is still beautiful. Her eyes are exquisite, her *en bon point* delightful, her sensibility melting. Think of your friend (you know him well) reclined upon a sofa with her, while she read to him some of the finest passages of her *Louisa*. How enchanting! Many moments of felicity have I enjoyed. Let me be thankful.

He would continue to try to involve her in an affair.[37]

Boswell seems to have decided on the road south, once and for all, to try his luck at the London Bar. All he needed was support from his friends. 'Now that I am *resolved* to try my fortune at the English bar', he implored Temple en route in Carlisle,

you and all my friends must encourage me, as Dr Johnson mirabile dictu! does in his powerful manner ... You cannot imagine with what firmness I am prepared to live in London upon a small scale for some time ... What a triumph shall I have if I acquire wealth and grandeur to the ancient family of Auchinleck. The difficulties are to keep the family seat in good repair – to be once a year there for some months with my family ... to get my debts kept quiet, and gradually cleared off. To restrain my eagerness for variety of scenes – to conduct myself with prudence.

As he confided in Barnard, he also had good prospects of 'getting into Parliament'. From London he announced his decision to Margaret, who at that moment in Auchinleck was happier than she had been for years. This was the last thing she wanted to hear, but with brave devotion she supported him: 'wherever you go, I shall willingly accompany you and hope to be happy.' A pipe dream, she might have been tempted to call it, had Boswell not already invested so much time and emotion in thinking and talking about the plan. Johnson was against it; his brother David, who had taken to calling himself Thomas David or T.D. because of the Spanish prejudice against Old Testament names, was against it; Forbes was against it; as were many others who appreciated the riskiness of the venture. But the time had come to act and stop talking.[38]

TWENTY-SIX

From Death to Biography

I

Boswell was delighted to find Johnson in better health than he had expected, but everyone knew he was failing. His maladies included gout, asthma, dropsy, and kidney stones. Hester Thrale had abandoned him, except for correspondence from Bath. 'I could bear sickness better,' he had written at Christmas, 'if I were relieved from solitude.' News of Boswell's coming brightened him and his health improved. He later told Boswell he was convinced he had had a spiritual healing. From someone often tormented with the fearful subjects of Necessity and the future state, Johnson's testimony of divine intervention moved Boswell so much that he slipped this affirmation of his faith into the *Life*: 'I have no difficulty to avow that cast of thinking, which by many modern pretenders to wisdom, is called *superstition*. But here I think even men of dry rationality may believe, that there was an intermediate interposition of divine Providence, and that "the fervent prayer of this righteous man" availed.' For the two months they spent together this spring Boswell felt closer to Johnson than ever. They met on twenty-six of fifty-five days. His only regret was that he neglected to record their conversation, which was odd since he knew that once he left for Scotland he might never see Johnson again.[1]

He accompanied Johnson to Oxford to see Dr Adams on 3 June, returned to London for a service to commemorate Handel in Westminster Abbey on 5 June, featuring a performance of *The Messiah*, and then rode back to Oxford. When Johnson discovered that Boswell had gone to such trouble to bring him to Oxford, when he knew he would have to retrace his steps immediately for the concert, he greeted Boswell more merrily than ever on his return. The concert in the Abbey was memorable not just for the production of *The Messiah* by 513 performers, but also because Charles Burney, who was there with Sir Joshua and Mary Palmer, introduced him to another member of their party, twenty-eight-year-old Miss Mary Hamilton. She was a granddaughter of Lord Archibald Hamilton, for five years assistant sub-governess of the royal nursery, and a correspondent of Horace Walpole. She was also intimate with Mrs Montagu and several of the Blue Stockings. She described the meeting in her own diary:

> Sir Joshua introduced me to Mr Boswell (the Mr Boswell who wrote the history of Corsica). From nine to twelve passed away very agreeably in conversation with Miss Palmer and these three sensible men ... Mr Boswell is one of those people with whom one instantly feels acquainted. We conversed together with as much ease and pleasantry as if we had been intimate a long time ... I was so delighted that I thought myself in the heavenly regions ...

There is no doubt that Boswell himself felt charming and in heavenly regions. He was ashamed of the thought, but his companions and the brilliance of image, word, and sound in the Abbey made Margaret and Edinburgh seemed remote and ordinary.[2]

He moved through London without any sign of hypochondria, thrilled now that he had decided to reside there. As well as endless dinners there were at least two Club meetings to whet his appetites further, with Burke, Malone, Reynolds, and Johnson in attendance. At Paoli's on 22 June someone floated the idea of sending Johnson to Italy for the winter. One more London winter, they agreed, would very likely kill him. Moreover, Johnson had never realized his lifelong hope of travelling to that 'classic ground'. Keeping the idea secret from Johnson, Boswell volunteered to ask Lord Thurlow, Lord High Chancellor, to speak to the King about raising Johnson's pension so that he could travel in a manner befitting 'the first literary character of a great nation'. Sir Joshua told him to go ahead. 'Here then was a ticket in the lottery of royal favour,' he wrote in a passage he later decided not to include in the *Life*, 'which I put into the wheel for him; and while the effect of it was to be progressively discovered I continued to see him without any difference in my behaviour, but exactly as if nothing of the sort had been done.'[3]

On 28 June, when Thurlow confirmed that he would promote the idea vigorously, Reynolds suggested that Boswell should postpone his departure for Scotland for a day so that the three of them could dine together and discuss the Italian scheme. Boswell's account in the *Life* of his breaking the good news to Johnson is moving:

BOSWELL: 'I am very anxious about you, Sir, and particularly that you should go to Italy for the winter, which I believe is your own wish.' JOHNSON: 'It is, Sir.' BOSWELL: 'You have no objection, I presume, but the money it would require.' JOHNSON: 'Why no, Sir!' Upon which I gave him a particular account of what had been done, and read to him the Lord Chancellor's letter. – He listened with much attention; then warmly said, 'This is taking prodigious pains about a man.' – 'O! Sir, (said I, with most sincere affection,) your friends would do every thing for you.' He paused, – grew more and more agitated, – till tears started into his eyes, and he exclaimed with fervent emotion, 'GOD bless you all.' I was so affected that I also shed tears ... We both remained for some time unable to speak. – He rose suddenly and quitted the room, quite melted in tenderness.

Boswell then left the house, never to set foot in it again. At Sir Joshua's the next day the three of them met privately. When they floated warm and enticing images of Italy before Johnson, he playfully said, 'Nay, I must not expect that. Were I going to Italy to see fine pictures, like Sir Joshua, or to run after women, like Boswell, I might be sure have pleasure in Italy. But when a man goes to Italy merely to feel how he breathes the air, he can enjoy very little.' None the less, he was ecstatic at the prospect.[4]

Afterwards, Sir Joshua's coach took Boswell and Johnson to Bolt Court. The farewell scene enacted there tore at them both. Johnson wanted him to come in:

I declined it from an apprehension that my spirits would sink. We bade adieu to each other affectionately in the carriage. When he had got down upon the foot-pavement, he called out, 'Fare you well!' and without looking back sprung away with a kind of pathetic briskness (if I may use that expression), which seemed to indicate a struggle to conceal uneasiness, and was to me a foreboding of our long, long separation.

They never saw each other again.[5]

Boswell was gone on 2 July, leaving the Italian negotiations in Sir Joshua's capable hands. Johnson pined after him. Nobody could take his place now that Mrs Thrale had announced her scandalous marriage to Piozzi: 'They that have your kindness may want your ardour,' he wrote on 26 July. Finally, after a two-month-long wait, Sir Joshua heard from Thurlow that the King had decided against raising Johnson's pension. Thurlow was distraught and offered to provide the money himself. Touched, Johnson none the less declined. In his letter to Thurlow of 9

September, which Boswell published in the *Life*, he admitted that he had not expected a refusal, but since he had not had long 'to brood hope, and have not rioted in imaginary opulence, this cold reception has been scarce a disappointment'. Boswell was bitter about it, however, and on 26 February 1786 he made a point of asking Thurlow plainly whether the King had ever been told of the application. He had, Thurlow answered, and he had rejected it. With impressive restraint, in the *Life* Boswell simply wrote, 'I abstain from presuming to make any remarks, or to offer any conjectures.'[6]

2

When Boswell had arrived in London that spring, he had no knowledge of the extraordinary drama that had been playing itself out in Mrs Thrale's life as she lingered on in Bath. He only knew that Johnson had been visibly upset over Mrs Thrale when he had called to see him on 16 May. When she told Johnson on 30 June of her intention to marry Piozzi, he knew he had lost her for ever. He was numb with disbelief. He drove all thoughts of her from his mind, so far as he could, and after the marriage on 23 July he burned all her letters.

Boswell heard about the marriage in Scotland soon after. The immediate result was that Johnson turned to him for the love and comfort he had continued to hope might still come from her. He wrote to Boswell more often than ever that summer and winter, and he longed to see him again. He wrote feelingly on 5 August: 'Write to me often, and write like a man. I consider your fidelity and tenderness as a great part of the comforts which are yet left me, and sincerely wish we could be nearer to each other ... Love me as well as you can.'[8]

3

As usual, it was not long after his return home in July that Boswell fell into 'a dreary vapour'. All it took this time was a good hard look at his finances, which showed inescapably that his family could not afford to live in London. The 'airy scheme' seemed like a 'delirium'. The 'coarse vulgarity' all around him in Edinburgh was more than he could bear. For four months he was suspended in 'a cloud of inactivity', suffering from 'a long affliction of bad spirits'.[9]

As soon as the court rose, he and his family escaped to Auchinleck for two months until the winter Session. He kept no journal for the entire four months following his return from London. When it was resumed on 12 November in Edinburgh, he was still 'quite hypochondriac'. To make matters worse, although in July and August Johnson had somehow managed to visit his friends in Lichfield and Dr Taylor at Ashbourne, after he got home his health worsened – 'my legs are extremely weak, and my breath very short, and the water is now encreasing on me'. 'In this uncomfortable state your letters used to relieve,' he grieved; 'what is the reason I have them no longer? Are you sick, or are you sullen?'[10] In a frenzy, Boswell dashed a letter off to him which was so despairing that Margaret would not allow him to send it. On the 15th Boswell's spirits revived for the first time since his return and, except for too much wine and a scorbutic complaint that required him to shave his head again, he continued to feel better. He also continued, however, to withdraw into himself and shun Edinburgh society.

Although Margaret had taken it upon herself to write to Dundas about her husband's London scheme, the Solicitor-General did not help matters by sending Alexander Gordon (Lord Rockville) to tell them that if any place of two or three hundred a year had fallen vacant at the time of his *Letter to the People of Scotland*, Boswell would have received it. As it was, Dundas was reported as saying, his jocularity and 'antipathies' to people weighed against any appointment to the bench. Lord Rockville told Margaret that Dundas wished her husband had more 'sedate behaviour'. Margaret in turn exhorted him to be less abstracted and to mix more with genteel company. That would help the children and it would check his propensity to see people's faults.[11]

On Sunday morning, 12 December, Dundas finally invited Boswell to his house. The interview was a study in evasiveness, though everything Dundas said was plausible. He would speak to Pitt, Lord Thurlow, and others to see if anything could be found for him, but he was against a judge's place since that would be the kiss of death to Boswell's political and London ambitions. Seduced, Boswell left 'quite animated and full of manly hope, and saw no desponding objections'. Margaret shrewdly read the conversation differently: 'My wife thought all this might be artful, to keep me off from interfering with his numerous claimants of a seat on the bench.' She was right. In February, Dundas again denied him the office of Knight Marshal of Scotland (worth £400 a year) when it fell vacant. Boswell had sent him no fewer than thirty-eight applications for the post.[12]

On 17 December the news Boswell had long been dreading finally arrived from Langton and from Johnson's physician, Dr Richard Brocklesby: Johnson had died on the 13th. 'I did not shed tears. I was not tenderly affected. My feeling was just one large expanse of stupor.' However, as the monumental importance of his great friend's death sank in, he fell into such low spirits that he could scarcely stir out of the house except to the court. 'My chief satisfaction was a kind of obstinate firmness which despair makes us feel,' he wrote on Christmas Day. Langton wrote to him from Johnson's bedroom, with his body 'exhibiting a spectacle' in the bed, but declined to give vent to his feelings since Boswell's 'own sensations will paint it so strongly'. Not until he described Johnson's death in the *Life* did Boswell properly release his emotions into words:

I trust, I shall not be accused of affectation, when I declare, that I find myself unable to express all that I felt upon the loss of such a 'Guide, Philosopher, and Friend'. I shall, therefore, not say one word of my own, but adopt those of an eminent friend, which he uttered with an abrupt felicity, superior to all studied compositions: – 'He has made a chasm, which not only nothing can fill up, but which nothing has a tendency to fill up. – Johnson is dead. – Let us go to the next best: – there is nobody; – no man can be said to put you in mind of Johnson.'[13]

4

Johnson's death changed everything. For the next six years Boswell would persist with his political fantasies, but a larger mission now possessed him. He wrote on 18 December: 'My resolution was to honour his memory by doing as much as I could to fulfill his noble precepts of religion and morality. I prayed to GOD that now my much respected friend was gone, I might be a follower of him ...' The pressure was on. Brocklesby reported that six authors were already at work writing Johnson's Life. Barnard put the position in a nutshell: 'The public expects it from you: and I (as one of them) call upon you to perform your promise, and give to the world the memorables of the Modern Socrates for his honour as well as your own.' Dilly, 'in the true spirit of *the trade*', wanted a 400-page volume of Johnson's conversations by February, and a *Life* and edition of his works perhaps within a year. Boswell had no choice; he was in a box of his own making:

I answered him that I had a large collection of materials for his life, but would write it deliberately. I was now uneasy to think that there would be considerable expectations from me of memoirs of my illustrious friend, but that habits of indolence and dejection of spirit would probably hinder me from laudable exertion. I wished I could write now as when I wrote my *Account of Corsica*.[14]

He did inform Dilly, however, that as a prelude to the *Life* he would bring out his *Tour to the Hebrides* in the spring. Would Dilly like to go halves on it? To publish the Hebrides journal would be good for his morale. It was an accessible island in a large ocean, something to swim to nearby without a great risk of drowning. It would satisfy the immediate demand on Boswell for *something*, and thus lessen the daunting burden of his magnum opus. In the meantime, he wrote to a host of people asking for biographical details of Johnson.[15]

After Christmas, he slipped over to Auchinleck by himself, leaving Margaret and the older girls in Edinburgh. The boys and Elizabeth, lively and well for having spent all winter in the country, were as usual overjoyed to see him. Sandy slept with him. He attended to estate business, chiefly concerning the need to obtain higher rents for new tenancies. Not surprisingly, since he was by now earning little in his legal practice, Boswell was failing to reduce his debt although Forbes at the bank eased his mind by accepting his father's house in the New Town as security and allowing him to pay off the debt at his leisure. On the other hand, it was typical of his patriarchal and baronial enthusiasm that in the middle of cash-flow problems and trying to scrape together enough money to move to London, Boswell should buy a new property, Willockshill Farm, half a mile north of Auchinleck House. Before leaving for London in March, he drew up a settlement on his wife and children – life-rents for Margaret equal to one-quarter of the total estate income, an annuity of £150 for Jamie, and £100 for each of the girls. Sandy, of course, as the eldest son would inherit everything else. Now, come what may, they would be provided for.

5

He arrived in London on 30 March, thoroughly disoriented without Johnson there as his focus and anchor. This time he was to be parted from his family for seven long months. Evidence of his irresolution was his extravagant regimen of drunkenness, underworld sex, and public executions. On 13 May, in an intoxicated stupor, he strayed into St Paul's Churchyard, sang some ballads with two prostitutes in red cloaks, had his pocket picked, and fell down in the street. Continuing relations with Betsy Smith, a prostitute who turned out to be infected and for whom he arranged treatment at St Thomas's Hospital, or with any of a number of other streetwalkers, brought him his sixteenth gonorrhoeal infection in mid-May. At times he had sex with more than one woman at a time. On 28 April he attended the execution of nineteen prisoners. 'Not shocked,' he wrote, although bodies were still hanging as he walked to Betsy Smith's dwelling nearby. 'I have got a shocking sight in my head,' he said to her; 'take it out'. 'Her pleasing vivacity *did* remove it,' he wrote.[16]

Not all his sexual escapades were in the underworld. He seems to have had an affair during the summer with a beautiful young married Italian miniaturist, Maria Cosway, who was brought to London to study and became a friend of Paoli's. Though 'worn out with too hard living', in August he also renewed his dangerous liaison with Mrs Rudd, who 'looked as well as ever and was exceedingly agreeable'. Sir Joshua seemed to know something of this relationship because on 28 August, looking directly at Boswell, he said, 'If a man were known to have a connexion with her, it would sink him. "You," said he, "are known not to be formally accurate . . . in your conduct. But it would ruin you should you be known to have such a connexion."' Temple was mystified: 'You boast your principles are good; but what have good principles to do with Margaret Caroline Rudd. You forget your wife, you are estranged from your brother, you neglect your friend, and yet can amuse yourself with – alas! Jimmy Boswell!'[17]

He decided he could make some money if he wrote up executions for the papers. So on 6 July he attended another multiple hanging, this one with Sir Joshua, which he described anonymously for the *Public Advertiser* on 7 July under the heading, 'Execution Intelligence'.[18] One of the five convicts hanged that day happened to be Burke's old servant. In his account, Boswell featured himself prominently, but he also indiscreetly dragged in Reynolds and Burke. Burke, especially, would not have been pleased to find himself mentioned in this passage:

> while he [the convict] stood under the fatal tree and the awful moment was approaching, he observed Sir Joshua Reynolds and Mr Boswell, two friends of his old master, Mr Burke, placed by Mr Sheriff Boydell; upon which he

turned round, and with a steady but modest look made them a graceful bow.

An interesting twist to this particular article is that someone prefaced it with a paragraph clearly designed to ridicule him. The author of the paragraph had obviously noticed Boswell's fascination with executions:

> While a great concourse of spectators were assembled, the first person who appeared upon the scaffold yesterday morning was Mr Boswell. *That* was nothing extraordinary, but it was surprising when he was followed by Sir Joshua Reynolds. – 'Evil communications corrupt good manners.' It is strange how that hard Scot should have prevailed on the amiable painter to attend so shocking a spectacle.

Boswell may also have been the author of a report for the *London Chronicle* which described how a brother and sister were hanged together, hand-in-hand, 'in which state they remained till they were cut down'.[19]
From then on he wrote for the papers sporadically and became a regular correspondent for the *Public Advertiser*, covering Newgate trials as well as executions. From 1787 he scarcely missed a trial at the Old Bailey, where his familiarity with legal jargon made him an especially valued correspondent.[20]

6

By 29 April, when Edmond Malone invited him to his house in Queen Anne Street East, Boswell had made little progress with the *Tour to the Hebrides*. A mainstay of the Club since joining it three years before, Malone knew of course that Boswell was now a central figure in the Johnsonian biographical sweepstakes. Sir John Hawkins (a magistrate and music historian, and one of Johnson's executors) had already been chosen by the booksellers to write an official biography and it was rumoured that something was expected from Mrs Piozzi who was on a wedding trip in Italy that would last until the spring of 1787. The Johnsonian inner circle, however, was squarely behind Boswell. On this particular evening, Malone was surprised to hear that he had barely looked at the Hebrides journal since arriving in London. They talked until two in the morning about his London scheme and getting the journal into book shape and the very next day Boswell was at Dilly's with Henry Baldwin, the printer, arranging a schedule. 'You must *feed* the press,' he was told plainly, to which he replied, 'Alas! [with] dinners, etc. I *feed myself.*' He agreed, though, and was as good as his word. On 2 May he even managed to take over some copy to Baldwin's and 'had it fairly put to the press'.[21]

Thus began a deepening friendship between Boswell and Malone that turned into a successful literary collaboration. Malone was a year younger, yet possessed those steady and disciplined qualities without which Boswell now, in Johnson's absence, seemed bent on destroying himself. Disliking the law as much as Boswell, in 1776 Malone gave up a legal practice in Dublin when his uncle left him a legacy of £1,000 per year. Against his family's wishes, he made straight for London and threw himself body and spirit into literary research, chiefly on Shakespeare, helping George Steevens to prepare another edition of the so-called Johnson–Steevens Shakespeare. His research, when it was published in 1778, was heralded as the work of an exciting new scholar. He also became one of Johnson's close friends and, like Boswell, a true believer. He was aching to help Boswell preserve Johnson's memory and achievements.

What did Malone say in the small hours of that morning to spur Boswell into action? If his subsequent handling of him is any guide, Malone did not mince his words. Boswell felt his steadiness and Irish bluntness. He walked straight home and the next day set to work.

Boswell was lucky to find Malone. Others might comfort him, feed and entertain him, and sympathetically or stiffly admonish him from afar, but Malone devoted hundreds of hours of his precious time not only to raising his new friend's morale, but also to helping him write the *Tour* and then the *Life*. He was astonishingly selfless. He read or had read to him virtually every word Boswell wrote about Johnson, and his revisions and suggestions were an essential part of their collaboration. Boswell grew to depend on him more than he had ever depended on any other human being, even Johnson.

7

Just as he was gathering momentum, Boswell allowed himself to be distracted for almost a month by a literary–political caper that would demolish any remnants of a political future he might still have had. Dundas had thrown his weight behind the so-called Diminishing Bill introduced into the House of Commons on 27 April, which proposed a reduction in the number of Scottish Lords of Session from fifteen to ten.

Its objective was to raise the salaries of the remaining judges, but Boswell was angry because he saw it as another instance of English innovation or interference in Scottish institutions and traditions. Moreover, Dundas's role in this inflamed him, especially as he had so recently bared his soul to the man. His proud spirit of political independence from the party-politicking of the Dundases, Mountstuarts, Eglintons, Fergussons, and Montgomeries drove him to retaliate. In a letter to the *St James's Chronicle* and the *Edinburgh Advertiser* on 12 May, he first preened himself absurdly by telling his countrymen not to worry: 'I am *upon the spot*. I am *upon the watch*. The bill *shall not pass* . . . Collect your minds. Be calm; but be firm. You shall hear from me at large a few days hence.' Then on 26 May he published his second *Letter to the People of Scotland.*

He wrote it at a furious pace, in less than three weeks. It is much longer than the first and contains a good deal more virulent political attack and autobiography. It is an exercise in self-advertisement, a wild but fully conscious attempt to excite, or incite, public attention. As he wrote it he had second thoughts about including so much about himself, namely his old friendship with the Dundas family and Lord Eglinton, and his love for Margaret, but in the end he allowed most of it to stand. As for the politics, the advertisement for the pamphlet in the *London Chronicle* on the day of publication specified 'Mr Dundas's prodigious power; pusillanimity of the Scots; . . . view of the Court of Session', and a series of both complimentary and stinging sketches of people like Thurlow, Lonsdale, Dundas, Fergusson, Eglinton, Burke, Dempster, Wilkes, Fox, and Pitt.[22]

This pamphlet is so exuberant and reckless that one of Boswell's earliest biographers suggested he wrote most of it while drunk. It was well received – 'the best performance which has proceeded from the pen of Mr Boswell', the *English Review* wrote – the papers responding warmly to its satirical humour. He also backed it up by successfully lobbying against the Diminishing Bill in Ayrshire and in June presenting the King with an Address on the subject from the Auchinleck tenants. The pamphlet had its desired effect, rousing public indignation against the bill to such a pitch that Dundas decided to drop it.[23]

In personal terms, it was disastrous. In one fell swoop Boswell had alienated most of the political personalities from whom he hoped favours would one day come. His friend, 'honest Jack Lee', a barrister and coarse-tongued MP, said to him after publication what several others were thinking: 'You're a very odd fellow. You'll raise enmities in so many people in Scotland, and Dundas will be angry and think it not right to laugh at him and call him "Harry the Ninth" when you are on terms of friendship with him.' Boswell soon realized he might have gone too far and feared a challenge to a duel by either Dundas or Fergusson, news of which terrified Margaret. At the very least, he feared a rift with Dundas and his cronies. But almost a worse thing happened. Political giants like Pitt and Dundas pretty much ignored the *Letter*. The damage had been done and their silence was deafening.[24]

The autobiographical vein in the pamphlet primed the pump for personal invective and ridicule against him. He had a small taste of this in the *Public Advertiser* for 14 July when an anonymous 'Ayrshireman', a friend of his father's, castigated him for the 'petulant vanity and violent versatility' which marked him out 'so conspicuously an object of contempt and ridicule'. He also alluded to Lord Auchinleck's distrust of his son. The wit and eloquence of Boswell's angry reply to this, in the *Advertiser* for 27 July, makes one grateful for the attack. He reserved special rancour for the 'base' snide comment on his father: 'No son ever respected a father more, though we had some unhappy differences with which this writer has no business, and though (as happened to men of the finest minds) evil influence was ungenerously practised upon him in the decline of his life.'

8

On the day the *Letter* was published, Boswell was busily back at work on the *Tour*. By then Malone had become a fixture of most of his days. He was literary adviser, confidant, trusted friend, and social companion. Boswell's fears of a duel over his *Letter* had led him hastily to draw up a will and on 30 May he 'lodged' it with Malone, making him, Forbes, and Temple his literary executors. In the case of his death, they were to publish anything they thought was publishable among his writings, or likely to earn some money for his children. On 22 December he went a step further, making Malone the sole literary executor for the *Life of Johnson*, if it was ever written. Such was Boswell's remarkable faith in Malone's judgement that, in the event of his death, he gave him unlimited access to his journals.

For Malone, a bachelor and himself prone to mild depression in his lonely scholarly work, Boswell's exuberant, albeit mercurial, spirits were a shot in the arm. They went everywhere together and, with two other bachelors, Sir Joshua Reynolds and John Courtenay, a colourful and witty Member of the House of Commons, took to calling themselves 'the Gang'. They dined with each other, attended the playhouse together, picnicked and took excursions together – such as to Horace Walpole's villa at Strawberry Hill and Alexander Pope's famous grotto in Twickenham.

At the same time, Malone knew all about Boswell's hypochondria and the effect it had on his life and work. He saw it as his role, partly as a friend and partly in the Johnsonian cause, to encourage, humour, restrain, and if need be rebuke him. Nobody in Boswell's life had ever reproved him with Malone's mixture of strength, rigour, and love. A case in point occurred after months of work together on the *Tour*. Trying to steer through the maze of animosities towards Boswell, Malone momentarily lost his temper when he thought back to the irreparable damage the *Letter* had done:

> You cannot imagine how much mischief your own pamphlet has done you and how slow people are to allow the praise of good thinking and good writing to one whom they think guilty of such indiscretion in that pamphlet as a man of sound sense (they allege) would not be guilty of. I venture to tell you this, because perhaps you will not hear it from others; and it proves decisively my doctrine, that a man should in his writings have as few *weak* places as possible. Pray turn this to account hereafter.[25]

Boswell brought fresh manuscript copy to Malone's house where at any mutually convenient time of the day, from breakfast to midnight or later, they sat down and worked on it. They adopted Malone's trusty method in revising Shakespearean text, removing sheets of the journal from Boswell's notebook and entering revisions directly on to them or, if the revisions were too long, writing them on separate sheets, so-called 'papers apart', and cueing them to the text. Then they sent these sheets and 'papers apart' to Baldwin, whose compositor would do his best to decipher the labyrinthine notations and set them in type while the two collaborators went on to the next batch of copy.

Shakespeare was Boswell's great rival during the next three months, for these sessions on the journal had to be stolen from Malone's work on his important edition. Boswell at times felt like a jilted lover, resenting the Bard for taking Malone from him. But the task was immense and Malone was generous with his time: 'Malone devoted the whole of this day to me, that we might get forward with my *Tour*. I breakfasted, dined, drank tea, and supped with him, and sat till near two in the morning.

Yet we did not get a great deal winnowed, there was so very much chaff in that portion of it.'[26]

Boswell distrusted his ability to revise on his own because of the thousands of decisions needing to be made concerning the decorum and dignity of discreet published prose. Scotticisms, vulgar or crude expressions, obscurities, clumsy wording, inaccuracies, minute details, and offensive anecdotes and reporting had to be challenged and, if Malone had his way, often deleted. Johnson had called the Rev. Kenneth Macaulay 'the most ignorant booby and grossest bastard', but should the public be told that? How offensive should Boswell allow the sections on Alexander Macdonald's boorish hospitality to remain? What about the Duchess of Argyll's hostile reception at Inverary Castle? Malone also tried to get Boswell to rein in several of his autobiographical effusions, mindful of the censure of the extravagant and exhibitionist *Letter* on grounds of egotism and irrelevance. 'My *Journal* is revised by Mr Malone,' Boswell wrote gratefully to Barnard, 'who I really think is the best critick of our age; and he not only winnows it from the chaff which in the hurry of immediate collection could not but be in it, but suggests little elegant variations which though they do not alter the sense, add much grace to the expression.'[27] He did not always agree with Malone's suggestions, however, often putting his foot down when his attempts to remove detail or his tendency to fussiness or pedantry threatened to emasculate the colour and vividness of scenes.

On 7 September Boswell had a woodcut from his family crest made for the title page. The revision was finished by 20 September. On that day, he paid Malone the honour of composing the dedication of the *Tour* to him. He knew that without him there would have been no book at all. Malone could vouch for its 'strict fidelity', he wrote, since 'he had taken the trouble to peruse' the manuscript. This was somewhat disingenuous since Malone had done vastly more than 'peruse' it.

9

The *Tour* was published on 1 October, two days before Boswell arrived home at Auchinleck. If he had any fears for its prospects, Malone's letter to him on 5 October laid them to rest: 'I heartily congratulate you on the astonishing success of your labours. Dilly called upon me yesterday, and told me that before the end of this week a thousand copies will probably have been issued; so that there will [be] an immediate call for

a second edition, which must be put to press before you return to town.'
By 17 October the first impression had sold out. Dilly was eager for them
to get on with a revised second edition but since Boswell did not plan to
return to London until well after it was needed, Malone took charge. He
drew up several pages of 'Errata' and suggestions about Scotticisms,
wordiness, and inelegant phrasing, to which Boswell was to respond
immediately. He did so on 13 and 15 October, with even more pages,
sometimes resisting Malone's criticisms regarding language and style. His
comments reveal a confidence in his own authorship, a belief in his
talents, that seldom appears in his journal and correspondence. And that
confidence was in the face of some severe censure in the press that Malone
immediately reported to him, although the reviews were on the whole
favourable and sometimes celebrative. Whether positive or negative, the
papers were 'living on you', Malone told him, and they continued to do
so for the rest of the year and well into the next.[28]

Malone reported that Sir Joshua was 'lavish' in his praise and that all
their friends had devoured the book, but there were a few demurrals. Sir
William Windham, MP, a member of the Club since 1778 and a good
friend of Malone, claimed that Boswell had not been 'sufficiently warm
and hearty' towards Johnson. Boswell thought that was nonsense, though
Wilkes joked that he had 'now fired a pocket pistol at Johnson's reputation' and, when he wrote the *Life*, would 'discharge a blunderbuss'.
Rumour had it, Wilkes added, that Mrs Piozzi would soon 'stab' Johnson
'with a stiletto'. What Windham, Wilkes and many others had difficulty
accepting about the *Tour* was that it was an entirely new genre of
biography, itself a legacy from Johnson, revolutionary in its attention to
anecdote and the kind of minute detail that Boswell once described as
creating a 'Flemish picture'. Wilkes told Boswell candidly that he thought
much of that detail was 'a horrid deal of trash'. He was not alone. Malone
had persuaded him to delete some of it, but apparently not enough for
a public with no previous exposure to biographical writing that was, after
all, drawn from a private journal.[29]

The papers also attacked Boswell for his public parading. Malone had
tried to cut down on this, too, in the second edition, but rarely successfully. One anecdote that especially came in for criticism was the one
about fourteen-month-old Veronica making 'a little infantine noise' on
seeing Johnson, which Boswell interpreted as showing her fondness for
him. Malone wrote that he and Courtenay wished that Veronica had
been 'left quietly in her nursery'. But Boswell insisted on retaining the
passage; Veronica was fond of it, he said. In any case, taking it out would

invite yet more attacks as he would be seen to be 'flying' from criticism.

Another large objection, voiced mostly in private, was to Boswell's faithfulness and accuracy in recording what Johnson had said about various people. Reynolds, Percy, Courtenay, Windham, Langton, Burney, Burke, Hamilton, Wilkes – all friends – and a host of others not so friendly suggested or demanded that in the second edition this should be toned down. Burke, for example, was offended to read that Johnson did not think much of his sense of humour. From this point on, his feelings for Boswell began to turn cold. Malone, caught in the middle, tried to help by writing a long explanatory footnote for the second edition, but it only made matters worse and Burke told Boswell icily on 4 January, 'I shall be well content to pass down to a long posterity in Doctor Johnsons authentick Judgement, and in your permanent record, as a dull fellow and a tiresome companion, when it shall be known through the same long period, that I have had such men as Mr Boswell and Mr Malone as my friendly counsel in the Cause which I have lost.'[30]

Alexander Macdonald actually threatened Boswell with violence over the treatment he received for his hospitality on the isle of Skye. Boswell, filled with remorse, would cancel a leaf or two in the second edition to placate him, but Macdonald inched closer to a duel: 'Damn me if with a heavier weapon [than a pen] I do not tickle your ass's head, till the blood flows down and the bare skull reeks horridly where I have ripped off the hide.' Panicked, Boswell turned in desperation to Courtenay for some coaching on shooting pistols. All Macdonald wanted, however, was to make him shake in his boots and cut the offending passages from the next edition. He succeeded with the former, only partially with the latter.[31]

Boswell's penitence could not have been more equivocal: 'I shall henceforth *to a certain degree* be more cautious to leave as few *weak* places (in the opinion of my friends) in what I publish.' He was genuinely if naïvely disappointed that more people did not understand and appreciate his genius for recording conversation and portraying character. Could they not discern the service he had performed for posterity? 'I am now amidst narrow-minded prejudiced mortals,' he complained.[32]

By the end of October Margaret could see that Boswell needed to be in London to complete work on the second edition. In spite of her unhappiness every time he went away, she urged him to go. 'My wife says my spirits are like brandy set on fire,' he wrote to Malone on 30 October. 'If not constantly stirred the flame will go out.'[33] He need not have hurried. By the time he reached London on the 17th, Malone had seen to virtually everything. The new edition appeared at the end of the month.

The revisions improved the book but not the reviews. The *Critical Review* thought his 'good-humoured vanity generally pleases': 'Excuse us, Mr Boswell; though we sometimes smile *at* your volubility, yet we go with you cheerfully along. Life has too many grave paths; let us catch the fluttering butterfly occasionally in the flowery meadows.' The *English Review* pounced on him for exposing Johnson's follies and weaknesses, and it spoke of the 'trifles and trash' littering the volume; but it was entertained by the feast of Johnson's 'solid and manly observations' that Boswell had served up. The December issue of the *Gentleman's Magazine* was one of the most unkind, attacking him for his vanity, forwardness, impertinence, absurdity and even for his nationality. Boswell and Malone suspected that Steevens had written it in pique partly over the new Shakespeare edition that Malone had suddenly decided to produce in protest over Steevens's inferior collations and inadequate historical commentary and his jealous dismissal of much of Malone's criticism. The review also claimed that Johnson had told Boswell the journal was not fit to be printed. The *Public Advertiser* for 21 December said flatly that the *Tour* should never have been published.

Malone was so incensed by several of the reviews that he moved swiftly to defend both Boswell and Johnson. His strident 5,000-word article appeared in the *Gentleman's Magazine* for January. 'I have, you see, worked hard for you,' he wrote on 1 February to Boswell.[34]

10

In preparing the text for the first edition of the *Tour*, Boswell had graciously deleted Mrs Thrale's name from Johnson's remark that he, Beauclerk, and she had not been able to get to the end of Elizabeth Montagu's *Essay on the Writings and Genius of Shakespeare*. However, Courtenay pointed out that to be quoted as an authority by Johnson was an honour for Mrs Thrale, so Boswell restored her name to the passage, deeply offending her and opening up a rupture in their relationship. 'It is hard upon me that I am not at home to defend myself,' she wrote bitterly on 31 December to her friend Samuel Lysons, the well-known antiquary, 'but Mr Boswell is well qualified to be witty on the *Dead* and the *Distant*.'[35]

In March 1786 her long-awaited *Anecdotes of the Late Samuel Johnson* were published, drawn from her 'Thraliana'. In a single day all one thousand copies of the book were sold. Most of the reviews were favourable and accompanied by large excerpts, whereas no newspapers had printed excerpts from the *Tour*. As for the Johnsonians, Boswell in particular, Mrs Piozzi was under no illusions about their likely response to her book. While she made some effort to be generous, there is an undercurrent of resentment towards Johnson throughout. Horace Walpole, certainly no friend of Johnson or Boswell, remarked that her 'panegyric is loud in praise of her hero – and almost every fact she relates disgraces him'. Malone thought the book was a 'high treat' and that she had 'caught something' but that she had spoiled it all with her theme that eighteen years with Johnson were a bondage she had endured to please her husband. Boswell agreed she was 'a little artful impudent malignant devil' who 'seems to have no *affection* for our great friend'.[36]

His strong language reflects her treatment of him, however, rather than of Johnson: 'It is *clear* that she *means* to bite me as much as she can, that she may curry favour with Mrs Montague.' She did so by virtually ignoring Boswell and his important relationship with Johnson. He is mentioned only once by name. She even ignores his role as Johnson's biographer and presents herself as the more obvious and capable person to write the *Life*, even though it was well-known in their circle that she neither recorded conversations nor approved of Boswell's doing so. In a Postscript, she denied having criticized Mrs Montagu's book, but Boswell had a letter from her in which she had indeed spoken against Mrs Montagu and which he was determined to use to defend his 'strict fidelity' to truth.[37]

He hit back at her hard, supported by Malone and Courtenay. In effect, the three of them wrote the counter-attack, which appeared in several papers and in a footnote to the third edition of the *Tour* published in October 1786. It would be open warfare between them in the public press for years to come.

Boswell kept up the attack. For the *London Chronicle* (18–20 April) he wrote some scurrilous *Piozzian Rhimes*[38] (under the title 'Old Salusbury Briar') mocking and deriding her style, 'Drest with Italian *goût* so nice, / With sugar now, and now with spice', and indicting her for her ingratitude to Johnson – 'Ah, luckless JOHNSON, hadst thou thought / Thou shouldst be thus to market brought ...' Even more uncalled for were some unpublished lines that he had her speak on her more delectable connubial delights. It was small wonder that she and Piozzi did not return from Italy until March 1787 when the fuss had died down and at which point she embarked on her second large Johnsonian project, an edition of his *Letters*.

II

The public quarrel with Mrs Piozzi delighted Horace Walpole, who had little use for either of the combatants. On 28 March, a few days after the *Anecdotes* appeared, Walpole described the fracas:

> Signora Piozzi's book is not likely to gratify her expectation of renown. There is a Dr Woolcot, a burlesque bard, who had ridiculed highly and most deservedly another of Johnson's biographic zanies, one Boswell; he has already advertised an eclogue between Bozzi and Piozzi, to be published next week and indeed there is ample matter. The Signora talks of her Doctor's *expanded* mind, and has contributed her mite to show that never mind was narrower. In fact, the poor man is to be pitied – he was mad, and his disciples did not find it out, but have unveiled all his defects – nay, have exhibited all his brutalities as wit, and his lowest conundrums as humour.

Walpole alludes here to Dr John Wolcot's first shot at Boswell in February, *A Poetical and Congratulatory Epistle to James Boswell* (written under the pseudonym Peter Pindar), a riotous burlesque on the *Tour*. Wolcot called Boswell 'a mighty shark for anecdotes and fame', a 'jackal, leading lion Johnson forth', 'a curious scrapmonger', and many other delights. He followed this on 25 April with *Bozzy and Piozzi; or, the British Biographers, a Town Eclogue*. Savouring these, Walpole wrote to Horace Mann on the 30th, 'She and Boswell and their hero are the joke of the public. A Dr Woolcot ... has published a burlesque eclogue, in which Boswell and the Signora are the interlocutors, and all the absurdest passages in the works of both are ridiculed. The print-shops teem with satiric prints on them: one, in which Boswell as a monkey is riding on Johnson the bear, has this witty inscription, "My friend *delineavit*" – but enough of these mountebanks!'[39]

In the choppy seas of derision and burlesque through which Boswell navigated over the next few years, Wolcot's mockery was singular in throwing him off-balance. Both the *Congratulatory Epistle* and *Bozzy and Piozzi* were so hilarious in ridiculing passages in Boswell's and Mrs Piozzi's books that they each went into ten editions over the next two years. The ridicule trivialized Boswell's character and he felt the injury.

When John Taylor, editor of the *Morning Post*, offered to introduce Boswell to Wolcot several years later, he indignantly turned him down.

None the less, he knew that such publicity was bound to increase sales of the *Tour* and, later, the *Life of Johnson*. Another spur to demand was a series of ten 'prints in burlesque' of the *Tour* that appeared in early June under the title, *The Picturesque Beauties of Boswell*, drawn by Samuel Collings and engraved by Thomas Rowlandson. Ten more were published in a second volume in late June. Collings's ribald and popular caricatures drew on certain faintly absurd scenes in the *Tour* such as 'Walking up the High Street', when Johnson whispered to Boswell, 'I smell you in the dark!'; 'Sailing Among the Hebrides', showing Boswell holding on to the useless rope in the storm; 'The Contest at Auchinleck', picturing Johnson about to bash Lord Auchinleck on the head with a large liturgical tome while Boswell frantically looks on with two fingers in his mouth; and 'Scottifying the Palate' in which Boswell is cramming a fish into Johnson's mouth. The only one Boswell probably disliked was 'Revising for the Second Edition', which features Lord Macdonald holding him by the throat and demanding that he strike out incriminating passages. Other stray caricatures appeared in addition to this series, mocking either the *Tour* itself, or its author, or the biographical competition which Johnson's death had launched.[40]

Boswell was now public property. He had always courted public attention. Now he enjoyed an embarrassment of riches. The criticism and ridicule, especially in the *Morning Post*, far outweighed any praise and it would scarcely let up for the rest of his life. Indeed, if his damaging posthumous reputation as a buffoon had its source in any one thing in Boswell's lifetime, it was the treatment he received in the papers during these last years.

TWENTY-SEVEN

'Oh, If This Book of Mine Were Done!'

I

Boswell should have been happy during the five weeks in London in November and December 1785. His *Tour* put him ahead of the other Johnson biographers who had yet to break into print and had even appeared in a second edition. He had updated his literary reputation from 'Corsica Boswell' to 'Johnson Boswell', even if not all the publicity pleased him. He enjoyed a close and loyal circle of friends, centred on 'the Gang'; he had quit the Court of Session and was on the verge (with only one more term to keep in the Inner Temple) of being called to the English Bar and making the longed-for move to London.

But happy he was not. Almost from the moment he arrived in London he was melancholic and confused. 'Was as ill as ever in a Scotch kirk,' he wrote on 20 November.[1] Despite his friends and all the dinners, he was terribly lonely without Margaret and the children and, astonishingly, after two weeks in the city wanted to go home. Moreover, hovering over him was indecision. Did he have enough money to live in London, and with his imperfect knowledge of English law could he command a successful London practice? Would he be betraying Auchinleck and the trust invested in him to promote family and estate?

On 20 December he wrote to Margaret that he was coming home, 'not for *relief* but for the *pleasure* of being with her and the children'. He left London two days later and was in his family's arms on the 28th. For the whole month of January in Edinburgh he deliberated about London as a place to live: 'The truth is that *imaginary* London, gilded with all the brilliancy of warm fancy as I have viewed it, and London as a scene of real business, are quite different.' This was what Johnson had told him all along. Before leaving London he had opened his heart in a letter to the Lord High Chancellor, hoping to persuade him to take him on as a small Scottish fish in London's predatory waters. Thurlow's support would virtually ensure his success at the Bar and perhaps could even be used to win him a seat in the Commons. Thurlow must tell him what to do. In Scotland, Boswell received his reply. Thurlow declined to offer a safety net, nor did he propose any other kind of succour or comfort. He pointed out that it would be an uphill climb at the English Bar, and that any 'advantage' would have to be won from Boswell's own efforts, not from those in high places.[2]

Both Temple and his brother, T.D., also argued against moving his family from Auchinleck. But Boswell preferred to listen to those who thought there would be no problem returning to the Court of Session, if he had to. He strode through the court one day in January, with hat and stick 'as a gentleman', shaking hands and talking confidently of having two strings to his bow, that of English barrister as well as Scottish advocate. As a last hurrah, he donned his wig and gown and even argued a cause eloquently on 19 January, for which he received a hearty public commendation from the Lord President, who then invited him to dinner. This public praise and invitation, he noted in his journal, 'had a wonderful effect'. The Court of Session was not so bad after all, in spite of the narrow-minded and begrudging few who were baffled that he could be so well-received after his *Letter* on the Diminishing Bill. Still, the 'vulgar familiarity' irritated him as much as ever, and he was miffed that his 'literary superiority' seemed to count for nothing.[3]

Do not make such heavy weather of the move to London, advised Malone, 'you consider it much too deeply'. Boswell replied, 'If I do succeed as an English Barrister, and add something to my family, I shall owe it to you; you *held* me to it. If I do not succeed I shall owe to you the tranquillity produced by having made the trial.' Malone had 'held' him to it because he knew the *Life* was not likely to be written anywhere but in London. The die in any case was cast. Boswell left Edinburgh on 27 January and arrived in London on 1 February.[4]

The journal that he began immediately and continued intermittently in London, Edinburgh, Auchinleck, Carlisle and elsewhere over the next five years does not make pleasant reading. It is the record of an unfulfilled and divided consciousness, of a man torn apart by the rival demands of art, life, and ambition. On the one hand, he had a split allegiance between the *Life of Johnson* and his craving to succeed as a London lawyer, perhaps eventually to enter the House of Commons. On the other hand, he oscillated pitifully between London and Auchinleck. Caught in the middle was his family, who at times suffered from his conflict of spirit as much as, or more than, he did. This is a period during which his last lingering hopes began to fade, when the objects that he had always told himself would one day bring him happiness receded from view even as he frantically and despairingly pursued them. This was the disturbed mental state in which he must devote himself to the one task that the artist in him told him must supersede all others. Only Malone and his own sense of mission kept him at it.

2

Boswell was now a resident of London, though as yet without his family. The first priority was to find a home where Margaret and the children could join him later in the year. By then he would have made a trial at Westminster Hall, so the reasoning went, and if it proved disastrous he could head north before they came south. He found an attractive if 'old-fashioned' and dark house at No. 56 Great Queen Street, Lincoln's Inn Fields, with a study that Malone thought was 'formed exactly for writing the life of Johnson'. The painter Sir Godfrey Kneller had owned the house earlier in the century, so it had fertile associations with the leading wits of Alexander Pope's era. Its chief virtue was that it could comfortably accommodate the whole family. It was also in a wide, well-aired street, healthy for Margaret, in a fashionable and central location. He stayed with Paoli until moving in on 16 May. Then the house had to be furnished, to which end on 11 April Margaret shipped him no fewer than twenty-one parcels of furnishings and goods, from chairs and tables to silver, fireplace grates, books, linen, and 'a small box containing marmalade and honey . . . and four coffee or chocolate cups which will serve you in the afternoon'. It all came from the Edinburgh house which she gave up that month. Now there was no haven in Edinburgh to which they could return if this London experiment failed and Boswell was forced to resume his career in the Court of Session. It was an expensive business as well. The house at first depressed him. 'My dearest life,' he wrote to Margaret on 18 May,

I have been two nights in the Queen Street house, the solitude of which is very dreary and gives room for very uneasy thought. Your illness distresses me deeply; and the situation of my affairs is really wretched. I begin to apprehend that it was very ill-judged in me to venture to come to the English bar at my time of life. I see numbers of barristers who I really believe are much better qualified for the profession than I am languishing from want of employment. How then can I reasonably hope to be more successful than they?[5]

After eating his last dinner at the Temple on 9 February, Boswell was admitted to the Bar as a barrister with almost complete ignorance of English law. Despite some early success, for most of his time at Westminster Hall and Guildhall he watched the proceedings at the King's Bench, took notes assiduously of the cases in a forlorn attempt to learn English law, and otherwise just twiddled his thumbs.

Hoping to generate some business and establish himself as a barrister, he left on his first Northern Circuit to York and Lancaster from 10 March to 9 April. In York, he took his place as a junior member of the Bar on the Circuit and proceeded to fill many pages in his legal notebook with minutes at the Lent Assizes. 'I am *learning* wonderfully,' he wrote to Malone, though these notes were pathetically random and hardly a useful substitute for methodical study of English law. He did not expect any briefs yet but was assured that at the Summer Assizes they would begin to come his way. He was in a 'patient and hopeful frame'. As a junior member, it was his lot to perform certain menial tasks like writing letters and keeping records, but he found plenty of time to dance with the ladies and enjoy a social life. If anything, he enjoyed himself too much. On 23 March he wrote to Malone about an 'unfortunate matter', his seventeenth gonorrhoeal infection, doubtless picked up in York. Malone urged him to return to London immediately and take care of his health, but he stayed on and took medicines. He could reassure his friend on 31 March that 'all is wonderfully well in this *last* excursion into the *wilds* of Venus'. His symptoms lasted for two months. From York he moved on to Lancaster where Mrs Piozzi's recently published *Anecdotes*, sent to him by Malone, seem to have commanded as much of his attention as the Assizes. He danced at the assembly, played whist, and drank with the ladies, pleased with their 'sweet tone': 'Here now did I *perfectly* and *clearly* realize my *ideas* of being a counsel on the Northern Circuit, and being an easy gentleman with Lancashire ladies, with no gloom, no embarrassment. *How* I was so well I know not.' He returned to London in early April.[6]

3

He attended the House of Lords as counsel on behalf of Margaret's nephew at Lainshaw who was owed money by the purchaser of that estate, but mostly he drifted, rudderless. His mood was not right for getting down to the *Life*. Gnawing doubts of his ability to succeed at the Bar gave him sleepless nights, and he was ill. Whenever he met someone with obvious mastery of English law, he shrank in his own estimation. He socialized too much and frequently was 'heated'. At other times, he hid in his house in 'gloomy solitude'.[7]

His depression was compounded by his lengthy separation from Margaret and the children. 'I am quite cast down.' Then there was the problem of how to educate the boys. London public schools seemed too severe for their delicate constitutions; he shied away from boarding them with 'strangers amongst many boys'. And yet he could not have them at home if he was going to get anything done on the *Life*. He was permeated with guilt: 'At this moment it seems to me a curse that I ever saw London, since it has occasioned so much vexation to my family and may estrange us from our own fine Place.' There would not be that much shame in returning to Scotland, he reasoned; he could put a good face on it.[8]

In a letter of 3 July, he wrote to Margaret despairingly that for some time his 'constitutional melancholy has been grievous'. The house was still lonely and dark. He ought to have followed his first instincts against it, for what he needed was plenty of light to counter the cloud in his mind: 'The solitude of this house has frightened me into constant dissipation. I do not mean vice but a perpetual succession of company; and my mind has been quite unhinged.' Vice however had certainly been one element of his dissipation from the moment he returned to London in February. As a 'strange prescription for illness', he noted on 14 April, he took up again with Polly Wilson; and there were other streetwalkers.[9]

His most insistent sexual diversion was with his enchantress Margaret Caroline Rudd. The sexual satisfaction he obtained from her remained unparalleled in his life. Dressed in her 'satin *couleur de rose*, her hair in perfect taste', and with her intelligence, elegant beauty, and (not to be underestimated) notoriety, she had absolute power over him. 'I am quite another man with M.C.,' he wrote.[10]

Most of his friends who knew of his continuing relations with her were disgusted. Margaret Stuart, in whom he confided, thought Mrs Rudd an ideal partner for a desert island but an offence to the laws of society. She thought Boswell's conduct was particularly cruel, given

Margaret's ill-health and her anxiety about leaving Auchinleck for London. In November 1788, Boswell had to reassure his wife, in her jealous suspiciousness: 'I told you [she] was totally dismissed from my attention, and I solemnly protest that I have not corresponded. How shameful would it have been if I had, after what I assured you, or indeed in any view!' But Margaret still was suspicious four months later. 'You really do not know me well enough,' he wrote in March, 'otherwise you would give more credit to me.' She did, of course, know him very well."

For some unknown reason, the affair came to a sudden end in early summer. He mentioned her for the last time in his journal on 29 May 1787, when he dreamed that the two Margarets were 'contending for me', which 'heated his fancy'. He hastened to her house only to find she had fled nobody knew where. He never saw her again. She died in 1797."

4

The Gang was Boswell's lifeline in the spring of 1786. He, Malone, Sir Joshua, and Courtenay were constantly in each other's company and homes. Courtenay, who during these months worked closely with Malone on his celebrative *Poetical Review of the Literary and Moral Character of the Late Dr Samuel Johnson* and finally published it on 6 April, threw in a few lines on his fellow Gang members that testify to their intimacy, their bond in Johnson's constellation. The lines on Boswell read,

> Amid these names can BOSWELL be forgot,
> Scarce by North Britons now esteemed a Scot?
> Who to the Sage devoted from his youth,
> Imbibed from him the sacred love of truth;
> The keen research, the exercise of mind,
> And that best art, the art to know mankind.

Elsewhere in the poem, 'fervent Boswell' is praised for his portrait of Johnson in the *Tour*:

> The master rises by the pupil's hand;
> We love the writer, praise his happy vein,
> Grac'd with the naïveté of the sage Montaigne.

Would not this help to cheer him up and encourage him to get on with the *Life?* The only sour note among old friends was Burke, whom he had a knack of irritating. Burke's coolness confused him. Malone had a theory about it: 'The true cause I perceive, of B[urke's] coldness, is that he thinks your habit of recording throws a restraint on convivial ease and negligence. I think after once your great work is done ... it will be of consequence to declare, that you have no thoughts of that kind more.'[13]

Malone, who was at the centre of Boswell's recreation and diversion, understood that Boswell had to be handled properly if the *Life* was ever to be written. If he were denied all wine and women, the cheering influence of happy company and varied activity, and forced to divide his time between fruitless attendance at Westminster Hall and work on the *Life* in that dark and silent house in Great Queen Street, his hypochondria would take over and the *Life* would be stillborn. With his own melancholic tendencies, engendered by a forlorn love affair with a woman who was now in a madhouse in Hoxton, Malone was sensitive to Boswell's moods. He was the perfect midwife for the magnum opus. He knew when to push him and when to desist, when to rebuke and when to praise.

On 3 June, after a letter from T.D. pleading with him not to bring his family to London, Boswell was 'much cast down'. He fled to Malone's where 'good eating and wine and conversation revived me'. Malone, Boswell wrote, 'with ability showed me that I had no reason to be discontented, and that making a trial in London was right. He raised my spirits to a manly pitch, and I came home at three in the morning quite resolved to stay in London at least a term or two more.' But the mysteries of English law continued to elude him, as on 27 June when he fretfully slammed shut his notebook, unable to understand what he was hearing at the King's Bench. Malone brought him home with him, gave him bread, wine and water, and got him to read some Johnsoniana aloud. 'He argued clearly with me not to be uneasy, for that I might be at the English bar, or the Scotch bar, or no bar at all, and nobody would trouble their heads about what I did.' While others, like Paoli, urged him to go home, 'You are past the age of ambition. You should determine to be happy with your wife and children,' Malone kept at him to persevere. As he saw it, the Bar was a means to an end, a necessary evil, for he was more certain than ever that Boswell could write the *Life* nowhere but in London.[14]

5

Boswell had continued to collect materials for the *Life*, writing to people all over Britain for Johnson anecdotes and letters.[15] In late April he went to Oxford for three days with Malone to gather anything that either Dr Adams at Pembroke or Thomas Warton, the Poet Laureate, could add to his already massive pile of papers and notes. Warton had recently sent him a windfall of nineteen Johnson letters. Until the summer, however, Boswell did virtually nothing with the material. Then on 5 June he began 'sorting' through it. On the 9th Malone advised him to make 'a skeleton with references to the materials, in order of time'. On 12 July, he and Malone tracked down all of Johnson's publications in the *Gentleman's Magazine*, arranging the titles by year. Then suddenly it all came to a stop.[16]

After a week's interruption on the Home Circuit to Kent and Surrey in late July, which Malone had urged him to take and on which he again felt annoyingly like the junior barrister, Boswell returned to London and the distressing news of Grange's death. It was the end of a precious link with his youth and 'a loss that never can be made up to me', he wrote feelingly to his eleven-year-old son Sandy. The 'melancholy weight' of it hung on him for months and made him severely homesick for Auchinleck. Abandoning Malone and the *Life*, he arrived there on 21 August with the idea of returning to London in a month with his entire family.[17]

Duly on 25 September, two post-chaises clattered into London. The family filed into the Great Queen Street house, unpacked and settled into their new lives. Here at last Boswell had them all with him in the one place on earth where he loved life most. There were difficult decisions to make about the children's schooling – he finally decided on a school in Soho Square for Sandy and a boarding school for Veronica and Euphemia which they could attend as day-scholars. Margaret took London in her stride, perfectly at ease in the shops; his friends were delighted to meet her. But whatever jubilation and excitement she may have felt initially soon turned to depression. Neither she nor the children were happy. The sudden exchange of the rolling acres of Auchinleck and the familiar streets of old Edinburgh for a dark and cold house in London, where they knew nobody, seemed unfair. And with his family around him, London now seemed no different from Edinburgh to Boswell. He became despondent, partly the effect of a stomach disorder and 'scurvy in my blood'. He feared, as he had many times in the past, that he would never be able to relish anything again.

It was not until November that Malone could again settle him down to the *Life*, but the hypochondria lingered on. Margaret did her best to rouse him but he was so 'sick and peevish' that he moped around the house, hunched over in the drawing room where he 'shut out the light and brooded over my supposed wretchedness'. Perhaps, they thought, a change of house was the answer, so in March they scoured London for something they could afford, with no success. On 9 April 1787, Boswell broke down in a fit of weeping, confusing and distressing Sandy, who 'comforted me like a man older than myself, saying, "O Papa, this is not like yourself."' He cursed the day he had brought Margaret to London, but he could not bear to send her and the children back, leaving him alone in this desperate mental state. Not even Malone and the Gang would be able to rescue him if that happened.[18]

6

On 1 November, Malone got him to start writing. He drew on a number of psychological tactics to keep him interested. Knowing, for example, the shot in the arm that seeing his writing set in type could give a struggling author, on the 7th Malone surprised Boswell with a page of sample copy printed in two typefaces. It was exhilarating. Day after day, they met. 'I cannot dine with you for ever,' Boswell told him, 'I had better board with you.'[19]

They made good progress but on 23 November, again just as the momentum was building up, Boswell answered a call from Sir James Lowther, the Earl of Lonsdale, puppet-master of nine Members (so-called 'Lowther's Ninepins') of the House of Commons. Sensing that Lonsdale might pave his way into Parliament, Boswell had made a calculated pitch for patronage in his *Letter to the People of Scotland*, addressing him as 'HE whose soul is all great – whose resentment is terrible; but whose liberality is boundless'. The resentment was not in doubt, for Lonsdale was famous as a megalomaniac, tactless, arrogant, tyrannical, and a rather boorish political manoeuvrer. Less certain was his liberality.

In July Lonsdale had finally responded to Boswell's flattery in the *Letter* by inviting him to dine. 'This was truly a stirring of my blood,' Boswell wrote; 'I strutted and said to myself, "Well, it is right to be in this metropolis ... The great LOWTHER himself has now taken me up."' He had a dinner engagement that night at Malone's with Reynolds and Wilkes and therefore declined, unwilling in any case to appear as a breathless, over-eager supplicant with his hat in his hand. He preferred to meet the 'bad Earl' on his own terms, as 'an ancient Baron'. He heard nothing more from the 'Potentate' for several months. Then, on 9 November, he wrote to Lowther asking to be made Recorder of Carlisle, the city's chief legal officer. Soon afterwards came Lowther's invitation to ride up with him to Carlisle to be Mayor's Counsel in the forthcoming election there. It would be a test.[20]

Not long after arriving in Carlisle, perhaps even on the three-day journey there, Boswell discovered that working for the overbearing Lonsdale was as demeaning to his dignity and spirit as he had heard it might be. Boswell liked to 'shine' at the dinner table and when he first dined with Lonsdale he was shocked to discover that the Earl '*harangued*, and when anyone began to speak, even to express agreement, he said, "You shall hear." ' At dinner on the second night, Lonsdale was still lecturing them, a pompous, penny-pinching boor. Once or twice Boswell attempted to disagree but soon learned that it was best to keep quiet. The others cowered. Lonsdale took madeira only for himself, with everyone else forced to drink bad port. Claret was definitely out of the question at six shillings. It was the miser's feast, treatment recalling Macdonald's hospitality on Skye. Occasionally, a smile would break over Lonsdale's stern face and, miracle of miracles, he would grace his little senate with one glass of madeira each. But on one of the last nights, when Boswell insisted on stating his own opinion, Lonsdale 'could not bear it'. He yearned to be home with his family, getting on with the *Life*.[21]

In the election for Carlisle's Member of Parliament, Lonsdale fielded a candidate against a far more popular opponent. Indeed, the fact that the candidate was Lonsdale's man made him unpopular. But Lonsdale's dubious tactic was to create 407 honorary freemen or 'mushroom' votes by importing that number of colliers and farmers into the election. Technically, this was a violation of borough rules, but that had never stopped Lonsdale. Lawyers for the two candidates argued over the matter. The Mayor, Sir Joseph Senhouse, as the Returning Officer was supposed to remain neutral, but since Lonsdale had hired Boswell specifically to advise the Mayor and speak on the issue, and since Boswell was eager to please the Earl, it was plain that Lonsdale was stacking the cards in his candidate's favour.[22]

Electoral manipulation was anathema to Boswell. Yet here he was in Carlisle, rising on 7 December to defend Lonsdale's position that the Corporation of Carlisle had the right instantly to create any number of honorary freemen. When he sat down again, his audience was stunned into 'quietness', probably by his boldness. His speech was well received and later that evening, he basked in the warmth of the inn's fire, snug in the thought that Lonsdale had heard favourable accounts of it.[23] Lonsdale won that legal battle and his candidate went on to win the election, though a couple of months later a Select Committee in the House of Commons overthrew the result and gave the seat to his opponent.

Although Boswell was paid handsomely for his efforts, he returned to London on 22 December feeling sullied. Others, to be sure, noticed his duplicity. There were squibs against him, caricaturing the famous defender of liberty and the Corsican cause as fallen among the thorns of petty politicking. It was not a promising start to his relationship with Lonsdale, but he knew he had to persevere with it. There was nothing else. As she told Barnard, the Carlisle experiment was enough to justify his first year at the London Bar; surely it must lead to something grand, at long last, via the Recordership. Barnard was delighted: 'So Corragio, my friend; something will turn up trumps yet at Westminster Hall, and a fico for Sweet Edinburgh.' Percy, too, over in Dublin had heard of his 'deluding tongue' in softening the 'iron hearts of the north' and felt it was only a matter of time before Boswell would find himself in Parliament.[24]

7

Lonsdale's fee helped, but Boswell's finances were generally deplorable and no word of the Recordership came. His first cousin, Captain Robert Preston, MP for Dover, wanted him to repay a loan of £500, for which later in the year he was reduced to borrowing a further £300 from Dilly and £200 from Baldwin, more or less as advances on the *Life*. He even tried to collect on a debt from Temple, who had no money to give him and was grieving the death of his son in January. He still had no practice at the Bar. Margaret began to spit blood again, feeling 'no comfort in view but being at home at Auchinleck' but she was now too ill to travel. They both feared her death would be accelerated by the London air. None the less, how could he leave his friends, the intellectual stimulation. Malone, the creative vortex of the *Life*? Dundas, still smarting from the infamous *Letter*, was not about to grant him a judge's place in Edinburgh, and the narrow sphere of an Edinburgh advocate would inevitably suffocate him. He was 'miserably cast down'. Malone tried to prop him up, throwing his weight firmly behind London. 'He said if I should quit London and return to Scotland, I would hang myself in five weeks. I begged he would prevent me.'[25]

The months passed and they stayed. In August, the need to collect rents combined with Margaret's unceasing pining for home induced them to retreat to Auchinleck for five weeks. They arrived on the 20th but Boswell did no work on the *Life*, even though Malone wrote to him twice about newly received Johnson letters. Instead he collected his rents, took in the society of the neighbourhood, attended the Auchinleck Lamb Fair, gave a large dinner for his tenants which put him in the baronial mood, and served as assistant chairman at the Circuit court dinner in September in Ayr – Lords Hailes and Braxfield had come to open the court. Even if he said nothing, which is hard to believe, one can imagine Hailes's mocking disapproval of this prodigal son who had irresponsibly given up his Scottish law practice and turned his back on Auchinleck in pursuit of vain dreams in London. Boswell kept no journal during this period and wrote only one letter (now lost) to Malone. Temple complained about his silence: 'In all the six weeks you were at Auchinleck, could you not sit down and give me half an hour?' On 24 September the family uprooted itself again and set off back to London. London had become Margaret's cross to bear. 'May Mrs Boswell's health still improve,' Temple added, 'and tell her she must have patience a little longer in London. She knows I always opposed your removal thither, but your credit requires that you be not precipitate ... She can be Lady Auchinleck whenever she pleases.' But that was not true. Margaret's time was running out and she and Boswell both knew it. As they set their course south, however, he was not thinking of his family: 'I am now a barrister-at-law of the Inner Temple, have a house in London, am one of the distinguished literary men of my age. And at the same time [I] have an extensive estate, a number of tenants all depending upon me; in short, have, when I please, the *potentiality* of a prince.'[26]

They were back in London on the 29th. After attending the Sessions at Chelmsford on 2–4 October, where Boswell managed to earn the princely sum of three guineas, he fell hard to the *Life* again. Almost every day for the next ten weeks he buried himself in it. According to his journal, he was either 'at *Life*', doing 'some *Life*', or with the *Life* all day'. The only real obstacle was a bad attack of hypochondria which set in shortly after his return from Chelmsford, brought on by the daunting task that still lay ahead of him. 'We'll set you up again,' Malone told him on 13 October. Young Jamie now emerged as one of his few undiluted delights, with his natural vivacity and obvious relish for learning. But he could not shake the gloom and 'absolute pain of mind'. Margaret badgered him about the expensiveness of London, its ill-effects on her and the boys' health, and the obscurity in which it was placing the girls who had little of the social advantages they could enjoy at Auchinleck and in Edinburgh. He worried that what he was writing was no good. He could not have found much pleasure in his journal either, for recording conversations seemed beyond him. Such writing as he did had to be channelled into the *Life*. Malone advised him to attend Westminster Hall 'laxly' this term. The effect of this monomania was to reduce his own life to a narrow sameness, soul-destroying for a man of Boswell's temperament.[27]

Two events in March served as temporary diversions: Mrs Piozzi's return to London to prepare the well-advertised edition of her correspondence with Johnson, and the publication of Hawkins's *Life of Johnson*. While Mrs Piozzi appeared more of a threat than Hawkins, the latter infuriated Boswell by rarely mentioning him in his biography, and then only as a person of little significance.

Hawkins's ponderous 600-page *Life* turned out to be scarcely readable. Courtenay joked in a letter to Boswell, 'Don't think of quitting the joys of wine – as you threaten in your last; if you do – your life of Johnson will resemble – Sir J. Hawkins.' Hugh Blair thought it was 'miserably stupid'. The papers also attacked Hawkins for his malevolence towards Johnson. Malone was furious on that account and later briefed Boswell on how to denigrate Hawkins in the *Life*. His tactic, which fortunately Boswell largely resisted, was to attack the book by discrediting the man. Boswell, of course, was relieved that Hawkins's book was so flawed. After consulting with Malone and Courtenay, he reminded the public that his own *Life* was 'in great Forwardness' and judged that Hawkins's offering contained little of that sort of 'authentic precision' that is the hallmark of important biography. He could not imagine it satisfying anyone's appetite for Johnsoniana. The King obviously shared this view. At the levee on 11 May he thought of another question for the Scotsman besides the usual one of when he was going north: 'How does writing go on . . . when will you be done?' Not for some time yet, Boswell replied: 'I have a good deal to do to correct Sir John Hawkins.'[28]

To fill out her slender collection of letters, Mrs Piozzi was pursuing much of the same material as Boswell, but she had offended many of the Johnsonians with her marriage and *Anecdotes* and all of them backed Boswell instead. Neither the Burneys, for example, nor Burke, nor

Reynolds, wanted to have anything to do with her. Not even her daughter Queeney would loan her Johnson's letters. And when she and Piozzi visited Lichfield in the summer, she found that Boswell had already raided all the sources, including Anna Seward who later shifted her allegiance back to her. Yet she persevered in the chase, delaying publication until the following year and succeeding here and there in obtaining papers Boswell would have dearly liked to lay his hands on. As the race heated up between them, the press was awash with updates, rumours, and ridicule, many of them planted by Boswell himself who unlike Mrs Piozzi enjoyed the publicity and thought it would sustain interest in his book. There was also a flood of pamphlets, books and ballads, several of them malicious, deriding the spectacle of these profiteers cashing in on Johnson's fame.[29] It was an irresistibly entertaining, gossipy literary carnival.

The newspapers tended to take sides, though these allegiances were as shifting as the finances that kept them in business. On the whole, Mrs Piozzi had the most support because her publisher Thomas Cadell paid for it – the *Morning Post*, to which Boswell's nemesis John Wolcot was a regular contributor, *World, Morning Herald, Public Advertiser*, and *General Evening Post*, all claimed she was the best biographer of Johnson. The *Morning Post* enjoyed taunting Boswell. After Mrs Piozzi's *Letters to and from the Late Samuel Johnson* appeared in March 1788, the paper mischievously asked, 'What is JEMMY BOSWELL about; where is his Life and Adventures of the *great Lexicographer*, the ATLAS of obscure sentiment, and pompous phraseology? Mrs Piozzi's last work hath been read and re-read with avidity and admiration. If the man doth not look sharp, the woman will run off with all the biographic laurels.'[30]

8

As 1788 drew to a close, Boswell wrote to Lonsdale again asking for the Recordership. Finally, on 20 December, Lonsdale told him he could have it.

A dilemma presented itself right away. Lonsdale was leaving the following day for the north and wanted Boswell to drop everything and come with him. That way he could be introduced to important people without delay and be elected Recorder in Carlisle. But, as Boswell told Lonsdale, he had several engagements, wanted 'to finish' the *Life*, and felt unhappy about abandoning his wife and children so suddenly.

Nothing could have interested the great man less. Boswell was told he could think about it overnight. Margaret and T.D. both encouraged him to jump at the chance, so the next morning he appeared at Lonsdale's house, twenty-five minutes late, having overslept, and unshaven. Lonsdale deliberately took his time about getting ready, but eventually Boswell climbed into the coach with his lordship and two of his 'Ninepins', John Lowther and Captain James Satterthwaite, and set off at a furious pace.

The journey was cold and uncomfortable and every step of the way Lonsdale added to his reputation as a skinflint. When they arrived at his seat, the ruined Lowther Hall, just south of Penrith, on the freezing and snowy night of the 23rd, they found their rooms 'cold, cold'. There was little food and drink and no fire in the unfurnished dining room. Smuggling extra food into their rooms under Lonsdale's nose, the three victims grumbled and gossiped about their patron's unbelievable parsimony. With horror Boswell heard them say that 'no man of parts' ever submitted to this bullying and that the Earl never placed his underlings in positions where they could be independent. In his journal, which he kept faithfully for the three weeks of this sojourn,[31] he wrote dejectedly, 'All this struck a damp upon me, and I saw how fallaciously I had imagined that I might be raised by his interest, for I never would submit to be dependent.' On Christmas Day, they sought refuge in the housekeeper's room and managed some good tea and breakfast. That night they had to sit by and listen to Lonsdale's lecturing for three hours at a stretch. 'I was quite dull and dispirited and gloomy, for we all sat in vile, timid restraint.'

Boswell felt disgraced, subjected to treatment no self-respecting man would endure, much less a laird and famous author with a happy family and brilliant friends back in London. How could he have attached himself to such a 'savage'? Impatient to escape the 'cold imprisonment' of this 'dreary waste' of a country house, he agonized over how to decline the Recordership. On the snowy morning of the 28th, he packed his bag and quietly walked out, hopping on a cart that slowly clattered along to Clifton. Thoughts of returning to his dear 'Peggie Montgomerie' made him glow all over, though he feared she might 'despise my impatience' and the childish manner of his escape. At the George Inn, Penrith, where wistfully he remembered that Margaret and he had stayed happily on their way to London just over a year earlier, he feasted on a pot of coffee and muffin and toast, his first decent meal in several days. Feeling himself gradually restored, he suddenly decided to go back, realizing how angry Lonsdale would be at his desertion. So he walked the four miles back to

Lowther Hall, arriving exhausted and 'all in a sweat'. However, he spoke frankly with Lonsdale, explaining that he was proving to be a failure at the Bar, on the Northern and Home Circuits, and suggesting that Lonsdale would do much better to appoint someone more at home with English law. Lonsdale agreed there were many more able barristers he could have chosen; none the less, he could also say to the Corporation in Carlisle, 'Here is a man of great sense, of talents, who when a thing is properly prepared can judge of it with ability.' Besides, all the legal details had now been finalized by the Town Clerk. After a wonderful meal with wine flowing freely, Boswell was won over: 'I am now ambitious to have it,' he declared. The prospect of moving on to Whitehaven Castle the following day also cheered him. 'Such is the human mind', he wrote – his, at least.

They drove through the heart of the sublime Lake District to White-haven where Lonsdale gave Boswell a personal tour of the enormous castle. The meal, however, was shockingly sparse and Lonsdale harangued them as usual. Letters arrived with reports of Margaret's alarming coughing. 'But what could I do? To break off now, when I was confident my election must soon come on, would have been losing all my time and expense and sore labour, as *hanging on* most certainly is to me.' With some unexpectedly warm weather, Lonsdale also warmed up, and he and Boswell began to strike up a friendship. On the 6th a letter from T.D. warned him of Margaret's deterioration and urged him not to linger in the north. Lonsdale told him he could leave if he liked; the Recordership could be left open for him until the summer. Indecision tore him apart. He hung on. Not until five days later in Carlisle was he duly elected Recorder, with a large majority. Afterwards, accompanied by the mayor and several friends, Boswell walked up the street to the Bush Inn where they all toasted him as 'Mr Recorder'. Then he bolted for London, fearing he might find Margaret dead.

9

To his infinite relief he found her almost recovered, but she was distraught. She had spent her days 'in almost constant solitude' except for the occasional visit by Malone and other friends. Escalating money worries had made her 'feverish': she had no idea how they would pay their bills until the summer and autumn when more rental income would come in at Auchinleck. She was now adamant that they should return home, arguing that Boswell was disgracing his father's memory and the estate, subjecting his family to the 'miserable consequences' of deprivation and strict economy, and wasting his time at Westminster. She insisted that his 'flow of spirits', the 'dissipation' and intemperance of endless dinners with his narrow circle – Malone, Reynolds, Courtenay, Windham, Burney, Langton, and Burke – in addition to the regular Club dinners, was preventing him from writing. Indeed, for most of February he had made no progress with the *Life*, which as she saw it was his only hope of 'fame and profit'. Not only that, but his children were suffering from the bad air and lack of exercise. It was madness to remain in London. Blame her bad health, she suggested, if he felt he needed a face-saving excuse for leaving.[32]

Boswell could see that by living at Auchinleck he could 'float' between Scotland and London and earn more money, but how could he leave London before finishing the *Life*? What a shame it would be also to pluck the boys out of their fine English education of which he was inordinately proud. And could he bear 'descending' to the narrowness of Scotland?

In March, just as he was taking heart from his writing, Margaret's health seriously worsened. The doctor ordered a blister on her breast and blood-letting, both of which she dreaded. 'Oh, Mr Boswell, I fear I'm dying,' she cried one day pitifully. He could not help her much, for he was now in the grips of another attack of hypochondria.[33]

On 9 February he was ashamed to have to admit to Percy that he still had seven years of Johnson's life to write. He owned that his delay was the subject of some ridicule, but he would not be hurried. Moreover, Mrs Piozzi's edition of the *Letters* was about to appear, 'a rich addition to the Johnsonian Memorabilia' from which he was sure his book would benefit. Yet when Dilly sent him an advance copy of the two-volume *Letters* on 7 March and he read it with 'assiduity', he was disappointed and angry. There were many more Johnson letters than he expected, but on a first reading he did not think they contained as much good writing as he had anticipated. Malone thought he rated them too low: 'I would not have one of them omitted.' But what hurt him most, and somewhat damaged his incentive to continue with the *Life*, was the evidence of Johnson's strong affection for Mrs Thrale. As in Hawkins's *Life*, Boswell was almost invisible in the letters; and when he did make an appearance, the impression given was that Johnson loved her more than him. Boswell knew the warmth of Johnson's love for him, but the public did not. He vowed to go on the offensive and put matters right in the *Life*. He would expose Mrs Piozzi, her *Anecdotes* and *Letters*, and her shabby treatment of their hero in the last months of his life. She thus became inadvertently a major impetus behind the rest of his work.[34]

Malone's greatest concern was that his friend was wasting time, that he should finish the *Life* and be done with it. Dilly was impatient, too; he dropped in on Boswell on 18 March and 'was very desirous that I should put it fairly into the press'. But between March and October of 1788 his magnum opus was overtaken by hypochondria, Margaret's illness, and Auchinleck – and also by politics and his dream of entering Parliament.

10

In May 1788 Margaret decided she had had enough. She was returning to Auchinleck, with or without her husband. Her health demanded it, but essentially she refused to put up any longer with his behaving as if he were still a London bachelor. Feeling guilty and defensive in equal measure, Boswell decided to go with her. At least he could take his journal with him and work on the *Life* at Auchinleck. By squeezing in the Northern Circuit and attending the Michaelmas Sessions at Carlisle, he could also build on his connection with Lonsdale. All the children were to come with them except for Veronica (now sixteen) who loved London and could not bear the thought of leaving it. They deposited her in a fashionable boarding school kept by the Misses Stevenson in Queen Square and left on 15 May.[35]

The collection of badly needed rents at Auchinleck, as well as a host of other aspects of estate management and some canvassing for the coming election, consumed Boswell's time from the moment they arrived. On 1 July he rode off to York to join the Northern Circuit for no fewer than six weeks, an unimaginably long period given the illness of his wife.[36] He flinched at the 'rough vulgarity' of the barristers, although he did his share of drinking and gambling. His eyes also took in quite a few pretty young women at sundry dances.

Probably the highlight of the Circuit was the Archbishop of York's invitation to spend the night at his residence, Bishopthorpe, near York. This restored some of Boswell's self-esteem even as it frustrated him: 'It was remarkable that he never talked to me as a writer, nor of Johnson, except that he merely asked if I had been in any of the Western Islands besides those in which I had been with Johnson.' In the widening wasteland of his hopes for patronage and wealth, his achievements as an author stood out in his mind as the only proud certainties. If people, especially eminent people, did not acknowledge his literary efforts, there was precious little left to show for his talents. After the coarse raillery of his fellow barristers in town, however, the affectionate and unpretentious nature of the Archbishop touched him:

> We had a little plain supper, a leg of roast lamb and some cold dishes. When the ladies were gone a servant came and helped his Grace to put on a night-gown and black nightcap, and he then said, 'Mr Boswell, will you walk this way?' I begged he might not take the trouble. He said, 'I go this way,' and he accompanied me to the door of my apartment, a handsome bedroom and dressing-room looking upon the garden and river.

Back at Auchinleck on 15 August, he still found every excuse for not getting on with his writing in spite of promising Malone to 'set apart so much time for the *Life*, that the rough draught shall be all done, and brought with me to town early in October'. By 18 September, he realized he would make no further progress on it until he was back in London. Again, Malone was his confessor:

> It will require an exercise both of your philosophy and indulgent friendship to make allowance for me ... I see that *the Whole* will be of London Manufacture ... I shall then set myself *doggedly* to my task ... I even think of *resolving* not to taste wine till it be done; and *that* I think will make me work hard indeed ... I beg of you to comfort me, instead of scolding me.

'Your neglect of Johnson's *Life* is only what I expected,' Malone replied.[37]
   After one week in Carlisle in early October where he met up with Lonsdale at the Quarter Sessions, he was once more at Auchinleck successfully raising the £500 he had to repay to Dilly and Baldwin by 1 November. He knew he should return to London to finish the *Life* and have one more go at the Bar. But Margaret was much too ill and weak to travel. How could he leave her alone in such a state? It would be the grossest neglect. He must have wept over his lot. He did not really have a choice. On 20 October, with Sandy and Jamie whom he was determined to place in good London schools, he set off with a leaden heart for 'the great Wheel of the Metropolis', leaving Margaret, Phemie, and Betsy behind. He knew he might never see Margaret again, 'but *reason* acquits

me from any blame in this separation', he rationalized. He would be gone for six months.[38]

With his much reduced family and mounting debts, Boswell decided to look around for a smaller house. Several months later he settled on 'a very small but neat' house at 38 Queen Anne Street West, Cavendish Square, just a stone's throw from Malone. For the time being, Sandy was tutored at home in preparation for Eton while Jamie, who sorely missed his mother, began as a day pupil at the Soho Academy, where his brilliance soon put him at the head of his class. Veronica had changed her tune about her boarding school and, not surprisingly, now envied Euphemia at Auchinleck. Feeling like an outcast in her own family, she wrote to her mother, 'I pray for the preservation of you my dearest mama and my father and sisters and brothers if it please him to grant my prayer and if we all meet again I hope to pass some more happy days.' Boswell, in short, had his hands full. One day, when he was sunk in hypochondria, Veronica cried, 'How melancholy is it to see you so ill and that I cannot help you!' 'Oh, that I had never come to settle in London!' he wrote to Margaret. 'Miserable I must be wherever I am. Such is my doom. Oh, if I could but have the boys placed under proper care.' But he could not bear to deepen his debt by sending them to a boarding school. There was another poignant moment in this sadly divided family when Jamie said to him, 'Papa, you say that I'm a great charge trusted by Mama to Sandy and you. But you are the charge trusted to us, for she writes to both of us to take care of you.'[39]

Boswell needed Malone more than ever, but for six months Malone was staying with his beloved Irish relatives in Surrey and unavailable. Crowded by family cares, then, still under 'the delusion of Westminster Hall, of brilliant reputation and splendid fortune as a barrister', and feeling very much alone with his magnum opus, Boswell set to work with a vengeance. By mid-November there was only a year-and-a-half left to cover. 'Papa is continuing to write his life of the great Dr Johnson,' Jamie wrote to his mother in December, 'and hopes to have it done by Christmas.' In January 1789 Boswell wrote the Introduction and composed a dedication to Sir Joshua, which he found very difficult, but still had not finished the book at the end of the month: 'Oh, if this book of mine were done! Job says, "Oh, that mine enemy *had written* a book!"' In early March he wrote the last word of the first draft. 'Well! The Magnum Opus is sent to the press,' he announced to Temple on the 18th, meaning simply that as he revised it with Malone (now back in London) he could 'feed' the press. If the moment of triumph went unrecorded in his journal or any known correspondence, at least the King provided the fanfare by timing the royal illuminations on 10 March celebrating his return to health, to coincide with it. As London burned with 'a general blaze of light ... coloured lamps, transparent figures', Veronica, Sandy, and Jamie rode gracefully in a coach with their father through the brilliant streets, all of them probably glowing with the thought that at long last the bitter cup, the writing of his monumental biography, was at an end. 'How much do I regret that we were not all here to see it altogether', he wrote to Margaret. 'Every street was crowded with people all rejoicing. The effect was to make me forget all anxious uneasiness for the time.' Thoughts of Margaret's illness quickly brought back his night, however: 'But, alas, when it was over, my former feelings recurred, and though they distress me, I should be most unworthy if I had them not.'[40]

Now surely the time was at hand when they could all be reunited in Auchinleck. Boswell's love for Margaret was 'perpetually pressing' on his heart and the ominous reports from James Bruce and others were that her health had seriously declined. But he lingered on in London, hoping for the sun to break through his gloomy political prospects. All such thoughts evaporated at the end of the month when he heard from Margaret, 'my fever still continues, and I waste away daily'. The idea of being four hundred miles away when she died was more than he could bear: 'Though she with admirable generosity bids me not to be in a haste to leave London (knowing my extreme fondness for it) I should have a heart as hard as a stone were I to remain here.' He left with Veronica, but without the boys, on 2 April, arriving on the 6th, after six long months apart, to find her even worse than he expected, 'emaciated and dejected' and unable to digest her food.[41]

The doctors gave her no hope of recovery and such medication as she was taking multiplied her problems. As Boswell looked at his wife, he was awed by her courage and fortitude and overwhelmed with remorse and a sense of tragic injustice. A lifetime of indiscretions flooded in on him. He had married her out of an 'attachment truly romantic', but 'the frequent scenes of what I must call *dissolute* conduct are inexcusable':

Often and often when she was very ill in London have I been indulging in festivity with Sir Joshua Reynolds, Courtenay, Malone &c. &c. &c. and have come home late, and disturbed her repose. Nay when I was last at Auchinleck on purpose to soothe and console her, I repeatedly went from home and both on those occasions, and when neighbours visited me, drank a great deal too much wine.

His conduct, failures, and family problems put him in mind of Johnson's lines in *The Vanity of Human Wishes*:

> Shall helpless man in ignorance sedate
> Roll darkling down the torrent of his fate?

Yet even now, Margaret's suffering was so painful to watch that he spent much of his time in the houses of friends, eating, drinking, and cavorting into the early hours; or out talking with tenants and catching up on estate matters with Bruce. Then, on 17 May, while he lay in bed recovering from a drunken fall, with his wife dying in the next room, he received word that Lonsdale wanted him at Lowther Hall. From there they would proceed together to London so that he could appear as Recorder of Carlisle in a lawsuit against the Corporation in the King's Bench. A seat in Parliament beckoned. Margaret urged him to go and bring back Sandy and Jamie when he returned. On the road on the 19th, he broke down in tears.[42]

At Lowther, Lonsdale typically dithered and for several days Boswell was forced to endure the man's insufferable pronouncements. It was time stolen from his wife. In London, they waited a further week for the suit to commence. Suddenly, letters from Euphemia and Bruce Campbell arrived urging him to return home at once. Margaret was on the verge of death. He swept Sandy and Jamie up into a coach and they were off, arriving at Auchinleck sixty-four hours later. He later told Temple what happened:

> But alas! our haste was all in vain. The fatal stroke had taken place before we set out. It was very strange that we had no intelligence whatever upon the road, not even in our own parish, nor till my second daughter came running out from our house, and announced to us the dismal event in a burst of tears ... When on my return ... I found that by my going away at that unlucky time, I had not been with her to soothe her last moments, I cried bitterly and upbraided myself for leaving her, for she would not have left me.[43]

He feared that his guilt would haunt him to the grave.

Four days later, her body was still in the house and still not disfigured: 'I could hardly bring myself to agree that the body should be removed, for it was still a consolation to me to go and kneel by it, and talk to my dear dear Peggie.' A large number of people attended the funeral – there were nineteen carriages and many horsemen, not to mention all the Auchinleck tenants. Breaking with convention, Boswell conducted the service himself.

When he returned with his children to the emptiness of the house that all his life had been the focus of his baronial dreams, the realization hit him that his children were now not only without a mother but would also have to be separated from each other. He wanted the girls to attend schools anywhere but in Scotland, so that they would not grow up 'Edinburgh-mannered' and afford him 'no satisfaction in their company'. For the time being, though, he hoped Lady Auchinleck, with whom he was now on friendlier terms and was consulting regarding the upbringing of the girls, would allow the headstrong Euphemia (now fifteen) to stay with her in Edinburgh. She quickly declined, however, pleading frequent headaches and Euphemia was instead deposited in an Edinburgh board-ing school. Veronica (sixteen) wanted to board in the London home of her friend Miss Buchanan, to be supervised by her widowed mother. Boswell agreed to this since he thought she still had too much of a Scottish manner about her. As for Betsy (nine), with Temple's encouragement he considered sending her to a boarding school near his friend in Cornwall, but when it came to it he could not bear to place her so far away. She would stay in London for the moment. Sandy (fourteen), who was becoming a little hard for him to handle, was earmarked for Eton if his hernia complaint did not prove an obstacle. A school had yet to be chosen for Jamie (eleven) – 'I can manage him as I choose,' he wrote to Malone. At least Boswell could thank Providence that all his children adored him and each other; in the dark times that lay ahead, they would remain his hope and comfort.[44]

Without Margaret, he would have to pursue his political ambitions, such as they were, on his own. There would be no check on his sexual life either, or on his drinking. Worst of all, when he published his *Life*, the object of so much of Margaret's patience, she would not be with him to rejoice. There was of course the memory of Johnson to consider, and all their friends to gratify with the crowning biography. Also the book would earn him money and his fame would accrue to Auchinleck. But the most important reader was never going to see it. The *Life of Johnson* was nigh to becoming something of an anticlimax.

TWENTY-EIGHT

Painful Progress

I

Boswell lingered on at Auchinleck until the beginning of October. He made vigorous efforts to keep himself socially active but that only worsened his grief. He had let it be known in March 1788 that he intended to be a candidate for the Ayrshire seat in the Parliamentary election of the following year. The allegiances, alliances, resentments, and jealousies that swirled through the county's politics involved Dundas, Fergusson, Eglinton, Pitt, two or three other candidates, and even the Prince of Wales. But the simple truth was that Boswell had little or no chance of winning. Dundas and Pitt either snubbed or ignored him. His only hope was that certain alliances would fall apart and the votes would rain on him, waiting in the wings. He spoke on certain issues, keeping himself in the picture, but his move to London had isolated him from the independent noblemen from whom he might expect support. They thought he was too rash. For 'conspicuousness', he had composed an 'Address' to the Prince of Wales in May 1789, congratulating him on his conduct during the King's madness. Perhaps on the strength of that, he thought, Eglinton would introduce him into the Prince's circle. But Eglinton ignored him, too. Langton thought he had a chance at the election, but Temple as usual sized up his prospects accurately and succinctly: 'Oh, why will you suffer the impatience of your temper to hurry you into such imprudencies? You show every one how eager you are for office and preferment, and yet by your own rashness throw obstacles in your way.' When the election was held on 3 August 1789, Boswell made a poor showing, coming in last with only a handful of votes.[1]

Later in the month he planned to take in the Northern Circuit at Carlisle, after spending a few days with Lonsdale and his 'myrmidons' at

Lowther Castle. There he witnessed the '*rough* scene of the roaring ban-
tering society of Lawyers' and had his wig stolen so that he was reduced to
spending an entire day in his nightcap and was forced to miss several of the
festivities. 'I suspected a wanton trick,' he wrote to Temple, 'which some
people think witty: but I thought it very ill timed to one in my situation.'
After that he retreated to Rose Castle for a few days, in the genial and
protective hospitality of his friend John Douglas, the Bishop of Carlisle.[2]

The rest of his letter to Temple from Rose Castle is as dismal as any
he ever wrote. Melancholy and grief preyed upon him day and night. 'I
have an *avidity* for death. I *eagerly* wish to be laid up by my dear Wife.
Years of life seem insupportable.' A procession of spectres haunted him:
Eton might make Sandy 'expensive and vicious'; it seemed cruel to send
Elizabeth to Cornwall; he was fit for no employment whatever; the
'vulgar familiarity' of life as a lawyer in Edinburgh would destroy him;
he could not for the life of him learn English law; to enter Parliament
under Lonsdale's thumb would 'gall' his spirit; and to live out his days
in the country at Auchinleck would 'sink me into a gloomy stupor'. The
only thing that bore him up was the *Life of Johnson*, after which he felt
he might lapse into 'total obscure indifference'.

He returned to Auchinleck on 28 August where, barring a few days in
September when his duties as Recorder took him back to Carlisle, he
stayed until 1 October, when he left for London with all the children
except Euphemia. On arrival, Sandy was promptly packed off to Eton,
Veronica to Mrs Buchanan's, Elizabeth to a boarding school in Chelsea,
and Jamie for another term at the Soho Academy. That left Boswell alone
at home either to brood or work.

Mostly he brooded. He drank too much wine and flew to 'every mode
of agitation', including prostitutes. Like all his friends except Courtenay,
he was distraught over developments in France since the storming of the
Bastille in July. He worried about money: each child would be costing
him about £100 annually, which meant he had to make do with only
£350 or so a year for himself. He could only hope that some overdue
rents and debts would come in to see him through. The children also
soon began to complain about feeling lonely and abandoned, especially
Sandy at Eton who wrote that he never before knew 'what it is to want
both father and mother'. 'O my dear Papa,' he pleaded, 'have pity on
poor little Jamie and do not make him to suffer what I do.' Boswell was
sympathetic but roused himself enough to tell Sandy in plain terms to
stop acting 'like a spoiled child'.[3]

After a hiatus of more than six months, the task of revising his enormous manuscript almost overwhelmed him. Racing ahead to complete his own great edition of Shakespeare, Malone, whom Boswell called 'John-sonianissimus', none the less gave him huge blocks of his time. Sir Joshua, who during the summer had lost the sight of one eye and was courageously coping with his fear of losing the sight of the other, sat with him quietly at home and cheered him on. By 30 November, having finished revising a third of the work, Boswell was suddenly hopeful of having the completed *Life* in the press by the following summer or early autumn. 'You cannot imagine what labour, what perplexity, what vexation,' he reported to Temple, 'I have endured in arranging a prodigious multiplicity of mater-ials, in supplying omissions, in searching for papers buried in different masses – and all this besides the exertion of composing and polishing. Many a time have I thought of giving it up.' It would all be worth it in the end, he thought, a 'peculiar' form of biography, 'full of literary and characteristical anecdotes . . . told with authenticity and in a lively manner'. If only it were behind him and already in the bookshops.[4]

From these remarks, and many others like them, it is clear that this process of revision involved much more than merely polishing the style, removing Scotticisms, and pruning. If that had been all there was to it, the task would not have come so near to defeating Boswell. All along as he composed he had been revising extensively, adding and altering, so that it is impossible to fix on any existing draft as completely original. The systematic revision he began in October 1789, however, was infinitely more complex. The revised manuscript that was fed to the printing house over a year and a half, beginning in January 1790, consists of more than a thousand leaves together with at least as many that the compositor was to 'take in' at marked places in the manuscript. This was an unenviable job, so much so wrote Boswell that Baldwin, the printer, 'was a little gruff about my mode of carrying on the work'. These materials, or 'papers apart', consisted of original and copied letters, essays composed even while Boswell was writing, excerpts from newspapers and books, and a host of additions and emendations too extensive to be squeezed on to the manuscript leaves themselves. He was so resourceful and diligent in following up sources of information – quite at odds with his self-denigration in the journal about his failure to work – that the new material necessitated a constant reworking of portions that had long since been revised, hence the 'multi-layered' nature of much of the manuscript. The one area where Boswell was clearly less scrupulous than he should have been was in checking the proof sheets against the manuscript, which allowed many printer's errors to pass undetected.[5]

There was also the seemingly endless task of establishing the accuracy of his sources, for which he wrote innumerable letters or often walked right across London to expedite matters. And not least, given the sensitive nature of much of the material and its reflection on many who were still living, he had to deal with the time-consuming, complex and delicate issues of attribution. Indeed, while posterity has given Malone ample credit for scholarly rigorousness and authenticity in his own work, it has been reluctant, to put it mildly, to give Boswell credit for the same qualities in his revisions. In the clutches of hypochondria and dissipation, it is one of the wonders of literary history that he found the strength and resolution to persist, even with Malone's help.

Most of the cumbersome revision work had to be done in his study at the house in Queen Anne Street West, where mountains of paper waited to greet him every morning after his invariably late nights. The finer revisions involving tact and style took place in Malone's study in nearby Queen Anne Street East. Partly in deference to Malone's worsening eyesight, their method was for Boswell to read the manuscript aloud and enter alterations on it according to Malone's comments. As Malone's edition of Shakespeare neared completion towards the end of 1790, Boswell grew concerned, for Malone had left him in no doubt that as soon as his own project was finished he would be leaving for several months in Ireland. It would be a disaster, Boswell thought, if that happened before they had worked their way through the entire *Life*. He had no confidence that on his own he could tackle the dizzying assortment of stylistic and substantial revisions that, in Marshall Waingrow's words, occupied them in their regular sessions together:

> the weeding out of verbiage, colloquialisms, and gratuitous references to himself, replacing nearby repeated words with variations; frequent toning down of expressions ...; refinements for the sake of delicacy ...; and conversions of indirect to direct discourse and the casting of conversations in stage-dialogue form ... [Additions of] information acquired after the first draft of an account was written; efforts at greater precision through elaboration or qualification; the cancellation of material suspected of being inauthentic ... and various suppressions – mainly of the identity of persons mentioned but also of some facts and opinions – from various motives ...[6]

Boswell's poor spirits took a turn for the better in the new year, in spite of a plethora of problems and the desolate emptiness in his life. 'I cannot account for my "healthful mind" at this time,' he puzzled:

There is no change to the better in my circumstances ... but my spirits are vigorous and elastick. I dine in a different company almost every day, at least scarcely ever twice running in the same company, so that I have fresh accessions of ideas. I drink with Lord Lonsdale one day; the next I am quiet in Malone's elegant study, revising my Life of Johnson, of which I have high expectations both as to fame and profit. I surely have the art of writing agreably.[7]

His optimism must have been due to the fact that at last he was making swift progress with Malone.

He was also stimulated by the process of taking copy to the press and arranging the format of his book. In mid-January, he, Malone, Baldwin, and Dilly agreed that at over four hundred thousand words the quarto volume would be too thick if printed in English font. Pica was therefore chosen instead, but when it was realized that even in that font the book would be too bulky, they reverted to English font and decided to publish in two quarto volumes. But would the public want to pay for two volumes, especially as Johnson's life had already been picked over by Hawkins and Piozzi? When Boswell suggested a single volume in folio (the largest size for a book), 'Malone said I might as well throw it into the Thames, for folio would not now be read.' John Nichols, with his considerable experience as a bookseller, publisher, and editor, came to the rescue by vouching for the rapid sale of two volumes and urging a print run of 1,500 copies.[8]

By July one-third of the revised material had been sent to the printer. Then Boswell was obliged to spend a dismal month of 'time-wasting' in Carlisle performing his onerous duties as Recorder. 'What vexes me,' he wrote to Forbes, 'is that all this time the hours which Mr Malone could have given me for the revisal of my manuscript, more than 350 pages of which are yet unconsidered by his acute and elegant mind ... I heartily wish the book were fairly *in boards*, for in my desponding hours, I am apt to imagine with a *blue* apprehension that I shall die before it is concluded.'[9]

2

From time to time over the next few years, Boswell considered remarrying some young woman or other of means. He still fancied himself able to charm females, and to some extent this was true. As he put it, 'my scheme was entirely *convenience* and *ambition* – and to satisfy his appetites. He discussed the matter with Temple and mentioned several potential wives, with 'flattering notions that I might be successful', but 'I wavered so, and was so much satisfied that my attachment to my valuable departed spouse, and my habits of living without restraint, unfitted me for a fair connection with any woman, that I doubted if I could as an honest man marry again'. He had a point.[10]

Yet this spring he wrote an experimental letter to Miss Isabella Wilson, his 'Newcastle flame', whom he had met two years earlier – to which she replied pleasantly – and he composed chivalrous verses to Lady Mary Lindsay, daughter of Margaret's dear friend Jean Hamilton, the Countess of Crawford, with whom (as with Mrs Stuart) he had for years enjoyed a platonic and flirtatious friendship. Nothing came of either of these overtures. Then there was forty-year-old Harriet Lister, a landscape painter, with whom he spoke 'very frankly' one night at Ranelagh in May, later 'in a still more frank style ... showing her my singular character', for which he was rewarded with an invitation to supper. There were several others, like young Jane Upton whom he saw one day at St George's Church in Hanover Square. He versified her, too, as 'Creation's fairest work'. Harriet Milles, the daughter of the late Dean of Exeter, who had a fortune of £10,000, kept putting off a meeting with him in spite of, or perhaps because of, a remarkably effusive, confessional letter to her. But his longest-standing infatuation was with Wilhelmina Alexander, sister of Claud Alexander of Ballochmyle, his neighbour at Auchinleck. It had begun long ago, in 1784, when he spotted her in a chaise, after which her eyes and beauty captivated him every time he saw her. It became a 'fondness [that] was gone too deep'. He even kept a separate mini-diary of his several meetings with her over the years, and when he saw her in the autumn of 1791 after a space of three years she struck him as being as beautiful as ever. However, like all such 'pleasing imaginations', this one could not survive Margaret's magnetism from the grave. As for marrying a fortune, he knew it was sheer vanity to think that any of these women would marry him.[11]

Temple was disgusted with these efforts and suggested that he focus his affections on his daughters instead: 'I perceive you are unwilling to abandon the thoughts of a union with some female, young, fair and wealthy; but where will you find such an one, who will resign herself to fifty, and a family of almost grown men and women? It is vain to dream ...' Was it not better to 'amuse your girls and endeavour to procure them suitable husbands?'[12]

3

Sandy had finally reconciled himself to Eton but after the Christmas holidays he contracted scarlet fever and missed several weeks of school. Then Jamie, who was more frail, also came down with it and for a time was in some danger from feverish after-effects. After much soul-searching, Boswell decided to send James to Westminster School but his worst fears for his favourite son's happiness were realized when in the first week the older boys got him drunk on burgundy. Boswell had nightmares about it, waking up from one shouting, 'Oh my poor son'. The bullying apparently did not let up for the remainder of the term, and he agonized over the summer before deciding to send Jamie back in the autumn. He also had to deal with Veronica's jealousy of Euphemia and growing suspicion that he loved her brothers more than her. 'Your sensible and affectionate attention during my absence and in my distress,' he wrote to her at school, 'have endeared you to me very much.' As Temple saw it, the real problem was still that Boswell spoiled the children:

> You are by much too unguarded and familiar in your family. Children should have respect as well as love for their parents: but how can they if we say every thing we think before them? I do not even approve of your indulgence to your favourite: it is pleasing yourself, at possibly his great loss.

Temple never seemed to understand that his friend's treatment of his children was the product of the injuries done to him by his own father. Moreover, without Margaret he was now turning to them, especially Veronica and Jamie, during attacks of depression and hypochondria. It is touching that their love for him was so complete and unreserved that they dropped everything to lift his spirits when they saw him suffering. Their tender relationship with him, in fact, was one of the most affecting themes of his closing years. If that was being 'unguarded and familiar', so be it. There was no other way he could be with them.[13]

Amid such anxieties he plodded on through the spring. With Reynolds, Malone, Burke and a few others he made up a 'committee' to raise money for a monumental statue of Johnson to be set up in Westminster Abbey. This fund-raising dragged on for years until the monument was put in place at St Paul's, not the Abbey, in February 1796. His relations with Burke happily showed some signs of warming up. At least they shared a revulsion for the current atrocities in France, which were getting worse by the day. Boswell's violent antipathy towards the radical republican principles of French revolutionaries, which were horrifying much of the world, prompted him to begin writing a heroic tragedy about the Marquis de Favras who was executed in February for allegedly trying to help Louis XVI and his family escape. It was never finished.[14]

Boswell's disgust also complicated his response to Paoli's unexpected decision to return to Corsica to take up the leadership of the island, which was now a French province. Was this not joining the enemy? Paoli eventually brought him round by explaining that in returning to Corsica he would guarantee the island's freedom from French oppression. Boswell gave a farewell dinner for his old friend in late March, and Paoli departed soon afterwards. Here was another diminution of London's appeal. They never saw each other again. As a final homage to the man who had first helped him to fame over twenty years earlier, Boswell published in the *London Chronicle* of 30 November a translation of Paoli's recent address to the General Assembly of Corsica. The great irony was that Paoli soon fell foul of the French revolutionaries, and led the Corsicans in a revolt against them in 1793. He sought and obtained the protection of the British to expel the French and then in 1795 was abandoned by the British themselves. In October of that year he returned to England for the rest of his life, soon after which the Corsicans threw out the British, thus allowing the French once more to make the island their province.

On 14 May, Temple came to London with his daughter Nancy to spend a few weeks with his oldest friend. It was their first meeting in seven years and, like the last one in London, far from successful. The very next day Lonsdale ordered Boswell to accompany him to his seat in Middlesex for a couple of days. Boswell left so suddenly he had no chance to explain his absence to Temple and worried that he would take offence and leave in a huff. With irritated nerves and a ruffled temper, Boswell was back home with Temple on the 17th and that night they all went off to Ranelagh Gardens. But Boswell neglected Temple by talking too much to Miss Lister, and Nancy Temple was finding Veronica's uncouthness a trial. She wrote home to her mother. 'You cannot conceive a more unpolished girl than Miss B. is. She is really vulgar, speaks broad Scotch, but appears very good-humoured. I am really surprised at Mr Boswell's keeping her so secluded: he never scarce permits her to go out. She seems now like a bird got out of her cage.' On 1 June they visited Vauxhall Gardens, by which time Nancy (writing to her mother again) had given up on Veronica and what she saw as her vulgarity and unpredictability: 'You cannot conceive how disagreeable Miss Boswell is at these places. She is so vulgar and uncouth and such a strange figure that she keeps one in continual dread of what she will say or do.' Temple's patience with Boswell was also wearing thin. He told his friend he had never seen anyone so idle. Revision of the *Life* continued spasmodically and he seemed to be doing little else except dining out with his cronies.[15]

4

In mid-June Lonsdale commanded Boswell to travel to Carlisle immediately to see to business and attend the Carlisle election.[16] He pleaded with the wicked 'Potentate' to let him remain in London until Temple left, but the great man would not hear of it. Temple and T.D. urged him to resign the Recordership immediately, assert his independence, and leave for Auchinleck. Malone advised caution: he should perform his duties at Carlisle, see if there was a seat in Parliament in the offing, and if not, resign. Malone would continue the revising on his own. When Boswell told Lonsdale he would go, but not until he was needed, Lonsdale insisted that he leave immediately. This finally provoked Boswell to offer his resignation, which Lonsdale was prepared to accept, but not until he had fulfilled his duties in Carlisle – for a paltry twenty pounds.

As they set off from Oxford Street in Lonsdale's coach on 17 June, they promptly fell into a furious quarrel that Boswell recreated vividly in his journal. He provoked his patron by talking 'too freely of my liberal and independent views', at which Lonsdale flew into a rage:

> he used shocking words to me, saying, 'Take it as you will. I am ready to give you satisfaction.' 'My Lord,' said I, 'you have said enough.' I was in a stunned state of mind, but calm and determined. He went on with insult: 'You have kept low company all your life. What are *you*, Sir?' 'A gentleman, my Lord, a man of honour; and I hope to show myself such.' He brutally said, 'You will be settled when you have a bullet in your belly.'

At the next inn, Lonsdale demanded a duel immediately. He had pistols ready but refused Boswell the use of one of them. As no other was to be had, they fell to talking instead of shooting. 'Looking on him really as a madman, and wishing upon principle never to have a duel if I could avoid it with credit', Boswell stepped back, insisting that Lonsdale had misinterpreted his words. Lonsdale finally relented and held out his hand: 'Boswell, forget all that is past.' But the relationship was at an end.

Carlisle was undiluted misery. Boswell's letters and journal (which he

called 'a lazar-house ... the journal of a diseased mind') during the
interminable three weeks he languished there are painful to read. For
one thing, he was ill from another sexual infection, having 'rashly'
gone to a prostitute three times on 14 June. A genital abscess made it
increasingly difficult for him to walk. 'I was sensible that I *deserved* that
part of my unhappiness occasioned by my complaint, for *what* can be
more culpable at any time of life, and in my situation as the head of a
family, than the wild conduct of a licentious youth?' He felt himself 'a
despicable being'. He was also 'devoured' by hypochondria so that 'all
was dull and dead within me'. One night he dreamed that Veronica had
consumption. What on earth was he doing in Carlisle, serving a ruthless
tyrant, when his scattered family needed him so much, his *Life* was still
unfinished, and Auchinleck lay neglected? What haunted him was the
thought that he was no better now than thirty years earlier, that not even
Johnson, a succession of eminent men, his European tour, Corsica or
two successful books had made any difference to his conduct and self-
perception: 'I was a board on which fine figures had been painted, but
which some corrosive application had reduced to its original nakedness.'
'You have had distress of mind,' he wrote to Malone on the 30th,

> but your active spirit never failed within you. I have heard you say that you
> never sat listless by the fire. I have during these wretched days sat so, hours
> and hours ... My dear friend! for GOD'S sake, if you possibly can let me
> have some consolation. The melancholy to which I am subject cannot be
> helped. But I beseech you try to alleviate ... my sufferings.

He promised that he would return to London by 18 July; tremblingly, he
asked his friend if he would have left for Ireland by then? Malone replied
with avuncular rigour and impatience: 'The being well or not being well
with [Lonsdale] has nothing to do with your changing Scotland for
London, with the embarrassments of your fortune, with the difficulty of
educating your children, and twenty other circumstances, that you have
enumerated by way of aggravating the account.' Think about the future,
not the past, Malone counselled. In any case, he had continued to
'superintend the press' and the compositor had also pushed ahead 'very
smartly'. So there was nothing to worry about. He did not tell Boswell
this, but he had resolved to stay in London longer than he needed so
that they could continue with the revisions and perhaps even finish
them.[17]

The days wore on and Euphemia joined him in Carlisle on the 11th.

Lady Auchinleck had usefully suggested that she should attend school in London and live with the rest of the family. They left Carlisle together on the 15th, Boswell escaping the sphere of Lonsdale's 'savage injustice' for ever.

Temple had long since departed London, but Malone was still there. Several dinners with him, Sir Joshua, and other friends put Boswell's spirits right again. He was also over the worst of his venereal infection and ready to start work. On 10 September he wrote, 'My life at present, though for some time my health and spirits have been wonderfully good, is surely as idly spent as can almost be imagined. I merely attend to the progress of my *Life of Johnson*, and that by no means with great assiduity, such as that which Malone employs on Shakespeare.'[18] Over the holidays he had all the children except Elizabeth in his cramped house with him, which surely explains his inability to get down to work. His mood remained bright for the rest of the year, however, and Malone was on hand to help with the revisions until as late as November. With his great edition complete and at the printer, Malone left for Ireland the following month. Boswell still had half of the second volume to revise on his own.

5

A pleasantly comic interlude occurred one day in February 1791, illustrating how eccentric Boswell was deemed to be in certain circles. On a visit to Sandy at Eton College, Boswell wandered over to Windsor where Fanny Burney was then living with the Royal Family as Second Keeper of the Queen's Robes. By appointment, he met her at the gate of St George's Chapel and, according to her account of the encounter in her colourful diary, what took place was worthy of a scene in one of her novels.[19] One must keep in mind that, with her sense of fun and instinct for the burlesque, she was unlikely to be fair to him. She had after all observed him at Mrs Thrale's, not the most neutral of environments, and referred to him in her diary as 'that biographical, anecdotical memorandummer'.

He made much of her need to be rescued from slavery at court, saying that he would lead a delegation to her father and 'harangue' him on the subject: 'Why, I would farm you out myself for a double, treble the money! I wish I had the regulation of such a farm, – yet I am no farmergeneral. But I should like to farm you . . .' She moved nervously away from the chapel, embarrassed lest anyone hear such 'treasonable' nonsense. But he pressed on until he came to his main theme – her Johnson letters and anecdotes:

> madam, you must give me some of your choice little notes of the Doctor's ... I want to show him in a new light. Grave Sam, and great Sam, and solemn Sam, and learned Sam, – all these he has appeared over and over. Now I want to entwine a wreath of the graces across his brow: I want to show him as gay Sam, agreeable Sam, pleasant Sam; so you must help me with some of his beautiful billets to yourself.

She had nothing to give him, she replied, and tried to escape. He followed, dancing along beside her and drawing the puzzled attention of members of the court. She was about to dart into the Queen's Lodge when he pulled from his pocket a proof sheet of the *Life* and began to read it to her loudly. Just then the King and Queen appeared, and with her 'now weakened limbs' she hurried into her apartment. Johnson's tender letters, she wrote in her diary, were too 'sacred' for her to allow Boswell to use them in such a public way. She had denied Mrs Thrale the use of them, too.

When the *Life* came out, she felt that her lack of co-operation had been vindicated. She was upset that Boswell's portrait of Johnson was not as benign as she felt it should have been, and concerned that people who did not know his 'intrinsic worth' would misunderstand his remarks. The King came to her several times, having seen her name in the book's index, cordial and eager for more information as there was little about her in Boswell's narrative. She was glad of it, she told him. Johnson's letters to her never did appear in editions of the *Life* until after her death.

6

Money was still a problem, two debts in particular haunting Boswell. The £500 he had borrowed in 1781 to lend to his impecunious cousin Bruce Boswell, a former East India captain, came due to a London merchant in January and he had little idea where that money would come from. He never did repay it. And in mid-October he imprudently bought the estate of Knockroon from his uncle John Boswell for the high price of £2,500, determined as he was to restore the property to Auchinleck and leave it as 'a patrimony to a younger son', Jamie. He borrowed £1,500 of that amount from his Auchinleck neighbour and agricultural mentor Alexander Fairlie, but in the new year he must somehow come up with the remaining £1,000.

The previous August he had lost his old friend and overseer James Bruce, who had been ill for some time and annoyingly inattentive to estate matters. Now with the young and energetic Andrew Gibb as the new overseer, he expected greater efficiency: 'You will collect both the half year's rents and feuduties of the village before the end of this month ... and you will take care to put what you collect into a safe place, and send every day's collection to the bank at Ayr the next morning in broad daylight. I indeed reckon that in three days the whole may be collected.' He insisted on being sent regular accounts.[20]

But the best he could expect to clear from the estate was only £900 annually. He needed a large amount right away and in September began to reconsider his decision to refuse an offer of 'a cool thousand' from the bookseller George Robinson for the copyright of the *Life*. It would 'go to my heart' to sell it for such a low price, he wrote to Malone in Ireland, but he was desperate and, besides, the book might not make that much money anyway. 'Pray decide for me,' he implored his friend: 'I am all timidity. Your absence has been a severe stroke to me. I am at present quite at a loss what to do.' Perhaps he could let him have £1,000 in credit for four or five years? Malone replied immediately that he had no money to lend, which was true. He suggested that Boswell might be able to convince Dilly or Baldwin to give him an advance. In March, Dilly and Baldwin did just that, each giving him £200, which with £600 from his bank in Ayr on credit for his rents saw him through.[21]

7

In spite of his money worries, Boswell's morale remained high through to the end of the year. He was present at the Lord Mayor's splendid banquet at the Guildhall on 9 November and used the occasion, attended also by Pitt, to sing his flattering ballad, 'William Pitt: The Grocer of London', to the assembled guests. They asked for five encores and toasted Boswell 'with three cheers standing'. According to one account, Pitt left before the singing; according to another, he melted and joined 'in the general laugh at the oddity of Mr Boswell's character'. Boswell made one final effort in April 1791 to be noticed by Pitt by publishing his lively poem on the Slave Trade Bill, 'No Abolition of Slavery; or the Universal Empire of Love'. It was an odd way to gain Pitt's attention since the

poem attacked him along with Burke, Wilberforce, and other supporters
of the Bill. Perhaps Boswell thought the novelty of the poem would
charm the Abolitionists. Instead he realized that any hopes of encouragement from that quarter, with a view to a Commons seat or some
other government post, were now extinct. His only political consolation
was that at last he prevailed on Dundas to fulfil his promise to the
dying Lord Auchinleck in 1782 to grant T.D. a salaried government
appointment. In February, his brother became a clerk in the Navy Pay-
Office with the modest salary of £100 per year.[22]

In January, Boswell still had one hundred pages of copy to prepare,
many insertions to make, and the death of Johnson to write. 'Indeed, I
go sluggishly and comfortlessly about my work. As I pass your door I
cast many a longing look,' he wrote to Malone. The second volume was
becoming embarrassingly big and the end seemed to recede just when
he thought it was within his grasp. To make things worse, he succumbed
to a severe bout of depression, one of the worst in his life. He could
scarcely bear to be in company, and when he was he looked cheerless.
His friends all noticed his gloom and his worsening health. Hoping to
hasten Malone's return, Courtenay wrote to him full of concern:

> Poor Boswell is very low and dispirited and almost melancholy mad – feels
> no spring, no pleasure in existence – and is so perceptibly altered for the
> worse that it is remarked everywhere. I try all I can to rouse him but he
> recurs so tiresomely and tediously to the same cursed, trite, commonplace
> topics about death, etc. – that we grow old, and when we are old we are not
> young – that I despair of effecting a cure ... You would be of more service
> to him than anybody is ...

On 19 January he moved to a still smaller house at 47 Great Portland
Street which he immediately disliked, though it pleased the children well
enough. His bedroom was at the front of the house and some nights he
could not sleep for the noise in the street.[23]

The gloom lifted briefly in late February and descended again in mid-
March, blanketing him in a mental darkness even more opaque than
before. Old demons had joined forces with new ones to haunt him, he
told Temple. 'The *possibility* of a *disturbed imagination* reducing me to
the mode of existence in my youth frightens me.' While it was a comfort
to him that Jamie had finally reconciled himself to Westminster School
and that Sandy was thriving at Eton, he was now beginning to be harassed
by the poor behaviour of his motherless daughters, especially Euphemia,

who he felt had little respect for him – 'as indeed how could they for a sickly-minded wretch'. They both lived with him and he wished them away.[24]

As for the *Life*, in expectation of its imminent appearance the newspapers were having some more fun at his expense. 'Dr *Johnson's* fate resembles that of the *Great Ox*,' wrote the *Morning Post* in April – 'They were both gigantic ... both shewn by their *friends* for a time, and both, after being knocked on the head, have *cut up well*!' Warming to the sport, a few days later the *Post* added, '*Bozzy*, and the owner of the great *Lincolnshire Ox*, have acted in the same manner towards their respective friends ...; they extolled them when living, and *cut them up* after their decease!'[25] The publicity was perfectly timed, and Boswell himself attempted to keep up the public's interest with a stream of anonymous announcements and observations relating to the *Life*. He looked forward longingly, once his book was launched, to freedom from incarceration as an author. He dreamed of furnishing the chambers at the Temple he had recently taken and sitting there hour after hour studying law and attending Westminster for legal work. In early April he could almost imagine himself free of the weight of his mighty literary albatross. The last proof sheet was in his hands on 9 April. On the 19th he fixed a firm publication date, 16 May, the twenty-eighth anniversary of his first meeting with Johnson. It would soon be revealed whether the world agreed with his remark to Dempster that the *Life* 'will be the most entertaining collection that has appeared in this age'.[26]

TWENTY-NINE

The Life of Johnson *and Its Aftermath*

I

The world did agree. Sales were swift from the moment the *Life of Johnson* was officially published on 16 May, in two quarto volumes. But even before publication, on the 13th, forty-one London booksellers purchased around 400 copies, rushing them into their shops in anticipation of an eager public. One of them sold twenty sets on the first day. Eight hundred of the total first printing of 1,750 copies were sold within two weeks. By December all but 300 were gone and sales continued briskly into the new year. The King led the way, praising the book highly at his levee at St James's Palace on 15 June. Burke was there and later told Boswell of how the King spoke of 'that excellent work'. He himself announced to the King that it was 'the most entertaining book he had ever read'.[1]

Although a vigorous public and private debate ensued over the *Life's* often forceful deprecation of the living as well as the recently dead, Boswell was now invited out to dinner more than he had been for years and the dominant theme of what he heard was praise. Charles Burney's was unstinting:

> If all his writings which had been previously printed were lost, or had never appeared, your book would have conveyed to posterity as advantageous an idea of his character, genius, and worth as Xeonophon has done of those of Socrates. I have often found your own reflections not only ingenious and lively but strong; and the latter part of your narrative, though I already knew its chief circumstances, has in it so much pathos that it renovated all my sorrows [over Johnson's death] and frequently made me weep like a tender-hearted female at a tragedy.

Temple was relieved and insightful: 'Perhaps no man was ever so perfectly painted as you have painted your hero ... under every shade and under every colour.' Charlotte Lennox, author of the famous novel *The Female Quixote* (1752) and admired by Johnson, wrote to him, 'At the same time that I hear from every mouth the highest praises of your *Life of Doctor Johnson*, I hear likewise of the honourable mention you make of me in that elegant performance.' Wilkes told him it was 'a wonderful book'. And his old friend and collaborator, Andrew Erskine, to whom he had sent complimentary copies, pronounced: 'I am fond of your style, it is not the solemn march of your friend, but the careless and easy walk of a gentleman ...'[2]

From Scotland, which had suffered quite a few insults at Johnson's hands, there was a muted response. Boswell's old friend Hugh Blair, who fared well in the *Life*, praised him for 'the balancing of good and bad' in his portrait of Johnson but also reproved him for having 'depicted yourself sometimes too graphically and unnecessarily'. As in their reviews of the *Tour*, the newspapers accused Boswell of vain and irrelevant intrusion into the narrative and of casting himself as a naïve stooge and target for Johnson's barbed wit. Most of the criticism, however, was political, either from friends of the Pitt government who were mortified by Boswell's clumsy praise (as in 'The Grocer of London' and other ballads) or by an Opposition delighted to burlesque him as a government toady. Horace Walpole, who resented Johnson's dislike of his dear friend Gray's poetry and boasted that he had never spoken to him or been in the same room with him more than six times, epitomized the mocking *ad hominem* criticism in one of his letters:

> Often indeed Johnson made the most brutal speeches to living persons, for though he was good-natured at bottom, he was very ill-natured at top. He loved to dispute to show his superiority. If his opponents were weak, he told them they were fools; if they vanquished him, he was scurrilous – to nobody more than to Boswell himself who was contemptible for flattering him so grossly, and for enduring the coarse things he was continually vomiting on Boswell's own country, Scotland.

The papers also disparaged Boswell for depicting Johnson's brutality and burlesqued him for his supposed frivolousness of detail and conversation. The reviewer in the *Oracle* for 23 June wrote:

> The general complexion of the work is, to us, infinitely too minute ... Many of his Anecdotes are surely frivolous, and contribute not a particle to the

development of either opinion or character. Such for instance as JOHN-
SON'S clearing rubbish with a pole, that obstructed a streamlet; and *how,*
when he was tired, he threw down the pole, and told BOZZY (we beg
pardon, we mean Mr Boswell) to labour in his turn; and *how* Mr B. *did*
labour; and *how,* being a *fresh man,* he succeeded in supplanting a dead cat
from her situation, and fairly threw her down the River!

There was too much gold dust scattered about which should have been
'ingotted' before it was given to the public.[3]

The *Oracle* review was also one of those that decried Boswell's open
attack on Hawkins and Piozzi. In fact, with Courtenay's help he had
deleted many passages in which, incited by years of hostility, he had
accused Mrs Piozzi of financial exploitation of Johnson, mis-
representation, inaccuracy, flightiness, flippancy, social climbing, duplicity, and ingratitude. What was left took aim 'reluctantly' at the wilful
inaccuracies in her *Anecdotes* and her disapproval of instant recording of
conversation. He also quoted Johnson's derogatory comments about her.
Mrs Piozzi's own view of his attack on her was self-pitying:

> I have been now laughing and crying by turns for two days over Boswell's
> book: That poor man should have a *Bon Bouillon* and be put to bed, – he is
> quite light-headed. Yet madmen, drunkards, and fools tell truth they say: –
> and if Johnson was to me the ... friend he has represented – let it cure me
> of ever making friendship more with any human being – let it cure me![4]

She had won the earlier battles for possession of Johnson, but Boswell,
chiefly with Malone's help, had triumphed in the war, if not in an
especially noble manner.

One of the most hilarious attacks on the *Life*, damaging because
it was so funny, was a lengthy anonymous parody of the recorded
conversations, 'Lessons in Biography or How to Write the Life of One's
Friend', that first appeared in the *Morning Herald* on 5 July and later was
reprinted in several of the papers. Boswell squirmed as he read the
brilliant adaptation of his naïvety and Johnson's philosophical talk to
such trivial subjects as the history of *Tommy Trip*, the squeezing of a
lemon, Boswell's verses on the making of breeches, green spectacles,
wind, small beer, and so on. Boswell and Johnson were compared to two
figs stuck together; or Johnson was depicted as a dog and Boswell as a
canister tied to his tail.

Negative notices in the papers were balanced by an almost equal number of positive reviews. The *Gentleman's Magazine* for May praised Boswell for completing his arduous task and having perfectly satisfied and pleased Johnson's followers with 'the MAN HIMSELF'. The *St James's Chronicle* on the day of publication applauded the *Life* as 'authentic, very amusing, and . . . very interesting', though it allowed there were a few 'superfluous' pages. It singled out Boswell's 'peculiar excellence' in preserving Johnson's conversation, his vivacity, and naïvety, and his introduction of a 'vast number of well-known characters in many spheres of life'. The *English Review* pitied grave and fastidious readers unable to appreciate Boswell's 'banquet of amusement' and the 'airy garrulity' with which he served it up.

2

The *Life* celebrates not only Johnson's mental powers, but also Boswell's zest for living. His delight in spinning out stories, anecdotes, and conversations – the antithesis of Johnson's bent for aphoristic suppression and contraction – is matched by his energy, his agitation, his eagerness to leave no stone unturned. To some extent, Johnson was an excuse for celebrating his own nature and psyche. Viewing the *Life* as Boswell's involuntary autobiography may help to explain why it embarrassed and exasperated so many critics. But it is also the first great modern biography, helped into existence by Malone, the greatest scholar of the age who defined his scholarship in terms of authenticating documents and facts, not impressionistic hearsay.

Boswell knew he was not writing a character sketch of a public figure, as in classical biography, but an exploration of the landscape of his subject's mind. It would not be an 'ethical' portrait of the man, aspiring to teach and make moral judgements. Thus he could claim that Johnson would 'be seen in this work more completely than any man who has ever yet lived. And he will be seen as he really was', an individual whose life provides detailed, anecdotal illustrations of the human experience. What he 'privately wrote, and said, and thought' would be far more important than chronological events and didactic generalizations. As Frank Brady put it, Boswell was determined that Johnson should emerge as 'a moral hero of everyday life'.[5] 'Had his other friends been as diligent and ardent as I was,' Boswell wrote in his preliminary remarks, 'he might have been almost entirely preserved.' Moreover, he did not intend a panegyric, for Johnson's life, 'great and good as he was, must not be supposed to be entirely perfect'. He would delineate him 'without reserve', with shade as well as light.

His portrait would be of a man who did not have all the answers though he sometimes sounded as if he did. Indeed Boswell himself did not have all the answers about Johnson. His commitment to authenticity and veracity prevented him from finding an explanation for everything and the uncertainty and interrogative mood this creates is very Shakespearean. Boswell often confesses himself baffled by his subject, leaving readers to draw their own conclusions about Johnson's physical eccentricities, unpredictability, psychic and emotional state, unhappiness, roughness, and irrationality. Much of his portrait, in fact, is of a man in the decline of old age, although he does not say so in as many words because that would have worked against his theme of the greatness of Johnson's mind during the time he knew him.[6]

The great link between Johnson and Boswell in the *Life* was provided by Johnson's 'diseased imagination', his morbid melancholy. Ever since his teenage years, when as a university student in Edinburgh he discovered the *Rambler*, Boswell had been fascinated and helped by Johnson's efforts to 'manage' his mind in order to survive. It was clear to him as a boy, and was to become increasingly so over the next twenty-five years, that Johnson was engaged in a heroic struggle to conquer or at least control his melancholy and tendencies to madness. For Boswell, who himself struggled incessantly with hypochondria, this was what made Johnson a sage.[7] The *Life* is a history of 'the progress of his mind', but it is also a record of Boswell's own efforts to be healed by Johnson, to attach and subject himself to his philosophy and personal magnetism in order to manage his own mind. While Johnson quietly tried to suppress and extinguish the foul fiend by cultivating sanity, Boswell talked and wrote about it. Writing the biography was the climax of his painful journey through the metaphoric hell of hypochondria. The *Life* is restlessly full of himself partly because he is using it to define his indefinable self, in the archetypal pattern of a Romantic egotist.

One of the controversies surrounding the *Life* concerns whether or not Boswell has written a biography at all in the modern sense, or at least an accurate one, as he boasted. This is not Johnson at all, but Boswell's Johnson, it is sometimes argued. Mention is made of Boswell's not meeting his mentor until the latter was fifty-four and had risen to eminence. Eighty per cent of the biography is about only the last twenty-two years of Johnson's life. The total number of days on which Boswell saw him amounts to a mere four hundred. How could he really know Johnson or what made him what he was?[8]

It is true that the most important parts of the *Life*, the conversations as well as many anecdotes, are taken from the journals, but where Johnson is concerned the journals are in themselves biographies. The art of biography that Boswell revealed to the world in his *Tour to the Hebrides*, and then in the *Life*, he had been practising ever since he first met Johnson. The journals are rich with biographical experimentation. One of the reasons he considered writing biographies of several people besides Johnson, including Hume, Kames, Reynolds, and Burke, was that he had already written much about them in his journals. As with Johnson, he could easily have rounded up material about them and read their works, but his greatest contribution to biography would have rested in what the journals had to offer by way of insight into their characters. That Boswell used himself in interviews and conversations to uncover truth, not distort it, is evident in the rich detail of countless living moments in the journals on which he drew exhaustively for his *Life* – 'little touches that give life to objects' and enable the reader to 'live o'er each scene'.[9] Indeed, a succession of such 'scenes', through which Johnson will present himself, is exactly what Boswell promises the reader. And the scenes triumph in the *Life* because of what Brady called their 'presentness' or immediacy. Physical detail achieves this. Boswell was the first 'mimetic biographer'.

Are the conversations in the journals, however, 'authentic'? To what extent can we rely on them as accurate transcriptions of what Johnson and others said? As Frederick Pottle has argued, the sophistication in Boswell's manner of remembering and recording dialogue was precisely the source of the unity in the *Life*.[10] His method was to preserve at least the 'heads [topics] and many of the words' of conversations when he did not have time to record them at length. With the help of these and, after he had become '*impregnated with the Johnsonian aether*', an intuitive understanding of Johnson's diction and modes of expression, he was able to turn long conversations with him into 'authentic' reconstructions. This sometimes involved conflating two or more utterances on a single topic or condensing long conversations, but he was always scrupulous about not fabricating material or violating chronology for the sake of artistic unity. As Pottle put it, this meant that while in both the journals and the *Life* Boswell never wrote all of what Johnson said, neither did he write what Johnson did not say. Thus the conversations are imaginative recreations that are faithful both to Johnson's style and sense.

The conversations in the *Life* also defend the work from the charge
that it is essentially a collection of random anecdotes and discourse, or a
mere compilation of a large number of Johnson's letters. A compilation
is not a biography at all, for it has no coherent theme or argument; it
is an anthology of disconnected statements. Boswell's organizational
instincts made certain that the letters did not overwhelm his imagination
or 'vision' of Johnson. Moreover, he chose to include many conversations
because they were about subjects in which he himself was deeply interested, endowing the work with a personal urgency that heightens the
drama of his account of Johnson's life. The *Life* is in effect a double-
drama, a double-plot in which Boswell is a principal player along with
Johnson. He was always his own most interesting subject, but in the *Life*
he used himself to help illuminate his subject. Over and over, just as the
reader begins to think that Boswell has thrown himself intrusively into
the narrative, it is revealed that he is only there to project on to his
biographical screen further images and colours of Johnson's personality
and psyche. It is extraordinary how resourceful he was in bringing himself
on stage in order to achieve this. And he is rarely put off from doing so
simply because a scene makes him the butt of Johnson's anger, sarcasm,
or humour.

3

Boswell was now famous. People recognized him and jumped to their
feet when he entered a room. He was inundated with dinner invitations.
On the recommendation of Sir Joshua, to whom he had dedicated the
Life, he was elected Secretary for Foreign Correspondence of the Royal
Academy, an honour that gave him much pleasure. He was warmly
received by fellow lawyers when he rejoined the Home Circuit in Sussex,
during which he found time to visit Brighton and Portsmouth. 'Though
I did not get a single brief,' he wrote philosophically to Temple, 'do not
repent of the expense as I am showing myself desirous of business and
imbibing legal knowledge.'[11] His money troubles were eased by the success
of his book and, with his new sense of importance, he began to consider
'matrimonial schemes' again. Nothing would come of them, but at last
they engaged some of his energy. He even felt his importance enough to
write his 'Memoirs of James Boswell, Esquire' for the *European Magazine*,
which appeared in May and June. In this he reviewed his life and writings
chronologically, down to his wife's death and the publication of his 'great

literary work . . . which has been received by the world with extraordinary approbation'.

The sensation of freedom after the publication of the *Life* was glorious, but release also meant that he could now drink freely. Friends warned him that it would ruin his health and reawaken hypochondria. He saw much more danger in the spectacle of atrocities against the monarchy in France, over which he worked himself into a frenzy, writing sundry paragraphs and songs for the papers attacking eruptions of British republican support for that 'horrible anarchy'. He joined two right-wing societies to counter the proliferation of pro-French reform societies. His hatred of the French anarchy over the next three years, keeping pace with Temple and Malone's even more furious outrage, at times seemed almost unbalanced.[12]

As long as he remained in London, and kept busy enough, he was able to fool himself that he was as happy as he deserved to be with his literary triumph. But his exhilaration was muted from the start. He relished literary fame, but it had never been his chief objective. Wealth, position and social prestige – all for the aggrandizement of Auchinleck and his venerable family – were what he had wanted most ever since he could remember. He could claim, as he did in the 'Memoir', 'as extensive and varied an acquaintance as any man of his time', but that had brought him little money. Moreover, there was tiredness and the emptiness of anticlimax at his heart's core.

At the end of August 1791, instead of visiting Temple in Cornwall, he returned to Auchinleck for six weeks – his first visit since Margaret's death – where he busied himself with estate matters and local politics. Sandy had preceded him there to do some grouse shooting, but his son's company was not enough to defend Boswell from hypochondria, which suddenly engulfed him. He left for London on 18 October. 'I had a very unhappy time in Ayrshire,' he told Temple on 22 November. 'My house at Auchinleck seemed deserted and melancholy; and it brought upon my mind with increased force the recollection of my having lost my dear and valuable wife.' He also continued to drink heavily. Temple was aghast. 'I feel for you, I pity you, I wish I could suggest any thing to comfort you. Ever dissatisfied, ever repining.'[13]

In London, Boswell threaded himself in and out of 'jovial scenes' but told Temple that he felt 'no pleasure in existence except the mere gratification of the senses. O my friend this is sad.' He kept to his chambers in the Temple and hoped for business, but nothing came. There was also the alarming condition of Reynolds who was tormented by the fear that he might go totally blind. Boswell sat with him in the evenings and tried to cheer him up, at the same time taking 'notes for a Life of Sir Joshua Reynolds', his idea for the next great book. Boswell had had plenty of encouragement from the Academy, which wanted the biography interwoven with a history of the arts during Reynolds's lifetime. The disincentive was Reynolds's character, which 'had not those prominent features which can be seized like Johnson's'. In Boswell's present mental state, even if he had wanted to proceed, not even the encouragement of Malone (who was himself preparing an edition and 'Memoir' of Reynolds) would have been enough to make him start work on it.[14]

Then, in January, a liver ailment caused Reynolds to take to his bed. He avoided his friends, took laudanum, and dozed in 'tranquil despondency'. The thought of his death 'hangs heavy upon my mind', Boswell wrote to Barnard, as it did on Club members like Burke, Courtenay, Malone, and Windham who feared they were about to lose 'the common cement that first united them', not to mention the dearest of friends. On 23 February the dreaded event occurred. 'This sad event damps the spirits much,' Boswell wrote to Sandy a couple of days later. Reynolds was the last of the 'old school'. In Malone's words, he had been a 'point of concentration'. Reynolds's body was carried to St Paul's Cathedral in a magnificent procession, Boswell walking proudly with the Royal Academy members as its Secretary of Foreign Correspondence, not with the Club members. In his will, Reynolds left him £200 with which to purchase one of his paintings as a remembrance.[15]

He compensated for his feeling of purposelessness by drinking too much and socializing in, as he put it, 'a feverish manner'. That in turn drove him to embarrassing buffoonery not especially becoming for a man of his years or for the greatest biographer of his era. An example occurred at the London Tavern on 26 June during the anniversary celebration of Alderman William Curtis's election to Parliament. In front of 250 distinguished guests, Boswell mounted a chair and repeated his song for the occasion several times, following it with a political harangue which had to be cut unceremoniously short by the chairman for the evening. In the *St James's Chronicle* for 26–8 June, under the heading 'Notoriety', he read:

> Nothing, says a literary friend, can be a stronger evidence of the force of this passion than that a man of real wit, learning, and genius, endowed with qualities to ensure him the respect of the wise and the worthy, should court

popularity by what might be almost called gross buffoonery at a City feast.

What would Dr Johnson have thought? the author asked. Boswell must have flinched. He was even more ashamed when Sandy wrote from Eton asking if he had seen the notice. There were further squibs against his performance in other newspapers, most of them politically motivated. For his poetical-political songs at celebrative dinners, the *Oracle* mockingly dubbed him the 'City Poet'. He had one defender, however, in the *World*: 'No man is honoured with more abuse than JEMMY BOSWELL – and no man, to do him justice, seems to value it less. He would not give an *old Sang* for all *they can say*.' In a limited sense, this writer was correct: Boswell still saw such attention as excellent publicity for his book.[16]

By February, it was clear that a second edition of the *Life* was called for. With all the suggestions and complaints he had received since publication, he had a good deal to change; and there were many more letters to add. Malone helped him as usual, and Baldwin began the printing in April as Boswell fed him copy. But this work was too insubstantial to sustain a positive mood, and he became restless to travel, to escape from the city. In early spring he played with the idea of accompanying the distinguished diplomat and member of the Club, Lord Macartney, who had recently been appointed Ambassador to China, to Peking. Temple was horrorstruck: 'At our time of life the climate would kill you either there or here.' In the spring he thought of visiting Barnard in Dublin, but decided against it. 'I had prepared you a good reception when you came among us,' Barnard chided him, 'and you would have met it, I can assure you.' On 21 June, having been chosen to serve on the London Committee of the Margate General Sea-bathing Infirmary, he ventured to the seaside town on the Kent coast for two or three days to attend the opening ceremonies. On 25 June he gave a dinner and musical party for Veronica to which he invited Franz Joseph Haydn, who had been in London since January 1791 and was about to return to Vienna. Unfortunately, he recorded nothing of this in his journal.[17]

He also travelled to Australia and the South Seas, even if only in his imagination. In 1788 William Bryant, a Cornish fisherman convicted of smuggling, had been transported to Botany Bay, Australia. On 28 March 1791 Bryant, Mary Broad, the woman he married there, their two young children, and seven convicts (all of whom had committed petty crimes) escaped and launched themselves on a daring ten-week, 3,000-mile journey to the island of Timor in a small boat with one sail and six oars.

Miraculously, they arrived safely but were later captured on the island and sent back to England. Bryant, his two children, and several of the convicts died on the return voyage. Mary Broad and the rest of the convicts survived the journey and were committed to Newgate, though they might easily have been hanged for escaping transportation. Their story was published in the *London Chronicle* and immediately caught the public's imagination. In the spirit of the old days when he went to such lengths on behalf of unfortunate criminals like John Reid, Boswell rushed to help them. He requested an interview with Dundas, now Home Secretary, which Dundas did not keep. He wrote again, pleading that they be pardoned. He also raised money for Mary. She was pardoned eventually, though the convicts remained in prison where on one occasion Boswell interviewed them after taking tea (with echoes of *The Beggar's Opera*) in the company of the new keeper, his wife, and other ladies: 'It was a curious thought that I was in *Newgate*; for the room was handsome and everything in good order as in the drawing-room of any good middle-rank family in any part of London.' Probably due to a petition he drafted to the Under-Secretary of State for the Home Department on 14 May 1793 the prisoners were released without being prosecuted for escaping when their first term expired in November.[18]

4

Temple had been urging Boswell to come to Cornwall during the summer of 1792. It was a long overdue trip. At last he set off with Veronica and Euphemia on 17 August, taking a new journal in which to record the six weeks he was away. 'I find I *journalize* too tediously. Let me try to abbreviate,' he wrote on the 20th, but he kept it up. They made their way to Wilton House, his first visit since 1775, and he again hit it off well with Lord Pembroke: 'I was delighted to find him walking about with me familiarly arm in arm and chatting freely as formerly.' He apologized to Pembroke that his daughters, deprived of Margaret's influence, had not grown into 'fine ladies', but his lordship thought that was all to the good and gave them a splendid dinner that evening:

> it was truly a *sight* to me ... to behold *my daughters Veronica and Euphemia* sitting with the Earl of Pembroke in his immense drawing-room, under the family picture by Van Dyck, undoubtedly the most capital work in portrait-painting that the world has to show. How many *Scotch lairds* are there whose

daughters could have such an honour? They behaved very well.

In spite of Pembroke's pressing, they could not stay even for the night and left soon after dinner.[19]

Arriving at Temple's vicarage of St Gluvias on the 24th, Boswell was pleasantly surprised to find it less provincial than he expected, 'prettily situated on a bank which my friend had dressed and planted with real taste'. They embraced on the spot, the young people got acquainted, and they all settled down to a few weeks of pleasant rural pastimes and excursions. The two fathers had a fine time, congratulating themselves on their 'friendship being now the same as ever', meeting the locals who were thrilled to see 'the *great Boswell*', and looking over Temple's huge collection of Boswell's letters since 1758. They agreed that it was 'wonderful' how he had made himself into 'the man I was, considering the extreme narrowness of my education; for he remembered me the most puritanical being, and the most timid in society . . .' And they chuckled over how he had pulled the wool over the eyes of so many, 'displaying extraordinary symptoms of learning and knowledge, when I had read so little in a regular way' – although, to be fair to himself, he observed that he did know many books and, like Johnson, had the knack of 'quickly seizing a general notion from perusing a small part'.[20]

With the ladies it was a different story. Before Boswell left London, Temple had warned him of his wife's temper – 'years do not improve it'. Even so, Boswell was taken aback by her peevishness. 'I was glad to turn my back on Mrs Temple,' he wrote at the end of his stay. Boswell seemed to think the girls got on famously, but Nancy Temple, who still harboured a dislike for Veronica and her impetuosity, now added an antipathy for Euphemia. She wrote to a friend: 'These girls are so boisterous and unpleasant that I think the strongest nerves would feel a shock from being with them.' It is hard to credit it, given the girls' rural life at Auchinleck, but Nancy made them out to be ridiculous, frivolous, delicate, blubbering, and trembling city girls, frightened of horses, the water, hiking, and whatever else might be lurking around the next hedge. She may have been influenced by her mother's views of the Boswells, especially of the 'great biographer' who was certainly 'a curious genius':

> He is perpetually falling in love, as he calls it, and then he can do nothing but talk of the angelic creature. In a man of more than fifty such behaviour is folly. In short, I am truly weary of them all, and if the truth were known, I believe they are full as weary of this (to them) stupid place.[21]

The Boswells left on the 11th, Temple accompanying them on a Cornish jaunt for several days. It had been a 'wonderful tour', Boswell wrote to Malone from Port Eliot on the 16th, though 'when I say *wonderful* I am not boasting of *happiness*. Would to God I were safe in London! which I hope to be on Saturday the 29th.'[22]

5

He scarcely had time to unpack once back in London, for on 1 October he sped off on the Home Circuit, on which as usual his expenses exceeded his income. At Chelmsford the black mood swallowed him up – 'my wretched hypochondria still continued,' he wrote on 10 December, 'I having never yet since 4 October at Chelmsford, when this fit began, had any fair remission.' This protracted attack, coupled with yet another unsuccessful Circuit, was the beginning of the end of his lingering delusion that one day he would succeed as a London barrister. It was an ugly realization because he had given up so much for it and an English legal career was his only remaining hope that he could one day earn good money, live well, and hold his head up in a wider London society than he presently enjoyed. In November, to save forty pounds per year, Boswell reluctantly gave up his chambers at the Temple, rationalizing that he would still cut enough of a figure of a lawyer as 'was consistent with ... a gentleman of estate and extensive acquaintance – and an author'. At Westminster Hall he shrank more than ever from the 'brisk and hearty salutations of some of my brother barristers' and was 'fretted' by seeing them all with briefs in their hands while he had little prospect of any. Malone reminded him of the truth he always ducked, that his character had forced him to choose the wider path of authorship and that this should be 'enough' for him.[23]

In late February 1793, he escaped to Auchinleck. His 'serious duty' was to see to the appointment of a new parish minister to replace the Rev. John Dun who had died the previous September. While there he flirted again to no effect with Wilhelmina Alexander and briefly recovered his health and spirits. He also visited Edinburgh for ten days, for the first time since moving to London in 1786. But otherwise it was a hollow homecoming, especially without the children. Back in London by 8 April, he complained that he no longer had a taste for the theatre, a telling hint that he was losing his relish for life in general. One night in June, he was mugged in Titchfield Street. According to a report in the

London Chronicle, he was 'knocked down, robbed, and left lying in the street quite stunned ... [with] a severe cut on the back of his head and a contusion on both his arms'. He was drunk at the time. A passer-by helped him home where for several days he was confined to bed with a fever. It was weeks before he could write again. In mid-July after another fruitless Circuit to Chelmsford, he dropped in at Warley Camp where Langton, serving as Major in the Royal North Lincolnshire Militia, promised to spread out sheets in the hot sun on which he could lie to convalesce from his wounds. After one sleepless night in a tent where he caught cold, he beat a hasty retreat to London, sicker than when he had left it.[24]

Nine months of hypochondria and vexation later, in September 1793, Temple whose wife had tragically died in March after an illness of three weeks, came to visit him with his son whom he was placing at Eton. The sight of him 'soothed my weary soul', Boswell wrote on 14 September, but it made no difference to his mental health. If anything, Temple's pitying and well-meaning presence brought his frustrations to the surface:

> My uneasiness of mind continued. Temple saw how unhappy I was, both from increased irritability and from finding myself disappointed in all my high views of rising in life and having no occupation, nor even any reasonable prospect of obtaining promotion ... Yet my friend, upon considering my unhappy constitution and long habits, thought that I must continue on, living with economy and hoping that something good might happen to me.

That was Malone's advice, too. What else could they say? They knew that his permanent return to Auchinleck now would probably kill him. Scurvy, innumerable colds, constant nervousness, and other ailments, had been undermining his health for months. Joseph Farington saw him on 6 October and wrote in his diary, 'Met Boswell, who, I think, is much altered for the worse in appearance.'[25]

Temple observed that Boswell's temper had dramatically deteriorated, epitomized by constant quarrels with his contradictory daughters: 'He saw that they did not treat me with the respect due to a parent. But he imputed this to the unsteadiness of my behaviour ...' Rebelliously, they went out too often unsupervised and brought a constant stream of friends through the house in the evening without asking him first. It also hurt that they scarcely observed their 'religious duties', made no effort to cultivate English pronunciation, and associated with 'Scotch people who could do them no credit'. They were, in short, out of control. But then so was Boswell's own life. 'I was in truth in a woeful state of depression in every respect ... Temple kindly said that he found me more wretched than he could have imagined; that he thought if I retired to Scotland, there was danger that I would sink into deep melancholy, or take to hard drinking.' It was best to steer the present course and be on the lookout for unexpected blessings, like the love and money of a good woman.[26]

A sense of inevitability crept into his journal in 1793: that London had nothing new to offer him; that he would never again live at Auchinleck, certainly not as a Lord of Session; that he would not write anything more of significance – though he gave some thought to publishing the journals of his Continental travels; and that his future days would follow each other monotonously, tolling like a muffled bell, heralding nothing and leading nowhere. The 'most beautiful prospects and all other circumstances of enjoyment when a man is well in body and mind, avail nothing'. He also began to imagine he was falling into ill-health.[27]

The most humiliating blow of all was Dundas's rejection of his application for a diplomatic appointment in Corsica, as a Minister or Commissioner to help work with Paoli on some sort of annexation of the island to Britain. He had written to Dundas on 17 March 1794: 'My knowledge of Corsica, and my having been the first man by whose means authentic information was obtained, my long and continued intimacy with General Paoli ... seems, I cannot help thinking, to have such weight as almost to preclude competition.' Dundas did not see it that way. Britain did not need a new Minister, he replied. 'It hurt me to think that Dundas, after his apparently cordial professions, was minded to neglect me totally,' Boswell noted in his journal.[28]

6

The one bright spot was the *Life*. After settling several debts, including those to Dilly and Baldwin and what was due on his purchase of Knockroon, he had earned £608 from the book by November 1792. And it was still selling. Now he planned a three-volume second edition. The first two volumes were put to the press so speedily 'in order to supply the public demand' that additional letters of Johnson's (notably thirteen to Langton) had to be tucked in awkwardly at the beginning of the first and end of the second volumes, making the pagination both chaotic and confusing.

Asked to prepare an Advertisement for the new edition, he added five more paragraphs of self-flattery, the last of which harked back to the memorable conversation he had had with the King in May 1785.

It is impossible for me an enthusiastic *Tory*, not to tell the world what I feel, and shall express with that reverential fondness which characterises a true royalist. Soon after the death of my illustrious friend, HIS MAJESTY one day at the levee, after observing that he believed Dr Johnson was so good a man as ever lived; was graciously pleased to say to me, 'There will be many lives of Dr Johnson: do you give the best.' I flatter myself that I have obeyed my SOVEREIGN'S commands.

Malone discovered these additions only by accident at the printer's in May. He exploded and wrote angrily to Boswell:

You have an undoubted right over your own reputation, and to expose yourself in any way you think proper; but you certainly have no right whatsoever over the reputation of others. If therefore you should persevere in printing the wild Rhodomontade which by accident I yesterday saw at the press ... I entreat, not as a favour, but a *right*, that you would cancel whatever relates to me in the former Advertisement ... You cannot degrade yourself without injuring at the same time the characters of those whom you mention as your friends. Poor Sir Joshua is in his grave, and *nothing can touch him further*, otherwise he could not but blush, that his name should appear at the head of a dedication, followed by such an Advertisement.

He added that he had no desire to be 'pilloried' in public with him.[29]

Boswell disagreed, 'for surely every man is at liberty to put himself forward in the style he likes best and his praise of his friends in a very different style must not be confounded with his own personal Rhodomontade'. But he was willing to consult Courtenay and Douglas, who evidently also advised him to drop the paragraph about the King. It did not appear in the new edition. Malone also wanted him to delete the other four paragraphs, but Boswell defiantly refused. He even added, unknown to Malone, a defence of his literary persona, including this sentence, 'I confess, that I am so formed by nature and by habit, that to restrain the effusion of delight, on having obtained such fame, to me would be truly painful. Why then should I suppress it?' Malone remembered this contretemps poignantly in 1798: 'I expressed myself so strongly, that for the only time I think in the whole course of our acquaintance, he lost his good humour. Of course I gave the matter up.'[30]

Two years after the first, the second edition was published on 17 July 1793. Shortly afterwards appeared *The Principal Corrections and Additions to the First Edition*. It was the last pamphlet or book Boswell ever published. The third or 'definitive' edition would not appear until after his death, when brought to press in 1799 by Malone who with great labour rearranged the text into a seamless chronology in a manner of which Boswell presumably would have approved, added the Johnson letters that had continued to trickle in, and made corrections that were drawn to his attention. His judgement was a model of tact and modesty. He continued to add, correct, and refine until 1811, when he brought out the sixth edition the year before he died. It could be argued that one of the reasons Malone never completed his own monumental Variorum edition of Shakespeare was because of the time and energy he devoted to the *Life of Johnson*. With a beautiful appropriateness and justice, it fell to young Jamie Boswell to bring Malone's edition to press in 1821.

Four hundred copies of the second edition were sold in one week. It earned Boswell a further £1,000, raising the total from the two editions to about £2,500, a huge sum given the size of the contemporary market.

7

Boswell's labours on the second edition created a temporary oasis of industry in the desert that London had become to him. 'I reflected how sadly London was changed to me of late,' he wrote on 10 August, 'no General Paoli – no Sir Joshua Reynolds – no Sir John Pringle – no Squire Godfrey Bosville – no General Oglethorpe.' He still found his 'theatrical taste gone', except for *The Beggar's Opera* which continued to 'animate' him, and he was made wretched by a 'total want of relish for literature'. As if that were not enough, Euphemia began to cough in a manner ominously like his wife's 'dismal disease'. The chaos in France demoralized and worried him as it did much of the country – the 'horrible murder of the Queen of France' was reported in late October – but he was struck by a more personal horror when he heard that Andrew Erskine, one of his oldest friends, had killed himself. One December night Boswell 'sallied out foolishly into the street' drunk, broke into a run and injured his elbow when he slipped on the mire on the pavement. He also became again a regular participant in the grosser pleasures of the city's underworld.[31]

There were none the less a few genteel comforts remaining – the occasional dinner out, Malone, the Club (though 'it was not as in the days of Johnson'), Dilly and Baldwin, Wilkes, T.D., the Royal Academy, and Farington. In the Academy's deliberations on how to celebrate its twenty-fifth anniversary, Boswell gave a speech which received 'so much applause that it vexed me to think I could not have an opportunity of being heard in the courts in Westminster Hall'.[32] His greatest comfort was young Jamie, who was growing into the apple of his father's eye even as the two older girls increasingly perturbed him. Whenever Jamie was home from Westminster School, which was too often owing to his fragile health, they played at draughts (sometimes the whole day), attended plays, and generally delighted in each other's company. Boswell played the part well of the supportive father for both his boys at school events, but he worried about Jamie to an excessive degree. Jamie worried about his father too, encouraging and advising him in his now constant and desperate struggle against depression and aimlessness.

The winter and spring months of 1793–4 rolled by uneventfully and deadeningly. Fed up with Boswell's droning discontent, in February Malone gave him a brisk lecture on gratitude: he should not forget he was educating his children 'in a most laudable manner', he was not as poor as he thought, and he had enough money at least to give ten dinners a year to his friends. He also enjoyed literary fame. What more did life have to offer? Boswell took heart momentarily: if he raised the rents in Ayrshire by one-third, he could see out his days as 'no unworthy *Laird*'. He continued to sustain a remarkable level of interest in Auchinleck affairs, if his frequent letters to Andrew Gibb are any clue. But that he was clearly running down is borne out by his neglect of his journal. 'I have lost the faculty of recording conversations,' he wrote in March 1794, and in April he stopped writing the journal altogether. If, as he said when he began to keep a journal, he would not wish to live any more of life than he could record, then the end of the journal was a subconscious signal to himself that he had little relish left for living. He thought himself a failure. 'I will try to avoid repining,' he confided in Jamie, 'yet at the same time, I cannot be contented merely with literary fame...'[33]

At the end of June, he left London for Auchinleck with Veronica and Euphemia, leaving Jamie and Elizabeth at their schools in London. He did not want the expense of taking the older girls with him but Jamie encouraged him to do so because they were more likely to attract husbands in their own country and should therefore be 'properly established'. During the six months he spent there he wrote every week to Jamie. The letters took the place of his journal and related his innermost thoughts to the fifteen-year-old boy. They were tender and honest, and Jamie, rising to the occasion, was every inch the man in returning succour to his father. The letters may be taken as Boswell's written farewell to his feverish life.

8

Affecting a superiority now that they were Londoners, the girls at first looked down their noses at the 'naked and wild' country, the provinciality of the scene, but within a few days they had reconciled themselves to Auchinleck and behaved better. They rode the little piebald pony to their heart's content and made raspberry and strawberry preserves and blackcurrant jelly. As for their father, the Auchinleck air and scene were a tonic. There were estate affairs to see to with Gibb and country pleasures without the burden of heavy entertaining. His spirits were 'wonderfully good'. After Jamie replied advising him to relax and to accept the girls as they were for the time being, Boswell wrote back to him gratefully, taking on the persona of the dependant in need of counsel. Jamie's advice was just what he needed, he told his son:

> you will be glad to know that I act in conformity to it in a degree far beyond what I expected I could do. I now and then have broke forth a little, but I assure you not often and by no means with that violence which you have observed in London. I have not drunk half a bottle of wine any day since I came here.

Sandy, who had been studying law in Edinburgh during the winter and had now joined them, was a fresh cause for concern with his 'familiarity of manner and a very broad pronunciation' from too much contact with his 'inferiors'. But Boswell hoped that reading Greek and Latin with him every day would remind him who he was.[34]

As always, however, the quiet and boredom of Auchinleck wore him down. 'I have very little inclination to visit, and to tell you the truth, am heartily weary,' he wrote to Jamie on 30 July. Although he took pleasure in being kind to his tenants, he became idle and listless. By September, he was doing virtually no reading, stagnating with 'a kind of deadness as to all intellectual pursuits'. Jamie recommended that he think of a 'Lord of Sessionship' and stay at Auchinleck at last until after Christmas, which he promised to do, but there was no way around his 'long-continued and rooted way of thinking':

> I must be as long at Auchinleck as I can, and do the estate and the people as much good as may be in my power. But truly the manners of England and the infinite variety of acquaintance and of important objects in the metropolis give me such a gratification that I may at least say that 'the load of life', as Johnson calls it ... is three-fourths lighter to me [there].

Lord Eglinton named him as one of his deputies as Lord Lieutenant of Ayrshire, but Boswell declined to accept any appointment under a man 'of whom I have a sorry opinion', and in any case there was little distinction in the offer. 'I never was in a more stupid state of mind,' he told Jamie in October.[35]

Alone in London, Jamie knew exactly what his father was going through and touchingly did his best to help. On 18 October he pleaded, 'Pray, Sir, do not suffer yourself to be melancholy.' He should consider that his lifestyle had never been compatible with 'a man of business' and that all those who obtained places and pensions 'have not the fame of having been the biographer of Johnson or the conscious exultation of a man of genius. They have not your happy and convivial hours.' Would he have enjoyed the company of the likes of Johnson, Voltaire, Rousseau, Garrick, and Goldsmith if he had been 'a rich, though dull, plodding lawyer'? 'You cannot expect to be both at the same time. Every situation in life has its advantages and disadvantages.'[36] Remarkable advice from a fifteen-year-old.

In his reply Boswell acknowledged that his son 'reasonest well' but went on to construct a coda on his life's frustrations, an outburst of protest against the pack of cards that had been dealt him. At the root of his disappointment was that all his 'fond' hopes of raising himself and his family through some kind of preferment had come to nothing, but most of all his 'constitutional melancholy' ever lurking about him to which 'perhaps I should impute ... the chief part of my unhappiness'. Add to that his dislike of rural life, irreconcilable with his lairdship of a Scottish estate, and in retrospect it seemed to him there was never any way his life could have turned out happily.[37]

Jamie sprang to the challenge of this bleak recapitulation. Did Boswell really want to be like Dr Warren rising in the middle of the night to visit a patient, or like Lord Mansfield going to bed at night with a stack of papers at his bedside? Did he really envy these people their money –

'such is the life that must be led by those who acquire money'. As for the hypochondria, there was no denying it:

> But who so merry and gay as you in company, though at times gloomy at home? Why may it not be so their happiness may be as much put on as yours is? I have since your absence been pretty frequently at my uncle's and I know that he (for one) is very far from being happy ... With such a share of felicity as you have now, and have had, I see no reason why you should be discontented.

Read something, Jamie advised, or write a play – how about *The Pawnbroker* or *The Improver* (two of Boswell's projects)? Most important, 'don't give way to your melancholy but drive it off; there are a thousand ways'.[38]

For all his Boethian consolatory philosophy, Jamie naturally did not have much insight into hypochondria. He had never suffered from it. Still, Boswell loved his youngest son for his help. Here was comfort indeed in these dark months. Temple warned him not to indulge 'your favourite Jimmy' too much – 'few natures will bear it' – but there was no risk of that.

To reverse his deepening depression as autumn passed and to give the girls more society, Boswell took to inviting many guests to Auchinleck. This increased turbulence only depressed him the more. In December, he struck off a few verses, 'Pathetic Song', which include the lines,

> 'Tis o'er, 'tis o'er, the dream is o'er,
> And Life's delusion is no more.

His gloss on the verses was, 'The subject must be the gay hopes indulged in youth, and the apathy which years and disappointment produce.' Once he had seen the last of the guests, and Sandy and the girls had returned to Edinburgh – Sandy to study and the girls to visit Lady Auchinleck – he recovered. He ate his Christmas dinner quietly, alone in the big house, happier than he had been for months.[39]

9

Having 'weathered' it out at Auchinleck for six months, he returned to London. The good mood he had recovered at Christmas carried him down through a freezing England and into the metropolis, where he threw himself with abandon into what life still had to offer him there. He drank heavily, seemingly without a thought for the morrow, agitated by the '*intellectual* luxury of London' after his long absence. He gave several jubilant dinners for his friends and family that lasted well into the morning.

His bold mood persisted until April. 'What a varied life do I lead!' he announced to Sandy. He drank so much wine and brandy that it became common gossip. After one particularly boisterous night with his daughters at the home of Charlotte Ann Francis, Fanny Burney's youngest sister, Miss Francis wrote in her journal:

> We left the gentlemen a quarter before eight and they were so merry and jovial that we could not get them up till past ten . . . Boswell [was] indisputably drunk. He hauled Veronica out of her seat that he might sit and have a quarter of an hour by Mrs Frances, he said. He began by attempting to make love to me, but I was so grave that happily the love-fit wore off.

His last service on behalf of Johnson was to write to Malone rejecting the pompous Dr Samuel Parr's demand that his epitaph for the Johnson monument to be erected at St Paul's be accepted without criticism from the Club: 'We are answerable to the memory of our illustrious friend, to the present age, and to posterity.'[40]

The next day, 14 April, at a meeting of the Club, Boswell was suddenly taken ill with a fever, severe shivering, violent headache, and a disordered stomach. After three weeks of acute suffering from progressive kidney failure and uraemia, on 8 May he dictated a letter to Jamie for Temple, unaware of the seriousness of his condition: 'The pain, which continued for so many weeks, was very severe indeed, and when it went off, I thought myself quite well, but I soon felt a conviction that I was by no means as I should be, being so excessively weak as my miserable attempt to write to you afforded a full proof.' Unknown to his father, Jamie enclosed a note to Temple: 'You will find by the foregoing, the whole of which was dictated to me by my father, that he is ignorant of the dangerous situation in which he was, and I am sorry to say still continues to be.' A week later Boswell was much the same. Then, on the 18th, when he asked to be lifted out of bed he fainted. Jamie wrote to Temple that there was little or no hope of recovery. Dr James Earle, the surgeon from St Bartholomew's Hospital, could do nothing for him. By the following day Boswell was dead. T.D. informed Temple: 'My dear brother expired this morning at two o'clock; we have both lost a kind, affectionate

friend, and I shall never have such another. He has suffered a great deal
during his illness, which has lasted five weeks, but not much in his last
moments ... He is to be buried at Auchinleck, for which place his sons
will set out in two or three days.' All the children behaved in 'the most
affectionate, exemplary manner' during his illness.[41]

Suddenly, Boswell's life had closed behind his journal. All his friends
were caught by surprise. Malone wrote most movingly about the loss felt
by the remaining Johnsonians in a letter to Windham two days later:

> I shall miss him more and more every day. He was in the constant habit of
> calling upon me almost daily, and I used to grumble sometimes at his
> turbulence, but now miss and regret his noise and his hilarity and his
> perpetual good humour, which had no bounds. Poor fellow, he has somehow
> stolen away from us, without any notice, and without my being at all prepared
> for it.

Barnard, Boswell's spiritual father, wrote to Forbes that when they had
last parted, in 1793, he had had forebodings they would never meet again.
He was in no doubt that Boswell would go to heaven, for 'his Principles
were those of a Christian, and *not lightly* taken up'. Boswell was buried
in the family vault at Auchinleck on 8 June, finally at rest in a place
where all his adult life it was his fate to be restless.[42]

Epilogue: The Children

Boswell left his family vulnerable. Malone came to the rescue, immediately taking on the responsibility of acting as the children's guardian. 'We shall never forget Mr Malone's kindness to us,' Euphemia wrote to Forbes a few weeks after her father's death, 'he has given us much good advice and that in the most pleasing manner.' Tragically, Veronica, who had nursed her father in his last illness, died four months later aged 22. Sandy was of the opinion that the fatigue of caring for her father proved to be too much – 'her affection exceeded her strength' – but the real reason was the sudden overpowering by consumption. After that, Euphemia, who was no longer at school and had no occupation, was most in need of Malone's assistance. In later years, she became an embarrassment to her father's friends, but in those early months after Veronica's death, Malone sorted out her finances and found her somewhere to live. She died unmarried in 1837.

Sandy inherited Auchinleck and his father's considerable debts. He married and proved to be a worthy landowner, proud of his father's literary achievements. He was elected a Member of Parliament, a fact over which his father would have rejoiced without ceasing. In 1821 he received a baronetcy. Ironically, in 1822, he was accidentally killed in a duel, the very fate his father dreaded and was so artful in avoiding. He was heavily in debt when he died. Elizabeth remained at school and later married against her elder brother's wishes. She died in 1814, estranged from her family. Jamie, who also never married, became a dear friend to Malone, almost a son, a scholar in his own right who spent the nine years following Malone's death in 1812 turning his incomplete enlarged edition of Shakespeare into the triumphant twenty-one-volume third Variorum edition (1821). His father would have been immensely proud of him. Like his brother, he died in 1822 and also in debt.

Acknowledgements

Any biographer of Boswell after Frederick A. Pottle and Frank Brady is deeply indebted to them for their exhaustive research and long years of immersion in the Yale Papers that bore such rich fruit in their own works. Moreover, the published Yale Boswell Papers, consisting of the Trade Editions of the journals (now complete in thirteen volumes) and the series of Research Editions of the correspondence and other documents that continue to appear, offering a wealth of annotations and insightful introductions, have made available a vast resource on which I have drawn freely. I am also indebted to the Yale Boswell Office at Yale University for helpful advice and assistance on several visits over the past few years, especially to Irene Adams and the chief editor of the Boswell Papers, Gordon Turnbull, who has made available to me edited and annotated material for the Research Editions, only part of which has yet been published. Their guidance has been a model of generosity. Irma Lustig and Thomas Crawford have kindly sent my way numerous publications of theirs that have helped me sort out knotty problems. And Thomas Crawford and Heather Barkley have generously let me use their typescript for the second Yale Research Edition volume of the Temple–Boswell correspondence in advance of its publication.

I would also like to acknowledge the helpfulness of the staffs at the Beinecke Rare Book and Manuscript Library at Yale, the Bodleian Library in Oxford, the British Library, the National Library of Scotland, the Pierpoint Morgan Library, and the John Rylands Library (Manchester University), as well as their permission to quote from their collections. To Viscountess (Mary Hyde) Eccles, I am especially grateful for permission to quote from the Hyde Collection, U.S.A. For permission to draw upon copyright texts and editions, I am grateful to Yale University Press, McGraw-Hill, Heinemann, Cambridge University Press, Oxford University Press, Weidenfeld & Nicolson, and University of Kentucky

Press. At Weidenfeld & Nicolson, Ion Trewin, Rebecca Wilson and Catherine Hill have provided encouragement and skilful practical help, as has the copy editor, Jane Birkett. Henry Hamlin also helped me with some photographic work as have Ned and Paula Bradley with some translations. For permission to publish certain illustrations, I should like to thank the Hyde Collection, U.S.A., National Portrait Gallery, the Scottish National Portrait Gallery, the British Museum, the British Library, the Museum of London, Dr Johnson's House in London, the Historic Scottish Buildings Trust, the Mellon Collection, Yale Center for British Art, and the New York Public Library. I am also grateful to Principia College for funds from the Faculty Development Fund to pay for illustrations.

From Andrew and Claire's sense of fun and purposefulness I have drawn much resolution. And finally, as usual, my wife Cynthia has always been there warmly, in the midst of her own busy work and study, to talk about Boswell and literature in general.

Note on quotations: For the sake of clarity, in many cases I have used modern spelling, punctuation, and capitalization in prose quotations. This is the method adopted in the Trade Editions of Boswell's journals, and it seems the best policy for this book, too. There are exceptions in the correspondence and only when the personality of the particular writer or the character of a document is blurred by doing so. Poetry is quoted as it was originally written or published.

Abbreviations

MANUSCRIPT SOURCES

BM: British Museum

Bodleian: Bodleian Library, Oxford University

BP: Private Papers of James Boswell, Beinecke Rare Book and Manuscript Library, Yale University

Hyde Collection: the Hyde collection of books and manuscripts at Four Oaks Farm, Somerville, New Jersey

NLS: National Library of Scotland

PML: Pierpont Morgan Library, New York

Rylands: John Rylands Library, University of Manchester

WRITINGS BY BOSWELL

(1) Books and miscellaneous

Account: Boswell's *An Account of Corsica, The Journal of a Tour to that Island; and Memoirs of Pascal Paoli*, 1768; Part II published in *GT(ii)*, pp. 156–216

Boswelliana: *Boswelliana: The Commonplace Book of James Boswell*, ed. Rev. Charles Rogers, LL.D., 1874

Column: *Boswell's Column 1777–1783* (70 'Hypochondriack' essays in *London Magazine* 1777–83), ed. Margery Bailey, 1951

Douce Poems: Boswell's manuscript poems, Bodleian Library, MS. Douce 193, ed. Jack Werner in *Boswell's Book of Bad Verse*, 1974

Life of Johnson: *Boswell's Life of Johnson*, eds. G. B. Hill and L. F. Powell, 1934

'Memoirs': 'Memoirs of James Boswell, Esq.', in *European Magazine* and *London Review*, May 1791

'Sketch': 'Sketch of the Early Life of James Boswell, Written by Himself for Jean-Jacques Rousseau, 5 December 1674' (pub. in *Earlier Years*, pp. 1–6; rough drafts and outlines of the final version are in BP: L1109–L1112)

Tour: *The Journal of a Tour to the Hebrides, with Samuel Johnson, LL.D.*, 1785, eds. G. B. Hill and L. F. Powell, in *Boswell's Life of Johnson*, vol. V (2nd edn, 1964)

Waingrow: *James Boswell's 'Life of Johnson': An Edition of the Original Manuscript in Four Volumes*, vol. I: 1709–65, ed. Marshall Waingrow, 1994

(2) Journals

Applause: Boswell: The Applause of the Jury 1782–1785, eds. Irma S. Lustig and Frederick A. Pottle, 1981

Defence: Boswell for the Defence 1769–1774, eds. William K. Wimsatt, Jr., and Frederick A. Pottle, New York 1959, London 1960

Experiment: Boswell: The English Experiment 1785–1789, eds. Irma S. Lustig and Frederick A. Pottle, 1986

Extremes: Boswell in Extremes 1776–1778, eds. Charles McC. Weis and Frederick A. Pottle, 1970

Great Biographer: Boswell: The Great Biographer 1789–1795, eds. Marlies K. Danziger and Frank Brady, 1989

GT(i): Boswell on the Grand Tour: Germany and Switzerland 1764, ed. Frederick A. Pottle, 1953

GT(ii): Boswell on the Grand Tour: Italy, Corsica, and France 1765–1766, eds. Frank Brady and Frederick A. Pottle, 1955

'Harvest Journal': 'Journal of My Jaunt, Harvest 1762' in deluxe edn. of *London Journal*, ed. Frederick A. Pottle, 1951

Hebrides Journal: Boswell's Journal of a Tour to the Hebrides with Samuel Johnson, LL.D., 1773, eds. Frederick A. Pottle and Charles H. Bennett, 1961

Holland: Boswell in Holland 1763–1764, ed. Frederick A. Pottle, 1952

Laird: Boswell: Laird of Auchinleck 1778–1782, eds. Joseph W. Reed and Frederick A. Pottle, 1977; rpt Edinburgh University Press 1993

London Journal: Boswell's London Journal 1762–1763, ed. Frederick A. Pottle, New York, 1950, London 1951

Ominous: Boswell: The Ominous Years 1774–1776, eds. Charles Ryskamp and Frederick A. Pottle, 1963

Wife: Boswell in Search of a Wife 1766–1769, eds. Frank Brady and Frederick A. Pottle, 1956

(3) Letters

E-B: Letters Between the Honourable Andrew Erskine and James Boswell, Esq., 1763

GBM: The Correspondence of James Boswell with David Garrick, Edmund Burke, and Edmond Malone, ed. Thomas W. Copeland, Peter S. Baker, Rachel McClellan, George M. Kahrl, James M. Osborn, et al., 1986 (includes a definitive introduction on Burke and Boswell by Frank Brady)

Gen. Corr. (i): The General Correspondence of James Boswell 1766–1769, vol. I: 1766–7, eds. Richard C. Cole, with Peter S. Baker and Rachel McClellan, etc., 1993

Gen. Corr. (ii): The General Correspondence of James Boswell 1766–1769, vol. II: 1768–9, eds. Richard C. Cole, with Peter S. Baker and Rachel McClellan, and with the assistance of James J. Caudel, 1997

Grange: The Correspondence of James Boswell and John Johnston of Grange, ed. Ralph S. Walker, 1966

Letters: The Letters of James Boswell, ed. Chauncey B. Tinker, 2 vols, 1924

Making of the 'Life': The Correspondence and Other Papers of James Boswell Relating to the Making of the 'Life of Johnson', ed. Marshall Waingrow, 1969

Members: The Correspondence of James Boswell with Certain Members of the Club, ed. Charles N. Fifer, 1976

Temple: The Correspondence of James Boswell and William Johnson Temple 1756–1795, vol. I: 1756–77, ed. Thomas Crawford, 1997

SECONDARY WORKS

Burney Diary: *Diary and Letters of Madame D'Arblay*, 6 vols, ed. Charlotte Barrett, with Preface and Notes by Austin Dobson, 1904–5

Citizen: *Boswell: Citizen of the World, Man of Letters*, ed. Irma S. Lustig, 1995

Clifford, *Piozzi*: James L. Clifford, *Hester Lynch Piozzi (Mrs Thrale)*, 1941

Earlier Years: Frederick A. Pottle, *James Boswell: The Earlier Years 1740–1769*, 1966

Impossible Friendship: Mary Hyde, *The Impossible Friendship: Boswell and Mrs Thrale*, 1973

JL: *The Letters of Samuel Johnson*, 5 vols, ed. Bruce Redford, 1992

Johnson's *Journey*: Samuel Johnson, *A Journey to the Western Islands of Scotland* (1774), ed. J. D. Fleeman, 1985

Later Years: Frank Brady, *James Boswell: The Later Years 1769–1795*, 1984

Literary Career: Frederick A. Pottle, *The Literary Career of James Boswell, Esq.*, 1929

New Light: New Light on Boswell: Critical and Historical Essays on the Occasion of the Bicentenary of 'The Life of Johnson', ed. Greg Clingham, 1991

Political Career: Frank Brady, *Boswell's Political Career*, 1965

Temple Diaries: *Diaries of William Johnson Temple*, ed. Lewis Bettany, 1929

Thraliana: *The Diary of Mrs Hester Lynch Thrale (later Mrs Piozzi) 1776–1809*, 2 vols, ed. Katharine C. Balderston, 1951

Walpole Corr.: *The Yale Edition of Horace Walpole's Correspondence*, 48 vols, ed. W. S. Lewis, 1937–81

Werkmeister: Lucyle Werkmeister, *Jemmie Boswell and the London Daily Press, 1785–1795*, 1963

Bibliography

This is a selective list of Boswell's most important works and those modern editions and writings on him that have most influenced this biography. Unless otherwise stated, place of publication is London.

WORKS BY BOSWELL

(1) Selected books and miscellaneous items

An Account of Corsica, The Journal of a Tour to that Island, and Memoirs of Pascal Paoli, 1768; Part II published in *GT(ii)*, pp. 156–216

Boswelliana: The Commonplace Book of James Boswell, ed. Rev. Charles Rogers, LL.D., 1874

Boswell's Column 1777–1783 (70 'Hypochondriack' essays in *London Magazine*) ed. Margery Bailey, 1951

Boswell's Book of Bad Verse, ed. Jack Werner, 1974

The Cub at New-Market: A Tale (1762)

Dorando, A Spanish Tale, 1767

James Boswell's 'Life of Johnson': An Edition of the Original Manuscript in Four Volumes, vol. I: 1709–65, ed. Marshall Waingrow, Edinburgh and New Haven, 1994

The Journal of a Tour to the Hebrides, with Samuel Johnson, LL.D., 1785. This is the first edition; the third is published in *Boswell's Life of Johnson*, vol. V, eds. G. B. Hill and L. F. Powell (2nd edn., 1964).

A Letter to the People of Scotland on the Alarming Attempt to Infringe the Articles of Union . . . by diminishing the number of Lords of Session, 1785

A Letter to the People of Scotland on the Present State of the Nation, Edinburgh, 1783

Letters between The Honourable Andrew Erskine, and James Boswell, Esq., 1763

The Life of Samuel Johnson, LL.D., ed. G. B. Hill, rev. L. F. Powell, 6 vols, Oxford, 1934–64

'Memoirs of James Boswell, Esq.', in *European Magazine* and *London Review*, May 1791

'Sketch of the Early Life of James Boswell, Written by Himself for Jean-Jacques Rousseau, 5 December 1764' (pub. in *Earlier Years*, pp. 1–6; rough drafts and outlines of the final version are in BP: L1109–L1112)

(2) Journals (listed chronologically)

Boswell's London Journal 1762–1763, ed. Frederick A. Pottle, 1951

Boswell in Holland 1763–1764, ed. Frederick A. Pottle, 1952

Boswell on the Grand Tour: Germany and Switzerland 1764, ed. Frederick A. Pottle, 1953

Boswell on the Grand Tour: Italy, Corsica, and France 1765–1766, eds. Frank Brady and Frederick A. Pottle, 1955

Boswell in Search of a Wife 1766–1769, eds. Frank Brady and Frederick A. Pottle, 1956

Boswell for the Defence 1769–1774, eds. William K. Wimsatt, Jr., and Frederick A. Pottle, 1960

Boswell's Journal of a Tour to the Hebrides with Samuel Johnson, LL.D., 1773, eds. Frederick A. Pottle and Charles H. Bennett, 1961

Boswell: The Ominous Years 1774–1776, eds. Charles Ryskamp and Frederick A. Pottle, 1963

Boswell in Extremes 1776–1778, eds. Charles McC. Weis and Frederick A. Pottle, 1970

Boswell: Laird of Auchinleck 1778–1782, eds. Joseph W. Reed and Frederick A. Pottle, 1977; rpt Edinburgh, 1993

Boswell: The Applause of the Jury 1782–1785, eds. Irma S. Lustig and Frederick A. Pottle, 1981

Boswell: The English Experiment 1785–1789, eds. Irma S. Lustig and Frederick A. Pottle, 1986

Boswell: The Great Biographer 1789–1795, eds. Marlies K. Danziger and Frank Brady, 1989

(3) Letters (Yale Research Editions, listed by date of publication)

The Correspondence of James Boswell and John Johnston of Grange, ed. Ralph S. Walker, New York and Toronto, 1966

The Correspondence and Other Papers of James Boswell Relating to the Making of the 'Life of Johnson', 2nd edn., Marshall Waingrow, New York and Toronto, 2000

The Correspondence of James Boswell with Certain Members of the Club, ed. Charles N. Fifer, New York and Toronto, 1976

The Correspondence of James Boswell with David Garrick, Edmund Burke, and Edmond Malone, ed. Thomas W. Copeland, Peter S. Baker, Rachel McClellan, George M. Kahrl, James M. Osborn, et al., 1986. Includes two introductions by Brady on Boswell–Burke and Boswell–Garrick, and one by Peter S. Baker on Boswell–Malone

The General Correspondence of James Boswell 1766–1769, vol. I: 1766–7, eds. Richard C. Cole, with Peter S. Baker and Rachel McClellan, with the assistance of James J. Caudle, Edinburgh, New Haven, and London, 1993

The Correspondence of James Boswell and William Johnston Temple 1756–1795, vol. I: 1756–77, ed. Thomas Crawford, Edinburgh, New Haven, and London, 1997

The General Correspondence of James Boswell 1766–1769, vol. II: 1768–9, eds. Richard C. Cole, with Peter S. Baker and Rachel McClellan, and with the assistance of James J. Caudle, Edinburgh, New Haven, and London, 1997

SECONDARY WORKS

(1) Biographies

Brady, Frank, *James Boswell: The Later Years, 1769–1795*, London and New York, 1984

Craik, Roger, *James Boswell, 1740–1795: The Scottish Perspective*, Edinburgh, 1994

Daiches, David, *James Boswell and His World*, 1976

Pottle, Frederick A., *James Boswell: The Earlier Years, 1740–1769*, New York and London, 1966

Tinker, Chauncey Brewer, *Young Boswell*, 1922

(2) Miscellaneous

Alkon, Paul K., 'Boswell's Control of Aesthetic Distance', in *University of Toronto Quarterly*, 38 (January 1969), pp. 174–91

Arnot, Hugo, *The History of Edinburgh*, 1788

Balderston, Katharine C., ed., *Thraliana: The Diary of Mrs Hester Lynch Thrale (later Mrs Piozzi) 1776–1809*, 2 vols, 1951

Barrett, Charlotte, ed., *Burney Diary: Diary and Letters of Madame D'Arblay*, with Preface and Notes by Austin Dobson, 6 vols, 1904–5

Baruth, Philip E., 'The Problem of Biographical Mastering: The Case for Boswell as Subject', *Modern Language Quarterly*, 52:4 (December 1991), pp. 376–403

Bate, Walter Jackson, *Samuel Johnson*, 1978

Bettany, Lewis, ed., *The Diaries of William Johnson Temple 1780–1796*, Oxford, 1929

Bleakley, Horace, *Some Distinguished Victims of the Scaffold*, 1905

Bloom, Harold, ed., *James Boswell's 'Life of Johnson'*, Modern Critical Interpretations, New York, New Haven, and Philadelphia, 1986

Brady, Frank, *Boswell's Political Career*, Yale Studies in English, no. 155, New Haven, CT, and London, 1965

Brewer, John, *The Pleasures of the Imagination: English Culture in the Eighteenth Century*, 1997

Bronson, Bertrand H., 'Boswell's Boswell', *Johnson Agonistes and Other Essays*, Berkeley and Los Angeles, 1965, pp. 53–99

Brooks, A. Russell, *James Boswell*, Twayne's English Authors Series, vol. 122, New York, 1971

Browne, Anthony E., ed., *Boswellian Studies: A Bibliography*, 2nd edn., Hamden, CT, 1972; 3rd edn. available from Edinburgh University Press.

Buchanan, David, *The Treasure at Auchinleck: The Story of the Boswell Papers*, New York, 1974

Clifford, James L., ed., *Boswell's Life of Johnson: A Collection of Critical Essays*, Twentieth Century Interpretations, Englewood, NJ, 1970

Clifford, James L., *Hester Lynch Piozzi (Mrs Thrale)*, Oxford, 1941

Clingham, Greg, ed., *New Light on Boswell: Critical and Historical Essays on the Occasion of the Bicentenary of 'The Life of Johnson'*, Introduction by David Daiches, Cambridge, 1991

Collecting and Recollecting James Boswell 1740–1795. A Bicentenary Exhibition from the Collections of Yale University and Four Oaks Farm, New York, 1995

Courtney, C. P., *Isabelle de Charrière (Belle de Zuylen)*, Voltaire Foundation, Taylor Foundation, Oxford, 1993

Crawford, Thomas, 'Boswell's Houses', in *Writers and Their Houses*, ed. Kate Marsh, 1993, pp. 31–38

Crawford, Thomas, 'Lowland and Popular Tradition in the Eighteenth Century', in *The History of Scottish Literature*, II (1660–1800), ed. Andrew Hoole, pp. 123–38. Aberdeen, 1987

Crawford, Thomas, 'Boswell and the Tensions of Enlightenment', in *The Science of Man in the Scottish Enlightenment*, ed. Peter Jones, Edinburgh, 1989

Crawford, Thomas, *Boswell, Burns, and the French Revolution*, Edinburgh, 1990

Crawford, Thomas, 'Boswell and the Rhetoric of Friendship', in *New Light on Boswell*, ed. Greg Clingham (1991), pp. 11–27

Daiches, David, *The Paradox of Scottish Culture*, 1964

Daiches, David, *James Boswell and His World*, 1976

Danziger, Marlies K., 'Self-restraint and Self-display in the Authorial Comments in the *Life of Johnson*', in *New Light on Boswell*, ed. Greg Clingham (1991), pp. 162–73

Danziger, Marlies K., 'Boswell's Travels through the German, Swiss, and French Enlightenment', in *Boswell: Citizen of the World, Man of Letters*, ed. Irma S. Lustig (1995), pp. 13–36

Danziger, Marlies K., 'James Boswell and Frederick of Prussia', *Studies on Voltaire and the Eighteenth Century*, 305 (1992), pp. 1654–57

Dowling, William C., *The Boswellian Hero*, Athens, GA, 1979

Dowling, William C., *Language and Logos in Boswell's 'Life of Johnson'*, Princeton, NJ, 1981

Duff, Montstuart E., ed. *Annals of the Club 1764–1914*, 1914

Fitzgerald, Percy, *Boswell's Autobiography*, 1912

Fleeman, J. D., ed., *A Journey to the Western Islands of Scotland by Samuel Johnson*, 1985

Foladare, Joseph, *Boswell's Paoli*, published for Connecticut Academy of Arts and Sciences, Hamden, CT, 1979

Fry, Michael, *The Dundas Despotism*, Edinburgh, 1992

Fry, Michael, 'James Boswell, Henry Dundas and Enlightened Politics', in *Boswell: Citizen of the World, Man of Letters*, ed. Irma S. Lustig (1995), pp. 87–100

Graham, Henry Grey, *The Social Life of Scotland in the Eighteenth Century*, 5th edn, 1969

Greig, J. Y. T., ed., *The Letters of David Hume*, 2 vols, Oxford, 1932

Grundy, Isobel, ' "Over Him We Hang Vibrating": Uncertainty in the *Life of Johnson*', in *Boswell: Citizen of the World, Man of Letters*, ed. Irma S. Lustig (1995), pp. 184–202

Hart, Francis R., 'Boswell and the Romantics: a Chapter in the History of Biographical Theory', *ELH*, 27 (1960), pp. 44–65

Heiland, Donna, 'Swan Songs: The Correspondence of Anna Seward and James Boswell', in *Modern Philology* (1993), pp. 381–91

Hill, G. Birkbeck, *Footsteps of Dr Johnson (Scotland)*, 1890

Hyde, Mary, *The Impossible Friendship: Boswell and Mrs Thrale*, 1973

Ingram, Allan, *Boswell's Creative Gloom: A Study of Imagery and Melancholy in the Writings of James Boswell*, 1982

Jackson, Stanley W., *Melancholia and Depression: From Hippocratic Times to Modern Times*, New Haven and London, 1994

Kerslake, John, *Mr Boswell*, exhibition catalogue, National Portrait Gallery, 1967

Korshin, Paul J., 'Johnson's Conversation in Boswell's *Life of Johnson*', in *New Light on Boswell*, ed. Greg Clingham (1991), pp. 174–93

Lascelles, Mary, ed., *Samuel Johnson's A Journey to the Western Islands of Scotland*. New Haven, 1971

Leask, Keith, *James Boswell*, Famous Scots Series, Edinburgh and London, 1896

Lewis, Wilmarth S., *The Yale Edition of Horace Walpole's Correspondence*, 48 vols, New Haven, CT, 1937–81

Lustig, Irma S., 'Boswell at Work: The "Animadversions" on Mrs. Piozzi', *Modern Language Review*, 67: 1 (January 1972), pp. 12–30

Lustig, Irma S., ed., *Boswell: Citizen of the World, Man of Letters*, Lexington, KY, 1995

Lustig, Irma S., 'Fact Into Art: James Boswell's Notes, Journals, and the *Life of Johnson*', in *Biography in the Eighteenth Century,* ed. J. D. Browning, New York and London, 1980, pp. 128–46

Lustig, Irma S., 'Boswell and Zélide', *Eighteenth-Century Life,* 13, n.s. 1 (February 1989), pp. 10–15

Lustig, Irma S., ' "My Dear Enemy": Margaret Montgomerie Boswell in the *Life of Johnson*', in *Boswell: Citizen of the World, Man of Letters,* ed. Irma S. Lustig (1995), pp. 228–45

Lustig, Irma S., 'The Myth of Johnson's Misogyny in the *Life of Johnson*: Another View', in *Boswell in Scotland and Beyond,* ed. Thomas Crawford, Glasgow, 1997, pp. 71–88

Maitland, William, *The History of Edinburgh,* 1753

Martin, Peter, *Edmond Malone, Shakespearean Scholar: A Literary Biography*, Cambridge, 1995

McLaren, Moray, *Corsica Boswell: Paoli, Johnson, and Freedom,* 1966

Ober, William B., *Boswell's Clap and Other Essays,* New York, London, 1978

Porter, Roy, *London: A Social History,* 1994

Pottle, Frederick A, 'Bozzy and Yorick', *Blackwood's Magazine,* CCXVII (March 1925), pp. 298–313

Pottle, Frederick A., *The Literary Career of James Boswell Esq.,* Oxford, 1965

Pottle, Frederick A., 'Boswell's University Education', in *Johnson, Boswell, and Their Circle,* Essays presented to Lawrence Fitzroy Powell, Oxford, 1965, pp. 230–51

Pottle, Frederick A., *Pride and Negligence: The History of the Boswell Papers,* 1981

Pottle, Frederick A., 'The Power of Memory on Boswell and Scott', in *Essays on the Eighteenth Century Presented to David Nichol Smith,* 1945

Pottle, Frederick A., 'The Life of Johnson: Art and Authenticity' in *Twentieth-Century Interpretations of Boswell's 'Life of Johnson',* ed. James L. Clifford, Englewood NY, 1970, pp. 66–73

Pottle, Marion S., ed., with Claude Colleer Abbott and Frederick A. Pottle, *Catalogue of the Papers of James Boswell at Yale University,* 3 vols, Edinburgh, New Haven, and London, 1993

Radner, John B., 'Pilgrimage and Autonomy: The Visit to Ashbourne' in *Boswell: Citizen of the World, Man of Letters,* ed. Imra S. Lustig, 1995, pp. 203–27

Rae, Thomas I., and William Beattie, 'Boswell and the Advocates' Library', in *Johnson, Boswell, and Their Circle,* Oxford, 1965, pp. 254–67

Redford, Bruce, 'Boswell as Correspondent; Boswell as Letter-Writer', *Yale University Library Gazette* (April 1982), pp. 40–52

Redford, Bruce, *The Letters of Samuel Johnson,* 5 vols, Princeton, NJ, 1992

Rogers, Pat, 'Boswell and the Scotticism', in *New Light on Boswell,* ed. Greg Clingham (1991), p. 56–71

Scott, Geoffrey, *The Portrait of Zélide,* 1925

Scott, Geoffrey, and Frederick A. Pottle, eds., *The Private Papers of James Boswell from Malahide Castle, in the Collection of Lt.-Colonel Ralph Heyward Isham,* 18 vols, Mount Vernon, 1928–34

Seecombe, Thomas., ed., *Letters of James Boswell to the Rev. W. J. Temple,* 1908

Sher, Richard B., *Church and University in the Scottish Enlightenment: The Moderate Literati of Edinburgh.* Princeton, NJ, and Edinburgh, 1985

Sher, Richard B., 'Scottish Divines and Legal Lairds: Boswell's Scots Presbyterian Identity', in *New Light on Boswell,* ed. Greg Clingham (1991), pp. 28–55

Sher, Richard B., ' "Something that Put Me in Mind of My Father": Boswell and Lord Kames', in *Boswell: Citizen of the World, Man of Letters* ed. Irma S. Lustig (1995), pp. 64–86

Siebenschuh, William R., *Form and Purpose in Boswell's Biographical Works*, Berkeley, CA, 1972

Smith, Janet Adam, 'Some Eighteenth-Century Ideas of Scotland', in *Scotland in the Age of Improvement*, ed. N. T. Phillipson and Rosalind Mitchinson, Edinburgh, 1970

Smith-Dampier, J. L., *Who's Who in Boswell?*, Oxford, 1935

Spacks, Patricia, *Imagining a Self: Autobiography and Novel in Eighteenth-Century England*, Cambridge, MA., 1977

Stauffer, Donald A., *The Art of Biography in Eighteenth-Century England*, Princeton, NJ, 1941 (pp. 411–55 on Boswell)

Steuart, A. Francis, *The Douglas Cause*, 1909

Stone, Lawrence, *The Family, Sex and Marriage in England, 1500–1800*. London, 1979

Strawhorn, John, 'Master of Ulubrae: Boswell as Enlightened Laird', in *Boswell: Citizen of the World, Man of Letters*, ed. Irma S. Lustig (1995), pp. 117–34

Suwabe, Hitoshi, 'Appendix: Boswell's Meetings with Johnson', in *Boswell: Citizen of the World, Man of Letters*, ed. Irma S. Lustig (1995), pp. 246–58

Tinker, Chauncey Brewer, ed., *The Letters of James Boswell*, 2 vols, 1924

Tinker, Chauncey Brewer, and F. A. Pottle, *A New Portrait of James Boswell*, Cambridge, MA, 1927

Turberville, A. S., ed., *Johnson's England: An Account of the Life & Manners of His Age*, 2 vols, Oxford, 1965 (first published 1933)

Turnbull, Gordon, 'Criminal Biographer: Boswell and Margaret Caroline Rudd', in *Studies in English Literature*, 26, 1986

Turnbull, Gordon, 'Boswell and Sympathy: The Trial and Execution of John Reid', in *New Light on Boswell*, ed. Greg Clingham (1991), pp. 104–15

Vance, John A., ed., *Boswell's Life of Johnson: New Questions, New Answers*. Athens, GA, 1985

Wain, John, *The Journals of James Boswell*. London, 1991

Wendorf, Richard, *The Elements of Life: Biography and Portrait-Painting in Stuart and Georgian England*. Oxford, 1990

Werkmeister, Lucyle, *Jemmie Boswell and the London Daily Press, 1785–1795*. New York Public Library, 1963

Werner, Jack, ed., *Boswell's Book of Bad Verse: Love Poems and Other Verses*. London, et al. 1974

Younger, A. J., *The Making of Classical Edinburgh 1750–1840*. Edinburgh, 1968

Notes

Preface

1 Thomas Babington Macaulay, review of John Wilson Croker's 5-volume edition of *The Life of Johnson* (1831), in *Critical and Historical Essays, contributed to the Edinburgh Review*, 3 vols (1843), I, pp. 404, 407.

2 The fascinating story of the discovery of the papers has been told twice very well: in Frederick A. Pottle, *Pride and Negligence* (1982) and David Buchanan, *The Treasure at Auchinleck* (1974). The latter especially is my source for so much of the summary of the history of the papers that follows that it is impractical to cite individual pages.

3 Buchanan, *Treasure at Auchinleck*, p. 53.

4 C. Colleer Abbott, *A Catalogue of Papers Relating to Boswell, Johnson & Sir William Forbes Found at Fettercairn House*... (Oxford, 1936), p. xxiii (cited in Buchanan, *Treasure at Auchinleck*, p. 128).

5 Buchanan, *Treasure at Auchinleck*, p. 262.

6 Ibid., p. 279.

Prologue

1 'Sketch of the Early Life of James Boswell, Written by Himself for Jean-Jacques Rousseau, 5 December 1764', *Earlier Years*, pp. 1–6.

2 For an excellent recent history of melancholia, see Stanley W. Jackson, *Melancholia and Depression: From Hippocratic Times to Modern Times* (1994). I have relied on his chapter, 'Melancholia in the Eighteenth Century', for much of my summary here. I also have benefited much from Alan Ingram's study, *Boswell's Creative Gloom* (1982), chapter 2, 'Melancholy and the Imagination', for a survey of the progress of the disease in the eighteenth century.

3 'Life of William Collins', in *Lives of the Poets* (2nd edn., 1783).

4 *An Essay on the Life and Genius of Samuel Johnson, LL.D.* (1793), pp. 80–1.

5 *Grange*, p. 72 (to Grange, 25 April 1763).

6 *Column*, p. 46 (no. 5, February 1778).

7 Cited in Jackson, *Melancholia and Depression*, pp. 301–2.

8 *London Journal*, p. 245 (23 April 1763).

9 Ibid., p. 44.

10 Ingram, *Boswell's Creative Gloom*, p. 14.

11 *Column*, p. 42 (no. 5, February 1778).

12 *Grange,* pp. 14–16 (to Grange, 13 September 1762).

13 *Column,* p. 43 (no. 5, February 1778).

14 *Holland,* p. 377.

15 *Column,* p. 44 (no. 5, February 1778).

16 *Grange,* p. 75 (to Grange, 17 May 1763).

17 *Column,* pp. 207–10 (no. 39, December 1780).

18 Ibid., pp. 208–10.

19 *Temple,* p. 99 (to Temple, *c.* 11 June 1764). For some interesting ideas on the relationship between Boswell's melancholy and his writing about it, I am indebted to Susan Manning, ' "This Philosophical Melancholy": Style and Self in Boswell and Hume', *New Light,* pp. 132–40.

ONE A World of Chimeras

1 *Laird,* p. 252 (21 September 1780).

2 'Sketch', p. 1. Boswell intended this 'Sketch' as a way of introducing himself to Rousseau. He tried to create particular impressions of himself in it that he thought would appeal to the philosopher, so it cannot in all respects be trusted as an accurate statement. But its facts are correct, as are the general outlines of how he represented himself emotionally.

3 *Laird,* p. 220 (4 June 1780).

4 Ibid., pp. 234 (26 August 1780), 164 (9 January 1780).

5 Ibid., pp. 163–4 (8 January 1780), 244 (9 September 1780).

6 By far the most complete description of Boswell's ancestry may be found in *Earlier Years,* pp. 7–12, 449–55.

7 'Sketch', pp. 2–3.

8 *London Journal,* p. 331 (30 July 1763).

9 *A Journey to the Western Islands of Scotland* (1775), ed. Mary Lascelles (New Haven, 1971), p. 161; *Tour,* pp. 372–4.

10 Ibid.

11 C. B. Tinker, *Young Boswell* (1922), pp. 180–90.

12 *Tour,* pp. 373, 440–41.

13 'Sketch', BP: L1108 (translated by Ned and Paula Bradley). For a more detailed account of James, the seventh Laird of Auchinleck, see *Earlier Years,* pp. 9, 453–4.

14 BP: L127 (17 July 1754), cited in *Earlier Years,* p. 26.

15 Cited in Roger Craik, *James Boswell 1740–1795: The Scottish Perspective* (1994), p. 4. I am indebted to this work for several details about the architecture and layout of Auchinleck House. The house is presently being renovated.

16 *Wife,* p. 118 (24 December 1767).

17 *London Journal,* p. 134 (10 January 1763); letter to John Wilkes (31 July 1765), BP: L1287.

18 *London Journal,* p. 294 (6 July 1763).

19 David Daiches, review of Frank Brady, *James Boswell: The Later Years 1769–1795* (1984), *Eighteenth-Century Studies,* 19: 3 (Spring 1986), p. 414.

20 Smollett's passage from *Humphry Clinker* is cited (p. 53) by A. J. Youngson in his excellent portrait of the old and new towns, *The Making of Classical Edinburgh 1750–1840* (1966); see especially chapters I–III. See also *A Tour Through the Whole Island of Great Britain* (1724–6), eds. P. N. Furbank, W. R. Owens, and A. J. Coulson (1991), p. 310. My brief description of Edinburgh in Boswell's day is based, in addition to

Youngson, on William Maitland, *History of Edinburgh* (1753); Craik, *Boswell*; Hugo Arnot, *The History of Edinburgh* (1788); and J. Grant, *Old and New Edinburgh* (1882).

21 The 'Proposals' are cited in Youngson, *Classical Edinburgh*, pp. 5–6.

22 Topham, *Letters from Edinburgh* (1776), pp. 8–9; Defoe, *A Tour Through the Whole Island of Great Britain*, eds. P. N. Furbank and W. R. Owens (New Haven and London, 1991), p. 311.

23 *GT*, (i), p. 151 (22 October 1764); *Life of Johnson*, I (14 July 1763), p. 431, n. 1; to Erskine, Letter XXVII (4 May 1762), *E-B*.

24 *Laird*, p. 467 (3 and 1 August 1782); 3 March [?] (BP: M 78).

25 Cited in Craik, *Boswell*, p. 22.

26 See *Earlier Years*, p. 17.

27 Ibid., p. 16.

28 Ibid., pp. 1–2; 'Sketch', BP: L1109; *Earlier Years*, p. 16.

29 'Sketch', BP: L1108.

30 *Earlier Years*, p. 2.

31 Ibid., p. 2; BP: L1108. Boswell cancelled several of these passages because he realized he had digressed from autobiography into the more abstruse area of religious education.

32 *Scots Magazine* (April 1749), pp. 206–7, announced James Boswell's death and that Alexander Boswell inherited Auchinleck and became Lord Auchinleck. On 4 October 1748 Old James drew up a document (BP: A10.9), 'Settlement Mr James Boswell in favour of his Children and others'. *Scots Magazine* (March 1748) announced Lord Auchinleck's appointment as Sheriff Depute by Royal 'Warrant', pp. 54–5. It was a two-year appointment, but well before its expiration Lord Auchinleck wanted to resign; however, he saw out his term (BP: C1330.57).

33 *Boswelliana*, p. 229.

34 'Sketch', p. 3; BP: L1108.

35 See 'Sketch', BP: L1109.

36 'Sketch', p. 3; *Grange*, pp. 47 (15 February 1763), 94–5 (21 July 1763); 'Sketch', pp. 3–4.

37 'Sketch', p. 4.

38 *Holland*, p. 44 ('French Theme', 12–14 October 1763).

39 *Applause*, p. 69 (14 March 1783); BP: L1109.

40 *London Journal*, p. 118 (3 January 1763); BP: L1111.

TWO Edinburgh Gloom

1 For 'surly tutor', see *Holland*, p. 45 (ten-line poem on 14 October 1763). On Edinburgh University, see Grant, *Old and New Edinburgh*, III, p. 20; Youngson, *Classical Edinburgh*, pp. 123–32; Craik, *Boswell*, pp. 23–4; Daiches, *James Boswell and His World*, p. 13.

2 'Sketch', p. 4; BP: L1111; to Alexander Boswell, Jr. (7 February 1794), BP: L108.

3 See Frederick A. Pottle, 'Boswell's University Education', in *Johnson, Boswell, and Their Circle* (1965), pp. 230–53.

4 Ibid.

5 Pottle, 'Boswell's University Education', pp. 237–9.

6 *Temple*, p. 33 (to Temple, 1 May 1761).

7 BP: L1109 (cited in *Earlier Years*, p. 31); to Grange, 24 July 1765 (*Grange*, pp. 178–9).

8 Carlyle, *Autobiography* (1860), pp. 42–3.

9 On Stevenson, see also James Somerville, *My Own Life and Times*, pp. 12–14. For Stevenson's influence on Boswell in the context of the Enlightenment, see Thomas Crawford, 'Boswell and the Tensions of Enlightenment', in *The Science of Man in the Scottish Enlightenment*, ed. Peter Jones (1989), p. 182.

10 'Sketch', BP: LIIII.

11 *Grange*, pp. xi–xiii.

12 *Grange*, pp. 45–6 (to Grange, 15 February 1763), 91–2 (to Grange, 19 July 1763).

13 Thomas Crawford, 'Boswell and the Rhetoric of Friendship', in *New Light*, pp. 16–17.

14 *Grange*, p. 14.

15 *Grange*, pp. 48–9 (to Grange, 22 February 1763).

16 BP: M215. There are two leaves of this fragment in Boswell's hand. The date, 1755, is tentative.

17 *London Journal*, pp. 296–7 (7 July 1763). For the following discussion of Temple and his relationship with Boswell, I am indebted especially to Thomas Crawford's Introduction to his recent edition of the Boswell–Temple letters, and to his essay, 'Boswell and the Rhetoric of Friendship'.

18 BP: C2650, C2647.

19 *Temple*, p. 6 (to Temple, 29 July 1758); 'Memoirs of James Boswell, Esq.', *Literary Career*, p. xxx; *Temple*, p. 1 (from Temple, 24 October 1756).

20 *Temple*, pp. 17 (from Temple, Spring 1759), 10 (from Temple, 5 December 1758), 14–15 (to Temple, 16 December 1758).

21 *Wife*, p. 148 (20 March 1768).

22 *London Journal*, p. 77 (11 December 1762); 'Sketch', p. 4.

23 'Sketch', p. 4; *Experiment* (29 November 1786), p. 103; *Applause*, p. 259 (to Temple, 8 July 1784: PML).

24 See Tinker, *Young Boswell*, pp. 181–90; David Daiches, *The Paradox of Scottish Culture* (1964); and Crawford, 'Boswell and the Tensions of Enlightenment' in *The Science of Man in the Scottish Enlightenment*, ed. Peter Jones (1989), p. 182. See also Daiches, *Robert Burns: The Poet* (1950, 1981), chapter 1.

25 *Boswelliana*, pp. 233, 272; *Temple*, p. 148 (to Temple, 17 May 1766).

26 Boswell quoted from John Armstrong's *The Art of Preserving Health* (1744), in 'On Hypochondria', *London Magazine* (February 1778). See *Column*, p. 45.

27 'Memoirs of James Boswell', *Literary Career*, p. xxx; BP: M264; *Life of Johnson*, IV, p. 50, n. 2.

28 *Temple*, pp. 7 (to Temple, 29 July 1758), 15 (to Temple, 16 December 1758).

29 *London Journal*, p. 85 (14 December 1762). For a history of the Edinburgh theatre, see J. C. Dibdin, *The Annals of the Edinburgh Stage* (1888).

30 The *London Magazine* for August, September, and October 1770; reprinted in a modern edition, *On the Profession of a Player* (1929), pp. 3, 32–3, 36, 37.

31 BP: C1038 (from Digges, April 1757).

32 *London Journal*, p. 62 (1 December 1762); to Garrick, 3 March 1778 (*GBM*, p. 77).

33 *Temple*, p. 15 (to Temple, 16 December 1758); *London Journal*, pp. 85–6 (14 December 1762).

34 See *Literary Career* for the list of Boswell's poems (and essays) published in the *Scots Magazine*, pp. 215–21.

35 *Temple*, pp. 6–7 (to Temple, 29 July 1758), 18 (from Temple, 8 July 1759). The epigram is in a manuscript collection of (mostly) his poems that Boswell seems to have prepared for the press, but never published: 'Plan of a Volume of Poems to be published for me by Becket and Dehondt' (Bodleian, Douce 193, f. 62). The poems

include songs, odes, epigrams, epistles, prologues, dramatic speeches, satires, hymns, and paraphrases of Scripture. Most of them date 1758–62.

36 *Temple*, p. 6 (to Temple, 29 July 1758).
37 *Temple*, pp. 3 (to Temple, 17 June 1758), 15 (to Temple, 16 December 1758).
38 *Temple*, p. 21 (from Temple, September 1759).
39 Bodleian, MS Douce 193, f. 91; from Temple, 25 December 1759–14 January 1760 (*Temple*, p. 30).
40 'Epistle to Temple' and 'Sequel to Lavinia', Douce Poems, fs. 82–83v. For a complete transcription of these poems, see *Temple*, pp. 23–8.
41 *Temple*, p. 21 (from Temple, September 1759); *Original Poems by Scotch Gentlemen*, published by A. Donaldson in 1762, II, 77; Pottle put his case for Boswell as their author in *Literary Career*, pp. 263, 284–91.
42 *Temple*, p. 19 (from Temple, 3 August 1759).
43 *Grange*, p. 7 (to Grange, 11 January 1760).
44 Ibid.; to Andrew Erskine, 8 December 1761 (BP: L509). Pottle argues against Boswell's lodging with Smith, *Earlier Years*, p. 43.

THREE Escape to London

1 *Temple*, p. 31 (from Temple, 22 March 1760).
2 Newhailes MS. These and all following excerpts from the letter of 22 March 1760 are discussed by Andrew G. Hoover, 'Boswell's First London Visit', *The Virginia Quarterly*, 29 (1953), pp. 242–56. But for Boswell's flirtation with Catholicism, the reader is referred to *Earlier Years*, Appendix, pp. 569–74.
3 *Wife*, p. 148 (20 March 1768); Jortin to Dalrymple, 27 April 1760, *Boswelliana*, p. 13.
4 *London Journal*, pp. 161 (20 January 1763), 236, 277 (10 June 1763), 228 (28 March 1763). In his *Life of Johnson*, Boswell identifies Derrick more kindly as a 'poet' and acknowledges his role in introducing him to Davies (I, 385).
5 *London Journal*, p. 167 (25 January 1763).
6 Letter to Eglinton, 25 September 1761, published in *Scots Magazine* (September 1761) under the title, 'AN ORIGINAL LETTER, From a GENTLEMAN OF SCOTLAND to the EARL of *** in London'.
7 *Holland*, p. 62 ('French Theme', 9–10 November 1763).
8 Boswell's meeting with Sterne is reconstructed by Pottle in 'Bozzy and Yorick', *Blackwood's Magazine* (March 1925), CCXVII, pp. 297–313.
9 *Tristram Shandy*, vol. IV.
10 'A Poetical Epistle to Doctor Sterne, Parson Yorick, and Tristam Shandy', printed in Douce Poems, pp. 131–40.
11 Boswell may have tried to publish the *Cub* before he left London. Later, he had difficulty getting Dodsley to publish it, who held on to the manuscript for months without doing anything about it. He finally had it printed at his own expense in March 1762.
12 *London Journal*, pp. 167–8 (25 January 1763).
13 *Temple*, p. 33 (to Temple, 1 May 1761).
14 *London Journal*, pp. 61–62 (1 December 1762).

FOUR Early Scribblings

1 *London Journal*, p. 164 (21 January 1763).
2 Ibid., p. 167 (25 January 1763); to Temple, 1 May 1761 (*Temple*, p. 33); to Grange, 22 September 1760 (*Grange*, p. 11). William B. Ober feels Boswell's second attack may have been complicated by epididymitis (*Boswell's Clap and Other Essays*, 1978, p. 40).
3 The unfinished manuscript is in BP: M116; to Scott, autumn 1760? (BP: L1139). See also *Earlier Years*, pp. 68–70.
4 To Lady Northumberland, 1 April 1761 (BP: L987); see Jack Werner's edition of the Douce Poems.
5 *London Journal*, p. 189 (14 February 1763).
6 *London Journal*, p. 191 (16 February 1763). For valuable insight into Boswell's friendships with Erskine and Dempster, see Thomas Crawford, 'Boswell and the Rhetoric of Friendship', in *New Light*, pp. 11–15.
7 BP: J1.
8 See *Literary Career*, p. 6; *E-B*, pp. 64–5. For much background information to the Erskine–Boswell letters, I am indebted to J. D. Hankins' annotations in his forthcoming Research Edition of these letters in the Yale Boswell Editions. I am most grateful to the Yale Boswell Editions for permission to see and cite from his anotations.
9 Douce Poems, p. 161.
10 BP: C2500, C811, C1432. Colquitt was a priest in one of the 'qualified' or legal Church of England chapels in Edinburgh, not a priest in the Scottish Episcopal Church which was repressed because of its loyalty to the exiled Stuart line. That Colquitt did make a deep impression on Boswell is evident from the latter's particular mention of him in his 1791 *Memoirs* (*Literary Career*, p. xxxii). At the start of their Hebridean journey in 1773, Boswell took Dr Johnson to a service at one of these 'qualified' chapels.
11 *Literary Career*, p. xxxii.
12 David Daiches writes tellingly of the social and literary character of Edinburgh clubs in *Paradox of Scottish Culture*, pp. 90–91; and *Robert Burns*, pp. 28–30. See also Thomas Crawford, 'Lowland Song and Popular Tradition in the Eighteenth Century', *History of Scottish Literature*, II, pp. 123–38.
13 Daiches, *Paradox of Scottish Culture*, p. 90.
14 Scotland's schizophrenia of language and culture in the late eighteenth century has been the subject of much study. Pat Rogers touches on the embarrassments of the Scots language in 'Boswell and the Scotticism', in *New Light*, pp. 56–71. Also, in addition to Daiches' *Paradox of Scottish Culture*, the reader may wish to look at the following studies: *Scotland in the Age of Improvement*, ed. N. T. Phillipson and Rosalind Mitchison (1970), essays by Janet Adam Smith, 'Some Eighteenth-Century Ideas of Scotland' (pp. 107–24), and John Clive, 'The Social Background of the Scottish Renaissance' (pp. 225–44); and Richard B. Sher, *Church and University in the Scottish Enlightenment: The Moderate Literati of Edinburgh* (1985).
15 Sheridan's lectures were publicized in the *Scots Magazine*, XXIII (July 1761), pp. 389–90. Sheridan's fussiness, pedantry, and jealousy spoiled an effort by the Select Society in 1762 to establish, under his direction, a 'Society for promoting the Reading and Speaking of the English Language in Scotland'. Boswell became progressively more impatient with him over the next few years.
16 BP: L1156 (to Sheridan, 27 September 1761).

17 BP: C2484 (from Sheridan, 21 November [1761]); BP: L1157 (to Sheridan, 25 November 1761); BP: 1158 (to Sheridan, 9 December 1761).
18 BP: L506 (to Erskine, August 1761).
19 To Eglinton, 25 September 1761 (*Scots Magazine*, XXIII, p. 470); to Katharine Colquhoun, 11 December 1761 (BP: L376); *E-B*, p. 81.
20 *E-B*, pp. 67–8, 5–6. See Thomas Crawford on Boswell and Erskine's epistolary 'talk', 'Boswell and the Rhetoric of Friendship', pp. 11–15.
21 BP: L510 (to Erskine, 17 December 1761).
22 *E-B*, pp. 57, 143 (5 July 1762).
23 See *E-B*, pp. 49–50, 68, 72–3, 75; BP: L526 (23 July 1762). Boswell's 'Ode to Gluttony' escaped censure, but when (stretching his luck) he printed it again the following year in his published correspondence with Erskine, the *Critical Review* impatiently nailed it and Erskine's 'Ode upon a Jew's Harp' as specimens of the age's poetic malaise: 'As to fun and rhyming, or what our two correspondents, probably, will call poetry, they are the cheapest and most nauseous drugs of this press-surfeited age and country' (May 1763, pp. 343–5).
24 *E-B*, 20 November 1762, pp. 155–6.
25 *E-B*, p. 72; to Grange, 23 September 1763 (*Grange*, p. 115).
26 *E-B*, p. 92.
27 *London Journal* (25 January 1763), pp. 168–9; BP: C2333.8.
28 Agreements dated 7 March 1762 (BP: M16) and 2 April 1762 (C210).
29 BP: L517 (to Erskine, 22 April 1762); *E-B*, p. 105; 29 May 1762 (*E-B*, pp. 131–2; BP: L520).
30 BP: J1.43.

FIVE Harvest Jaunt

1 *Grange*, p. 13 (to Grange, 17 August 1762).
2 Ibid., pp. 14–15 (to Grange, 13 September 1762).
3 *London Journal*, p. 191 (16 February 1763); to Grange, 13 September 1762 (*Grange*, p. 16); 'Harvest Journal', p. 43.
4 'Harvest Journal', pp. 43–4.
5 Ibid., pp. 44–7.
6 Ibid., pp. 49–50.
7 'Sketch', p. 5; Douce Poems.
8 'Harvest Journal', p. 53.
9 Ibid., pp. 54–5, 63.
10 Ibid., pp. 55–6.
11 Ibid., pp. 58–61.
12 Ibid., p. 68 (3–4 October).
13 Ibid., p. 73.
14 Ibid., pp. 97, 92, 106 (6 November 1762).
15 Ibid., pp. 76–7 (12 October).
16 Ibid., pp. 78–80 (13 October).
17 Ibid., p. 81 (14 October).
18 'Harvest Journal', pp. 83–4.
19 'Harvest Journal': pp. 86, 88–9 (22 October), 89–90 (23 October).
20 Ibid., pp. 94–7.
21 Ibid., p. 95; *London Journal*, p. 120 n. 1.

22 'Harvest Journal', pp. 106–7 (6 November).

23 Ibid., pp. 100, 102–4 (4 November), 109 (9 November), 110 (11 November).

24 Ibid., pp. 104, 109 (8 November), 105–6.

25 Ibid., p. 108 (7 November).

26 Ibid., pp. 110 (10–11 November); *London Journal*, pp. 40–41 (15 November); 'Harvest Journal', p. 111 (13 November).

SIX London: The Promised Land

1 *Grange*, p. 104 (2 August 1763); *London Journal*, pp. 41–2 (15 November 1762).

2 Roy Porter, *London: A Social History* (1994), pp. 168–9; see especially chapter 7, 'Culture City: Life Under the Georges'. Another good overview of eighteenth-century London is provided by M. Dorothy George, 'London and the Life of the Town', in *Johnson's England* ed. A. S. Turberville (1965), I, pp. 160–96.

3 *Grange*, p. 23 (20 November 1762); *E-B*, pp. 155–6 (20 November 1762).

4 *London Journal*, pp. 45–7 (19–21 November 1762).

5 Ibid., pp. 49–50 (25 November 1762).

6 Ibid., p. 50 (26 November 1762).

7 *Holland*, p. 53 ('French Theme', 26 October 1763).

8 Ibid., pp. 52–3 (27 November 1762).

9 Ibid., pp. 54–5; to Grange, 4 January 1763 (*Grange*, p. 37); *London Journal*, pp. 150–52 (18 January 1763). Boswell describes this Johnson–Sheridan quarrel in the *Life of Johnson*, I, pp. 385–9.

10 *London Journal*, p. 152 (18 January 1763).

11 *Grange*, pp. 31–2 (to Grange, 14 December 1762); *London Journal*, p. 62 (1 December 1762); to Grange, 30 June 1763 (*Grange*, p. 81). Boswell's angst in the face of the pressures of society is discussed by Ingram, *Boswell's Creative Gloom*, pp. 67–71.

12 *London Journal*, p. 61 (1 December 1762).

13 Ibid., p. 39.

14 *Life of Johnson*, III, p. 228; Bertrand H. Bronson, 'Boswell's Boswell', in *Johnson Agonistes and Other Essays* (1965), p. 65.

15 *London Journal*, p. 269 (25 May 1763).

16 Ibid., p. 39.

17 Ibid., p. 40. See Ingram, *Boswell's Creative Gloom*, pp. 126–7.

18 *London Journal*, p. 224 (21 March 1764).

19 *Wife*, p. 311 (16 September 1769).

20 *Grange*, p. 26 (to Grange, 6 December 1762).

21 *London Journal*, pp. 54 (28 November), 83–5. Little more is known about Louisa than what Boswell tells us. Her real name was Mrs Lewis.

22 Ibid., pp. 84–5 (14 December 1762), 88–9 (16–17 December 1762).

23 Ibid., pp. 94–5 (18 December 1762), 96–8 (20 December 1762).

24 Ibid., pp. 96–102 (20–21 December 1762), 107 (26 December 1762).

25 Ibid., pp. 105–6 (25 December 1762), 176 (3 January 1763), 287–8 (1 July 1763).

26 Ibid., pp. 116–18 (2 January 1763).

27 Ibid., pp. 120 (4 January 1763), 137–40 (12 January 1763).

28 Ibid., pp. 139–40 (12–13 January 1763).

29 Ibid., pp. 142 (14 January 1763), 149 (18 January 1763). Pottle identifies the lady as Lady Mary Coke, daughter of the second Duke of Argyll and a countrywoman of Boswell's (*London Journal*, p. 142 n. 5; in *Earlier Years*, pp. 484–5, he rescinds this).

30 Ibid., pp. 156, 158 (20 January 1763).
31 Ibid., pp. 158–61 (20 January 1763).
32 Ibid., pp. 164–5 (21 January 1763).
33 Ibid., pp. 161 (20 January 1763), 256–7.
34 Ibid., pp. 179 (6 February 1763), 186–7 (9 February 1763). See *Literary Career*, p. 19.
35 Ibid., pp. 197 (20 February 1763), 204–5.

SEVEN 'The Johnsonian Aether'

1 *Grange*, p. 82 (30 June 1763); *London Journal*, pp. 205 (27 February), 107 (26 December 1762).
2 *London Journal*, pp. 109 (27 December 1762), 111–12 (30 December).
3 Ibid., p. 223 (21 March 1763); from Cochrane, 20 December 1762 (BP: C798); *London Journal*, p. 200 (24 February).
4 *London Journal*, pp. 200, 194 (18 February 1763).
5 *Grange*, p. 65 (5 April); from Euphemia Boswell, 7 March 1763 (BP: C332).
6 *Grange*, p. 78 (16 June); *London Journal*, p. 274 (6 June 1763).
7 From Lord Auchinleck, 30 May 1763 (*London Journal*, pp. 338–41).
8 *Grange*, pp. 58–62 (to Grange, 22 March 1763).
9 BP: C214.
10 BP: J3.
11 From Dalrymple, 21 April 1763 (BP: C1419), 30 May 1763 (BP: C1421); *Public Advertiser*, 15 and 28 April; *Monthly Review*, XXVIII, 476–7; *London Chronicle*, 27 April 1763.
12 *London Journal*, p. 188 (10 February 1763); from Dalrymple, 16 June 1763 (BP: C1422).
13 *London Journal*, pp. 165 (22 January 1763), 213, 228, 245; to Grange, 25 April 1763 (*Grange*, p. 72).
14 *London Journal*, pp. 252–4 (3–6 May 1763). On public executions in London, see Porter, *London*, pp. 153–4.
15 *Grange*, p. 75 (to Grange, 17 May 1763); *London Journal*, pp. 227, 231–2 (31 March 1763), 255–6.
16 *London Journal*, p. 263 (19 May 1763).
17 Ibid., p. 260; *Life of Johnson*, I, pp. 392–3. Boswell's account of this first meeting is much fuller in his *Life* than in his journal.
18 *London Journal*, pp. 268 and n 6.
19 *Life of Johnson*, I, 395–99; *London Journal*, p. 268.
20 *Life of Johnson*, II, pp. 451–2; I, pp. 401–10.
21 *London Journal*, pp. 282–85.
22 Ibid., pp. 327, 291–4 (6 July).
23 Ibid., p. 293 (6 July 1763); *Life of Johnson*, I, p. 421; *London Journal*, p. 305 (16 July); to Dalrymple, 23 July 1763 (*Letters*, I, p. 30); to Dalrymple, 16 July 1763 (*Letters*, I, p. 24); from Dalrymple, 28 July 1763 (BP: c1428); cited in *Life of Johnson*, I, pp. 432–3; from Temple, 16 July 1763 (*Temple*, p. 45).
24 *London Journal*, pp. 303 (14 July 1763), 304 (15 July 1763), 332–3 (3 August 1763).
25 Ibid., pp. 311 (19 July 1763), 327–8 (28 July 1763), 332.
26 *Grange*, pp. 86 (9 July 1763), 83 (2 July 1763); to Dalrymple, 16 July 1763 (*Letters*, I, pp. 24–5); from Temple, 16 July 1763 (*Temple*, p. 45).
27 *Grange*, pp. 85–6, 83 (to Grange, 9 and 2 July 1763).
28 Ibid., pp. 82, 102–3 (to Grange, 30 June and 30 July 1763).

29 *London Journal*, pp. 327–30 (28–30 July 1763); *Life of Johnson*, I, pp. 457–62.

30 *London Journal*, p. 331 (30 July 1763); *Life of Johnson*, I, p. 462; to Dalrymple, 23 July 1763 (*Letters*, I, p. 31).

31 *London Journal*, pp. 331, 333 (4 August 1763); to Grange, 4 August 1763 (*Grange*, pp. 106–7).

32 *Life of Johnson*, I, pp. 464–72.

EIGHT   Utrecht: Acquiring a Noble Character

1 *Wife*, p. 68.

2 *Holland*, pp. 3–4; to Grange, 23 September 1763 (*Grange*, p. 112).

3 *Grange*, pp. 112–13 (to Grange, 23 September 1763); to Temple, 16 August 1763 (*Temple*, p. 62).

4 *Grange*, p. 114 (to Grange, 23 September 1763).

5 From Stewart, 7 September 1763 (BP: C 2553); from Dempster, 29 October 1763 (BP: C932); from Dempster, 23 August 1763 (BP: C931); from Dalrymple, 26 September 1763 (BP: C1429).

6 *Holland*, pp. 21, 39 (5 October 1763).

7 Ibid., pp. 46 (16 October 1763), 375–8, 63 (12 November 1763).

8 Ibid., pp. 37 (27 September 1763), 50 (23 October 1763).

9 *Temple*, p. 82 (to Temple, 6 December 1763); *Holland*, pp. 45 (14 October 1763), 82–3 (7–8 December 1763).

10 *Holland*, pp. 83–4 (9 December 1763).

11 *Holland*, p. 93 (20 December 1763). See *Life of Johnson*, V, p. 25 n. 2. Boswell's great-grandmother was Sommelsdyck's great-aunt Veronica, after whom he named his first daughter.

12 *Holland*, pp. 109 (30 December 1763), 95–103 ('Dialogues at The Hague'), 98 (21 December 1763), 113 (6 January 1764), 114 (9 January 1764).

13 *Temple*, pp. 87 (to Temple, 23 March 1764); to Grange, 20 January (*Grange*, pp. 118–20); *Holland*, pp. 122 (21 January 1764), 123 ('French Theme', ?22 January 1764).

14 *Temple*, p. 87 (to Temple, 23 March 1764); to Grange, 9 April 1764 (*Grange*, pp. 121–2); *Holland*, p. 173 (8 March 1764).

15 *Holland*, p. 233 (6 May 1764); to Temple, 22 May 1764 (*Temple*, pp. 97–8).

16 *Temple*, pp. 99–100 (to Temple ?11 June 1764).

17 *Holland*, p. 168 (4 March 1764); Moore is cited in Ingram, *Boswell's Creative Gloom*, p. 71.

18 *Temple*, pp. 94 (to Temple, 17 April 1764), 84–5 (from Temple, ?7 January 1764).

19 *Holland*, pp. 128–9 (1 February 1764) and n. 1, 132, 138–9 (9 February 1764).

20 Ibid., pp. 150–3; to Grange, 9 April 1764 (*Grange*, p. 123); *Holland*, pp. 207–8 (10 April 1764).

21 From Gronovius, 9 June 1764 (BP: C1404).

22 *Holland*, pp. 226 (23 April 1764), 231 (3 May 1764), 252–5 (25–27 May 1764).

NINE   Zélide

1 There are a number of biographies of this remarkable woman, among them Geoffrey Scott's charming and impressionistic *The Portrait of Zélide* (1925), and C. P. Courtney, *Isabella de Charrière (Belle de Zuylen)* (1993), a recent full-scale biography. See also

Irma S. Lustig, 'Boswell and Zélide', *Eighteenth-Century Life*, 13, n.s. 1 (February 1989), pp. 10–15. See *Holland*, pp. 285–9.

2 *Madame de Charrière et ses amis*, I, pp. 1–3 (quoted in *Holland*, p. 257 n. 2).

3 *Holland*, pp. 54–5 (31 October 1763), 62 (9 November 1763), 72–3 (26 November 1763).

4 Ibid., pp. 160–61 (24 February 1764).

5 Ibid., pp. 134 (7 February 1764), 136 (8 February 1764), 137 (9 February 1764).

6 Ibid., pp. 165 (25 February 1764), 170 (7 March 1764), 171 (8 March 1764), 180–84.

7 Ibid., p. 195 (28 March 1764), 211 (11 April 1764); from Lord Auchinleck, 2 April 1764 (BP: C225).

8 Ibid., pp. 215 (14 April 1764), 230 (28 April 1764); to Temple, 17 April 1764 (*Temple*, pp. 93–4).

9 *Temple*, p. 96 (from Temple, 15 May 1764); *Holland*, pp. 252–3.

10 Godet, *Madame de Charrière et ses amis*, I, p. 3 (cited in *Holland*, p. 257 n. 2); *Holland*, pp. 257, 269 (7 June 1764), 270, 272 (11 June 1764).

11 *Holland*, pp. 279–80 (17 June 1764); to Temple, 17 June 1764 (*Temple*, p. 103). Irma S. Lustig has some interesting thoughts on Boswell's anxieties over an intellectually superior wife in 'Boswell and Zélide', pp. 10–15. For her correspondence with Constant d'Hermenches about Boswell's courtship, see *Lettres de Belle de Zuylen (Madame de Charrière) à Constant d'Hermenches*, ed. Philippe Godet (1909); cited in *Holland*, pp. 368, 289–90 (14 June 1764).

12 *Temple*, p. 126 (to Temple, 28 December 1764); from Monsieur de Zuylen, 17 August 1764 (BP: C3174; cited in *Holland*, pp. 311–12); to Monsieur de Zuylen, 25 December 1764 (BP: L1322; cited in *Holland*, p. 317).

13 *Temple*, p. 125 (28 December 1764); to Belle de Zuylen, 25 December 1764 (BP: L1317; cited in *Holland*, p. 319); from Belle de Zuylen, 27 January 1765 (BP: C3166; cited in *Holland*, pp. 321–2); to Belle de Zuylen, ?3 April 1764 (BP: L1318; cited in *Holland*, p. 324).

14 BP: C3167 (cited in *Holland*, pp. 329–30, from Belle de Zuylen, 25 May 1765).

15 *GT(ii)*, p. 60 (17 March 1765); to Temple, 19 March 1765 (*Temple*, p. 132); *GT(ii)*, p. 282 (14 January 1766).

16 BP: L1324 (cited in *Holland*, pp. 333–42, from Monsieur de Zuylen, 16 January 1766).

17 BP: C3178 (cited in *Holland*, p. 343, from Monsieur de Zuylen, 30 January 1766); from Lord Auchinleck, 30 January 1766 (BP: C231; cited in *Holland*, pp. 344–5).

TEN 'Let Me Be Boswell': Touring Germany and Switzerland

1 Ibid., p. 265 (25 May 1764).

2 *Temple*, p. 108 (to Temple, 23 July 1764); to Grange, 10 September 1764 (*Grange*, p. 134); *GT(i)* p. 98 (19 September 1764).

3 *Temple*, p. 96 (from Temple, 5 May 1764); *Holland*, pp. 261–2 (4 June 1764); to Grange, 11 June 1764 (*Grange*, pp. 126–7).

4 *Holland*, p. 276.

5 BP: C1945 (cited in *Holland*, pp. 262–3, from Marischal, 25 May 1764).

6 *GT(i)*, p. 7; to Temple, 23 July 1764 (*Temple*, p. 104); *GT(i)*, pp. 10–11.

7 For a discussion of Boswell's response to the Continental landscape, see Peter F. Perreten, 'Boswell's Response to the European Landscape', *Citizen*, pp. 37–63.

8 To Monsieur de Zuylen, 30 July 1764 (BP: L1320; cited in *Holland*, p. 309); *GT(i)*, p. 10 (24 June 1764).

9 *Grange*, pp. 138, 137 (to Grange, 12 and 6 October 1764).

10 *GT(i)*, pp. 56 (11 August 1764), 140 (18 October 1764).

11 Ibid., p. 152 (24 October 1764).

12 There is a brief summary of the German states in the eighteenth century by F. A. Pottle in *GT(i)*, pp. 3–4; for a comprehensive and enticing portrait, see Thomas Carlyle's *History of Frederick II of Prussia* (6 vols, 1858–65). Carlyle obtained much of his information from the letters of Sir Andrew Mitchell, who befriended Boswell in Berlin.

13 *Temple*, p. 105 (to Temple, 23 July 1764). Marlies K. Danziger considers the theme of the Enlightenment in Boswell's travels in her helpful essay, 'Boswell's Travels Through the German, Swiss, and French Enlightenment', *Citizen*, pp. 13–36.

14 *GT(i)*, p. 12 (27 June 1764); to Temple, 23 July 1764 (*Temple*, p. 105); *GT(i)*, pp. 59, 15 (13 August, 28 June 1764).

15 *GT(i)*, p. 15 (28 June 1764).

16 Ibid., pp. 15–18 (30 June–3 July 1764); to Temple, 23 July 1764 (*Temple*, p. 106).

17 *GT(i)*, p. 20 (6 July 1764).

18 Ibid., pp. 21, 48, 27, 22 (10 July, 4 August, 18 and 12 July 1764).

19 Ibid., pp. 88–9, 132, 134 (11 September, 11 and 15 October 1764).

20 *Temple*, p. 106; *GT(i)*, p. 23 (13 July 1764).

21 *GT(i)*, pp. 42–5 (31 July 1764).

22 In her article on Boswell's efforts to meet Frederick, in 'James Boswell and Frederick of Prussia', *Studies on Voltaire and the Eighteenth Century*, 305 (1992), pp. 1654–7, Marlies K. Danziger analyses the letter from Burnet for perspectives on Boswell's failure to meet Frederick the Great.

23 Burnet archive, Kemnay House, Aberdeenshire, cited in Danziger, 'Boswell and Frederick'; Sir Andrew Mitchell, 'Memories of Ayrshire about 1780', *Miscellany of the Scottish History Society*, 33 (1939), VI, p. 264; *GT(i)*, p. 99.

24 *Grange*, p. 133 (to Grange, 10 September 1764).

25 To Kames, 27 September 1764 (BP: L817); *GT(i)*, p. 116 (1 October 1764); to Marischal, 30 October 1764 (BP: L951; cited in *GT(i)*, pp. 158–9).

26 *GT(i)*, pp. 170–79 (9–17 November 1764).

27 Ibid., pp. 307–8.

ELEVEN 'Above the Vulgar Crowd': Meeting Rousseau and Voltaire

1 *GT(i)*, pp. 210–11 (3 December 1764).

2 Ibid., pp. 212–13.

3 BP: L1105–6 (cited in *GT(i)*, pp. 213–15, to Rousseau, 3 December 1764).

4 Boswell's account of the first interview is in *GT(i)*, pp. 216–20 (3 December 1764).

5 Rousseau to Alexandre Deleyre, 20 December 1764 (BP: C2416): to Dempster, 3 December 1764 (BP: L418).

6 *GT(i)*, pp. 222–4 (4 December 1764).

7 Ibid., pp. 224–6 (5 December 1764).

8 Ibid., p. 226.

9 Ibid., p. 229 (see also *Earlier Years*, p. 5).

10 BP: C1432 (cited in *GT(i)*, pp. 236–41, from Hailes, 10 October 1764); *GT(i)*, p. 233 (6 December 1764).

11 *GT(i)*, pp. 245–7 (14 December 1764).

12 Ibid., pp. 247–50.

13 Ibid., pp. 251–9 (15 December 1764).

14 On the complexities of Buttafaco's negotiations with Rousseau, see Joseph Foladare, *Boswell's Paoli* (1979), pp. 24–8.

15 *GT(i)*, p. 256.

16 Ibid., pp. 272–4 (24 December 1764); to Temple, 28 December 1764 (*Temple*, p. 124).

17 *GT(i)*, p. 175 (25 December 1764); to Louise (Mignot) Denis, 25 December 1764 (BP: L424).

18 *GT(i)*, pp. 279–93 (27–28 December 1764); to Temple, 28 December 1764 (*Temple*, pp. 124–5).

19 *GT(i)*, p. 279 n.

20 Frederick Pottle reminds us that most such notes and memoranda of his very long conversations with Johnson, Rousseau, Voltaire, Hume, Wilkes, and many others did remain as notes, except where, as in the *Life of Johnson*, he wrote them up for publication.

21 *GT(i)*, p. 296 (29 December); to Voltaire, 29 December 1764 (BP: L1261).

TWELVE O Italy!

1 *GT(ii)*, p. 21; to Rousseau, 3 October 1765 (BP: L1115; cited in English, *GT(ii)*, p. 3); to Temple, 28 December 1764 (*Temple*, p. 125); to Grange, 15 January 1765 (*Grange*, p. 152); *GT(ii)*, pp. 23–4 (6–7 January 1765).

2 G. M. Trevelyan, 'The Age of Johnson', *Johnson's England*, ed. A. S. Turberville, I, p. 2.

3 *The Wealth of Nations*, cited by H. L. Beales, 'Travel and Communications', *Johnson's England*, I, pp. 157–8.

4 BP: L1117 (cited in *GT(ii)*, pp. 3–4, to Rousseau, 3 October 1765).

5 *GT(ii)*, pp. 25–6, 30 (8, 10–11 January 1765).

6 Ibid., pp. 29–31 (10–11 January 1765).

7 Ibid., pp. 32–3, 36 (12–13, 14 January 1765).

8 Ibid., pp. 40–41 (21 January 1765).

9 Ibid., pp. 43–4 (22, 24 January 1765).

10 *Grange*, p. 166 (to Grange, 11 May 1765); *GT(ii)*, pp. 45–6 (26 January 1765).

11 Deleyre to Rousseau, 18 February 1765, *Correspondence générale de J.-J. Rousseau*, XIII, pp. 18–24 (BP: C293; cited in English, *GT(ii)*, p. 50).

12 *GT(ii)*, pp. 53–4 (20 February 1765).

13 To Alexander Dick, 22 May 1765 (*Letters*, I, pp. 79–80); to Grange, 19 March 1765 (*Grange*, p. 159).

14 *Grange*, pp. 159–60 (to Grange, 19 March 1765); to Rousseau, 3 October 1765 (BP: L1117; cited in *GT(ii)*, p. 6).

15 *GT(ii)*, pp. 63–6 (25–30 March 1765).

16 *Temple*, p. 134 (to Temple, 22 April 1765); *GT(ii)*, p. 67 (4 April 1765).

17 *GT(ii)*, pp. 78, 80 (4, 10 May 1765); to Grange 11 May 1765 (*Grange*, pp. 164–5). On Willison's portrait and Alves' miniature, see Chauncey B. Tinker and Frederick A. Pottle, *A New Portrait of James Boswell* (1927). Boswell had a miniature done of the portrait for Grange by another Scot in Rome, James Alves, which unhappily has gone missing.

18 *Grange*, pp. 164–5; *GT(ii)*, p. 4.

19 To Rousseau, 3 October 1765; *GT(ii)*, pp. 78 (2 May 1765), 11.

20 Ibid., pp. 68, 86 (5 April, 14 May 1765); to Rousseau, 3 October 1765.

21 Boswell's political leanings in these early days are taken up by Frank Brady, *Boswell's Political Career* (1965), chapter 2.

22 BP: L1280 (cited in *Letters*, I, pp. 68–9, to Wilkes, 9 January 1765); to Rousseau, 3 October 1765; to Temple, 22 April 1765 (*Temple*, p. 133); to Wilkes, ?March 1765 (BP: L1282; cited in *Letters*, I, p. 71); *GT(ii)*, p. 62 (19 March 1765).

23 From Wilkes, 27 April 1765 (BP: C3088; cited in *GT(ii)*, p. 75); to Wilkes, 22 April 1765 (BP: L1283; cited in *Letters*, I, pp. 72–3).

24 To Wilkes, 15 June 1765 (BP: L1285; cited in *Letters*, I, p. 81); to Rousseau, 3 October 1765.

25 *GT(ii)*, pp. 88–92 (24 May–4 June 1765); to Rousseau, 3 October 1765.

26 To Rousseau, 3 October 1765.

27 *GT(i)*, pp. 113–14 (27 July 1765).

28 Ibid., pp. 142 ('Sienese Reflections'); to Porzia Sansedoni, 25–31 August 1765 (BP: L1128, L1129; cited in *GT(ii)*, pp. 124–5, 6 September 1765 (BP: L1132–1133; cited in *GT(ii)*, p. 133); to Grange, 28 September 1765 (*Grange*, p. 188).

29 *GT(ii)*, pp. 137, 16 (to Rousseau, 3 October 1765); to Grange, 28 September 1765 (*Grange*, p. 188).

30 BP: C2250, 2251 (cited in *GT(ii)*, pp. 141, 144, from Piccolimini, ?18 September 1765).

31 *GT(ii)*, pp. 86, 121 (from Rousseau, 30 May 1765, BP: C2417), 145 (29 September 1765), 229–35 (from Piccolimini, 3–21 October 1765, BP: C2252–2255).

32 From Lord Auchinleck, 10 August, 16 September, 1 October 1765 (BP: C227–229; cited in *GT(ii)*, pp. 222–8).

33 *Grange*, p. 190 (to Grange, 9 October 1765).

34 For his political instincts in Corsica, see Brady, *Boswell's Political Career*, pp. 37–44.

35 On Boswell's journey to Corsica, see *Earlier Years*, pp. 244–50. For the pre-Romanticism in Boswell's enthusiasm for Corsica, see also, more recently, Thomas M. Curley's 'Boswell's Liberty-Loving *Account of Corsica* and the Art of Travel Literature', in *New Light*, pp. 89–103.

36 *GT(ii)*, p. 158 (6–11 October 1765).

37 Ibid., pp. 160, 162 (12–13 October 1765).

38 Ibid., pp. 164–8 (14–18 October 1765).

39 Ibid., pp. 168–9, 170 (19–20 October 1765).

40 Ibid., p. 171 (21 October 1765); *Burney Diary*, II (1904–5), p. 100.

41 *GT(ii)*, pp. 173 (22–27 October 1765), 185 (22–27 October 1765).

42 Ibid., pp. 185, 179, 199.

43 Ibid., p. 201 (28 October 1765); *Boswelliana*, p. 328 (27 May 1783).

44 *GT(ii)*, pp. 209–14 (9–20 November 1765); to Grange, 14 November 1765 (*Grange*, p. 191).

45 *Grange*, pp. 191–2 (to Grange, 24 November 1765); *GT(ii)*, p. 221 (21–28 November 1765).

46 *GT(ii)*, pp. 236–7 (1–9 December 1765). Count Antonio Rivarola, Sardinian Consul in Leghorn and a friend of Sir John Dick, British Consul in Leghorn, who befriended Boswell and provided him with valuable letters of introduction for Corsica, was also having him tracked. He sent a number of reports on him to the King of Sardinia.

47 Ibid., p. 222.

48 *GT(i)*, p. 261; *GT(ii)*, pp. 239–40 (10–11 December 1765).

49 *GT(ii)*, pp. 243 (12 December 1765), 250 (17 December 1765).

50 Ibid., pp. 251–2 (18 December 1765).

51 Ibid., pp. 252, 254 (18, 21 December 1765); to Grange, 27 December 1765 (*Grange*, p. 203); *GT(ii)*, p. 272 (2 January 1766).

52 BP: L1119 (cited in *GT(ii)*, p. 275; *Letters*, I, pp. 85–7); from Piccolomini, 12 December 1765 (BP: C2256; cited in *GT(ii)*, pp. 277–81); *GT(ii)*, p. 255 (21 December 1765); to Temple, 26 January 1766 (*Temple*, p. 138).

53 Walpole to Gray, *Walpole Corr.*, XIV, pp. 170–71 (18 February 1768), 174 (25 February).

54 *GT(ii)*, p. 287 (27–28 January 1766); from Lord Auchinleck, 11 January 1766 (BP: C230; cited in *GT(ii)*, pp. 288–9; *GT(ii)*, p. 292 (30 January 1766); to Temple, 29 January 1766 (*Temple*, p. 139); to Wilkes, 6 May 1766 (BP: L1290; cited in *Letters*, I, pp. 89–90).

55 *GT(ii)*, p. 290 (29 January 1766). David Buchanan has summarized the controversy over these missing pages in *The Treasure of Auchinleck*, Appendix IV. One of Pottle's objections to Isham's account was that he makes no mention of a violent storm that for days delayed the packet from Calais and wrecked many ships along the Channel coasts. Pottle insisted that this is just the sort of detail Boswell would never have omitted. Another objection is that much of the language and emphasis is Ishamesque, not Boswellian (*Earlier Years*, p. 277).

56 Ibid., pp. 293–4.

57 Ibid., pp. 313–18. For another viewpoint on Rousseau's relations with Boswell, see R. A. Leigh, 'Boswell and Rousseau', *Modern Language Review*, 47 (1952), pp. 289–318. Hume did not know Boswell was the inspiration for the print when he wrote as follows about it: 'M. Rousseau is represented as a Yahoo, newly caught in the woods; I am represented as a farmer, who caresses him and offers him some oats to eat, which he refuses in a rage; Voltaire and D'Alembert are whipping him up behind; and Horace Walpole making him horns of *papier-mâché*. The idea is not altogether absurd' (*The Letters of David Hume*, ed. J. Y. T. Greig, 1932, II, p. 120).

THIRTEEN 'Like Embroidery upon Gauze': *Corsica*, Law, and Propaganda

1 *GT(i)*, pp. 115–16; *GT(ii)*, p. 313 (23 February 1766).

2 *GT(ii)*, p. 298 (13 February 1766); *Wife*, p. 43 (March 1767).

3 *GT(ii)*, pp. 300–3 (16 February 1766); to Temple, 17 March 1766 (*Temple*, p. 143).

4 *GT(ii)*, pp. 299–300 (15 February 1766).

5 Ibid., p. 300 (16 February 1766).

6 *Gen. Corr. (i)*, p. 2 (to Pitt, 19 February 1766).

7 Ibid. *(i)*, pp. 2 (from Pitt, 16 February 1766), 139 (to Pitt, 8 April 1767); *GT(ii)*, pp. 308–11; to Temple, 17 May 1766 (*Temple*, pp. 150, 170 n. 34).

8 *GT(ii)*, pp. 258–60. Boswell kept a file of his contributions to the *London Chronicle*; see *Literary Career*, pp. 236–47.

9 *Gen. Corr. (i)*, p. 75 (to Sir Alexander Dick, 23 October 1766); to Temple, 1 February 1766 (*Temple*, p. 167).

10 From Johnson, 21 August 1766 (*JL*, I, p. 73).

11 *Life of Johnson*, II, pp. 58–9. See Thomas M. Curley's fertile essay on the synthesis of Boswell's libertarian radicalism and pursuit of greatness in *An Account of Corsica*, in *New Light*, pp. 89–103.

12 *Gen. Corr. (i)*, pp. 139–40 (to Pitt, 8 April 1767); to Temple, 30 March 1767 (*Temple*, p. 182); to Sir Alexander Dick, 27 August 1767 (*Gen. Corr. (i)*, p. 205); from Hailes, 29 August 1766 (BP: C1433).

13 *Gen. Corr. (i)*, pp. 205, 83 (from Davies, 15 November 1766), 193 (to Edward Dilly, 6 August 1767).

14 *Temple*, pp. 206 (to Temple, 9 September 1767), 214 (to Temple, 9 November 1767).

15 Ibid., p. 227 (to Temple, 24 March 1768); Gray to Walpole, 25 February 1768 (*Walpole Corr.*, XIV, p. 174).

16 *JL*, I, pp. 328–9 (from Johnson, 9 September 1769); *Wife*, p. 177 (2 May 1768).

17 See *Literary Career*, pp. 63–75.

18 *Temple*, p. 242 (to Temple, 24 August 1768); to Dick, 7 May 1768 (*Letters*, I, p. 157); *Literary Career*, pp. 76–85.

19 'Memoirs', *Literary Career*, p. xxxviii; *Wife*, pp. 288 (2 September 1769), 291; to Margaret Montgomerie, 5 September 1769 (BP: L169).

20 *Wife*, pp. 297–8 (6 September 1769).

21 Ibid., p. 300 (7 September 1769); from Temple, 22 September 1769 (*Temple*, p. 258); *Wife*, pp. 301–2 (7–8 September 1769).

22 *Wife*, p. 307 (12 September 1769).

23 Ibid., pp. 319–21 (22 September 1769).

24 Ibid., p. 325 (24 September 1769); to Sir Alexander Dick, 3 October 1769 (*Gen. Corr. (ii)*, p. 246).

25 *Temple*, p. 142 (to Temple, 6 March 1766); to Grange, 31 March 1766, 4 May 1766 (*Grange*, pp. 211, 214–15).

26 *Temple*, p. 153 (from Temple, 28 May 1766); to Johnson, 21 August 1766 (*JL*, I, p. 272); *Life of Johnson*, III, p. 357.

27 *Wife*, p. 310 (15 September 1769).

28 Ibid., p. 125 (16 January 1768); to Temple, 22 June 1767 (*Temple*, p. 190); to Sir Alexander Dick, 9 December 1766 (*Gen. Corr. (i)*, p. 93); *Wife*, p. 245 (15 July 1769); *Gen. Corr. (i)*, p. xlv.

29 *Boswelliana*, p. 242.

30 For a lucid and brief explanation of the Scots legal system, see *Defence*, pp. 364–72. I draw on these pages for most of my background to Boswell's legal work.

31 *Wife*, pp. 32–3 (21, 25 February 1767).

32 Ibid., p. 35 (3 March 1767); to Temple, 22 June 1767; from Temple, 24 June 1767; to Temple, 26 June 1767 (*Temple*, pp. 189, 191, 192).

33 *Gen. Corr. (i)*, pp. 93 (to Sir Alexander Dick, 9 December 1766), xl; *Wife*, p. 60 (14 April 1767).

34 *Gen. Corr. (i)*, pp. 82 (from John Reid, 13 November 1766), 86 (from John Johnstoun, 20 November 1766).

35 Ibid., pp. 95 (from Sir Alexander Dick, 17 December 1766), 118 (from Pringle, 10 February 1767).

36 *Wife*, pp. 69–70 (4 May 1767), 72 (11 May 1767); from James Maitland, 18 May 1767 (*Gen. Corr. (i)*, pp. 165–6). See also *Gen. Corr. (i)*, pp. 160–1 n.

37 From Hailes, 13 April 1768 (BP: C1436); *Wife*, pp. 27–8, 30, 56 (10–11, 15 February 1767; 2 April 1767). The reader is referred to a brilliant analysis of the psychology of Boswell's 'sympathy' for John Reid and other sufferers in society in Gordon Turnbull's 'Boswell and Sympathy: The Trial and Execution of John Reid', *New Light*, pp. 104–15.

38 Ibid., pp. 139–41 (21–24 February 1768), 150–51 (23 March 1768).

39 *Tour to the Hebrides*, in *Life of Johnson*, V, p. 28; 'Memoir', *Literary Career*, p. xxxv.

40 *Wife*, p. 29 (14 February 1767). See *Literary Career*, p. 27, and to Grange, 28 May 1767 (*Grange*, pp. 229–30).

41 *Wife*, pp. xvi, 60 (15 April 1767). On the complication publication details of *Dorando*, see *Literary Career*, pp. 32–7.

42 *Dorando: A Spanish Tale*, pp. 41–2.

43 *Wife*, p. 101 (8 October 1767); *Early Career*, p. 333.

44 *Grange*, p. 232 (Erskine to Grange, 4 August 1767).

45 *Literary Career*, pp. 238–63 passim.

46 *Wife*, pp. 180–86 (20–22 May 1768). Boswell visited Mansfield twice, on 20 and 22 May.

47 Ramsay to Charles Yorke, 23 March 1769 (Add. Ms. 35,639, d. 42, Hardwicke MSS), *Scotland and Scotsmen*, ed. Alexander Allardyce (1888), I, pp. 172–3. Pottle describes the riots, *Earlier Years*, pp. 398–9.

48 From Hailes, 4 March 1769 (BP: C1439); from Marischal, 26 August 1769 (*Gen. Corr. (ii)*, p. 226); from Dempster, 12 March 1769 (*Gen. Corr. (ii)*, p. 156). The confusion of 2 March was reported in the *Scots Magazine*, XXXI, p. 109.

FOURTEEN 'Happy as an Unmarried Man Can Be'

1 *Wife*, pp. 147 (20 March), 149 (22 March 1766).

2 *Temple*, p. 146 (to Temple, 28 April 1766).

3 Ibid., pp. 149 (to Temple, 17 May 1766), 159 (from Temple, 20 November 1766).

4 Ibid., p. 165 (to Temple, 1 February 1767).

5 Ibid., p. 166 (to Temple, 4 March 1767).

6 Ibid., pp. 166–8.

7 *Temple*, p. 168; Ober, *Boswell's Clap*, p. 13.

8 *Temple*, pp. 192 (to Temple, 26 June 1767), 195 (from Temple, 27 June 1767).

9 *Wife*, p. 68 (27 April 1767).

10 *Gen. Corr. (i)*, pp. 211–12 (from Marischal, 1 September 1767), 217 (from Marischal, 12 September 1767).

11 *Temple*, p. 219 (to Temple, 24 December 1767). Ober writes as follows about Boswell's infections at this point: 'By this time his urethral infection was so firmly established in its chronicity that he was probably never without some form of discharge, usually clear' (*Boswell's Clap*, p. 15).

12 Ibid., p. 181 (to Temple, 30 March 1767).

13 *Wife*, pp. 59–61.

14 Ibid., pp. 72–3 (28 May–2 June); to Temple, 12 and 22 June (*Temple*, pp. 187, 190).

15 *Temple*, pp. 192–3, 197 (to Temple, 26 June and 29 July 1767), 198 (from Temple, 7 August 1767).

16 Ibid., pp. 201, 204 (from Temple, 25 August and 3 September 1767), 205, 202, 203 (to Temple, 9 September, 28 August, 29 August 1767).

17 Ibid., pp. 212–13 (to Temple, 8 November 1767).

18 Ibid., p. 214 (to Temple, 9 November 1767); from Pringle, 4 December 1767 (*Gen. Corr. (i)*, p. 261).

19 *Temple*, pp. 217–19 (to Temple, 24 December 1767).

20 Ibid., p. 220 (from Temple, 8 January 1768); *Wife*, p. 131 (27 January 1768); to Temple, 8 February 1768 (*Temple*, pp. 222–3).

21 *Wife*, pp. 195–6 (9 December 1768).

22 Ibid., p. 126 (16 January 1768).

23 *Temple*, p. 167 (to Temple, 1 February 1767).

24 *Gen. Corr. (i)*, p. 242 (from Brown, 22 October 1767); to Temple, 8 November 1767 (*Temple*, p. 213).
25 *Holland*, pp. 357–9 (from Zélide, 16 February 1768).
26 Ibid., pp. 359–61 (to Zélide, 26 February 1768).
27 Ibid., p. 372 (2 June 1768). Geoffrey Scott writes entertainingly about Zélide's rejection, *Portrait of Zélide*, pp. 41–2.

FIFTEEN 'The Rage for Matrimony'

1 *Wife*, p. 150–54 (22–25 March 1768).
2 Ibid., pp. 157–67 (26–28 March 1768).
3 Ibid., p. 169 (29 March 1768).
4 *Temple*, pp. 232, 142 (to Temple, 26 April, 24 August 1768).
5 *Wife*, p. 174; to Temple, 14 May 1768 (*Temple*, p. 236).
6 *Wife*, pp. 186–9 (7 June 1768). Unfortunately, Boswell uncharacteristically failed to record much of the talk. Richard B. Sher analyses Boswell's own complex responses to Scottish authors like Robertson, Blair, and Kames in 'Scottish Divines and Legal Lairds', *New Light*, pp. 28–55.
7 See *Life of Johnson*, I, p. 495; II, p. 77. For a complete picture of Boswell's relationship with Mrs Thrale, written sympathetically from her point of view, see Mary Hyde's entertaining book, *The Impossible Friendship: Boswell and Mrs Thrale* (1973); see also Clifford, Piozzi, pp. 63–78, and *Life of Johnson*, Appendix F.
8 *Temple*, pp. 190–92 (to Temple, 24 August 1768).
9 *Temple*, p. 246 (to Temple, 3 May 1769).
10 Ibid.
11 Ibid.
12 Ibid.
13 *Wife*, pp. 226–7 (?21 June 1769).
14 *Gen. Corr. (ii)*, p. 178 (to Sir Alexander Dick, 29 May 1769).
15 *Wife*, p. 222 (12–13 June 1769).
16 *Wife*, pp. 222–46 passim (12 June–17 July 1769).
17 *Temple*, pp. 164 (to Temple, 1 February 1767), 213 (to Temple, 8 November 1767); from Pringle, 4 December 1767 (*Gen. Corr. (i)*, pp. 261–2).
18 *Wife*, p. 231 (1 July 1769).
19 Ibid., p. 232 (4 July 1769); from Margaret Montgomerie, 1 July 1769 (BP: C421).
20 *Wife*, pp. 232 (4 July 1769), 240–41 (13 July 1769), 245 (16 July 1769); to Margaret Montgomerie, 17 July 1769 (BP: L165; cited in *Wife*, p. 247). In an essay, 'On Second Marriages', which he may have written for a magazine but never sent out, he fictionalized this family quarrel as an indictment of his father (*Wife*, pp. 248–50).
21 Ibid., pp. 240, 244–5 (13, 14 July 1769), 270, 280 (26 August 1769).
22 To Margaret Montgomerie, 20 July 1769 (BP: L166; cited in *Wife*, pp. 252–3); from Margaret Montgomerie, 22 July 1769 (BP: C423; cited in *Wife*, p. 256); *Wife*, p. 262 (4 August 1769); from Temple, 28 July 1769 (*Temple*, p. 251).
23 From Margaret Montgomerie, 10 August 1769 (BP: C426; cited in *Wife*, pp. 267–70).
24 *Wife*, pp. 270–71 (13 August 1769).
25 Ibid., pp. 305, 308, 337 (11, 14 September; 16 October 1769); to Grange, 16 October 1769 (*Grange*, p. 258). On the treatments for gonorrhoea available in London, see Stone, *The Family, Sex and Marriage in England, 1500–1800*, (1979), pp. 582–3, 600.

26 *Temple*, p. 260 (from Temple, 6 October 1769); from Margaret Montgomerie, 10 August 1769; to Grange, 5 September 1769 (*Grange*, p. 253).

27 From Johnson, 9 September 1769 (*JL*, I, p. 329); to Margaret Montgomerie, 2 October and 23 November 1769 (BP: L170, L172; cited in *Wife*, pp. 328–30, 369).

28 Boswell to Hester Thrale, 5 September 1769, MS Hyde; cited in *Impossible Friendship*, pp. 14–15; *Wife*, pp. 332–4 (6 October 1769).

29 *Life of Johnson*, II, pp. 93–4, 107.

30 *Wife*, p. 318 (21 September 1769).

31 Ibid., pp. 321–2, 334–6 (22 September, 6–10 October 1769).

32 From Margaret Montgomerie, 31 October 1769 (BP: C429; cited in *Wife*, pp. 361–2).

33 *Life of Johnson*, II, pp. 109–10.

34 To Margaret Montgomerie, 5 November 1769 (BP: L171; cited in *Wife*, pp. 365–6).

35 From Margaret Montgomerie, 24 October 1769 (BP: C428; cited in *Wife*, pp. 358–9).

36 To Margaret Montgomerie, 23 November 1769, BP: L172; *Ominous*, p. 54 (9 January 1775).

37 *Temple*, p. 267 (from Temple, 15 December 1769).

SIXTEEN Settling Down: 'The Antechamber of His Mind'

1 *Temple*, p. 275 (from Temple, ?25 May 1770).

2 To Margaret Boswell, 7 February 1770 (BP: L173); to Temple, 6 October, 7 May 1770 (*Temple*, pp. 287, 273).

3 *Temple*, pp. 269 (from Temple, 15 December 1769), 284 (to Temple, 6 September 1770), 286 (from Temple, 30 September 1770).

4 *Grange*, p. 260 (to Grange, 31 May 1770). See Thomas Crawford, 'Boswell's Houses', *Writers and Their Houses*, ed. Kate Marsh (1993), pp. 31–8, and *Edinburgh*, Buildings of Scotland Series (1984), p. 211.

5 *Grange*, p. 264 (to Grange 29 August 1770); to Temple, 6 September 1770 (*Temple*, p. 284).

6 *Grange*, pp. 264 (to Grange, 22 May 1771), 273 (to Grange, 20 October 1771); to Temple, 27 December 1771 (*Temple*, p. 304).

7 *Grange*, p. 265. See Crawford, 'Boswell's Houses', *Writers and Their Houses*.

8 *Grange*, pp. 267–72 (to Grange, 27 August 1771).

9 *Temple*, pp. 271 (from Temple, 26 April 1770), 277 (to Temple, 19 June 1770), 279 (from Temple, 5 July 1770), 293 (from Temple, 26 April 1771).

10 *Grange*, pp. 264 (to Grange, 22 May 1771), 273 (to Grange, 20 October 1771); from Hailes, 23 September 1771 (BP: C1442).

11 *Grange*, pp. 266–7 (to Grange, 22 May 1771).

12 *Life of Johnson*, II, p. 172; 'The Moderator's Advice to James Boswell Esq. ... on his first appearance as a Lawyer at the Bar of the General Assembly' (BP: C1110).

13 *Grange*, p. 261 (to Grange, 31 May 1770).

14 *Life of Johnson*, II, pp. 47–8.

15 See *Literary Career*, pp. 215–58.

16 *Temple*, p. 318 (from Temple, 5 October 1772).

17 *London Magazine* (September 1770). His interest in the *London Magazine* was worth £240 in 1777. See *Wife*, p. 336 (14 October 1769); *Defence*, p. 17; and *Literary Career*, p. 221.

18 *Wife*, pp. 344–6 (19–20 October 1769); J. C. Dibdin, *Annals of the Edinburgh Stage* (1888), p. 153; to Garrick, 30 March 1771 (*GBM*, p. 31).

19 *GBM*, pp. 32, 35 (from Garrick, 30 March, 18 April 1771); *Defence*, p. 124 (15 April 1772).

20 *Literary Career*, p. 88; to Garrick, 18 September 1772, from Garrick, 2 March 1772 (*GBM*, pp. 39, 42).

21 *GBM*, pp. 5–9.

22 He wrote up the article from condensed journal notes (BP: J22).

23 *Literary Career*, p. 247; New Hailes Ms.

24 *Life of Johnson*, II, pp. 139–40 (to Johnson, 18 April 1771); from Johnson, 20 June 1771 (*JL*, I, pp. 362–3); to James Beattie, 27 July 1771 (*Letters*, I, p. 181).

25 *Letters*, I, p. 186 (to Johnson, 3 March 1772); from Johnson, 15 March 1772 (*JL*, I, p. 388); *Life of Johnson* (Limited Editions Club, London, 1938), I, p. 465.

26 *Letters*, I, p. 186; from Johnson, 15 March 1772 (*JL*, I, p. 389).

SEVENTEEN 'The Down upon a Plum'

1 *Defence*, pp. 30, 32–3 (14, 16 March 1772).

2 Ibid., pp. 36–7, 69, 90–91 (19, 26, 31 March 1772).

3 Ibid., p. 95 (2 April 1772); from Grange, 18 April 1772 (*Grange*, p. 280).

4 *Temple*, pp. 364 (to Temple, 4 April 1775), 375 (to Temple, 22 May 1775); *Defence*, p. 79 (29 March 1772); Notes, BP: J25.

5 *Grange*, pp. 280–81; *Defence*, pp. 34, 46, 83 (19, 21, 30 March 1772).

6 *Defence*, pp. 108 (10 April 1772), 104 (7 April 1772).

7 Ibid., pp. 108–12 (10 April 1772).

8 Ibid., pp. 133–5, 114, 136, 86 (19, 11, 20 April 1772; 31 March 1772).

9 Ibid., pp. 123–4; *Life of Johnson*, II, p. 192.

10 Notes, BP: J24, J27 (*Defence*, p. 139).

11 *Defence*, pp. 137–8 (20 April 1772).

12 Ibid., pp. 117, 134 (13, 19 April 1772), 86–7; Notes, BP: J25 (11 May 1772).

13 *Defence*, pp. 127–8 (15 April 1772).

14 Ibid., p. 128.

15 Ibid., pp. 58–60, 113 (23 March, 11 April 1772); *Life of Johnson*, II, pp. 183–5.

16 *Defence*, pp. 118–23 (14 April 1772); from Temple, 2 May 1772 (*Temple*, pp. 312–13).

17 *Defence*, pp. 122, 125, 128 (14, 15 April 1772).

18 Ibid., pp. 100, 103 (6 April 1772).

19 Ibid., pp. 45–6 (21 March 1772).

20 Ibid., pp. 55, 131–2 (22 March, 17 April 1772).

21 See Brady, *Boswell's Political Career*, pp. 52–4.

22 From Johnson, 25 December 1772 (*Letters*, I, p. 90); *Life of Johnson*, III, pp. 321–2; to Garrick, 10 September 1772 (*GBM*, pp. 44–5).

23 *Members*, pp. 16 (from Percy, 24 August 1772), 18 (to Percy, 1 March 1773).

24 *Defence*, p. 53 (21 March 1772); from Pringle, 19 September 1772 (BP: C2302, cited in *Defence*, p. 144); from Temple, 5 October 1772 (*Temple*, pp. 317, 319).

25 *Defence*, pp. 146, 153–6.

26 Ibid., pp. 147, 153 (8, 9 January 1773).

27 *Members*, p. 19 (to Percy, 1 March 1773).

28 *Defence*, pp. 162–3 (30 March 1773), 167–8 (5 April 1773).

29 Ibid., p. 157; Goldsmith, 29 March 1773 (*Members*, p. 25).

30 *Defence*, pp. 165–6 (3 April 1773), 95–6 (3 April 1772); *Life of Johnson*, II, pp. 210, 501; from Goldsmith, 4 April 1773 (*Members*, p. 26).
31 *Defence*, pp. 174–5 (7 April 1773).
32 *Life of Johnson*, II, p. 257.
33 *GBM*, p. 60 (to Garrick, 11 April 1774); Sir James Northcote, *Memoirs of Sir Joshua Reynolds* (1813), I, p. 327. In his tribute to Goldsmith, Boswell published for the first time several lines of a song Goldsmith wrote for but left out of *She Stoops to Conquer*. 'As I could sing the tune,' he writes, 'and was fond of them, he was so good as to give me them about a year ago just as I was leaving London and bidding him adieu for that season, little apprehending that it was a last farewell.' He had preserved it since 'with an affectionate care'.
34 *Members*, p. 27 (to Percy, 16 April 1773); Johnson to Goldsmith, 23 April 1773 (*JL*, II, p. 27).
35 *Defence*, p. 172 (7 April 1773); *Life of Johnson*, II, p. 240; *Hebrides*, p. 53 (21 August 1773).
36 *Defence.*, p. 169 (5 April 1773).
37 Ibid., pp. 174–5 (7 April 1773); Clifford, *Piozzi*, pp. 97–9.
38 *Defence*, pp. 179–80, 181–3 (9, 11 April 1773).
39 *Life of Johnson*, II, p. 242. On Boswell's ambivalence about his accent, see Rogers, 'Boswell and the Scotticism', *New Light*, pp. 56–71.
40 *Defence*, p. 194; *Life of Johnson*, p. 247.
41 *GBM*, p. 56 (from Garrick, 14 September 1773); from Temple, 14 June 1773 (*Temple*, p. 329).
42 *Members*, p. 34 (to Langton, 14 August 1773); *Defence*, pp. 200–2.
43 *Literary Career*, pp. 98–100.
44 *Impossible Friendship*, p. 20 (Rylands: Eng. MS. 539/30); *Life of Johnson*, II, p. 264; Rylands: Eng. MS 542/1.
45 *Members*, p. 33 (to Langton, 14 August 1773).

EIGHTEEN The Hebrides

1 *Hebrides*, p. 11 (14 August). All citations from *Hebrides* are dated 1773.
2 Ibid., p. 10; Janet Adam Smith, 'Some Eighteenth-Century Ideas of Scotland', *Scotland in the Age of Improvement*, ed. N. T. Phillipson and Rosalind Mitchison (1970), p. 115.
3 *Hebrides*, pp. 13, 27 (14 August); Johnson to Hester Thrale, 17 August 1773 (*JL*, II, p. 52).
4 *Life of Johnson*, II, p. 269 n. 1; Johnson to Hester Thrale, 3 November 1773 (*JL*, II, p. 111). Boswell wrote in his journal that when they left Edinburgh, Johnson entrusted to Margaret's care a volume of 'a pretty full and curious Diary of his Life, of which I have a few fragments, but the book has been destroyed. I wish female curiosity had been strong enough to have had it all transcribed, which might easily have been done; and I should think the theft, being *pro bono publico*, might have been forgiven. But I may be wrong. My wife told me she never once looked into it' (*Hebrides*, pp. 33–4, 18 August 1773).
5 Ibid., p. 17 (15 August); Johnson to Hester Thrale, 17 August 1773 (*JL*, II, p. 53).
6 *GBM*, pp. 53–4, 56 (to Garrick, 29 August, 1773), 56 (from Garrick, 14 September 1773); *Hebrides*, p. 86 (26 August); Johnson's *Journey*, p. 18.

7 Peter Levi's introduction to his Penguin edition of Johnson's *Journey to the Western Islands of Scotland* and Boswell's *Journal of a Tour to the Hebrides* (1984), p. 12.

8 Johnson's *Journey*, pp. 1, 8, 61, 90.

9 *Hebrides*, p. xi.

10 Ibid., pp. 165, 188, 226 (13, 19, 27 September); 241–2 (2 October), 245 (3 October).

11 Ibid., pp. 33–4, 46 (18, 19 August).

12 Ibid., pp. 37 n. 9, 51–7 (21 August).

13 Ibid., p. 58 (21 August).

14 Ibid., p. 59.

15 Ibid., pp. 59–61 (22 August); Johnson's *Journey*, p. 13.

16 *Hebrides*, pp. 71–2 (24 August); Johnson's *Journey*, p. 14.

17 *Hebrides*, pp. 81, 84 (26 August).

18 *Hebrides*, p. 95 (28 August).

19 Ibid., pp. 95–6 (29 August).

20 Johnson's *Journey*, p. 21.

21 *Hebrides*, p. 100 (30 August).

22 Johnson's *Journey*, p. 31; Johnson to Hester Thrale, 6 September 1773 (*JL*, II, p. 66).

23 *Hebrides*, pp. 105–6 (31 August).

24 Ibid., pp. 107–9 (1 September).

25 Ibid., p. 110.

26 Ibid., pp. 111–12; Johnson to Hester Thrale, 21 September 1773 (*JL*, II, p. 76); Johnson's *Journey*, p. 39.

27 Ibid., pp. 114–15.

28 Ibid., pp. 116–17 (3 September).

29 Ibid., pp. 119–27 (6–8 September).

30 Ibid., p. 127 (8 September).

31 Ibid., pp. 131–55 (8–12 September).

32 *JL*, II, p. 70 (Johnson to Hester Thrale, 14 September 1773); Johnson's *Journey*, p. 47.

33 *Hebrides*, pp. 158–64 (12–13 September).

34 Ibid., p. 165 (13 September).

35 Ibid., pp. 166–99 (13–22 September).

36 Ibid., p. 204 (22 September).

37 Ibid., pp. 213, 217 (23, 24 September).

38 Ibid., pp. 221–31 (25–28 September).

39 Ibid., pp. 243–4 (2 October).

40 Ibid., pp. 246–50 (3 October).

41 Ibid., pp. 298, 300 (14 October).

42 Ibid., pp. 302–3, 349 (14, 23 October).

43 Ibid., pp. 312–24 (17–19 October).

44 *JL*, II, p. 104 (to Hester Thrale, 23 October 1773).

45 *Hebrides*, pp. 324–38 (19–20 October).

46 Ibid., pp. 344 (21 October).

47 Ibid., pp. 351–6 (24–25 October).

48 *London Journal*, p. 331, (30 July 1763).

49 *Tour*, p. 376 (6 November).

50 *Life of Johnson*, II, pp. 268–9.

51 *Hebrides*, p. 394; *Life of Johnson*, II, p. 272 (29 January 1774).

NINETEEN Post-Hebrides: Ominous Edinburgh Flatness

1 *Defence*, pp. 207 (June 1774), 226 (25 June 1774).
2 Ibid., p. 224 (20 June 1774); from Johnson, *c.* 19 March 1774 (*JL*, II, p. 133).
3 Henry Dundas is a figure that continues to haunt Boswell in the following pages. For a recent assessment of their relationship, see Michael Fry, 'James Boswell, Henry Dundas, and Enlightened Politics', *Citizen*, pp. 87–100.
4 BP: C2308 (from Pringle, 2 February 1774); from Temple, 15 February 1774 (*Temple*, p. 340).
5 Frank Brady's review of this political skirmish is as good as they come – see *Political Career*, pp. 59–74.
6 *Boswelliana*, pp. 283–4.
7 *JL*, II, p. 133 (from Johnson, *c.* 19 March 1774); from Pringle, 2 February 1774 (BP: C2308).
8 *JL*, II, p. 123 (from Johnson, 29 January 1774); *Life of Johnson*, II, p. 285; to Johnson, 19 January 1775 (*Letters*, I, p. 207).
9 BP: C1451 (from Hailes, 9 March 1775).
10 *Defence*, pp. 220 (15 June 1774), 280 (11 August 1774).
11 Ibid., pp. 221 n. 3 (30 May 1774), 237 (14 July 1774), 239 (17 July 1774).
12 Ibid., pp. 224–5 (21 June 1774), 234–5 (9 July 1774), 242 (22 July 1774), 292 (24 August 1774), 334 (17 September 1774).
13 Ibid., p. 245 (28 July 1774).
14 Ibid., pp. 235 (10 July 1774), 242 (22 July 1774).
15 Ibid., pp. 247–363 passim (30 July–21 September 1774).
16 *Ominous*, pp. 48 (23 December 1774), 70 (23 February 1775).
17 *Defence*, pp. 264–5 (1 August 1774); from Nasmith, 6 September [1774] (BP: C2070).
18 *Defence*, pp. 278–9 (11 August 1774).
19 Ibid., pp. 304–5 (1 September 1774).
20 Ibid., pp. 296–303 (29–31 August 1774).
21 Gordon Turnbull, 'Boswell and Sympathy: The Trial and Execution of John Reid', *New Light*, pp. 104–15.
22 *Ominous*, p. 32 (31 October 1774).
23 Ibid., pp. 7, 27, 26, 30, 32 (21, 19, 28, 31 October), 251 (12 March 1776).
24 The Miller fiasco is unfolded in *Ominous*, pp. 11–15, 17–25, 38–9 (6 October–17 November 1774).
25 Ibid., pp. 63–4 (from Johnson, 7 February 1775). Boswell left out of the *Life of Johnson* the sensitive portion of the letter that he cited in his journal – see *JL*, II, p. 178 n. 9.
26 *Ominous*, pp. 34–5 (4 November 1775).
27 Ibid., p. 35 (9 November 1775).
28 Ibid., p. 64 (12 February 1775).
29 Ibid., p. 54 (10 January 1775).
30 Ibid., pp. 56 (18 January 1775), 218 (12 January 1775), 176 (7 November 1774).
31 Ibid., p. 48 (24 December 1774).
32 Ibid., p. 72 (5 March 1775); to Temple, 18 March 1775 (*Temple*, p. 359).
33 *Ominous*, pp. 74 (8 March 1775), 82 (19 March 1775).
34 Ibid., pp. 43–4 (9–11 December 1774), 78 (16 March 1775).
35 Ibid., p. 86 (21 March 1775).
36 Ibid., pp. 86–7.

TWENTY Picking Up Fragments

1 *Ominous*, p. 168 (19 October 1775).
2 Ibid., pp. 147–8 (16 April), 203 (22 December), 283 (20 March 1776); to Temple, 18 March 1775 (*Temple*, p. 358).
3 *Ominous*, p. 283.
4 *Temple*, pp. 375 (to Temple, 22 May 1775), 378 (from Temple, 27 May 1775).
5 *Ominous*, pp. 103, 90, 89, 97–8 (27, 23, 22, 26 March 1775).
6 Ibid., pp. 95, 111, 115, 139 (24, 31 March; 2, 11 April 1775).
7 Ibid., pp. 141–2 (13 April 1775).
8 Ibid., p. 88 (21 March 1775).
9 Ibid., pp. 109–10 (31 March 1775).
10 Ibid., p. 141 (12 April 1775).
11 *Temple*, pp. 375 (to Temple, 22 May 1775), 382 (from Temple, 16 June 1775), 414 (to Temple, 1 May 1776).
12 *JL*, II, p. 270 (from Johnson, 14 September 1775).
13 *Ominous*, pp. 103 (27 March, 1775), 144 (14 April 1775).
14 *Letters*, I, pp. 209–10 (to Johnson, 2 February 1775).
15 *JL*, II, pp. 176–7 (from Johnson, 7 February 1775); to Johnson, 18 February 1775 (*Letters*, I, pp. 210–11); from Johnson, 25 February 1775 (*JL*, II, pp. 180–81); *Ominous*, p. 87 (21 March 1775).
16 *JL*, II, p. 170 (from Johnson, 21 January 1775); to Johnson, 27 January 1775 (*Letters*, I, pp. 208–9); to Temple, 18 March 1775 (*Temple*, pp. 358–9).
17 *Temple*, p. 394 (to Temple, 12 August 1775).
18 *Ominous*, pp. 145–6 (14 April 1775).
19 Ibid., p. 150 (18 April 1775).
20 Ibid., pp. 151, 153 (18 April 1775), 138 (10 April 1775).
21 Ibid., p. 136 (7–8 April 1775); to Hester Thrale, 30 August 1776 (BP: L1072; cited in *Letters*, I, p. 255).
22 *Ominous*, pp. 101–2 (27 March 1775); to Temple, 10 May 1775 (*Temple*, p. 372).
23 BP: C2265 (from Hester Thrale, 18 May 1775); Johnson to Hester Thrale, 22 May and 11 June 1775 (*JL*, II, pp. 209, 223); from Johnson, 27 August 1775 (*JL*, II, p. 266). For a sensitive assessment and chronicle of these murky Hebridean waters, see *Impossible Friendship*, pp. 29–32.
24 *JL*, II, p. 270 (from Johnson, 14 September 1775); to Johnson, 24 October 1775 (*Letters*, I, p. 244); Johnson to Levett, 22 October 1775 (*JL*, II, p. 273).
25 *JL*, II, p. 274 (from Johnson, 16 November 1775); *Life of Johnson*, II, pp. 389–406.
26 *Ominous*, pp. 154–7 (19–23 April 1775).
27 One of the more interesting things that happened to Boswell at Wilton was to have himself weighed by Pembroke who apparently was obsessed with weighing 'man and beast'. He weighed 166 pounds.
28 *Temple*, p. 373 (to Temple, 17 May 1775); to Wilkes, 26 May 1775 (BP: L1291; cited in *Letters*, I, pp. 226–7).
29 *Temple*, pp. 379 (to Temple, 3 June 1775), 394 (to Temple, 12 August 1775); *Ominous*, pp. 158–9.
30 *Temple*, pp. 386 (to Temple, 19 June 1775).
31 Ibid., p. 396 (to Temple, 2 September 1775).
32 Ibid., p. 401 (to Temple, 10 October 1775); *Ominous*, pp. 168, 177 (19 October, 10 November 1775).
33 *Ominous*, pp. 180, 182–4 (13, 17–18 November 1775).

34 Ibid., pp. 209, 245 (31 December 1775, 6 March 1776).

35 *Temple*, p. 375 (to Temple, 22 May 1775).

36 *Grange*, pp. 286–8 (from Grange, 15 March 1776); *Ominous*, p. 247 (9 March 1776). See *Political Career*, pp. 79–80.

37 *Ominous*, pp. 247–8 (10 March 1776).

38 Ibid., pp. 177–8 (10 November 1775).

39 Ibid., pp. 173, 195 (30 October, 9 December 1775).

40 Ibid., pp. 188, 191–2 (26 November, 4 December 1775).

41 Ibid., pp. 233–49 (27 February 1776); from Johnson, 5 March 1776 (*JL*, II, p. 299).

42 Ibid., pp. 249–50 (10–11 March 1776).

43 Ibid., pp. 251–2 (12 March 1776).

44 Ibid., pp. 258–63 (16–17 March 1776).

45 Hannah More, *Memoirs*, ed. William Roberts (1834), I, p. 213; *Life of Johnson*, II, p. 326; *Letters of Hannah More*, ed. R. B. Johnson (1925), p. 36.

46 *Ominous*, pp. 276–301 (19–27 March 1776).

47 *Ominous*, pp. 303–7 (29 March–1 April 1776). Much of Boswell's description of this seamy descent to the London underworld is scored out in twentieth-century ink, but it has been carefully reconstructed.

48 Ibid., pp. 315, 320, 319 (4–5 April 1776).

49 Ibid., pp. 308–10 (2–3, 18 April 1776), 341.

50 *Temple*, p. 412 (to Temple, 28 April 1776); *Ominous*, pp. 323–4 (10 April 1776).

51 *Temple*, pp. 411–12 (to Temple, 28 April 1776); *Impossible Friendship*, p. 39; *Life of Johnson*, III, pp. 50–51.

52 There are two versions of the Wilkes–Johnson meeting: *Ominous*, pp. 345–50 and *Life of Johnson*, III, pp. 64–79. Boswell's 'Negotiation' of the meeting is found only in the *Life*. The manuscript first draft of the meeting is printed in *Ominous* and is the one used here.

53 *Temple*, p. 412 (to Temple, 28 April 1776). The background to Boswell's meeting with Mrs Rudd, and his account of two interviews with her, are provided in *Ominous*, pp. 351–61. See also *Temple*, pp. 412–13. The traditional authority on Mrs Rudd has been Horace Bleackley, in *Some Distinguished Victims of the Scaffold* (1905); but Gordon Turnbull has recently analysed Boswell's biographical fascination with this woman, 'Criminal Biographer: Boswell and Margaret Caroline Rudd', *Studies in English Literature*, 26 (1986).

54 *Extremes*, p. 304 (21 April 1778).

TWENTY-ONE 'Inexplicable Dilatory Disease'

1 *Extremes*, pp. 84, 120 (8 May, 3 February 1777).

2 *JL*, II, p. 348 (from Johnson, 2 July 1776); *Extremes*, pp. 26, 81 (23 August 1776, 24 January 1777).

3 *Extremes*, pp. 91 (6 March 1776), 202–3 (5 January 1778).

4 Ibid., pp. 19, 61 (5 August, 25 November 1776).

5 Ibid., pp. 53, 65 (10 November, 9 December 1776); 'Uxoriana'.

6 Ibid., pp. 66, 69–70, 39 (17 and 25 December, 4 October 1776), 112 (14 April 1777).

7 Ibid., pp. 19–20 (6 August 1776).

8 Ibid., p. 26 (25 August 1776); from Johnson, 6 July 1776 (*JL*, II, p. 349).

9 *Extremes*, pp. 76, 88 (9 January, 21 February 1777); to Johnson, 9 June 1777 (*Letters*, I, p. 261); from Johnson, 22 July 1777 (*JL*, III, p. 41).

10 *Extremes*, p. 6 (17 June 1776).

11 *Extremes*, pp. 11–15 (3 March 1777).

12 Ibid., pp. 55 (15 November 1776), 80, 83, 92 (24 January, 3 February, 10 March 1777).

13 *JL*, III, p. 20 (from Johnson, 3 May 1777); *Extremes*, pp. 103–4 (29 March 1777).

14 Ibid., pp. 104–5 (30 March 1777), 105 (31 March 1777).

15 Ibid., pp. 106–7 (7 April 1777).

16 Ibid., pp. 115–16, 119, 121 (23–24 April, 2 May, 7 May 1777).

17 Ibid., pp. 121–6, 207, 361–78.

18 *JL*, III, pp. 8–9 (from Johnson, 18 February 1777); to Johnson, 24 February 1777 (*Letters*, I, p. 259).

19 *JL*, III, pp. 11–12 (from Johnson, 11 March 1777); *Life of Johnson*, III, p. 109; to Johnson, 9 June 1777 (*Letters*, I, pp. 261–2).

20 *Extremes*, pp. 144–5 (11 September 1777).

21 Ibid., pp. 149–86 (14–24 September 1777).

22 Ibid., p. 155 (16 September 1777).

23 For the following theme regarding Boswell's changed relations with Johnson, I am indebted to an essay by John B. Radner on the Ashbourne visit, 'Pilgrimage and Autonomy: The Visit to Ashbourne', in *Citizen*, pp. 203–27.

24 *Life of Johnson*, III, p. 206; *Extremes*, pp. 183 (23 September 1777), 225 (20 March 1778).

25 *Extremes*, p. 186 (26–27 September 1777).

26 Ibid., pp. 187–216 (28 September 1777–12 March 1778).

27 Ibid., p. 58 (21 November 1776).

28 Ibid., p. 270 (12 April 1778).

29 *Column*, pp. 23, 25 (October 1777).

30 *Column*, pp. 42–51 (February–March 1778).

31 *Column*, p. 357 (August 1783).

32 *Column*, p. 332 (March 1783).

33 For Boswell's use of the Advocates' Library, see Thomas I. Rae and William Beattie, 'Boswell and the Advocates' Library', *Johnson, Boswell and Their Circle* (1965), pp. 262–3.

34 *Members*, p. 278 (26 February 1778).

35 *Extremes*, p. 217 (13 March 1778).

TWENTY-TWO Later Thirties: 'The Author and the Gentleman United'

1 *Life of Johnson*, III, p. 225.

2 To Hester Thrale, 30 August 1776 (NLS); copy in BP: L1078.

3 Hester Thrale to Johnson, 2 August 1777 (Rylands: Eng. MS. 540/66. Letter 532.a); Hester Thrale to Johnson, 16 September 1777 (Rylands; Eng. MS. 540/71. Letter 547.a); Johnson to Hester Thrale, 4 August 1777 (*JL*, III, p. 46).

4 *Life of Johnson*, III, pp. 228–9; *Extremes*, pp. 246, 301 (7, 18 April 1778).

5 *Thraliana*, I, pp. 257 (April 1773), 195.

6 *Extremes*, p. 250 (7 April 1778); *Thraliana*, I, pp. 329–30.

7 *Extremes*, pp. 287 (15 April), 230.

8 Ibid., pp. 336, 338 (12 May 1778).

9 *Laird*, p. 102 (30 April 1779).

10 *Extremes*, pp. 264, 343–4 (10 April, 12 May 1778); *Life of Johnson*, III, p. 350.
11 *Extremes*, pp. 254, 256, 328 (9 April, 2 May 1778); to Temple, 8 May 1779 (*Letters*, II, p. 285).
12 *Extremes*, pp. 328–9, 297 (8 May, 17 April 1778).
13 Ibid., p. 222 (18 March 1778).
14 Ibid., pp. 226, 242 (21 March, 5 April 1778).
15 Ibid., p. 257 (9 April 1778).
16 Ibid., pp. 350, 299 (19 May, 18 April 1778).
17 Ibid., pp. 243, 311, 286 (6, 25, 15 April 1778).
18 Ibid., p. 350 (19 May 1778).
19 Ibid.
20 Ibid., p. 354 (23 May 1778).
21 *Laird*, pp. 11, 5, 14, 8 (23, 21, 24, 22 August 1778).
22 Ibid., pp. 45–6 (3 January 1779).
23 *Laird*, pp. 17–18, 24 (16–18, 24 September 1778).
24 *Column*, pp. 70, 73, 81.
25 *Laird*, pp. 21–5 (22–28 September 1778).
26 Ibid., pp. 33–44 (23 October–11 November 1778).
27 Ibid., p. 49 (2 February 1779).
28 *Column*, p. 87.
29 *Letters*, II, p. 280 n. 2.
30 *Letters*, II, p. 281 (to Johnson, 2 February 1779); *Life of Johnson*, III, p. 371 n. 1; to Langton, 25 February 1779 (*Members*, p. 88).
31 *JL*, III, pp. 156–7 (from Johnson, 13 March 1779).
32 *Life of Johnson*, III, p. 376.
33 *Laird*, pp. 100–1 (25–26 April 1779); *Life of Johnson*, III, p. 391; from Temple, 8 May 1779 (*Letters*, II, p. 285).
34 *Laird*, pp. 61 (31 March), 69–70, 99, 92 (7, 24, 18 April 1779).
35 Ibid., pp. 83, 90–91, 92 (15, 16, 18 April 1779).
36 Ibid., pp. 72–3, 86–9, 95, 100 (20, 24 April 1779).
37 Ibid., p. 80 (14 April 1779).
38 *Letters*, II, pp. 283–8 (to Temple, 3–8 May 1779).
39 Ibid., p. 301. Thomas Crawford has a recent essay on Boswell and Temple's political differences, 'Politics in the Boswell–Temple Correspondence', *Citizen*, pp. 101–16.

TWENTY-THREE No Considerable Figure: Politics, Family, and Hypochondria

1 *Laird*, p. 106 (3 June 1779).
2 Ibid., pp. 116 (28 June 1779), 118 (5, 8 July 1779).
3 Ibid., p. 121 (15 July 1779).
4 Ibid., pp. 114 (20 June 1779), 126 (31 July 1779).
5 Ibid., pp. 106–7 (4 June 1779).
6 *JL*, III, pp. 178 (from Samuel Johnson, 13 July 1779), 181 (from Johnson, 9 September 1779).
7 *Letters*, II, pp. 294–5 (to Samuel Johnson, 7 November 1779); *Life of Johnson*, III, pp. 399–400.
8 *Letters*, II, p. 292 (to Johnson, 22 October 1779).

9 *Laird*, pp. 148–9; to Johnson, 22 November 1779 (*Letters*, II, p. 297).
10 BP: L1296 (to Wilkes, 14 March 1780); *Laird*, pp. 236 (30 August 1780), 162 n. 6.
11 *Laird*, pp. 160–61 (6 January 1780).
12 Ibid., p. 166 (11 January 1780).
13 Ibid., pp. 168–9 (14 January 1782), 467 (1 August 1782), 154 (26 December 1779).
14 Ibid., p. 172 (23 January 1780).
15 Ibid., pp. 169 (14 January), 180, 181, 182, 184 (15, 16, 20, 26 February 1780).
16 *JL*, III, p. 232 (from Samuel Johnson, 8 April 1780); *Laird*, p. 199 (12 April 1780).
17 *Laird*, pp. 167, 171, 173, 176 (12, 18, 24, 31 January 1780).
18 *Column*, p. 168 (no. 29, February 1780).
19 *Laird*, pp. 198, 199.
20 Ibid., pp. 221–3.
21 Ibid., pp. 228–48 (16 August–13 September 1780).
22 *Column*, pp. 199–200 (no. 37, October 1780).
23 *Laird*, p. 249 (19 September 1780).
24 Ibid., p. 237 (1 September 1780).
25 Ibid., pp. 148–9, 151 (21 December 1779); *Life of Johnson*, III, p. 331.
26 *Laird*, pp. 197, 203–6 (6, 24 April 1780).
27 Ibid., pp. 265–6 (21–22 October 1780).
28 Michael Fry, 'James Boswell, Henry Dundas, and Enlightened Politics', *Citizen*, pp. 87–100; Brady, *Political Career*, pp. 56–96, passim.
29 See F. A. Pottle's description of the *Letter to . . . Braxfield* in *Literary Career*, pp. 101–5.
30 *Laird*, pp. 207, 211.
31 Ibid., pp. 285–90 (23 February–10 March 1781).
32 Ibid., p. 403 (22 October 1781).
33 *JL*, III, pp. 303 (from Samuel Johnson, 21 August 1780), 317–18 (17 October 1780).
34 *Laird*, pp. 270 (17 November 1780), 283.

TWENTY-FOUR The Road to Ulubrae–Auchinleck

1 *JL*, III, pp. 328–9 (from Johnson, 14 March 1781); *Laird*, p. 292 (21 March 1781). Mysteriously, the manuscripts of the *Lives of the Poets* did not surface in the Malahide papers.
2 *Laird*, pp. 352, 347 (13, 17 May 1781).
3 *Laird*, pp. 342–5, 352–4 (5, 13 May 1781).
4 Ibid., pp. 356–7 (16 May 1781).
5 Ibid., pp. 361–6 (24, 27, 30 May 1781); *GBM*, p. 118 (to Burke, 18 March 1782).
6 *Members*, p. 113 (to Reynolds, 27 February 1781); *Laird*, pp. 310–12 (BM: Egerton MSS. 3700B).
7 *Memoirs of Dr Burney* (1832), II, p. 190. Since Fanny Burney edited this edition of her father's papers, she may have wished to conceal her identity in this ridicule of his good friend.
8 *Walpole Corr.*, XXIX (22 May 1781), pp. 144–5; *Experiment*, p. 217 (25 April 1788).
9 *Laird*, p. 324 (15 April 1781); Clifford, *Piozzi*, p. 200.
10 Published version, 1788 (the MS is in BP: M302); *Life of Johnson*, IV, p. 387 n. 1.
11 *Laird*, pp. 373 (2 June 1781), 412 (3 December 1781).
12 Ibid., pp. 429 (26 February 1782), 389–90 (9 August 1781); *Column*, p. 263; *Members*, p. 127 (from Reynolds, 1 October 1782).

13 Ibid., pp. 384–5 (22 July 1781).
14 Ibid., pp. 314 (9 April 1781), 396 (11 September 1781).
15 Ibid., pp. 397–8 (20 September 1781), 400 (5 October 1781), 429 (27 February 1782).
16 *Column*, pp. 221, 223, 225.
17 *Laird*, pp. 454 (4 July 1782), 473 (19 August 1782).
18 BP: J83.
19 *Laird*, pp. 418, 462 (21 July 1782), 473 (20 August), 474 (23 August).
20 Boswell wrote out a 'State of My Affairs on 1 September 1782' (*Laird*, p. 478 n. 5).
21 *JL*, IV, pp. 4, 27–8 (from Johnson, 5 January and 28 March 1782).
22 *Laird*, p. 481 (to Johnson, 1 October 1782); from Johnson, 21 September 1782 (*JL*, IV, p. 73); Johnson to Margaret Boswell, 7 December 1782 (*Life of Johnson*, IV, p. 156). See Irma S. Lustig's analysis of Margaret's nine-year antipathy towards Johnson until it was healed in 1783, ' "My Dear Enemy": Margaret Montgomerie Boswell in the *Life of Johnson*', in *Citizen*, pp. 228–45.
23 *GBM*, p. 117 (to Burke, 18 March 1782).
24 *Laird*, p. 436 (14 April 1782); to Burke, 18 April 1782 (*GBM*, pp. 119–20); from Burke, 23 April 1782 (*GBM*, pp. 121–2); *Laird*, p. 442 (4 May 1782).
25 *GBM*, pp. 126–7 (to Burke, 19 July 1782).
26 BP: L448 (to Dundas, 20 April 1782), C1133 (from Dundas, 12 May 1782); *Laird*, pp. 460–61 (16 July 1782).
27 *Column*, pp. 286–7 (no. 56, 'On Penuriousness and Wealth').
28 *Laird*, pp. 456 (8 July 1782), 414 (11 May 1782).
29 Ibid., p. 477 (29 August 1782).
30 Ibid., p. 479.
31 *JL*, IV, pp. 71–3 (from Johnson, 7 September 1782).

TWENTY-FIVE The Cracked Enamel

1 *Laird*, p. 481 (to Johnson, 1 October 1782: BP: L673). John Strawhorn, in his interesting essay, 'Master of Ulubrae: Boswell as Enlightened Lord', in *Citizen*, pp. 117–34, has described Boswell's preparations to take on his role as laird of his large estate. I am indebted to this essay for many of the estate details.
2 *Laird*, pp. 257 n. 8.
3 Ibid., p. 482 (to Johnson, 1 October 1782).
4 *Applause*, p. 10 (15 October 1782).
5 Strawhorn, 'Master of Ulubrae', p. 121.
6 *Applause*, p. 19 (18 November 1782).
7 *Great Biographer*, p. 105 (23 August 1790).
8 *Letters*, II, p. 473 (to Gibb, 6 November 1790). Much of Boswell's meticulous correspondence with Gibb is printed in the *Letters*, II, Appendix I.
9 *Applause*, Introduction, pp. xii–xiii; *Letters*, II, p. 483 (to Gibb, 4 June 1791); *Life of Johnson*, IV, p. 163.
10 *Letters*, II, pp. 504, 517 (to Gibb, 10 January 1794 and 19 March 1795). See Strawhorn, 'Master of Ulubrae', pp. 124–5.
11 *Experiment*, pp. 255–6 (Burns to Bruce Campbell, 13 November 1788).
12 *Applause*, p. 29 (2 December 1782); from Barnard, 2 March 1783, to Barnard, 14 February 1783 (*Members*, pp. 132, 129–30); *Applause*, p. 64 (25 February 1783).
13 *Applause*, pp. 17–23, 24–8, 30–31, 31–3, 35–9, 42–4, 44–6 (18, 29 November; 4, 5, 10, 20, 21, 22 December 1782).

14 Ibid., p. 53 (18 January 1783).

15 *Column*, pp. 325, 332, 336, 341.

16 *Applause*, pp. 77–8 (22 March 1783).

17 *Letters*, II, pp. 313–14 (to Hester Thrale, 9 July 1782); *Applause*, pp. 74–5, 83, 84 (21, 23, 24 March 1783), 96 (3 April 1783). Boswell's memorandum is in the Hyde Collection.

18 Ibid., pp. 110–13 (20 April 1783).

19 Ibid., pp. 97, 140, 142, 148, 144.

20 Ibid., pp. 89–90 (31 March 1783).

21 *Applause*, pp. 93–4 (3 April 1783).

22 Ibid., pp. 113, 116 (21 April 1783), 155–7 (29 May 1783).

23 *Grange*, pp. 299–300 (to Grange, 28 April 1783); from Temple, 16 July 1782 (BP: C2806); *Temple Diaries*, p. 41.

24 *Applause*, p. 152 (29 May 1783).

25 Ibid., p. 165 (19 October 1783).

26 Ibid., pp. 166–7 (30 October 1783), 169 (10 November 1783).

27 Ibid., pp. 171 (13 December), 176 (7 January 1784), 180–81 (21 January 1783).

28 Ibid., pp. 174 n. 9, 183, 187 (20 and 4 February 1783).

29 BP: C2820 (15 December 1782).

30 *GBM*, pp. 135–6 (to Burke, 8 August 1783).

31 Ibid., pp. 137–8 (from Burke, 13 August 1783); *Applause*, p. 162 (11 September 1783).

32 See Pottle, *Literary Career*, pp. 107–8, for background and details of publication.

33 *Applause*, pp. 193, 197–9.

34 Ibid., pp. 181, 184–5 (21 January, 9 February 1783); *Life of Johnson*, IV, p. 261 n. 3; from Johnson, 27 February 1784, Johnson to Langton, 8 April 1784 (*JL*, IV, pp. 291, 310).

35 *Members*, p. 152 (to Barnard, 8 March 1784); *Applause*, pp. 202–6 (10 April 1783); to Burke, 10 and 12 April 1783 (*GBM*, pp. 142–4).

36 See *Political Career*, pp. 108–14.

37 BP: L1143 (to Seward, 18 May 1784); from Seward, 20 June 1784 (BP: C2469); to Temple, 6 July 1784 (BP: L1236.9).

38 BP: C348 (from Margaret, 26 May 1784; cited in *Applause*, p. 222); BP: C440 (from Margaret, 8 June 1784; cited in *Applause*, p. 246); to Barnard, 14 May 1784 (*Members*, p. 159).

TWENTY-SIX From Death to Biography

1 *JL*, IV, p. 263 (from Johnson, 24 December 1783); *Life of Johnson*, IV, p. 331 (25 June).

2 *Applause*, pp. 228–9 (5 June 1784).

3 Manuscript draft of the *Life of Johnson*, ibid., pp. 248–9.

4 *Life of Johnson*, IV, pp. 336–7; *Applause*, p. 255 (30 June 1784).

5 *Applause*, p. 255.

6 *JL*, IV, p. 354 (from Johnson, 26 July 1784); from Reynolds, 2 September 1784 (*Members*, pp. 172–3); *Life of Johnson*, IV, pp. 350, 543.

7 *Applause*, p. 213 (15 May 1784).

8 *JL*, IV, p. 359 (from Johnson, 5 August 1784).

9 Register of Letters August–November 1784 (BP: M255).

10 *JL*, IV, p. 434 (from Johnson, 3 November 1784).

11 *Applause*, p. 268 (9 December 1784).

12 Ibid., pp. 269–70 (12 December 1784); from Dundas, 30 March 1785 (BP: C1135). See *Political Career*, pp. 117–19.

13 *Applause*, p. 271 (17 December 1784); from Langton, 13 December 1784 (*Members*, p. 174); *Life of Johnson*, IV, pp. 420–21.

14 *Applause*, pp. 271–2 (18 December 1784); from Brocklesby, 27 December 1784 (BP: C582); from Barnard, 10 February 1785 (*Members*, p. 181).

15 For the extensive steps Boswell took in gathering materials for his *Life of Johnson*, see *Making of the 'Life'*.

16 *Applause*, pp. 304–5.

17 *Applause*, pp. 335–6, 337, 339, 340 (9, 14, 28 August and 9 September 1785); from Temple, 31 August 1785 (BP: C2835).

18 *Applause*, p. 318.

19 Ibid., pp. 319, 338 and n. 1.

20 The best review of Boswell's newspaper activities after 1785 is by Lucyle Werkmeister, *Jemmie Boswell and the London Daily Press, 1785–1795* (New York, 1963).

21 *Applause*, pp. 288–9. For an account of Boswell and Malone's collaborations and friendship, see Peter Martin, *Edmond Malone, Shakespearean Scholar: a Literary Biography* (Cambridge, 1995), pp. 95–111, 144–64.

22 *London Chronicle*, LVII (2 June 1785). For background to the inflammatory *Letter to the People of Scotland*, see *Political Career*, pp. 120–30; *Literary Career*, pp. 108–12; and *Applause*, p. 292 n. 1.

23 Percy Fitzgerald, *Life of Boswell*, II, pp. 18–19; *English Review*, V, pp. 441–4.

24 *Applause*, p. 303.

25 *GBM*, p. 271 (to Boswell, 5 November 1785).

26 *GBM*, p. 197 (from Malone, 9 August 1785); *Applause*, p. 336 (11 August 1785).

27 *Members*, p. 196 (to Barnard, 1 July 1785).

28 *GBM*, p. 200–7 (from Malone, 5 October 1785), 207–20 (to Malone, 13 October 1785), 220–26 (to Malone, 15 October 1785).

29 Ibid., p. 235 (from Malone, 19 October 1785). See *Applause*, p. 345, and Irma S. Lustig, 'Fact into Art: James Boswell's Notes, Journals, and the *Life of Johnson*', IV, pp. 128–46.

30 *GBM*, p. 149 (from Burke, 4 January 1786).

31 *GBM*, p. 278 (to Malone, 11 November 1785); from Macdonald, 8 December 1785 (BP: C1831).

32 *GBM*, pp. 276, 279.

33 Ibid., p. 262 (to Malone, 30–31 October 1785).

34 Ibid., p. 294 (from Malone, 1 February 1786).

35 MS Letter: Hyde.

36 *Walpole Corr.*, XXV, p. 636 (Walpole to Mann, 28 March 1786); from Malone, 27 March 1786, to Malone, 31 March 1786 (*GBM*, pp. 311, 314–17).

37 There is some useful insight into Mrs Piozzi's attitude towards Boswell in the *Anecdotes* in *Impossible Friendship*, pp. 106–15.

38 BP: M310.

39 *Walpole Corr.*, XXV, pp. 634, 638, 640–41 (Walpole to Mann, 16 and 28 March, 30 April 1786).

40 *Experiment*, p. 69.

TWENTY-SEVEN 'Oh, If This Book of Mine Were Done!'

1 *Experiment*, p. 7 (20 November 1785).
2 Ibid., pp. 18 (20 December 1786), 31 (27 January 1786); from Thurlow, 5 January 1786 (BP: C2992; cited in *Experiment*, pp. 289–92).
3 BP: C2837 (from Temple, 4 January 1786); *Experiment*, pp. 28–9 (17–20 January 1786).
4 *GBM*, pp. 286–7 (from Malone, 13 January 1786); to Malone, 12 March 1786 (*GBM*, p. 298).
5 BP: C447 (from Margaret, 11 April 1786); to Margaret, 1 May 1786 (BP: L178; cited in *Experiment*, p. 63).
6 *GBM*, pp. 305 (to Malone, 22 March 1786), 306 (to Malone, 23 March 1786), 313 (to Malone, 31 March 1786); *Experiment*, p. 56 (5 April 1786).
7 *Experiment*, p. 68 (6–8 June 1786).
8 Ibid., p. 64 (18 May 1786).
9 BP: L179 (from Margaret, 3 July 1786; cited in *Experiment*, p. 7).
10 *Experiment*, p. 51 and n. 50 (9 March 1786).
11 Ibid., pp. 50 (7 March 1786), 67 n. 8; to Margaret, 9 November 1788 (BP: L181; cited in *Experiment*, p. 253).
12 Ibid., p. 137 (29 May 1787).
13 Ibid., p. 34 (7 February 1786); from Burke, 9 February 1786 (*GBM*, p. 153); from Malone, 14 September 1787 (*GBM*, p. 330); from Burke, 20 July 1791 (*GBM*, pp. 161–2).
14 *Experiment*, pp. 66–7, 75–6, 80 (3 and 27 June, 6 July 1786).
15 For an exhaustive record of Boswell's prodigious labours in preparing the *Life of Johnson*, and a lucid introduction to Boswell as editor and biographer, see *Making of the 'Life'*.
16 Ibid., pp. 68, 69, 83 (8 and 9 June, 13 July 1786).
17 BP: L73 (to Alexander Boswell, Jr., 4 August 1786).
18 *Experiment*, pp. 94–6 (25 September–31 October 1786).
19 Ibid., pp. 96–7 (7–8 November 1786).
20 Ibid., pp. 86 (21 July), 101–2. On Boswell's painful relationship with Lonsdale, see Brady's comprehensive treatment in *Political Career*, pp. 131–79; and Brady, *Later Years*, pp. 344–413 passim.
21 Ibid., pp. 103–19 (29 November–11 December 1798).
22 *Political Career*, pp. 142–3.
23 *Experiment*, p. 113 (7 December 1786).
24 *Members*, pp. 239–40 (to Barnard, 6 January 1787), 242 (from Barnard, 23 January 1787).
25 *Experiment*, pp. 140 (11 June 1787), 123 (22 March 1787).
26 BP: C2852 (from Temple, 30 November 1787); *Experiment*, p. 146.
27 *Experiment*, p. 147–8 (16–22 October 1787).
28 *GBM*, p. 356 (from Courtenay, 29 September 1788); from Blair, 25 August 1788 (*Making of the 'Life'*, p. 232); Sir James Prior, 'Maloniana', *Life of Edmond Malone*, p. 393; *Experiment*, p. 134.
29 *Impossible Friendship*, pp. 118–20.
30 Cited in Werkmeister, p. 16.
31 *Experiment*, pp. 160–85 (21 December–14 January 1787).
32 Ibid., pp. 190–91 (20 February 1788).
33 Ibid., pp. 201 (17 March 1788), 196–7 (9 March 1788).

34　*Making of the 'Life'*, p. 265; *GBM*, p. 332 (from Malone, 8 March 1788); *Impossible Friendship*, pp. 123–30.

35　*Experiment*, pp. 222–5 (5–16 May 1788).

36　He kept a copious journal while on the Circuit, ibid., pp. 227–50.

37　*GBM*, p. 353 (to Malone, 18 September 1788); from Malone 29 September 1788 (*GBM*, pp. 353, 357).

38　*Letters*, II, pp. 358–9 (to Temple, 5 March 1789; MS PML).

39　*Experiment*, pp. 262 (Veronica to Margaret, 7 December 1788), 254; to Margaret, 28 November 1788 (BP: L183; cited in *Experiment*, p. 258).

40　*Letters*, II, p. 353 (to Temple, 10 January 1789; MS PML); *Experiment*, pp. 262 (5 December 1788), 269 (28 January 1789); to Temple, 18 March 1789 (BP: C2868); to Margaret, 11 March 1789 (BP: L190; cited in *Experiment*, p. 276).

41　*Letters*, II, p. 363 (to Temple, 31 March 1789; MS PML).

42　Ibid., pp. 369–70 (to Temple, 22 May 1789; MS PML).

43　Ibid., p. 373 (to Temple, 3 July 1789; MS PML).

44　BP: C317 (from Lady Auchinleck, 16 July 1789); to Malone, 8 July 1789 (*GBM*, p. 364).

TWENTY-EIGHT　Painful Progress

1　See *Political Career*, pp. 149–58; BP: C2871 (from Temple, 28 May 1789).

2　*Letters*, II, pp. 376–8 (to Temple, 23 August 1789; MS PML).

3　BP: C236 (from Alexander Boswell, Jr., *c.* 23 October 1789).

4　*Letters*, II, pp. 381–2 (to Temple, 30 November 1789; MS PML).

5　*Great Biographer*, p. 27 (1 January 1790). See *Making of the 'Life'*, especially pp. xxii–xxv. For an excellent summary of Boswell's progress on the *Life*, see *Literary Career*, pp. 161–6.

6　*Making of the 'Life'*, p. xxxiii.

7　*Letters*, II, p. 390 (to Temple, 13 February 1790; MS PML).

8　*Great Biographer*, pp. 32–3 (13 January 1790).

9　Ibid., p. 79 (to Forbes, 2 July 1790).

10　Ibid., pp. 60 (10 June 1790), 51.

11　Ibid., pp. 52 (21 May 1790), 115, 215–16.

12　BP: C2892 (from Temple, 18 October 1790).

13　*Great Biographer*, pp. 35, 82 (5 July 1790), 88–9 (to Veronica, 9 July 1790); to Temple, 8 September 1790 (MS PML).

14　Ibid., pp. 34 (15 January 1790), 36–7 (23 January 1790), 42.

15　*Temple Diaries*, pp. 70, 71, 62.

16　For the final Carlisle fiasco, see *Great Biographer*, pp. 62–6.

17　*GBM*, pp. 369–70 (to Malone, 30 June 1790), 371–4 (from Malone 8 July 1790).

18　*Great Biographer*, p. 108 (10 September 1790).

19　*Burney Diary*, III, p. 219 (26 February 1787); IV, pp. 431–3.

20　*Letters*, II, p. 477 (to Gibb, 16 December 1790).

21　*GBM*, pp. 389–90, 394–5, 410 (to Malone, 18 and 29 January and 9 March 1791).

22　John Taylor, *Records of My Life*, I, pp. 89–90; *Great Biographer*, p. 121. See *Literary Career*, pp. 141–9; Werkmeister, pp. 22–6; and Thomas Crawford, *Boswell, Burns, and the French Revolution* (1990), pp. 36–9.

23　*GBM*, p. 395 (to Malone, 29 January 1791); *Great Biographer*, pp. 125 (Courtenay to Malone, 22 February 1791), 127 (21 February 1791).

24 MS PML (to Temple, 2 April 1791).
25 *Morning Post,* 23 and 26 April 1791. See Werkmeister, pp. 29–30.
26 *Great Biographer,* p. 127; to Dempster, 30 April 1791 (BP: L423).

TWENTY-NINE The *Life of Johnson* and Its Aftermath

1 *GBM,* p. 162 (from Burke, 20 July 1791).
2 *Members,* pp. 343–4 (from Burney, 16 July 1791); from Temple, 4 July 1791 (BP: C2912); to Wilkes, 25 June [1791] (*Letters,* II, p. 437).
3 BP: C165 (from Blair, summer 1791); Walpole to Mary Berry, 26 May 1792 (*Walpole Corr.,* XI, p. 275).
4 *Thraliana,* II, pp. 809–11. On Boswell's treatment of Mrs Piozzi in the *Life,* see *Impossible Friendship,* pp. 147–62.
5 See Frank Brady's elegant assessment of Boswell's place in the history of biography, *Later Years,* pp. 423–31.
6 *Life of Johnson,* I, p. 30. On Boswell's uncertainty about Johnson, see Isobel Grundy, ' "Over Him We Hang Vibrating": Uncertainty in the *Life of Johnson',* *Citizen,* pp. 184–202.
7 Marshall Waingrow is excellent on Boswell's fascination with Johnson's management of his mind, *Making of the 'Life',* pp. xlv–l.
8 Hitoshi Suwabe has recently come up with this number, revising Donald Greene's earlier count of 327, in 'Boswell's Meetings with Johnson, A New Count', *Citizen,* pp. 246–57. See Donald J. Greene, 'Reflections on a Literary Anniversary', *Queen's Quarterly,* LXX (Summer, 1963), pp. 198–208.
9 *Life of Johnson,* I, p. 30.
10 See Frederick Pottle's fine essay, 'The *Life of Johnson:* Art and Authenticity', *Twentieth-Century Interpretations of Boswell's 'Life of Johnson',* ed. James L. Clifford (1970), pp. 66–73. See also Ralph W. Rader, 'Literary Form in Factual Narrative: The Example of Boswell's *Johnson',* *Essays in Eighteenth-Century Biography,* ed. P. B. Daghlian (1968). On Boswell's type of memory, see Pottle, 'The Power of Memory in Boswell and Scott', in *Essays on the Eighteenth Century Presented to David Nichol Smith* (Oxford, 1945), pp. 185–6. For a more recent and innovative assessment of the nature and function of Johnson's conversation in the *Life,* see Paul J. Korshin, 'Johnson's Conversation in Boswell's *Life of Johnson',* in *New Light,* pp. 174–93.
11 *Letters,* II, p. 439 (to Temple, 22 August 1791).
12 *Great Biographer,* p. 206 (16 December 1792). See Crawford, *Boswell, Burns, and the French Revolution,* pp. 39–50.
13 *Letters,* II, p. 440 (to Temple, 22 November 1791); from Temple, 6 December 1791 (BP: C2915).
14 *Letters,* II, pp. 440–41.
15 *Members,* pp. 356 (to Barnard, 12, 15 February 1792), 368 (from Barnard, 4 July 1792); to Alexander Boswell, Jr., 29 August 1792 (BP: L101); from Malone's 'Account' of Reynolds in his edition of Reynolds's *Works* (1798), I, pp. ci–cii.
16 *Great Biographer,* pp. 155–6; Werkmeister, pp. 40–49.
17 BP: C2920 (from Temple, 30 March 1792); from Barnard, 4 July 1792 (*Members,* p. 369); from Erskine, 14 January 1793 (*Making of the 'Life',* p. 511).
18 *Great Biographer,* pp. 156–8, 226–7 (19 August 1793).
19 Ibid., pp. 162–4 (20 August 1792).
20 Ibid., pp. 171–2. Temple allowed Boswell to take back to London the letters he wrote

during his travels abroad, with a view to using them for his proposed book on Continental travel. He never returned them. It is a great shame he did not take with him all his letters to Temple, for they were later removed to France where many of them were lost. Many were found there, however, in the mid-nineteenth century in another of those sensational and lucky discoveries of Boswell papers. See *Temple*, vol. I, pp. xxxi–xxxiii; MS. Somervell Papers, National Library of Scotland (from Temple, 27 April 1796).

21 BP: C2912, C2925 (from Temple, 4 July 1791, 11 July 1792); *Great Biographer*, pp. 181 (11 September 1792), 179 (Nancy Temple to Padgy Peters, 8 September 1793).
22 *GBM*, p. 421 (to Malone, 16 September 1792).
23 *Great Biographer*, pp. 194 (5–6 November 1792), 204 (8 December 1792), 205.
24 Ibid., pp. 221–2; to Langton 24 July 1793 (*Members*, p. 387).
25 Ibid., p. 233 (16 September 1793); Joseph Farington, *Diary*, I (6 October 1793).
26 *Great Biographer*, pp. 236–7 (24, 25, 26 September 1793).
27 *Great Biographer*, p. 223 (4 August 1793).
28 BP: L48 (to Dundas, 17 March 1794); *Great Biographer*, p. 297.
29 *GBM*, p. 423 (from Malone, 13 May 1793).
30 Ibid., p. 424 (to Malone, 17 May 1793); Malone to Forbes, MS. Fettercairn (Acc. 4796, Box 87), National Library of Scotland.
31 *Great Biographer*, pp. 224, 245 (25 October 1793).
32 Ibid., p. 257 (3 December 1793).
33 Ibid., pp. 287 (13 February 1794), 295 (22 March 1794), to James Boswell, Jr., 21 November 1794 (BP: L152).
34 BP: L130–L132 (to James Boswell, Jr., 30 June and 7 and 14 July 1794).
35 BP: L141, L145 (to James Boswell, Jr., 6 September, 6 October 1794).
36 BP: C353 (from James Boswell, Jr., 18 October 1794).
37 BP: L148 (to James Boswell, Jr., 27 October 1794).
38 BP: C354 (from James Boswell, Jr., 10 November 1794).
39 *Great Biographer*, pp. 308–10.
40 BP: L123 (to Sir Alexander Boswell, 18 March 1795); to Malone, 13 April 1795 (*GBM*, p. 431).
41 MS. PML (to Temple, 8 May 1795); James Boswell, Jr to Temple, 18 May 1795 (*Letters*, II, pp. 467–8); Thomas David Boswell to Temple, 19 May 1795 (*Letters*, II, p. 468).
42 *Windham Papers*, ed. Lewis Melville (1913), I, pp. 297–8 (Malone to Windham, 20 May 1795); Barnard to Forbes, 27 March 1796 (*Members*, p. 406).

Index

Adams, Dr William 368, 468, 495
Alexander, Wilhelmina (sister of Claud Alexander of Ballochmyle) 516
Amsterdam 154
Argyll, Elizabeth Gunning, Duchess of, hostility toward JB 324–5
Argyll, John Campbell, 5th Duke of, JB and SJ visit 324–5
Auchinleck, Alexander Boswell, 8th Laird of (father of JB) 63–5, 126–7, 161–2, 223–4, 256–7, 329
  temperament 23, 24–5, 28, 38, 380–81, 408, 420
  Lord of the Justiciary 29–30, 33, 38, 428
  Blair's Land, Edinburgh 33, 35–6, 48, 101, 381
  moves to gain JB a commission 72–3, 84, 104
  irritated by JB's behaviour 80, 126–8, 234
  financial provisions for JB 89, 101, 164, 362
  attitude to JB's travels abroad 136–7, 164, 171, 181, 200, 203
  ill-health 203, 268, 380, 384, 408, 415
  improved relations with JB 223, 226–7, 380, 384, 386
  disapproval of JB's choice of wife 253–4
  marriage to Elizabeth Boswell 254, 262
  agrees to JB's marriage 255
  ballot-rigging in Ayrshire election 329–30
  death and funeral 445–6
  financial provisions for second wife Elizabeth 449–50

Auchinleck (estate)
  Old Castle 25–7, 28, 29
  entail problems 227, 256–7, 288, 333, 342, 362–3, 380–1, 408
  JB's and David's ritual oath of allegiance 424
  collection of rents 461, 474, 499, 503, 505, 523
Auchinleck House 5, 29, 30, 75, 91
Auchinleck, James (Old James), 7th Laird of (grandfather of JB) 28–9, 37

Baldwin, Henry, printer 476, 498
Barnard, Thomas 453, 467, 473, 481, 498, 535
Beattie, James 87, 275, 276, 288
  An Essay on the Nature and Immutability of Truth 275
  The Minstrel 275, 288
Beauclerk, Topham 293–4, 347, 411–12, 423, 484
Bellegarde, suitor of Zélide 159, 160, 161
Berlin 168–71
Blair, Catherine (the 'Heiress'; the 'Princess') 30, 239–40, 242
Blair, Dr Hugh 248, 355, 527
Bosville, Elizabeth Diana (daughter of Godfrey) 216, 235, 240, 243, 286, 312, 313
Boswell, Alexander, 8th Laird of Auchinleck see Auchinleck (Alexander Boswell)
Boswell, Alexander 'Sandy' (son of JB) 362, 397, 406, 419–20, 495, 533, 544
  Eton 507, 510, 512, 516, 521, 524

Boswell, Charles (illegitimate son of JB) 109, 137, 150

Boswell, Dr John (uncle of JB) 99, 257

Boswell, Elizabeth 'Betsy' (daughter of JB) 424, 510, 512, 549

Boswell, Elizabeth (later 2nd Lady Auchinleck) 254, 510, 521
  JB's dislike of (*noverca*) 255, 258, 265, 386, 445
  hostility toward JB 386, 416, 420, 450
  financial benefits accrued from Auchinleck estate 449–50

Boswell, Euphemia (daughter of JB) 331, 385, 397, 406, 419, 520–1, 549, 543–4
  boarding schools 495, 510
  poor behaviour 524–5
  Nancy Temple comments on 537

Boswell, Euphemia (Erskine) (mother of JB) 23, 24, 27, 35–7, 126, 192, 203, 211

Boswell, James
  affairs
    Mrs Cowper 61–2
    Mrs Love 85, 91, 99, 367, 404–5, 459
    Peggy Doig 85, 91
    Jean Heron 94–5, 98, 180, 182
    Louisa 115–17, 118–21
    Mrs Dodds 236–9
    Mrs Rudd 376, 475, 492–3
    Liberton's Wynd landlady 424, 440
    Maria Cosway 475
  Auchinleck
    agriculture and estate management 224, 268–9, 451–2, 505, 523, 543–4
    visits from Edinburgh 267, 268, 274, 296, 325, 361–2, 384, 386, 396, 408, 424
    James Bruce 408, 415, 425–6, 449, 451, 452, 508–9, 523
    takes possession of ancestral seat 449
    Andrew Gibb 451–2, 523, 543, 544
    relationship with estate tenants 451–2
    visits from London 495, 499, 505–6, 508–12, 533, 538–9, 543–6
  conversations
    with David Hume 60, 383–4

Boswell, James – *contd*
  conversations – *contd*
    with SJ 246–7, 259–60, 283–4, 294–5, 301, 316, 355–6, 367–9, 373, 388–91, 411, 418
    with Lord Mansfield 233
    with Rousseau 177–80, 182–5
    with Margaret Stuart 351–22
    with Mrs Rudd 375–6
    with Voltaire 186, 187–9
  correspondence
    Temple 4, 45, 50–1, 59, 63, 73, 137, 223, 236, 251, 265, 413, 533
    Dalrymple 66–7, 129, 135–6, 181, 225, 274
    Erskine 79, 86, 87–8, 127–8
    Zélide 159–61, 169, 243–4
    Rousseau 185, 186, 190, 197, 198, 199, 202, 213
    Wilkes 199, 200
    Piccolimini ('Moma') 203, 208
    Marischal 224, 239
    Margaret Montgomerie 254–5
    Johnson 217, 219, 258, 274–5, 326, 328, 378, 381, 387, 417, 421–2, 442, 446, 471
    Goldsmith 290–1
    Burke 393–4
    Jamie 543–6
  drinking to excess
    beginning of 238
    developing pattern of drink and sex 238
    in London 280, 349, 432, 462, 475, 512, 533, 534, 539, 542, 547
    in Edinburgh 289, 343, 364, 379, 407, 416
    relief from boredom 289, 327
    at Coirechatachan 319
    Iona 325
    daily problem 331–2
    after-effects 332, 333
    in company of Synod 341
    Paoli attempts to curb 360, 389, 404, 410, 432–3
    discussion with SJ 389
    sobriety 393, 400, 404, 406, 418, 453
  education
    school 34, 35
    home schooling 39–40

Boswell, James – *contd*
  education – *contd*
    tutors 39–40, 43–4
    lack of knowledge and book reading 348–49, 396, 537
  excursions
    Moffat spa 40–2, 52, 236
    Carlisle 52
    'Journal of my Jaunt, Harvest 1762' 92–102
    trip to Greenwich with SJ 138
    Twickenham with SJ 355–6
    Oxford 367–8
    Birmingham 368
    Lichfield 368–9
    Bath 371–2
    Ashbourne 388–92
  executions attended
    Tyburn 130, 229, 259, 412–13, 459, 475
    Turin 194
    Edinburgh 229–30, 270, 289, 329, 337
    thoughts on resuscitation of hanged persons 335–7
    John Reid 337
    writes reports of 475
  family affairs
    ambivalent attitude to mother 24
    beaten for telling lies 25, 36
    birth 33
    spoilt by mother 35–6
    ambivalent feelings for father 38, 53, 64, 84
    tutors 39–40, 43–4
    affected by death of son John 150–1
    mother's death 211
    poor relationships with father 234, 239, 251, 252, 254–6, 288, 296, 361
    fear of disinheritance 254, 288–9
    reaction to father's remarriage 254–5
    improved relations with father 268–9
    protecting inheritance 268–9
    feelings of guilt on leaving Margaret 277–8, 289, 314
    father's pressure for entail on estate 329
    threat of duel with William Miller 339–41

Boswell, James – *contd*
  family affairs – *contd*
    conversation with stepmother 363–4
    death and funeral of JB's father 445–6
  finances after father's death 457
    investment in *London Magazine* 271, 279–80
    debts incurred earlier 422, 442, 498, 522
    loan to Margaret's nephews 422
    restricted by stepmother's inheritance 449–50
    bank credit exhausted 463
    insufficient to support family in London 471
    earning little from legal practice 474
    property purchases 474, 522, 540
    settlement on wife and children 474
    borrowing to repay debts 498
    repaying debts to Dilly and Baldwin 506
    costs of children's education 507, 512
    advances from Dilly and Baldwin 523, 540
    offer for copyright of *Life* 523
    income from *Life* 532, 540, 542
  flirtations
    Mrs Love 61
    Miss Dallas 78
    Lady Kenmure 93–4
    at Brampton puppet show 97
    Annie Cunninghame 380, 386
    Anna Seward 466
    Lady Mary Lindsay 516
    Wilhelmina Alexander 538
  health
    final illness and death 3, 547
    in childhood 35–6, 40–1, 43–4
    psychosomatic illness 40–41
    depression 51–2
    nervous breakdown 52
    sexual infections 73, 75, 120–3, 198, 201, 238–40, 242, 247–8, 255, 257, 370, 393, 424, 440, 463, 475, 491, 520
    malaria (ague) 208, 268
    ingrown toenail 209, 247, 410, 416, 418, 421

Boswell, James – *contd*
  health – *contd*
    operations 247, 257, 421
    scurvy 40–1, 418, 472, 539
    temper deteriorating 539
    kidney failure and uraemia 547
    see also hypochondria (melancholia)
  Hebridean tour
    Macbeth's blasted heath 302–3
    motivation behind journey 303–4
    SJ praises journal 305
    call on Lord Monboddo 306
    gloomy feelings 306, 308
    inspects body of executed robber 308
    criticism of hospitality at Armadale 312
    fear at sea 314, 319–20, 323
    trek around Raasay 314
    emotionally and physically exhausted 327
  hypochondria 3, 23, 52, 110, 195, 278–9, 339, 381, 416, 421–2, 430–1, 462, 471–2
    self-examination 13, 15–20
    essays in *London Magazine* 15, 17, 18, 394, 407
    irritability caused by 19
    triggers 39, 89–90, 121, 124–6, 129–31, 228
    alleviated by military fancies 45
    private language for 48
    at Kirroughtrie 95
    journals as antidotes 113–14
    associated with sexual dissipation 130–1
    on arrival in Utrecht 144–5
    eased by SJ's *Rambler* essays 145
    advice from friends 146
    struggle against in Utrecht 146–7, 150–1
    religious origins 151
    on German tour 163, 165
    Hebridean tour 308, 312, 318, 321
    after Reid trial 342
    while visiting Wilton 359–60
    after London visit 360–1
    regularity of occurrence 364–55, 377
    discussion between JB and SJ 367–8, 389
    thoughts of suicide 438

Boswell, James – *contd*
  hypochondria – *contd*
    after move to London 492, 496–7, 499, 504, 507
    after death of wife 512, 520, 524
    after publication of *Life* 533, 538–40
  Journals
    Northern Circuit 78
    'Journal of My Jaunt, Harvest 1762' 92–102
    'Boswelliana' 95, 226, 287
    character sketching 95–7
    first London journal 110–15
    lost journals 143, 295, 417
    on German tour 165–6
    pages burnt by Lady Talbot 211–12
    advice from SJ 295
    Hebridean tour 304–5, 320, 321
    left around for Margaret to read 364, 440
    JB has doubts of value 378, 416, 455
    'Journal of my Jaunt with the Honourable Colonel James Stuart' 417
    journal of Margaret's illness 441
    method of recording conversation 531, 543
    ceases to write journal 543
  law studies 45, 51, 54, 61, 90
    Edinburgh University 43, 44–5, 51, 54, 61
    Glasgow University 64
    at home 73, 75, 84–5, 88
    plan to study at Inner Temple 84
    Utrecht 143–54
    Latin thesis 223, 224
    ignorance of English law 491, 494
  legal affairs
    admitted to Faculty of Advocates 224
    Court of Session 226, 230, 232, 296, 488, 489
    defence of John Reid 227–8, 334–8
    entail of family estates through male line 227, 256–7, 288
    defence of rioters 228–9, 289
    southern Justiciary Circuit with father 228
    defence of John Raybould 229
    defence of Robert Hay 229
    emotional ties with clients 229

Boswell, James – *contd*
 legal affairs – *contd*
  thoughts of escaping to English Bar
  253, 275, 285, 330, 338, 345, 357,
  390–1
  practising at Bar of General Assembly of Church of Scotland 269, 296
  defence of William Harris 270
  defence of John Hastie 275, 285–6
  defence of Adam sisters 328
  growing reputation 328
  increasing business 331
  attempts to have Reid's sentence reduced 335–6
  letter attacking bias of Lord Justice-Clerk Miller 337
  cause of Alexander Rule v. Smith 386–7
  speaks at bar of House of Commons 403
  Assizes at Carlisle 406
  decline in income 416, 421
  one of counsel representing Hugh Montgomerie 429
  decision to try at London Bar 467
  called to English Bar 488, 491
  Northern Circuit 491, 505, 511
  counsel for Margaret's nephew in House of Lords 492
  Home Circuit 495, 532, 538, 539
  defence of Lonsdale's electoral manipulation 497–8
  Chelmsford Sessions 499
  Quarter Sessions 506
 Life of Johnson
  seeking details of SJ's life 283–4, 288, 296
  starts writing 496
  collaboration with Edmond Malone 489–90, 494, 495, 496, 506, 513–15, 520–21, 535, 541–2
  continued application to writing 499, 507, 521
  printer's errors 513
  process of revision 513–15
  format of book 515
  revision completed 525
  public reception 526–9
  sales 526
  reviews 527–9

Boswell, James – *contd*
 Life of Johnson – *contd*
  parodied in 'Lessons in Biography' 528
  autobiographical component 529, 530
  a new form of biography 529–32
  conversational authenticity 530, 531
  dedicated to Sir Joshua Reynolds 532
  second edition 535, 540, 541–2
  third edition 542
 in love
  Miss Mackay 41–2
  unnamed actress 53
  Martha Whyte 59–60
  Peggy Stewart 88
  Jean Heron 94
  Jeanie Dempster 100
  Lady Betty Erskine 100
  Catherina van Geelvinck 152–3
  Zélide 152, 153–4, 155–62
  Girolama Piccolimini ('Moma') 202–3
  gardner's daughter 236
  Mrs Dodds 236–9
  Mary Ann Boyd 250
  Margaret Montgomerie 251–7
 marriage to Margaret Montgomerie
  marriage contract 261
  Paoli wishes to attend ceremony 261
  coincident with father's marriage 262
 married life
  mutual devotion 265–6, 268, 381
  apartments 266, 267, 381–2
  jaunt together into northern England 267–8
  devotion to Veronica 332
  verbal and physical violence toward Margaret 333, 364, 380, 463
  after-effects of Reid trial 338–40
  deterioration of compatibility 344–5
  lack of realistic conversation 344
  JB purchases suit of laces for Margaret 351
  reckless and boorish behaviour upsets Margaret 379–80
  reactions to death of son David 385

Boswell, James – *contd*
  married life – *contd*
    change in JB's feelings 440
    problems within marriage 441
    will 479
    return to Auchinleck to be with wife 508
    guilt at not being at wife's death 509
    returns to London after wife's death 512
    thoughts of remarriage 515–16
    affection for the children 517
    daughters out of control 539, 543
    close relationship with Jamie 543
    see also Boswell, Margaret; children under own names
  metaphysical preoccupations 51, 339, 382, 384, 419
    degree of immorality in concubinage (fornication) 135, 182, 269, 277, 344, 350
    death 259–60, 382–3, 453–5
    morality of pleading for guilty client 270
  military ambitions 45, 72–3, 84, 88–9, 104, 124–6
    quest for Guards commission 72–3, 84, 88–9, 104–5, 109, 124–5
  move to London
    discouragement of friends 489, 494
    indecision 489–90
    house in Great Queen Street 490, 494, 495
    family arrives 495
    Margaret wants to go back 498–9, 503–4, 505
    family break in Auchinleck 499
    house in Queen Ann Street West 507, 514
    house in Great Portland Street 524
    chambers in Temple 525, 533, 538
  personal attributes
    descriptions and opinions of 1–2, 210, 211, 304, 434–6, 461–2, 469
    lack of confidence 19, 44, 53
    superstitions 24, 35–6
    romanticism 26–7, 29–30, 176–7, 391
    pride in royal ancestry 27–8
    timidity as child 35, 37, 48

Boswell, James – *contd*
  personal attributes – *contd*
    intellectual curiosity aroused 46
    love of theatre 49, 53, 54, 56–8, 62, 106, 538, 542
    misanthropy 52
    dislike of law 53, 72, 226
    singing 53, 80, 108, 231, 523
    talent for mimicry 100, 112, 127
    cultivation of reserved behaviour (*retenu*) 110, 123, 144, 146–51, 154, 155, 349
    fluency in French and Dutch 143, 147
    Inviolable Plan 147–9
    gambling at cards 250, 289, 333, 342, 364, 424
    acting, psychological appeal of 272
    patriotic feelings 301, 304–5
    ability to lead conversation 318, 319
    indiscriminate criticism of others 343
    interest in science 370
    poor understanding of women 374
    affected by music 389
    reaction to death of SJ 473
    buffoonery 534–5
  personal papers
    at Malahide Castle 1, 2, 5–8, 10–11, 304
    discovered at Fettercairn House 2, 8–9
    discovered in Boulogne 4
    sent to Willam Forbes by Edmond Malone 4
    transferred from Auchinleck to Malahide 5
    sold at Sotheby's 8
    Cumberland Infirmary 9–11
  political ambitions
    search for patronage 359–60, 367, 427–30, 433, 442–4, 459–61, 464–6, 472, 488–9
    cultivation of Henry Dundas 426–30
    remote from political reality 464
    denied office of Knight Marshal of Scotland by Dundas 472
    ended by Diminishing Bill affair 477–9, 489

Boswell, James – *contd*
  political ambitions – *contd*
    candidate for Ayrshire Parliamentary seat 511
    attempts to attract William Pitt's attention 523–4
    application for diplomatic post in Corsica rejected 540
    see also Recorder of Carlisle
  political leanings
    toward social despotism 184
    committment to Corsican liberty 207, 209, 216–22
    interview with William Pitt to discuss Corsica 216
    propagandist in Douglas cause 230–4
    support for oppressed Americans 356
    antipathy toward French revolutionaries 517–18, 533, 542
  prostitutes
    London 69, 73, 106, 107, 115, 130–1, 133, 135–6, 246, 247, 367, 370, 459, 475, 492, 512, 520–1, 542
    abroad 169, 193–4, 195, 196, 198, 201, 252, 255
    after witnessing executions 230, 475
    Edinburgh 235, 238–9, 290, 333, 343, 379, 393, 416, 418, 424
    dalliance with 350–1, 459
  Recorder of Carlisle 503, 519
    journeys to Carlisle with Lonsdale 502–3, 519
    duties in Carlisle 512, 515
  religion
    Presbyterian upbringing 23–4, 36–7, 46, 53
    Calvinistic fears of afterlife 24
    Christian Humanist influences 39
    Anglicanism 52, 53, 80–1, 181
    Methodism 52
    Roman Catholicism 65, 66–8, 74, 179–80, 182, 191, 194–5
    Christian doubts 151
    prayers at Inchkenneth chapel 323
    piety and resolutions at Iona 323–4
  sexuality
    development 41, 52, 54, 69
    sensuality 41–2
    illegitimate children 109, 137, 150, 239, 242, 238–9

Boswell, James – *contd*
  sexuality – *contd*
    anxiety-driven impotence 116–17, 212
    dissipation associated with hypochondria 130–1
    moral implications of concubinage (fornication) 135, 182, 269, 277, 344, 350
    voracious sexual appetite 236, 344
    see also health; prostitutes
  social intercourse
    Select Society membership 81–3
    developing friendship with SJ 131–6, 137, 138–9
    visits SJ in chambers for first time 132–3
    farewell to SJ at Harwich 139–40
    letter of introduction to Rousseau 176–7
    visits to Rousseau 177–85
    meetings with Voltaire 186–9
    paintings commissioned by 196–7
    friendship with Wilkes 199–200
    as Corsican Chief at Shakespeare Jubilee 220–1
    visits to Sir Alexander Dick 225
    visit to Boyd family in Ireland 251–2
    visit to Temple in Devon 261
    relationship with Garrick 273, 281–2
    meeting with Lord Mansfield 292
    visit to Goldsmith 292
    affected by death of Goldsmith 292
    reunion with SJ after Hebridean tour 348–51, 353, 355–6
    visit to Pembroke at Winton 359–60
    joins SJ and Thrales in Bath 371–2
    accomplishes meeting between SJ and Wilkes 372–4
    presentation at Court 433–4
    farewell to SJ at Bolt Court 470
    'the Gang' (JB, Malone, Reynolds, Courtenay) 479–80, 488, 493
    meeting with Fanny Burney 521–2
    visit to Temple with Veronica and Euphemia 536–8

Boswell, James – *contd*
  Tour to the Hebrides
    plan to publish with Dilly 474
    start of collaboration with Malone
      476–7, 479–81, 483–4, 496
    continuing progress 479
    revision methods 480–1
    dedicated to Malone 481
    public reception 481–3, 484
    second edition 482, 483–4
    objections to reporting of SJ's
      personal comments 483
    see also Malone, Edmond
  travels abroad
    Utrecht 143–54, 155–62
    Amsterdam 154
    German tour 164–74
    Brunswick 165, 167–8
    Berlin 168–71
    Karlsruhe 172–4
    Switzerland 175–89
    Neuchâtel 181
    Geneva 186–9
    Italy 190–210
    Turin 190–4
    Milan 194–5
    Naples 195–6, 199
    Rome 195, 196
    Venice 198, 201
    Siena 201–3
    Corsica 203–8
    Genoa 208–9
    France 210–11
    Paris 210–11
    Ireland 250–2
  visits to England
    London (1759) 65–73
    London (1762) 103–139
    London (1768) 246–62
    London (1772) 277–287
    London (1775) 347–60
    London (1776) 366–76
    Ashbourne (1777) 378, 388–92
    London (1778) 396, 398–405
    Carlisle (1778) 406
    London (1779) 410–14
    London and Chester (1780) 417–18
    London (1781) 432–8
    London (1783) 456–61
    London (1784) 466–7, 468–71

Boswell, James – *contd*
  visits to England – *contd*
    London (1785) 474–81, 483–7,
      488
  writings
    Account of Corsica 1, 6, 204, 211, 217–
      20, 240, 244
    Journal of a Tour to the Hebrides 1,
      8, 26–7
    Life of Johnson 1, 6, 10, 111, 217, 259,
      281, 292, 300–1, 348, 359, 489
    'Hypochondriac' essays 15, 17, 18,
      287, 394–6, 404, 407, 409–11, 412,
      416, 423–5, 438, 444, 455
    'October' 55
    poetry 55, 58–9, 60–3, 71, 76–80,
      79–81, 172
    'On the Profession of a Player' 1770
      56, 271–2
    'Epistle to Temple' 62
    *A View of the Edinburgh Theatre
      During the Summer Season, 1759* 63
    The Cub at Newmarket 71, 117
    'Poetical Epistle to Doctor Sterne'
      71
    Give Your Son His Will 76
    *An Elegy on the Death of an Amiable
      Young Lady* 79
    'Ode to Gluttony' 86
    'Ode to Tragedy' 86
    prologue to Mrs Sheridan's *The
      Discovery* 109
    *Critical Strictures on the New Tragedy
      of Elvira* 122
    correspondence with Erskine 127–8
    Dorando, A Spanish Tale 231–2
    The Douglas Cause 231
    The Essence of the Douglas Cause
      232–3, 244
    Letters of Lady Jane Douglas 233
    opening night prologue for Theatre
      Royal 272
    article on patronage in Church of
      Scotland 287
    *Reflections on the Bankruptcies in
      Scotland, 1772* 288
    *The Decision of the Court of Session
      upon the Question of Literary
      Property* 297
    'A Review of my Life' 361

Boswell, James – *contd*
  writings – *contd*
    'Account of my Last Interview with
    David Hume, Esq.' 382–3
    abortive search for literary subjects
    394, 409
    account of Highlander's mutiny
    408
    articles on Hackman case 412
    *Letter to Robert Macqueen, Lord
    Braxfield* 428
    'Ode by Dr Samuel Johnson to Mrs
    Thrale' 437–8
    Letter to the People of Scotland (1783)
    464–6, 472
    reports of executions 475–6
    trial reports 476
    Letter to the People of Scotland (1785)
    478–9, 480
    Piozzian Rhimes 485–6
    ballad 'William Pitt: The Grocer of
    London' 523
    poem 'No Abolition of Slavery: or
    the Universal Empire of Love'
    523–4
    'Memoirs of James Boswell,
    Esquire' 532
    *The Principal Corrections and
    Additions to the First Edition*
    542
    see also Boswell, James, *Life of
    Johnson*; Boswell, James, *Tour of the
    Hebrides*
Boswell, James Jr. 'Jamie' (son of JB) 406,
  419, 499, 507, 510
  schools 507, 512, 517, 524, 543
  completes Malone's edition of Shakespeare 542, 549
  close relationship with JB 543–6
  correspondence with JB 543–6
Boswell, John (brother of JB)
  mental illness 99, 223, 345, 392
  in London 122, 130
  at Auchinleck 253
  living with father and stepmother
  262
  in Newcastle 267, 345, 365
  visits from JB 267, 345, 365, 392
  visits JB in Edinburgh 420
  at father's funeral 445

Boswell, Margaret (Montgomerie), wife
  of JB 267, 271, 415, 490
  in Edinburgh
    irritation with SJ 289, 300, 326, 387,
    442
    death of son David 385
  health
    ill-health (non-specific) 266, 275,
    277, 343–4, 351, 379, 420, 445
    consumption 379, 393, 420, 429,
    423, 441, 450, 498, 503, 504, 508–9
    too ill to travel 498, 506
    death 509
  in London
    homesick for Auchinleck 495,
    498–9
    disadvantages of London life 500,
    503–4
    determined to return to Auchinleck
    503–4, 505
  pregnancies and births
    first child 266
    second child, stillborn 267, 268
    Veronica 288, 289–90
    Euphemia, nicknamed 'Effie' 331
    Alexander, nicknamed 'Sandy' 342,
    362
    David 379, 384
    James Jr., nicknamed 'Jamie' 393,
    406
    Elizabeth, nicknamed 'Betsy' 420,
    424
    miscarriage 440
  relations with JB
    concern with JB's drinking and
    gambling 270, 289–90, 332
    forgives JB's infidelities and
    drunkenness 289, 333, 416, 440
    fear of JB's duelling 339–40, 479
    growing unhappiness with JB 342–
    4, 380
    decreasing interest in sex 344, 351
    finds clues to sexual episodes in
    journal 364, 380
    supportive 421, 467, 467
    letter to Dundas about employment
    for JB 472
    see also Boswell, James, married life
Boswell, Sally (illegitimate daughter of
  JB) 239, 242

Boswell, Thomas, 1st Laird of Auchinleck *see* Auchinleck (Thomas Boswell)
Boswell, Thomas David 'T.D.' (brother of JB)
  Valencia 23–4, 257, 424
  possible career 127, 223, 275, 424
  JB's and David's ritual oath of allegiance at Auchinleck 424
  irritating personality 424–5
  advice on deportment to JB 425
  clerk in Navy Pay Office 524
Boswell, Veronica (daughter of JB) 290–1, 331, 332, 335, 380–2, 385, 387, 397, 406, 419, 510, 512, 543–4
  boarding school in London 495, 505, 507
  jealousy of Euphemia 517
  description by Nancy Temple 518–19, 537
  poor behaviour 524–5
  musical evening with Haydn 535
  dies of consumption 549
Boyd, Mary Ann 250
Braxfield, Robert Maxqueen, Lord 428, 429
Broad, Mary, escaped convict 535–6
Brown, Robert 143, 151–2, 384
Bruce, James 408, 415, 449, 451, 452, 508–9, 523
Brunswick 165, 167–8
Bryant, William, escaped convict 535–6
Burgaretta *see* Borgaretto
Burke, Edmund 280, 293–4, 393–4, 411, 413, 493–4, 517
  Philosophical Enquiry into the Sublime and Beautiful 416
  approached by JB for patronage 442–3, 464
  Paymaster-General 443, 459
  urges JB to approach Henry Dundas 443
  advises JB to fix mind on Scotland 460–1
  invites JB to Chelsea Hospital dinner 460
  invites JB to Gregories 460
  JB rides to Glasgow to meet 465
  fondness for JB abated 483
  offended by SJ's comments in *Tour* 483

Burney, Charles (father of Charlotte and Francis) 469, 526
Burney, Charlotte Ann (sister of Fanny) 434–5
Burney, Francis ('Fanny') 206, 280, 435–6, 521–2
Burns, Robert, poet, letter to JB 452–3
Bute, John Stuart, 3rd Earl of 68, 69, 104, 124, 125–6, 199, 432, 433

Carlisle 502, 512, 515, 519
Catch Club 108, 167
Chambers, Sir Robert 34–5, 246, 298
Clement XIII, Pope 196, 198
Cochrane, Basil, Commissioner of Customs 125, 340, 345, 445
Cook, James 370–1
Corradini, Gertrude, mistress of John Wilkes 199
Corsica 184, 207–9
  struggle for liberty 184
  JB's visit 203–8
  JB known as Corsica Boswell 207, 220, 221
  JB suspected of spying 208–9
  JB's campaign for 216–22
  defeated by French 221, 253
  JB rejected for diplomatic post 540
  see also Paoli, Pasquale di
Cosway, Maria 475
Courtenay, John (nephew of Lord Bute) 479–80, 484, 500
  Poetical Review of the Literary and Moral Character of the late Dr Samuel Johnson 493
Cowper, Mrs 61–2, 65, 66
Crosbie, Andrew 284, 285, 301, 329, 334
Cunninghame, Annie (niece of JB's wife) 380, 415

Dalrymple, Sir David (later Lord Hailes) 54–5, 80–1, 137, 217, 231, 331
  correspondence with JB 66–7, 129, 181, 225
  attempts to divert JB from Catholicism 68
  critical of JB's indiscretions 128
  approves JB friendship with SJ 135
  mediator between JB and father 136–7
  advice against hypochondria 146

Dalrymple, Sir David – *contd*
  constructive comments on *Account of Corsica* 218, 219
  furious with JB over attack on Lord Provost 274
Davies, Thomas 68, 117, 131–2, 217, 218, 248
Deleyre, Alexander 178, 185, 195
Dempster, George 77–8, 86, 100, 122, 145, 146, 443
Dempster, Jeannie 100
Desmoulins, Elizabeth 398, 457
Dick, Sir Alexander 195, 218, 225, 228, 252, 301, 381, 385, 409, 439
Dick, Sir John, British Consul at Leghorn 217
Digges, West 57–8, 63, 110
Dilly, Charles (brother of Edward) 413, 473–4, 505
  loans to JB 422, 498
Dilly, Edward, publisher of *Account of Corsica* 218, 219, 248, 271, 280, 281, 372–4, 413
Dodd, Sir William, execution of 388–9
Dodds, Mrs 237–9
Doig, Peggy 91, 92, 99, 109, 137
Donaldson, Alexander, *A Collection of Original Poems . . .* 77, 78–9, 84, 85–7, 297, 330
Douglas, Andrew 107, 370, 403
Douglas, Archibald James Edward (previously Stewart; later 1st Baron Douglas) 230, 253, 262, 275, 324, 431
Douglas, Lady Jane (wife of Sir John Stewart) 230, 233
Dun, John 39, 416, 538
Dundas, Henry, Solicitor-General 328, 334, 386
  political rise resented by JB 363
  duel planned by JB for father's honour 364
  JB initiates reconciliation 426–7
  invites JB and Maclaurin to Melville 427
  JB seeks political patronage 427–8, 443–4, 460
  sees JB as risky political appointee 427–8
  apology and advice to JB 429
  sharp words to JB in court 429

Dundas, Henry – *contd*
  Lord Advocate 459, 464
  Treasurer of the Navy 459, 466
  quotes from JB's pamphlet in Commons 465
  sees JB as unfitted for appointment to bench 472
  Diminishing Bill 477–8
  offended by *Letter to the People of Scotland* 478–80, 498
  ignores JB in elections 511
  salaried appointment for David Boswell 524
  Home Secretary 536
  rejection of JB for diplomatic post in Corsica 540
Dundas, Robert, Lord President of Court of Session 230, 232, 234

Eglinton, Alexander Montgomerie, 10th Earl of 68–70, 71, 72, 74, 108–9, 322
  JB's letter published 69–70, 85
  JB's search for a commission 88–9, 105, 109
  accidental death 261–2
Eglinton, Archibald Montgomerie, 11th Earl of 329, 422, 545
Erskine, Andrew 77–8, 79, 86–7, 100, 110, 253, 422, 527
  correspondence with JB 79, 86, 87–8, 127–8
  suicide 542
Erskine, Elizabeth ('Betty') (later Macfarlane) 100, 107, 110
Evans, Thomas, publisher 291, 292

Fergusson, Joseph 39–42, 101
Fergusson, Sir Adam 230, 329, 427, 429, 466
Fettercairn House 2, 8–9
Forbes, Sir William (JB's executor) 4, 9, 301, 381, 393, 422, 463, 474, 479, 528
Fox, Charles James 350, 443, 459, 464
France 210–11
Francis, Charlotte Ann (Burney) (sister of Fanny Burney) 546
Franklin, Benjamin 224, 248, 280
Frederick William II 'the Great', King of Prussia 167, 170–1

Froment, Madame de 165
Fullarton, William (the 'Nabob') 240–2

Garrick, David 58, 68–9, 114, 121–2, 248, 280, 347, 404
    Shakespeare Jubilee 220–1
    JB's articles on 271–2, 273
    strained relationship with SJ 273, 281–2
    death and funeral procession 409–10
Geelvinck, Catherina Elizabeth van, ('La Veuve') 152
Geneva 186–9
Genoa 208–9
Gentleman, Francis 58, 64, 68
George III, King of England 215, 222, 433–4, 500, 526
Germany 165–6
Gibb, Andrew, estate overseer 451–2, 523, 543, 544
Gilpin, Kitty 96–7
Goldsmith, Oliver 117, 280
    liking for JB 118, 292
    dinner with JB and SJ at the Mitre 134
    with SJ at General Oglethorpe's 279
    She Stoops to Conquer 280, 290, 291–2
    death of kidney infection 292, 330
Grange (John Johnston) 17, 47, 39, 47, 48–50, 64, 66, 91, 92, 114–15, 126, 137, 495
Gronovius, Abraham 149, 154

Hackman, James, murderer of Martha Ray 411–12
Hailes, Lord see Dalrymple, Sir David
Hamilton, Archibald 469
Hamilton, Douglas Hamilton, 8th Duke of 403
Hamilton, Elizabeth Gunning, Duchess of see Argyll, Duchess of
Hamilton, James George Hamilton, 7th Duke of 230, 325
Hanni, Jacob, JB's Swiss servant 164, 205, 208–10
Hawkins, Sir John, official biographer of SJ 476, 500
Hebridean tour
    Inverness 302, 306, 308–9
    Dunvegan Castle 305, 316, 315–17

Hebridean tour – contd
    Aberdeen 306–7
    call on Lord Monboddo 306
    leave Edinburgh 306
    St Andrews 306
    Bullers of Buchan 307
    horse transport 309, 311, 316
    Loch Ness 309
    Auchnasheal 310
    Fort August 310
    Glen Moriston 310
    Glen Shiel 310
    Glenelg 311
    Skye 312–19
    Coirechatachan 313, 318
    Raasay 313–14
    Kingsburgh 315
    Portree 315
    Talisker 317–18
    storm on way to Mull 319–20
    Coll (island) 320
    Mull 321–2
    Inchkenneth 322–3
    Inverary 324–5
    Iona 324
Hector, Dr Edmund 357, 368
Hermenches, David-Louis, Baron de Constant de Rebecque, Seigneur d' 186, 244
Heron, Jean (Jeany), wife of Patrick 94–5, 98
Hume, David 20, 33, 60, 81, 82, 100, 173, 212, 248, 267
    religious scepticism 275, 301, 382, 384
    deathbed discussion of afterlife with JB 382–3
hypochondria (melancholy) 13–20
    Boswell family trait 13, 28, 35, 36
    The Anatomy of Melancholy (Robert Burton) 13
    famous victims of 14
    Samuel Johnson 14–15
    compounded by religious guilt 15
    definition in Johnson's Dictionary 15
    subject of JB essays for London Magazine 15, 17, 18, 394, 407
    alternation with manic exuberance 17, 18
    see also Boswell, James

Ireland 250
Isham, Ralph Heyward
  acquisition of JB's papers 6–8, 10, 11
  recollection of destroyed Journal pages
    211–12
Italy 190–210

Jachone, Corsican boar-hunting dog 208,
    209–10
Johnson, Samuel
  advice
    to JB not to publish *Account of
      Corsica* 217
    against vows 223, 405
    to JB on father's remarriage 258
    to JB on behaviour toward father
      289
    on avoiding hypochondria 418,
      421–2
    to JB to be frugal 442, 446, 457
    to JB to care for Margaret 442
  health
    Hebridean tour cancelled 288
    breathing troubles 387, 456, 468,
      472
    weak ankles and bad toe 417
    gout, dropsy and kidney stones 468,
      472
    struggle against hypochondria 530
  Hebridean tour
    cancelled for bad health 288
    joins JB in Edinburgh 298
    arrival in Scotland 299
    letters to Mrs Thrale 300, 304, 311,
      316, 321
    motivation behind journey 303
    comments on JB as travelling
      companion 304
    praises JB's journal 305
    sleeps in bed of Bonnie Prince
      Charlie 315
    horror at dead men's bones 323
    visit to Auchinleck 325
    see also Hebridean tour
  Hester Thrale
    taken up by 249
    journey through Wales with 330, 358
    proposed journey with to Italy 358,
      363, 365, 371
    relationship with 358, 468

Johnson, Samuel – *contd*
  Hector Thrale – *contd*
    journey to France with 359
    abandoned by 468
    emotional effects of her marriage
      471
  miscellaneous
    mentioned by Sheridan to JB 83, 109
    opinion of *Account of Corsica* 219
    apprehensions of death 259, 390
    friendship with James Beattie 275,
      276, 286
    intolerance of Methodists 283
    opinion of Margaret Boswell 300,
      301, 325–6
    mimics Lady Macdonald 313
    Ossian controversy 313, 317, 353–4
    stylistic revision of Lord Hailes's
      manuscript 331
    support for policy of American
      taxation 354
    moves to Bolt Court 366
    dinner with Wilkes at Dilly's 372–4
    efforts on behalf of Sir William
      Dodd 388–9
    sex life discussed by JB and
      Elizabeth Desmoulins 457–8
    plan to send to Italy for winter
      469–70
    memorial statue at St Pauls 517, 547
  moral viewpoint
    disapproval of concubinage 135
    views on adultery 247
    disapproval of Lady Diana Beau-
      clerk 296
  relations with JB
    visit to Auchinleck 26, 27, 30
    developing friendship with JB
      131–6, 137, 138–9
    meets JB first in bookshop 131–2
    understanding of JB's hypochon-
      dria 137
    visit to Greenwich with JB 138
    reunited with JB after Grand Tour
      215
    JB visits in Oxford 246–7
    assists JB to prepare for Hastie cause
      284–5
    nominates JB for Literary Club
      293–4

Johnson, Samuel – *contd*
  relations with JB – *contd*
    outbursts against JB 296, 341, 369,
      391–2, 400–3, 457
    good wishes to JB's wife 326, 387
    sends books to JB 349, 378
    discourages JB from publishing
      Hebridean journal 357–8, 378
    at Ashbourne with JB 388–92
    views on JB's proposed move to
      London 390–1
    final farewell to JB at Bolt Court
      470
  writings
    The Vanity of Human Wishes 11
    essays in *Rambler* and *Idler* 95, 132,
      145
    Dictionary of the English Language
      132, 217
    Lives of the English Poets 132, 387,
      400, 413, 430, 432
    Rasselas 132
    *Journey to the Western Islands of Scot-
      land* 303–4, 316, 330, 353
    Taxation No Tyranny 354
Johnston, John *see* Grange

Kames, Agatha Drummond, Lady 95, 98,
  453–5
Kames, Henry Home, Lord 81, 82, 85,
  94–5, 171
    advice to JB 98
    trial of John Reid 334, 335
    potential subject for biography 394,
      454
    interviews with JB just prior to death
      453–5
Karlsruhe 172–4

Langton, Bennet 248, 283–4, 288, 347
Le Vasseur, Thérèse 176, 177, 179, 182,
  185, 186, 211–12
Levett, Dr Robert 136, 367, 398, 456
Lindsay, Lady Margaret 516
Lister, Harriet 516, 518
Literary Club 117, 248, 284, 347, 367,
  403–4, 409, 411
    JB nominated and elected 293–4
London, *see* Boswell, visits to England,
  Boswell, John *and* Boswell, Mar-
  garet

Lonsdale, James Lowther, 1st Earl of
    character 406, 496–8, 502, 503, 506,
      518, 519
    JB and Recordership of Carlisle 497,
      501, 519
Love, James (Dance) 55, 58, 63
Lumisden, Andrew 196–7
Lyttelton, George Lyttelton, 1st Baron
  248, 285

Macaulay, Kenneth, minister at Cawdor
  308, 309
Macdonald, Alexander, of Kingsburgh
  315
Macdonald, Flora (wife of Alexander of
  Kingsburgh) 315
Macdonald, Sir Alexander, of Armadale
  243, 286, 311
    poor hospitality shown to JB and SJ
      312
    threat of violence to JB 483
Mackay, Miss 41–2
Mackinnon, Lachlan, of Coirechatachan
  313, 318
Maclaurin, John (later Lord Dreghorn)
  269, 297, 301, 343
Maclean, Donald, of Coll ('Young Coll')
  317–18, 319–22
Maclean, Dr Hector, of Erray 321
MacLeod, Anne (Martin) (wife of
  Norman MacLeod) 316
Macleod family of Raasay 313–14
Macleod, John, of Talisker 316, 317
Macleod, Malcolm, of Raasay 313
MacLeod, Norman, 19th Laird of
  MacLeod 316, 317
Macpherson, James, *Ossian* 87, 288, 313,
  317, 353–4
Macpherson, Lauchlan 168, 170
McQuhae, William 92, 110, 126
Malahide Castle 1, 2, 5–8, 10–11, 304
Malone, Edmond (JB's executor)
    sends JB papers to William Forbes
      3–4
    Literary Club 423, 456
    JB introduced to 433
    collaboration with JB (*Life of
      Johnson*) 489–90, 494, 495, 496,
      506, 513–15, 520–21, 535,
      541–2

Malone, Edmond – *contd*
  collaboration with JB (*Tour of the Hebrides*) 476–7, 479–81, 483–4, 496
  literary research into Shakespeare 477
  literary executor to JB 479
  management of JB's moods 480, 494, 520
  new Shakespeare edition 484, 513, 514, 521
  urges JB to move to London 489
  Poetical Review of the Literary and Moral Character of the Late Samuel Johnson 493
  hypochondria 494
  furious with Hawkins 500
  deteriorating eyesight 514
  helps JB with second edition of *Life* 535
  quarrel with JB over second edition Advertisement 541
  feelings on JB's death 548
  acts as guardian to JB's children 549
Mansfield, William Murray, 1st Earl of 233, 280, 284, 285, 292, 347, 430
Marchmont, Hugh Hugh-Campbell, 3rd Earl of 98–9, 400–1, 413
Marischal, George Keith, 10th Earl of 164–5, 175, 176, 178, 224, 239
melancholy *see* hypochondria
Milan 194–5
Millar, Andrew, publisher 217, 218
Miller, Thomas, Lord Justice-Clerk 334, 337, 339–41
Moffat, spa town 40–2, 52, 236
Monboddo, James Burnett, Lord 253, 254, 306, 330, 431
Monro, Alexander 328, 335–6
Montague, Elizabeth (Robinson) 285, 404, 469, 484
Montgomerie family of Lainshaw (cousins of JB) 215, 250
Montgomerie, Hugh 427, 429
Montgomerie, Margaret (later wife of JB) 250
  accompanies JB to Ireland 250–2
  JB declares love for 251
  accepts JB's proposal of marriage 255
  portraits of 255–6
  JB's trip to London before marriage 257–8
  see also Boswell, Margaret

Montgomery, James William, Lord Advocate 334, 386
Mountstuart, John Stuart, Viscount (later 4th Earl) 200–1, 275, 347, 459

Nairne, William 100, 301, 428
Naples 195–6, 199
Nasmith, Michael 334, 336, 337
Neuchâtel 181
Newgate prison 106, 130, 412, 536
Nichols, John 515
Northumberland, Elizabeth, Duchess of 30, 104, 120, 124

Oglethorpe, General James Edward 248, 278, 279

Palmer, Mary (niece of Sir Joshua Reynolds) 456, 463, 469
Paoli, Pasquale di, Corsican patriot 184, 204, 217, 280–1, 286
  JB meets in Corsica 206–7
  flees Corsica 221, 253
  reunion with JB in London 221–2
  JB introduces SJ 258, 260
  visits JB in Edinburgh 273–4
  visited by JB and SJ 281
  has JB to stay 347, 360, 366, 410, 456, 490
  accompanies JB to Wilton 359–60
  lectures JB on drinking 410, 432–3
  return to Corsica 518
Paris 210–11
Pembroke, Henry Herbert, 10th Earl of 335, 347, 443, 536–7
Percy, Dr Thomas 248, 267–8, 280, 288, 347, 498
Piccolimini, Girolama ('Moma') 202–3
Piozzi, Gabriel, Italian music teacher 436, 456, 470
Piozzi, Hester (wife of Gabriel; previously Hester Thrale) 476, 482
  Anecdotes of the Late Samuel Johnson 485
  treatment of JB and SJ in book 485
  Letters to and from the Late Samuel Johnson 501, 504
  evidence in *Letters* of SJ's affection for Mrs Thrale 504
  in *Life of Johnson* 528

Pitt, William 104, 216, 464, 465, 511
Pope, Alexander 400–1
Pottle, Frederick A. 2, 3, 8, 10, 212, 304, 531
Preston, Sir George, of Valleyfield 381, 409, 439
Pringle, Dr John 107, 216, 224, 228, 243, 248, 253, 289, 329, 347, 366, 438

Queensberry, Charles Douglas, 3rd Duke of 89, 104–5, 124, 260, 275

Reid, John, sheep-stealer, defended by JB 227–8, 333–7
Reynolds, Sir Joshua 260, 280, 469–70, 475
    attends execution with JB 475
    comments on Mrs Rudd 475
    approves of *Tour* 482
    loses sight of one eye 513
    fears of going blind 533–4
    death 534
    JB plans biography of 534
Robertson, William 43, 81, 82, 248, 301, 428
Rome 195, 196
Rousseau, Jean-Jacques 13, 23, 26, 169, 175–85, 190
    Emile 175, 190
    Nouvelle Héloïse 175, 177
    meetings with JB 177–80, 182–5
    letter to Deleyre 178–9, 185
    Christian beliefs 180
    Social Contract 184
    impressed by JB 185
    going to England 210
    no longer impresses JB 212–13
    physical and mental decline 212–13, 214
    paranoid 213
Rowlandson, Thomas, cartoons depicting scenes from Hebridean tour 299, 320, 325, 487
Rudd, Margaret Caroline 374–6, 475, 492–3

San Gillion, Caterina Maria Theresa, Countess di 192, 193
Sansedoni, Porzia, mistress of Mountstuart 201–2

Scott, Geoffrey 7–8, 111, 192, 212
Seward, Anna 369, 405, 466, 501
Sheridan, Frances (Chamberlaine) (wife of Thomas) 109, 118
Sheridan, Thomas (actor) 83–4, 109
Siena 201–3
Smith, Adam 64–5, 191–2
Soaping Club, founded by JB 79–81, 100–1, 128
Sommelsdyck family 149
Spaen, Alexander Sweder, Baron de 150
Spaen, Elisabeth Agnes Jacoba, Baroness von 157, 159
Steevens, George 350, 423, 477, 484
Stevenson, John 46, 51
Stewart, Archibald 144, 146, 149
Stobie, John 381, 408, 445, 462
Stow, Anne, (later wife of William Temple) 215, 241, 261, 266, 296, 537, 539
Stuart, Charles Edward ('Young Pretender') 311, 313, 315
Stuart, James Archibald (Earl of Bute's second son) 278, 351–2, 417
Stuart, Margaret ('Peggie' Cunynghame) (wife of James Archibald) 278, 351–2, 374, 404, 492
Switzerland 175–89

T. D. *see* Boswell, Thomas David
Talbot, Lady, wife of 6th Lord 5–8, 10, 12
Taylor, Dr John 366, 387–8, 472
Temple, Nancy (daughter of William Temple) 518–19, 537
Temple, William 47, 49–50, 135, 261, 266, 413
    correspondence with JB 4, 45, 50–1, 59, 63, 73, 137
    letters discovered in Boulogne 4
    Trinity Hall, Cambridge 49, 50, 61
    affection for JB 50–1, 223
    concern for JB's Catholocism 66
    views on JB's journals 112
    JB's tour of Germany 163–4
    meets SJ 215
    advice to JB on *Account of Corsica* 218
    opinions of Catherine Blair 240–1
    visits to Auchinleck 240, 296
    reaction to JB's proposed marriage 254
    visits to JB and wife 265, 296